P9-BYB-048

READING CRITICALLY, WRITING WELL

A Reader and Guide

SECOND EDITION

READING CRITICALLY, WRITING WELL

A Reader and Guide

SECOND EDITION

RISE B. AXELROD

California State University, San Bernardino

CHARLES R. COOPER

University of California, San Diego

ST. MARTIN'S PRESS
New York

Senior editor: Mark Gallaher
Managing editor: Patricia Mansfield
Editorial assistant: Robert Skiena
Production supervisor: Katherine Battiste
Text design: Nancy Sugihara
Graphics: G&H Soho Ltd.
Cover design: Celine Brandes

Library of Congress Catalog Card Number: 88-63068
Copyright © 1990 by St. Martin's Press, Inc.
All rights reserved. No part of this publication may be reproduced, stored in a retrieval system, or transmitted by any form or by any means, electronic, mechanical, photocopying, recording, or otherwise, except as may be expressly permitted by the 1976 Copyright Act or in writing by the Publisher.
Manufactured in the United States of America.
 321
fe

For information, write:
St. Martin's Press, Inc.
175 Fifth Avenue
New York, NY 10010

ISBN: 0-312-02109-7

Acknowledgments

Agee, James, "The Treasure of the Sierra Madre" by James Agee, reprinted by permission of Grosset & Dunlap from *Agee on Film*, Vol. 1, copyright © 1958 by the James Agee Trust, copyright renewed © 1986 by Teresa, Andrea, and John Agee.

Baker, Carlos, "The Way it Was." Carlos Baker, *Hemingway—The Writer as Artist*, 4th ed. Copyright 1952, © 1980 renewed by Carlos Baker. Excerpts, pp. 48–54, reprinted by permission of Princeton University Press.

Baker, Russell, "Saving America from Herbert Hoover" from *Growing Up* by Russell Baker. Copyright © 1982 by Russell Baker. Reprinted by permission of Congdon & Weed.

Bok, Sissela, "Intrusive Social Science Research." From *Secrets: On the Ethics of Concealments and Revelation* by Sissela Bok. Copyright © 1982 by Sissela Bok. Reprinted by permission of Pantheon Books, a division of Random House, Inc.

Bruce-Novoa, Juan, "Interlingualism." Reprinted from *Chicano Authors: Inquiry by Interview* by Juan D. Bruce-Novoa (1980) by permission of University of Texas Press.

Christensen, Kathryn, "Steno Pool's Members, Buried by Paper Flood, Yearn for Other Things." Reprinted by permission of the *Wall Street Journal*, © Dow Jones & Company, Inc., 1981. All Rights Reserved worldwide.

Cole, K. C., "Why Are There So Few Women in Science?" Copyright © 1981 by The New York Times Company. Reprinted by permission.

Acknowledgments and copyrights are continued at the back of the book on pages 598–600, which constitute an extension of the copyright page.

From Rise in loving memory of her father, Alexander Borenstein.

From Charles for Suzy and her writing, Laura and her painting, and Vince and his music.

Preface

Like the first edition, this second edition of *Reading Critically, Writing Well* is more than simply a collection of readings for a college writing course; our goal throughout continues to be to teach students specific strategies for critical reading, thereby enabling them to analyze thoughtfully the readings in this text and in their other college courses. We assume that college students should learn to think and read critically and that as they become better critical readers, they will also become more effective writers. To this instruction in reading, we add comprehensive guidance in writing, helping students to understand and manage the composing process—from invention through planning and drafting to revision.

This text attempts to bring reading and writing together in an ideal relationship: students learn to read a type of discourse with a critical eye and then practice writing that same kind of discourse. It suggests specific questions a good reader uses to analyze each kind of discourse and the criteria for evaluating it—questions and criteria students can apply to the readings in this book as well as to their own writing.

We believe that if students have specific strategies for reading and careful guidance with writing, they can study seriously and compose confidently the types of discourse written by academics and professionals. Instead of exercises in the conventional modes of writing, this text offers real-world writing tasks; students read and write the kinds of discourse they will encounter during college and on the job. They practice the forms of critical analysis, inquiry, and knowledge-making central to research and learning in college. In this way, the text introduces them to writing and learning across the college curriculum.

Reading Critically, Writing Well opens with a chapter presenting nine critical reading strategies: previewing, annotating, summarizing, outlining, taking inventory, analyzing arguments, identifying and evaluating basic features, comparing and contrasting related readings, and exploring personal responses. (The final three of these represent additions to this second edition, providing students with greater opportunities for exploratory writing about their reading; in addition, the discussion of analyzing arguments has been expanded to include more attention to fallacies and to breaking arguments down into their logical components in outline form.) Models are included here of a critical analysis of an excerpt from Martin Luther King, Jr.'s "Letter from Birmingham Jail," and students are guided through their own critical reading of a further short argument, Amitai Etzioni's "When Rights Collide." Chapter 1 can be studied carefully when the course begins or sampled as it proceeds.

Chapters 2 through 9, then, focus on reading and writing particular forms of discourse: two types of personal discourse—autobiography and reflection; two types of explanatory discourse—observation and explanation; and four types of argumentative discourse—evaluation, analysis of cause and effect, proposal, and position paper. These eight chapters provide students with comprehensive support for reaching the goals stated in our title: reading critically and writing well. Each begins by introducing the type of writing being considered and offers a sample excerpt, annotated to demonstrate how its basic features can be analyzed. Students are then guided through their own annotation and critical analysis of a brief, representative essay; this guide refers to the general critical reading strategies introduced in Chapter 1 and includes a further list of questions to help students focus on particular basic features so they can analyze, evaluate, and write the type of discourse under discussion.

Next in Chapters 2 through 9, six or seven published readings and one student piece, of varying length and difficulty, illustrate the wide range of writing situations typical of that type of discourse. Well over half of these readings are new to the second edition, and our goal has been to choose new readings that—in terms of subject matter, rhetorical structure, and representativeness of discourse type—will be interesting and readable and at the same time benefit from close, critical analysis. Each reading is preceded by headnotes that discuss the author and the context in which the selection was written and is followed by questions for analysis. These questions attempt to transcend the division between form and content common in writing courses. They ask students to examine textual features as reflections of the writer's decisions, decisions that encompass the writer's understanding of the subject, the rhetorical situation, and the possibilities and constraints of the discourse. The questions for analysis particularize the critical reading questions introduced at the beginning of the chapter. Ideas for writing also accompany each selection and invite students to compose the type of discourse they have been studying in the chapter. Each chapter concludes with a brief but comprehensive guide to writing that helps students through each stage of the writing process for that particular genre—from finding a topic to revising for readability.

Chapter 10—which is new to this edition—provides a casebook of further readings that encompass a variety of discourse types and that are all centered on the issue of civil liberties vs. the values of an orderly society. Included here are classic philosophical statements, an adaptation of Sophocles' *Antigone*, Thoreau's famous essay, "Civil Disobedience," and a selection of writing by twentieth-century authors. Accompanied by minimal apparatus, this casebook can provide the basis for a thematically focused assignment involving controlled research; the readings can also supplement appropriate rhetorical chapters.

The text concludes with an appendix that discusses library and field research. It includes MLA and APA guidelines for documenting sources, and it offers advice to help students integrate research materials into their own writing.

An Instructor's Resource Manual outlines various course plans for using this text and offers suggestions for presenting each reading. It includes, as well, discussion of general teaching strategies that became central to our work as we taught the first edition and an annotated bibliography of recent research and theory on learning from text, sources that influenced our choice of critical reading strategies for Chapter 1.

Acknowledgments

We first want to thank our students. Students in the Third College Writing Program at the University of California, San Diego, and at California State University, San Bernardino, have been generous and frank with their advice, and some of them contributed essays to this text. Their instructors also have had a major role in shaping the book.

We owe a debt of gratitude to the many reviewers and questionnaire respondents who made suggestions for the revision. They include James H. Atchison, Hawaii Loa College; Bioly Dee Bailey, Maysville Community College; Anna Battigelli, SUNY, Plattsburgh; Conrad S. Bayley, Glendale Community College; Sandra Bennett, Winona State University; J. David Boocker, University of Nebraska, Lincoln; Anne L. M. Bowman, University of San Francisco; Lynne E. Martin Bowman, University of North Carolina at Greensboro; H. Eric Branscomb, Northern Essex Community College; Kathryn M. Burton, Florida State University; Lissette Carpenter, McLennan Community College; Donna M. Carter, University of Maine; Mary Casper, West Valley College; C. Lok Chua, California State University, Fresno; Helen Coleman, University of Connecticut, Avery Point; Thomas Cook, Russell Sage College; Marsha Cooper, California State University, Dominguez Hills; Elizabeth R. Curry, Slippery Rock University of Pennsylvania; Susan S. Davis, Arizona State University; Imogene H. Draper, Virginia Commonwealth University; Roman Druker, Hawaii Loa College; L. M. Dryden, California State University, Los Angeles; Chris Ellery, Texas A & M University; Marjorie Ford, Stanford University; Carolyn E. Foster, Clemson University; John C. Freeman, El Paso Community College; Marcia Gottschall, SUNY, Plattsburgh; Deborah A. Gutschera, Loyola University; Virginia Nees-Hatlen, University of Maine; Jackie Hayes, Arizona State University; Josephine Hays, Arizona State University; Karen Helgeson, University of North Carolina, Greensboro; Douglas Hesse, Illinois State University; Jennifer Hicks, Northeastern University; Anna R. Holston, McLennan Community College; Laurie J. Hoskin, University of Michigan; Thomas Hurley, University of Massachusetts; John L. Idol, Jr., Clemson University; Ted Johnston and his colleagues at El Paso Community College; Carole Kayne, SUNY, Buffalo; Cheryl Kroll, Loyola Marymount University; Cynthia B. Lewiecki-Wilson, University of Cincinnati; Nedra D. Lundberg, Kentucky State University; Jeanette D. Macero, Syracuse University; Sister Mary Denis Maher, Ursuline College; Sara McKinnon, Pueblo Community College; Michael J. Meils, El Paso Community College; A. A. Metz-Bundiy, Clemson University; Douglas Meyers, University of Texas at El Paso; George Miller, University of Delaware; Edmund O. Mintz, Norwalk Community College; K. Mitchell, Cypress College; Virginia R. Mollenkott, William Paterson College of New Jersey; LeRoy Mottla, William Rainey Harper College; Kath Pennararia, University of Missouri, Kansas City; Delma M. Porter, Texas A & M University; Mary Prindiville, University of Wisconsin— Green Bay; MeMe Riordan, City College of San Francisco; Judith Saunders, Marist College; Brenda Schildgen, University of San Francisco; Mareleyn Schneider, Fordham University; Cary Ser, Miami-Dade Community College; Diane Seskes, Lorain County Community College; Mary A. Shaughnessy, Glendale Community College; Anne Shifrer, Utah State University; Carolyn Shultz, Walla Walla College; Louise Noah Skellings, Miami-Dade Community College North; Michel Small, Shasta College; Louise M. Stone, Bloomsburg University; Jenny Sullivan, Northern Virginia Community College; Stephen E. Thomas, Maysville Community College; Barbara Thompson, University of Texas at El Paso; Sharon Walsh, Loyola University; Patricia Webb, Maysville Community College; Harriet S. Williams, University of South Carolina; Charlotte M. Wright, Utah State University; and Jeff Wylie, Maysville Community College.

To the crew at St. Martin's Press, we wish to convey our deepest appreciation. We thank Mark Gallaher for his several contributions (and his abiding patience), Patricia Mansfield for managing the project so deftly, Denise Quirk for her careful attention to detail, and Anne Sadowski Loomis for tying up so many loose ends.

Finally, we want to thank our families. The Cooper family provided unwavering enthusiasm and support. Every time one of them asked, "How's it going?" it seemed to come from the heart. The Axelrods, conversely, kept asking, "Are you done yet?"—and for that, too, we are grateful.

Rise B. Axelrod
Charles R. Cooper

Contents

CHAPTER FOUR

Observation

CHAPTER FIVE

Explanation

CHAPTER SIX

CHAPTER SEVEN

Analysis of Cause or Effect

A writer on science and women's issues argues that the under-
representation of women among scientists is rooted in pervasive
gender stereotyping.

A physicist explores possible reasons for the gradual expansion of
the human brain over the last five million years.

A leading economist argues that "the growth of real wages and
the expansion of the service sector" explain why more and more
married women with children are working outside their homes.

CHAPTER EIGHT

Proposal   353

CHAPTER NINE

Position Paper

417

A member of the World Health Organization makes a rigorous plea for restraint in legislative efforts to contain the spread of HIV, such as laws requiring quarantine or registration.

A researcher defends experimentation on animals in the service of advancing human welfare.

A philosophy professor argues against the death penalty, saying that even one "wrongful execution is a grievous injustice that cannot be remedied after the fact."

A philosophy professor argues that American schools, by failing to acquaint students with "classic" works, are turning Americans into "a culture without a culture, lacking fixed points of reference and a shared vocabulary."

A literature professor defends rock music's central place in contemporary culture, finding in it a "living lyric tradition" with

APPENDIX

Strategies for Research and Documentation   575

READING CRITICALLY, WRITING WELL

A Reader and Guide
SECOND EDITION

CHAPTER ONE

Strategies for Critical Reading

Serious study of a text requires a pencil in hand—how much pride that pencil carries. IRVING HOWE

Critical reading is a rigorous process. It is sometimes slow and always demanding. Reading actively, thoughtfully, and *critically* can be one of the most challenging human activities, for it tests the limits of our energy, patience, and intellect.

Reading critically is often harder than it needs to be, however, because so few readers know how to approach difficult reading. This chapter presents several proven strategies for reading critically, strategies that you can learn readily and then apply not only to the selections in this text but also to your other college reading. Although mastering these strategies will not make the critical reading process an easy one, it can make reading much more satisfying and productive and thus help you handle difficult material with confidence.

In order to read critically, you must be prepared to read actively, with pencil in hand, and to perform specific operations on the text as you read. These actions will slow down your reading, but they may save you time in the long run, especially if you must later discuss the reading in class or write about it. New research on how people learn from their reading shows that the active, pencil-in-hand strategies demonstrated in this chapter are far more productive than merely rereading or highlighting or underlining.

In college you will be reading new kinds of material, in forms you may not have had much experience with. Much of this new reading—books, essays, reports—will not have the familiar and helpful cues that textbooks provide, such as headings, summaries, and questions. Your instructors will expect you to handle these unfamiliar texts on your own, and they will assume that you are able to do more with them than you may be accustomed to:

summarize and outline complex material

evaluate a text, deciding whether it is accurate, authoritative, and convincing

gauge a text's importance or significance

compare and contrast different texts

synthesize information from several texts

apply concepts or principles in one text to other texts

analyze the way a text achieves its effects

critically examine a text's reasoning

These expectations call for critical, not casual, reading. When you read a text in this way you must think critically and become an active participant rather than a passive recipient. Instead of listening passively to the author's monologue, you should strive to become actively involved in a dialogue with the author and with other readers of the text.

This chapter will demonstrate nine strategies for critical reading to help you meet the demands of college studies:

- *Previewing*: looking over a text to learn everything you can about it before you start reading

- *Annotating*: marking up a text to record your reactions, questions, and conclusions

- *Outlining*: identifying the sequence of main ideas

- *Summarizing*: stating in your own words the essence of a reading

- *Taking Inventory*: looking for patterns of meaning

- *Analyzing an Argument*: evaluating the reasoning and persuasiveness of a text

- *Identifying Basic Features*: identifying and evaluating the special characteristics of the type of writing you are reading

- *Comparing and Contrasting Related Readings*: exploring likenesses and differences between readings in order to understand them better

- *Exploring Your Personal Responses*: composing an extended piece of writing presenting your insights about the meaning and significance of a reading

Throughout this chapter we will refer to "Letter from Birmingham Jail," a celebrated essay by Martin Luther King, Jr., to demonstrate each of the critical reading strategies.

Previewing

The first strategy is called previewing because it involves noticing certain features about a text *before* reading it, in order to establish a context and purpose for reading.

Previewing enables you to consider the following basic questions. You may not be able at this point to answer them all, but considering them will help you focus your reading.

What do I know about the author?

What does the title tell me?

What kind of text is it?

What else do I know about the context of this text?

What can I discover about this text by skimming it?

What Do I Know about the Author?

Knowing something about the author is not a prerequisite for critical reading, but it can help you determine how much to trust the information and judgments presented. A text's credibility or ethos derives in large part from the reader's willingness to accept the author's authority on the subject. The author's reputation, credentials, and other publications help establish his or her authority. Even the most highly respected expert, however, can be wrong. So, you should be sure to judge the reading on the basis of what it says rather than on who is saying it.

Occasionally a reading may be accompanied by a preface, headnote, or other biographical information. For each selection in this book, for example, a headnote presents vital facts about the writer. Often, however, no special information about the author will accompany an assigned reading. If the name is familiar, recall what you know about the author—the period and the place in which he or she lived, any other publications, anything about his or her life or work that might give clues about this particular reading. If the name is unfamiliar, you might want to learn more by consulting a biographical dictionary, encyclopedia, or index such as *Who's Who, Current Biography, Biographical Index, Dictionary of American Biography,* or *Annual Obituary.*

Take a moment to consider what you already know about Martin Luther King, Jr. When did he live? What is his reputation, credentials, other publications? What else do you know about his life and work? How does this information influence your attitude toward his essay? Do you expect to agree or disagree with him? Why?

What Does the Title Tell Me?

Paying some attention to the title before reading the whole selection may provide clues about the subject of the selection, the kind of writing it is, and the circumstances surrounding its composition.

The title of King's essay, "Letter from Birmingham Jail," indicates several things: that it is a letter, that it was written while the author was in jail, and that it was written from the city of Birmingham. Readers who know nothing about the author might discount the letter because it was written by someone in jail, but those familiar with King's career would be likely to assume that the author was imprisoned because of his protest against racial injustice. These readers might further recognize Birmingham as the city in Alabama where dramatic events took place in the civil rights movement.

What Kind of Text Is It?

Reading an unfamiliar text is like traveling in unknown territory. Wise travelers use a map, checking what they see against what they expect to find. In much the same way, previewing for genre equips you with a set of expectations to guide your reading. The word *genre* means "sort" or "type," and is generally used to classify pieces of writing according to their particular style, form, and content. Nonfiction prose genres include autobiography, reflection, observation, explanation, and various forms of argument, such as evaluation, speculation about causes or effects, proposal, and position on a controversial issue. These genres are illustrated in chapters 2 through 9 with guidelines to help you analyze and evaluate their effectiveness. After reading these chapters, you will confidently identify the genre of any unfamiliar piece of writing you encounter.

You can make a tentative decision about the genre of a text by first looking at why the piece was written and to whom it was addressed. These two elements—purpose and audience—constitute what is called the rhetorical or writing situation. Paying attention to the genre of a particular text leads you to consider how the writing situation affected the particular way the text was written. The title "Letter from Birmingham Jail" explicitly identifies this particular selection as a letter. We know that letters are usually written with a particular reader in mind, although they may be addressed to the public in general; that they may be part of an ongoing correspondence; and that they may be personal or public, informal or formal.

The opening of King's letter (p. 524) provides some insight into the situation in which he wrote the letter and some understanding of his specific purpose for writing. The first paragraph makes clear that King wrote the letter in order to refute or answer criticisms against him by other members of the clergy. The tone he establishes suggests that his refutation will not take the form of an angry counterattack but will attempt to explain and justify his position to critics he hopes ultimately to win over to his side. As a public letter written in response to a public statement, "Letter from Birmingham Jail" thus may be classified as a position paper, one that argues for a particular position on a controversial issue. In this case, the issue is racial segregation; King's position is that segregation must end.

Knowing that "Letter from Birmingham Jail" is a position paper allows you to appreciate the controversiality of the subject King is writing about and the sensitivity of the rhetorical situation. You can see how he sets forth his own position at the same time that he tries to bridge the gap separating him from his critics. You can then evaluate the kinds of points King makes and the persuasiveness of his argument.

When you think of a text as belonging to a particular genre, you may recall other examples of that genre. Some of these other texts may have influenced the writer you are reading. For instance, King probably knew of the famous public letter "J'accuse" by French author Emile Zola about the notorious Dreyfus case, and as a minister he most certainly knew the Epistles, or letters, in the New Testament. He also must have known some part of the long tradition of writing on civil disobedience: Plato's *Apology,* Thoreau's "Civil Disobedience," and Gandhi's *Nonviolent Resistance,* all advocating the duty to disobey unjust laws. King almost certainly knew, as well, Thomas Hobbes's *Leviathan* and Edmund Burke's *Reflections on the Revolution in France,* both arguing against civil disobedience. These famous documents on civil disobedience must have influenced King's decisions about how to address his readers, what argumentative strategies he might adopt, and the kinds of examples and evidence he might include as he argued the appropriateness of nonviolent direct action. You will have an opportunity to explore the intertextuality of

King's essay when you come to Chapter 10, "Casebook on Civil Disobedience." The chapter includes excerpts from many of the important documents on civil disobedience.

Whenever you begin a new reading, try to determine as soon as possible what genre you are encountering. You will then be able to read more confidently and productively.

What Else Do I Know about the Context?

The author, title, and genre provide a good deal of information about the particular context in which a text was written, but there may be still further contexts to be inferred by previewing a selection.

For example, you know that King is responding to a statement made by several clergymen. Although it is not necessary to read their statement, doing so would enlarge your understanding of the context for the letter and also furnish insight into King's argumentative strategy. With a little research, you could find the clergymen's statement, which is printed here:

Public Statement by Eight Alabama Clergymen

April 12, 1963

We the undersigned clergymen are among those who, in January, issued "An Appeal for Law and Order and Common Sense," in dealing with racial problems in Alabama. We expressed understanding that honest convictions in racial matters could properly be pursued in the courts, but urged that decisions of those courts should in the meantime be peacefully obeyed.

Since that time there has been some evidence of increased forebearance and a willingness to face facts. Responsible citizens have undertaken to work on various problems which cause racial friction and unrest. In Birmingham, recent public events have given indication that we all have opportunity for a new constructive and realistic approach to racial problems.

However, we are now confronted by a series of demonstrations by some of our Negro citizens, directed and led in part by outsiders. We recognize the natural impatience of people who feel that their hopes are slow in being realized. But we are convinced that these demonstrations are unwise and untimely.

We agree rather with certain local Negro leadership which has called for honest and open negotiation of racial issues in our area. And we believe this kind of facing of issues can best be accomplished by citizens of our own metropolitan area, white and Negro, meeting with their knowledge and experience of the local situation. All of us need to face that responsibility and find proper channels for its accomplishment.

Just as we formerly pointed out that "hatred and violence have no 5 sanction in our religious and political traditions," we also point out that such actions as incite to hatred and violence, however technically peaceful those actions may be, have not contributed to the resolution of our local problems. We do not believe that these days of new hope are days when extreme measures are justified in Birmingham.

We commend the community as a whole, and the local news media 6 and law enforcement officials in particular, on the calm manner in which these demonstrations have been handled. We urge the public to continue to show restraint should the demonstrations continue, and the law enforcement officials to remain calm and continue to protect our city from violence.

We further strongly urge our own Negro community to withdraw 7 support from these demonstrations, and to unite locally in working peacefully for a better Birmingham. When rights are consistently denied, a cause should be pressed in the courts and in negotiations among local leaders, and not in the streets. We appeal to both our white and Negro citizenry to observe the principles of law and order and common sense.

Signed by:

C. C. J. CARPENTER, D.D., LL.D., *Bishop of Alabama*

JOSEPH A. DURICK, D.D., *Auxiliary Bishop, Diocese of Mobile-Birmingham*

Rabbi MILTON L. GRAFMAN, *Temple Emanu-El, Birmingham, Alabama*

Bishop PAUL HARDIN, *Bishop of the Alabama-West Florida Conference of the Methodist Church*

Bishop NOLAN B. HARMON, *Bishop of the North Alabama Conference of the Methodist Church*

GEORGE M. MURRAY, D.D., LL.D., *Bishop Coadjutor, Episcopal Diocese of Alabama*

EDWARD V. RAMAGE, *Moderator, Synod of the Alabama Presbyterian Church in the United States*

EARL STALLINGS, *Pastor, First Baptist Church, Birmingham, Alabama*

King was already a prominent civil rights leader, and the clergymen knew that he was in Birmingham and had been jailed. Yet they do not mention him, referring only to certain "outsiders." Instead, the clergymen address their remarks to the "responsible citizens" of Birmingham. The date on the letter places the momentous events in Birmingham precisely in the larger historical context of the civil rights movement.

King's letter (printed in its entirety in Chapter 10) is dated just four days later.

Looking closely at the clergymen's titles, you can see that they represent a variety of American religious groups—Jewish, Catholic, and a range of Protestant denominations. Knowing this lets you know precisely who King means when he expresses his disappointment in "the church."

Other background information could also be brought to bear on a reading of King's letter. A general historical knowledge of the period and of the civil rights movement, particularly of the circumstances surrounding the Birmingham demonstrations, would be useful. It would help as well to know something about King's philosophy of nonviolent civil disobedience and to relate it to some of its sources—as illustrated in Chapter 10.

You can learn about these historical and cultural contexts through reading and library research; the amount you do, of course, depends on how much time you have. You might begin by consulting an encyclopedia under civil disobedience, the civil rights movement, or Martin Luther King, Jr. Other possible sources on any of these subjects can be found by consulting the subject card catalog for books, the *Reader's Guide to Periodical Literature* or a specialized index like *America: History and Life* for journal articles, and *The New York Times Index* for newspaper articles.

What Else Can I Discover by Skimming the Text?

Before reading a selection carefully, you should skim it to get a sense of what it is about and how it is organized. Skimming is especially useful for long and complicated texts with many headings, subheadings, charts, and figures. Many shorter readings do not provide these cues, but it is still a good idea to look them over quickly in order to get an overview. This kind of superficial first reading is good preparation for a more thoughtful close reading and can also suggest a particular purpose or set of questions to explore while reading.

Even a short text can be informatively skimmed, particularly if you pay attention to the way it unfolds. Since authors often place forecasting and transitional phrases at the beginnings of paragraphs to orient the reader, it is easy to get an overview simply by looking at the first sentence of each paragraph. A quick survey of even a small portion of "Letter from Birmingham Jail" gives a good indication of the main points King takes up: Paragraph 2 indicates why he came to Birmingham; paragraph 3 gives his basic reason for being in Birmingham; paragraph 4 expands on his reasoning; paragraph 5 acknowledges his critics' attitude; and paragraph 6 explains steps in a nonviolent campaign.

If you continue looking quickly at the first sentence of each paragraph, you will be surprised to see how much you can learn about the contents and plan of the essay.

A Checklist for Previewing

To orient yourself and get the most from your reading, try taking the following steps:

- Consider what you know about the author and how much you should trust him or her.
- Reflect on what the title suggests about the reading.
- Classify the text as to genre, and then speculate about what the piece will be like.
- Determine what the historical and cultural context indicates about the text.
- Skim the reading, noting your first impressions.

Exercise 1

The exercises in this chapter enable you to practice critical reading strategies on the following brief essay, "When Rights Collide," by Amitai Etzioni.

Using the Checklist for Previewing above, first follow the steps of previewing with Etzioni's essay. You may want to review the earlier discussion of each previewing step.

This essay was written in 1977 by Amitai Etzioni (b. 1929) and published in *Psychology Today*, a magazine presenting new developments in psychology for a general readership. Etzioni is a professor of sociology at Columbia University and director of the Center for Policy Research. Born in Germany in 1929, Etzioni was educated at Hebrew University and the University of California. He has written three books, all dealing with war: *A Diary of a Commando Soldier*, *The Hard Way to Peace*, and *Winning*

Without War. This essay, "When Rights Collide," concerns the conflict between individual rights and the rights of society.

[handwritten: Circle = metaphor, etc.]

When Rights Collide
Amitai Etzioni

[handwritten left margin: Americans have rights, but how far should these rights go]

The viewpoint, now gaining momentum, that would allow individuals to "make up their own minds" about smoking, air bags, safety helmets, Laetrile,[1] and the like ignores some elementary social realities. The ill-informed nature of this viewpoint is camouflaged by the appeal to values that are dear to most Americans. The essence of the argument is that what individuals wish to do with their lives and limbs, foolhardy though it might be, is their own business, and that any interference would abridge their rights.

[handwritten left margin: 1.) View is with dislike / Who are most Americans? / lives and limbs]

Mr. Gene Wirwahn, the legislative director of the American Motorcyclist Association, which is lobbying against laws requiring riders to wear helmets, put it squarely: "The issue that we're speaking about is not the voluntary use of helmets. It's the question of whether or not there should be laws telling people to wear them." State representative Anne Miller, a liberal Democrat in Illinois, favors legalization of Laetrile. She explains that she is aware that this apricot-pit extract is useless, but insists that "the government shouldn't protect people from bad judgment. They might as well bar holy water."

[handwritten left margin: 2. Supporting arguments to people's choices / wrong / Equipment is made for people to wear it / they don't, that's their problem]

U.S. representative Louis Wyman recently invoked much the same argument in leading the brigade that won adoption in the House of a resolution making seat belts voluntary. The 1974-model cars had been engineered not to start unless the seat belt was buckled. Wyman, a New Hampshire Republican, called the buckle-up system un-American, saying it made the government a Big Brother to auto drivers. Representative Abraham Kazen, Texas Democrat, summed it all up: "It is wrong to tell the individual what is good for him. . . . These are some of the things that the American people want to judge for themselves. Give them the equipment if they so desire, and if they do not, let them do whatever they want."

[handwritten left margin: 3. I disagree with / What is Big Brother / un-American]

No civil society can survive if it permits each person to maximize his or her freedoms without concern for the consequences of one's act on others. If I choose to drive

[handwritten left margin: I disagree with this. People are ignorant. They need help.]

[1]Laetrile: a drug made from apricot pits that was proven to be an ineffective treatment for cancer.

without a seat belt or air bag, I am greatly increasing my chances, in case of accident, of being impaled on the steering wheel or exiting via the windshield. It is not just my body that is jeopardized; my careening auto, which I cannot get back under control, will be more likely to injure people in other autos, pedestrians, or riders in my car. (Yes, my passengers choose their own fate when they decide to ride with me, but what about the infants who are killed and injured because they are not properly protected?)

American institutions were fashioned in an era of vast unoccupied spaces and preindustrial technology. In those days, collisions between public needs and individual rights may have been minimal. But increased density, scarcity of resources, and interlocking technologies have now heightened the concern for "public goods," which belong to no one in particular but to all of us jointly. Polluting a lake or river or the air may not directly damage any one person's private property or living space. But it destroys a good that all of us—including future generations—benefit from and have a title to. Our public goods are entitled to a measure of protection.

The individual who chooses to act irresponsibly is playing a game of heads I win, tails the public loses. All too often, the unbelted drivers, the smokers, the unvaccinated, the users of quack remedies draw on public funds to pay for the consequences of their unrestrained freedom of choice. Their rugged individualism rapidly becomes dependency when cancer strikes, or when the car overturns, sending the occupants to hospitals for treatment paid for at least in part by the public, through subsidies for hospitals and medical training. But the public till is not bottomless, and paying for these irresponsible acts leaves other public needs without funds.

True, totalitarian regimes often defend their invasions of individual liberties by citing public need or "national interest." One difference is that they are less concerned with protecting public goods than they are with building national power or new world orders. Instead of insisting on protection for some public rights, such regimes seek to put the national interest above all individual rights. The lesson is that we must not allow any claim of public or national need to go unexplained. But at the same time, we cannot allow simpleminded sloganeering (from "creeping Communism" to "Big Brother") to blind us to the fact that there are needs all of us share as a community.

Last but not least, we must face the truth about ourselves. Are we the independent, self-reliant individuals

[margin numbers: 6, 7, 8]

Handwritten margin annotations:

4. Are we in a non-civil society?

Repetition "I" as the reader.

An American's ignorance can kill himself and others who don't know otherwise

5. What is preindustrial technology?

Concerns of everyone, give me a break Human's bad habits may kill the generation Yes to come

6. Is our environment and use of it a game?

Certain freedoms kill others

What money?

Irresponsible acts by individuals is are payed for by the public

Rights or power

Regimines are interested mostly in national power than in saving the earth What is creeping Communism. a form of government ruled by 1 man

voluntary reg Government pec One person public funds to public that need inte Community ne

Experts:
Mr. Gene Wirwa
Anne Mill
Louis Wyma
Abraham Kaz

First Person
I

8 Individuals
need self-
Control

Individuals need
protection from
themselves.

What

9. Conclusion: We need
a balance of
individual rights and support
from the laws.
9. Conclusion:

Individual rights
Public rights
Government power

the politicians like to tell us we are? Or are we a human combination of urges and self-controls (impulses and rational judgments? Can we trust ourselves to make wise judgments routinely, or do we at times have to rely on the laws our elected representatives have fashioned, with our consent, to help guide us? The fact is that driving slowly saves lives, lots of lives; but until we are required to do so, most of us drive too fast. The same holds true for buckling our seat belts, buying air bags, and so on. Similarly, we need protection from quack cures. It sounds very libertarian to argue that each person can make up his or her own mind about Laetrile. But the fact is that when confronted with cancer and fearful of surgery, thousands of Americans are tempted to try a "painless medication" first, often delaying surgery until it is too late.

All in all, it is high time the oversimplifications about 9 individual freedom versus Big Brother government were replaced by a social philosophy that calls for a balance among the rights of various individuals, between individual rights and some public rights, and that acknowledges the support we fallible individuals need from the law.

Annotating

Previewing is valuable because it prepares you to read closely and critically, but the most fundamental of all critical reading strategies is annotating. As you will see, the subsequent critical reading strategies all grow out of and extend annotating. This process is essential to critical reading because it focuses your attention on the language of the text. As you read, annotate directly on the page, underlining key words, phrases, or sentences and writing comments or questions in the margins. You can also bracket important sections of the text, connect ideas with lines or arrows, and number related points in sequence. If writing on the text itself is impossible or undesirable to you personally, you can still write notes about the reading on a separate piece of paper.

Most readers annotate in layers, adding further annotations on second and third readings. Annotations can be light or heavy, depending on the reader's purpose and the difficulty of the material. Reading a textbook to prepare for an exam, for example, you might limit yourself to underlining (or highlighting with a colored marker) main ideas and defining new words in the margin. Analyzing a poem or story as a subject for an essay, on the other hand, you would almost certainly annotate more heavily, layering annotations from several readings. You may want to annotate some of the essays in this book heavily in order to analyze the strategies and processes each writer uses as well as to explore ideas and your reactions to them.

The annotating process is demonstrated here with an excerpt from "Letter from Birmingham Jail." A complete argument in itself, this excerpt expresses King's disappointment in whites who did not support his campaign of nonviolent direct action. We have annotated this excerpt as if we had read only the King headnote on page 524 and the clergymen's letter reprinted earlier in this chapter. We began with three questions to focus the reading: (1) As an outsider, how can King respond in a convincing way to these respected insiders? (2) Will he attack them or show them respect? (3) Will he rely on legal, personal, or historical arguments? The first time through the reading, we annotated with comments, reactions, and questions. Subsequent readings produced annotations of images and oppositions, definitions, and still more questions. In the margin, we outlined the main ideas of the excerpt. The questions that appear after the excerpt express our concluding reflections.

Read the excerpt first without looking at the annotations, and then reread slowly, paying attention to them. Remember that they were accumulated during several readings. The discussion that follows the excerpt comments on the annotations and disentangles the layers:

An Annotated Reading:
from *Letter from Birmingham Jail*
Martin Luther King, Jr.

1. White moderates' shallow understanding and lukewarm acceptance a barrier to racial justice.
WCC?
KKK: white sheets, nooses, burning crosses—founded after Civil War—white supremacy by terror

forecasts his main arguments here

. . . My Christian and Jewish brothers . . . I must confess that over the past few years I have been gravely disappointed with the <u>white moderate</u>. I have almost reached the regrettable conclusion that the Negro's [great stumbling block in his stride toward freedom] is not the White Citizen's Counciler or the Ku Klux Klanner, but the white moderate, who is more devoted to <u>"order"</u> than to justice; who prefers a <u>negative peace</u> which is the <u>absence of tension</u> to a positive peace which is the presence of justice; who constantly says: "I agree with you in the goal you seek, but I cannot agree with your <u>methods</u> of direct action"; who paternalistically believes he can set the timetable for another man's freedom; who lives by a mythical concept of time and who constantly advises the Negro to wait for a "more convenient season." Shallow understanding from people of good will is more frustrating than absolute misunderstanding from people of ill

1

not sure I agree

will. Lukewarm acceptance is much more bewildering than outright rejection.

Law and order

I had hoped that the white moderate would understand that law and order exist for the purpose of establishing justice and that when they fail in this purpose they become the dangerously structured dams that block the flow of social progress. I had hoped that the white

2. Tension is necessary for progress toward freedom.

moderate would understand that the present tension in the South is a necessary phase of the transition from an obnoxious negative peace, in which the Negro passively accepted his unjust plight, to a substantive and positive peace, in which all men will respect the dignity and worth of human personality. Actually, we who engage in nonviolent direct action are not the creators of tension.

Repetition and shorter sentences give emphasis.

We merely bring to the surface the hidden tension that is already alive. We bring it out in the open, where it can be seen and dealt with. Like a boil that can never be cured so long as it is covered up but must be opened with all its

Will light of human conscience and air of national opinion always produce justice?

ugliness to the natural medicines of air and light, injustice must be exposed, with all the tension its exposure creates, to the light of human conscience and the air of national opinion before it can be cured.

Repetition of sentence structure

In your statement you assert that our actions, even though peaceful, must be condemned because they precipitate violence. But is this a logical assertion? Isn't this like condemning a robbed man because his possession of money precipitated the evil act of robbery? Isn't this like

Who was Socrates? Greek philosopher and teacher, 5th c. B.C. Why refer to Socrates and Jesus?

condemning Socrates because his unswerving commitment to truth and his philosophical inquiries precipitated the act by the misguided populace in which they made him drink hemlock? Isn't this like condemning Jesus because his unique God-consciousness and never-ceasing devotion to God's will precipitated the evil act of crucifixion? We must come to see that, as the federal courts have

3. Peaceful actions justified even if they lead to violence.

consistently affirmed, it is wrong to urge an individual to cease his efforts to gain his basic constitutional rights because the question may precipitate violence. Society

Yes!

must protect the robbed and punish the robber.

Myth of time

I had also hoped that the white moderate would reject the myth concerning time in relation to the struggle for freedom. I have just received a letter from a white brother in Texas. He writes: "All Christians know that the colored people will receive equal rights eventually, but it is

4. Must take action now to ensure racial justice.

possible that you are in too great a religious hurry. It has taken Christianity almost two thousand years to accomplish what it has. The teachings of Christ take time to come to earth." Such an attitude stems from a tragic misconception of time, from the strangely irrational notion that there is something in the very flow of time that will inevitably cure all ills. Actually, time itself is neutral; it can be used either destructively or constructively. More and more I feel that the people of ill will have used time much more effectively than have the people of good will. We will have to repent in this generation not merely for the hateful words and actions of the bad people but for the appalling silence of the good people. Human progress never rolls in on wheels of inevitability; it comes through the tireless efforts of men willing to be co-workers with God, and without this hard work, time itself becomes an ally of the forces of social stagnation. We must use time creatively, in the knowledge that the time is always ripe to do right. Now is the time to make real the promise of democracy and transform our pending national elegy into a creative psalm of brotherhood. Now is the time to lift our national policy from the quicksand of racial injustice to the solid rock of human dignity.

You speak of our activity in Birmingham as extreme. 5 At first I was rather disappointed that fellow clergymen would see my nonviolent efforts as those of an extremist. I began thinking about the fact that I stand in the middle of two opposing forces in the Negro community. One is a force of complacency, made up in part of Negroes who, as a result of long years of oppression, are so drained of self-respect and a sense of "somebodiness" that they have adjusted to segregation; and in part of a few middle-class Negroes, who because of a degree of academic and economic security and because in some ways they profit by segregation, have become insensitive to the problems of the masses. The other force is one of bitterness and hatred, and it comes perilously close to advocating violence. It is expressed in the various black nationalist groups that are springing up across the nation, the largest and best-known being Elijah Muhammad's Muslim movement. Nourished by the Negro's frustration over the continued existence of racial discrimination, this movement is made up of people who have lost faith in America, who have absolutely repudiated Christianity, and who have concluded that the white man is an incorrigible "devil."

I have tried to stand between these two forces, saying 6 that we need emulate neither the "do-nothingism" of the complacent nor the hatred and despair of the black nationalist. For there is the more excellent way of love and nonviolent protest. I am grateful to God that, through the influence of the Negro church, the way of nonviolence became an integral part of our struggle.

"We" must be the white moderates. The clergymen who wrote the letter? Have they repented?

stagnation: not moving or flowing

Short words make this stand out. Ripe/right.

Alliteration, lots of images: dams, boils, light, wheels, quicksand, rock

Accused of being an extremist.

5. two opposing groups of Negroes: complacent and bitter, violent

Who was Elijah Muhammad?

**6. King stands between complacent and violent Negro groups.
How did nonviolence become part of King's movement? the church? How about Gandhi?**

7. King's movement has prevented racial violence.

solace: comfort
Did this scare tactic really work?

8. Protest is a natural result of yearning for freedom.

Zeitgeist: spirit of the times

Not a threat?

9. We need extremists for good causes.

Amos: 8th c. B.C.
Hebrew prophet
Paul: 1st c. Christian, now a Catholic saint
Luther: 16th c. German monk who founded Protestantism
Bunyan: 17th c. English preacher

If this philosophy had not emerged, by now many 7 streets of the South would, I am convinced, be flowing with blood. And I am further convinced that if our white brothers dismiss as "rabble-rousers" and "outside agitators" those of us who employ nonviolent direct action, and if they refuse to support our nonviolent efforts, millions of Negroes will, out of frustration and despair, seek solace and security in black-nationalist ideologies—a development that would inevitably lead to a frightening racial nightmare.

Oppressed people cannot remain oppressed forever. 8 The yearning for freedom eventually manifests itself, and that is what has happened to the American Negro. Something within has reminded him of his birthright of freedom, and something without has reminded him that it can be gained. Consciously or unconsciously, he has been caught up by the Zeitgeist, and with his black brothers of Africa and his brown and yellow brothers of Asia, South America and the Caribbean, the United States Negro is moving with a sense of great urgency toward the promised land of racial justice. If one recognizes this vital urge that has engulfed the Negro community, one should readily understand why public demonstrations are taking place. The Negro has many pent-up resentments and latent frustrations, and he must release them. So let him march; let him make prayer pilgrimages to the city hall; let him go on freedom rides—and try to understand why he must do so. If his repressed emotions are not released in nonviolent ways, they will seek expression through violence; this is not a threat but a fact of history. So I have not said to my people: "Get rid of your discontent." Rather, I have tried to say that this normal and healthy discontent can be channeled into the creative outlet of nonviolent direct action. And now this approach is being termed extremist.

But though I was initially disappointed at being cate- 9 gorized as an extremist, as I continued to think about the matter I gradually gained a measure of satisfaction from the label. Was not Jesus an extremist for love: "Love your enemies, bless them that curse you, do good to them that hate you, and pray for them which despitefully use you, and persecute you." Was not Amos an extremist for justice: "Let justice roll down like waters and righteousness like an ever-flowing stream." Was not Paul an extremist for the Christian gospel: "I bear in my body the marks of the Lord Jesus." Was not Martin Luther an extremist: "Here I stand; I cannot do otherwise, so help me God." And John Bunyan: "I will stay in jail to the end of my days before I make a butchery of my conscience." And <u>Abraham Lincoln</u>: "This nation cannot survive half slave and half free." And <u>Thomas Jefferson</u>: "We hold these truths to be self-evident, that all men are created equal . . ." So the question is not whether we will be extremists, but <u>what kind of extremists we will be</u>. <u>Will we be</u> extremists for hate or for love? <u>Will we be</u> extremists for the preservation of injustice or for the extension of justice? In that dramatic scene on Calvary's hill three men were crucified. We must never forget that all three were crucified for the same crime—the crime of extremism. Two were extremists for immorality, and thus fell below their environment. The other, <u>Jesus Christ,</u> was an <u>extremist for love, truth and goodness,</u> and thereby rose above his environment. Perhaps the South, the nation and the world are in dire need of creative extremists.

Will creative extremism work in every situation? Did Lincoln and Jefferson consider themselves extremists?

I had hoped that the white moderate would see this need. Perhaps I was too optimistic; perhaps I expected too much. I suppose I should have realized that few members of the oppressor race can understand the deep groans and passionate yearnings of the oppressed race, and still fewer have the vision to see that injustice must be rooted out by strong, persistent and determined <u>action</u>. I am thankful, however, that some of our white brothers in the South have grasped the meaning of this <u>social revolution</u> and committed themselves to it. They are still all too few in quantity, but they are big in quality. Some—such as Ralph McGill, Lillian Smith, Harry Golden, James McBride Dabbs, Ann Braden and Sarah Patton Boyle—have written about our struggle in eloquent and prophetic terms. Others have marched with us down nameless streets of the South. They have languished in filthy, roach-infested jails, suffering the abuse and brutality of policemen who view them as "dirty nigger-lovers." Unlike so many of their moderate brothers and sisters, they have recognized the urgency of the moment and sensed the need for powerful "action" antidotes to combat the disease of segregation.

Disappointed in the white moderate.

10

10. Some whites have supported King.

What did these people write?

Where are the eight clergymen now? What do they think now of their letter and their role in what happened?
What do my parents remember about these events and about the civil rights movement of the 1960s?
If this were 1963 and I were in Birmingham, what would I be thinking and doing?
Did King write his letter expecting immediate results, or was he just making a statement about racial prejudice?
Which earlier American writers did King admire?

As you can see, the annotations on this excerpt are quite diverse. Questions, definitions, reactions, and an outline, attending both to King's ideas and to his argumentative strategies and style, appear in the margin. Within the text itself, key words, phrases, and sentences are underlined, circled, bracketed, and boxed.

Layered annotations like these produce a comprehensive record of a critical reading, a record you can use in class discussion or for your own writing. Such annotations can give you confidence that you understand what a writer is saying and how it is being said. By persisting with demanding, time-consuming annotations and rereadings, you will gradually master the critical reading strategies and approach any difficult text confidently.

In the following analysis of the annotations, we comment separately on the marginal questions, definitions, reactions, outlining, and text markings. In this discussion, the numbers in parentheses indicate the paragraph number of the annotated text.

Questions

Questions are the most notable aspect of the annotations: the more than twenty questions in the margins help focus the reading, identify needed information and definitions, and express confusion. These questions emerged gradually through several readings. Three questions were written even before the first reading, in the previewing stage. During the first reading, most of the questions indicating lack of knowledge arose: WCC (1), Socrates (3), moderates' reaction (4), identity of white moderates (4), typicality of Birmingham (5), source of King's nonviolence (6), training for nonviolence (6), and identity and writings of whites who supported King (10). Questions written during later readings express doubts, observations, and reactions. These appear at many points. The five concluding questions, written after the last reading, identify final thoughts.

All these questions characterize the work of an inquiring, critical reader, one who is willing to admit what he or she does not know and unwilling to accept passively a revered American's argument. This questioning stance can lead to useful reflection—and to questions that may later suggest topics for writing.

Definitions

On our first reading, imagining ourselves to be college freshmen, we encountered several unfamiliar words and names; since none of them seemed essential to a general understanding of the reading, we did not stop to look them up. We did, however, write down impressions of the Ku Klux Klan (1) and ask "Who was Socrates?" (3). During the second reading, we looked up words and people in an unabridged college dictionary: Ku Klux Klan (1), Socrates (3), stagnation (4), solace (7), *Zeitgeist* (8), Amos, Paul, Luther, and Bunyan (9). Identifying the individuals revealed that King is relying in part on a wide range of historical figures to support his argument. The dictionary did not provide definitions of White Citizen's Counciler (1) or Elijah Muhammad (5), but these could be tracked down in the library.

Reactions

The annotations on this excerpt react to both ideas and style. Some annotations record agreement ("Yes!" in 3) or disagreement (1) with King's statements. At other times, annotations point out King's writing strategies, such as forecasting (1), contrast (5), or referring to authorities (3). Other annotations comment on aspects of his style: contrast of long sentences with short sentences used for emphasis (2), short words used for emphasis (4), and use of images (4). Within the text, several of King's attempts at concise, quotable statements are boxed (1, 3, 4, 8).

Outlining Main Ideas

An outline of the sequence of main ideas appears in the margin as a series of numbered points, one point for each paragraph. The next section will examine this outline and discuss the strategy of outlining. We mention it here as a reminder that annotating leads naturally to outlining, which can join other annotations in the margin.

Text Markings

Knowing that we eventually wanted to make an inventory of images and oppositions (strategies illustrated later in this chapter), we bracketed images and underlined oppositions. These annotations enable us to produce the word and phrase lists that are essential for taking inventory.

A Checklist for Annotating

To focus and sustain a critical reading, annotate as you read and reread. In the margin, write any:

- questions
- definitions
- comments and reactions
- main ideas for outline

On the reading itself, underline, circle, or box any:

- special uses of language, such as images or oppositions
- features of style
- words to be defined or people and events to be identified

Exercise 2

Read "When Rights Collide" at least two or three times. Annotate as you read in order to understand the reading more fully, using the annotating strategies from the checklist above. You may want to review our demonstration of each activity before you begin.

A thorough, productive annotation of this reading will help you complete the remaining critical reading exercises in this chapter.

Outlining

Outlining may be a part of the annotating process, or it may be a separate critical reading activity that follows and extends your annotation of a text. Making an outline on a separate piece of paper is especially helpful when you need to remember the reading or when it is complicated and hard to follow.

When you write, you probably do some outlining to sort through and organize your ideas. In the same way, outlining as you read leads you to focus on a text's most important ideas, separating what is central from what is peripheral. Outlining also reveals just how the selection is organized and may help you identify any shortcomings in its organization or logic. Since it displays just the main points, an outline presents only the framework of an essay and hence is quite general, even abstract.

Outlining a reading is a two-step process. First, you must identify the main ideas. Look for the sequence of main points that carries the reading along. Some paragraphs may contain no main ideas, while others may contain one or more. Then, you should underline (or otherwise highlight) the main ideas on the text or list them in your own words in the margin.

In the King excerpt on pages 13–17, the numbered list in the margins is a scratch, or informal, outline that captures the movement of King's argument and the main points of the essay. Listing it separately enables us to see the framework of the reading more easily. The outline is printed here, slightly reworded for consistency:

1. White moderates' shallow understanding and lukewarm acceptance are a barrier to racial justice.
2. Tension is necessary for progress toward freedom.
3. Peaceful actions can be justified even if they result in violence.
4. People must take action now to ensure racial justice.
5. There are two opposing groups of Negroes: complacent and violent.
6. King stands between complacent and violent Negro groups.
7. King's movement has prevented racial violence.
8. Protest is a natural result of yearning for freedom.
9. We need extremists for good causes.
10. Some whites have supported King.

The main ideas are expressed in our own sentences. This outline captures the movement of King's argument and the main points of the essay. A later section in this chapter will demonstrate a more formal and specialized kind of outline that results from a logical analysis of an argument.

Scratch outlining adequately identifies the sequence of main ideas or events in all kinds of writing. It can increase your understanding of a difficult reading and ensure that you will remember it longer. As you attempt to produce the kinds of writing you read in this book, outlining will enable you to reflect on the decisions other writers have made about organizing and ordering their materials.

Exercise 3

Make a scratch outline for "When Rights Collide."

Summarizing

Summarizing an unfamiliar, difficult reading is an excellent way to figure out what it means and to remember what you have read. Whereas previewing prepares you to read with a questioning attitude, annotating alerts you to the text's language and ideas, and outlining reveals the order of main points, summarizing a reading selection not only gives you its gist but also helps you to see how its meaning is constructed. Summarizing builds on all of the earlier critical reading strategies, but goes further. It includes synthesis and composing—putting together in your own words the important ideas and information to make a coherent meaning. The act of writing a summary or *abstract* (as it is sometimes called) requires the reader to make critical judgments and interpretations along the way. Therefore, one reader's summary is likely to differ in significant ways from another reader's. Comparing these summaries can lead to a deeper understanding of the reading selection and to fascinating insights into one's own reading process.

There is no exact formula about how long a summary should be in relation to the original. Some readings are dense with new concepts, while others intersperse concepts with quotations, charts and tables, and illustrations. A summary should be long enough to present the main ideas coherently. To summarize the King excerpt on pages 13–17, for example:

> King expresses his disappointment with white moderates who, by opposing tension-producing nonviolent direct action, become a barrier to racial justice. He explains that tension is often necessary for social progress and that nonviolent direct action can be justified even if it results in violence. He argues that racial justice will come about only by taking action now. Responding to charges of extremism from white moderates, King claims that he has actually prevented extreme racial violence by directing the frustrations of oppressed blacks into nonviolent protest. He asserts that extremism for a good cause is justified.

This summary relies on key words from King's writing, but all the sentences are our own. We have abstracted the main ideas and woven them into a coherent summary.

Since summarizing is time-consuming and challenging, you should reserve it for material that is unusually hard to understand, perhaps material on which you will be tested or material about which you must write convincingly.

A Checklist for Summarizing

To summarize a text in your own words in order to master difficult material or ideas, try the following steps:

- Read and reread the material, annotating as you go. At this stage you are trying to become thoroughly familiar with the material.
- Identify the main ideas, either by making a scratch outline or by underlining the main ideas.
- Write a summary that includes only the main ideas, not illustrations or examples or quotations, and make sure that it is coherent and reads smoothly. Although your summary will rely on key terms and concepts in the material, it must be stated entirely in your own words.

Exercise 4

Summarize "When Rights Collide."

Taking Inventory

Like outlining and summarizing, taking inventory builds on and extends annotating. Taking inventory involves analyzing and classifying your annotations, searching systematically for patterns in the text, and interpreting their significance. An inventory is basically a list. When you take inventory, you make various kinds of lists to explore their meaning. You will want to use this strategy when you are preparing to write about a reading, but you can also use it simply to read critically.

This section presents three basic kinds of inventories: (1) inventory of annotations to discover and interpret patterns, (2) inventory of oppositions to reveal contrasting perspectives within the text, and (3) inventory of figurative language to uncover the author's feelings and attitudes.

Inventory of Annotations

As you review your annotations on a particular reading, you may discover that the language and ideas cluster in various ways. Taking inventory of the patterns you've discovered while annotating allows you to explore their possible meaning and significance.

Inventorying annotations is a three-step process:

1. First, examine your annotations for patterns or repetitions of any
   kind. Here are some possibilities:

   recurring images

   noticeable stylistic features

   repeated descriptions

   consistent ways of characterizing people or events and of defining
   terms

   repeated words and phrases

   repeated subjects or topics

   repeated examples or illustrations

   reliance on particular writing strategies

2. List and group the items in the pattern.

3. Finally, decide what the pattern indicates about the reading.

The patterns you discover will depend on the kind of reading you are
analyzing and on the thoroughness of your annotations. In our annotations of the King excerpt on pages 13–17, we noted several different
patterns, including images, quotable statements, and authorities. To
learn more about why King cited these particular authorities, we listed
and grouped them as follows:

Philosopher: Socrates

Religious leaders: Jesus, Amos, Paul, Luther, and Bunyan

Political leaders: Lincoln and Jefferson

In an encyclopedia, we read the entry about each person on the list,
trying to connect the individual's particular philosophy to King's criticism of moderates and his justification for tension-producing direct
action. With just a little reading, we found enough material for a brief
paper analyzing King's argumentative strategy of quoting and aligning
himself with revered authorities. King relies on this strategy throughout
the letter (reprinted in its entirety in Chapter 10), mentioning and
quoting many more authorities.

Inventory of Oppositions

Another way to take inventory is to study the pattern of oppositions
within the text. All texts carry within themselves voices of opposition.

These voices may echo the views and values of critical readers the writer anticipates or predecessors to which the writer is responding in some way; they may even reflect the writer's own conflicting values. You may need to look closely for such a dialogue of opposing voices within the text.

When we think of oppositions, we ordinarily think of polarities such as *yes* and *no*, *up* and *down*, *black* and *white*, *new* and *old*. Some oppositions, however, may be more subtle. The excerpt from the "Letter from Birmingham Jail" is rich in such oppositions: *moderate* versus *extremist*, *order* versus *justice*, *direct action* versus *passive acceptance*, *expression* versus *repression*. These oppositions are not accidental; and they form a significant pattern that gives a critical reader important information about the essay.

A careful reading will show that one of the two terms in an opposition is nearly always valued over the other. In the King passage, for example, *extremist* is valued over *moderate*. This preference for extremism is surprising. The critical reader should ask why, when white extremists like the Ku Klux Klan have committed so many outrages against African-Americans, King would prefer extremism. If King is trying to convince his readers to accept his point of view, why would he represent himself as an extremist? Moreover, why would a clergyman advocate extremism instead of moderation?

Only by studying the pattern of oppositions can you answer these questions. Then you will see that King sets up this opposition to force his readers to examine their own values and realize that they are in fact misplaced. Instead of working toward justice, he says, those who support law and order maintain the unjust status quo. Getting his readers to think of the white moderate as blocking rather than facilitating peaceful change brings them to align themselves with King and perhaps even embrace his strategy of nonviolent resistance.

Taking inventory of oppositions is a four-step method of analysis:

1. Divide a piece of paper in half lengthwise by drawing a line down the middle. In the left-hand column, list those words and phrases from the text that you think indicate oppositions. Enter in the right-hand column the word or phrase that is the opposite of each word or phrase in the left-hand column. You may have to paraphrase or even supply this opposite word or phrase if it is not stated directly in the text.

2. For each pair of words or phrases, put an asterisk next to the one that seems to be preferred by the writer.

3. Study the list of preferred words or phrases, and identify what you think is the predominant system of values put forth by the text. Do the same for the other list, identifying the alternative system or systems of values implied in the text. Take about ten minutes to describe the oppositions in writing.

4. To explore these conflicting points of view, write for about five minutes presenting one side, and then for another five minutes presenting the other side. Use as many of the words or phrases from the list as you can—explaining, extending, and justifying the values they imply. You may also, if you wish, quarrel with the choice of words or phrases on the grounds that they are slanted or over-simplify the issue.

The following inventory and analysis of the King excerpt on pages 13–17 demonstrates the four-step method for inventorying oppositions.

LISTING OPPOSITIONS. This list of oppositions with asterisks next to King's preferred word or phrase in each pair demonstrates steps 1 and 2:

white moderate	*extremist
order	*justice
negative peace	*positive peace
absence of justice	*presence of justice
goals	*methods
*direct action	passive acceptance
*exposed tension	hidden tension
*robbed	robber
*individual	society
*words	silence
*expression	repression
*extension of justice	preservation of injustice
*extremist for love, truth, and justice	extremist for immo-rality

ANALYZING OPPOSITIONS. Step 3 produced the following description of the conflicting points of view:

In this reading, King addresses as "white moderates" the clergymen who criticized him. He sees the moderate position in essentially negative terms, whereas extremism can be either negative or positive. Moderation is equated with passivity, acceptance of the status quo, fear of disorder, perhaps even fear of any change. The moderates believe justice can wait, whereas law and order cannot. Yet, as King points out, there is no law and order for blacks who are victimized and denied their constitutional rights.

The argument King has with the white moderates is basically over means and ends. Both agree on the ends but disagree on the means that should be taken to secure those ends. What means are justified to achieve one's goals? How does one decide? King is willing to risk a certain amount of tension and disorder to bring about justice; he suggests that if progress is not made, more disorder, not less, is bound to result. In a sense King represents himself as a moderate caught between the two extremes—the white moderates' "do-nothingism" and the black extremists' radicalism.

At the same time, King substitutes the opposition between moderation and extremism with an opposition between two kinds of extremism, one for love and the other for hate. In fact, he represents himself as an extremist willing to make whatever sacrifices—and perhaps even to take whatever means—are necessary to reach his goal of justice.

CONSIDERING ALTERNATIVE POINTS OF VIEW. Step 4 entailed five minutes of writing exploring the point of view opposed to the author's and five more minutes of writing presenting King's possible response to this point of view:

> *The moderates' side*: I can sympathize with the moderates' fear of further disorder and violence. Even though King advocates nonviolence, violence does result. He may not cause it, but it does occur because of him. Moderates do not really advocate passive acceptance of injustice, but want to pursue justice through legal means. These methods may be slow, but since ours is a system of law, the only way to make change is through that system. King wants to shake up the system, to force it to move more quickly for fear of violence. That strikes me as blackmail, as bad as if he were committing violence himself. Couldn't public opinion be brought to bear on the legal system to move more quickly? Can't we elect officials who will change unjust laws and see that the just ones are obeyed? The *vote* should be the weapon in a democracy, shouldn't it?

> *King's possible response*: He would probably argue that this viewpoint is naive. One of the major injustices at that time was that blacks were prevented from voting, and no elected official would risk going against those who voted for him or her. King would probably agree that public opinion needs to be changed, that people need to be educated, but he would also argue that education is not enough when people are being systematically deprived of their legal rights. The very system of law that should protect people was being used as a weapon against blacks in the South. The only way to get something done is to shake people up, make them aware of the injustice they are allowing to continue. Seeing their own police officers committing violence should make people question their own values and begin to take action to right the wrongs.

Inventory of Figurative Language

Inventorying can also be used to analyze figurative language patterns in a text. Figurative language (metaphor, simile, and symbol), which takes words literally associated with one object or idea and transfers them to another object or idea, communicates more than direct statement can convey. Such language enhances meaning because it embodies abstract ideas in vivid images. For example, King uses the image of a dam to express the abstract idea of the blockage of justice. Figurative language also enriches meaning by drawing upon a complex of feeling and association. Connotations associated with one thing are transferred to the other, as when King compares the injustice suffered by blacks to a boil. Most people associate boils with throbbing pain and would do almost anything to relieve the discomfort.

As oppositions indicate relations of contrast and difference, figures of speech indicate relations of resemblance and likeness. Here are definitions and examples of the most common figures of speech:

Metaphor implicitly compares two different things by identifying them with each other. For instance, when King calls the white moderate "the Negro's great stumbling block in his stride toward freedom," he does not mean that the white moderate literally trips the Negro who is attempting to walk toward freedom. The sentence makes sense only if understood figuratively: the white moderate trips up the Negro by frustrating every effort to eliminate injustice.

Simile, a more explicit form of comparison, uses the word *like* or *as* to signal the relation of two seemingly unrelated things. King uses simile when he says that injustice is "like a boil that can never be cured so long as it is covered up." This simile makes several points of comparison between injustice and a boil. It suggests that injustice is a disease of society as a boil is a disease of the body and that injustice, like a boil, must be exposed or it will fester and worsen.

Symbolism compares two things by making one stand for the other. King uses the white moderate as a symbol for supposed liberals and would-be supporters of civil rights who are actually frustrating the cause.

How these figures of speech are used in a text reveals something of the writer's feelings about the subject and attitude toward prospective readers. It may even suggest the writer's feelings about the act of writing itself. Taking inventory of patterns of figurative language can provide insight into the tone of the writing and the text's emotional effect on its readers.

Taking inventory of figurative language is a three-step procedure:

1. List all the figures of speech you find in the reading—metaphor, simile, and symbol.
2. Group the figures of speech that appear to express similar feelings and attitudes, and label each group.

3. Write for ten to fifteen minutes, exploring the meaning of these patterns.

The following inventory and analysis of the King excerpt on pages 13–17 demonstrates the three steps for inventorying figurative language.

LISTING FIGURES OF SPEECH. Step 1 produced this inventory:

order is a dangerously structured dam that blocks the flow

social progress should flow

stumbling block in the stride toward freedom

injustice is like a boil that can never be cured

the light of human conscience and air of national opinion

time is something to be used, neutral, an ally, ripe

quicksand of racial injustice

the solid rock of human dignity

human progress never rolls in on wheels of inevitability

men are co-workers with God

groups springing up

promised land of racial justice

vital urge engulfed

pent-up resentments

normal and healthy discontent can be channeled into the creative outlet of nonviolent direct action

root out injustice

powerful action is an antidote

disease of segregation

GROUPING FIGURES OF SPEECH. Step 2 yielded three groups:

Sickness: segregation is a disease; action is healthy, the only antidote; injustice is like a boil

Underground: tension is hidden; resentments are pent-up, repressed; injustice must be rooted out; extremist groups are springing up; discontent can be channeled into a creative outlet

Blockage: forward movement is impeded by obstacles—the dam, stumbling block; human progress never rolls in on wheels of inevitability; social progress should flow

EXPLORING PATTERNS. Step 3 entailed about ten minutes of writing to explore the meaning of the groups listed in step 2:

> The patterns of blockage and underground suggest a feeling of frustration. Inertia is a problem; movement forward toward progress or upward toward the promised land is stalled. There seems to be a strong need to break through the resistance, the passivity, the discontent and to be creative, active, vital. These are probably King's feelings both about his attempt to lead purposeful, effective demonstrations and his effort to write a convincing letter.
>
> The simile of injustice being like a boil links the two patterns of underground and sickness, suggesting something bad, a disease, is inside the people or the society. The cure is to expose, to root out, the blocked hatred and injustice and release the tension or emotion that has so long been repressed. This implies that repression itself is the evil, not simply what is repressed.

A Checklist for Taking Inventory

To recapitulate, it is helpful when reading closely to make inventories of the following:

- your annotations, in order to summarize and expand your observations about the reading
- oppositions within the text, in order to discover the conversations taking place between the author and other writers and readers, and even between the author's own ideas and values
- figurative language, in order to uncover clues about the author's attitudes and feelings on the subject, the writing situation, and even about writing itself

---

Exercise 5

We have demonstrated three different inventories of annotations: (1) taking inventory of your own annotations on a text, (2) taking inventory of the oppositions within a text, and (3) taking inventory of the figurative language in a text. You may choose one of these inventories to complete for "When Rights Collide," or your instructor may assign one of them.

If you inventory your own annotations, you may not need to annotate further. If you inventory oppositions or figurative language, however, you will want to first annotate the text carefully for these special features. Review the steps and demonstration for the inventory you choose.

If you inventory oppositions, these first possible pairs will get you started:

*interference—individual wishes

voluntarism—*rules or laws

etc.

The first pair comes from paragraph 1, the second from paragraph 2. Another reader might word these oppositions somewhat differently or see another possible opposition in paragraph 2 (*government—the people). We have asterisked the word or phrase preferred by the author. Remember that sometimes the oppositions are only implied, requiring you to come up with your own words or phrases to identify them.

If you inventory figurative language, these first two images from paragraphs 1 and 2 will get you started:

camouflaged viewpoint

might as well bar holy water

etc.

Analyzing an Argument

All writing makes assertions, statements that the writer wants readers to accept as true. In autobiographical and explanatory writing, readers are generally willing to assume that writers know what they are saying—that autobiographers' self-disclosures are sincere and experts' explanations are authoritative and accurate. In argumentative and evaluative writing, the writer's assertions make up the argument of an essay. Because many topics discussed in these kinds of writing are open to debate, readers are reluctant to accept the writer's assertions at face value. In these situations, the writer must attempt to convince readers to accept his or her assertions as true. Readers expect writers not only to state their assertions but also to give reasons for believing their assertions and backing for their reasons.

An argument has basically two parts: a claim and support. The *claim* asserts an opinion, judgment, or point of view that the writer wants readers to accept as true or, at least, as reasonable. In an essay, the claim serves as the essay's thesis. The *support* is the heart of the argument, the reasoning that seeks to convince readers to accept the claim. Supporting material consists of reasons, backing to justify the claim on the basis of the reasons, and refutation of opposing arguments. The *reasons* explain why the writer thinks the claim should be acceptable to readers. The *backing* provides evidence, explanation, and further justification. The *refutation* acknowledges those opposing arguments that make sense, while rebutting those that do not.

Analyzing an argument involves first identifying its claim and support, and then evaluating the argument. You can identify the claim and support right on the text by annotating, or you can use a separate piece of paper to write out an outline like the one illustrated in the next section.

Identifying the Parts of the Argument

Argumentative writing can be quite complex. To examine an author's line of reasoning in an argument, the critical reader must read the text closely and set out its claims and support schematically. This kind of outline—whether it is written directly on the text or on a separate piece of paper—is more detailed and specialized than the scratch outline introduced earlier. However, once you've made a scratch outline of a selection, it might provide the basis for your argument outline.

In identifying the parts of an argument, you may quote the writer's words directly or use your own words to paraphrase the writer. Quoting has the advantage of allowing you to focus on the writer's key words and phrases, while paraphrasing is sometimes crucial because it enables you to make explicit those points that are only implied. Your argument outline does not have to cover every point or account for all nuances of meaning. The aim of this critical reading strategy is to give you a good sense of how the reasoning process proceeds so that you can understand and evaluate the argument.

Following is an overview of the process of identifying claims and supports (reasons, backing, refutations) central to analyzing any argument. In each case, we have provided a question to help you focus on the particular element.

IDENTIFYING THE WRITER'S CLAIM OR THESIS. Ask yourself: *What opinion, idea, or point of view is the writer trying to convince me to accept?*

In the King excerpt on pages 13–17, the claim appears in the first paragraph: "I have almost reached the regrettable conclusion that the Negro's great stumbling block in his stride toward freedom is not the White Citizen's Counciler or the Ku Klux Klanner, but the white moderate. . . ."

Notice that the quotation includes two key words—*almost* and *regrettable*—that are important to evaluating the effectiveness of this argument. The word *almost* serves as a qualifier to limit the certainty with which King asserts his claim: he is *almost* but not quite certain of it. Similarly, the word *regrettable* indicates that King takes no pleasure in having come to this conclusion and suggests that he and the reader might share common values and goals.

IDENTIFYING THE REASONS. Ask yourself: *What statements does the writer make that tell me why I should accept the claim?*

Locating the reasons in an argument is often a challenging task. Writers seldom announce their reasons with words like *because* and *since*. In most cases, readers have to tease out reasons that are stated indirectly or tossed in with other kinds of statements.

Occasionally a writer will make it easy for readers by announcing at least some of the reasons in the opening paragraph or by beginning each paragraph with a new reason. Few essays, however, are that formulaic. Be prepared to find reasons anywhere in a paragraph, and don't be surprised if more than one reason appears in a paragraph or if a single reason is developed over several paragraphs.

Identifying the reasons in an argument involves selection and interpretation. Therefore, the reasons one reader identifies may differ somewhat from the reasons other readers identify. For example, to support his claim that the white moderate is an obstacle to racial progress, King's first reason seems to be that "the white moderate . . . is more devoted to 'order' than to justice." Look at the argument outline on pages 35–37 for our list of his further reasons to support the claim. Based on your reading of the excerpt, do you identify the same reasons?

IDENTIFYING THE BACKING. Ask yourself: *What information or explanation does the writer give to justify acceptance of the claim on the basis of this reason?*

King's claim is that the white moderate is an obstacle in the progress toward racial justice. His first reason for this claim, we have noted, is that "the white moderate . . . is more devoted to 'order' than to justice." This reason asserts a fact about white moderates, that they value order over justice. King does not attempt to prove this fact explicitly, in part because his reference is directly to the language of the Alabama clergymen, who have advocated "law and order." But he uses this reason to introduce backing suggesting that those who value order over justice are wrong, backing that supports his original claim:

> I had hoped that the white moderate would understand that law and order exist for the purpose of establishing justice and that when they fail in this purpose they become the dangerously structured dams that block the flow of social progress. (paragraph 2)

The words, *I had hoped*, indicate King's disappointment that he and his opponents do not share the same values. He asserts that law and order should be the means to an end—justice—and not an end in themselves. Arguing by analogy (law and order is to progress toward justice as a dam is to water), he implies that when the means become the end, progress toward the true end is blocked.

From this example, you can see that reasons and backing may serve a variety of functions in supporting a claim. Backing must be clearly identified, however, if you are to understand how an argument works and evaluate it. Among the kinds of backing writers use to elaborate on reasons and support their claims are the following:

Asserting Fact: Statements can be proven objectively to be true. If a writer asserts that a statement is factual and if readers accept the statement as fact, then readers will be very likely to accept the claim supported by that fact. A special kind of assertion of fact uses statistics.

Arguing by Example: An example is an individual instance taken to be representative of a general pattern. In using one or more examples, the writer argues that if the examples are true, then readers should accept the more general reason or claim. An anecdote is a special kind of example that tells a story about a single episode asserted to be representative.

Arguing by Analogy: An analogy is a comparison to a parallel case. By using analogy, the writer argues that a claim reasonable for one case should also be reasonable for the analogous case.

Invoking Authority: An authority is a recognized expert. By invoking authority, the writer argues that because the claim is in agreement with the authority's words or actions, readers ought to accept the claim.

Arguing a Causal Relationship: A cause is the reason or motive for a particular result. By arguing that a causal relationship exists, the writer asserts that one thing actually results from another. A causal relation differs from a correlation: in a causal relation, one thing produces or brings about the other, whereas in a correlation, one thing is merely associated with the other.

Asserting Shared Beliefs: Shared beliefs or assumptions are often called common knowledge. By asserting shared beliefs, the writer argues that if something is widely believed, then readers also should accept it.

Asserting Shared Values: Many claims are based on values and judgments. By asserting shared values, the writer argues that if readers and the writer share certain values and those values underlie the claim, then readers also should accept the writer's claim.

IDENTIFYING THE REFUTATION. Ask yourself: *What opposing arguments does the writer anticipate, and how are they dealt with?*

"Letter from Birmingham Jail" can be seen as an extended refutation of the charges made against King and his supporters by the forces of "moderation." In the opening of the third paragraph of the excerpt, for example, King refers directly to the clergymen's statement:

> In your statement you assert that our actions, even though peaceful, must be condemned because they precipitate violence. But is this a logical assertion? Isn't this like condemning a robbed man because his possession of money precipitated the evil act of robbery?

King's refutation begins by restating the argument against him: that his actions must be condemned because they precipitate violence. He responds first by posing a rhetorical question, and then by answering the question with a series of analogies, many of which appeal to authority.

Like reasons, the refutation generally requires backing to provide justification for the claim. To be convinced, readers need to know *why* you offer a reason and *why* you refute a counterargument. These "why's" are supplied by inventive backing.

Following this process, we made an outline of the argument in the King excerpt, identifying the claim, reasons for the claim, refutation of counterarguments, and backing. Our written outline is illustrated below. Notice that we retained King's own language whenever possible and that we labeled the kinds of support offered. Follow this format when you write out an outline of an argument.

Claim: "The Negro's great stumbling block in his stride toward freedom is . . . the white moderate."

Reason 1: The white moderate is concerned more with preserving law and order than with achieving justice (paragraph 2)

Backing:

"Law and order exist for the purpose of establishing justice" (*assertion of shared values*)

"When they fail in this purpose they become the dangerously structured dams that block the flow of social progress" (*argument by analogy*)

Reason 2: The white moderate doesn't recognize that "the present tension in the South is a necessary phase" in the struggle for justice (paragraph 2)

Backing:

The tension results from injustice, not from King's activities (*assertion of fact*)

Nonviolent direct action helps cure tension by bringing injustice into the open as one would expose a boil (*argument by analogy*)

Refutation 1: King recognizes the white moderate may agree with the goal of justice, but he criticizes the white moderate for not supporting the means necessary to achieve it (paragraph 3)

Backing:

"Isn't this like condemning a robbed man because his possession of money precipitated the evil act of robbery?" (*argument by analogy*)

It seems unreasonable to condemn Socrates or Jesus for their commitment to truth and justice (*invocation of authority*)

Reason 3: White moderates believe that blacks are too impatient (paragraph 4)

Backing:

White moderates have a "tragic misconception of time" (*assertion of fact*)

Time itself will not "cure all ills," but is "neutral" (*assertion of shared beliefs*)

Progress is not inevitable, but results from tireless work and creativity (*assertion of shared beliefs*)

Refutation 2: King rejects the characterization of himself as an extremist (paragraph 5)

Backing:

King stands between complacent and violent blacks (*assertion of fact*)

Nonviolent protest has been the way of King's group (*assertion of fact*)

Nonviolent direct action has prevented bloodshed and violence (*assertion of fact*)

Reason 4: The white moderate has not recognized that "the yearning for freedom eventually manifests itself" (paragraph 8)

Backing:

Black and brown and yellow people around the world are struggling urgently for racial justice (*assertion of fact*)

"The Negro has many pent-up resentments" and must release them through nonviolent direct action (*argument by causal relationship*)

Refutation 3: King turns around and happily accepts the characterization of himself as an extremist (paragraph 9)

Backing:

Many great religious and political leaders have been considered extremist: Jesus, Amos, Paul, Luther, Bunyan, Lincoln, Jefferson (*invocation of authority*)

It is good to be an extremist for "love, truth, and goodness" (*assertion of shared values*)

Refutation 4: Some white moderates support King (paragraph 10)

Backing:

Some whites have participated in King's crusade: McGill, Smith, Golden, Dabbs, Braden, and Boyle (*invocation of authority*)

These whites recognize that action is necessary (*assertion of shared beliefs*)

Evaluating the Argument

Once you have identified the claim and support and have either annotated or outlined its structure, you may begin to evaluate it. A successful argument makes three kinds of appeals: an appeal to the readers' sense of *logic*; an appeal to their *emotions*; and an appeal to their sense of *ethics*. In evaluating an argument, you should examine how these appeals are made and decide how convincing they are. An argument need not make all three appeals, but those that do tend to be stronger and more convincing.

LOGICAL APPEAL. Logic refers to the quality of the reasoning in an argument. Three conditions must be met for an argument to be logically acceptable:

1. The support must be *appropriate* to the claim.
2. The support must be *believable*.
3. The support must be *consistent*.

We call these conditions the ABC's of sound reasoning: appropriateness, believability, consistency.

Testing for Appropriateness. By appropriateness, we mean that readers recognize the logical, if-then relationship between the support and the claim. In other words, if the support is acceptable, then acceptance of the claim must follow. To test for appropriateness ask: Is the support relevant to the claim? Does the support justify accepting the claim?

Appropriateness of support comes most often into question when the writer is arguing by analogy or invoking authority. In the King excerpt, for example, Reason 1 on our outline is backed by the analogy we paraphrased as "law and order is to progress toward justice what a dam is to water." If readers do not see any similarity between these two cases, then the analogy will fail the test of appropriateness.

In backing Refutation 1 on our outline, King argues by analogy and, at the same time, invokes authority: "Isn't this like condemning Socrates because his unswerving commitment to truth and his philosophical inquiries precipitated the act by the misguided populace in which they made him drink hemlock?" (paragraph 3). Readers not only must judge the appropriateness of comparing these two cases, but must also judge whether it is appropriate to accept Socrates as an authority on this subject. Since Socrates is generally respected for his teachings on justice, his words and actions are likely to be considered by readers appropriate to King's situation in Birmingham.

False analogy, then, occurs when two cases are not sufficiently parallel to lead readers to accept the claim; *false use of authority* occurs when writers invoke as expert in the field being discussed a person whose expertise or authority lies not in the given field but in another. Following are some other common flaws or fallacies in reasoning that cause an argument to fail the test of appropriateness:

Non sequitur (Latin, meaning "it does not follow"): Occurs when one statement is not logically connected to another.

Ad hominem (Latin, meaning argument "against the man"): Occurs when the writer personally attacks his or her opponents instead of finding fault with their argument.

Straw man: Occurs when the writer directs the argument against a claim that nobody actually holds or that everyone agrees is weak; often involves misrepresentation or distortion of the opposing argument.

Red herring: Occurs when a writer raises an irrelevant issue to draw attention away from the central issue.

Post hoc, ergo propter hoc (Latin, meaning "after this, therefore because of this"): Occurs when the writer implies that because one event follows another, the first caused the second. Chronology is not the same as causality.

Testing for Believability. By believability, we mean the degree to which readers are willing to accept the assertions supporting the claim. Whereas some assertions are self-evidently true, most depend on the readers' judgment of what to rely on. Common kinds of backing include necessary truths, facts, statistics, examples, and authorities.

Necessary truths are assertions that, by definition, cannot be denied. If you were to deny a necessary truth, you would be contradicting yourself.

King asserts a necessary truth early in his "Letter from Birmingham Jail" (page 525) when he tries to refute the opposing argument that as a resident of Atlanta, Georgia, he is an outsider who should not have come to Birmingham, Alabama: "Anyone who lives inside the United States can never be considered an outsider anywhere within its bounds." King asserts this statement as truth because the word *outsider* means someone who does not live inside. Readers may, however, question the appropriateness of it as a refutation because King has changed the meaning of the terms used by his opponents. Whereas they referred to his not being a resident of Birmingham, he refers to himself as being a resident of the United States. In other words, they are claiming that the issue is a local one, while he is claiming that it is a national one.

Facts are statements that can be proven objectively to be true. The believability of facts depends on their *accuracy* (they should not distort or misrepresent reality), *completeness* (they should not omit important details), and the *trustworthiness* of their sources (sources should be qualified and unbiased). In the excerpt on pages 13–17, for instance, King asserts as fact that the African-American will not wait much longer for racial justice (paragraph 8). His critics might question the factuality of this assertion by asking: Is it true of all African-Americans? How much longer will they wait? How does King know what the African-American will and will not do?

Statistics are often assumed to be factual but are really only interpretations of numerical data. The believability of statistics depends on the *comparability* of the data (apples cannot be compared to oranges), the *accuracy* of the methods of gathering and analyzing data (representative samples should be used and variables accounted for), and the *trustworthiness* of the sources (sources should be qualified and unbiased).

Examples and *anecdotes* are particular instances that if accepted as believable lead readers to accept the general claim. The believability of examples depends on their *representativeness* (whether they are truly typical and thus generalizable) and their *specificity* (whether particular details make them seem true to life). Even if a vivid example or gripping anecdote does not convince readers, it strengthens argumentative writing by clarifying the meaning and bringing home the point dramatically. In paragraph 5 of the excerpt, for example, King supports his generalization that there are black nationalist extremists motivated by bitterness and hatred by citing the specific example of Elijah Muhammad's Muslim movement. Conversely, in paragraph 9, he refers to Jesus, Paul, Luther, and others as examples of extremists motivated by love. These examples support his assertion that extremism is not in itself wrong, that any judgment must depend on what cause one is an extremist for.

Authorities are people to whom the writer attributes expertise on a given subject. Such authorities not only must be appropriate, as mentioned earlier, but they must be believable. The believability of authorities depends on their *credibility*, on whether the reader accepts them as experts on the topic at hand. King cites authorities repeatedly throughout the essay. In our brief excerpt, for instance, he refers not only to religious leaders like Jesus and Luther but also to American political leaders like Lincoln and Jefferson. These figures are certain to have a high degree of credibility among King's readers.

In addition, you should be aware of the following fallacies in reasoning that undermine the believability of an argument:

Begging the question: Occurs when the believability of the support itself depends upon the believability of the claim. Another name for this kind of fallacy is *circular reasoning*.

Failing to accept the burden of proof: Occurs when the writer asserts a claim but provides no support for it.

Hasty generalization: Occurs when the writer asserts a claim on the basis of an isolated example.

Sweeping generalization: Occurs when the writer fails to qualify the applicability of the claim and asserts that it applies to "all" instances instead of to "some" instances.

Overgeneralization: Occurs when the writer fails to qualify the claim and asserts that it is "certainly true" rather than that it "may be true."

Testing for Consistency. In looking for consistency, you should be concerned that all the support works together and that none of the supporting statements contradicts any of the other statements. In addition, the support, taken together, should provide sufficient reason for accepting the claim. To test for consistency ask: Are any of the supporting statements contradictory? Do they provide sufficient support for the claim? Are there opposing arguments that are not refuted?

A critical reader might regard as contradictory King's characterizing himself first as a moderate between the forces of complacency and violence, and later as an extremist opposed to the forces of violence. King attempts to reconcile this apparent contradiction by explicitly redefining extremism in paragraph 9.

Similarly, the fact that King fails to examine and refute every legal recourse available to his cause might allow a critical reader to question the sufficiency of his supporting arguments.

In evaluating the consistency of an argument, you should also be aware of the following fallacies:

Slippery slope: Occurs when the writer argues that taking one step will lead inevitably to a next step, one that is undesirable.

Equivocation: Occurs when a writer uses the same term in two different senses in an argument.

Oversimplification: Occurs when an argument obscures or denies the complexity of the issue.

Either-or reasoning: Occurs when the writer reduces the issue to only two alternatives which are polar opposites.

Double standard: Occurs when two or more comparable things are judged according to different standards; often involves holding the opposing argument to a higher standard than the one to which the writer holds his or her own argument.

Thus, in evaluating the logic of King's claim that white moderates are a primary obstacle in the progress toward racial justice, we consider the appropriateness, believability, and consistency of his supporting reasons and backing:

> King writes both to the ministers who published the letter in the Birmingham newspaper and also to the people of Birmingham. He seems to want to justify his group's actions. He challenges white moderates, but he also tries to avoid antagonizing them. Given this purpose and his readers, his supporting statements are generally appropriate. He relies mainly on assertions of shared belief with his readers and on memorable analogies. For example, he knows his readers will accept assertions like "law and order exist for the purpose of establishing justice"; it is good to be an extremist for "love, truth, and goodness"; and progress is not inevitable, but results from tireless work and creativity. His analogies seem appropriate for his readers. For example, he compares injustice to a boil that nonviolent action must expose to the air if it is to be healed. Several times, King invokes authorities (Socrates, Jesus, Amos, Paul, Luther, Bunyan, Jefferson) his readers revere. Throughout his argument, King avoids fallacies of inappropriateness. Likewise, his support is believable in terms of the well-known authorities he cites; the facts he asserts (for example, that racial tension results from injustice, not from nonviolent action); and the examples he offers (such as his assertion that extremism is not in itself wrong—as exemplified by Jesus, Paul, and Luther). If there is an inconsistency in the argument, it is the contradiction between King's portraits of himself both as a moderating force and as an "extremist for love"; but his redefinition of extremism as a positive value for any social change is central to the overall persuasiveness of his logical appeal to white moderates.

EMOTIONAL APPEAL. By appealing to readers' emotions, the writer tries to excite readers and involve them emotionally in the argument. Sometimes, however, a writer may use slanted, highly charged language to manipulate the reader's emotions. Even though this kind of manipulative argument might seem convincing, it is unacceptable because it is unfair.

All words have connotations, associations that enrich their meaning. These connotations give words much of their emotional power. In the preceding paragraph, for example, the word *manipulate* arouses an emotional response as well as an intellectual one. Being manipulated implies being treated like a puppet. No one wants to be manipulated. We used this word to make readers see why manipulative arguments are unfair even if they seem to be convincing.

When you evaluate an argument's emotional appeal, you are basically asking yourself: Do I feel manipulated by this argument? Knowing that figurative language can arouse strong emotions and that arguments based on such language may be questionable, we asked ourselves just this question in regard to King's use of the dam metaphor in paragraph 2. This is what our question produced:

> When King equates law and order with dams, he is trying to change his readers'
> understanding of the situation. The dam metaphor represents law and order

negatively rather than positively. Dams are holding places that serve a positive function but they can also be seen as obstacles that block the natural and free flow of water. When water is equated to social progress, the dams clearly become obstacles. Why he describes the dams as "dangerously structured" is unclear. Perhaps he wants to suggest the possibility that they are a threat to safety and peace. This would be a surprising turn since dams are supposed to protect us. Anyway, the dam metaphor makes the white moderate, who thinks of himself as advancing the cause of justice by upholding law and order, see himself instead as actually blocking progress. It doesn't seem to be an unfair or manipulative use of language, though the implied threat could be seen as unfair.

ETHICAL APPEAL. Through this appeal, writers try to persuade readers to respect and believe them. Because readers may not know them personally or even by reputation, they must present an image of themselves in their writing that will gain their readers' confidence. This image cannot be made directly but must be made indirectly, through the arguments, language, and the system of values and beliefs implied in the writing.

One way to gauge the author's credibility is to identify the tone of the argument. Tone is concerned not so much with what is said as with how it is said. It conveys the writer's attitude toward the subject and toward the reader. By reading sensitively, you should be able to evaluate the writer's stance and attitude through the tone of the writing. To identify the tone, list whatever descriptive adjectives come to mind in response to either of these questions: How would you characterize the tone of this selection? Judging from this piece of writing, what kind of person does the author seem to be? Here is an answer to the second question, based on the excerpt from "Letter from Birmingham Jail":

> I know something about King from television programs on the civil rights movement. But if I were to talk about my impression of him from this passage, I'd use words like patient, thoughtful, well educated, moral, confident. He doesn't lose his temper, but tries to convince his readers by making a case that is reasoned carefully and painstakingly. He's trying to change people's attitudes; no matter how annoyed he might be with them he treats them with respect. It's as if he believes that their hearts are right, but they're just confused. If he can just set them straight, everything will be fine. Of course, he also sounds a little pompous when he compares himself to Jesus and Socrates, and the threat he appears to make in paragraph 8 seems out of character. Maybe he's losing control of his self-image at those moments.

A Checklist for Analyzing an Argument

To identify the *claim*, ask:

- What opinion, idea, or point of view is the writer trying to get me to accept?

To identify the *reasons*, ask:

- What statements does the writer offer that tell me why I should accept the claim?

To identify the *backing*, ask:

- What information or explanation does the writer give to justify acceptance of the claim on the basis of this reason?

To identify the *refutation*, ask:

- What opposing arguments does the writer anticipate, and how are they dealt with?

To evaluate the *logical appeal* of the argument, remember the ABC's of sound reasoning.

- Test for *appropriateness* by asking:
    Is the support relevant to the claim?
    Does the support justify accepting the claim?
- Test for *believability* by asking:
    Are the facts accurate, complete, and trustworthy?
    Are the statistics based on comparability? Are they accurate and trustworthy?
    Are the authorities credible?
- Test for *consistency* by asking:
    Are the supporting statements contradictory?
    Do they provide sufficient support for the claim?

To evaluate the *emotional appeal*, ask:

- Do I feel manipulated by slanted or highly charged language?

To evaluate the *ethical appeal*, ask:

- How would I characterize the tone of this argument?
- What kind of person does the writer seem to be?

Exercise 6

Analyze the logical appeal of "When Rights Collide." Begin by identifying the parts of the argument either by annotating on the text or

In Notebook

writing out an outline. If you write out an outline, follow the format of our sample outline. Give the paragraph numbers of claims, reasons, and refutations. Classify each piece of backing by type using our classifications on pages 34–35. Then, evaluate the logic by applying the ABC test of sound reasoning to this essay.

Identifying and Evaluating Basic Features

Sometimes readers want to understand the basic features of the kind of writing they are reading and discover how that kind of writing achieves its purpose for its particular readers. Writers often read in this way in order to improve their own writing. In fact, a basic purpose of this text is to enable you to become a better writer by analyzing the kinds of discourse you will be writing. Consequently, this critical reading strategy—identifying and evaluating basic features—will be central to your work throughout this book. In the introductions to each of the remaining chapters, one exercise (Exercise 3) guides you in reading a particular type of writing in order to understand its basic features more fully.

Here you can practice this critical reading activity by identifying and evaluating the basic features of position papers—the kind of writing in the King excerpt on pages 13–17 and the kind you may write in Chapter 9. The following are the questions about basic features from Chapter 9:

1. How does the writer define the issue? Is it clearly arguable? What is at stake?

2. What exactly is the writer's position on this issue? How well is this position distinguished from opposing positions? Are the opposing positions presented fairly?

3. How effectively does the writer argue for the position? What are the main reasons, and how well are they supported?

4. How effectively does the writer handle objections and counterarguments? Are valid objections acknowledged and invalid ones refuted?

5. What tone does the writer adopt? How appropriate is this tone for the subject and audience?

6. How well organized is the essay?

Here are possible answers to these questions for the King excerpt:

1. The issue in this excerpt—whether white moderates are supporting King's movement as they should—is certainly arguable. It is arguable because it can't be settled with facts or by assertions of religious beliefs. It can only be understood and perhaps resolved by convincing arguments. King fully defines "white moderates" and their beliefs in the first paragraph. This paragraph, along with the clergymen's letter, gives readers a good sense of the issue. What is at stake is racial justice.

2. King clearly states his position: he believes that the white moderates who oppose his group's nonviolent protest as extremist are the primary obstacle to racial justice. He distinguishes his position from that of his opponents by refuting individually each of his critics' charges. King presents fairly the white moderates' position by quoting them directly and stating each of their criticisms: they consider him an outsider, deplore the violence, hold him responsible, and regret his impatience.

3. King's argument overall seems very convincing, although it is hard to know for certain just how convincing the white moderates to whom it is addressed found it. His main reasons for challenging the white moderates are as follows:

   • the white moderate is more concerned with preserving law and order than with achieving justice
   • the white moderate doesn't recognize that "the present tension in the South is a necessary phase" in the struggle for justice
   • white moderates believe that blacks are too impatient
   • King is disappointed that white moderates see him as an extremist
   • like all oppressed people, blacks yearn for freedom and equality
   • few white moderates have the vision to see that "injustice must be rooted out by strong, persistent, determined action"

   All of these reasons are supported effectively by various devices: analogy, figurative language, authorities, history, moral arguments.

4. Throughout the excerpt, King considers what the white moderate's objections will be to his letter, and responds to these objections. This seems to be a special strength of his argument. A good

example is his careful attempt to convince readers that he is not a violent and dangerous extremist.

5. King's tone is serious and restrained. He has been jailed for organizing nonviolent demonstrations against racial injustice. His cause is personal, religious, political, and social and the stakes are high. Still, he adopts a tone that will not anger or alienate his readers before they have heard him out. He avoids name-calling. He must have been angry himself, and yet he approaches his readers in a very restrained way.

6. King's argument is well organized and easy to follow. In the first paragraph, he forecasts his main points about method and timing. His continual reference to his readers and their letter help unify the argument. He begins by addressing his readers directly and defining "white moderates." Then, in order, he presents his arguments about tension, violence, timing, balancing opposing forces, protest, and extremism. He concludes by naming some whites who have supported his movement, contrasting them with the clergymen and other white moderates.

Exercise 7

Turn to Analyzing the Basic Features of Position Papers in Chapter 9 and read the questions about basic features and the discussion of each. Write a few sentences answering each question for "When Rights Collide."

Comparing and Contrasting Related Readings

Comparing and contrasting are essential to our intellectual development. Our brains and our language ensure that we notice how things are alike and different. Comparison and contrast enable us to make sense of the world and to accumulate knowledge about it.

It is no surprise, then, that comparing or contrasting related readings enables us to understand them more fully and to see how they work as texts. College professors value compare-and-contrast writing assignments because they believe such assignments enable students to understand important ideas of each essay in a larger context. You will encounter such assignments as you work through this book.

The analysis below illustrates one kind of contrast of two position papers. It contrasts the King excerpt on pages 13–17 and paragraphs 14–19 of the Van Dusen essay, "Civil Disobedience: Destroyer of Democracy," in Chapter 9. Before you read the analysis, reread the King excerpt and then read the Van Dusen excerpt (paragraphs 14–19 only).

> King and Van Dusen present radically different views of legal, nonviolent direct action, such as parades, demonstrations, boycotts, sit-ins, or pickets. Although Van Dusen acknowledges that direct action is legal, he nevertheless fears it; and he challenges it energetically in these paragraphs. He seems most concerned about the ways direct action disturbs the peace, infringes on others' rights, and threatens violence. He worries that even though some groups make gains through direct action, the end result is that everyone else begins to doubt the validity of the usual democratic procedures of relying on legislation and the courts. He condemns advocates of direct action like King for believing that the end (in this case, racial justice) justifies the means (direct action). Van Dusen argues that demonstrations often end violently and that an organized movement like King's can in the beginning win concessions through direct action but then end up extorting demands through threats and illegal uses of power.
>
> In contrast, King argues that nonviolent direct action preserves the peace by bringing hidden tensions and prejudices to the surface where they can be acknowledged and addressed. Direct action enhances democracy by changing its unjust laws and thereby strengthening it. Since direct action is entirely legal, to forego it as a strategy for change would be to turn one's back on a basic democratic principle. Although it may inconvenience people, its end (a more just social order) is entirely justified by its means (direct action). King would no doubt insist that the occasional violence that follows direct action results always from aggressive, unlawful interference with demonstrations, interference sometimes led by police officers. He might also argue that neither anarchy nor extortion followed from his group's actions.

Notice that the analysis does not rely on King's or Van Dusen's language. Instead of quoting, it paraphrases. Notice, too, that the analysis first presents Van Dusen's side and then King's. An alternative would be to contrast the two writer's positions point by point.

Every comparison or contrast has a specific *basis*. This basis limits the comparison and provides its focus. For example, the basis for the King–Van Dusen contrast is the authors' positions on the issue of legal, nonviolent direct action, not their styles of writing or their arguments' structures. Because any two or three related essays can be compared in many ways, writers of comparisons always select one basis (or a very few bases) that seems appropriate for their purpose and readers.

Exercise 8

Read and then write a brief comparison-and-contrast analysis of two essays in Chapter 10: "It's Our Right to Offend and Outrage" and "What About U.S. Unity?"

Assume that your readers have not read either essay. Begin by summarizing the position each essay takes, and then examine the points on which the two essays agree and disagree. Avoid taking a position yourself or saying which of the two essays you find more convincing.

Exploring Your Personal Response

Writing an extended response to a reading can be a particularly satisfying way to conclude the process of reading critically. The satisfaction can be personal as well as intellectual. On a personal level, extended writing enables you to probe your own thoughts about the reading, to consider what it means to you and how it might affect your life, to review your past experience and understanding in light of your reading, and to come to some sense of closure on the reading experience. On an intellectual level, writing gives you the opportunity to reflect on what you have learned from your reading, to organize your insights, to make new connections and discoveries, to test your assumptions, to discover how the reading selection works, and to determine whether or not it works effectively.

There are many different purposes and occasions for extended writing about your reading. You may write primarily for yourself, to see how well you understand a reading or to explore its new and challenging ideas. You may write for a class, to demonstrate your critical acuity or to relate what you have read to other material you have studied. You may also write on the job, to pass along information or to make evaluations. In each of these situations, the critical reading strategies presented in this chapter will prepare you to write thoughtfully about your reading.

Exercises throughout this book invite you to write 300–400-word responses to your reading. Depending on your purpose or your instructor's advice, you may write a quick draft to try out some ideas, a more carefully planned draft that reflects a period of note-making or organizing, or a draft with revision that benefits from advice from other students and your instructor.

Following is a list of some of the kinds of extended writing exercises you can expect to find in later chapters:

1. Write about your personal associations with something in the reading, such as an image, idea, event, or character.

2. Write to explore the meaning and implications of a particular point made in the reading.

3. Write in the format of a letter to the author in which you respond to anything in the essay that you found particularly unusual, interesting, or intriguing.

4. Play devil's advocate and challenge the writer's ideas or argument.

5. Compare what the writer says with what others have said about the subject.

6. Explain the reading to your classmates, friends, or family.

7. Write about the history of your reading of an essay. That is, tell a story about your impressions and reactions during first and later readings. Reflect on how your response to the essay changed.

8. Write about this essay and another reading, book, or movie it reminded you of.

Exercise 9

Choose an assignment from the list above, and write 300–400 words about the excerpt on pages 13–17 from King's "Letter from Birmingham Jail."

Exercise 10

Choose an assignment from the list above, and write 300–400 words about Etzioni's "When Rights Collide" on pages 10–12.

Looking Ahead

In this chapter, you have practiced a wide range of critical reading strategies, strategies that rely on anticipating a reading, rereading it thoughtfully, and writing in various ways about it:

Previewing

Annotating

Outlining

Summarizing

Taking Inventory

Analyzing an Argument

Identifying and Evaluating Basic Features

Comparing and Contrasting Related Readings

Exploring Your Personal Response

Now, with your pencil in hand, you can approach any reading assignment with greater confidence. In the chapters that follow, as you learn about the basic features of different types of writing, you will be able to make good use of these critical reading strategies. In each chapter, you will annotate a sample reading and explore it further through appropriate critical reading strategies. The Questions for Analysis and Ideas for Your Own Writing following each reading invite you to use relevant critical reading strategies. In all of these ways, this chapter's critical reading strategies will enable you to understand a kind of writing and to write it yourself with greater confidence and satisfaction.

CHAPTER TWO

Autobiography

Everyone enjoys hearing a story. Nearly every day we encounter stories in one form or another—a friend's account of something that happened, a television soap opera, a prime-time television drama, a movie, a novel, a short story.

Autobiographers are storytellers too. They share their remembered experience of events, people, and places significant in their lives. This form of writing is important to both writers and readers. Writers value the way autobiography records and clarifies their experience. They treasure the insight that comes from exploring their personal histories through writing. Readers take special pleasure in the engaging stories offered in autobiography. They enjoy comparing others' lives to their own, and they savor the reflections on human experience such accounts inspire.

Autobiography is a centuries-old form of writing. Literary scholars have studied it respectfully, tracing its changes through time and describing its modern variations. Many autobiographies, like those of Benjamin Franklin, Frederick Douglass, Mark Twain, Henry Adams, Zora Neale Hurston, Richard Rodriguez, Maya Angelou, Lillian Hellman, and Russell Baker, are important works of American literature.

In addition to its value to individual readers and writers and its importance as literary art, autobiography plays a role in documenting cultural and intellectual history. In business, the arts, and academic disciplines, influential persons describe in their autobiographies what it was like to engage in a particular kind of work and professional life. Here, autobiography shades off into memoir, which is not so frankly personal as autobiography. Still, most memoirs reveal something of a person's values and character.

Autobiography derives from a particular way of reflecting on experience. Relying on memory, autobiographers try to recall in detail what happened at key points in their lives; from these details they hope to discover the *significance* of what happened. Their central purpose, then, is to discover what their experience means and why it is important or memorable, in order to convey this significance to their readers.

Participating in this ancient and valued form of writing, you will be creating art from your life, shaping a story that can give great pleasure to readers. By vividly recalling an important event in your life, you may discover how it contributed to making you the person you are.

A GUIDE TO READING AUTOBIOGRAPHICAL WRITING

To begin your work with autobiography, you will first look closely at a piece of autobiographical writing by a highly regarded journalist and autobiographer, Russell Baker. Closely analyzing Baker's writing will provide a foundation for the serious study of autobiography this chapter encourages. As you become a more critical, insightful reader of autobiographical writing, your own writing will become more vivid and engaging.

As the initial step in your analysis, you will annotate the Baker selection. The next exercise asks you to take inventory of your annotations in order to disclose a pattern of meaning you have discovered. In the third exercise, guided by special questions, you will report what you have learned in analyzing the unique features of autobiographical writing. Finally, the concluding exercise invites you to write a brief exploratory essay, consolidating what you have learned about the Baker selection and trying out your own ideas about it or extending your personal response to it.

The time you invest now in annotating, analyzing, and writing will pay off richly as you read, write about, and discuss the essays in this chapter. It will also give you confidence that you can successfully write your own autobiographical essay.

Annotating As You Read

Perhaps the most basic, and most useful, strategy for reading attentively and critically is annotating. Pencil in hand as you read, you are ready to record on the page any comments, questions, definitions, or insights—whatever crosses your mind—about a piece of writing. As an illustration, note how we have annotated the following brief passage from an autobiographical essay by Alice Walker that appears in its entirety later in this chapter:

note descriptive details	It is Easter Sunday, 1950. I am dressed in a <u>green, flocked, scalloped-hem dress</u> (handmade by my adoring sister, Ruth) that has its own smooth satin petticoat and tiny hot-pink roses tucked into each scallop. My <u>shoes,</u>
really with a biscuit?	<u>new T-strap patent leather,</u> again highly <u>biscuit-polished.</u> I am six years old and have learned one of the longest Easter speeches to be heard that day, totally unlike the speech I said when I was two: "Easter lilies / pure and
almost floating	white / blossom in / the morning light." When I <u>rise</u> to give my speech I do so <u>on a great wave of love and pride and expectation.</u> People in the church stop rustling their
crinolines: stiff fabric	new crinolines. They seem to hold their breath. I can tell they admire my dress, but it is my spirit, bordering on
Mean the same? →	sassiness, womanishness, they secretly applaud.
Why *pleased?* **Mess = pleasing?**	"That girl's a little mess," they whisper to each other, pleased. Naturally I say my speech without stammer or
still sassy	pause, unlike those who stutter, stammer, or, worst of all, forget. This is before the word "beautiful" exists in people's vocabulary, but "Oh, isn't she the *cutest* thing!"
Self-image defined by response of others	frequently floats my way. "And got so much sense!" they gratefully add . . . for which thoughtful addition I thank them to this day.

For more on annotating, pause now to review the guidelines in Chapter 1 and the model annotations on the excerpt from "Letter from Birmingham Jail." Note particularly the Checklist for Annotating.

Exercise 1

Annotate Russell Baker's "Saving America from Herbert Hoover" as you read. Reread it at least one time, continuing to annotate as you reread. Your purpose is to focus your attention on the text, to read as thoughtfully—as critically—as possible. Annotate details you admire as well as things you question or challenge; mark noteworthy stylistic devices or writing strategies; write down any personal responses. Record your insights and reactions directly on and around the text itself.

The following selection comes from Russell Baker's *Growing Up*, winner of the Pulitzer Prize for Autobiography in 1983. For many years Baker was a journalist for the *Baltimore Sun* and the *New York Times*, covering the White House, Congress, and national politics. Since 1962 he has written a column for the *Times*, meriting the Pulitzer Prize for Distinguished Commentary in 1979.

Baker was born in 1924 and grew up in small towns in Virginia and in the cities of Newark and Baltimore. When his father died, he and his mother and sister lived for a short time with his Uncle Allen and Aunt Pat. The incident described in this excerpt, which concerns the awakening of political awareness, occurs at Uncle Allen's house when Baker was eight, a presidential election year when America was in the depths of a great economic depression. Pause for a moment to reflect on the first sitting president you were aware of and the first presidential election that caught your attention. If you briefly preview the selection, you'll notice that Baker includes a good amount of dialogue. Why do you suppose an autobiographer would include dialogue?

Saving America from Herbert Hoover
Russell Baker

Uncle Allen moved us out of Newark and up to Belleville in 1932. I liked Belleville. There were big grassy lawns and streets canopied with trees. We lived on the first floor of a two-family house across the street from Public School Number 8. The landlady lived on the second floor. Aunt Pat detested her for being a landlady. The propertied classes ranked high in Aunt Pat's catalogue of natural enemies. 1

Coming in from play one evening at dusk, I heard Aunt Pat shouting in the kitchen. 2

"She's got her nerve!" 3

Uncle Allen tried his customary soothing refrain. "Calm down now, Pat. Just calm down." 4

"Calm down! Not with that thing on the front door! Jesus, Mary, and Joseph, Allen! What are the neighbors going to think?" 5

I tiptoed outside to see what terrible thing was on the front door. In fact there were two front doors side by side. One opened directly into our parlor, the other opened onto a staircase that led up to the landlady's quarters. Our front door looked the same as always, but fixed to the landlady's door was a large head-and-shoulders portrait of a genial-looking man with hair parted down the middle. 6

imagine that he is smart

There was printing under the picture. I could read 7
easily now. My mother had spent so much time teaching
me to read that the principal at P.S. Number 8 had agreed
to let me skip second grade and go on to the third, which
didn't satisfy my mother, who thought I should have
been skipped at least to the fourth. Reading the material
under the picture gave me no trouble, but I couldn't
understand why it should anger Aunt Pat.

It identified the man in the picture as Herbert Hoover. 8
It said something to the effect that he should be reelected.
I studied the picture carefully and was impressed by the
gentleness of Herbert Hoover's expression. He had
round, chubby cheeks that reminded me of babies. He
certainly didn't look like a man to make your blood boil. I
went back in the house, where Uncle Allen was trying to
focus Aunt Pat's mind on making supper.

fiercely angry

"How can I cook with that damn thing on the front 9
door?" she cried.

My mother was sitting at the table smiling and enjoy- 10
ing the excitement. As meekly as possible, I asked her,
"What's wrong about Herbert Hoover?"

"Great mother of God!" cried Aunt Pat. "You poor 11
child!" And she told me what was wrong about Herbert
Hoover. He was destroying America, that was one thing
wrong about him.

"Now just a second, Pat—" 12

idea what Herbert Hoover was bad for

But Uncle Allen's plea for calm was lost in the gale. 13
People were starving because of Herbert Hoover. My
mother was out of work because of Herbert Hoover. Men
were killing themselves because of Herbert Hoover, and
their fatherless children were being packed away into
orphanages—Aunt Pat's dread of orphanages made this
the worst offense of all to her—because of Herbert
Hoover.

"Now, Pat, be fair—" 14

"I'll be fair. I'm going to tear that thing off the front 15
door."

She was in motion now. Uncle Allen stepped between 16
her and the parlor. "You can't do that, Pat. It's her house.
She has a right to put up a poster if she wants."

"We pay the rent that keeps her, it's our house too," 17
Aunt Pat roared, but for the first time she seemed ready
to defer to Uncle Allen's sense of what was right.

Seeing that he had averted a crisis for the moment, 18
Uncle Allen adopted the foxy-grandpa style he sometimes used when he wanted to win a point by persuasion.
Taking a toothpick out of his vest pocket, he chewed it
thoughtfully for the longest while, a gesture we all recog-

nized. He was thinking; he had an idea aborning. When all was silent, he smiled a canny smile and spoke in his deepest down-home southern drawl.

"Waal, Pat, I'll tell you," he said. "Down in Lancaster 19 Court House where I come from, we always liked to settle things peaceable. Kind of keep the blood cool, y'know. I remember one time old Mr. Charlie Nickens had a fight with a fellow down there whose cows kept getting into his orchard"—Uncle Allen remembered nothing of the sort. He was making it up out of the whole cloth, hoping to get Aunt Pat soothed sufficiently to get on with making the chipped-beef gravy for supper—"and old Mr. Nickens swore he was going to shoot the next cow he caught in there eating his apples off the ground, because he fed those apples to his hogs, you know. But I had a better idea. 'Lord, Mr. Nickens, you don't want to shoot that man's cows,' I told him. 'A hole in the fence is a two-way street. If his cows come over to your side, why don't you encourage your hogs to go over to his side and wallow around in his vegetable garden?' I think that's what we ought to do about Mr. Hoover out front."

"I don't get it," said Aunt Pat. I didn't either.   20

"We've got a front door too," Uncle Allen said. "It's a 21 two-way street. Instead of tearing down her Hoover poster, why don't we get a Roosevelt poster and stick it up right alongside hers on our own door?"

Aunt Pat was delighted with the idea. She headed for 22 the door.

"Where are you going, Pat?" he asked.   23

"To talk to the Dunleavys," she said. "I want to find 24 out where to get a Roosevelt poster."

"Can't it wait till after supper?"   25

It couldn't. Aunt Pat headed out to canvass the neigh- 26 bors. The Dunleavys, the O'Connells, the Quinns, the O'Learys. They were all rabid Democrats. One of them would guide her to the source of Franklin Roosevelt posters. We had no telephone; telephones were luxuries for the rich. She traveled from neighbor to neighbor in search of someone wise in the mechanics of politics and came back with the address of a storefront campaign office where posters were available free.

The office lay a mighty distance, down on Washington 27 Avenue, and we had no car. Cars were also luxuries for the rich. That was all right; Aunt Pat would walk.

"Supper," Uncle Allen pleaded.   28

My mother could cook the chipped beef, Aunt Pat 29 said, and have it ready on her return.

leads to main idea

"It's dark," Uncle Allen said. "It's too far to go alone." 30
By now I was totally involved. I too wanted to save 31
America from Herbert Hoover. I wanted to defeat the
landlady upstairs who lived off Uncle Allen's money.
Above all I wanted to be part of the excitement. "I'll go
with her," I cried.

Off we went. The walk seemed endless, the trip back 32
even longer, but when we returned and Aunt Pat taped
the picture of Franklin Roosevelt to our front door I
forgot exhaustion. I felt like a hero of liberty. I had
discovered the joys of politics. If I had lived upstairs with
the landlady I would probably have become a hard-
money Republican, but chance had put me on the lower
level where the Depression stirred such passion that even

main idea

a child could not resist. In my first venture into politics, I
became a Roosevelt Democrat.

Inventorying Your Annotations

Once you have annotated a reading with your observations and
insights, you'll want to analyze your annotations to discover their special
meaning. The best way to do this is by taking inventory of your annotations to identify any patterns or key repetitions.

Before completing Exercise 2, review the guidelines and illustration for
the Inventory of Annotations in Chapter 1.

Exercise 2

Inventory the annotations you made on "Saving America from Herbert Hoover," looking for meaningful patterns.

Analyzing the Basic Features
of Autobiographical Writing

In addition to annotating a text to record your initial impressions and
inventorying your annotations for their patterns of meaning, you can
analyze the basic features of a piece of writing, in this case those qualities
that make it distinctively autobiographical.

Look back at Identifying and Evaluating Basic Features in Chapter 1. Although the questions there are different from the ones you will find in this chapter, the answers illustrate what a thoughtful analysis of basic features might look like.

Exercise 3

Analyze "Saving America from Herbert Hoover" by answering the following questions. You will want to reread the selection with each question in mind, and you may want to annotate further.

Write out your answers to the questions.

1. *How does the writer present the story?* Story is a complex feature of fictional and autobiographical texts, involving a good deal more than the simple narrative line, the basic statements that assert what happened.

To answer this question, notice as you read and reread an essay how the writer creates tension or suspense, making you anxious (or eager or just curious) to know what will happen. Observe how the writer uses dialogue and specific narrative action (people moving or gesturing). Notice where the pace of the story seems to quicken or slow, and consider what the writer is doing at those points. Finally, decide whether the writer presents a full, comprehensive narrative, one that answers all your questions about what happened.

2. *What is the scene (or scenes), and how does the writer present the scene?* Identify the scene or scenes in the essay. Notice the actual physical location for the event, person, or place. Observe the size of the scene. Consider whether the writer remains located in one scene or shifts from one scene to another. Decide which scene is the most important one in the essay.

Consider first the point of view from which the writer presents the scene (or scenes), viewing it from one fixed position, moving through the scene, or alternating between fixed and moving points of view. Notice whether the writer provides a distant, panoramic view of the scene as well as a close-up view of particular objects in the scene. Notice the extent of the exact details provided—color, size, texture, location.

Reflect on what you have observed, and conjecture why the writer has presented the scene in just this way. Imagine the writer deciding what to leave out, what to put in, whether to mention an object or describe it in detail, whether to shift point of view and when to do it, whether to stay at a distance or move in close. Remember that the writer chose to present the scene in a way that would support his or her larger purpose of sharing a personally significant incident. Remember, too, that writers choose details not randomly but systematically to create a particular mood or impression of the scene. What dominant impression do you get of the scene? Which details contribute most notably to your impression? Which ones, if any, seem extraneous?

3. *Who are the significant people and how does the writer present them?* Notice how many people other than the writer play a role in the essay, and observe the relations of these people to the writer and to each other. Where are the antagonistic, the loving, and the indifferent relations?

Notice whether the writer describes people or merely identifies them. Observe the kind of description the writer offers: looks or dress, movements or gestures or postures, ways of talking. Consider how much the writer leaves to the reader to infer about the person and how much is offered directly.

From these observations, decide how successfully the writer has presented other people. Keep in mind that, except in autobiographical essays concerned mainly with significant other people, the writer will be the central figure, with other people having only minor roles. Do you want to know more about a person? Do you remain puzzled about a person even though the writer describes this person in some detail? Are you uncertain about the motives for a person's actions? Are you unclear about the relations between people or about the writer's attitude toward them?

4. *What do I learn about the writer, and how is the autobiographical significance disclosed?* Consider all the cues available to you about the writer. What different kinds of information do you have about the writer? How much do you learn? What seems to be the significance for the writer of the event? (Autobiographical significance reveals the meaningfulness and importance of the incident in the writer's life. You can think of it as the theme of the essay.)

Consider just how the writer discloses autobiographical significance in the material you are reading. Must you infer it, or is it stated? (It may be inferred from the writer's selection of details and events and from the writer's interactions with other people.) Are you satisfied that the writer has realized the significance? Is it possible the writer has distorted or overlooked certain personal meanings of the event, person, or place? In general, what can you conclude about the writer's handling of autobiographical significance?

Exploring Your Personal Response

One other way of focusing your response to an autobiographical text is by taking the time to record your thoughts in a more extended piece of your own writing. Basically, such an exercise can help you to consider how the piece reminds you of your own experience, to explore your impressions and define further your unique perspective on what you've read.

Exercise 4

Write 300–400 words (two or three handwritten pages) about "Saving America from Herbert Hoover." Choose one of the suggestions listed in Exploring Your Personal Response in Chapter 1.

Annie Dillard

Annie Dillard (b. 1945) is a poet, reporter, essayist, and literary theorist. Since 1974, when she won the Pulitzer Prize for *Pilgrim at Tinker Creek*, she has been considered one of America's finest nonfiction prose writers. She has published a book of poems, *Tickets for the Prayer Wheel* (1982), and a book of literary theory, *Living by Fiction* (1982), and an autobiography, *An American Childhood* (1987).

A Chase

Like the Baker selection at the beginning of this chapter, this selection from Dillard's autobiography focuses on a single incident in the writer's life, an incident occupying less than a day. Book-length autobiographies include narratives of such brief incidents, along with characterizations of unforgettable people, descriptions of memorable places, narratives of meaningful phases of time, and presentation of significant recurring activities. The readings in this chapter illustrate the autobiographer's focus on incidents, on people, and on phases.

Here, from the vantage point of her forties, Dillard vividly recalls a snowy morning when she was seven and with a friend was chased relentlessly by an adult stranger at whom they were throwing snowballs. She admits that she was terrified, and yet she asserts that she has "seldom been happier since." As you read, try to arrive at an explanation for this paradox and make a note of it along with your other annotations.

Some boys taught me to play football. This was fine sport. You thought up a new strategy for every play and whispered it to the others. You went out for a pass, fooling everyone. Best, you got to throw yourself mightily at someone's running legs. Either you brought him down or you hit the ground flat out on your chin, with your arms empty before you. It was all or nothing. If you hesitated in fear, you would miss and get hurt: you would take a hard fall while the kid got away, or you would get kicked in the face while the kid got away. But if you flung yourself wholeheartedly at the back of his knees—if you gathered and joined body and soul and pointed them diving fearlessly—then you likely wouldn't get hurt, and you'd stop the ball. Your fate, and your team's score, depended on your concentration and courage. Nothing girls did could compare with it.

Boys welcomed me at baseball, too, for I had, through enthusiastic practice, what was weirdly known as a boy's arm. In winter, in the snow, there was neither baseball nor football, so the boys and I threw snowballs at passing cars. I got in trouble throwing snowballs, and have seldom been happier since.

On one weekday morning after Christmas, six inches of new snow had just fallen. We were standing up to our boot tops in snow on a front yard on trafficked Reynolds Street, waiting for cars. The cars traveled Reynolds Street slowly and evenly; they were targets all but wrapped in red ribbons, cream puffs. We couldn't miss.

I was seven; the boys were eight, nine, and ten. The oldest two Fahey boys were there—Mikey and Peter—polite blond boys who lived near me on Lloyd Street, and who already had four brothers and sisters. My parents approved Mikey and Peter Fahey. Chickie McBride was there, a tough kid, and Billy Paul and Mackie Kean too, from across Reynolds, where the boys grew up dark and furious, grew up skinny, knowing, and skilled. We had all drifted from our houses that morning looking for action, and had found it here on Reynolds Street.

It was cloudy but cold. The cars' tires laid behind them on the snowy street a complex trail of beige chunks like crenellated castle walls. I had stepped on some earlier; they squeaked. We could have wished for more traffic. When a car came, we all popped it one. In the intervals between cars we reverted to the natural solitude of children.

I started making an iceball—a perfect iceball, from perfectly white snow, perfectly spherical, and squeezed perfectly translucent so no snow remained all the way through. (The Fahey boys and I considered it unfair actually to throw an iceball at somebody, but it had been known to happen.)

I had just embarked on the iceball project when we heard tire chains come clanking from afar. A black Buick was moving toward us down the street. We all spread out, banged together some regular snowballs, took aim, and, when the Buick drew nigh, fired.

A soft snowball hit the driver's windshield right before the driver's face. It made a smashed star with a hump in the middle.

Often, of course, we hit our target, but this time, the only time in all of life, the car pulled over and stopped. Its wide black door opened; a man got out of it, running. He didn't even close the car door.

He ran after us, and we ran away from him, up the snowy Reynolds sidewalk. At the corner, I looked back; incredibly, he was still after us. He was in city clothes: a suit and tie, street shoes. Any normal adult would have quit, having sprung us into flight and made his point. This man was gaining on us. He was a thin man, all action. All of a sudden, we were running for our lives.

Wordless, we split up. We were on our turf; we could lose ourselves in 11
the neighborhood backyards, everyone for himself. I paused and considered. Everyone had vanished except Mikey Fahey, who was just rounding
the corner of a yellow brick house. Poor Mikey, I trailed him. The driver
of the Buick sensibly picked the two of us to follow. The man apparently
had all day.

He chased Mikey and me around the yellow house and up a backyard 12
path we knew by heart: under a low tree, up a bank, through a hedge,
down some snowy steps, and across the grocery store's delivery driveway.
We smashed through a gap in another hedge, entered a scruffy backyard
and ran around its back porch and tight between houses to Edgerton
Avenue; we ran across Edgerton to an alley and up our own sliding
woodpile to the Halls' front yard; he kept coming. We ran up Lloyd Street
and wound through mazy backyards toward the steep hilltop at Willard
and Lang.

He chased us silently, block after block. He chased us silently over 13
picket fences, through thorny hedges, between houses, around garbage
cans, and across streets. Every time I glanced back, choking for breath, I
expected he would have quit. He must have been as breathless as we
were. His jacket strained over his body. It was an immense discovery,
pounding into my hot head with every sliding, joyous step, that this
ordinary adult evidently knew what I thought only children who trained
at football knew: that you have to fling yourself at what you're doing, you
have to point yourself, forget yourself, aim, dive.

Mikey and I had nowhere to go, in our own neighborhood or out of it, 14
but away from this man who was chasing us. He impelled us forward; we
compelled him to follow our route. The air was cold; every breath tore
my throat. We kept running, block after block; we kept improvising,
backyard after backyard, running a frantic course and choosing it simultaneously, failing always to find small places or hard places to slow him
down, and discovering always, exhilarated, dismayed, that only bare
speed could save us—for he would never give up, this man—and we were
losing speed.

He chased us through the backyard labyrinths of ten blocks before he 15
caught us by our jackets. He caught us and we all stopped.

We three stood staggering, half blinded, coughing, in an obscure 16
hilltop backyard: a man in his twenties, a boy, a girl. He had released our
jackets, our pursuer, our captor, our hero: he knew we weren't going
anywhere. We all played by the rules. Mikey and I unzipped our jackets. I
pulled off my sopping mittens. Our tracks multiplied in the backyard's
new snow. We had been breaking new snow all morning. We didn't look
at each other. I was cherishing my excitement. The man's lower pants

description of man legs were wet; his cuffs were full of snow, and there was a prow of snow beneath them on his shoes and socks. Some trees bordered the little flat backyard, some messy winter trees. There was no one around: a clearing in a grove, and we the only players.

It was a long time before he could speak. I had some difficulty at first 17 recalling why we were there. My lips felt swollen; I couldn't see out of the sides of my eyes; I kept coughing.

"You stupid kids," he began perfunctorily.   18

We listened perfunctorily indeed, if we listened at all, for the chewing 19 out was redundant, a mere formality, and beside the point. The point was that he had chased us passionately without giving up, and so he had caught us. Now he came down to earth. I wanted the glory to last forever.

shows that extent the excitement would have dies down because anything on top of this excitement
But how could the glory have lasted forever? We could have run 20 through every backyard in North America until we got to Panama. But when he trapped us at the lip of the Panama Canal, what precisely could he have done to prolong the drama of the chase and cap its glory? I brooded about this for the next few years. He could only have fried Mikey Fahey and me in boiling oil, say, or dismembered us piecemeal, or staked us to anthills. None of which I really wanted, and none of which any adult was likely to do, even in the spirit of fun. He could only chew us out there in the Panamanian jungle, after months or years of exalting pursuit. He could only begin, "You stupid kids," and continue in his ordinary Pittsburgh accent with his normal righteous anger and the usual common sense.

If in that snowy backyard the driver of the black Buick had cut off our 21 heads, Mikey's and mine, I would have died happy, for nothing has required so much of me since as being chased all over Pittsburgh in the middle of winter—running terrified, exhausted—by this sainted, skinny, furious redheaded man who wished to have a word with us. I don't know how he found his way back to his car.

He likes to see how far she can push people.

QUESTIONS FOR ANALYSIS

1. Between paragraphs 9 and 15 Dillard narrates the chase. When you first read these paragraphs, what held your attention? How did Dillard keep you reading? Reread these paragraphs and move beyond a general impression of Dillard's technique to look at the sentence-by-sentence details of her narrative. What can you conclude about the way autobiographers narrate fast-moving action?

2. Dillard describes the scene in detail, but gives us very few specific details about herself and the man in the Buick. Review the essay, annotating every detail you can find about the man and about

Dillard's attitude toward him. Inventory these details in order to discover how much you can learn about him. (Review the Inventory of Annotations in Chapter 1.) What can you conclude about autobiographers' strategies for presenting secondary characters?

3. Within the context of all the details and events of the essay, how would you assess the importance of Dillard's assertion in paragraph 16, "We all played by the rules"?

4. Why do you think this incident is so memorable and significant for Dillard? What does she tell you explicitly about its significance and what can you infer?

5. Review Exploring Your Personal Response in Chapter 1. Then write a 300–400 word personal response to the Dillard selection, choosing one of the following topics:

> Write about your personal associations with something in the Dillard selection, such as an image, idea, event, or character.
>
> Write about the Dillard selection and a movie or another piece of writing you are reminded of.

After you have written your response, reread it thoughtfully. In two or three sentences, say what you learned about the Dillard selection by writing an extended response to it.

IDEAS FOR YOUR OWN WRITING

Consider childhood incidents that frightened or excited you. Choose one and recall who was present and what happened. Did everyone play by the rules or break the rules? How might you tell this story? Why is it memorable and significant?

Richard Rodriguez

Richard Rodriguez (b. 1944) describes himself as "a full-time writer." He is also a popular lecturer. His essays have appeared in the *American Scholar, College English*, the *Los Angeles Times*, and *Change*, and *Saturday Review*. An autobiography of his school years, *Hunger of Memory: The Education of Richard Rodriguez* (1982), won the Christopher Award.

My Parents

Russell Baker and Annie Dillard narrate significant incidents from their childhoods. Autobiographers also characterize significant people in their lives, exploring relationships to discover their meanings; as Rodriguez does in this selection and Vivian Gornick does in the next.

In *Hunger of Memory*, Rodriguez explores his gradual alienation from his parents because of his academic success. As a child attending Catholic schools, he was singled out as a "scholarship boy," a minority or working-class student with special promise. In this selection, Rodriguez portrays his parents in terms of their own educational histories and their aspirations for him. As you read, notice that Rodriguez discloses a good deal about himself while telling us about his parents. What does he disclose about himself and his relationship with his parents?

'Your parents must be very proud of you.' People began to say that to me about the time I was in sixth grade. To answer affirmatively, I'd smile. Shyly I'd smile, never betraying my sense of the irony: I was not proud of my mother and father. I was embarrassed by their lack of education. It was not that I ever thought they were stupid, though stupidly I took for granted their enormous native intelligence. Simply, what mattered to me was that they were not like my teachers.

But, 'Why didn't you tell us about the award?' my mother demanded, her frown weakened by pride. At the grammar school ceremony several weeks after, her eyes were brighter than the trophy I'd won. Pushing back the hair from my forehead, she whispered that I had 'shown' the *gringos*. A few minutes later, I heard my father speak to my teacher and felt ashamed of his labored, accented words. Then guilty for the shame. I felt such contrary feelings. (There is no simple roadmap through the heart of the scholarship boy.) My teacher was so soft-spoken and her words were edged sharp and clean. I admired her until it seemed to me that she spoke too carefully. Sensing that she was condescending to them, I

1

2

68

became nervous. Resentful. Protective. I tried to move my parents away. *It was Ricardo's da not the res of the childr* 'You both must be very proud of Richard,' the nun said. They responded quickly. (They were proud.) 'We are proud of all our children.' Then this afterthought: 'They sure didn't get their brains from us.' They all laughed. I smiled.

3.
3 contrat the irony: not proud of his parents again

Tightening the irony into a knot was the knowledge that my parents were always behind me. They made success possible. They evened the path. They sent their children to parochial schools because the nuns 'teach better.' They paid a tuition they couldn't afford. They spoke English to us.

4 Parents are childre backbone,

For their children my parents wanted chances they never had—an easier way. It saddened my mother to learn that some relatives forced their children to start working right after high school. To *her* children she would say, 'Get all the education you can.' In schooling she recognized the key to job advancement. And with the remark she remembered her past.

4. Parents want an easier way for their children

As a girl new to America my mother had been awarded a high school diploma by teachers too careless or busy to notice that she hardly spoke English. On her own, she determined to learn how to type. That skill got her jobs typing envelopes in letter shops, and it encouraged in her an optimism about the possibility of advancement. (Each morning when her sisters put on uniforms, she chose a bright-colored dress.) The years of young womanhood passed, and her typing speed increased. She also became an excellent speller of words she mispronounced, 'And I've never been to college,' she'd say, smiling, when her children asked her to spell words they were too lazy to look up in a dictionary.

5. Mother's background Determined & smart in her own wa

Typing, however, was dead-end work. Finally frustrating. When her youngest child started high school, my mother got a full-time office job once again. (Her paycheck combined with my father's to make us—in fact—what we had already become in our imagination of ourselves—middle class.) She worked then for the (California) state government in numbered civil service positions secured by examinations. The old ambition of her youth was rekindled. During the lunch hour, she consulted bulletin boards for announcements of openings. One day she saw mention of something called an 'anti-poverty agency.' A typing job. A glamorous job, part of the governor's staff. 'A knowledge of Spanish required.' Without hesitation she applied and became nervous only when the job was suddenly hers.

6.
6. Mom's work comes to an end, but soon she hung her end of the stability

X.

'Everyone comes to work all dressed up,' she reported at night. And didn't need to say more than that her co-workers wouldn't let her answer the phones. She was only a typist, after all, albeit a very fast typist. And an excellent speller. One morning there was a letter to be sent to a

7

[handwritten margin notes, left side:]
7. One mistake cause her her job. She wouldn't become anymore except a mother.

8. Back to Ricardo, his future to make mom proud

9. Father cares about a good working life.

10.

Father tries out cannot go further in his educ. He works hard labor forever.

11. Tired of living his hard life

Washington cabinet officer. On the dictating tape, a voice referred to urban guerrillas. My mother typed (the wrong word, correctly): 'gorillas.' The mistake horrified the anti-poverty bureaucrats who shortly after arranged to have her returned to her previous position. She would go no further. So she willed her ambition to her children. [Get all the education you can; with an education you can do anything.] (With a good education *she* could have done anything.)

When I was in high school, I admitted to my mother that I planned to   8
become a teacher someday. That seemed to please her. But I never tried to explain that it was not the occupation of teaching I yearned for as much as it was something more elusive: I wanted to be like my teachers, to possess their knowledge, to assume their authority, their confidence, even to assume a teacher's persona.

In contrast to my mother, my father never verbally encouraged his   9
children's academic success. Nor did he often praise us. My mother had to remind him to 'say something' to one of his children who scored some academic success. But whereas my mother saw in education the opportunity for job advancement, my father recognized that education provided an even more startling possibility: It could enable a person to escape from a life of mere labor.

In Mexico, orphaned when he was eight, my father left school to work   10
as an 'apprentice' for an uncle. Twelve years later, he left Mexico in frustration and arrived in America. He had great expectations then of becoming an engineer. ('Work for my hands and my head.') He knew a Catholic priest who promised to get him money enough to study full time for a high school diploma. But the promises came to nothing. Instead there was a dark succession of warehouse, cannery, and factory jobs. After work he went to night school along with my mother. A year, two passed. Nothing much changed, except that fatigue worked its way into the bone; then everything changed. He didn't talk anymore of becoming an engineer. He stayed outside on the steps of the school while my mother went inside to learn typing and shorthand.

By the time I was born, my father worked at 'clean' jobs. For a time he   11
was a janitor at a fancy department store. ('Easy work; the machines do it all.') Later he became a dental technician. ('Simple.') But by then he was pessimistic about the ultimate meaning of work and the possibility of ever escaping its claims. In some of my earliest memories of him, my father already seems aged by fatigue. (He has never really grown old like my mother.) From boyhood to manhood, I have remembered him in a single image: seated, asleep on the sofa, his head thrown back in a hideous corpselike grin, the evening newspaper spread out before him.

'But look at all you've accomplished,' his best friend said to him once. My father said nothing. Only smiled.

It was my father who laughed when I claimed to be tired by reading and writing. It was he who teased me for having soft hands. (He seemed to sense that some great achievement of leisure was implied by my papers and books.) It was my father who became angry while watching on television some woman at the Miss America contest tell the announcer that she was going to college. ('Majoring in fine arts.') 'College!' he snarled. He despised the trivialization of higher education, the inflated grades and cheapened diplomas, the half education that so often passes as mass education in my generation.

It was my father again who wondered why I didn't display my awards on the wall on my bedroom. He said he liked to go to doctors' offices and see their certificates and degrees on the wall. ('Nice.') My citations from school got left in closets at home. The gleaming figure astride one of my trophies was broken, wingless, after hitting the ground. My medals were placed in a jar of loose change. And when I lost my high school diploma, my father found it as it was about to be thrown out with the trash. Without telling me, he put it away with his own things for safekeeping.

These memories slammed together at the instant of hearing that refrain familiar to all scholarship students: 'Your parents must be very proud. . . .' Yes, my parents were proud. I knew it. But my parents regarded my progress with more than mere pride. They endured my early precocious behavior—but with what private anger and humiliation? As their children got older and would come home to challenge ideas both of them held, they argued before submitting to the force of logic or superior factual evidence with the disclaimer, 'It's what we were taught in our time to believe.' These discussions ended abruptly, though my mother remembered them on other occasions when she complained that our 'big ideas' were going to our heads. More acute was her complaint that the family wasn't close anymore, like some others she knew. Why weren't we close, 'more in the Mexican style'? Everyone is so private, she added. And she mimicked the yes and no answers she got in reply to her questions. Why didn't we talk more? (My father never asked.) I never said.

QUESTIONS FOR ANALYSIS

1. Writers sometimes "frame" essays by referring at the end to something at the beginning. How does Rodriguez frame this essay about his parents? What advantages do you see in framing an essay like this?

2. In paragraphs 6, 7, 12, and 13, Rodriguez combines general, recurring events with specific, one-time incidents.

   For example, in paragraph 6 the general events are his mother's working full time and looking for a more interesting job, while the specific incident is her applying for and moving to a new job.

   In paragraphs 7, 12, and 13, mark the specific incidents with brackets. What contribution does each make to the essay? What can you conclude about the function of incidents in essays about remembered people?

3. In paragraph 3, Rodriguez refers to the irony of his relationship with his parents. Explain in your own words what this irony is. In what ways does he reveal this irony throughout the selection? How does his acknowledging this irony permit him to achieve an unsentimental perspective?

4. Annotate Rodriguez's presentation of one of his parents, concentrating on his "contradictory feelings." Inventory your annotations to discover autobiographers' strategies for presenting significant people in their lives. (Review the Inventory of Annotations in Chapter 1.)

IDEAS FOR YOUR OWN WRITING

If you wrote about a parent or guardian, could you do it with perspective, with some emotional distance, and without sentimentality? Consider which anecdotes you might tell to reveal to your readers what your parent or guardian is like.

Vivian Gornick

From 1969 to 1977, Vivian Gornick (b. 1935) was a staff writer for the *Village Voice*, an influential weekly newspaper published in New York City's Greenwich Village neighborhood. During this period, Gornick also published *In Search of Ali Mahmoud: An American Woman in Egypt* (1973) and *Essays in Feminism* (1979). Her most recent book is an autobiography, *Fierce Attachments* (1987).

Mrs. Kerner

Like Rodriguez, Gornick writes about a significant person from her childhood. She writes about an unusual and memorable neighbor in the Bronx apartment house where she grew up. The mother of her best friend, Mrs. Kerner offered a fascinating contrast to Gornick's own more settled family life. As you read, notice how the accumulating details about Mrs. Kerner present her fully and with all her contradictory aspects.

Every neighborhood had a village idiot or a holy fool; we had three. 1
There was Tom, the sixty-year-old delivery boy who worked for the butcher. He'd carry a package of meat on the run, stop suddenly, throw the package down on the sidewalk, shake his finger at it, and announce: "I'm not going to carry you anymore, you lousy thing you!" There was Lilly, a mongoloid child of forty who wandered about in little-girl dresses, a pink satin bow in her greasy hair, crossing on the red light, cars screeching to a halt all around her. And there was Mrs. Kerner, a tiny, birdlike woman who ran around with her hair wrapped in a cleaning rag, her gestures wild, her manner crazily abrupt. She would stop people she didn't know in the grocery store or the butcher shop or at the druggist's, bring her hands together in a pair of loose fists in front of her face and, her brown eyes shining madly, say, "Oy, I was reading just today a bee-*yoo*-tee-ful story from Russian literature! A story of the heart to make the most miserable of souls cry out against the injustice of this life!" Then she would forget why she was in the store, turn and fly out the door.

Mrs. Kerner was Marilyn Kerner's mother. Marilyn was my best friend. 2
The Kerners lived one floor below us, in the apartment next door, and were as different, my mother thought, from our family as it was possible to be. The difference eluded me. The Kerners were simply the family downstairs, and I thought: Well, that's how they do it in *their* house.

73

Marilyn was an only child. The Kerners had a three-room apartment.   3
Marilyn and her mother slept on twin mahogany bedsteads in the
bedroom; her father slept on a cot beside the couch in the living room.
Mr. Kerner, like my father, worked in the garment district. He was a
handsome, silent man with thick gray hair and cold blue eyes, who lived
in my imagination as a perpetual source of fear and anxiety. His wife and
daughter welcomed his departure and dreaded his arrival. His presence
not only put an immediate stop to afternoon good times in the Kerner
apartment, it was perceived as threatening. When Mrs. Kerner went stiff
and alert at five-thirty, put her forefinger up in the air, and said, "Quiet!
He's coming!" it was as though Bluebeard were about to walk through the
door.

I preferred spending the afternoon in the Kerner apartment to spend-   4
ing it anywhere else. It was like having no parent in the house. Mrs.
Kerner might be masquerading as an adult out on the street, but Marilyn
and I knew better. With Mrs. Kerner it was so obvious that authority was
an acquired position I began to suspect that perhaps more than one
mother was assuming it, not earning it. Mrs. Kerner was enchanting and
irritating: more interesting to be with than any regular mother, and more
oddly instructive. My mother's presence was powerful, but Mrs. Kerner's
was touching. Her distress was so open, so palpable, I would feel a finger
pressing on my heart as she laid herself open to the ridicule and dismissal
of a pair of street-smart twelve-year-olds.

She was a terrible housekeeper who never stopped keeping house. At   5
all times she had a rag tied around her head, a feather duster in her
hand, and an expression of confusion in her eyes. She would wander
around the house, aimlessly flicking the duster here and there. Or she'd
drag out an iron monster of a vacuum cleaner, start it up with a terrific
whining noise that made you think a plane was about to land in the
living room, push it across the threadbare carpet a few times, lose
interest, and leave the vacuum cleaner standing where she turned it off,
sometimes for two or three days.

She baked also: the most godawful stuff, a kind of breadcake loaf,   6
always the same unyielding mass of half-raw dough. She'd break off a
piece, lift it dramatically to her nose, inhale deeply, declare it am-
brosia, and feed it to me or Marilyn. "Tasty, isn't it?" she'd say, beam-
ing, and I'd nod, chewing as fast as I could to get it down (that took a
good three, four minutes), knowing it would weigh on my chest for the
rest of the day. But I wanted to get it down. I knew Mrs. Kerner would
be more confused than usual if I didn't (what was she doing wrong
now?), and I think I felt protective toward her from our earliest time
together.

She never finished vacuuming because halfway through a push across   7
the rug she would stop, jerk about (sometimes forgetting to turn off the
machine), rush into the bedroom or the kitchen, where Marilyn and I
were reading or drawing, and, with her hands on her face and her eyes
shining, exclaim, "Oy, girls! Only this afternoon I was reading a story in
the paper. A woman—poor, good, beautiful—was rushing across the
street, her last penny in her hand to buy milk for a sick child she left
upstairs, only a minute she left it, just to buy milk, a car comes rushing
around the corner, hits her, knocks her down, crushes and destroys her.
A *gevalt*! People come running. Blood everywhere! The world is drenched
in her blood. They take her away. And guess what? You'll never believe
this. It is impossible that the human mind should have imagined what
actually happened. Are you ready? An hour later they find her hand in
the gutter. Still clutching the penny."

Marilyn, if she was drawing, would forget to put down her charcoal   8
stick. I, if I was reading, would remain sitting with a page between my
fingers. Irritated at first by her appearance in the doorway, we invariably
found ourselves drawn in by her urgent, lilting voice. My heart would
beat faster as she spoke, my attention press itself against the unexpected-
ness of her details. Mrs. Kerner was a spellbinder. Hers was the power of
the born storyteller—that is, the one for whom every scrap of experience
is only waiting to be given shape and meaning through the miracle of
narrative speech.

It wasn't a philosophic need to make sense of it all that drove Mrs.   9
Kerner to storytelling. It was, rather, that she treasured feeling, and for
her the arts—music, painting, literature—were a conduit for pure emotion. She told stories because she pined to live in a world of beauty
among cultured people who had feeling. And feeling, girls, was everything. A person's life was made rich or poor, worth a ransom or something to throw away in the gutter, if it was enhanced by or stripped of
feeling.

Mrs. Kerner would generally deliver this impassioned speech about   10
art, life, and feeling after she had told us a story. Sometimes she would
then push up her sleeves and run to the piano, which had been bought
for forty dollars over Mr. Kerner's protest so that Marilyn who hated it,
never touched it, would be able to bring into the house, right into the
house, Chopin, Rachmaninoff, Mozart. The piano stood unused in the
foyer except for the two or three times a week Mrs. Kerner rushed at it,
wiped the bench with her skirt, sat down with the exaggerated motions
of an artist at the piano, raised her arms high in the air, and brought her
fingers down hard into the opening bars of "The Volga Boatmen." That
was it. That was all she could play. The opening bars of "The Volga

Boatmen." These she repeated ten or twenty times with no diminution of interest on either her part or ours.

The piano urge frequently overtook her during the last moments of the afternoon when, feverish with our shared storytelling rapture, she would lose track of the time. As she was crashing about on the piano keys the door would open and we would all freeze. Mr. Kerner would look silently at us. Then he would walk past us into the apartment, take a turn around the living room, come back into the foyer, hang his coat up carefully in the hall closet (he was the most fastidious man I ever knew), say, "The house is a pigpen. What have you been doing all day?" walk back into the living room, sit down in the one upholstered chair, and begin reading the paper. We would all scatter immediately: Mrs. Kerner to the kitchen, Marilyn to the bedroom, I out the door.

One Saturday morning Marilyn and I were on our way to Tremont Avenue, the major shopping street in our neighborhood. Just out the front door, Marilyn remembered that she had forgotten her wallet. We ran back upstairs, rushed into the Kerner apartment, and pushed into the bedroom, Marilyn first me right behind her. She stopped abruptly on the threshold and I rammed into her. With my hands on her back I looked past her shoulder into the room. Mr. and Mrs. Kerner were in one of the mahogany bedsteads, he on top of her, both of them covered with a blanket, only their naked upper bodies visible. His face was buried, hers thrown back, her eyes closed, her mouth twisted in a silent moan. Her hands pressed strongly into his back, his mouth sucked at her neck. The convulsion was violent and, I knew instantly, mutual. A rush of heat and fear went through my body from my throat to my groin. It was that mutuality.

So there were the Kerners, riddled with hate, secretly locked together in sexual spasm, and there were my parents, loving each other, while their bed rode chastely about in open space. Downstairs the house was a shambles, the husband exiled to the living room, the wife a half-mad dreamer; upstairs all was barracks-clean, the husband at the fixed center, the wife impassioned and opinionated. These differences refused to imprint on me. They felt neither striking nor crucial. What did register was that both Mrs. Kerner and my mother adored romantic emotion, and both were married women.

QUESTIONS FOR ANALYSIS

1. Gornick's conclusion startles us, just as it startled her to see the Kerners "locked together in sexual spasm." Her aim in the essay is not

to titillate us with a sexual scene, however, but rather to show the importance of Mrs. Kerner in her life, an aim to which the vividly remembered sexual scene contributes. What would you say was the significance of Mrs. Kerner in Gornick's life? Consider carefully the contrast in the last paragraph between the Kerners and Gornick's parents. Reflect on Gornick's concluding insights about what "refused to imprint" and what "did register."

2. In portraying significant people, autobiographers alternate between specific one-time incidents and generalized recurring events or activities. (Gornick concludes with a single incident, for example, while Rodriguez includes several.) List the generalized activities by which Gornick reveals Mrs. Kerner. What can you conclude about the role of generalized activities in autobiography? Why do you suppose Gornick relies on generalized activities rather than one-time incidents?

3. Novelists and autobiographers are said to emphasize *showing* over *telling*. Gornick, for example, tells us that Mrs. Kerner was an unusual woman (she was "masquerading as an adult," was "enchanting and irritating"), but she goes well beyond *telling* to provide vivid, concrete *showing*. Annotate the essay for two kinds of *showing*: (1) visual details about Mrs. Kerner's appearance and (2) descriptions of her specific actions (movements, expressions, gestures, dialogue). Inventory your annotations. (Review the Inventory of Annotations in Chapter 1.) What does your inventory reveal about Mrs. Kerner, and what can you conclude about Gornick's strategies for *showing*?

4. Because they know that serious readers resist oversimplified views of human experience, autobiographers search out surprising or unusual aspects of experience. They are especially interested in paradoxes and ironies. (A *paradox* brings together seemingly contradictory aspects of a person's actions and motives; *irony* refers to an incongruity or gap between what we expect people to do and what they actually do.) Compare instances of paradox and irony in the Dillard, Rodriquez, and Gornick essays. Consider paradoxes and ironies in the narrator's behavior as well as in the behavior of other people in the essay. How do you respond to the paradoxes and ironies in these essays? What role do you think they play in each essay? Write up the results of your analysis and interpretation. (See Comparing and Contrasting Related Readings in Chapter 1.)

5. Review Exploring Your Personal Response in Chapter 1. Then write a 300–400-word personal response to the Gornick selection, choosing one of the following topics:

Write about the history of your reading of the Gornick selection. That is, tell a story about your impressions and reactions during first and later readings. Reflect on how your response to the selection changed.

Write a letter to Gornick, responding to anything in the selection that you found particularly unusual, interesting, or intriguing.

After you have written your response, reread it thoughtfully. In two or three sentences, say what you learned about the Gornick selection by writing an extended response to it.

IDEAS FOR YOUR OWN WRITING

Choose a person outside your family who had a significant influence on you in your childhood. Which recurring activities and one-time incidents would you choose to characterize this person for your readers? Were there any paradoxes or ironies in your relationship with this person?

Victor Perera

Victor Perera (b. 1934) was born in Guatemala City, Guatemala, and moved as a child to the United States. From 1963 to 1966 he was a member of the *New Yorker* magazine's editorial staff. He has taught writing at several colleges and has published stories and articles in a variety of magazines. He has also translated for publication the poems of the renowned Nobel Prize–winning Chilean writer, Pablo Neruda. Perera's books include a novel, *The Conversion* (1970), and an autobiography, *Rites: A Guatemalan Boyhood* (1986).

Kindergarten

Autobiographers write about specific incidents, and about particular people. They also write about longer, meaningful phases in their lives, phases lasting several weeks or months. In this selection from his autobiography, Perera writes about a time when he was barely five years old and just entering kindergarten, a time when he was first moving out into the world beyond his home. You will see that in his progress he encounters unusual people and strange events. Consider how these seem to affect his development as a person.

My earliest images are geometrical: the narrow bars of the bedstead that I amazed everyone by squeezing through one windy night when I was frightened by a sheet flapping on a clothesline and wanted my mother; the perfect rectangle of Parque Central, with its octagonal tiled benches, encircled fountains, chequered flagstones. And across the way the twin towers of the cathedral, housing a dark mystery of candles and painted idols that would forever be barred to me. *why would it be barred*

In my pedal-car I explored the limits of my universe, always certain that beyond our doorstep and the park's four borders lay unnamed terrors. I was especially fond of a wooded labyrinth in the park's northern end, a dark, sinuous place where I could act out my heroic reveries unseen by Chata, the Indian girl with long braids and sweet-smelling skirts who looked after me. To my five-year-old's eyes Chata seemed a rare beauty; she dressed in the vivid, handwoven *huipil* blouse and skirt of her region, and had unusually fine olive skin. Chata was a spirited and mischievous young woman who let me eat forbidden sweets from street vendors and who would gently tease me into fondling her firm round breasts under the thin blouse. *they had a special re-lationship*

79

I made friends in Parque Central, the year before my second branding. 3
The first I can recall was Jorge, an idiot boy with gray drooping eyes that
did not disguise his sunny nature. I liked Jorge because he was
affectionate—indeed, he was little else—and disarmed my budding defenses by hugging me uninhibitedly and stroking my face. Jorge taught
me to touch another without shame or ulterior motive, and for this I am
forever indebted to him. I grew to love Jorge and had begun to interpret
his grunts and noises into a modest vocabulary when he stopped coming
to the park. Chata found out from his *china* that Jorge had been placed
in a home.

That year I acquired my first heroes, the platoon of uniformed guards 4
who marched past every afternoon on their way to the Palacio. I would
follow them the length of the park, beating my hands to the beat of the
drum, pumping my legs as high as I could to their stride. At the curb I
would stop and mark time until they turned the corner and disappeared.

Chata had an admirer, a tall Indian laborer named Ramiro who 5
courted her in the afternoons and on weekends, when Chata would take
me to the park. Ramiro wore a straw hat and leather shoes, and used to
flash a gold tooth when he smiled or smirked. Chata kept Ramiro on
tenterhooks, encouraging his advances and then rebuffing him with a
toss of her head, or mocking his confusion with a whinnying giggle that
appeared to goad and arouse him. He looked at her at times with a cold,
hungering menace that I recognized even then as lust. I disliked and
feared Ramiro, but I never dared to intrude on their lovers' play or their
frequent spats in the park. Instead, I would retaliate by making Chata
admit, when she tucked me into bed at night, that I was her favorite.

I was some weeks short of five, and small for my age, the first time 6
Chata took me to school and abandoned me in the hands of a tall, gaunt
woman with hard eyes and a pursed mouth. Her name was Miss Hale,
and I detected from her accent that she was foreign.

"Aren't we a little small to be starting school?" she said, in slow, badly 7
slurred Spanish. I understood this to be a taunt, which, on top of my
desertion by Chata, brought tears to my eyes. I feared and distrusted
Miss Hale all the more when I realized this was the exact reaction she
wanted, and my tears had placated her.

The room she led me into was musty and dim. I was presented to my 8
classmates, most of whom seemed strange to me, and very large. Even
their names, Octavio, Gunter, Michel, Loretta, had a foreign ring. From
my earliest consciousness I had known I was a foreigner in this strange
place, Guatemala. Now, in the kindergarten room of the English-
American School, I felt an alien among aliens.

"My mother says you are a Jew." It was Arturo, a dark, thickset boy 9
with hooded eyes and hairy legs below his short trousers. Within a week

he and Gunter, a tall blond boy with smudged knees who made in his pants, established themselves as the class bullies. We were at recess, which meant I could play with my new friends, plump-cheeked Grace Samayoa and Michel Montcrassi, who was French, and wore sandals on his stockinged feet and a round blue cap. There was a fountain in the patio with goldfish in it, and a rising nymph with mossy green feet who poured water from her pitcher. In each corner of the patio (Mother said it had once been a convent) was a large red flowerpot, with pink and white geraniums. I sensed the question was critical and I must reply with care.

"Yes," I said. 10

"My mother says the Jews killed Christ." 11

Now this was a trickier question. Who was Christ? "They did not," I 12 said, but all I could be certain of was that I, at least, had not killed Christ—whoever he was—because I had never killed anyone, at least not knowingly. Then I remembered stepping on a cockroach once, and stomping on ants in the kitchen. Maybe I had killed Christ by accident.

"Prove it," Octavio said. 13

I told him I would ask Father about it and give him a reply the next 14 day.

That night I asked Father why I was a Jew. He hoisted me up by the 15 armpits, sat me on his knee, and told me a long and complicated story about God, the Bible, and a Jew named Moses. When I asked if it was true that the Jews had killed Christ he frowned and said the Romans had done it. He said I should pay no attention to Arturo.

When Arturo approached me next day Father's story had gone clear 16 out of my head. All I remembered was that the Romans had done it.

"The Romans killed Christ," I said. 17

"Who are the Romans?" Arturo asked. 18

I said I wasn't sure, but would ask Father and let him know. 19

When I asked Father in the evening he was reading a newspaper. He 20 said the Romans did it and that was that, and I was to pay no heed to Arturo. Father was not in a talkative mood, and I did not press the matter. But I was confused, and feared my next encounter with Arturo.

Several days passed, and Arturo did not mention the Jews and Christ. 21 I dared hope the whole subject had been forgotten. In the meantime my friendship with Michel grew. He let me call him "Coco," which was his nickname, because his head was round and hard like a coconut; even his curly blond hair resembled a coconut husk. Coco was as much a foreigner in the school as I was. He was Protestant, and the bigger boys mocked his French accent and played catch with his cap.

Grace Samayoa was a little shy of me, although she liked me to tell her 22 stories I'd made up in the labyrinth. Now and again she gave me an approving smile when I answered Miss Hale's questions correctly—and once she let me stroke her hair. Grace Samayoa was the most attractive female I knew next to Chata and my mother. But Grace was also my own size, which made her a challenge. I longed to hug her.

One afternoon Chata failed to pick me up at school. That morning Ramiro had followed us to school, as usual, although they had quarreled in the park the day before when he caught her flirting with a young chauffeur.

"He's following us. Don't turn around," I recall Chata saying, glancing behind her without turning her head. They were the last words of Chata's I would ever hear.

It had grown dark outside and my knees were cold when Father finally came for me, after closing the store.

"Chata has gone away," was all he would say. "We will get you another *china*."

After dinner I went into the kitchen and wormed the truth out of Clara, the cook. She said Chata and I had been followed by Ramiro. After she deposited me at the school he waylaid Chata a block away and gave her "*siete puñaladas en el mero corazón*" (seven knife stabs in the very heart). I accepted Clara's story on faith, not at all concerned that her description matched word for word the title of a popular song. I stamped about the house, pumping my legs high like the palace guards and chanting the song title aloud: "*Sié-te Puña-ládas en El Mero Corazón. Sié-te Puña-ládas en El Mero Corazón.*" The resonance of the phrase, its hard metric beat, gave Chata's disappearance a finality I could comprehend.

The fuller import of Chata's death did not dawn on me until the following day, when I was taken to school by her older sister, Elvira, whose braids were neither as long nor as glossy as Chata's, and whose skirts did not smell half as good.

In the days that followed, Chata's violent death and Arturo's hard questions got mixed together in my dreams, and my apprehension grew that Chata had been murdered because of me, and because I was a Jew.

Unlike her younger sister, Elvira was a practicing Catholic, and one Sunday afternoon she sneaked me into the Cathedral across from the park.

"You must pray to our Lord," she whispered, pointing to the pale naked statue, with bloodied ribs and thorns on his head, that hung with arms outstretched from the front wall, in the same place where the Ark would stand in our synagogue; only this place was a lot bigger and scarier.

When I balked at reciting the Pater Noster she had taught me, Elvira rebuked me, "You must pray to our Lord to be forgiven for your

[margin note:] Was Chata really killed

[margin line numbers:] 23 24 25 26 27 28 29 30 31 32

ancestors' sins against him. That way you can go to Heaven, even if you're not Catholic."

Choking back tears, I mumbled the Pater Noster, not for myself so *really* much but for Chata, who Elvira said had been punished for her sins. *I loved Chata*

During recess one noon Arturo again brought up the Jews and Christ. This time Gunter was with him, and there was something in his face I had not seen there before. Gunter's blue eyes never looked right at yours.

"My mother says all Jews have tails and horns," Arturo said, with an accusing look. Now this I knew was absurd, because I had seen myself in the mirror.

"They do not," I said.

"Jews have bald-headed pigeons," Gunter said, with a smirk.

I flushed, because this was true—at least I did, Father did and Uncle Mair, and Mr. Halevi at the Turkish baths, but not Señor Gonzales and the others there that day—their pigeons weren't bald. . . . But then— what business was it of Gunter's anyway?

"It's none of your business," I said. My face was hot.

"My mother says Jews are the devil," Arturo said, and gave me a shove.

Gunter called the other boys over and said, "Look at the Jew who killed Christ." Then they all gathered behind him and Arturo and stared at me.

"Leave him alone," called a thin, furry voice from the back. "He's not the devil." It was Coco.

"You keep still, dirty Frenchy," Gunter said.

"Dirty Frenchy, dirty Frenchy," chorused the other boys. Someone snatched the beret from Coco's head and they all stomped on it, one by one.

"Let's look at his bald-headed pigeon," Gunter said, turning toward me, without looking in my eyes.

I was growing frightened now, but not of Gunter, whom I suspected to be the instigator of all this. I feared the mob.

"He killed Christ," Gunter said, in a rising voice, and the group behind him grew tighter. Arturo shoved me again, harder. Torn between fear and anger, I wanted to punch Gunter in the face. But Gunter was a head taller than I, and out of reach.

I stretched to my full height. "At least I don't make in my pants," I said, and looked Gunter straight in the eye.

He made a grab for my suspenders and I swung at his face. But Arturo held me fast and then all the other boys fell on top of me. I kicked and scratched and defended myself, but they were too many. When they had stripped off all my clothes—except my shoes and socks—they stepped back to look at me.

"He lost his tail," Arturo said, almost in relief.   50

"But he has a bald-headed pigeon," Gunter said. A giggle came out of   51
his face that was unlike any sound I had ever heard from a boy, or anyone else.

I turned toward the wall. My chest ached from the effort to hold back   52
tears. Several of the boys had drifted away, as if they wished to distance themselves from the two leaders.

Silence, except for the trickle of the fountain and the heaving of my   53
chest. Coco came forward and offered me his crushed beret so I could cover myself.

More boys moved away and I saw that the girls had all gathered at the   54
far end of the patio, behind the fountain—all except Grace Samayoa. She sat on the rim of the fountain, and stared at me.

"Don't look," I said to Grace Samayoa, and turned to one side. But she   55
kept on looking.

Then Grace Samayoa said, "I hate you," and walked toward the girls at   56
the far end of the patio.

I covered myself with Coco's cap, and I cried. I cried at the top of my   57
lungs until Miss Hale came. She cleared everyone from the patio and told me to get dressed.

The following year I was left back in kindergarten. Miss Hale and my   58
parents agreed I was underage for the first grade.

QUESTIONS FOR ANALYSIS

1. How does Perera present the key people from this phase in his life? Choose one person—Chata, Ramiro, Gunter, or Grace—and annotate and then inventory all of the material in the selection presenting that person. (Review the Inventory of Annotations in Chapter 1.) What do you discover about the autobiographer's strategies for presenting people?

2. Perera relies in large part on dialogue to present the most dramatic incident he relates (paragraphs 34–57). Reread this incident, noticing especially the dialogue. How do you think Perera went about reconstructing this long-ago talk? What do you learn from it about the people and events? What can you conclude about the role of dialogue in autobiography?

3. How does Perera organize his essay about this phase in his life? You can see the organization easily if you outline the essay. (Take a

moment to review Outlining in Chapter 1.) What advantages or disadvantages do you find in Perera's organization?

4. What might be the relation among the three grim events in Perera's narrative: the disappearance of Jorge, the murder of Chata, and the attack at the school?

5. Perera comments very little from his adult perspective. Instead, he attempts to remember and reveal his feelings and perceptions as a young child. How successful is he at presenting a five-year-old's experience? Which parts ring truest?

6. What seems to be the significance of this kindergarten phase in Perera's life? Search the story for evidence to support your conclusions.

IDEAS FOR YOUR OWN WRITING

What are your earliest memories of your neighborhood and school? Who were your first friends outside your family? What places and incidents can you recall from your first moments of venturing out into the world? How would you write about this crucial phase in your life? Which people and events would you include?

Alice Walker

Alice Walker was born in 1944 in the small town of Eatonton, Georgia. She has taught for short periods at Jackson State College, Wellesley College, Brandeis University, and the University of California at Berkeley. She is best known for her Pulitzer Prize–winning novel, *The Color Purple* (1982), and the movie based on it. Some consider her first novel, *Meridian* (1976), the best novel of the civil rights movement. Her most recent novel is *The Temple of My Familiar* (1989). She has published two collections of short stories, *In Love and Trouble: Stories of Black Women* (1973) and *You Can't Keep a Good Woman Down* (1981), and four collections of poems, *Once* (1968), *Revolutionary Petunias and Other Poems* (1973), *Goodnight, Willie Lee, I'll See You in the Morning* (1979), and *Horses Make a Landscape Look More Beautiful* (1984). Her essays, written between 1967 and 1982, have been published in *In Search of Our Mothers' Gardens* (1983). Her stories, poems, and essays are often anthologized.

Beauty: When the Other Dancer Is the Self

This selection is the final chapter in Walker's *In Search of Our Mothers' Gardens*. In this essay, Walker ranges across many years of her life, from her early childhood to her mid-thirties, when she is writing the selection. Though she moves around in time, she keeps returning to a single traumatic incident that influenced her life.

It is a bright summer day in 1947. My father, a fat, funny man with beautiful eyes and a subversive wit, is trying to decide which of his eight children he will take with him to the county fair. My mother, of course, will not go. She is knocked out from getting most of us ready: I hold my neck stiff against the pressure of her knuckles as she hastily completes the braiding and then beribboning of my hair.

My father is the driver for the rich old white lady up the road. Her name is Miss Mey. She owns all the land for miles around, as well as the house in which we live. All I remember about her is that she once offered to pay my mother thirty-five cents for cleaning her house, raking up piles of her magnolia leaves, and washing her family's clothes, and that my mother—she of no money, eight children, and a chronic earache—refused it. But I do not think of this in 1947. I am two and a half years old. I want to go everywhere my daddy goes. I am excited at the prospect of riding in

86

a car. Someone has told me fairs are fun. That there is room in the car for only three of us doesn't faze me at all. Whirling happily in my starchy frock, showing off my biscuit-polished patent-leather shoes and lavender socks, tossing my head in a way that makes my ribbons bounce, I stand, hands on hips, before my father. "Take me, Daddy," I say with assurance; "I'm the prettiest!"

Later, it does not surprise me to find myself in Miss Mey's shiny black 3 car, sharing the back seat with the other lucky ones. Does not surprise me that I thoroughly enjoy the fair. At home that night I tell the unlucky ones all I can remember about the merry-go-round, the man who eats live chickens, and the teddy bears, until they say: that's enough, baby Alice. Shut up now, and go to sleep.

It is Easter Sunday, 1950. I am dressed in a green, flocked, scalloped- 4 hem dress (handmade by my adoring sister, Ruth) that has its own smooth satin petticoat and tiny hot-pink roses tucked into each scallop. My shoes, new T-strap patent leather, again highly biscuit-polished. I am six years old and have learned one of the longest Easter speeches to be heard that day, totally unlike the speech I said when I was two: "Easter lilies / pure and white / blossom in / the morning light." When I rise to give my speech I do so on a great wave of love and pride and expectation. People in the church stop rustling their new crinolines. They seem to hold their breath. I can tell they admire my dress, but it is my spirit, bordering on sassiness (womanishness), they secretly applaud.

"That girl's a little *mess*," they whisper to each other, pleased. 5

Naturally I say my speech without stammer or pause, unlike those who 6 stutter, stammer, or, worst of all, forget. This is before the word "beauti-ful" exists in people's vocabulary, but "Oh, isn't she the *cutest* thing!" frequently floats my way. "And got so much sense!" they gratefully add . . . for which thoughtful addition I thank them to this day.

It was great fun being cute. But then, one day, it ended. 7

I am eight years old and a tomboy. I have a cowboy hat, cowboy boots, 8 checkered shirt and pants, all red. My playmates are my brothers, two and four years older than I. Their colors are black and green, the only difference in the way we are dressed. On Saturday nights we all go to the picture show, even my mother; Westerns are her favorite kind of movie. Back home, "on the ranch," we pretend we are Tom Mix, Hopalong Cassidy, Lash LaRue (we've even named one of our dogs Lash LaRue); we chase each other for hours rustling cattle, being outlaws, delivering damsels from distress. Then my parents decide to buy my brothers guns. These are not "real" guns. They shoot "BBs," copper pellets my brothers say will kill birds. Because I am a girl, I do not get a gun. Instantly I am relegated to the position of Indian. Now there appears a great distance between us. They shoot and shoot at everything with their new guns. I try to keep up with my bow and arrows.

One day while I am standing on top of our makeshift "garage"—pieces 9 of tin nailed across some poles—holding my bow and arrow and looking out toward the fields, I feel an incredible blow in my right eye. I look down just in time to see my brother lower his gun.

Both brothers rush to my side. My eye stings, and I cover it with my 10 hand. "If you tell," they say, "we will get a whipping. You don't want that to happen, do you?" I do not. "Here is a piece of wire," says the older brother, picking it up from the roof; "say you stepped on one end of it and the other flew up and hit you." The pain is beginning to start. "Yes," I say. "Yes, I will say that is what happened." If I do not say this is what happened, I know my brothers will find ways to make me wish I had. But now I will say anything that gets me to my mother.

Confronted by our parents we stick to the lie agreed upon. They place 11 me on a bench on the porch and I close my left eye while they examine the right. There is a tree growing from underneath the porch that climbs past the railing to the roof. It is the last thing my right eye sees. I watch as its trunk, its branches, and then its leaves are blotted out by the rising blood.

I am in shock. First there is intense fever, which my father tries to 12 break using lily leaves bound around my head. Then there are chills: my mother tries to get me to eat soup. Eventually, I do not know how, my parents learn what has happened. A week after the "accident" they take me to see a doctor. "Why did you wait so long to come?" he asks, looking into my eye and shaking his head. "Eyes are sympathetic," he says. "If one is blind, the other will likely become blind too."

This comment of the doctor's terrifies me. But it is really how I look 13 that bothers me most. Where the BB pellet struck there is a glob of whitish scar tissue, a hideous cataract, on my eye. Now when I stare at people—a favorite pastime, up to now—they will stare back. Not at the "cute" little girl, but at her scar. For six years I do not stare at anyone, because I do not raise my head.

Years later, in the throes of a mid-life crisis, I ask my mother and sister 14 whether I changed after the "accident." "No," they say, puzzled. "What do you mean?"

What do I mean?   15

I am eight, and, for the first time, doing poorly in school, where I have 16 been something of a whiz since I was four. We have just moved to the place where the "accident" occurred. We do not know any of the people around us because this is a different county. The only time I see the friends I knew is when we go back to our old church. The new school is the former state penitentiary. It is a large stone building, cold and drafty, crammed to overflowing with boisterous, ill-disciplined children. On the third floor there is a huge circular imprint of some partition that has been torn out.

"What used to be here?" I ask a sullen girl next to me on our way past 17
it to lunch.

"The electric chair," says she. 18

At night I have nightmares about the electric chair, and about all the 19
people reputedly "fried" in it. I am afraid of the school, where all the students seem to be budding criminals.

"What's the matter with your eye?" they ask, critically. 20

When I don't answer (I cannot decide whether it was an "accident" or 21
not), they shove me, insist on a fight.

My brother, the one who created the story about the wire, comes to 22
my rescue. But then brags so much about "protecting" me, I become sick.

After months of torture at the school, my parents decide to send me 23
back to our old community, to my old school. I live with my grand-parents and the teacher they board. But there is no room for Phoebe, my cat. By the time my grandparents decide there *is* room, and I ask for my cat, she cannot be found. Miss Yarborough, the boarding teacher, takes me under her wing, and begins to teach me to play the piano. But soon she marries an African—a "prince," she says—and is whisked away to his continent.

At my old school there is at least one teacher who loves me. She is the 24
teacher who "knew me before I was born" and bought my first baby clothes. It is she who makes life bearable. It is her presence that finally helps me turn on the one child at the school who continually calls me "one-eyed bitch." One day I simply grab him by his coat and beat him until I am satisfied. It is my teacher who tells me my mother is ill.

My mother is lying in bed in the middle of the day, something I have 25
never seen. She is in too much pain to speak. She has an abscess in her ear. I stand looking down on her, knowing that if she dies, I cannot live. She is being treated with warm oils and hot bricks held against her cheek. Finally a doctor comes. But I must go back to my grandparents' house. The weeks pass but I am hardly aware of it. All I know is that my mother might die, my father is not so jolly, my brothers still have their guns, and I am the one sent away from home.

"You did not change," they say. 26

Did I imagine the anguish of never looking up?   27

I am twelve. When relatives come to visit I hide in my room. My   28
cousin Brenda, just my age, whose father works in the post office and
whose mother is a nurse, comes to find me. "Hello," she says. And then
she asks, looking at my recent school picture, which I did not want
taken, and on which the "glob," as I think of it, is clearly visible, "You
still can't see out of that eye?"

"No," I say, and flop back on the bed over my book.   29

That night, as I do almost every night, I abuse my eye. I rant and rave   30
at it, in front of the mirror. I plead with it to clear up before morning. I
tell it I hate and despise it. I do not pray for sight. I pray for beauty.

"You did not change," they say.   31

I am fourteen and baby-sitting for my brother Bill, who lives in   32
Boston. He is my favorite brother and there is a strong bond between us.
Understanding my feelings of shame and ugliness he and his wife take me
to a local hospital, where the "glob" is removed by a doctor named O.
Henry. There is still a small bluish crater where the scar tissue was, but
the ugly white stuff is gone. Almost immediately I become a different
person from the girl who does not raise her head. Or so I think. Now that
I've raised my head I win the boyfriend of my dreams. Now that I've
raised my head I have plenty of friends. Now that I've raised my head
classwork comes from my lips as faultlessly as Easter speeches did, and I
leave high school as valedictorian, most popular student, and *queen*,
hardly believing my luck. Ironically, the girl who was voted most beautiful in our class (and was) was later shot twice through the chest by a male
companion, using a "real" gun, while she was pregnant. But that's
another story in itself. Or is it? Male violence towards
women —
"You did not change," they say.   33

It is now thirty years since the "accident." A beautiful journalist comes   34
to visit and to interview me. She is going to write a cover story for her
magazine that focuses on my latest book. "Decide how you want to look
on the cover," she says. "Glamorous, or whatever."

Never mind "glamorous," it is the "whatever" that I hear. Suddenly all   35
I can think of is whether I will get enough sleep the night before the
photography session: if I don't, my eye will be tired and wander, as blind
eyes will.

At night in bed with my lover I think up reasons why I should not   36
appear on the cover of a magazine. "My meanest critics will say I've sold
out," I say. "My family will now realize I write scandalous books."

"But what's the real reason you don't want to do this?" he asks.   37

"Because in all probability," I say in a rush, "my eye won't be straight." 38

"It will be straight enough," he says. Then, "Besides, I thought you'd 39 made your peace with that."

And I suddenly remember that I have. 40

I remember:

I am talking to my brother Jimmy, asking if he remembers anything 41 unusual about the day I was shot. He does not know I consider that day the last time my father, with his sweet home remedy of cool lily leaves, chose me, and that I suffered and raged inside because of this. "Well," he says, "all I remember is standing by the side of the highway with Daddy, trying to flag down a car. A white man stopped, but when Daddy said he needed somebody to take his little girl to the doctor, he drove off."

I remember:

I am in the desert for the first time. I fall totally in love with it. I am so 42 overwhelmed by its beauty, I confront for the first time, consciously, the meaning of the doctor's words years ago: "Eyes are sympathetic. If one is blind, the other will likely become blind too." I realize I have dashed about the world madly, looking at this, looking at that, storing up images against the fading of the light. *But I might have missed seeing the desert!* The shock of that possibility—and gratitude for over twenty-five years of sight—sends me literally to my knees. Poem after poem comes—which is perhaps how poets pray.

ON SIGHT

I am so thankful I have seen
The Desert
And the creatures in the desert
And the desert Itself.

The desert has its own moon
Which I have seen
With my own eye.
There is no flag on it.

Trees of the desert have arms
All of which are always up
That is because the moon is up
The sun is up
Also the sky
The stars
Clouds
None with flags.

If there *were* flags, I doubt
the trees would point.
Would you?

But mostly, I remember this:

I am twenty-seven, and my baby daughter is almost three. Since her   43
birth I have worried about her discovery that her mother's eyes are
different from other people's. Will she be embarrassed? I think. What will
she say? Every day she watches a television program called "Big Blue
Marble." It begins with a picture of the earth as it appears from the
moon. It is bluish, a little battered-looking, but full of light, with whitish
clouds swirling around it. Every time I see it I weep with love, as if it is a
picture of Grandma's house. One day when I am putting Rebecca down
for her nap, she suddenly focuses on my eye. Something inside me
cringes, gets ready to try to protect myself. All children are cruel about
physical differences, I know from experience, and that they don't always
mean to be is another matter. I assume Rebecca will be the same.

But no-o-o-o. She studies my face intently as we stand, her inside and   44
me outside her crib. She even holds my face maternally between her
dimpled little hands. Then, looking every bit as serious and lawyerlike as
her father, she says, as if it may just possibly have slipped my attention:
"Mommy, there's a *world* in your eye." (As in, "Don't be alarmed, or do
anything crazy.") And then, gently, but with great interest: "Mommy,
where did you *get* that world in your eye?"

For the most part, the pain left then. (So what, if my brothers grew up   45
to buy even more powerful pellet guns for their sons and to carry real
guns themselves. So what, if a young "Morehouse man" once nearly fell
off the steps of Trevor Arnett Library because he thought my eyes were
blue.) Crying and laughing I ran to the bathroom, while Rebecca
mumbled and sang herself off to sleep. Yes indeed, I realized, looking into
the mirror. There *was* a world in my eye. And I saw that it was possible to
love it: that in fact, for all it had taught me of shame and anger and inner
vision, I *did* love it. Even to see it drifting out of orbit in boredom, or
rolling up out of fatigue, not to mention floating back at attention in
excitement (bearing witness, a friend has called it), deeply suitable to my
personality, and even characteristic of me.

That night I dream I am dancing to Stevie Wonder's song "Always"   46
(the name of the song is really "As," but I hear it as "Always"). As I
dance, whirling and joyous, happier than I've ever been in my life,
another bright-faced dancer joins me. We dance and kiss each other and
hold each other through the night. The other dancer has obviously come
through all right, as I have done. She is beautiful, whole and free. And
she is also me.

QUESTIONS FOR ANALYSIS

1. How would you explain the significance for Walker of the central
   incident in this selection?

2. What impression do you get of Walker from this selection? Point to specific parts of the selection that support your impression.

3. Outline this selection by listing each specific incident and indicating Walker's approximate age at the time of that incident. Why do you think Walker chose each of these incidents? What seems to be the relevance of each incident to Walker's autobiographical disclosure?

4. Choose the one incident that for you is most memorably presented. How exactly does Walker present this incident? Explain why you find it so effective.

5. Analyze how Walker uses the repeated phrases "You did not change" and "I remember." When does Walker use these phrases, and to what effect? What advantages or disadvantages do you see in this strategy of repetition?

6. How does Walker begin (paragraph 1) and end (paragraph 46) this essay? What relation do you see between the beginning and ending?

7. Select at least three paragraphs from the selection that contain dialogue. Keeping in mind that Walker could have summarized rather than quoted, decide why she might have chosen to use dialogue in each of these paragraphs.

IDEAS FOR YOUR OWN WRITING

Think about the crucial events in your childhood and adolescence. Which one might you write about? How would you go about presenting this event for your readers and showing them how it has continued to be important in your life?

Brad Benioff

Brad Benioff was a freshman at the University of California at San Diego when he wrote the following essay for his composition class.

Rick

Like the Gornick selection earlier in this chapter, Benioff's essay focuses on a single memorable person. Benioff writes about his high-school water polo coach, Rick Rezinas. As you read, notice how Benioff uses dialogue to dramatize his relation to Rick and how he discloses Rick's significance in his life.

I walked through the dawn chill, shivering as much from nervousness 1 as from the cold. Steam curled up from the water in the pool and disappeared in the ocher morning light. Athletes spread themselves about on the deck, lazily stretching and whispering to each other as if the stillness were sacred. It was to be my first practice with the high school water polo team. I knew nothing about the game, but a friend had pushed me to play, arguing, "It's the most fun of any sport. Trust me." He had awakened me that morning long before daylight, forced me into a bathing suit, and driven me to the pool.

"Relax," he said. "Rick is the greatest of coaches. You'll like him. You'll 2 have fun."

The mythical Rick. I had heard of him many times before. All the 3 older players knew him by his first name and always spoke of him as a friend rather than a coach. He was a math teacher at our school, and his classes were very popular. Whenever class schedules came out, everyone hoped to be placed in Mr. Rezinas's class. He had been known to throw parties for the team or take them on weekend excursions skiing or backpacking. To be Rick's friend was to be part of an exclusive club, and I was being invited to join. And so I looked forward with nervous anticipation to meeting this man.

My friend walked me out to the pool deck and steered me toward a 4 man standing beside the pool.

"Rick," announced my friend, "I'd like you to meet your newest 5 player."

Rick was not a friendly looking man. He wore only swim trunks, and 6 his short, powerful legs rose up to meet a bulging torso. His big belly was solid. His shoulders, as if to offset his front-heaviness, were thrown back, creating a deep crease of excess muscle from his sides around the small of his back, a crease like a huge frown. His arms were crossed, two medieval maces placed carefully on their racks, ready to be swung at any moment. His round cheeks and chin were darkened by traces of black whiskers. His hair was sparse. Huge, black, mirrored sunglasses replaced his eyes. Below his prominent nose was a thin, sinister mustache. I couldn't believe this menacing-looking man was the legendary jovial Rick.

He said nothing at first. In those moments of silence, I felt more inadequate than ever before in my life. My reflection in his glasses stared back at me, accusing me of being too skinny, too young, too stupid, too weak to be on his team. Where did I get the nerve to approach him with such a ridiculous body and ask to play water polo, a *man's* game? Finally, he broke the silence, having finished appraising my meager body. "We'll fatten him up," he growled.   7

Thus began a week of torture. For four hours a day, the coach stood beside the pool scowling down at me. I could do nothing right.   8

"No! No! No!" He shook his head in disgust. "Throw the damn ball with your whole arm! Get your goddamn elbow out of the water!"   9

Any failure on my part brought down his full wrath. He bellowed at my incompetence and punished me with push-ups and wind sprints. Even when I was close to utter exhaustion, I found no sympathy. "What the hell are you doing on the wall?" he would bellow. "Coach . . . my side, it's cramped."   10

"Swim on it! If you can't take a little pain, then you don't play!" With this, he would push me off the wall.   11

He seemed to enjoy playing me against the older, stronger players. "Goddamn it, Brad! If someone elbows or hits you, don't look out at me and cry, 'It's not fair.' Push back! Don't be so weak!" I got elbowed around until it seemed that none of my internal organs was unscathed. He worked me until my muscles wouldn't respond, and then he demanded more.   12

"You're not trying! Push it!"   13

"Would you move? You're too slow! Swim!"   14

"Damn it! Get out and give me twenty!"   15

It took little time for me to hate both the game and the man who ruled it.   16

I reacted by working as hard as I could. I decided to deprive him of the pleasure of finding fault with me. I learned quickly and started playing as flawlessly as possible. I dispensed with looking tired, showing pain, or complaining of cramps. I pushed, hit, and elbowed back at the biggest of players. No matter how flawless or aggressive my performance, though,   17 he would find fault and let me know it. He was never critical of other players. He would laugh and joke with the other players; but whenever he saw me, he frowned.

I decided to quit.   18

After a particularly demanding practice, I walked up to this tyrant. I   19 tried to hold his gaze, but the black glasses forced me to look down.

"Coach Rezinas," I blurted, "I've decided that I don't want to play   20 water polo." His scowl deepened. Then after a moment he said, "You can't quit. Not until after the first game." And he walked away. The dictator had issued his command.

There was no rule to keep me from quitting. Anger flushed through   21 me. Somehow I would get revenge on this awful man. After the first game? Okay. I would play. I would show him what a valuable player I was. He would miss my talents when I quit. I worked myself up before the first game by imagining the hated face: the black glasses, the thin mustache, the open, snarling mouth. I was not surprised that he placed me in the starting lineup because I was certain he would take me out soon. I played furiously. The ball, the goal, the opposition, even the water seemed to be extensions of Rick, his face glaring from every angle, his words echoing loudly in my ears. Time and time again I would get the ball and, thinking of his tortures, fire it toward the goal with a strength to kill. I forgot that he might take me out. No defender could stand up to me. I would swim by them or over them. Anger and the need for vengeance gave me energy. I didn't notice the time slipping by, the quarters ending.

Then, the game ended. My teammates rushed out to me, congratulat-   22 ing and cheering me. I had scored five goals, a school record for one game, and shut out the other team with several key defensive plays. Now I could get revenge. Now I could quit. I stepped out of the pool prepared with the words I would spit into his face: "I QUIT!"

As I approached him, I stopped dead. He was smiling at me, his glasses   23 off. He reached out with his right hand and shook mine with exuberance.

"I knew you had it in you! I knew it!" he laughed.   24

Through his laughter, I gained a new understanding of the man. He   25 had pushed me to my fullest potential, tapping into the talent I may never have found in myself. He was responsible for the way I played that day. My glory was his. He never hated me. On the contrary, I was his apprentice, his favored pupil. He had brought out my best. Could I really hate someone who had done that much for me? He had done what he had promised: he had fattened me up mentally as well as physically. All this hit me in a second and left me completely confused. I tried to speak, but only managed to croak, "Coach . . . uh . . . I, uh . . ." He cut me off with another burst of laughter. He still shook my hand.

"Call me Rick," he said.   26

QUESTIONS FOR ANALYSIS

1. How would you explain the significance of Rick in Benioff's life?

2. Benioff includes scenes, incidents, and people. Which one of these features receives most emphasis? Given Benioff's purpose, how do you assess this emphasis?

3. Benioff includes typical interactions with his coach as well as specific one-time dramatic confrontations. Identify these one-time confrontations. What role do they play in the essay? What is Benioff's strategy in presenting them?

4. Compare or contrast the Benioff and Gornick essays, both written about a memorable adult from the writer's adolescence. First, review Comparing and Contrasting Related Readings in Chapter 1. Then reread each essay, deciding on one or two main likenesses or differences as the focus for your comparison or contrast. Once you have chosen the basis for comparison or contrast—perhaps organization, or strategies of presenting the subject, or paradoxes and ironies (see question 4 following Gornick's essay), or some other feature— annotate that feature in both essays. Write up the results of your analysis. Your purpose is not to argue that one essay is better but only to report the likenesses or differences in the one or two features you have singled out.

IDEAS FOR YOUR OWN WRITING

Consider school coaches and other coaches who have influenced your life. Choose one of these people, and think about how you might describe what the individual taught you and how he or she went about it. How would you reveal your reaction and what you learned about the person and about yourself? Or consider the adults with whom you had continuing disagreements or conflicts when you were a child or teenager. Choose one of these people—a parent, relative, teacher, or neighbor, for example—and speculate about how you might present this adult and show the nature of the disagreement through specific incidents. How might you disclose what you learned about the adult and about yourself?

A GUIDE TO
AUTOBIOGRAPHICAL WRITING

From the autobiographical selections you have read and analyzed in this chapter, you have learned that autobiographical essays include engaging stories; vivid scenes; memorable people; and personal disclosure by the writer, indicating the autobiographical significance of the events, phases, or people. Having learned to question, evaluate, and appreciate autobiography as a reader, you can now approach autobiography more confidently as a writer. You can more readily imagine the problems autobiographers must solve, the materials and possibilities they have to work with, the choices and decisions they must make. This section offers specific guidelines for writing autobiographical essays and suggestions to help you solve the special problems this kind of writing presents.

The Writing Task

Write an autobiographical essay about a significant event, phase, or person in your life. Choose a subject that will be engaging for your readers. Write about your subject dramatically and vividly, giving a clear indication of its autobiographical significance.

Invention

The following activities will help you to find an autobiographical topic to write about, to recall details of this topic, and to explore its significance in your life. Completing these activities will produce a record of remembered details and thoughts that will be invaluable as you draft your essay.

FINDING AN AUTOBIOGRAPHICAL TOPIC. The readings in this chapter illustrate many possible autobiographical topics, as do the ideas for your own writing that follow each reading. You might want to review these quickly before you begin.

It is more likely that you will find a promising topic if you have many diverse possibilities to choose from. You might therefore begin your search by listing potential subjects, using the three autobiographical categories illustrated in this chapter as a starting point. List as many specific topics as you can under each of these categories: event, phase, person. The growing list may suggest still further topics that might not have come to mind immediately.

For *events*, list especially memorable brief events of a few hours or, at most, a day in length. Think of the first time you did something; of accidents, surprises, victories, defeats; of moments of discovery or awareness.

For *phases*, list periods of several weeks or months when something important was happening in your life, when you were changing in a significant way. Perhaps participating in a particular group, class, or team challenged you in some way or changed your beliefs or ideas. You may have moved to a new city or school and had to make a difficult adjustment, or you may have been ill for a long time. Maybe you learned something new or developed a new interest. Think of recent phases as well as ones much earlier in your life.

For *persons*, list significant people in your life. Think of people who taught you something about yourself, who surprised or disappointed you, or who had authority over you.

This list-making process will almost certainly produce a number of possible topics for your autobiographical essay. The topic you ultimately choose should be one you truly care about, one that will give you the pleasure of recalling past experience and deciding what it means to you. Your topic should also be one that is likely to engage your readers, who will enjoy reflecting on their own lives as they read about yours. Finally, and of the greatest importance, your topic should have rich autobiographical significance. In autobiographical writing, you will describe events, phases, and people; but you will do so in an expressive and revealing way. Readers expect to hear a personal voice in autobiography. They expect personal disclosure—even risky and surprising disclosure—not just amiable reporting. Fulfilling this expectation is the special challenge of autobiographical writing.

PROBING YOUR TOPIC. Once you have selected a topic, probe your memory to recall details and feelings. You should explore your present perspective on this topic and attempt to establish its autobiographical significance. The following activities will guide you in probing your subject, in order to produce a fuller, more focused draft. Each activity takes only a few minutes to complete.

Recalling First Impressions. Write for a few minutes about your very first thoughts and feelings about the event, phase, or person. What happened? Who was there? How did you react? What thoughts did you have? What feelings can you remember? What do your first impressions reveal about you as a person?

Exploring Your Present Perspective. Next, shift your focus from the past to the present. From your present perspective, what ideas do you have about the event, phase, or person? Write for a few minutes, trying to express your present thoughts and feelings. How have your feelings changed? What insights do you now have? What does your present perspective reveal about you as a person?

Stating Autobiographical Significance. Readers want not only to hear your story but also to know what it means to you, what you learned from it, how it changed you. Now that you have explored your first impressions and present perspective of the event, phase, or person, try writing two or three sentences that state its significance in your life. These sentences may eventually help you to focus your draft, providing a purpose and a main point for your writing.

Identifying Particulars of the Scene. If readers are to imagine the particulars of your story, you must show them who was there and what the scene looked like. Think of your topic and the important people and particular objects in the scene (or scenes). In your mind's eye, survey the location of your topic, trying to visualize again all the important particulars. List the most important objects and people.

Detailing the Scene. In order to make the scene vivid and memorable for readers and to understand its significance for you, try moving in close and presenting details of some particulars in the scene. Choose two or three objects or people from your list, and write about each for a few minutes, detailing each object or person as fully as you can. Try to recall specific sensory details: size, appearance, dress, way of walking and gesturing, posture, and mannerisms of a person; size, shape, color, condition, and texture of an object. Imagine the object or person seen from the side, from behind, from a distance, and close up. Write down what you see.

Reconstructing Dialogue. Reconstructed conversations are often important in modern autobiography. If another person plays a role in your topic—even a minor role—reconstruct what the two of you might have said to each other. Keep your dialogue as close to informal talk as you can, and use the following format:

[Your name]: [What you said]

[Other person's name]: [What the other person said]

[Continue alternating contributions down the page.]

Restating Autobiographical Significance. Now that you have explored your topic in several ways, write two or three sentences restating its significance in your life. Why is this event, phase, or person still important to you? What do you think you might learn about yourself as you write? What do you want to disclose about yourself to your readers?

This final restatement of autobiographical significance will help you to focus your thoughts before you begin drafting. It will also guide you in selecting details to include in your essay.

Drafting

Before you begin drafting, review the invention writing you have completed. Reread your notes, searching for promising ideas and notable details; then jot down any further ideas and details your notes suggest to you.

You are now ready to proceed to your first draft. The following guidelines will help you set goals to focus your writing, make specific plans for your essay, and decide how to begin.

SETTING GOALS. Establishing specific goals before you begin and keeping them in mind as you write will enable you to draft more confidently. The following questions may help you to set goals for your draft: What do I want to accomplish with this autobiographical essay? How can I present my topic vividly and memorably to my readers? Like Baker and Benioff, should I rely on reconstructed conversation to dramatize an incident or a relationship with another person? To describe a person, should I attempt Gornick's variety of details about Mrs. Kerner—her manner, movements, dress, repetitive piano playing, dramatic stories, and her relationship with her husband?

How will I tell readers why this event, phase, or person is important to me? For example, Benioff leaves us to infer how Coach Rick Rezinas has been a significant influence in his life. Walker in part presents the significance of her struggle with disfigurement through a dream. Gornick tells us directly what she learned from Mrs. Kerner, just as Baker states explicitly the significance of the incident involving Herbert Hoover's campaign poster.

How will I begin engagingly and hold my reader's interest? How can this essay about my experience lead readers to reflect on their own experience?

How can I avoid superficial or one-dimensional presentations of myself and my relations with others? Readers are turned off by predictable stories and people. They expect surprises, contradictions, paradoxes, ironies—signs that the writer is thinking deeply, freshly, and honestly, probing remembered experience in a way that may teach both the writer and the reader something about the human condition. Recall the paradox in Dillard's feeling both terror and pleasure when she was chased by the man in the black Buick, the paradox of the Kerners' repulsion and attraction to each other in Gornick's essay, the irony of romance with violence and the shame of discrimination in Perera's essay, Rodriguez's disclosure of guilt for being ashamed of his parents, and Walker's admission of the effects on her childhood of a disfiguring wound.

PLANNING YOUR ORGANIZATION. The particular goals you have established will determine the plan of your draft. Although this plan can unfold as you write, many writers find it helpful to sketch out a tentative plan before they begin drafting. If you plan to narrate a single event, for example, you could outline briefly what happens from beginning to end. If you plan to describe a person, you might plan the order in which major features of your description will appear. Reviewing plans of selections in this chapter will suggest possibilities. Be prepared to depart from your plan once you have started writing, since drafting nearly always produces unexpected discoveries that may make it necessary to change direction.

BEGINNING. A strong beginning will immediately engage readers' interest, so consider beginning your essay with dialogue, with an unusual detail of a person or scene, or with an action. You might also begin by presenting the context for your essay, orienting readers in a general way to the event, phase, or person. For example, Walker begins with activity—getting ready for the county fair, competing with brothers and sisters for a place in the car, driving off down the road. Benioff begins with a specific scene, the school's swimming pool in the early morning light.

   Gornick begins with offbeat characterizations of three of her neighborhood's "holy fools." Dillard begins more conventionally, though no less successfully, by giving us a context for the story she will tell.

   You might have to try two or three different beginnings before finding a promising way to start, but do not agonize for too long over the first sentence. Try out any possible beginning and see what happens.

CHOOSING RELEVANT DETAILS. If you have had a successful period of invention, you probably already have more particular details than you can use in one essay. Well-prepared writers must spend a great deal of time deciding which details and information to leave out. As you draft, remember to include enough details so that readers can imagine the person or scene but only those details that support the autobiographical disclosure you are making.

Revising

Once you have completed a first draft, you should try to find ways to strengthen it so that it comes closer to achieving your goals. The questions for analyzing basic features at the beginning of this chapter will guide you in reading your draft critically and determining how it can be improved. You should also try to have someone else read your draft in light of these questions.

As you revise an autobiographical essay, concentrate on clarifying the autobiographical significance, strengthening particularity, and improving readability.

REVISING TO CLARIFY AUTOBIOGRAPHICAL SIGNIFICANCE. Remember that readers of autobiography want to know why the event, phase, or person was important in the writer's life. They also want to reflect on similar episodes in their own lives. Try to clarify and focus the autobiographical significance in your draft, and remove any details that do not contribute to it. Reconsider your tone of voice and perspective. Consider adding further details, scenes, or anecdotes to demonstrate the importance of the episode in your life.

REVISING TO STRENGTHEN PARTICULARITY. Reconsider how well you have presented the scene and people to your readers. You may need to reduce the number of particular details in order to keep the essay in focus, or you may want to add details to enable readers to imagine the scene and people more vividly. Keeping in mind that any additional details should support the autobiographical significance, try to identify other objects or people in the scene and provide specific details about them. Consider whether you should include a fuller range of sensory details—sounds and smells, in addition to sights. Decide whether you should recreate dialogues to particularize your summaries of conversations or to dramatize relations between people.

REVISING TO IMPROVE READABILITY. Imagine a reader reading your essay for the first time, sentence by sentence. This reader's inevitable first question will be, do I really want to read this? Decide whether you can improve your beginning to engage this reader immediately. Look for any gaps in your essay, and think about how you might smooth the transition from one part to the next. Find any overly complicated or slow sections from which you could delete unnecessary material. Look for sentences that could be clarified or perhaps combined with adjacent sentences. Decide whether you can improve your ending to provide a more dramatic, memorable, and satisfying conclusion.

When you have a final version of your essay, proofread it closely for mistakes in spelling, usage, and punctuation. If possible, have someone else examine your essay for such mistakes too.

CHAPTER THREE

Reflection

The reflective essay is an exercise in the art of inquiry—informal, exploratory, often inconclusive. It can be traced back to 1580, when the French nobleman Michel Eyquem de Montaigne published a collection of reflections he called *Essays*, a word which in French means "tests" or "trials." Although the word *essay* is used more generally now to refer to nonfiction prose written for many different purposes, the reflective essay remains true to its original purpose: to test or try out ideas.

Written for the sheer pleasure of exploring a question or pursuing an insight, the reflective essay typically moves from experience to idea, from particular to general. An ordinary thing seen, heard, read, or felt triggers the reflections. From there on, one idea leads to another as the writing moves toward insights about the way people are and the way things happen.

The subjects of reflective essays—self-esteem, intimacy, fear—tend to be far-reaching. Yet, writers of reflection have relatively modest goals. They do not attempt to exhaust their subjects, nor do they set themselves up as experts. They simply try, as Montaigne explains, to see what they have to say about the subject:

> I take the first subject that chance offers. They are all equally good to me. And I never plan to develop them completely. For I do not see the whole of anything, nor do those who promise to show it to us. Of a hundred members and faces that each thing has, I take one, sometimes only to lick it, sometimes to brush the surface, sometimes to pinch it to the bone. I give it a stab, not as wide but as deep as I know

how. And most often I like to take them from some unaccustomed point of view.
. . . I want to be seen in my simple, natural, ordinary fashion, without straining or
artifice; for it is myself that I portray.

When Montaigne writes "it is myself that I portray," he reminds us of
the central role self-presentation plays in the reflective essay. Reflective
essayists present themselves not only by what they say but also by how
they say it. Their essays give readers a strong image of the writer, what we
call the *persona* or voice of an essay.

Whatever his or her persona, the reflective essayist typically addresses
readers directly and openly, making us want to know what the writer is
thinking. It is as if the writer were sitting across from the reader talking
about what happened and what it might mean. This conversational tone
characterizes the reflective essay and can be quite seductive, as we hope
you will discover in reading the essays included in this chapter.

A GUIDE TO
READING REFLECTIVE WRITING

To begin to understand how the reflective essay works, you will first
look closely at an example by essayist Phyllis Theroux. Closely analyzing
Theroux's work will provide a foundation for the serious study of reflective writing this chapter encourages. As you become a more critical,
insightful reader of reflection, your own writing will become more vivid
and engaging.

As the initial step in your analysis, you will annotate Theroux's essay.
The next exercise asks you to take inventory of your annotations in order
to disclose the pattern of meaning you have discovered. In the third
exercise, guided by special questions, you will report what you have
learned in analyzing the unique features of the reflective essay. Finally,
the concluding exercise invites you to write a brief exploratory essay,
consolidating what you have learned about Theroux's essay and trying
out your own ideas about it or extending your personal response to it.

The time you invest now in annotating, analyzing, and writing will pay
off richly as you read, write about, and discuss the essays in this chapter.
It will also give you confidence that you can write your own engaging,
imaginative reflective essay.

Annotating As You Read

As we have discussed, the most basic, and most useful, strategy for
reading attentively and critically is annotating. Pencil in hand as you

read, you are ready to record on the page any comments, questions, definitions, or insights—whatever crosses your mind—about a piece of writing. As an illustration, note how we have annotated the following brief passage from a reflective essay by Joan Didion that appears in its entirety later in this chapter.

Sets up opposition:
With self-respect:
freedom to choose

[To have] that sense of one's intrinsic worth which constitutes self-respect is potentially to have everything: the ability to discriminate, to love and to remain indifferent. [To lack] it is to be locked within oneself, paradoxically incapable of either love or indifference. If we do not respect ourselves, we are on the one hand forced to despise those who have so few resources as to consort with us, so little perception as to remain blind to our fatal weaknesses. [On the other,] we are peculiarly in thrall to everyone we see, curiously determined to live out—since our self-image is untenable—their false notions of us. We flatter ourselves by thinking this compulsion to please others an attractive trait: a gist for imaginative empathy, evidence of our willingness to give. Of course I will play Francesca to your Paolo, Helen Keller to anyone's Annie Sullivan: no expectation is too misplaced, no role too ludicrous. At the mercy of those we cannot but hold in contempt, we play roles doomed to failure before they are begun, each defeat generating fresh despair at the urgency of divining and meeting the next demand made upon us.

Without self-respect:
compulsion to
please others

untenable: **can't be**
maintained or
defended

Paradox: need
approval of those we
despise

Depressing

For more on annotating, pause now to review the guidelines in Chapter 1 and the model annotations on the excerpt from "Letter from Birmingham Jail." Note particularly the Checklist for Annotating.

Exercise 1

Annotate Phyllis Theroux's "Fear of Families" as you read. Reread the essay at least one time, continuing to annotate as you reread. Your purpose is to focus your attention on the text, to read as thoughtfully—as critically—as possible. Annotate details you admire as well as things you question or challenge, mark noteworthy stylistic devices or writing strategies, write down any personal responses. Record your insights and reactions directly on and around the text itself.

Phyllis Theroux (b. 1939) is a professional writer whose reflective essays appear regularly in newspapers like the *Washington Post* and the *New York Times* and in magazines like *Mademoiselle* and *Reader's Digest*. She has published two collections of essays, *California and Other States of Grace* (1980) and *Peripheral Visions* (1982).

Reprinted in *Peripheral Visions*, "Fear of Families" originally appeared in an early January issue of the *Times*, shortly after the Christmas and New Year's holidays. Preview the essay briefly. What do you think Theroux's title means? What might be the difference in calling the essay "Fear *in* Families" instead of "Fear *of* Families"?

Fear of Families
Phyllis Theroux

As life goes on and independence becomes necessary 1 for survival, pride of family can turn into fear of family, and during this past Christmas and New Year's season, which I celebrated with a number of other people's relatives, it appeared that fear of families is not a unique problem. To sit around a table with all those faces that give back the truth, the whole truth, and quite possibly nothing but the truth about ourselves, can give one a "so help me God" feeling.

Twelve months of apartness culminating in a week of 2 togetherness can turn a family reunion into a family face-off. The odds are that somebody will "say something," a stiffness will descend over the table, and several people will excuse themselves to make early plane reservations home. At one family dinner it got so hot that I retreated into the kitchen, only to be followed by a couple who squared off before the microwave oven, where he said to her, "You want to know what really tees me off about you . . .?" I went back into the dining room where his mother had just said, "Well, I don't think that Sadat acted like a politician but a statesman!" To which her mother replied archly, "And what's wrong with that?"

There were a lot of small vignettes like these going on 3 all over town during the holidays, and the first conclusion to draw is that relatives are better off not relating to each other if blood is going to gush all over the rug. But I can't help but think that beneath all the double-edged remarks and devastating toasts was a lot of anxiety that had no place to go.

If the son is threatened by his mother, so also is the 4 mother threatened by the son. Her loneliness, his unwillingness to identify with it, his guilt, her bitterness—

this is only one of the combinations that sit above and below the salt, and I wonder whether family reunions don't turn into disasters so quickly because we're only willing to relate to each other when it's safe.

To embrace the whole of another person is to take the   5 risk that their dam will break and overwhelm us with responsibility and anxiety. To recognize another person's frailty may somehow sap whatever strength we've managed to build up for ourselves. The anger comes from sensing the support we need is not so different from the support the other person needs. But to acknowledge that is so painful that some people would rather drink themselves into the bottom of a bottle of Old Grand-Dad and count the hours left before everyone will go home.

The strain of not relating is what provokes the blood-   6 shed, and some people will kill each other for love, particularly during the holidays when we're supposed to love each other to death. But perhaps the reason it's so hard to relate is because it's so hard to be disappointed, to know that the schizoids, compulsive cleaners, alcoholics, and dullards, all the relatives who come home to roost, are not so different from us.

To embrace them is to embrace these tendencies in   7 ourselves, which is a difficult task. And so anger deflects love, hands are clenched behind backs, and we walk the tightrope of the holidays praying the wrong prayer for the wrong reason, instead of saying, "What the hell, we're all in this together. . . ."

Inventorying Your Annotations

Once you have annotated a reading with your observations and insights, you'll want to analyze your annotations to discover their special meaning. The best way to do this is by taking inventory of your annotations to identify any patterns or key repetitions.

Before completing Exercise 2, review the guidelines and illustration for Inventory of Annotations in Chapter 1.

Exercise 2

Inventory the annotations you made on Theroux's "Fear of Families," looking for meaningful patterns.

Analyzing the Basic Features of Reflective Writing

In addition to annotating a text to record your initial impressions and inventorying your annotations for their patterns of meaning, you can analyze the basic features of a piece of writing, in this case those qualities that enable us to recognize an essay as distinctively reflective.

Look back at Identifying and Evaluating Basic Features in Chapter 1. Although the questions there are different from the ones you will find in this chapter, the answers illustrate what a thoughtful analysis of basic features might look like.

Exercise 3

Analyze "Fear of Families" by answering the following questions. You will want to reread the selection with each question in mind, and you may want to annotate further.

Write out your answers to the questions.

1. *What occasioned the writer's reflections, and how is this particular occasion presented?* Notice the particular occasion: is it a one-time event or a recurring activity, a personal experience or simply something the writer has observed? Look at whether the writer develops anecdotes dramatically by describing the scene and people in some detail and even including dialogue, or if the writer presents quick, suggestive vignettes or arresting images to catch the reader's attention. Whatever the case, evaluate how the particular occasion is used to make the writer's abstract ideas more understandable.

2. *What subject does the particular occasion lead the writer to explore, and what questions or insights about the human condition emerge from the reflections?* In addition to being vivid, the particular occasion also must be suggestive. Consider how it leads the writer—and, consequently, you as reader—to reflect on some aspect of human experience: virtues and vices (such as vanity, compassion, and jealousy); social customs and problems (such as those related to dating and child rearing); hopes and fears (such as the desire for intimacy and the fear of it).

Rather than trying to grasp the whole, writers follow Montaigne's example and focus their reflections on some special concern, insight, or question suggested by the subject. These may or may not be stated explicitly. Pinpoint the central question or insight, either by noting the writer's explicit statement or by summarizing it in your own words.

3. *How inventive are the writer's reflections on the subject suggested by the particular occasion?* Successful reflective writing enables us, as readers and writers, to see even the most familiar things in new ways. Avoiding the obvious, resisting the impulse to moralize, revealing a contradiction rather than trying to paper it over—these are some of the characteristics that make reflective essays interesting to read and fun to write. What gives us pleasure is witnessing a limber mind at work, flexing its muscles, exploring its own associations, trying to understand the meaning and significance of what it has seen, heard, or felt.

Writers of reflection need to have a large repertoire of invention strategies. They might examine an incident, for example, by imagining how it would look from different people's perspectives. They might compare and contrast it to other incidents, trace it back to its origins, or place it in a larger context. Notice carefully the methods the writer has used. Consider how the writer develops the subject, and whether its development is predictable or inventive. Most reflective essays try to recreate the unpredictability and excitement of the thinking process. Writers of reflection extend themselves to be inventive in order to surprise and please their readers.

4. *How would you describe the essay's voice or persona, and is it appropriate to the essay?* Reflective essayists unabashedly use the first-person pronoun, *I*, to portray themselves in their writing. The use of *I* invites readers into intimacy, making us feel as if the writer were present, speaking directly to us. This sense of presence is referred to as voice or as persona. Whatever term you use, think about the personality that comes across as you read and consider how it influences your response to the reading.

5. *What stylistic devices does the writer use to enliven the writing and make it memorable?* When composing reflective essays, writers regularly use language in ways that capture readers' attention. Playing with ideas seems to lead them to playing with language. As you read, notice stylistic devices like these: memorable or surprising phrasing; striking word choice; puns, metaphor, simile, or other figures of speech; precisely described details; sentences that have unusual but effective patterns; sentences that repeat the patterns of other sentences or repeat patterns within themselves.

Exploring Your Personal Response

One other way of focusing your response to a reflective essay is by taking the time to record your thoughts in a more extended piece of your own writing. Basically, such an exercise can help you to follow up on an insight, to compare your own experience and understanding with the writer's, to explore your impressions and define further your unique perspective on what you've read.

Exercise 4

Write 300–400 words (two or three handwritten pages) about "Fear of Families." Choose one of the suggestions listed in Exploring Your Personal Response in Chapter 1.

Ellen Goodman

Like Phyllis Theroux, Ellen Goodman (b. 1941) makes a profession of writing reflective essays. A graduate of Radcliffe College, Goodman writes the widely syndicated column "At Large" for the *Boston Globe*. In 1980, she won a Pulitzer Prize in distinguished commentary for this column, and in 1988, she was given the Hubert H. Humphrey Civil Rights Award for dedication to the cause of equality. She has published four collections of essays: *Close to Home* (1979), *At Large* (1981), *Keeping in Touch* (1985), and *Making Sense* (1989), as well as a collection of interviews, *Turning Points* (1979).

Nouvelle Nutrition

Goodman is noted for her witty style and attention to contemporary social issues and concerns. Among the topics she treats are staples of the reflective essay: values, relationships, gender roles, families, and change. "Nouvelle Nutrition," which appeared in May 1989, is about a current change in attitudes toward food.

Read and reread the essay, annotating your observations and responses. As you do, consider whether Goodman's observations correspond to your own. Do you think of food in the way she describes? Do people you know? What do you think such a change in attitude signifies?

A friend and I go through the lunch line together. We pause at the 1
salad bar, while she carefully picks up six green flowerettes. "Calcium," she explains. I thought it was broccoli.

I sit down at a table with a colleague who is deliberately spearing beige 2
flakes of food with his fork. "Protein," he says. I could have sworn it was tuna.

I am on the subway when a student next to me reaches into a bag, 3
grabs something yellow and peels it. As if to explain her intense, even desperate chewing, she utters one word: "Potassium." It looked like a banana to me.

Forget about Paul Prudhomme and Julia Child.[1] Never mind the 4
sauces of France and the spices of Mexico. This is what eating is like in America today. Like taking medicine.

---

[1] Paul Prudhomme and Julia Child are famous chefs. [Eds.]

The haute cuisine of the body-conscious culture has become Nouvelle 5
Nutrition. We don't exchange recipes as much anymore as we exchange
information. Pleasing our palates has become a secret vice, while fiber-
fueling our colons has become a most public virtue.

If we had a menu for the way we now think about food, it would look 6
like a prescription pad. Any day now I expect even the supermarkets to
arrange their aisles: complex carbohydrates to the right, simple to the
left.

I cannot date the precise moment when we began to think of food as 7
medicine. I know for sure that the nutrition I learned in school was as
circumscribed as the four basic food groups. I got the general idea that as
long as there were different color foods on our plates, we were okay. The
only certified culinary cure of my childhood was chicken soup for the
common cold.

For the most part, good nutrition was a synonym for bad taste. Cod 8
liver oil and cooked spinach carried the evil tracers of wellness. Things
that were healthy came with a maternal stamp of approval. An occasional piece of liver. Endless glasses of milk. Please.

But somewhere along the way, we became a far more sophisticated, far 9
more suspicious, food-fixated culture. The oldest anxiety about food—is
there enough?—was translated into this new anxiety. The body is now
regarded as a complicated, even fragile item—a human Jaguar—that
won't operate right unless it is cared for with utmost precision by its
owner.

The more we learn, the more we fine-tune our diet. Going to run 10
tomorrow? Load up on some carbohydrates tonight. Got a test at two?
Proteins at noon. Feel the 4 p.m. blues? Have a nice big piece of fructose.
Trouble sleeping? You never should have had that amino acid.

Nouvelle Nutrition is more complex than a bowl of beans and rice. 11
Even the television ads today read like entries in a medical journal. The
caring American family is shown as they begin the day with a bowlful of
antidotes for rectal cancer. That is followed almost immediately by a
potion to prevent osteoporosis. We have legumes for lunch and balance
our electrolytes with dinner. And we haven't even gotten to vitamins.

The epitome, or piece de resistance, of food as medicine is of course, 12
oat bran. This is the good grain you should ingest to counter the bad
cholesterol you ingest. Oat bran is the current four-star item on the
Nouvelle Menu, having barely and recently edged out calcium among
the most culinary cautious.

Admittedly, there are some advantages to the food-is-medicine school, 13
although the taste of oat bran isn't one of them. It offers a balanced diet
of worries. We don't just concentrate on the bad things in our food—from

fat to Alar—we get obsessed with the good.[2] It also, as a comedian noted the other night, offers a new set of excuses when you get caught with the munchies. I couldn't help it. I needed the zinc.

But there is something missing in any cuisine that asks us to think of a 14 banana as a portion of potassium. There is something skewed about an eating regimen designed to do the most for every part of your body except the tip of your tongue.

What I need, creature of comfort that I am, is a regular dose of 15 chocolate truffles. It has all the necessary ingredients for my health. My mental health. Put it before me and I promise to take my medicine.

QUESTIONS FOR ANALYSIS

1. Whereas Phyllis Theroux describes only one specific family dinner to arrive at her general reflections, Goodman offers a series of separate incidents. Identify these brief anecdotes with a vertical line in the margin. What makes them effective as the particular occasion for a reflective essay?

2. Goodman's reflection centers on the insight that today many Americans regard food as medicine. What is the basis for this analogy between food and medicine? How does Goodman develop it?

3. Find one place in the essay where you get a clear sense of Goodman's voice or *persona*. Describe it as precisely as you can. How does your attitude toward the author influence your response to her reflections?

4. Notice how Goodman paragraphs this essay—how many paragraphs there are, how many sentences they include, where she makes the paragraph breaks. In this essay, which was written originally as a newspaper column, Goodman's paragraphing conforms to conventional newspaper paragraphing style. What advantages and disadvantages for reflective writing do you find in this newspaper paragraphing style?

5. Review Exploring Your Personal Response (Chapter 1). Then write a 300–400-word personal response to the Goodman essay, choosing one of the following topics:

    Write about the history of your reading of Goodman's essay. That is, tell a story of your reactions during first and subsequent readings. Reflect on how your response to the essay changed.

    Write about your personal associations with something in the essay, such as an image, idea, or character.

---

[2] Alar is a cancer-causing chemical used to make apples appear shiny. [Eds.]

After you have written your response, reread it thoughtfully. In two or three sentences, say what you learned about the Goodman essay by writing an extended response to it.

IDEAS FOR YOUR OWN WRITING

Organizing reflections around a central analogy (such as food is like medicine) is a common strategy of reflective essays. By yourself or with your classmates, write a list of analogies that bring unlikely or surprising subjects together. Here are a few to get you started: memories are like a painting, history is like an amusement park, clothes are like armor, a building is like a body. Choose one analogy from your list that seems promising, and explore it in writing. Consider it from several different perspectives: think of examples that illustrate it; think of its implications; think of how people you know would react to your ideas.

Brent Staples

Brent Staples (b. 1951) received his Ph.D. in psychology from the University of Chicago. He has written for several magazines and newspapers, including the *Chicago Sun-Times*. In 1985, he joined the *New York Times* as first assistant metropolitan editor.

Black Men and Public Space

Whereas Phyllis Theroux reflects on families and how they interact, Staples writes in this essay about strangers. He is especially interested in how people, especially women, react when they see him on the street late at night. He has noticed that he seems to have the ability to "alter public space in ugly ways" simply because he is an African-American and a man. As you read the essay, consider the implications of the experience Staples describes.

This selection was originally published in September 1986 in *Ms.* magazine under the title "Just Walk on By," and was slightly revised and reprinted under the present title in December 1987 in *Harper's*.

My first victim was a woman—white, well dressed, probably in her late 1 twenties. I came upon her late one evening on a deserted street in Hyde Park, a relatively affluent neighborhood in an otherwise mean, impoverished section of Chicago. As I swung onto the avenue behind her, there seemed to be a discreet, uninflammatory distance between us. Not so. She cast back a worried glance. To her, the youngish black man—a broad six feet two inches with a beard and billowing hair, both hands shoved into the pockets of a bulky military jacket—seemed menacingly close. After a few more quick glimpses, she picked up her pace and was soon running in earnest. Within seconds she disappeared into a cross street.

That was more than a decade ago. I was twenty-two years old, a 2 graduate student newly arrived at the University of Chicago. It was in the echo of that terrified woman's footfalls that I first began to know the unwieldy inheritance I'd come into—the ability to alter public space in ugly ways. It was clear that she thought herself the quarry of a mugger, a rapist, or worse. Suffering a bout of insomnia, however, I was stalking sleep, not defenseless wayfarers. As a softy who is scarcely able to take a knife to a raw chicken—let alone hold one to a person's throat—I was surprised, embarrassed, and dismayed all at once. Her flight made me feel like an accomplice in tyranny. It also made it clear that I was indistinguishable from the muggers who occasionally seeped into the area from the surrounding ghetto. That first encounter, and those that followed, signified that a vast, unnerving gulf lay between nighttime pedestrians—particularly women—and me. And I soon gathered that being perceived as dangerous is a hazard in itself. I only needed to turn a corner into a dicey situation, or crowd some frightened, armed person in a foyer somewhere, or make an errant move after being pulled over by a policeman. Where fear and weapons meet—and they often do in urban America—there is always the possibility of death.

In that first year, my first away from my hometown, I was to become   3 thoroughly familiar with the language of fear. At dark, shadowy intersections, I could cross in front of a car stopped at a traffic light and elicit the *thunk, thunk, thunk, thunk* of the driver—black, white, male, or female— hammering down the door locks. On less traveled streets after dark, I grew accustomed to but never comfortable with people crossing to the other side of the street rather than pass me. Then there were the standard unpleasantries with policemen, doormen, bouncers, cabdrivers, and others whose business it is to screen out troublesome individuals *before* there is any nastiness.

I moved to New York nearly two years ago and I have remained an avid   4 night walker. In central Manhattan, the near-constant crowd cover minimizes tense one-on-one street encounters. Elsewhere—in SoHo, for example, where sidewalks are narrow and tightly spaced buildings shut out the sky—things can get very taut indeed.

After dark, on the warrenlike streets of Brooklyn where I live, I often   5 see women who fear the worst from me. They seem to have set their faces on neutral, and with their purse straps strung across their chests bandolier-style, they forge ahead as though bracing themselves against being tackled. I understand, of course, that the danger they perceive is not a hallucination. Women are particularly vulnerable to street violence, and young black males are drastically overrepresented among the perpetrators of that violence. Yet these truths are no solace against the kind of alienation that comes of being ever the suspect, a fearsome entity with whom pedestrians avoid making eye contact.

Over the years, I learned to smother the rage I felt at so often being   6 taken for a criminal. Not to do so would surely have led to madness. I now take precautions to make myself less threatening. I move about with care, particularly late in the evening. I give a wide berth to nervous people on subway platforms during the wee hours, particularly when I have exchanged business clothes for jeans. If I happen to be entering a building behind some people who appear skittish, I may walk by, letting them clear the lobby before I return, so as not to seem to be following them. I have been calm and extremely congenial on those rare occasions when I've been pulled over by the police.

And on late-evening constitutionals I employ what has proved to be   7 an excellent tension-reducing measure: I whistle melodies from Beethoven and Vivaldi and the more popular classical composers. Even steely New Yorkers hunching toward nighttime destinations seem to relax, and occasionally they even join in the tune. Virtually everybody seems to sense that a mugger wouldn't be warbling bright, sunny selections from Vivaldi's *Four Seasons*. It is my equivalent of the cowbell that hikers wear when they know they are in bear country.

QUESTIONS FOR ANALYSIS

1. Staples begins his essay with a dramatic anecdote. Look closely at this opening paragraph, and underline the words or phrases that heighten the suspense or feeling of danger and foreboding. How effectively does Staples create suspense in this paragraph?

2. Throughout the essay, Staples contrasts the way others view him with the way he sees himself. Make two lists of words and phrases that indicate how Staples views himself and how he thinks others see him. Then compare these opposing images with the persona that comes across to you in the essay. What can you conclude about Staples's dilemma from your analysis of these images?

3. Staples explains in paragraph 6 that he used to feel enraged by the way others view him, but that he has "learned to smother the rage." What seems to be the dominant feeling expressed in the essay? Find one place where this feeling comes through.

4. Staples's reflections center on the paradox that even though he is no threat to women, "the danger they perceive is no hallucination." What do you think he means? What does this paradox and Staples's way of resolving it imply about our society?

5. A stylistic device Staples uses effectively in this essay is alliteration, repeating consonant sounds as in "woman—white, well dressed." Skim the essay, marking an *A* in the margin wherever you find alliteration. What can you conclude about the effect repeated use of alliteration has on you as one reader?

6. Review Exploring Your Personal Response in Chapter 1. Then write a 300–400-word personal response to the Staples essay, choosing one of the following topics:

Write a letter to Staples, responding to anything in the essay that you found particularly noteworthy.

Write about your personal association with the situation Staples describes.

After you have written your response, reread it thoughtfully. In two or three sentences, say what you learned about the Staples essay by writing an extended response to it.

IDEAS FOR YOUR OWN WRITING

In this essay, Staples refers to the notion of public space. As a society, we have many conventions about when we can touch another person or come close. Unless two people are close friends or family members, they usually sit some distance apart on the same sofa, being careful not to touch. When people meet, they may shake hands, but they have to reach across a gulf of space to do so. Take some time to observe the people around you. Can you identify any patterns in the way they relate to one another and in how they honor or break down the spatial boundaries between one another? Then, taking an instance you observed, reflect on what it says about the way people relate to each other.

Laurence Shames

A free-lance writer, Laurence Shames has had articles published in such diverse journals as *World Tennis* and *Saturday Review*. In 1982, he was a contributing editor for *Esquire*, writing the monthly "Ethics" column. Some of the subjects he touched upon were success and failure, fidelity, the fear of losing, and the desire to win. He recently published a collection of essays entitled *The Hunger for More: Searching for Values in an Age of Greed* (1989).

The Eyes of Fear

As the title of this selection indicates, Shames—like Theroux—is writing about the general subject of fear. While Theroux treats fear in families, Shames focuses on fear in sexual relationships, but both are ultimately concerned with fear of intimacy. Reflective essays often deal with similar subjects, but they approach these subjects from different angles because of the subjective nature of reflective writing. The occasions out of which reflections arise are bound to differ, as are the conclusions that writers draw from their reflections.

Reflective essays also differ from one another because they are written for different purposes and audiences. "The Eyes of Fear" (1982), for example, was originally written for the "Ethics" column in *Esquire*, a magazine with a well-defined audience composed primarily of young professional men. As you read this essay, consider how writing on ethics for this particular audience may have shaped Shames's essay. What seems to you to be his immediate purpose? How might this essay have been different if Shames had written it for another magazine, such as *Ms.* or *Family Circle*?

Remember how they did it in *1984*? 1

They studied you until they'd learned your deepest fear—rats, bats, 2 darkness, whatever—and then they used that fear to turn you. The premise was that while human beings might be expected to behave with some degree of dignity and moral sense under normal circumstances, they'd crumble when confronted with their personal demons; courage and resolve would slip away, and people would become abject, malleable, capable of any sort of betrayal.

A sobering proposition—but one that, in Orwell's nightmare world, 3 proved only too accurate. How about in our world?

We, too, occasionally have our worst fears thrown in our face, are $_4$
confronted with situations in which the choice is between staring down
our private bogeymen and skulking away in safe but ignoble retreat.
True, most of us will never have to deal with the primordial horror of
having rodents nibble at us, but we will face other fears: the fear of
intimacy, which, for many of us, is truly scarring and which can lead us
to be dishonest, unfair, and self-defeating in our relationships; the fear of
taking an uncharted course in a career—a fear that can turn us into
morally hollow yes-men or cause us to be untrue to our real ambitions;
and, in every aspect of our lives, the basic fear of change—a timidness
about growth and risk that, in the long haul, can make us bitter,
disappointed, and mean.

Consider, for example, the fear of intimacy. Intimacy offers itself as $_5$
one of life's great comforts, but for all its tender appeal, many of us find it
terrifying. And not without reason: intimacy means reckless self-
exposure, a bold baring of the soft white underbelly, an offering of the
jugular. It demands more trust than many of us grow up believing the
world deserves. Yet few of us choose to be hermits or celibates; the
difficulty, then, is in reconciling our need for closeness with our fear of it.
And, ethically, the danger is that we may go halfway, then balk, inevitably hurting people in the process, deceiving them without intending to,
being helplessly dishonest to others because we're being untrue to ourselves.

In college I hung around with a group of guys for whom meeting $_6$
women was a major preoccupation. Some of us liked having one
girlfriend at a time, in a sort of puppy-love version of what has come to
be known as serial monogamy. Others preferred to juggle several en-
tanglements at once, with results that ranged from the comical to the
cruel. Then there was this fellow I'll call Arty. Arty had a style all his
own. Forward, eccentric, and dapper, he insinuated himself into the
favor of more young ladies than any of us could win. Yet he never seemed
the slightest bit entangled. He was the consummate hit-and-run man, as
adept at ending things as at starting them.

For a while, of course, this capacity of his impressed the rest of us no $_7$
end. Compared with the blistering pace of Arty's escapades, our humble
efforts seemed sluggish and mundane. Gradually, however, even to us
die-hard adolescents, it became clear that the fellow had a problem. His
fear of getting close to women was so pronounced that it led him to all
sorts of caddish behavior. Whatever his intentions may have been, he
ended up misleading every woman he met, and he left behind, if not
exactly a string of broken hearts, then certainly a number of ladies who

had good reason to feel baffled, angry, and used. Arty was a classic case of a guy letting himself be bullied into shabbiness by his fears, not even truly enjoying his encounters because they were laced with so much anxiety. After a while, the rest of us didn't know whom to feel sorrier for—the women who crossed Arty's path, or Arty himself. *They* were victimized by Arty's fear only once; *he* was doomed to repeat the pattern again and again.

After college, some of us old friends stayed in touch, staging informal 8 reunions at various taverns in the cities where we'd ended up. True to form, we'd still discuss, among other things, our dealings with women, but the emphasis was different now. In spite of ourselves, we were getting serious. We were at the age when the question of marriage was beginning to bear down on us with the slow portentousness of a distant but oncoming train. We'd flirt with the subject and sometimes make goading conjectures about who would be the first to take the plunge. There was no consensus on this point; as to who would be the *last*, however, there was general and confident agreement.

We were wrong, of course. Arty was the first of us to wed. To me, this 9 was more than a surprise; it represented a moral victory of a high order.

I still remember when he told me of his plans. The revelation literally 10 took my breath away. This was *Arty*—the guy so scared of closeness that he'd hardly leave an imprint on a paramour's pillow. But people change—or *can* change. "Look," Arty said to me, "don't you think I know what I've been doing all these years? I've just been jerking around, wasting everybody's time, acting like the kind of person I really hope I'm not. I've got to take the chance and try to be different. I think I've found someone who understands how tough it's gonna be for me and who'll be able to handle it, and I've got to take a shot."

That was around three years ago, and Arty and his wife are still 11 fighting the good fight against Arty's fear of intimacy. It hasn't been easy. It's not the sort of fear you stand up to once and conquer; it requires a more durable sort of courage, the sort that renews itself every day.

Arty—so he admits—is still clutched at times by the old terrors; he 12 clams up, broods, gets moody and aloof. His wife, when frustrated, throws tantrums. The two of them have been known to make scenes and to indulge in extended sulks. Yet, beneath the turbulent surface of their marriage, there is a true adventure going on.

It's an adventure whose basis is a moral contract, a mutual pledge not 13 to retreat into halfheartedness. And while the contract's demands are unyielding, its rewards are rich and irreplaceable. "I no longer try to get away with the sort of evasions that I never *wanted* to get away with in the first place," Arty says. "Marriage is like boxing: you can run but you can't hide. Sooner or later, you're going to end up in a clinch—and it's in the clinches where you learn the most about yourself, where your strength is really tested."

But the challenge of marriage is one that Arty still wonders if he's 14 equal to. "You know," he said to me a while back, during a particularly bumpy phase, "I didn't exactly pave the way for this. I mean, I'd always been too scared even to really have a girlfriend, and all of a sudden this little voice starts telling me that maybe I should take this giant leap all the way to marriage, and I *listen*. Maybe it was just a crazy thing for me to do."

I disagreed with him, and told him so. To me, it was his finest hour. 15 Because if duking it out with our personal demons is full of potential pitfalls, it also offers opportunities for real self-transcendence, for genuine heroics. Where's the virtue, after all, in taking a stand when we're *not* afraid? What's the value of a moral contract that doesn't cost us anything?

Big Brother, in his perverse wisdom, was correct in his assumption that 16 every person has his private fear, his exposed nerve. But it doesn't take an all-seeing autocrat to discover that vulnerable point and to probe it— the circumstances of ordinary life will do that just as well. The way we hold our ground when that sensitive place is tweaked, when that anxiety-drenched subject is foisted on us, is the surest test of what we're made of.

QUESTIONS FOR ANALYSIS

1. Writers of reflective essays sometimes use a strategy called framing. Framing simply involves referring at the end of the essay to something mentioned in the beginning. How does Shames frame this essay? What purpose does this frame serve?

2. What is the particular occasion for Shames's reflections on the fear of intimacy? Put a vertical line in the margin wherever the particular occasion is described. Then do the same for any other reflective essay you've read in this chapter.

   Compare the way the two writers develop their particular occasions and the amount of space they devote to them. What can you conclude from this comparison about the way particular occasions are presented in reflective essays? (For advice on Comparing and Contrasting Related Readings, see Chapter 1.)

3. What question or insight does this particular occasion suggest to Shames?

4. Find one place in the essay where you get a clear sense of the authorial voice. What adjectives would you use to characterize Shames's voice or *persona*? Why do you think this voice is appropriate or inappropriate for this essay?

5. Even though the essay deals with fear of intimacy, it contains references to conflict—for example, the simile "Marriage is like boxing." Skim the essay, annotating language that refers to intimacy as well as to conflict. Then ask yourself why Shames might be concerned with conflict in an essay on intimacy. What do you think the connection is between the two?

IDEAS FOR YOUR OWN WRITING

In the beginning of this essay, Shames identifies several kinds of private fears: the fear of intimacy, the fear of taking an uncharted course, the fear of change. Make a list of other fears people commonly have. Using one or more of the items on your list, consider any occasions in your past that might have led you to reflect on the nature of such fear.

Joan Didion

Joan Didion is a novelist, a screenwriter, and an essayist. Her most successful novels have been *Play It As It Lays* (1971), *The Book of Common Prayer* (1977), and *Democracy* (1984). With her husband John Gregory Dunne, Didion wrote the screenplays for *A Star Is Born* (1976) and *True Confessions* (1981). In addition to the controversial book-length essays *Salvador* (1983) and *Miami* (1987), she has published two collections of essays: *Slouching towards Bethlehem* (1968) and *The White Album* (1979).

After graduating from college, Didion wrote for *Mademoiselle, Saturday Evening Post*, and *Life*. She even worked for a time on the editorial staff of *Vogue*, where a senior editor taught her how to write: "Every day I would go into her office with eight lines of copy or a caption or something. She would sit there and mark up with a pencil and get very angry about extra words, about verbs not working. . . . In an eight-line caption everything had to work, every word, every comma."

On Self-Respect

The following selection may seem unusual in that it was occasioned by something that did not happen. In this piece, Didion writes about the memory of her failure to be elected to Phi Beta Kappa, the college honorary society. As you read this essay, ask yourself what question or insight this particular occasion suggests to Didion.

A recognized master of the reflective essay, Didion writes occasionally about her art. In one essay, she commented: "We live entirely, especially if we are writers, by the imposition of a narrative line upon disparate images, by the 'ideas' with which we have learned to freeze the shifting phantasmagoria which is our actual experience." As you read this selection, consider how Didion uses ideas to order and understand her experience.

Once, in a dry season, I wrote in large letters across two pages of a notebook that innocence ends when one is stripped of the delusion that one likes oneself. Although now, some years later, I marvel that a mind on the outs with itself should have nonetheless made painstaking record of its every tremor, I recall with embarrassing clarity the flavor of those particular ashes. It was a matter of misplaced self-respect.

I had not been elected to Phi Beta Kappa. This failure could scarcely have been more predictable or less ambiguous (I simply did not have the grades), but I was unnerved by it; I had somehow thought myself a kind of academic Raskolnikov, curiously exempt from the cause-effect relationships which hampered others. Although even the humorless nineteen-year-old that I was must have recognized that the situation lacked real tragic stature, the day that I did not make Phi Beta Kappa nonetheless marked the end of something, and innocence may well be the word for it. I lost the conviction that lights would always turn green for me, the pleasant certainty that those rather passive virtues which had won me approval as a child automatically guaranteed me not only Phi Beta Kappa keys but happiness, honor, and the love of a good man; lost a certain touching faith in the totem power of good manners, clean hair, and proven competence on the Stanford-Binet scale. To such doubtful amulets had my self-respect been pinned, and I faced myself that day with the nonplused apprehension of someone who has come across a vampire and has no crucifix at hand.

Although to be driven back upon oneself is an uneasy affair at best, rather like trying to cross a border with borrowed credentials, it seems to me now the one condition necessary to the beginnings of real self-respect. Most of our platitudes notwithstanding, self-deception remains the most difficult deception. The tricks that work on others count for nothing in that very well-lit back alley where one keeps assignations with oneself: no winning smiles will do here, no prettily drawn lists of good intentions. One shuffles flashily but in vain through one's marked cards—the kindness done for the wrong reason, the apparent triumph which involved no real effort, the seemingly heroic act into which one had been shamed. The dismal fact is that self-respect has nothing to do with the approval of others—who are, after all, deceived easily enough; has nothing to do with reputation, which, as Rhett Butler told Scarlett O'Hara, is something people with courage can do without.

To do without self-respect, on the other hand, is to be an unwilling audience of one to an interminable documentary that details one's failings, both real and imagined, with fresh footage spliced in for every screening. *There's the glass you broke in anger, there's the hurt on X's face; watch now, this next scene, the night Y came back from Houston, see how you muff this one.* To live without self-respect is to lie awake some night, beyond the reach of warm milk, phenobarbital, and the sleeping hand on the coverlet, counting up the sins of commission and omission, the trusts betrayed, the promises subtly broken, the gifts irrevocably wasted through sloth or cowardice or carelessness. However long we postpone it, we eventually lie down alone in that notoriously uncomfortable bed, the one we make ourselves. Whether or not we sleep in it depends, of course, on whether or not we respect ourselves.

To protest that some fairly improbable people, some people who *could not possibly respect themselves*, seem to sleep easily enough is to miss the point entirely, as surely as those people miss it who think that self-respect has necessarily to do with not having safety pins in one's underwear. There is a common superstition that "self-respect" is a kind of charm against snakes, something that keeps those who have it locked in some unblighted Eden, out of strange beds, ambivalent conversations, and trouble in general. It does not at all. It has nothing to do with the face of things, but concerns instead a separate peace, a private reconciliation. Although the careless, suicidal Julian English in *Appointment in Samarra* and the careless, incurably dishonest Jordan Baker in *The Great Gatsby* seem equally improbable candidates for self-respect, Jordan Baker had it, Julian English did not. With that genius for accommodation more often seen in women than in men, Jordan took her own measure, made her own peace, avoided threats to that peace: "I hate careless people," she told Nick Carraway. "It takes two to make an accident."

Like Jordan Baker, people with self-respect have the courage of their   6
mistakes. They know the price of things. If they choose to commit adultery, they do not then go running, in an excess of bad conscience, to receive absolution from the wronged parties; nor do they complain unduly of the unfairness, the undeserved embarrassment, of being named corespondent. In brief, people with self-respect exhibit a certain toughness, a kind of moral nerve; they display what was once called *character*, a quality which, although approved in the abstract, sometimes loses ground to other, more instantly negotiable virtues. The measure of its slipping prestige is that one tends to think of it only in connection with homely children and United States senators who have been defeated, preferably in the primary, for reelection. Nonetheless, character—the willingness to accept responsibility for one's own life—is the source from which self-respect springs.

Self-respect is something that our grandparents, whether or not they   7
had it, knew all about. They had instilled in them, young, a certain discipline, the sense that one lives by doing things one does not particularly want to do, by putting fears and doubts to one side, by weighing immediate comforts against the possibility of larger, even intangible, comforts. It seemed to the nineteenth century admirable, but not remarkable, that Chinese Gordon put on a clean white suit and held Khartoum against the Mahdi; it did not seem unjust that the way to free land in California involved death and difficulty and dirt. In a diary kept during the winter of 1846, an emigrating twelve-year-old named Narcissa Cornwall noted coolly: "Father was busy reading and did not notice that the house was being filled with strange Indians until Mother spoke about it." Even lacking any clue as to what Mother said, one can scarcely fail to be impressed by the entire incident: the father reading, the Indians filing

in, the mother choosing the words that would not alarm, the child duly recording the event and noting further that those particular Indians were not, "fortunately for us," hostile. Indians were simply part of the *donnée*.

In one guise or another, Indians always are. Again, it is a question of recognizing that anything worth having has its price. People who respect themselves are willing to accept the risk that the Indians will be hostile, that the venture will go bankrupt, that the liaison may not turn out to be one in which *every day is a holiday because you're married to me*. They are willing to invest something of themselves; they may not play at all, but when they do play, they know the odds.

That kind of self-respect is a discipline, a habit of mind that can never be faked but can be developed, trained, coaxed forth. It was once suggested to me that, as an antidote to crying, I put my head in a paper bag. As it happens, there is a sound physiological reason, something to do with oxygen, for doing exactly that, but the psychological effect alone is incalculable: it is difficult in the extreme to continue fancying oneself Cathy in *Wuthering Heights* with one's head in a Food Fair bag. There is a similar case for all the small disciplines, unimportant in themselves; imagine maintaining any kind of swoon, commiserative or carnal, in a cold shower.

But those small disciplines are available only insofar as they represent larger ones. To say that Waterloo was won on the playing fields of Eton is not to say that Napoleon might have been saved by a crash program in cricket; to give formal dinners in the rain forest would be pointless did not the candlelight flickering on the liana call forth deeper, stronger disciplines, values instilled long before. It is a kind of ritual, helping us to remember who and what we are. In order to remember it, one must have known it.

To have that sense of one's intrinsic worth which constitutes self-respect is potentially to have everything: the ability to discriminate, to love and to remain indifferent. To lack it is to be locked within oneself, paradoxically incapable of either love or indifference. If we do not respect ourselves, we are on the one hand forced to despise those who have so few resources as to consort with us, so little perception as to remain blind to our fatal weaknesses. On the other, we are peculiarly in thrall to everyone we see, curiously determined to live out—since our self-image is untenable—their false notions of us. We flatter ourselves by thinking this compulsion to please others an attractive trait: a gist for imaginative empathy, evidence of our willingness to give. *Of course* I will play Francesca to your Paolo, Helen Keller to anyone's Annie Sullivan: no expectation is too misplaced, no role too ludicrous. At the mercy of those we cannot but hold in contempt, we play roles doomed to failure before they are begun, each defeat generating fresh despair at the urgency of divining and meeting the next demand made upon us.

It is the phenomenon sometimes called "alienation from self." In its advanced stages, we no longer answer the telephone, because someone might want something; that we could say *no* without drowning in self-reproach is an idea alien to this game. Every encounter demands too much, tears the nerves, drains the will, and the specter of something as small as an unanswered letter arouses such disproportionate guilt that answering it becomes out of the question. To assign unanswered letters their proper weight, to free us from the expectations of others, to give us back to ourselves—there lies the great, the singular power of self-respect. Without it, one eventually discovers the final turn of the screw: one runs away to find oneself, and finds no one at home. 12

QUESTIONS FOR ANALYSIS

1. As the title suggests, this essay centers on the question "What is self-respect?" To get a clear sense of how Didion goes about defining this concept, make a scratch outline of the essay's main ideas. (To review the procedures for outlining, refer to Chapter 1.)

2. Throughout the essay, Didion contrasts what it is like to have self-respect and what it is like to lack it. Make an inventory of these oppositions in two lists, one headed "With Self-Respect," the other "Without Self-Respect." (Chapter 1 contains a plan for taking inventory of annotations.) What can you conclude about Didion's strategy of contrast? How does she use it to develop her ideas?

3. Didion consistently surprises us with references to common objects and everyday events: lights turning green, crossing a border, well-lit back alleys, marked playing cards, for example. Make an inventory of these references. What can you conclude about their role in the essay?

4. In this essay, Didion regularly presents examples in threes: in paragraph 2, for example, she asserts that she lost faith in "good manners, clean hair, and proven competence on the Stanford-Binet scale [an intelligence test]." Skim the essay, underlining other instances where examples come in threes. Why do you think Didion relies on this strategy? What advantages or disadvantages do you see in it?

5. Didion relies on her reading as well as her personal experience to develop her ideas about self-respect. Underline all of the references to books and authors. Choose one reference that you recognize and explain what it contributes to the essay.

IDEAS FOR YOUR OWN WRITING

Reflective essays often meditate on the meaning of an abstract concept like self-respect. Make a list of possible concepts, and then identify one for which you can recall specific occasions to spur reflection. Here are a few possibilities to get your list started: love, greed, conformity, depression.

John McMurtry

John McMurtry (b. 1939) earned a B.A. at the University of Toronto and a Ph.D. in philosophy at the University of London. He teaches social and political philosophy at the University of Guelph in Canada, and has written a scholarly book entitled *The Structure of Marx's World-View*.

McMurtry played football as an undergraduate and, after graduating, played professionally for a short time with the Calgary Stampeders of the Canadian Football League.

Kill 'Em! Crush 'Em! Eat 'Em Raw!

McMurtry seems to love football, yet is able at the same time to look at it critically. As you read and annotate the essay, consider the specific incident that occasions his reflections and ask yourself what question or insight helps him focus his thoughts about the sport.

"Kill 'Em! Crush 'Em! Eat 'Em Raw!" first appeared in the Canadian newsmagazine *Maclean's* in 1971.

A few months ago my neck got a hard crick in it. I couldn't turn my 1
head; to look left or right I'd have to turn my whole body. But I'd had cricks in my neck since I started playing grade-school football and hockey, so I just ignored it. Then I began to notice that when I reached for any sort of large book (which I do pretty often as a philosophy teacher at the University of Guelph) I had trouble lifting it with one hand. I was losing the strength in my left arm, and I had such a steady pain in my back I often had to stretch out on the floor of the room I was in to relieve the pressure.

A few weeks later I mentioned to my brother, an orthopedic surgeon, 2
that I'd lost the power in my arm since my neck began to hurt. Twenty-four hours later I was in a Toronto hospital not sure whether I might end up with a wasted upper limb. Apparently the steady pounding I had received playing college and professional football in the late Fifties and early Sixties had driven my head into my backbone so that the discs had crumpled together at the neck—"acute herniation"—and had cut the nerves to my left arm like a pinched telephone wire (without nerve stimulation, of course, the muscles atrophy, leaving the arm crippled). So I spent my Christmas holidays in the hospital in heavy traction and

much of the next three months with my neck in a brace. Today most of the pain has gone, and I've recovered most of the strength in my arm. But from time to time I still have to don the brace, and surgery remains a possibility.

Not much of this will surprise anyone who knows football. It is a sport   3
in which body wreckage is one of the leading conventions. A few days after I went into hospital for that crick in my neck, another brother, an outstanding football player in college, was undergoing spinal surgery in the same hospital two floors above me. In his case it was a lower, more massive herniation, which every now and again buckled him so that he was unable to lift himself off his back for days at a time. By the time he entered the hospital for surgery he had already spent several months in bed. The operation was successful, but, as in all such cases, it will take him a year to recover fully.

These aren't isolated experiences. Just about anybody who has ever   4
played football for any length of time, in high school, college or one of the professional leagues, has suffered for it later physically.

Indeed, it is arguable that body shattering is the very *point* of football,   5
as killing and maiming are of war. (In the United States, for example, the game results in 15 to 20 deaths a year and about 50,000 major operations on knees alone.) To grasp some of the more conspicuous similarities between football and war, it is instructive to listen to the imperatives most frequently issued to the players by their coaches, teammates and fans. "Hurt 'em!" "Level 'em!" "Kill 'em!" "Take 'em apart!" Or watch for the plays that are most enthusiastically applauded by the fans. Where someone is "smeared," "knocked silly," "creamed," "nailed," "broken in two," or even "crucified." (One of my coaches when I played corner linebacker with the Calgary Stampeders in 1961 elaborated, often very inventively, on this language of destruction: admonishing us to "unjoin" the opponent, "make 'im remember you" and "stomp 'im like a bug.") Just as in hockey, where a fight will bring fans to their feet more often than a skillful play, so in football the mouth waters most of all for the really crippling block or tackle. For the kill. Thus the good teams are "hungry," the best players are "mean," and "casualties" are as much a part of the game as they are of a war.

The family resemblance between football and war is, indeed, striking.   6
Their languages are similar: "field general," "long bomb," "blitz," "take a shot," "front line," "pursuit," "good hit," "the draft" and so on. Their principles and practices are alike: mass hysteria, the art of intimidation, absolute command and total obedience, territorial aggression, censorship, inflated insignia and propaganda, blackboard maneuvers and strategies, drills, uniforms, formations, marching bands and training camps.

And the virtues they celebrate are almost identical: hyper-aggressiveness, coolness under fire and suicidal bravery. All this has been implicitly recognized by such jock-loving Americans as media stars General Patton and President Nixon, who have talked about war as a football game. Patton wanted to make his Second World War tank men look like football players. And Nixon, as we know, was fond of comparing attacks on Vietnam to football plays and drawing coachly diagrams on a blackboard for TV war fans.

One difference between war and football, though, is that there is little ₇ or no protest against football. Perhaps the most extraordinary thing about the game is that the systematic infliction of injuries excites in people not concern, as would be the case if they were sustained at, say, a rock festival, but a collective rejoicing and euphoria. Players and fans alike revel in the spectacle of a combatant felled into semiconsciousness, "blindsided," "clotheslined" or "decapitated." I can remember, in fact, being chided by a coach in pro ball for not "getting my hat" injuriously into a player who was already lying helpless on the ground. (On another occasion, after the Stampeders had traded the celebrated Joe Kapp to BC, we were playing the Lions in Vancouver and Kapp was forced on one play to run with the ball. He was coming "down the chute," his bad knee wobbling uncertainly, so I simply dropped on him like a blanket. After I returned to the bench I was reproved for not exploiting the opportunity to unhinge his bad knee.)

After every game, of course, the papers are full of reports on the day's ₈ injuries, a sort of post-battle "body count," and the respective teams go to work with doctors and trainers, tape, whirlpool baths, cortisone and morphine to patch and deaden the wounds before the next game. Then the whole drama is reenacted—injured athletes held together by adhesive, braces and drugs—and the days following it are filled with even more feverish activity to put on the show yet again at the end of the next week. (I remember being so taped up in college that I earned the nickname "mummy.") The team that survives this merry-go-round spectacle of skilled masochism with the fewest incapacitating injuries usually wins. It is a sort of victory by ordeal: "We hurt them more than they hurt us."

My own initiation into this brutal circus was typical. I loved the game ₉ from the moment I could run with a ball. Played shoeless on a green open field with no one keeping score and in a spirit of reckless abandon and laughter, it's a very different sport. Almost no one gets hurt and it's rugged, open and exciting (it still is for me). But then, like everything else, it starts to be regulated and institutionalized by adult authorities. And the fun is over.

So it was as I began the long march through organized football. Now   10
there was a coach and elders to make it clear by their behavior that
beating other people was the only thing to celebrate and that trying to
shake someone up every play was the only thing to be really proud of.
Now there were severe rule enforcers, audiences, formally recorded
victors and losers, and heavy equipment to permit crippling bodily
moves and collisions (according to one American survey, more than 80%
of all football injuries occur to fully equipped players). And now there
was the official "given" that the only way to keep playing was to wear
suffocating armor, to play to defeat, to follow orders silently and to
renounce spontaneity for joyless drill. The game had been, in short,
ruined. But because I loved to play and play skillfully, I stayed. And
progressively and inexorably, as I moved through high school, college
and pro leagues, my body was dismantled. Piece by piece.

I started off with torn ligaments in my knee at 13. Then, as the   11
organization and the competition increased, the injuries came faster and
harder. Broken nose (three times), broken jaw (fractured in the first half
and dismissed as a "bad wisdom tooth," so I played with it for the rest of
the game), ripped knee ligaments again. Torn ligaments in one ankle and
a fracture in the other (which I remember feeling relieved about because
it meant I could honorably stop drill-blocking a 270-pound defensive
end). Repeated rib fractures and cartilage tears (usually carried, again,
through the remainder of the game). More dislocations of the left shoulder than I can remember (the last one I played with because, as the
Calgary Stampeder doctor said, it "couldn't be damaged any more").
Occasional broken or dislocated fingers and toes. Chronically hurt lower
back (I still can't lift with it or change a tire without worrying about
folding). Separated right shoulder (as with many other injuries, like badly
bruised hips and legs, needled with morphine for the games). And so on.
The last pro game I played—against Winnipeg Blue Bombers in the
Western finals in 1961—I had a recently dislocated left shoulder, a more
recently wrenched right shoulder and a chronic pain centre in one leg. I
was so tied up with soreness I couldn't drive my car to the airport. But it
never occurred to me or anyone else that I miss a play as a corner
linebacker.

By the end of my football career, I had learned that physical injury—   12
giving it and taking it—is the real currency of the sport. And that in the
final analysis the "winner" is the man who can hit to kill even if only half
his limbs are working. In brief, a warrior game with a warrior ethos into
which (like almost everyone else I played with) my original boyish
enthusiasm had been relentlessly taunted and conditioned.

In thinking back on how all this happened, though, I can pick out no   13 villains. As with the social system as a whole, the game has a life of its own. Everyone grows up inside it, accepts it and fulfills its dictates as obediently as helots. Far from ever questioning the principles of the activity, people simply concentrate on executing these principles more aggressively than anybody around them. The result is a group of people who, as the leagues become of a higher and higher class, are progressively insensitive to the possibility that things could be otherwise. Thus, in football, anyone who might question the wisdom or enjoyment of putting on heavy equipment on a hot day and running full speed at someone else with the intention of knocking him senseless would be regarded simply as not really a devoted athlete and probably "chicken." The choice is made straightforward. Either you, too, do your very utmost to efficiently smash and be smashed, or you admit incompetence or cowardice and quit. Since neither of these admissions is very pleasant, people generally keep any doubts they have to themselves and carry on.

Of course, it would be a mistake to suppose that there is more blind 14
acceptance of brutal practices in organized football than elsewhere. On the contrary, a recent Harvard study has approvingly argued that football's characteristics of "impersonal acceptance of inflicted injury," an overriding "organization goal," the "ability to turn oneself on and off" and being, above all, "out to win" are of "inestimable value" to big corporations. Clearly, our sort of football is no sicker than the rest of our society. Even its organized destruction of physical well-being is not anomalous. A very large part of our wealth, work and time is, after all, spent in systematically destroying and harming human life. Manufacturing, selling and using weapons that tear opponents to pieces. Making ever bigger and faster predator-named cars with which to kill and injure one another by the million every year. And devoting our very lives to outgunning one another for power in an ever more destructive rat race. Yet all these practices are accepted without question by most people, even zealously defended and honored. Competitive, organized injuring is integral to our way of life, and football is simply one of the more intelligible mirrors of the whole process: a sort of colorful morality play showing us how exciting and rewarding it is to Smash Thy Neighbor.

Now it is fashionable to rationalize our collaboration in all this by 15
arguing that, well, man *likes* to fight and injure his fellows and such games as football should be encouraged to discharge this original-sin urge into less harmful channels than, say, war. Public-show football, this line goes, plays the same sort of cathartic role as Aristotle said stage tragedy does: without real blood (or not much), it releases players and audience from unhealthy feelings stored up inside them.

As an ex-player in this seasonal coast-to-coast drama, I see little to 16 recommend such a view. What organized football did to me was make me *suppress* my natural urges and re-express them in an alienating, vicious form. Spontaneous desires for free bodily exuberance and fraternization with competitors were shamed and forced under ("If it ain't hurtin' it ain't helpin'") and in their place were demanded armored mechanical moves and cool hatred of all opposition. Endless authoritarian drill and dressing-room harangues (ever wonder why competing teams can't prepare for a game in the same dressing room?) were the kinds of mechanisms employed to reconstruct joyful energies into mean and alien shapes. I am quite certain that everyone else around me was being similarly forced into this heavily equipped military precision and angry antagonism, because there was always a mutinous attitude about full-dress practices, and everybody (the pros included) had to concentrate incredibly hard for days to whip themselves into just one hour's hostility a week against another club. The players never speak of these things, of course, because everyone is so anxious to appear tough.

The claim that men like seriously to battle one another to some sort of 17 finish is a myth. It only endures because it wears one of the oldest and most propagandized of masks—the romantic combatant. I sometimes wonder whether the violence all around us doesn't depend for its survival on the existence and preservation of this tough-guy disguise.

QUESTIONS FOR ANALYSIS

1. Since this essay is somewhat long and complicated, begin your critical reading by making a scratch outline of the main ideas. (To review the procedures for scratch outlining, refer to Chapter 1.)

2. How does McMurtry make the particular occasion for his reflections vivid and dramatic? What does the story about his brother's surgery add?

3. McMurtry develops over several paragraphs an analogy between football and war. How does he develop the analogy? What special purpose do you think it serves, given that the essay was originally published in 1971 at the height of the Vietnam War?

4. McMurtry also spends several paragraphs recounting the history of his football experiences. Why do you think he inserts this autobiographical information into a reflective essay? How does it fit?

5. Review the other essays in this chapter, looking for one that you can compare or contrast to this essay by McMurtry. Then choose a single

basis for either comparison or contrast. You can focus on anything: a particular idea, a stylistic device, the personas projected by the two writers, their use of autobiography or narrative detail—any aspect of the two essays that captures your interest. Once you've chosen a point of comparison or contrast, annotate both essays noting that particular feature. Then write a brief essay reporting on what you have discovered. (For further suggestions, see Comparing and Contrasting Related Readings in Chapter 1.)

6. Review Exploring Your Personal Response (Chapter 1). Then write a 300–400-word personal response to the McMurtry essay, choosing one of the following topics:

Play devil's advocate and challenge one of McMurtry's ideas.

Write about the history of your reading of McMurtry's essay. That is, tell a story of your reactions during first and later readings. Reflect on how your response to the essay changed.

After you have written your response, reread it thoughtfully. In two or three sentences, say what you learned about the McMurtry essay by writing an extended response to it.

IDEAS FOR YOUR OWN WRITING

As this essay indicates, popular enthusiasms like football, rock music, and sports cars can be good subjects for reflective essays. Add to this list as many popular pastimes as you can. Then choose one that interests you, and try to recall a single memorable experience you strongly associated with it. How might you use this memory as a particular occasion for a reflective essay? What ideas or insights does it lead you to reflect on?

Matt Paschall

Matt Paschall wrote this essay for a freshman composition class at the University of California, San Diego.

Dare to Dream

Previewing this essay, you will see that it includes a poem. Read the poem now before reading the essay itself. Then write down your reflections on it. What does it say to you about your own dreams? about the American dream itself?

Camera in hand, I must have looked like a blind person who had been granted sight. The grand tour—six countries in nineteen days demanded that the essentials of Europe be compacted into a handful of thirty-six-exposure rolls of film and some generic souvenirs made in Hong Kong. France was the midway point of our sojourn, and Paris the main attraction. I was sixteen, in Paris, and on my way to the Louvre to see the *Mona Lisa*. To me, she was the mecca of all artistic reprobates seeking absolution and enlightenment.

Outside the Louvre, a large crowd gathered around a man sitting on the ground. The center of attention was a street painter working in colored chalks. He was copying from a small three-by-five postcard laying next to him. The scene struck me as comical—a grown man sitting on the sidewalk like a child with his assortment of Crayolas filling in the spaces of a coloring book.

He was scraggly and unshaven. His toothless grin and smudged hands were stained from hours of painstaking sketching. The T-shirt he wore had a *Mona Lisa* on the back, rainbow fingerprints and food stains on the front. His palette, a small box of chalks grated down like slivers of cheese, sat next to a felt hat begging at his side.

So intently did he work that he seemed unconscious of the noisy crowd that looked down on him. He never spoke and his eyes did not look up from the portrait; the only thing that acknowledged our presence was the hat containing the day's earnings. At times, he drew in long sweeping motions, but to add detail he would bend down inches from the ground. It was as if he were whispering secrets to the woman he was drawing—secrets we all wanted to hear. Each time he fell prostrate, the crowd leaned forward with him, then back again when he sat upright.

139

As I watched, I could not escape the beauty of the woman he created.   5
She had dark, flowing hair, deep-set eyes, and fair skin. I cannot forget
her facial expression. Sad and confused, with her head slightly cocked,
she seemed to be pleading—to be admired, loved, listened to, remembered, I wasn't sure.

"Who is that he's drawing?" I asked the man in a bright Hawaiian shirt   6
standing next to me.

"That's supposed to be Leonardo's *Woman of the Rocks*. The original is   7
inside. Much better on canvas. You should see it."

"Is he a professional artist?"   8

"No," the man laughed abruptly, "he's only a con-artist."   9

Con-artist or not, the man seemed to me to possess talent I could only   10
dream of. I envied his ability. I also hated him for stooping so low, for
prostituting himself like a floozy on a streetcorner.

Once, I had imagined myself an artist. From as far back as I can   11
remember, layers of dark gray pencil lead smeared along my southpaw
pinky and the side of my palm where my hand dragged across the page. I
believed that someday I would be able to paint like Leonardo, but as I
grew older my confidence and interest dissolved. My expectations were
so high that they rose like a helium balloon only to pop on the limbs of
the lowest branch. I became frustrated with drawing. It seemed that the
connection between my hands and my brain was incomplete. Impatient,
angry, and hypercritical, I would wad up hours of work.

We are much alike, the street artist and I. Like me, he is mediocre, but   12
he dares to dream. Fear of our own mediocrity steals our dreams from us.
We seem to have gotten our priorities turned upside down. It used to be
that what counted was how you play the game; now winning is everything. Growing up in a land of heroes and hero worshippers, we have
come to believe that all that counts is coming in first. We seem to have
forfeit our dreams.

That raises the question Langston Hughes asked in his poem entitled,   13
"What happens to a dream deferred?"

> Does it dry up
> like a raisin in the sun?
> Or fester like a sore—
> And then run?
> Does it stink like rotten meat?
> Or crust and sugar over—
> like a syrupy sweet?
>
> Maybe it just sags
> like a heavy load?
>
> Or does it explode?

I remember leaving the street artist and running all the way to the 14 *Mona Lisa*. When I got there, I joined the crowd standing in front of the bulletproof shell in which she was encased. Fluorescent lights haloed her head. Two armed guards stared stolidly at us as we stared reverently at her. I waited impatiently but no revelation came. It took me an hour to find Leonardo's *Woman of the Rocks*. There were no crowds, guards, or bulletproof glass to come between us. I felt she was almost within my reach, and I admired the street artist even more for choosing her over the *Mona Lisa*.

QUESTIONS FOR ANALYSIS

1. Paschall ends the opening paragraph with this comment about the *Mona Lisa*: "To me, she was the mecca of all artistic reprobates seeking absolution and enlightenment." What do you think he means by this statement? How does he contrast the two paintings, *Mona Lisa* and *Woman of the Rocks*? How does this contrast enable him to focus his insights and reflections?

2. Reread paragraphs 1–10 that present the particular occasion and underline anything—details, images, stylistic devices, word choices— that you think makes the writing especially effective. Then, make an inventory of your annotations following the procedures in Chapter 1. What patterns do you find? What meanings do they suggest?

3. Paschall doesn't generalize about his experience until paragraph 12. What question or insight has the particular incident led him to reflect on? Comment on the effectiveness of including in these reflections Langston Hughes's poem "What happens to a dream deferred?"

4. Describe the *persona* Paschall establishes in this essay. How appropriate is it, given the question or insight the essay reflects on?

5. Review Exploring Your Personal Response in Chapter 1. Then write a 300–400-word personal response to Paschall's essay, choosing one of the following topics:
   Write a letter to Paschall, responding to anything in the essay that you found particularly unusual, interesting, or intriguing.
   Write about your personal associations with something in the essay, such as an image, idea, or character.
   After you have written your response, reread it thoughtfully. In two or three sentences, say what you learned about the Paschall essay by writing an extended response to it.

IDEAS FOR YOUR OWN WRITING

Think of poems or paintings, films or stories, or songs or television shows that mean something to you. List several of these, and then choose one or two to explore further. Write about each one for five minutes, recalling as many specific details as you can. Then reread your exploratory writing, and in a sentence or two, try to say what insight or idea your reflections have led you to.

A GUIDE TO REFLECTIVE WRITING

As the selections in this chapter suggest, reflective essays can make for engaging reading. They are interesting, lively, insightful—like good conversation—and at the same time focus on basic human and social issues that concern us all. Writers of reflection, while never pretentious or preachy, are not reluctant to say what they think, to express their most personal observations.

Because reflective essays broaden personal experience into exploration of larger issues, they can be particularly enjoyable to write. This section guides you through the various decisions you will need to make as you plan, draft, and revise a reflective essay.

The Writing Task

Write a reflective essay exploring a question or insight you have about the human condition. Ground your general reflections in a particular occasion. Present the occasion vividly and explore inventively its meaning and implications.

Invention

The following activities should spur your thinking, helping you to find a particular occasion and general subject, develop your subject, and identify your controlling idea. Taking some time now to consider a wide range of possibilities will pay off later when you draft your essay because it will give you confidence in your choice of subject and in your ability to develop it effectively.

FINDING A PARTICULAR OCCASION AND GENERAL SUBJECT. As the readings in this chapter illustrate, writers usually begin their essays with a particular event or observation that occasions their reflections upon a general subject. In the process of invention, however, the particular occasion does not always come before the general subject. Sometimes writers set out to reflect upon a general subject such as envy or friendship and must search for just the right image or anecdote with which to particularize it.

To help you find an occasion and subject for your essay, make a chart like the one that follows by matching particular occasions to general subjects. In the left-hand column, list particular occasions—a conversation you have had or overheard, a scene you have observed, a quotation you recall, an incident in your own or someone else's life—that might lead you to reflect more generally. In the right-hand column, list general subjects—human qualities like compassion, vanity, jealousy, faithfulness; social customs and mores for dating, eating, working; abstract notions like fate, free will, the imagination—that suggest themselves to you.

Move from left to right and also from right to left, making your lists as long as you can. You will find that a single occasion might suggest several subjects and that a subject might be particularized by a variety of occasions. Each entry will surely suggest other possibilities for you to consider. If you are having trouble getting started, review the Ideas for Your Own Writing following each reading in this chapter. Your chart of possibilities is likely to become quite messy, but do not censor your ideas. A full and rich exploration of topics will give you confidence that the one you finally choose is the most promising.

Particular Occasions	*General Subjects*
Saw jr. high girls wearing makeup as thick as a clown's	Make-up: make-over, mask the real self; Ideas of beauty;
Punk styles of the 80s/ zoot suits of the 40s	Changing fashions: conformity or rebellion?
Rumor of Paul McCartney's death	Rumors: Sources? Purpose? Malicious
Rumor about Diane and Tom spread by a friend of theirs	like gossip? How do they start? stop?
Saw film called *Betrayal*	Friendship & betrayal

Buying clothes, I couldn't decide and let salesperson pressure me. Take friends to help me make a decision	Decisions & indecisiveness; Bowing to outside pressure; Low self-esteem; Can't or won't think of self— conformity again!
Saw bumper sticker: "Don't Californicate Oregon" "Truckers Do It On the Road" "Nuke the Gay Whales"	Bumper stickers—a kind of writing, very expressive Political, sexual, just funny Propaganda, offensive

As further occasions and subjects occur to you over the next two or three days, add them to this chart.

CHOOSING A SUBJECT. Review the chart and select an occasion and subject you now think looks promising.

To test whether this selection will work, write for fifteen minutes exploring your thoughts on it. Do not make any special demands on yourself to be profound or even to be coherent. Just put your ideas on paper as they come, letting one idea suggest another. Your aim is to determine whether you have anything to say and whether the topic holds your interest. If you discover that you do not have very much to say or that you quickly lose interest in the subject, choose another one and try again. It might take you a few preliminary explorations to find the right subject.

DEVELOPING THE PARTICULAR OCCASION. These activities will help you recall details about the occasion for your reflection that will make your narrative vivid and dramatic.

Identifying Particulars of the Event. Write for five minutes, narrating what happened during the event. Include as many details as you can recall. What did the people look like? How did they act toward one another? Recall sensory details about the scene: its look, sound, smell, feel, taste. Speculate about what people were feeling at the time.

Reconstructing Dialogue. Try adding one or two snippets of conversation to your narrative. You may decide, later, to include dialogue because it helps make anecdotes dramatic. You might also discover, as Ellen Good-man did, that what was said is basically what happened.

DEVELOPING THE SUBJECT. As a means of developing your subject, try the invention activity called cubing. Based on the six sides of a cube, this activity leads you to turn over your subject as you would a cube, looking at it in six different ways. Complete these activities in any order you want, writing five minutes on each. Your goal is to invent new ways of considering your subject.

Define It. Identify the key terms you used to state and restate your subject, and then define them. What other key terms could you use, and what do they imply?

Compare It. Compare and contrast your subject to other related subjects. Look for differences as well as similarities.

Extend It. Take your subject to its logical limits. Speculate about its implications. Where does it lead?

Analyze It. Take apart your subject. What is it made of? How are the parts related to one another? Are they all of equal importance?

Apply It. Think about your subject in practical terms. How can you use it or act on it? What difference would it make to you and to others?

Argue about It. Think of others who might disagree with you about your subject. What objections might they have? How could you respond to their arguments?

Drafting

After completing the preceding invention activities, you should feel confident in your choice of particular occasion, knowing that it suggests a subject that you can develop in interesting ways. The following sugges-tions for setting goals, planning, and deciding how to begin your essay prepare you to write your first full draft.

SETTING GOALS. Writers need to set goals—specific (or local) goals as well as general (or global) ones—to guide them as they draft their essay.

These goals ought to be determined by a consideration of who will be reading the essay and what the writer wants to get across to these readers.

Before establishing your specific goals, consider what your general ones should be. Ask yourself what your purpose is: What main point do you want your readers to come away with? Ask yourself how you want your readers to view you: What voice or persona will you try to present to them?

If, for example, you think your readers are likely to have some thought about what you are saying, you might try to give your essay a surprising turn, as Staples does when he acknowledges that people, especially women, are right to fear him or as Shames does when he tells us that Arty understood what was going on the whole time.

If you expect readers to have a simple answer to one of your questions, you might push them to probe the point more deeply, as Theroux does in explaining why family members tend to get into petty disputes during holiday gatherings.

If you assume readers are satisfied with their own understanding, you might come at your subject from a unique angle, as Didion does when she acknowledges that having self-respect does not guarantee that you'll act morally but only that you'll take responsibility for your actions.

If you are afraid readers won't be interested by what you have to say, you could use the particular occasion to catch their attention, as Goodman does by opening with amusing snippets of conversation.

PLANNING YOUR ORGANIZATION. Your invention writings will probably have given you many ideas. In fact, you might feel overwhelmed by the richness of your own invention. A good way to sort through your ideas and find ways of grouping them is to use clustering. In this process, you will need to refer repeatedly to what you have written thus far, and you may also need to generate more material to fill out some points.

First, decide on a single word or phrase that summarizes your subject (such as "food-medicine"). Put it in the center of the page and circle it. Second, skim your invention writings to find key ideas or questions. Label and circle these and place them at various points around the central idea, connecting them with a line to the center. Third, look again at your invention writing to find material—ideas, questions, facts, examples—relating to each of these subordinate points. Cluster these around the relevant point.

BEGINNING. Most reflective essays begin with the particular occasion, but they present it in a variety of ways. Goodman uses amusing dialogue to catch our attention, while Staples uses drama, opening his narrative with the arresting statement: "My first victim was a woman. . . ." Theroux announces her topic with the epigrammatic statement: "As life goes on and independence becomes necessary for survival, pride of family can turn into fear of family. . . ." Didion confides in the reader, telling about something that embarrassed her. Shames sets the particular occasion within a general frame by alluding at the beginning and end of his essay to Orwell's *1984*.

Revising

Even if you start out with a clear sense of purpose, drafting can take you in unexpected directions. In the process of putting ideas down on paper, you are likely to gain new insights and raise questions you had not anticipated. Reflective writing, more than other types of writing, depends on serendipity such as this.

Discovering new ideas as you write makes writing fun and creative, but it also can add to the work of revising your draft. You might find that some of your ideas need to be clarified, extended, or connected. You might recognize ways to make your train of thought easier for readers to follow. The advice below focuses on ways to develop your ideas and to improve the readability of your essay.

To revise, you will need to read your own draft critically; to do so, you need to get some distance from it. Using the questions for analyzing basic features at the beginning of this chapter will help you see the draft more objectively. Having someone else respond to your writing—a classmate or your instructor—will help you see where it works for others and where it doesn't.

REVISING TO DEVELOP YOUR IDEAS. Your purpose has probably changed somewhat as you've explored your ideas, so you might begin by writing down the main point you now want to get across to readers. Keep this idea in mind as you reread the draft, and then compare what the essay actually says to what you want it to say.

The following guidelines will help you identify the passages you need to revise and also suggest ways of revising them:

Look for ideas that now seem to you to be trite or predictable, simplistic or undeveloped, abstract or vague. On a separate piece of paper, write for five minutes about each of these ideas. Restate them in new terms, explain them in more detail, or apply them to different situations. Pair or group ideas to discover patterns you might have missed. Extend ideas you touched on briefly, speculating on their long-term implications or ferreting out their roots. Explain why certain ideas are important to you personally or in a larger context.

Make a scratch outline of the draft and look for ways to clarify connections, reorder points, and make the essay flow more smoothly.

Look at the way you present the particular occasion. Try to focus your narrative by making it more vivid and detailed. Intensify the drama with specific narrative action and dialogue. Clarify the connection between the particular occasion and your central insight or question. Then, make this point more explicit and develop it at greater length.

REVISING TO IMPROVE READABILITY. Reflective essays should be inviting and personable. Reading them should be like listening to good conversation—amusing as well as illuminating.

Think about the *persona* or voice you project in your essay. Try to make it more attractive by inserting humor, personal disclosure, straight talk. Be more playful with language. Make your writing style more vigorous by using action verbs and more vivid by using figurative language (images that appeal to the senses, similes, and metaphors).

Consider alternative ways of opening your essay. Cut more quickly to your anecdote by eliminating general or unnecessary introductory statements. Let the reader get a sense of you from the very start.

When you are satisfied with your revisions, carefully proofread your writing to eliminate errors in spelling, usage, and punctuation. If possible, have someone else examine your essay for such mistakes too.

Observation

Certain kinds of writing are based on direct investigation. Motivated by curiosity to learn about unusual subjects or to find a unique perspective on ordinary subjects, writers observe and then go on to share what they learn with their readers in order to inform and intrigue them.

Travel accounts, descriptions of natural phenomena, profiles of people or places, and original research reports are some familiar examples of such writing. In all of these, writers depend mainly, if not solely, on what they can learn for themselves. Whether by visiting a place, participating in an activity, or interviewing a person, writers carry out firsthand research to find the information they then present to readers. Travel writers, for example, may write about a place they have visited; naturalists may describe phenomena they have observed. Investigative reporters or clinical psychologists may write about a person they have talked to many times; anthropologists may write about a group with whom they have lived for several months or years.

A great deal of what we know about people and the world comes from this kind of writing—in fact, it establishes much of the basic knowledge in both the natural and social sciences. Because it often deals with unfamiliar subjects, it can be enormously interesting.

Writing up your own observations can offer special challenges and rewards. You can visit places on or off campus and interview people who interest you—and write extended profiles of those places or people.

This kind of writing allows you to understand better the complex relations among the activities of observing, taking notes, and writing them up. Essentially, you will be translating your own experiences and perceptions into writing to be shared with others—a profoundly important act. Moreover, such activities form the basic strategies of inquiry and knowledge-making in many of the academic disciplines you will study as a college student.

A GUIDE TO READING OBSERVATIONAL WRITING

To begin your study of observational writing, you will first look closely at an excerpt from a book by historian and journalist Frances FitzGerald. Closely analyzing FitzGerald's observations will provide a foundation for the serious study of observational writing this chapter encourages. As you become a more critical, insightful reader of observational writing, your own observational writing will become more vivid and engaging.

As the initial step in your analysis, you will annotate the FitzGerald selection. The next exercise asks you to take inventory of your annotations in order to disclose a pattern of meaning you have discovered. In the third exercise, guided by special questions, you will report what you have learned in analyzing the unique features of observational writing. Finally, the concluding exercise invites you to write a brief exploratory essay, consolidating what you have learned about the FitzGerald selection and trying out your own ideas about it or extending your personal response to it.

The time you invest now in annotating, analyzing, and writing will pay off richly as you read, write about, and discuss the essays in this chapter. It will also give you confidence that you can successfully write your own observational essay.

Annotating As You Read

As we have discussed, the most basic, and most useful, strategy for reading attentively and critically is annotating. Pencil in hand as you read, you are ready to record on the page any comments, questions, definitions, or insights—whatever crosses your mind—about a piece of writing. As an illustration, notice how we have annotated the following brief passage from a profile of a Brooklyn farmers' market by John McPhee that appears in its entirety later in this chapter.

Scene: long and short sentences mirror con man's confusing action and Rich's simplicity

A man who gave Rich Hodgson a ten-dollar bill for a ninety-five-cent box of brown eggs asks Rich to give the ten back after Rich has handed him nine dollars and five cents, explaining that he has some smaller bills that he wants to exchange for a twenty. Rich hands him the ten. Into Rich's palm he counts out five ones, a five, and the ten for a twenty and goes away satisfied, as he has every reason to be, having conned Rich out of nine dollars, five cents, and a box of brown eggs. Rich smiles at his foolishness, shrugs, and sells some cheese. If cash were equanimity, he would never lose a cent.

equanimity: **composure, even-tempered under stress**

One day, a gang of kids began taking Don Keller's vegetables and throwing them at the Hodgson truck. Anders Thueson threw an apple at the kids, who then picked up rocks. Thueson reached into the back of the truck and came up with a machete. While Hodgson told him to put it away, pant legs went up, switchblades came into view. Part of the gang bombarded the truck with debris from a nearby roof. Any indication of panic might have been disastrous. Hodgson packed deliberately, and drove away.

Escalation of conflict shown through weapons named

Two examples show Rich's personality

For more on annotating, pause now to review the guidelines in Chapter 1 and the model annotations on the excerpt from "Letter from Birmingham Jail." Note particularly the Checklist for Annotating.

Exercise 1

Annotate Frances FitzGerald's "Refugees" as you read. Reread it at least one time, continuing to annotate as you reread. Your purpose is to focus your attention on the text, to read as thoughtfully—as critically—as possible. Annotate details you admire as well as things you question or challenge, mark noteworthy stylistic devices or writing strategies, write down any personal responses. Record your insights and reactions directly on and around the text itself.

The following selection comes from the beginning of *Fire in the Lake*, Frances FitzGerald's remarkable study of the Vietnamese and of the American influence in Vietnam. FitzGerald was a free-lance journalist there in 1966, and she continued to study its history when she returned to the United States. Published in 1972, *Fire in the Lake* won the Pulitzer Prize, the National Book Award, and the Bancroft Prize for History.

This excerpt illustrates the important role firsthand investigation can play in historical writing about recent events. From the first paragraph—in which FitzGerald begins with a panoramic view of traffic entering Saigon (now Ho Chi Minh City), the capital and largest city in Vietnam, then zooms in close to a narrow bridge, piles of garbage, a mysterious girl in high heels, and a waiting Buick—we are aware that the writer has observed her subject directly.

Refugees
Frances FitzGerald

Before entering Saigon, the military traffic from Tan Son Nhut airfield slows in a choking blanket of its own exhaust. Where it crawls along to the narrow bridge in a frenzy of bicycles, pedicabs, and tri-Lambrettas, two piles of garbage mark the entrance to a new quarter of the city. Every evening a girl on spindle heels picks her way over the barrier of rotting fruit and onto the sidewalks. Triumphant, she smiles at the boys who lounge at the soft-drink stand, and with a toss of her long earrings, climbs into a waiting Buick. 1

Behind her, the alleyway carpeted with mud winds back past the facade of the new houses into a maze of thatched huts and tin-roofed shacks called Bui Phat. One of the oldest of the refugee quarters, Bui Phat lies just across the river from the generous villas and tree-lined streets of French Saigon. On its tangle of footpaths, white-shirted boys push their Vespas past laborers in black pajamas and women carrying water on coolie poles. After twelve years and recurrent tides of new refugees, Bui Phat is less an urban quarter than a compost of villages where peasants live with their city children. The children run thick underfoot. The police, it is said, rarely enter this quarter for fear of a gang of teen-age boys, whose leader, a young army deserter, reigns over Bui Phat. 2

Most of Bui Phat lives beyond the law, the electricity lines, and the water system, but it has its secret fortunes. Here and there amid the chaos of shacks and alleyways, new concrete buildings rear up in a splendor of pastelfaced walls, neon lights, and plastic garden furniture. In one of them there is a half-naked American who suns himself on a porch under a clothesline draped with military uniforms. He does not know, and probably never will know, that the house just down the alleyway is owned and inhabited by an agent of the NLF. 3

Bui Phat and its likenesses are what the American war has brought to Vietnam. In the countryside there is only 4 an absence: the bare brown fields, the weeds growing in the charred earth of the village, the jungle that has swept back over the cleared land. The grandest ruins are those of the American tanks, for the Vietnamese no longer build fine stone tombs as did their ancestors. The U.S. First Infantry Division has carved its divisional insignia with defoliants in a stretch of jungle—a giant, poisonous graffito—but the Vietnamese have left nothing to mark the passage of their armies and an entire generation of young men. In many places death is not even a physical absence. The villages that once again take root in the rich soil of the Delta fill up with children as quickly as the [holes] made by the five-hundred-pound and thousand-pound bombs fill up with paddy silt. The desire for survival has been greater than the war itself, for there are approximately two million more people in the south to-day than there were before the war. But the balance of the nation has changed, and Saigon is no longer the village, it is Bui Phat.

From Dong Ha in the north to Rach Gia, the slow port 5 at the base of the Delta, these new slums, these crushed villages, spread through all of the cities and garrisoned towns. They are everywhere, plastered against sandbag forts, piled up under the guns of the provincial capitals, overwhelming what is left of the Delta's yellow stucco towns. Seaward of Da Nang the tin huts of the refugee settlements lie between the ammunition and the garbage dumps, indistinguishable from either. These huts have been rebuilt many times during the war, for every year there is some kind of disaster—an airplane crash or an explosion in the ammunition depot—that wipes out whole hamlets. Around Qui Nhon, Bien Hoa, and Cam Ranh bay, where the Americans have built jetports and military installations to last through the twentieth cen-tury, the thatched huts crowd so closely that a single neglected cigarette or a spark from a charcoal brazier suffices to burn the settlements down. On the streets of tin shacks that run straight as a surrealist's line past the runways and into the sand, babies play naked in the dust and rows of green combat fatigues hang over the barbed wire like dead soldiers.

Out of a population of seventeen million there are now 6 five million refugees. Perhaps 40 or 50 percent of the population, as opposed to the 15 percent before the war, live in and around the cities and towns. The distribution is that of a highly industrialized country, but there is almost no industry in South Vietnam. And the word "city" and even "town" is misleading. What was even in 1965 a nation of villages and landed estates is now a nation of bidonvilles, refugee camps, and army bases. South Vietnam is a country shattered so that no two pieces fit together.

Inventorying Your Annotations

Once you have annotated a reading with your observations and insights, you'll want to analyze your annotations for their special meaning. The best way to do this is by taking inventory of your annotations, to identify any patterns or key repetitions.

Before completing Exercise 2, review the guidelines and illustration for the Inventory of Annotations in Chapter 1.

Exercise 2

Inventory the annotations you made on "Refugees," looking for meaningful patterns.

Analyzing the Basic Features
of Observational Writing

In addition to annotating a text to record your initial impressions and inventorying your annotations for their patterns of meaning, you can analyze the basic features of a piece of writing, in this case those qualities that enable us to recognize an essay as distinctively observational.

Look back at Identifying and Evaluating Basic Features in Chapter 1. Although the questions there are different from the ones you will find in this chapter, the answers illustrate what a thoughtful analysis of basic features might look like.

Exercise 3

Analyze "Refugees" by answering the following questions. You will want to reread the selection with each question in mind, and you may want to annotate further.

Write out your answers to the questions.

1. *How does the writer engage and sustain readers' interest in the subject?* Consider how effectively the writer draws you in from the very beginning. Look for places where the pace slows and your attention wanders. Does the writer present too much new information too fast? Are there any long factual stretches that need to be broken by descriptive details or anecdotes to make abstract facts more understandable and memorable?

2. *How are important scenes and people presented?* Decide how many actual places and people there are (you might want to list them), and then consider how the writer presents them. Are scenes described or merely mentioned? Does the writer point out any small parts of the scenes? Are you given many visual details? Look for information about size, shape, position, color, texture. Are people described or merely named? Do you see them moving, gesturing, and talking? Are you aware of what they're wearing? Do you have any sense of their personalities?

Try to assess how successfully the writer has presented scenes and people, and then analyze whether they seem relevant to the writer's purpose. Do details contribute to your understanding of the subject, or do they seem irrelevant? Identify key details that contribute to a dominant impression of the subject. Which details are especially telling?

3. *What vantage point does the writer use to present the scene or scenes?* Look to see whether the writer views a scene from a distance or moves in close. Also notice whether he or she presents a scene from a fixed vantage point (looking at it from one perspective), or takes you on a tour through a scene, or both. Consider why the writer chose this particular vantage point. Can you imagine a different vantage point or various sequential vantage points which the writer might have chosen instead? Do you think the writer's vantage point is the most appropriate one for his or her purpose?

4. *How does the writer organize the observations?* Scrutinize the way in which the writer has planned the piece. Of special importance is how the piece begins and ends. With these considerations in mind, decide whether the writer's plan produced a well-paced essay, easy and satisfying for you to follow. What are the strongest and weakest features of the organization? Consider ways the observations could have been organized differently. Might some alternative plan be just as effective or even more effective?

5. *What is the writer's controlling theme?* Observational writing achieves focus and purpose through a controlling theme. This theme may not be

stated explicitly, like a main point or thesis, but usually it is. The controlling theme can take various forms: a surprising insight (surprising to either writer or reader) into the subject of the observations, an interpretation of the subject, an incongruity or contradiction in the subject, or an angle on it (as in in-depth reportage). What seems to be the insight, incongruity, or angle in the writing? Look at how the various parts of the writing support this theme. Do any parts seem to lead away from it?

6. *What is the writer's purpose in presenting this subject to readers?* To understand the writer's purpose, consider the theme and tone of the piece. Is it playful? serious? angry? What seems to be the writer's attitude toward the subject? Can you guess what motivated the writer to address this subject? What does the writer seem to assume about his or her readers? From these conjectures, decide what you think the writer's purpose might be.

7. *What do I learn from the writer's observations?* Whatever the writer's purpose and strategies, your own aim as a reader of an observational piece is to be informed about subjects and to find satisfaction in their manner of presentation. Were you informed by this piece, and did you learn anything of importance? Are there any things you are likely to remember? What did you learn?

Exploring Your Personal Response

One other way of focusing your response to a piece of observational writing is by taking the time to record your thoughts in a more extended piece of your own writing. Basically, such an exercise can help you to follow up on an insight, to compare your own experience and understanding with the writer's, to explore your impressions and define further your unique perspective on what you've read.

Exercise 4

Write 300–400 words (two or three handwritten pages) about "Refugees." Choose one of the suggestions listed in Exploring Your Personal Response in Chapter 1.

Maxine Kumin

A novelist, poet, and essayist, Maxine Kumin (b. 1925) lives in New Hampshire. She won the Pulitzer Prize in 1973 and was Consultant in Poetry to the Library of Congress for 1981–82. She has taught at several universities, including Columbia and Princeton.

From a Journal

These journal selections appear in Kumin's most recent book, *In Deep: Country Essays* (1987). She writes these "country essays" from a farm which she and her husband cleared and fenced. She writes about her observations of wild and domestic animals, the change of the seasons, and the daily affairs of life on a nearly self-sufficient farm. Inserted occasionally among the essays are revised selections from Kumin's journals. The selections that follow are observations on three consecutive days of an impressive owl who suddenly appeared in a tree on her farm. Knowing that Kumin is a poet, how would you expect her to present her observations of this owl?

13 February 1978   Today, in the dying butternut tree that holds up the clothesline from which depend various suets and the main sunflower-seed feeder, an owl. Peterson's indicates it is a barred owl, not an unusual bird in these surroundings. He arrived, like a poem, unannounced. He squatted on the branch, puffed to an almost perfect roundness against the cold. His gray and brown and buff markings imitate the landscape of tree branch and caterpillar nest tatters against the snow. I could not, as the cliché has it, believe my eyes at first, and tried to make him into some recognizable artifact of nature—a clump of windblown leaves, for example. Like the notes for a poem, he would not go away but merely swelled there passively all through breakfast.

The squirrels did not show themselves, wisely. The chickadees are fearless, or at least know they have nothing to fear. The blue jays likewise. I note that our narrow-faced, downside-traveling nuthatches were absent all day.

14 February   The owl is a Cheshire cat of an owl, noiselessly appearing, disappearing, flapping off soundlessly on immense wings, returning, higher up than before. He swivels his head almost 360 degrees, like a Japanese puppet-balloon held aloft on a stick. The face is infinitely old, infinitely wise, very catlike. When perched, no wings or claws are evi-

157

[handwritten margin notes:]
1. Describes the owl, & come it cune to be there

3. The owl is descri as a cat & a Japanese pupple

dent, lending him even more mystery than is warranted. Like the finished poem, he makes it all seem easy. Not since last winter's wild turkeys, not since last summer's swallow nestling sideshow on the front porch stringers, has there been better indoor viewing.

15 February   This resident owl of ours, I muse on the third day of his tenure in the butternut, resembles nothing birdlike. Most of all he looks like a baseball pitcher in a tight spot, winding up, swiveling to check the runners at first and second, then . . . the balk. The old owls of my poems were of the furtive sort, night hooters. Whenever I did catch a daytime glimpse of them, they were in a hurry to get under cover and they seemed ragged, weary, diminished by a hard night's work. This one is larger than life-size. He has assumed the stature of a godhead in the birdfeeding zone, though today he and the squirrel eyed each other and nothing happened. Perhaps the owl is full of his nightly mice? I noticed that the squirrel took care, while cleaning up the spilled sunflower husks, not to turn his back on the owl. Although only a small red squirrel, perhaps he is too large to tempt even an enlarged owl.

QUESTIONS FOR ANALYSIS

1. Kumin relies mainly on figurative language to present the owl. Annotate her journal entries for figurative language, and then inventory what you find in order to discover the meaning of the figurative language. (Review Inventory of Figurative Language on pages 27–31 in Chapter 1.) Here are some early images to get you started: arrived "like a poem," "markings imitate [are like] the landscape of tree branch and caterpillar nest tatters against the snow."

2. What is Kumin's vantage point in these observations? That is, where is she in relation to the owl? Does her vantage point change as she observes the owl, or does it remain the same? What advantages or disadvantages do you see in her vantage point?

3. How would you describe Kumin's tone—her attitude towards the owl? Does she seem amused, bored, judgmental, or something else? What is there in the journal entries that influences your decision about her tone?

4. Observational writing is characterized by diversity and inventiveness of sentence patterns. Look closely at the sentences in the journal entry of February 14, and identify the different patterns or structures Kumin uses. (Even if you do not know grammatical concepts and terms, you can still recognize whether sentences look alike or different.) Look again at the first sentence and conjecture about how its pattern allows Kumin to present her observations of the owl.

5. Given all the details of Kumin's observations (figurative language, vantage point, tone, visual details), what seems to you the dominant impression she creates about the owl?

IDEAS FOR YOUR OWN WRITING

Consider starting an observation journal. To do so, record from five to ten daily observations of a bird or animal (pet, work animal, wild animal) or a person you see every day but who would not be aware of your observations (baby, neighborhood child, waiter, bus driver). Devote ten to fifteen minutes to each of your daily observations. Record your observations primarily in drawings, words, and phrases. You may use sentences, but they will slow you down. For each observation, record (1) a large number of concrete details (movements, appearance, dialogue, specific objects in the scene where you observe the animal or person, sounds, smells); (2) images, analogies, comparisons, contrasts—that is, what the animal or person reminds you of or suggests to you; and (3) quick impressions, ideas, or insights.

After completing one five-to-ten-day observation sequence, select two or three of your daily records and, like Kumin, rewrite them as observational reports.

The New Yorker

Written by an unidentified staff writer, the following selection appeared in the "Goings on about Town" section of the *New Yorker* magazine (January 1989). The *New Yorker*, which brings together fiction, poetry, observational writing, and reviews, is known for the detailed clarity of its reporting and the grace and precision of its editorial style. "Goings on about Town" is a weekly compendium of brief, anonymous observations of New York places and people in action.

Soup

The author of this piece reports firsthand observations of a Manhattan takeout soup kitchen and its creative and demanding owner, Mr. Albert Yeganeh. As you read, you can readily imagine the reporter interviewing the owner, writing down soup names and menu items, observing people in line, and even standing in line as well for a bowl of soup. As you preview this selection, notice that the writer relies on extended quotations from the interview in order to keep the focus on Mr. Yeganeh. Besides letting the owner speak for himself, what other strategies does the writer adopt for presenting the owner and his soup kitchen?

When Albert Yeganeh says "Soup is my lifeblood," he means it. And 1
when he says "I am extremely hard to please," he means that, too. Working like a demon alchemist in a tiny storefront kitchen at 259-A West Fifty-fifth Street, Mr. Yeganeh creates anywhere from eight to seventeen soups every weekday. His concoctions are so popular that a wait of half an hour at the lunchtime peak is not uncommon, although there are strict rules for conduct in line. But more on that later.

"I am psychologically kind of a health freak," Mr. Yeganeh said the 2
other day, in a lisping staccato of Armenian origin. "And I know that soup is the greatest meal in the world. It's very good for your digestive system. And I use only the best, the freshest ingredients. I am a perfectionist. When I make a clam soup, I use three different kinds of clams. Every other place uses canned clams. I'm called crazy. I am not crazy. People don't realize why I get so upset. It's because if the soup is not perfect and I'm still selling it, it's a torture. It's *my* soup, and that's why I'm so upset. First you clean and then you cook. I don't believe that ninety-nine per cent of the restaurants in New York know how to clean a tomato. I tell my crew to wash the parsley *eight* times. If they wash it five

160

or six times, I scare them. I tell them they'll go to jail if there is sand in the parsley. One time, I found a mushroom on the floor, and I fired the guy who left it there." He spread his arms, and added, "This place is the only one like it in . . . in . . . the whole earth! One day, I hope to learn something from the other places, but so far I haven't. For example, the other day I went to a very fancy restaurant and had borscht. I had to send it back. It was *junk*. I could see all the chemicals in it. I never use chemicals. Last weekend, I had lobster bisque in Brooklyn, a very well-known place. It was *junk*. When I make a lobster bisque, I use a whole lobster. You know, I never advertise. I don't have to. All the big-shot chefs and the kings of the hotels come here to see what *I'm* doing."

As you approach Mr. Yeganeh's Soup Kitchen International from a   3
distance, the first thing you notice about it is the awning, which proclaims "Homemade Hot, Cold, Diet Soups." The second thing you notice is an aroma so delicious that it makes you want to take a bite out of the air. The third thing you notice, in front of the kitchen, is an electric signboard that flashes, say, "Today's Soups . . . Chicken Vegetable . . . Mexican Beef Chili . . . Cream of Watercress . . . Italian Sausage . . . Clam Bisque . . . Beef Barley . . . Due to Cold Weather . . . For Most Efficient and Fastest Service the Line Must . . . Be Kept Moving . . . Please . . . Have Your Money . . . Ready . . . Pick the Soup of Your Choice . . . Move to Your Extreme . . . Left After Ordering."

"I am not prejudiced against color or religion," Mr. Yeganeh told us,   4
and he jabbed an index finger at the flashing sign. "Whoever follows that I treat very well. My regular customers don't say anything. They are very intelligent and well educated. They know I'm just trying to move the line. The New York cop is very smart—he sees everything but says nothing. But the young girl who wants to stop and tell you how nice you look and hold everyone up—*yah!*" He made a guillotining motion with his hand. "I tell you, I hate to work with the public. They treat me like a slave. My philosophy is: The customer is always wrong and I'm always right. I raised my prices to try to get rid of some of these people, but it didn't work."

The other day, Mr Yeganeh was dressed in chefs' whites with orange   5
smears across his chest, which may have been some of the carrot soup cooking in a huge pot on a little stove in one corner. A three-foot-long handheld mixer from France sat on the sink, looking like an overgrown gardening tool. Mr. Yeganeh spoke to two young helpers in a twisted Armenian-Spanish barrage, then said to us, "I have no overhead, no trained waitresses, and I have the cashier here." He pointed to himself theatrically. Beside the doorway, a glass case with fresh green celery, red and yellow peppers, and purple eggplant was topped by five big gray soup

urns. According to a piece of cardboard taped to the door, you can buy Mr. Yeganeh's soups in three sizes, costing from four to fifteen dollars. The order of any well-behaved customer is accompanied by little wax-paper packets of bread, fresh vegetables (such as scallions and radishes), fresh fruit (such as cherries or an orange), a chocolate mint, and a plastic spoon. No coffee, tea, or other drinks are served.

"I get my recipes from books and theories and my own taste," Mr.   6 Yeganeh said. "At home, I have several hundreds of books. When I do research, I find that I don't know anything. Like cabbage is a cancer fighter, and some fish is good for your heart but some is bad. Every day, I should have one sweet, one spicy, one cream, one vegetable soup—and they *must* change, they should always taste a little different." He added that he wasn't sure how extensive his repertoire was, but that it probably includes at least eighty soups, among them African peanut butter, Greek moussaka, hamburger, Reuben, B.L.T., asparagus and caviar, Japanese shrimp miso, chicken chili, Irish corned beef and cabbage, Swiss chocolate, French calf's brain, Korean beef ball, Italian shrimp and eggplant Parmesan, buffalo, ham and egg, short rib, Russian beef Stroganoff, turkey cacciatore, and Indian mulligatawny. "The chicken and the seafood are an addiction, and when I have French garlic soup I let people have only one small container each," he said. "The doctors and nurses love that one."

A lunch line of thirty people stretched down the block from Mr.   7 Yeganeh's doorway. Behind a construction worker was a man in expensive leather, who was in front of a woman in a fur hat. Few people spoke. Most had their money out and their orders ready.

At the front of the line, a woman in a brown coat couldn't decide   8 which soup to get and started to complain about the prices.

"You talk too much, dear," Mr. Yeganeh said, and motioned to her to   9 move to the left. "Next!"

"Just don't talk. Do what he says," a man huddled in a blue parka   10 warned.

"He's downright rude," said a blond woman in a blue coat. "Even   11 abusive. But you can't deny it, his soup is the best."

QUESTIONS FOR ANALYSIS

1. The writer presents Mr. Yeganeh in part by quoting him directly. Annotate this quoted material for specific details about Mr. Yeganeh as a person and soup chef. Inventory your annotations to discover what the quoted material reveals about Mr. Yeganeh. (Review the Inventory of Annotations in Chapter 1.)

2. Instead of quoting Mr. Yeganeh, the writer could have paraphrased the quoted material, presenting it indirectly. (For example, at the beginning of paragraph 2, instead of quoting, the writer might have written the following: Mr. Yeganeh said that he believed soup to be good for the digestive system. He claimed that he always used only fresh ingredients in his soups.) What do the quotations add to the essay? How would the essay be different if the writer had quoted less and paraphrased more?

3. Review the lengthy list in paragraph 6. Why do you think the writer lists so many types of soup? How does the list add to what you know about Mr. Yeganeh and his soup kitchen? Conjecture about why the writer might have chosen these particular soups from the eighty soups in Mr. Yeganeh's repertoire.

4. Do you think the writer visited Mr. Yeganeh once or several times? How can you tell?

5. The writer only once comments on or evaluates Mr. Yeganeh or his soup kitchen, by noting the "delicious aroma" of the soups. This lack of explicit evaluation seems appropriate, given that the piece is not designed to be a restaurant review. How is the writer able to lead you to make a judgment about Mr. Yeganeh's Soup Kitchen International? What is your judgment?

6. This writer never states his or her controlling theme or purpose. As we have mentioned, understatement or implicitness like this is not at all unusual in observational writing. Writers often prefer merely to show or present scenes and people, stopping short of telling readers what to think. Knowing that readers always try to infer meanings, writers trust alert readers to guess a theme or speculate about purpose. What would you say are the controlling theme (the angle or insight) and the writer's purpose?

IDEAS FOR YOUR OWN WRITING

If you were to write about an unusual place on campus or in your community, what place might you choose? Make a list of as many places as you can think of. Cull through your list, and concentrate on two or three possibilities. Who would you interview for each? What might interest your readers about each place? What appeals to you personally?

Gretel Ehrlich

Gretel Ehrlich (b. 1946) is a writer and rancher who lives in Wyoming. A former filmmaker, she first visited Wyoming to film a documentary on sheepherders and subsequently married a rancher there. Her prose has been published by a number of popular magazines, including *Harper's* and the *Atlantic*, and collected in the critically praised *The Solace of Open Spaces* (1985). She is also the author of *Heart Mountain* (1988), a novel.

Saddle Bronc Riding at the National Finals

In this selection from *The Solace of Open Spaces*, Ehrlich observes a classic American event, a rodeo, this one the National Finals in Oklahoma City. If you know rodeo, pause for a moment to remember its competitive events, specifically saddle bronc riding, in which a rider must stay on a wildly bucking horse for eight seconds, holding on to nothing but the reins. Ehrlich will remind you vividly of rodeos you have seen. If you have never been to a rodeo, you will be introduced memorably to one of its major events.

Rodeo is the wild child of ranch work and embodies some of what ranching is all about. Horsemanship—not gunslinging—was the pride of western men, and the chivalrous ethics they formulated, known as the western code, became the ground rules for every human game. Two great partnerships are celebrated in this Oklahoma arena: the indispensable one between man and animal that any rancher or cowboy takes on, enduring the joys and punishments of the alliance; and the one between man and man, cowboy and cowboy.

The National Finals run ten nights. Every contestant rides every night, so it is easy to follow their progress and setbacks. One evening we abandoned our rooftop seats and sat behind the chutes to watch the saddle broncs ride. Behind the chutes two cowboys are rubbing rosin— part of their staying power—behind the saddle swells and on their Easter-egg-colored chaps which are pink, blue, and light green with white fringe. Up above, standing on the chute rungs, the stock contractors direct horse traffic: "Velvet Drums" in chute #3, "Angel Sings" in #5, "Rusty" in #1. Rick Smith, Monty Henson, Bobby Berger, Brad Gjermudson, Mel Coleman, and friends climb the chutes. From where I'm sitting, it looks like a field hospital with five separate operating theaters, the cowboys, like surgeons, bent over their patients with sweaty brows and looks of concern. Horses are being haltered; cowboys are measuring out the long, braided reins, saddles are set: one cowboy pulls up on the swells again and again, repositioning his hornless saddle until it sits just right. When the chute boss nods to him and says, "Pull 'em up, boys," the ground crew tightens front and back cinches on the first horse to go, but very slowly so he won't panic in the chute as the cowboy eases himself down over the saddle, not sitting on it, just hovering there. "Okay, you're on." The chute boss nods to him again. Now he sits on the saddle, taking the rein in one hand, holding the top of the chute with the other. He flips the loose bottoms of his chaps over his shins, puts a foot in each stirrup, takes a breath, and nods. The chute gate swings open releasing a flood—not of water, but of flesh, groans, legs kicking. The horse lunges up and out in the first big jump like a wave breaking whose crest the cowboy rides, "marking out the horse," spurs well above the bronc's shoulders. In that first second under the lights, he finds what will be the rhythm of the ride. Once again he "charges the point," his legs pumping forward, then so far back his heels touch behind the cantle. For a moment he looks as though he were kneeling on air, then he's stretched out again, his whole body taut but released, free hand waving in back of his head like a palm frond, rein-holding hand thrust forward: "*En garde!*" he seems to be saying, but he's airborne; he looks like a wing that has sprouted suddenly from the horse's broad back. Eight seconds. The whistle blows. He's covered the horse. Now two gentlemen dressed in white chaps and satin shirts gallop beside the bucking horse. The cowboy hands the rein to one and grabs the waist of the other—the flank strap on the bronc has been undone, so all three horses move at a run— and the pickup man from whom the cowboy is now dangling slows almost to a stop, letting him slide to his feet on the ground.

Rick Smith from Wyoming rides, looking pale and nervous in his white [3] shirt. He's bucked off and so are the brash Monty "Hawkeye" Henson, and Butch Knowles, and Bud Pauley, but with such grace and aplomb, there is no shame. Bobby Berger, an Oklahoma cowboy, wins the go-round with a score of 83.

By the end of the evening we're tired, but in no way as exhausted as [4] these young men who have ridden night after night. "I've never been so sore and had so much fun in my life," one first-time bull rider exclaims breathlessly. When the performance is over we walk across the street to the chic lobby of a hotel chock full of cowboys. Wives hurry through the crowd with freshly ironed shirts for tomorrow's ride, ropers carry their rope bags with them into the coffee shop, which is now filled with contestants, eating mild midnight suppers of scrambled eggs, their numbers hanging crookedly on their backs, their faces powdered with dust, and looking at this late hour prematurely old.

In the rough stock events such as the one we watched tonight, there is no victory over the horse or bull. The point of the match is not conquest but communion: the rhythm of two beings becoming one. Rodeo is not a sport of opposition; there is no scrimmage line here. No one bears malice—neither the animals, the stock contractors, nor the contestants; no one wants to get hurt. In this match of equal talents, it is only acceptance, surrender, respect, and spiritedness that make for the midair union of cowboy and horse.

QUESTIONS FOR ANALYSIS

1. How many scenes (specific locations) does this selection present? Where does Ehrlich place herself to observe these scenes—and to present them to us? What advantages or disadvantages do you see in her vantage point?

2. Instead of referring generally to horses and riders, Ehrlich provides specific names in paragraphs 2 and 3. Look closely at these names. What do you learn from them? Are they necessary?

3. In addition to naming specific horses and riders, Ehrlich identifies and details many specific objects and people in the chutes, arena, and hotel. Review the selection carefully, annotating the specific objects and people. Also annotate any details Ehrlich provides about these objects or people. These examples from the first part of paragraph 2 will get you started: *chutes, saddle broncs, rosin, saddle swells, chaps (Easter-egg-colored, pink, blue, light green, with white fringe), chute rungs, stock contractors, reins (long, braided)*. From your annotations, what can you conclude about the function of identifying and detailing specific objects and people in observational writing?

4. Writers reporting their observations of people and activities rely on specific narrative action: they show people moving, gesturing, talking, taking certain postures, interacting with others. These are concrete actions that let readers see what is happening. Annotate the selection (using a different colored pen or pencil from the one you used to annotate objects and people in question 3) for instances of specific narrative action. Watch for action verbs and participles showing action. These examples in paragraph 2 will get you started: *rubbing rosin, standing on the chute rungs, direct horse traffic, climb the chutes, bent over their patients, looks of concern, horses haltered, measuring out reins,*

saddles set. From your annotations, what can you conclude about the function of specific narrative action in observational writing?

5. How has Ehrlich organized this report of her observations at the rodeo? To discover her plan, make an outline of the selection. (Pause to review Outlining in Chapter 1.) Given her subject and purpose, what advantages or disadvantages do you see in her plan?

6. Mark Twain once wrote: "The difference between the *almost right* word and the *right* word is really a large matter—'tis the difference between the lightning bug and the lightning. After that, of course, that exceedingly important brick, the *exact* word. . . ." Reread Ehrlich's profile, noting any words that seem to you *right* or *exact*. Select two or three of these words, and explain why you think Ehrlich chose them.

IDEAS FOR YOUR OWN WRITING

If you were asked to profile an unusual event, activity, or performance, which one would you choose? List as many possibilities as you can think of. Choose two or three to consider in more detail. What would you expect to see and learn at each place? How could you engage readers in your observations?

Kathryn Christensen

A native of Nebraska, Kathryn Christensen graduated from the University of Nebraska in 1971 with a degree in journalism. After college, she joined the staff of the Des Moines *Register* as a city reporter, later working for the *Chicago Daily News*, the *Chicago Sun-Times* as marketing columnist, and the Charlotte (N.C.) *News*.

In 1979 Christensen joined the *Wall Street Journal's* Dallas bureau as staff reporter and transferred a year later to the *Journal's* San Francisco bureau. In 1981 she was named Boston bureau chief, the first woman to be appointed to a bureau chief position by the *Journal*, and she has also served as bureau chief in London. Currently, she is senior editor/features on the News Desk in the *Journal's* New York headquarters.

Steno Pool's Members Buried by Paper Flood, Yearn for Other Things

In this piece, written in 1982 for the *Wall Street Journal*, Christensen reports on life in a stenographer (or typist) pool at a major corporation in the San Francisco Bay area. It is an excellent example of a profile of a workplace or type of job. The *Wall Street Journal* is read carefully every day by investors and by managers in businesses and corporations. As you read, imagine how Christensen went about collecting her observations: asking permission for the visit, arranging interviews, observing, taking notes. What kinds of questions do you think she would have asked in her interviews?

It's only midmorning, but the fancy electric typewriters and other machines are already pounding with the sound and rhythm of muffled jackhammers. Another boss in a vest enters the room, clips a blue work order to the six-page penciled memo he is carrying and—without a word or an expression—piles it on to the stack of paper on a supervisor's desk.

The man in the vest doesn't mean much to Teresita Clamucha, Jean Hill or Mimi Tong, one of whom will soon be typing his memo. He is just another contributor to the paper flood that constitutes daily life in the government-affairs stenography pool of Chevron USA Inc.'s public-affairs department.

168

Life in the pool—seven hours of typing and filing, broken up by 3
occasional dictation duties—is clean, safe and fairly well paid. It is also
dull, according to stenographer Jean Hill. "If I could possibly earn my
living any other way, I'd do it," she says. "Sheer necessity and lack of
education, that's why I'm here."

The pool is crowded and stuffy; rows of file cabinets eat up one-third of 4
the space, and two fans with aqua blades push the stale air around.
There aren't any windows; a mural with a forest scene provides the only
"view."

Each member of this Chevron pool harbors some fantasy about work- 5
ing elsewhere. On most corporate ladders, the steno pool remains only a
rung or two above the bottom. Few aspire to it, and it still is almost
exclusively the province of women. They are as likely to be former
teachers as they are to have barely finished high school. Some hope the
pool will be the first step toward becoming an executive's personal
secretary—as in the movies—but many more regard it simply as a steady
paycheck. The most common gripe is that management doesn't appreciate the work and rarely says thank you.

More Impersonal Now?   Although much of this complaint is as old as 6
the typewriter itself, the recent advent of sophisticated word-processing
technology has wrought considerable change—and some new
dissatisfaction—among the five million people in this country who,
according to the Labor Department, earn their livings as typists, stenographers and secretaries.

Steno work isn't restricted any longer to taking letters in shorthand 7
and typing them. Word processors capable of almost instantly turning
out hundreds of error-free "original" letters have transformed some
stenographers, at the pool here and at other offices, into computer
operators, too. And the processors have almost precluded the luxurious
old concept of providing every manager with his own secretary.

Many managers hail the increased productivity made possible by this 8
new technology. But some workers think their jobs have been made even
more impersonal than they were before. They feel they are beginning to
take on the traits of the machines they operate.

"We can't really spend any creative energy at our work; I guess you'd 9
say we're kind of like cogs in a machine," says Miss Tong, a senior clerk-
typist. "The best we can do is work quickly and not make mistakes."
Miss Clamucha, who is classified as a management stenographer, adds:
"They (the managers) do all the thinking around here, we just do the
punching."

That, of course, is as management intended. "Everything we do is to 10
serve management better," says Edward Coy, the Chevron executive in

charge of the office-services group that includes 17 mail clerks, typists and stenographers who work for the public-affairs department here. These support people form three pools that work for some 70 staff members.

Despite the clear demarcation line between "staff" and "support" 11 troops, Mr. Coy makes it clear that Chevron tries to make pool life in the 1980s less demeaning than it used to be. Chevron policy, he says, forbids "subservient jobs at any level." He winces upon hearing indirectly that managers occasionally ask stenographers to run their personal banking errands.

Such managers have to be reminded, Mr. Coy says, "that there are no 12 'go-fers' or servants around here."

Though they are protected from servitude, the members of the 13 government-affairs pool regard terms like "job satisfaction" as empty phrases for them. Still, they are grateful for their jobs, and they say they are lucky to be working for Chevron, particularly in its public-affairs department.

"I hate to say it because it's such a cliche," says Mrs. Hill, a 58-year-old 14 widow who has worked in many other offices, "but as far as this kind of work goes, this company is the cream of the crop. I get no sense of identity from my work, but for someone like me with minimum skills, this pays the best."

Salaries for employes in the pool members' classifications range from 15 $12,000 to $20,000 (compared with an average range of $11,000 to $16,000 for all such jobs in the San Francisco Bay area), and the atmosphere is relaxed enough that they aren't required to account for every break or trip to the coffee maker. Moreover, a slot at the public-affairs department means frequent free tickets to baseball games, plays and museum exhibits, and to charity luncheons that Chevron supports by buying tables. Some pool members even get roles in films produced by the department.

Personal Problems   Some others in the three public-affairs pools agree 16 with Mrs. Hill's assessment of the job, adding that the mix of personalities and backgrounds here helps to keep the routine from becoming oppressive. The 17 members of the pools range from 20 to 58 years old and from Vietnam veteran to aspiring gospel singer. Though they rarely socialize outside the office, they like one another well enough to arrange an occasional potluck "gourmet extravaganza," and they confide in one another about personal problems.

One woman is a victim of her husband's physical abuse. Another is 17 having trouble kicking a drinking habit. One lies awake nights worrying because a creditor is about to garnishee her wages. One way or another, all are concocting ways to defeat the monotony of their jobs, and about half are trying to figure a way out of their steno pool.

Even at 58, Mrs. Hill would do practically anything to escape office 18 work. Given to a theatrical style of makeup and described by one co-worker as "our mystery lady," she longs for work—however menial—in a more artistic field. Not long ago, she says, "I took one of those aptitude tests with the ink spots and everything. I was sure it would show some marvelously creative field I should study, but my only talents seems to lie in bookkeeping and accounting."

"Creatures on a Treadmill" The thought appalls her. Early widowhood 19 and five children to support drove her to the business world, she explains, and she can't shake her conviction that it is inhabited by "creatures on a treadmill. It's as though they're alien beings, and I'm working on their planet. I know they're human and they do valuable work, but I just can't put myself into it."

Since learning the discouraging results of her aptitude test, however, 20 Mrs. Hill is more resigned to her working life. "I'll just have to work with what I've got," she says. Now she spends nearly every lunch hour practicing her shorthand at Chevron's training center because "it tightens my mind." By quitting time, she says, she is eager to catch the bus to the residence hotel where she lives and has the time to "think about adventuring."

While not quite as restless as Mrs. Hill about office work, her col- 21 leagues also were looking for something more challenging or prestigious.

To Miss Clamucha, a career in accounting looks like the answer. "I 22 don't really want to be a secretary; I want to be on my own," says the 28-year-old Filipino. "That's why I go to school two nights a week; to better myself." A divorced mother of a seven-year-old boy, she says her other obligations mean that her education can't proceed as quickly as she would like.

For some, recognition of the impossible dream comes slowly. Miss Tong 23 studied criminology for two years before she realized that with little stamina, and weighing less than 100 pounds, she wasn't going to become the star of the San Francisco Police Department. Now her dreams turn to religion. Born a Buddhist but a convert to Christianity, the 28-year-old Chinese-American woman says that her idea of a dream job would be joining the staff of a Christian organization. But she is also hoping to move up a notch or two at Chevron, and, toward that end, she too is going to night school.

A Smile for a Mask A fourth member of the government-affairs pool, 24 37-year-old Sergio Alexandre, who handles the filing, photocopying and envelope-stuffing, also has his aspirations. A tall, husky man whose former jobs have included lifting boxes for supermarkets, Mr. Alexandre says he chose to work in an office because "at least you're around people with brains." But, he says, the smile he wears as he assembles and staples 30 copies of a report is just a mask for a wandering mind: He fantasizes about being a professional comedian or an actor. He is realistic enough, however, to be studying how to operate a word-processing machine.

The possibility of breaking out of the steno pool isn't just an illusion,   25 according to Carol Summers, the supervisor for the public-affairs department's office-services group. Nor, judging from Mrs. Summer's experience, must it take forever to accomplish. Now 25 years old, she began working in a steno pool two years ago. Her starting salary was about $11,800. Within a few months, she began receiving promotions and now earns more than $25,000. Though she does have a college degree, she points to other women in the company who have moved from a steno pool to jobs higher than hers with no college experience.

For a time Mrs. Summers moved her desk into the steno pool where   26 Mrs. Hill, Miss Clamucha, Miss Tong and Mr. Alexandre work. The group, she says, had been making too many errors, and there had been complaints from management. She felt that on-the-spot supervision would help, and she says it did. "Jobs like mine are often mothers' jobs," she says. "It's kind of like I have 17 kids to watch."

Mrs. Hill uses a different analogy to describe the role of stenographers   27 in the office. "It reminds me of a dinner party," she says. "The executives are giving it, and we're the kitchen help."

QUESTIONS FOR ANALYSIS

1. Christensen writes in the present tense about events she observed in the past. (Her report begins "It's only midmorning. . . . Another boss . . . enters the room. . . ."). Why do you think she chooses the present tense?

2. We can assume that Christensen began with a jumble of material in her observational notes—details of the scene, quotations from interviews, factual information, impressions. What arrangement did she decide on? To discover the arrangement, outline the piece. (Pause to review Outlining in Chapter 1.) For her publication source and readers, what advantages or disadvantages do you see in her arrangement? Can you imagine a different (even slightly different) arrangement?

3. Why do you think Christensen talks to both workers and managers? Review what she learns from the managers and supervisors. What does this particular information add to her report?

4. Christensen devotes more space to Mrs. Hill than to the others. Why do you suppose Christensen does this? Where might she have interviewed Mrs. Hill? What does Christensen learn from her and what does it contribute to the report?

5. How would you describe the dominant impression Christensen creates of the steno pool? Identify key details that create this dominant impression.

6. What would you say are Christensen's purpose and controlling theme?

IDEAS FOR YOUR OWN WRITING

You might consider writing an observational report on a workplace or a particular kind of job at a workplace. Which workplaces or jobs do you admire? Which do you have suspicions or reservations about? What kind of work would you like to do when you graduate? What kind of work on or off campus is related to the academic major you intend to pursue? List several possibilities and choose a likely one. Who would you need to interview at this workplace? How would you gain access? Who might be interested in reading your observational report on this workplace?

If you are presently working somewhere, you would want to write about a different workplace. Your own workplace would be entirely too familiar, making it difficult for you to separate yourself from it and see it freshly and observantly.

John McPhee

John McPhee (b. 1931) lives in Princeton, New Jersey, where he occasionally teaches a writing workshop in the "Literature of Fact" at Princeton University. He is very highly regarded as a writer of profiles—in-depth reporting about people, places, and activities—and is a shrewd observer and masterful interviewer. In his profiles he ingeniously integrates information from observations, interviews, and research into engaging, readable prose. Readers marvel at the way he explains clearly such complex subjects as experimental aircraft or modern physics and captures interest in such ordinary subjects as bears or oranges. Among his eighteen published books are *Oranges* (1967), *Coming into the Country* (1977), *In Suspect Terrain* (1983), and *Table of Contents* (1985).

The New York Pickpocket Academy

This selection comes from *Giving Good Weight* (1979), a long profile of the New Jersey farmers who sell produce at a farmers' market in Brooklyn. McPhee spent several weeks working at Rich Hodgson's produce stand, gathering material for his essay. Among other things, he observed pickpockets at work; from these observations came this profile of pickpocketing and other crimes, focusing on the criminals, their victims, and the reactions of the farmers.

Right away, as we begin reading, we meet two pickpockets and three farmers, Melissa Mousseau, Bob Lewis, and Rich Hodgson, who get the story—this "narrative of fact"—underway. The narrator of the story is McPhee himself, weighing and sacking produce, all the while looking beyond the zucchini and tomatoes for material that might interest readers.

As you read, notice the many details McPhee provides about the people and the scene: the vegetables and trucks and hats and colors and sounds of the market. Notice, too, the great variety of examples he presents of crime—and honesty. Do these diverse examples add up to anything special? What would you say McPhee's purpose is in sharing his observations with us?

Brooklyn, and the pickpocket in the burgundy jacket appears just   1
before noon. Melissa Mousseau recognizes him much as if he were an old
customer and points him out to Bob Lewis, who follows him from truck
to truck. Aware of Lewis, he leaves the market. By two, he will have made

another run. A woman with deep-auburn hair and pale, nervous hands clumsily attracts the attention of a customer whose large white purse she is rifling. Until a moment ago, the customer was occupied with the choosing of apples and peppers, but now she shouts out, "Hey, what are you doing? Your hand is in my purse. What are you doing?" The auburn-haired woman not only has her hand in the purse but most of her arm as well. She withdraws it, and with intense absorption begins to finger the peppers. "How much are the peppers? Mister, give me some of these!" she says, looking up at me with a gypsy's dark, starburst eyes. "Three pounds for a dollar," I tell her, with a swift glance around for Lewis or a cop. When I look back, the pickpocket is gone. Other faces have filled in—people unconcernedly examining the fruit. The woman with the white purse has returned her attention to the apples. She merely seems annoyed. Lewis once sent word around from truck to truck that we should regularly announce in loud voices that pickpockets were present in the market, but none of the farmers complied. Hodgson shrugged and said, "Why distract the customers?" Possibly Fifty-ninth Street is the New York Pickpocket Academy. Half a dozen scores have been made there in a day. I once looked up and saw a well-dressed gentleman under a gray fedora being kicked and kicked again by a man in a green polo shirt. He kicked him in the calves. He kicked him in the thighs. He kicked him in the gluteal bulge. He kicked him from the middle of the market out to the edge, and he kicked him into the street. "Get your ass out of here!" shouted the booter, redundantly. Turning back toward the market, he addressed the curious. "Pickpocket," he explained. The dip did not press charges.

People switch shopping carts from time to time. They make off with a loaded one and leave an empty cart behind. Crime on such levels is a part of the background here, something in the urban air, so many parts per million. The condition is accepted with a resignation that approaches nonchalance. . . . We lost . . . [a cash box] once in Brooklyn, with something like two hundred dollars. For various reasons, suspicion immediately attached itself to a part-time employee who was selling with us and probably handed the box in a bag to a confederate. The previous Wednesday, he had been working for another farmer, who discharged him for dishonesty. Now, just after our cash box disappeared, he began saying, and repeating, in an excited voice, "It's real, man. It's real. We don't like it but that's reality—reality, man—and there is nothing we can do." Rich felt there *was* something he could do. He said, "You're fired."

Politely, the man inquired if he could know the reason for his dismissal.

"Sure," Rich said. "I don't trust you." 4

"That's cool, man, cool," said our ex-employee. He took off his apron 5
and was gone.

Most thievery is petty and is on the other side of the tables. As Rich 6
describes it, "Brooklyn, Fifty-ninth Street, people rip off stuff everywhere. You just expect it. An old man comes along and puts a dozen eggs
in a bag. Women choosing peaches steal one for every one they buy—a
peach for me, a peach for you. What can you do? You stand there and
watch. When they take too many, you complain. I watched a guy one day
taking nectarines. He would put one in a plastic bag, then one in a
pocket, then one in a pile on the ground. After he did that half a dozen
times, he had me weigh the bag."

"This isn't England," Barry Benepe informed us once, "and a lot of 7
people are pretty dishonest."

Now, in Brooklyn, a heavyset woman well past the middle of life is 8
sobbing pitifully, flailing her arms in despair. She is sitting on a bench in
the middle of the market. She is wearing a print dress, a wide-brimmed
straw hat. Between sobs, she presents in a heavy Russian accent the
reason for her distress. She was buying green beans from Don Keller, and
when she was about to pay him she discovered that someone had opened
her handbag—even while it was on her arm, she said—and had removed
several books of food stamps, a telephone bill, and eighty dollars in cash.
Lewis, in his daypack, stands over her and tells her he is sorry. He says,
"This sort of thing will happen wherever there's a crowd."

Another customer breaks in to scold Lewis, saying, "This is the biggest 9
rip-off place in Brooklyn. Two of my friends were pickpocketed here last
week and I had to give them carfare home."

Lewis puts a hand on his forehead and, after a pensive moment, says, 10
"That was very kind of you."

The Russian woman is shrieking now. Lewis attends her like a working 11
dentist. "It's all right. It will be O.K. It may not be as bad as you think."
He remarks that he would call the police if he thought there was
something they could do.

Jeffrey Mack, eight years old, has been listening to all this, and he now 12
says, "I see a cop."

Jeffrey has an eye for cops that no one else seems to share. (A squad 13
car came here for him one morning and took him off to face a truant
officer. Seeing his fright, a Pacific Street prostitute got into the car and
rode with him.)

"Where, Jeffrey?" 14

"There." Jeffrey lifts an arm and points. 15

"Where?"   16

"There." He points again—at trucks, farmers, a falafel man.   17

"I don't see a policeman," Lewis says to him. "If you see one, Jeffrey, go   18
and get him."

Jeffrey goes, and comes back with an off-duty 78th Precinct cop who is   19
wearing a white apron and has been selling fruits and vegetables in the
market. The officer speaks sternly to the crying woman. "Your name?"

"Catherine Barta."   20

"Address?"   21

"Eighty-five Eastern Parkway."   22

Every Wednesday, she walks a mile or so to the Greenmarket. She has   23
lived in Brooklyn close to half her life, the rest of it in the Ukraine.
Heading back to his vegetables, the officer observes that there is nothing
he can do.

Out from behind her tables comes Joan Benack, the baker, of Rocky   24
Acres Farm, Milan, New York—a small woman with a high, thin voice.
Leaving her tropical carrot bread, her zucchini bread, her anadama
bread, her beer bread, she goes around with a borrowed hat collecting
money from the farmers for Catherine Barta. Bills stuff the hat, size 7—
the money of Alvina Frey and John Labanowski and Cleather Slade and
Rich Hodgson and Bob Engle, who has seen it come and go. He was a
broker for Merrill Lynch before the stock market imploded, and now he
is a blond-bearded farmer in a basketball shirt selling apples that he
grows in Clintondale, New York. Don Keller offers a dozen eggs, and one
by one the farmers come out from their trucks to fill Mrs. Barta's
shopping cart with beans and zucchini, apples, eggplants, tomatoes,
peppers, and corn. As a result, her wails and sobs grow louder.

A man who gave Rich Hodgson a ten-dollar bill for a ninety-five-cent   25
box of brown eggs asks Rich to give the ten back after Rich has handed
him nine dollars and five cents, explaining that he has some smaller bills
that he wants to exchange for a twenty. Rich hands him the ten. Into
Rich's palm he counts out five ones, a five, and the ten for a twenty and
goes away satisfied, as he has every reason to be, having conned Rich out
of nine dollars, five cents, and a box of brown eggs. Rich smiles at his
foolishness, shrugs, and sells some cheese. If cash were equanimity, he
would never lose a cent. One day, a gang of kids began taking Don
Keller's vegetables and throwing them at the Hodgson truck. Anders
Thueson threw an apple at the kids, who then picked up rocks. Thueson
reached into the back of the truck and came up with a machete. While
Hodgson told him to put it away, pant legs went up, switchblades came
into view. Part of the gang bombarded the truck with debris from a

nearby roof. Any indication of panic might have been disastrous. Hodgson packed deliberately, and drove away.

Todd Jameson, who comes in with his brother Dan from Farmingdale, 26 New Jersey, weighed some squash one day, and put it in a brown bag. He set the package down while he weighed something else. Then, reaching for the squash, he picked up an identical bag that happened to contain fifty dollars in rolled coins. He handed it to the customer who had asked for the squash. Too late, Todd discovered the mistake. A couple of hours later, though, the customer—"I'll never forget him as long as I live, the white hair, the glasses, the ruddy face"—came back. He said, "Hey, this isn't squash. I didn't ask for money, I asked for squash." Whenever that man comes to market, the Jamesons give him a bag full of food. "You see, where I come from, that would never, never happen," Todd explains. "If I made a mistake like that in Farmingdale, no one—no one—would come back with fifty dollars' worth of change."

Dusk comes down without further crime in Brooklyn, and the farmers 27 are packing to go. John Labanowski—short, compact, with a beer in his hand—is expounding on his day. "The white people are educating the colored on the use of beet greens," he reports. "A colored woman was telling me today, 'Cut the tops off,' and a white woman spoke up and said, 'Hold it,' and told the colored woman, 'You're throwing the best part away.' They go on talking, and pretty soon the colored woman is saying, 'I'm seventy-three on Monday,' and the white says, 'I don't believe a word you say.' You want to know why I come in here? I come in here for fun. For profit, of course, but for relaxation, too. I like being here with these people. They say the city is a rat race, but they've got it backwards. The farm is what gets to be a rat race. You should come out and see what I—" He is interrupted by the reappearance in the market of Catherine Barta, who went home long ago and has now returned, her eyes hidden by her wide-brimmed hat, her shopping cart full beside her. On the kitchen table, at 85 Eastern Parkway, she found her telephone bill, her stamps, and her cash. She has come back to the farmers with their food and money.

QUESTIONS FOR ANALYSIS

1. In order to evaluate McPhee's plan, make a brief outline of the selection, listing the separate crimes in the order they occur and noting key people and incidents. What advantages do you see in the way McPhee sequences the various crimes? What other order might he have tried?

2. Using your outline, review the separate crimes in the selection, noticing which ones McPhee relates in the present tense and which in the past tense. All the crimes, of course, occurred in the past. Why do you think he presents some in the present tense, and how does it influence your response?

3. This selection includes many remembered or reconstructed statements and conversations. Skim the selection, noticing how often direct dialogue (that set within quotation marks) is used. Instead of quoting exactly, McPhee could have paraphrased what people said. What contribution does direct dialogue make to the essay? (You might try paraphrasing one of the quotations to judge the different effects.)

4. The heavyset woman in the print dress, Catherine Barta, appears twice. What roles does she play in the selection? Why do you think McPhee gives her such prominence?

5. McPhee includes many specific details of the market scene—we learn people's names, see what they're wearing, hear their voices, and listen in on their conversations. Choose a brief part or episode that you think has especially notable and memorable details. Annotate all the details you notice. What do you think they contribute to the essay?

6. What do you think was McPhee's purpose in writing about crime at the Brooklyn market? What would you say is the controlling theme of this profile?

7. Compare McPhee's and Ehrlich's essays on two or three features unique to observational writing, such as engaging readers' interests, presenting scenes or people, or adopting a particular vantage point. You will want to analyze each essay closely and then report the results of your analysis, concentrating on how the essays are alike or different. Pause to review Comparing and Contrasting Related Readings in Chapter 1.

8. Review Exploring Your Personal Response in Chapter 1. Then write a 300–400-word personal response to the McPhee section, choosing one of the following topics:

   Write about your personal associations with anything McPhee describes or relates.

   Write about the history of your reading of the selection. That is, tell a story about your impressions and reactions during first and later readings. Reflect on how your response to the essay changed.

   After you have written your response, reread it thoughtfully. In two or three sentences, say what you learned about the McPhee selection by writing an extended response to it.

IDEAS FOR YOUR OWN WRITING

If you were to write about your observations of a scene filled with people and action, what scene would you choose? How would you go about visiting the scene and recording your observations? What vantage point or points would you choose? How could you present the scene vividly to your readers? Can you imagine a controlling theme and purpose for your profile of this active scene?

Kent Burbank

Kent Burbank wrote this essay as a freshman at the University of North Dakota in Grand Forks, North Dakota.

Production at WDAZ

Focusing on the preparation and production of a single newscast, Kent Burbank profiles a television studio. Like Ehrlich and McPhee, Burbank closely observes a single scene and reports his observations as a continuous narrative of one relatively brief event. (Notice, however, that even when observational writers appear to be reporting only one event, they may visit a place several times and then synthesize their observations into a single narrative.) Like all writers of profiles, Burbank hopes both to entertain and to inform readers. As you read, notice whether he presents enough new information about television studios to augment what you already know.

The control room is long, narrow, and dimly lit. Set into one of the long walls is a large window looking into the filming studio. The dim lights from inside the control room are reflected on the window glass. The room is packed with large, intimidating, dark metallic cabinets filled with dials, buttons, meters, lights, and different-sized television screens. The room would look almost futuristic if it were not so drab and colorless. The television show *The Facts of Life* can be heard clearly above the other voices in the room and seen on the various color and black-and-white monitors around the room.

It is Monday evening and I have just entered WDAZ–Channel Eight's control room. I will be following the production crew at WDAZ and will be observing the production of a newscast. As I look around, I realize that there are certain things that I, as a viewer, tend to expect to see when I go to a familiar, yet unfamiliar place. Already I am surprised and a little disappointed by the dull and dim atmosphere of the control room, which I had expected to be large, orderly, and well lit.

The members of the production crew are relaxing in their chairs, making idle conversation with the engineers and the camera operators, yet they are watching the television monitors at all times. One of the two crew members on duty, Don Arvidson, tells me to pull up a chair as he starts to explain some of his responsibilities. He begins by telling me that the production crew's main responsibility is running the local commercials at just the right moment during television programming breaks. As Don lifts a packet of papers off the control panel with its switches and blinking lights, he explains that this packet is the pre-made "log" that tells him the order in which the commercials are to be run for today. Don informs me that ABC, WDAZ's affiliated network, reserves a certain number of spots in the log for national commercials. All remaining commercial spots must be filled in by WDAZ or its sister station in Fargo, WDAY.

Carefully watching the clock while he talks, Don suddenly excuses himself, explaining that it is almost time for a commercial break and he must get to work. Sure enough, in just a few seconds *The Facts of Life* goes off the air and Don, quickly pushing a couple of buttons in front of him, sends the preloaded tapes in the back of the room spinning wildly. He repeats this process for several commercials and then one final time to get the second half of *The Facts of Life* rolling again.

Once the program has begun, Don sits back and relaxes, knowing he has approximately ten minutes before he must work again. Continuing where he left off, Don picks up the day's log and opens it to this time period. Showing the log, he begins to explain the process by which he determines the order in which to run the commercials. The log looks like this:

	LENGTH	TYPE		SENDER NAME
5:30 pm	*World News Tonight*			
	60 sec.	CM		Ford Motor Company
	90 sec.	CM		Pepsi-Cola
	60 sec.	CM		RJ Reynolds Tobacco Co.
	30 sec.	PR	Z	WDAZ–Station Ident.
6:00 pm	*WDAZ Six O'Clock News*			
	30 sec.	PS	Z	American Cancer Society
	60 sec.	CM	YZ	Coca-Cola
	60 sec.	PR	Z	WDAZ
6:30 pm	*Entertainment Tonight*			
	60 sec.	CM	YZ	Dakota Steele
	90 sec.	CM	YZ	Northwest Airlines
	60 sec.	PS	Z	United Way
	30 sec.	PR	Z	WDAZ

Pointing to the 5:30 program, Don explains that during the day the ABC network puts on most of the programs, such as *World News Tonight*; however, they also leave several time slots open that must be filled with either local programs, such as *WDAZ Six O'Clock News* or syndicated programs, such as *Entertainment Tonight*. Syndicated programs are bid upon by all the stations in one region, with the highest bidder receiving the sole rights to air the show.

Don then explains that the two letters in the second column stand for the type of commercial. "CM" stands for commercial, "PS" stands for a public service announcement, and "PR" stands for station promotion.

Continuing with the third column, Don tells me that a blank means commercials are coming from the network through WDAY into WDAZ. "YZ" means that WDAY is sending their commercials to Grand Forks and a "Z" means that WDAZ itself is showing a local commercial, 89 percent of which they film themselves, according to Don. He points out that during the national news only one local commercial is alloted space, while during the two local programs, *WDAZ Six O'Clock News* and *Entertainment Tonight*, all of the commercials come locally from WDAY or WDAZ.

The activity in the control room starts to pick up a bit as the clock nears 5:30. Don explains to me that every weekday "at precisely 5:27" one member of the anchor crew goes on the air and presents what they refer to as a "teaser"—a brief list of some of the major stories WDAZ will be covering at six o'clock. WDAZ presents these "teasers" to get viewers to tune into their newscast.

Walking hurriedly into the studio, coanchor Rose Brunsvold takes her place on the set where the news is filmed. Although I realize that the WDAZ news team is not internationally famous, I am still awed when I see her in person. After the initial shock, I am further startled by her everyday normality. Off camera, she walks, talks, and acts like anyone else on a typical day at work.

I stand back and watch this intriguing process. *World News Tonight* soon comes to an end, and Don starts a commercial. He uses headset microphones to tell the cameraperson to ready Brunsvold. The cameraperson then raises his hand and holds it there until he receives the cue from the production staff to drop it. The lowering of his hand tells Brunsvold that the commercial is over and the television picture is being switched to the studio cameras. As quickly as it began, the short teaser segment is over without a hitch.

Looking at the studio through the window, I am astonished at how different it looks from what I had expected. The two sets used at WDAZ, the one used for newscasts and the one used for *Town and Country*, appear full and real on television. In reality, the sets end abruptly, going from carpeting and wallpaper to cement and steel beams without any transition. The two sets appear out of place in separate corners of a large, one-and-a-half-story, square room that resembles a small indoor arena.

As a viewer, I realized beforehand that they were only sets, but I am still disappointed with what lies before me. Two large, moveable cameras, nearly as tall as a person, stand dormant in the center of the room. Contrasting with the neatness of the two sets, the other two corners are filled with various equipment and junk.

In the back of the control room, an engineer is loading tapes of 13 commercials and stories that will be presented on the six o'clock news. While carefully watching special graphs displayed on small screens, the engineer moves certain knobs that alter the graphs to adjust the color of the tapes. I follow the engineer to the front of the room where he instructs one of the camera operators in the studio to focus each camera, one at a time, on a card colored black and white with different shades of gray between. Using equipment at the front of the room similar to that in the back, he proceeds to adjust the colors in the same manner.

The production crew is looking over the logs, finishing some odds and 14 ends and relaxing before the six o'clock news. I ask Don where WDAZ stores its weather equipment. Much to my surprise, Don informs me that WDAZ does not do its own weather broadcast. Instead, they use the weather broadcast from WDAY. Setting his work down, Don explains that although the weather forecast is taped in Fargo, it is not the same one that is used by WDAY. WDAY's weather anchor tapes a special broadcast aimed specifically at the Grand Forks area. Don says that this is why the weather anchor on WDAZ's newscast never talks with the other anchors.

Recently the production crew has had to deal with unexpected prob- 15 lems. Normally, the broadcasts are taped in Fargo and sent by micro-waves to WDAZ where they are held until needed. Don explains that a couple days ago when the production staff was airing the weather report from Fargo, the transmission appeared shaky and distorted. Evidently, WDAY's taping machine was not working properly. Until WDAY gets its equipment fixed, Don explains, it will have to send the broadcast up to Grand Forks live and have WDAZ tape it as they receive it.

As the time nears 6:00, everyone is hurrying to get their tasks done on 16 time. In the studio, coanchors Rick Lockridge and Rose Brunsvold are organizing their materials, collecting their thoughts, and taking their places for the newscast. The camera operators are stationing themselves, adjusting their cameras, and prefocusing on their subjects.

Inside the control room, everyone works fast. The engineers are mak- 17 ing final color adjustments for the cameras and are preparing the tapes of stories and commercials that will be used during the newscast. The production staff is preparing the photos that appear on the television next to the anchor's head when he or she is introducing a story.

While working, Don explains that the production staff can determine 18
which picture they want to place in the box and how large the box will
appear just by pressing a few buttons. Although there are several sources
used to call up these pictures, the main source is a special slide machine
containing premade slides. Don holds up a slide he is currently working
on and explains that it is a letter M for the Minnesota Gophers and will
be used by Pat Sweeny, WDAZ's sports anchor, when introducing the
Gophers' hockey game. Don takes the slide and places it in one of the
slots in the machine. He then returns to the control table, brings up the
picture by pressing a few buttons, and alters the picture's screen size and
placement.

From my position in the control room it is easy to see everything 19
coming together. On the production crew's cue, the camera operators
signal the anchors and the television picture switches from film to studio
cameras. The first two stories deal with a fire that burned down a church
and an explosion that critically injured two firefighters. Both of these
stories had been sent up to WDAZ from WDAY earlier that day. WDAZ
then edited them for length and content. When presenting these stories,
the anchors begin by giving their own introduction to the story and then
the production crew switches from the studio cameras directly to the
prerecorded film.

Two feature stories are also presented today. Both stories were done by 20
reporters from WDAZ and were taped entirely while on assignment. The
first is a feature on small towns reported by Penny Walsh in Thompson,
ND. The second is a feature on children's books done by Terry Dullum.
The anchors present these stories in a manner similar to the stories from
WDAY.

Another story that Rose Brunsvold presents this evening is just camera 21
footage. When a film is just footage, the anchors write the story ahead of
time and then present it with the film. The anchors begin by introducing
the story, then the production crew switches over to the film and cues the
camera operators to signal the anchors to begin presenting their story.

Inside the studio is a monitor allowing the anchors to see what the 22
audience is viewing and to get an idea of the length of a break they have
during a prerecorded story.

After the news stories have been presented and a commercial break 23
has been taken, the production staff switches the television picture over
to the tape of the weather, which despite earlier difficulties, works
perfectly. After another commercial break, Pat Sweeny presents his
sportscast in a manner similar to the earlier newscast.

Throughout the broadcast, the production crew is constantly moving. 24
They are continuously switching from newscaster to picture to commer-

cial to story and back to newscaster. The production crew is responsible for keeping the newscast flowing smoothly through its many transitions. The final output that the audience views is completely dependent upon the production staff.

The production is soon over and the entire staff relaxes as the tension   25 of the broadcast seems to dissipate. Rick Lockridge, still hyped over the excitement of the newscast, can be seen dancing wildly down the hall. The studio quickly clears and the intense lights slowly dim to a soft glow. The control room staff gets up, stretches, and exits, leaving me to reflect on what I have seen. The control room itself, once alive with activity, is now empty and quiet, awaiting the return of the staff.

QUESTIONS FOR ANALYSIS

1. In contrast to the selection from the *New Yorker* about Albert Yeganeh's soup kitchen, this selection uses relatively few quotations. Review paragraphs 3–8, where Burbank talks to WDAZ production crew member Don Arvidson. Why do you think Burbank decided to paraphrase rather than quote Arvidson? On what basis do you think observational writers in general decide when to paraphrase and when to quote?

2. Burbank reproduces a section from WDAZ's log. What advantage or disadvantage do you see in Burbank's reproducing this material?

3. In observational writing, readers can perceive the pace as fast or slow. Review the selection, noting the paragraphs where the pace seemed slow to you. How can you account for your perception of slowness?

4. Observational writers sometimes frame their essays by referring at the end to something at the beginning. Compare Burbank's first and last paragraphs to discover how his frame works. What specific advantages do you see in this strategy?

5. How would you define Burbank's controlling theme? If you have trouble doing so, what causes you difficulty?

6. As a student writer like Burbank, what would you say are the strengths and weaknesses of this selection?

IDEAS FOR YOUR OWN WRITING

All of us are curious about what really goes on "behind the scenes" to produce those phenomena for which we are the audience—concerts, recording sessions, sporting events, and daily newspapers, for example.

Think of a familiar phenomenon you would like to investigate in order to find out what is really behind it. How would you arrange to visit and observe behind the scenes? What would you expect to learn? What surprises might be in store for you?

A GUIDE TO OBSERVATIONAL WRITING

From the readings in this chapter you have learned that observational writing centers on a controlling theme that makes the writing seem focused and purposeful. Observational writers try both to entertain and to inform readers. Not content with generalizations and summaries, they vividly present scenes and people to their readers. We can imagine specific details of a scene—objects, shapes, textures, colors, sounds, even smells. We see people dressed a particular way. We see them moving and gesturing, and we hear them talk. All the details contribute to a single dominant impression of the subject.

Observational writing presents special challenges. Since writers necessarily collect large amounts of original material of diverse kinds from visits and interviews, all of it must be sorted through, organized, and integrated into a readable draft. The guide to invention, drafting, and revising that follows is designed to assist you in solving the special problems you encounter in this kind of writing.

The Writing Task

Write an observational essay about an intriguing person, place, or activity in your community. You have several options for completing this assignment: a brief profile of an individual based on one or two interviews, or of a place or an activity observed once or twice; or a longer, more fully developed profile of a person, place, or activity based on several observational visits and interviews. Observe your subject closely and then present what you have learned in a way that both informs and engages readers.

Invention

The following activities can help you choose a subject, plan and carry through your observations, find a controlling theme, and analyze your readers. If you complete them all before you write your first draft, you will have collected all, or nearly all, the information you will need—and you will then be free to focus well on your actual writing.

CHOOSING A SUBJECT. Finding just the right subject is critical. A good way to begin is by listing the widest possible variety of subjects. It is advantageous to make the list cumulative, allowing yourself to add more items as they come to mind. After a while your list should be long enough to ensure that you have not overlooked a possible subject. Just laying it out on the page and scanning your options are a visual aid to choosing what subject you want to write about.

For an essay based on personal observation and interviews, your subject should be a person or a place. Each type of essay is illustrated by a reading in this chapter.

You might begin by listing possible subjects in each category. For a *person*, list activities or professions you want to study closely by profiling someone in the event or field. You need not have a particular person in mind. For a *place*, list places you are curious about and would be able to visit and study. If you can think of unusual places, fine, but consider also places from everyday life—a computer center, a weight-reduction clinic, a small-claims court, a nursery school. Some students find that they are unable to list subjects in all of these categories, so if this happens to you just concentrate on the ideas that do come to mind.

After reflecting on your lists, choose a subject you are genuinely curious about, one which will provide enough information for a week or two of study. Select one you can visit several times, observing closely and in detail. Most important, choose a subject that interests you—and that you think might appeal to your readers.

PROBING YOUR SUBJECT. Before you study your subject, it might be helpful to jot down everything you presently know and feel about it. You may discover that you know more than you think you do.

Start by writing for several minutes without stopping, putting down everything you know about your subject. Include personal memories, facts, anecdotes, statistics, visual details—anything that comes to mind. How would you define or describe this subject? What is its purpose or function? What does it remind you of?

Next, try to state something about your attitude toward your subject. What feelings do you have about it? Do you feel neutral, anxious, eager? Why does it interest you? What preconceptions do you have about it? How do other people feel about it?

Continue with your expectations. What do you expect to discover? Do you anticipate being surprised, amused, shocked? What kind of profile or report would you really like to write about this subject? What readers do you want to address?

This initial probing of your subject will probably help you decide whether you are interested enough to continue with it.

INVESTIGATING YOUR SUBJECT. This kind of writing requires that you go out and gather original information. To guarantee that you complete the information gathering within the time available, take time now to plan. Decide what times you have open within the next few days, then make phone calls to schedule visits. When you write down your appointments, be sure to include names, addresses, phone numbers, dates and times, and any special arrangements you have made for a visit. The Appendix provides helpful guidelines for observing, interviewing, and taking notes.

Visiting a Place. If you profile a place or a person engaged in an activity at a particular place, you will need to make one or more visits to the place to gather information. The Appendix on research and documentation provides useful guidelines for observing a place, taking notes on the spot, supplementing your notes later, and reflecting on what you have seen.

Interviewing a Person. If your profile requires that you interview someone, you will find the guidelines for interviewing in the Appendix to be invaluable. These guidelines will help you plan and set up an interview, take notes during an interview, supplement your notes immediately after an interview, and reflect on what you have learned.

Gathering Published Information. If you are profiling a person or place, you may be able to pick up appropriate fliers, brochures, or reports, and you may want to do background reading on a particular kind of work or activity. Take careful notes from your reading, and keep accurate records of sources.

DECIDING ON YOUR CONTROLLING THEME. You will need to find a focus in the material you have collected and then to decide on exactly what you want to say about it. Review all your notes and impressions, with the following kinds of questions in mind. What is the single most important thing you learned? What surprises or contradictions did you encounter? What larger social or personal implications do you see in your material? What do you most want readers to know about your subject? What will be your purpose in writing about this subject? What are your feelings about the subject? From your reflections on these questions, you should be able to write a few sentences that tentatively identify a controlling theme. Once you begin drafting, however, you may want to revise this theme or even consider a different one.

ANALYZING YOUR READERS. Before you begin drafting, you will find it helpful for planning and selecting material to analyze your readers carefully—who they are will very much influence your writing. You could try to write for several minutes about your readers, just to see what turns up. What do they know about your subject? What preconceptions are they likely to have? Why would they want to read about it? How can you interest them in it? What parts of your material might especially interest them?

Drafting

If you have completed the preceding invention activities, you will probably have made many discoveries about your subject and with your substantial notes in hand will be ready to proceed to a first draft. The following discussion describes how to set goals for drafting, plan your draft, and decide how to begin.

SETTING GOALS. Establish specific goals with your readers and purpose in mind. Consider how much your readers already know about the subject. If they are familiar with it, you will need to find an engaging angle to present it to them. If they are likely to be unfamiliar with the subject, you may need to define special terms or describe fully unusual procedures or activities. Considering how you will enable them to visualize the subject for themselves should lead you to determine a larger strategy for engaging and holding their interest throughout your essay. Notice, for instance, how Ehrlich emphasizes the drama of the rodeo and Burbank appeals to our curiosity about how a television station operates. Both writers count on our curiosity about the unfamiliar to pull us into their narrative.

Not only should you keep your readers' expectations in mind as you draft, but you should also make sure to include everything that serves your own purposes of presentation. McPhee, for example, chose from a wealth of sights and sounds just those details that serve his purpose: telling about crime at the farmers' market. Concentrating on your thesis or main point as you draft should help this process.

PLANNING YOUR ORGANIZATION. If you are profiling a person or place, you will have many choices of plans. You can organize around features (of a person or place), around subtopics, or around ideas. The *New Yorker* staff writer, for example, organizes "soup" around Mr. Yeganeh's values and attitudes. You can also organize narratively, taking the reader on a tour of a place in just the order you followed on your visit. Both McPhee and Burbank organize narratively. Whatever plan you decide on should reflect your purpose and your readers' needs.

Some writers find it helpful to outline a tentative plan before beginning to draft. You may change direction once you start drafting, but some sort of plan is necessary if your draft is to be well organized and coherent.

BEGINNING. It is sometimes difficult to know how to begin writing about personal observations. You may have so much interesting material that it could be difficult to decide how to lead the reader into it. As you begin to draft, you can start with any part of the material, but it is usually best to start with an easy part—something you know you want to include or information you understand particularly well. Eventually you will want to open with something that will capture readers' attention, but there's no reason you must write it first. Ehrlich opens her essay by asserting her controlling theme, but all the other writers in this chapter begin with specific scenes or actions: McPhee focuses immediately on two pickpockets at work; Burbank places us in the television studio control room.

Revising

Since a first draft is an initial attempt to discover the possibilities in your material, it will nearly always need substantial revision. A good starting point would be to read your draft critically (and have someone else read it, as well) in light of the questions for analyzing basic features at the beginning of this chapter. These questions should enable you to reconsider what you have achieved in your draft and to decide what you can do to strengthen it. When revising observational writing, you will want to be particularly concerned with the controlling theme and informativeness, as well as with readability.

REVISING TO FOCUS YOUR CONTROLLING THEME. To provide a clear focus for your revision, consider whether you want to make your purpose more explicit. Be sure that readers will see the point of your essay. Decide whether all the details in your draft support your purpose, and eliminate any material that does not. Consider whether any additional anecdotes, visual details, or dialogue might sharpen the focus.

REVISING FOR INFORMATIVENESS. Once you have a draft and perhaps some response to it from readers, you may see other ways you need to inform readers still further about your subject. Does anything still need clarification, explanation, or definition? Again, decide whether you want to revisit the place or reinterview the person or otherwise gather still more data. Consider whether you might have given readers more information than they need about parts of your subject, thereby blurring the focus of your essay.

REVISING TO IMPROVE READABILITY. Since a clear, engaging beginning is essential, consider alternatives to what you have chosen, on the chance that some other part of your information would make a stronger opening. You might look at the beginnings of the selections in this chapter to see whether one of them suggests a different way you might open your piece. Outline your draft to discover its basic plan, and then consider whether you can improve on the plan by moving or deleting any parts. Reread your draft, looking for gaps and slow spots. Finally, decide whether adding anything or taking out any details would help keep readers on track and hold their interest.

Once you have a revision, proofread it carefully for mistakes in usage, punctuation, and spelling. Careless errors will reduce the readability of your essay and undermine your authority with your readers.

CHAPTER FIVE

Explanation

Explanatory writing has a limited but very important purpose: to inform readers. It does not feature its writers' experiences and feelings as autobiography does, nor reveal its writers' exploratory insights into a subject as reflection does. Instead, explanatory writing confidently and efficiently presents information—the writing job, in fact, required most frequently every day of professionals in every field. Explanation may be based in firsthand observation but always moves beyond description of specific objects and scenes to general concepts and ideas. Since it deals almost exclusively with established information, explanatory writing need never argue for judgments or opinions or speculate about causes or effects. While often friendly, inviting, even engaging to readers, explanatory writing does not aspire to be more than it is: a way for readers to find out how to do something or to learn more about a particular subject. This is the writing we find in newspapers and magazines, encyclopedias, instruction manuals, reference books and textbooks, memos and research reports.

This chapter focuses on one important kind of explanatory writing: explaining a concept to readers in order to increase their understanding of it and its applications and consequences. The reading selections you will be analyzing all explain a single concept such as "the uncertainty principle" in physics or "anorexia" in medicine and psychology. Your own essay for this chapter will explain a concept that you choose from your current studies or special interests. This focus on explaining concepts has several advantages to you as a college student: it gives you strategies for reading critically the textbooks and other concept-centered explanatory material in your college courses; it enables you to learn to write confidently a common type of essay examination question and paper assignment; and it acquaints you with the basic discourse features—definition, classification, comparison, illustration, process narration—common to all types of explanatory writing, not just explanation of concepts.

By "concept," we mean a major idea or principle and its label or name. Every field of endeavor or study has its concepts: physics has "atom," psychiatry has "neurosis," business management has "corporate culture," literature has "irony," writing has "invention," sailing has "tacking," music has "harmony," and mathematics has "probability." From this brief list, you can see that concepts include abstract ideas, objects, processes, and activities. You can see, too, that concepts and their names are central to the understanding of virtually every subject. Indeed, much of human knowledge is made possible by concepts. Our brains evolved to do conceptual work—to create concepts, name them, communicate them, and think with them.

Although it need not trouble you much when you choose a concept to write about, you should be aware that concepts exist at different levels of abstraction; that is, certain concepts in a field are "larger," or more inclusive, than others. For example, in physics, "atom" is more abstract than "electron" or "ionization"; in filmmaking, "editing" is more abstract than "jump-cut." The level of abstraction of the concept you choose to write about will depend on your interest and knowledge and your readers' current understanding of your subject.

Keep in mind as you work through this chapter that we learn by connecting what we are presently learning to what we have previously learned. Good explanatory writing, therefore, must be incremental, adding bit by bit to the reader's knowledge base. It should also provide a scaffolding—a framework built around a central, focusing point—that holds together the disparate bits of information, giving them form and meaning.

Above all, explanatory writing should be interesting to readers. We read explanations either out of curiosity or out of necessity. But even when we are self-motivated, bad writing can turn us off. Explanatory writing goes wrong when the flow of new information is either too fast or too slow for the particular reader, when the information is above our heads or too far below, or when the writing is too abstract or just plain dull, lacking in vividness and energy.

A GUIDE TO READING EXPLANATORY WRITING

To begin your work with explaining concepts, you will first look closely at a piece of explanatory writing by Caroline Seebohm, a professional writer. Closely analyzing Seebohm's writing will provide a foundation for the serious study of explanation this chapter encourages. As you become a more critical, insightful reader of explanatory writing, your own writing will become more interesting and informative.

As the initial step in your analysis, you will annotate the Seebohm selection. The next exercise asks you to take inventory of your annotations in order to disclose a pattern of meaning you have discovered. In the third exercise, guided by special questions, you will report what you have learned in analyzing the basic features of explanatory writing. Finally, the concluding exercise invites you to write a brief exploratory essay, consolidating what you have learned about the Seebohm selection and trying out your own ideas about it or extending your personal response to it.

The time you invest now in annotating, analyzing, and writing will pay off richly as you read, write about, and discuss the essays in this chapter. It will also give you confidence that you can write an effective explanatory essay of your own.

Annotating As You Read

Perhaps the most basic, and most useful, strategy for reading attentively and critically is annotating. Pencil in hand as you read, you are ready to record on the page any comments, questions, definitions, or insights—whatever crosses your mind—about a piece of writing. As an illustration, note how we have annotated the following brief introductory passage from an essay by Lawrence Stone on "passionate attachments" that appears in its entirety later in this chapter:

Term defined; same as "passionate attachment"?

Central point is to discuss *causes*: cultural or chemical?

Historians and anthropologists are in general agreement that romantic love—the usually brief but intensely felt and all-consuming attraction toward another person—is culturally conditioned. Love has a history. It is common only in certain societies at certain times, or even in certain social groups within those societies, usually the elite, which have the leisure to cultivate such feelings. Scholars are, however, less certain whether romantic love is merely a culturally induced psychological overlay on libido = "sexual drive"

Nicely put!

top of the biological drive for sex, ⟨or⟩ whether it has <u>biochemical</u> roots that operate quite independently from the libido. Would anyone in fact "fall in love" if they had not read about it or heard it talked about? Did poetry invent love, or love poetry?

For more on annotating, pause now to review the guidelines in Chapter 1 and the model annotations on the excerpt from "Letter from Birmingham Jail." Note particularly the Checklist for Annotating.

Exercise 1

Annotate Caroline Seebohm's "Lateral Thinking" as you read. Reread it at least one time, continuing to annotate as you reread. Your purpose is to focus your attention on the text, to read as thoughtfully—as critically—as possible. Annotate details you admire as well as things you question or challenge, mark noteworthy stylistic devices or writing strategies, highlight important points and key terms, write down any personal responses. Record your insights and reactions directly on and around the text itself.

Published originally in 1974, "Lateral Thinking" introduces a concept that was familiar to specialists but new to general readers, such as those reading the popular magazine *House and Garden* in which the essay first appeared.

To explain the concept effectively, Seebohm must analyze what her readers need to know in order to grasp the concept and to appreciate its importance for them. Since she is herself a nonspecialist who has only just learned about the concept, Seebohm is in an excellent position to anticipate her readers' needs. As you read, consider whether Seebohm has successfully anticipated your needs. What questions has she answered? What questions still need to be answered?

Lateral Thinking
Caroline Seebohm

Why

ital, cized

What's

smallpox

The famous Dr. Edward Jenner was busy trying to solve the problem of ⟨smallpox.⟩ After studying case after case, he still found no possible cure. *He had reached an impasse in his thinking.* At this point, he changed his tactics.

Instead of focusing on people who had smallpox, he switched his attention to people who did *not* have small-pox. It turned out that dairymaids apparently never got the disease. From the discovery that harmless cowpox gave protection against deadly smallpox came vaccination and the end of smallpox as a scourge in the Western world.

We often reach an impasse in our thinking. We are looking at a problem and trying to solve it and it seems there is a deadend, an "aporia" (the technical term in logic meaning "no opening"). It is on these occasions that we become tense, we feel pressured, overwhelmed, in a state of stress. We struggle vainly, fighting to solve the problem.

Dr. Jenner, however, did something about this situation. He stopped fighting the problem and simply changed his point of view—from patients to dairymaids. Picture the process going something like this: Suppose the brain is a computer. This computer has absorbed into its memory bank all your history, your experiences, your training, your information received through life; and it is programmed according to all this data. To change your point of view you must reprogram your computer, thus freeing yourself to take in new ideas and develop new ways of looking at things. Dr. Jenner, in effect, by re-programming his computer, erased the old way of looking at his smallpox problem and was free to receive new alternatives.

That's all very well, you may say, but how do we actually *do* that? In *New Think*, philosopher Edward de Bono has come up with a technique for changing our point of view, and he calls it Lateral Thinking.

The normal Western approach to a problem is to *fight* it. The saying, "When the going gets tough, the tough get going," epitomizes this aggressive, combat-ready attitude toward problem-solving. No matter what the problem is, or the techniques available for solving it, the framework produced by our Western way of thinking is *fight*. Dr. de Bono calls this vertical thinking, the traditional, sequential, Aristotelian thinking of logic, moving firmly from one step to the next, like toy blocks being built one on top of the other. The flaw is, of course, that if at any point one of the steps is not reached, or one of the toy blocks is incorrectly placed, then the whole structure collapses. Impasse is reached, and frustration, tension, feelings of *fight* take over. Lateral thinking, according to Dr. de Bono, is a new technique of thinking about

[handwritten margin annotations:]
story of Jenner

I think this would be a great hunch + therefore hard to believe

Repetition of 1st para. Also a def. Aporia - defin. Can relate

Good point but change unbelievable maybe to patients is animals repetition

Better Explanation Good concept Good analogy

All about changing point of view

Exactly easy to say

general - Common saying

Title + reason

Opposite of lateral (to fight)

Concept of fighting is still alive today

another repeat

repetition expaning on why we have an impasse in our think

Definition - of lateral thinking

[handwritten: like talking to solve a problem instead of with fists]

things—a technique that avoids this fight altogether, and solves the problem in an entirely unexpected fashion.

[handwritten: I don't think it sounds simple]

Lateral thinking sounds simple. And it is. Once you 6 have solved a problem laterally, you wonder how you could ever have been hung up on it. The knack is making that vital shift in emphasis, that sidestepping of the problem, instead of grappling with it head-on. It could even be as simple as going to a special part of the house, which is quiet and restful; buying a special chair, an "escape" chair, where we can lose our day-to-day preoccupations and allow our computers to reprogram themselves and become free to take in new ideas, see things in a different light. *[handwritten: metaph; back to computer]*

[handwritten: cute metaphor]

[handwritten: or def. more support]

Dr. A. A. Bridger, psychiatrist at Columbia University 7 and in private practice in New York, explains how lateral thinking . . . "is simply approaching a problem with . . . an Eastern flanking maneuver. You know, when a zen archer wants to hit the target with a bow and arrow, he doesn't concentrate on the target, he concentrates rather on what he has in his hands, so when he lets the arrow go, his focus is on the end-result of the arrow, rather than the target. This is what an Eastern flanking maneuver implies—instead of approaching the target directly, you approach it from a sideways point of view—or laterally instead of vertically."

[handwritten: Compared to Western thinking (vertical)]

[handwritten: More of a comparison]

[handwritten: the same. the fight impasse]

Lateral thinking, in short, is most valuable in those 8 problem situations where vertical thinking has been unable to provide a solution. When you reach that impasse, and feel the fight upon you, quickly reprogram your thinking:

1. Is there any other way the problem can be expressed?
2. What random ideas come to mind when you relax and think about it?
3. Can you turn the problem upside down?
4. Can you invent another problem to take its place?
5. Can you shift the emphasis from one part of the problem to another?

[handwritten: back to reprogramming computer]

These are difficult questions, and it takes imagination 9 to ask and to answer them. But that is how we change our point of view—by being imaginative enough to think up new ideas, find new ways of looking at old problems, invent new methods for dealing with old patterns. Think laterally instead of vertically. Take the fight out of our lives. Move Eastward in our attitudes.

[handwritten: Use your imagination is lateral thinking]

[handwritten: Not Westward (smallpox)]

Inventorying Your Annotations

Once you have annotated a reading with your insights and thoughts, you'll want to study your annotations for their special meaning. The best way to do this is by taking inventory of your annotations, to discover any patterns or significant repetitions.

Before completing Exercise 2, review the guidelines and illustration for the Inventory of Annotations in Chapter 1.

Exercise 2

Inventory the annotations you made on "Lateral Thinking," looking for meaningful patterns in your response to the selection.

Analyzing the Basic Features of Explanatory Writing

In addition to annotating a text to record your initial impressions and inventorying your annotations to discover their patterns of meaning, you can analyze the basic features of a piece of writing, in this case those qualities that make it distinctively explanatory.

Look back at Identifying and Evaluating Basic Features in Chapter 1. Although the questions there are different from the ones you will find in this chapter, the answers illustrate what a thoughtful analysis of basic features might look like.

Exercise 3

Analyze "Lateral Thinking" by answering the following questions. You will want to reread the selection with each question in mind, and you may want to annotate further.

Write out your answers to the questions.

1. *What term does the writer use to name the concept, and how is it defined?* At the center of any explanation of a concept is the key term used to name the concept. Concepts, of course, frequently are called by more than one name. For example, this text uses the term *invention* to identify

the process of generating ideas for an essay, while others use *prewriting* or *discovering*. Although these terms are often used interchangeably, they have different connotations. Prewriting implies that you think of ideas before you begin writing, while invention and discovery can occur at any point in the writing process. Discovery implies that the ideas already exist and that you simply go out and find them, while invention implies that you actively invent or create the ideas. As a critical reader, you should ask yourself what other terms are used to identify the writer's concept and how they differ from the term the writer uses.

Essays that explain concepts naturally seek to define them. Defining a concept basically answers the question, What does it mean? Defining might involve giving the word's *etymology*, naming *synonyms* (words that have similar meanings) and *antonyms* (words that have opposite meanings), identifying the *general class* to which the word belongs, and presenting *specific examples*.

As you reread the essay, look for places where the concept is defined. Also look for other important words that are defined or that you think require definition. To determine the appropriateness of the definitions, consider which of the words are likely to be new for the intended readers of the selection. Beware particularly of circular definitions, which incompletely define a word by using the word itself in the definition (for example: *A circular definition goes around in a circle*).

2. *What is the main point or thesis?* The primary purpose for explaining is obviously to inform readers, but writers of explanation cannot possibly hope to say everything there is to say about a concept, nor would they want to. Instead, they must make choices about what to include, what to emphasize, and what to omit. These choices are made on the basis of what they think is important and interesting about the concept and what they expect their readers to gain from their explanation. The thesis asserts what is significant about the concept, implying why readers should make the effort to learn about it.

As a critical reader, you should identify the main point or thesis. Sometimes, identifying the thesis is easy because it is stated explicitly, but often it is only implied. Consider what the essay says about the concept's significance: Does its importance stem from its usefulness? Is it interesting because it is problematic, open to different interpretations? Does it have broader implications about how we see ourselves and organize our experience of the world?

3. *In addition to defining, which of the following strategies are used to explain the concept, and how effectively have the strategies been used?* Writers seldom use all of these strategies in a single essay. As you identify and evaluate the particular strategies that have been used, ask yourself

whether they are all necessary. Also consider what strategies that were not used could have added to the explanation.

- *Classifying or Dividing.* Classifying and dividing are reciprocal acts. We classify a concept by grouping it with related concepts to form a more inclusive, general class; we divide a concept by breaking it into its more specific subclasses. Classifying involves moving to higher levels of generalization, while dividing goes toward more specificity. For example, in this text we have divided the concept of nonfiction prose into eight subclasses or categories of discourse (autobiography, reflection, observation, explanation, evaluation, analysis, proposal, position paper) and then classified specific pieces of writing by grouping them within one of these subclasses. We classify and divide on the basis of something the elements under consideration have in common (in our case, the writer's purpose). This basis must be applied consistently to all the items. Furthermore, the items should not overlap one another, but be clearly differentiated.

  As you reread a piece of explanatory writing, look for ways the writer has classified or divided the concept into subclasses. Ask yourself: Is the basis for classification or division applied consistently? Are the items mutually exclusive?

- *Comparing and Contrasting.* Comparing identifies similarities, while contrasting highlights differences. In either case, the items compared or contrasted must be related and members of the same class. A related strategy often used in explanatory writing is *analogy*: whereas items compared and contrasted must be basically similar, items related by analogy must be basically dissimilar. For example, explanatory writing can be compared and contrasted to observation and analysis, while it can be related by analogy to programming a computer or laying out a garden. As you reread a piece of explanatory writing, look for ways the writer uses comparing and contrasting as well as analogy. These strategies help readers to understand a new concept by showing how it is similar to or different from concepts with which readers are already familiar. To evaluate these strategies, ask: What aspects of the concept are highlighted through comparing and contrasting? How does comparing and contrasting clarify the main point or thesis?

- *Illustrating.* Illustrating makes unfamiliar concepts understandable and memorable. It can take many forms such as giving examples, telling anecdotes, listing facts and details, and quoting, summarizing, or paraphrasing other texts. Illustrating brings abstract concepts down to earth by grounding them in concrete experience and observation. For illustrations to be effective, however, they must be appropriate to the writing situation, suiting the readers and purpose. Personal anecdotes, for example, may be out of place in explanations written for formal, academic purposes.

As you read and reread, locate any illustrations and consider how they are used. Ask yourself: How does each illustration contribute to your understanding of the concept? Does it make an abstract idea tangible or a new one memorable? Are each of the illustrations appropriate to the writing situation?

- *Narrating a Process.* Writers of explanation occasionally have to narrate how the concept or some aspect of it works or could be put into practice. To be effective, a process narrative must be divided into a clearly delineated sequence of steps or stages.

  As you reread, notice any process narrative and consider how clearly it is presented. Ask yourself: Is each step sufficiently explained? Are there any important steps or transitions left out? If the purpose of the process narrative is to explain how something should be done, are the instructions easy to follow? Also notice where including a process narrative would help readers better understand the concept or clarify the thesis.

- *Explaining Causes and Effects.* While some causes and effects can only be speculated on, others have been determined with certainty. Writers of explanation usually limit their discussion of causes and effects to those that are certain, although they may occasionally report the speculations of experts. Explaining known causal relationships—telling why something happened or what its consequences were—can play an important role in explaining concepts. As a critical reader, you will want to identify any causes or effects and ask yourself: How clearly is the causal connection explained? On what authority are readers being asked to accept a particular cause or effect? Which are asserted as fact or common knowledge, and which are based on speculation?

4. *How is the explanation organized?* The effectiveness of explanatory writing often depends on how well it is organized. Points should be sequenced in a way that incrementally builds readers' understanding of the concept. Cueing devices—*forecasting statements* (which let readers know beforehand what they will be learning and why), *transitions* (which make disparate parts of the essay hang together or cohere), and *summary statements* (which help readers consolidate what they have learned)—should be provided to help readers follow the essay's development from one point to another without getting lost or confused.

To discover the essay's organization, begin by outlining it. You can outline right on the text by noting where each new point is introduced, or you can construct an outline on a separate piece of paper. Either way, your aim is to set out schematically the sequence of points in the order that they appear in the essay. Also note on this outline where cueing devices are used.

To evaluate the essay's organization, ask yourself: Given the main point the writer wants to get across about the concept and the readers' needs and expectations, how appropriate is this sequence of points? Does it begin with information readers already know or with points they will be able to comprehend easily? Could the points be rearranged to build on one another more systematically? Identify any places where you, as one reader, feel that the pace needs to be slowed down and the information developed further or in more detail. Also identify slow spots where you are given more information than you need. Finally, check to see that the cueing devices are helpful and supplied where they are needed.

5. *What sources of information does the writer draw on to explain the concept, and are these sources acknowledged appropriately?* Writers of explanation gather information from many different sources. They often draw on their own firsthand experience and observation. In addition, they may research the concept, reading what others have said about it. Referring to secondary sources, particularly what experts have written, lends authority to an explanation and can be especially helpful with problematic concepts, where the meaning or importance is uncertain.

How writers treat secondary sources depends on the writing situation. In more formal situations, such as assignments for college instructors or papers for scholarly audiences, writers are expected to follow prescribed rules for citing and documenting their sources. Students and scholars are expected to cite their sources formally because readers judge their writing in part by what they've read and how they've used their reading. In our discussion of Acknowledging Sources in the appendix Strategies for Research and Documentation, we present two different ways of citing sources: the Modern Language Association (MLA) style used chiefly by English instructors and the American Psychological Association (APA) style used by many social and natural scientists. Both of these styles call for parenthetical citations within the essay keyed to a list of works cited at the end.

On more informal writing occasions—newspaper and magazine articles, for example—readers do not expect writers to include page reference or publication information, but they do expect writers to identify their sources in some way. As you read the selection, notice how much information each writer gives readers about the secondary sources. Ask:

Is enough information given, considering the formality of the writing situation?

6. *How knowledgeable and trustworthy does the writer appear to be?* The effectiveness of an explanation depends in large part on how the writer comes across to readers, what persona the writer presents. Some writers put their personality center stage. This kind of explanatory writing typifies the style of writing in some popular magazines. Other writers, particularly reporters and scientists for whom objectivity is a virtue, absent themselves from their writing. Both extremes present problems: intrusiveness can be grating, while aloofness can deaden writing.

As a critical reader, you need to judge the appropriateness of the persona. Notice especially whether the writer adopts the persona of an expert or of a nonspecialist interpreting what the specialists say. Be wary of writers who lecture, patronize, or talk down to readers. Ask yourself: Is the tone of this essay appropriate? Does the writer come across as authoritative and knowledgeable?

Exploring Your Personal Response

One other way of focusing your response to an explanatory text is by taking the time to record your thoughts in a more extended piece of writing. Basically, such an exercise can help you to consider how the explanation relates to your own experience, to explore your understanding and define further your unique perspective on what you've read.

Exercise 4

Write 300–400 words (two or three handwritten pages) about "Lateral Thinking." Choose one of the suggestions listed in Exploring Your Personal Response in Chapter 1.

Lawrence Stone

Lawrence Stone studied history at Oxford University in England, receiving his advanced degree in 1947. He is currently Director of the Shelby Cullom Davis Center for Historical Studies at Princeton University. A social historian, he has concentrated much of his research on British history from the Renaissance through the Reformation. Among his books are *Family, Sex, and Marriage in England 1500–1800* (1980) and *The Past and the Present* (1987).

Passionate Attachments

This selection was published originally in *Passionate Attachments: Thinking about Love* (1989), edited by Willard Gaylin and Ethel Person, and reprinted in *Harper's*. It is from a paper Stone delivered at a conference cosponsored by Columbia University Psychoanalytic Center and the Association for Psychoanalytic Medicine in New York City.

The title names the concept *passionate attachments*, but you can see from skimming the opening paragraph that *romantic love* is the term Stone uses in the essay. Pause before reading further to think about these two terms. What does each term mean to you? Is *passionate* the same as *romantic*, *attachment* the same as *love*? Write down your thoughts above the text.

Historians and anthropologists are in general agreement that romantic love—the usually brief but intensely felt and all-consuming attraction toward another person—is culturally conditioned. Love has a history. It is common only in certain societies at certain times, or even in certain social groups within those societies, usually the elite, which have the leisure to cultivate such feelings. Scholars are, however, less certain whether romantic love is merely a culturally induced psychological overlay on top of the biological drive for sex, or whether it has biochemical roots that operate quite independently from the libido. Would anyone in fact "fall in love" if they had not read about it or heard it talked about? Did poetry invent love, or love poetry?

Some things can be said with certainty about the history of the phenomenon. The first is that cases of romantic love can be found in all times and places and have often been the subject of powerful poetic expression, from the Song of Solomon to Shakespeare. On the other hand, as anthropologists have discovered, neither social approbation nor the actual experience of romantic love is common to all societies. Second,

205

historical evidence for romantic love before the age of printing is largely confined to elite groups, which of course does not mean that it may not have occurred lower on the social scale. As a socially approved cultural artifact, romantic love began in Europe in the southern French aristocratic courts of the twelfth century, and was made fashionable by a group of poets, the troubadours. In this case the culture dictated that it should occur between an unmarried male and a married woman, and that it either should go sexually unconsummated or should be adulterous.

By the sixteenth and seventeenth centuries, our evidence becomes quite extensive, thanks to the spread of literacy and the printing press. We now have love poems, such as Shakespeare's sonnets, love letters, and autobiographies by women concerned primarily with their love lives. The courts of Europe were evidently hotbeds of passionate intrigues and liaisons, some romantic, some sexual. The printing press also began to spread pornography to a wider public, thus stimulating the libido, while the plays of Shakespeare indicate that romantic love was a concept familiar to society at large, which composed his audience.

Whether this romantic love was approved of, however, is another question. We simply do not know how Shakespearean audiences reacted to *Romeo and Juliet*. Did they, like us (and as Shakespeare clearly intended), fully identify with the young lovers? Or, when they left the theater, did they continue to act like the Montague and Capulet parents, who were trying to stop these irresponsible adolescents from allowing an ephemeral and irrational passion to interfere with the serious business of politics and patronage?

What is certain is that every advice book, every medical treatise, every sermon and religious homily of the sixteenth and seventeenth centuries firmly rejected both romantic passion and lust as suitable bases for marriage. In the sixteenth century, marriage was thought to be best arranged by parents, who could be relied upon to choose socially and economically suitable partners. People believed that the sexual bond would automatically create the necessary harmony between the two strangers in order to maintain the stability of the new family unit. This assumption is not, it seems, unreasonable, since recent investigations in Japan have shown that there is no difference in the rate of divorce between couples whose marriages were arranged by their parents and couples whose marriages were made by individual choice based on romantic love.

In the eighteenth century, orthodox opinion about marriage began to shift from subordinating the individual will to the interests of the group, and from economic or political considerations toward those of well-tried personal affection. The ideal marriage was one preceded by three to six months of intensive courting by a couple from families roughly equal in social status and economic wealth; that courtship, however, took place only with the prior consent of parents on both sides. But it was not until the Romantic movement and the rise of the novel, especially the pulp novel in the nineteenth century, that society accepted a new idea—that it is normal and indeed praiseworthy for young men and women to fall passionately in love, and that there must be something wrong with those who fail to have such an overwhelming experience sometime in late adolescence or early adulthood. Once this new idea was publicly accepted, the arrangement of marriage by parents came to be regarded as intolerable and immoral.

Today, the role of passionate attachments between adults is obscured by a new development: the saturation of the whole culture—through every medium of communication—with the belief that sexuality is the predominant and overriding human drive, a doctrine whose theoretical foundations were provided by Freud. In no past society known to me has sex been given so prominent a role in the culture at large, nor has sexual fulfillment been elevated to such preeminence in the list of human aspirations—in a vain attempt to relieve civilization of its discontents. We find it scarcely credible today that in most of Western Europe in the seventeenth century, in a society in which people usually married in their late twenties, a degree of chastity was practiced that kept the illegitimacy rate—without contraceptives—as low as 2 or 3 percent. Today, individualism is given such absolute priority in most Western societies that people are virtually free to act as they please, to sleep with whom they please, and to marry and divorce when and whom they please. The psychic (and, more recently, the physical) costs of such behavior are now becoming clear, however, and how long this situation will last is anybody's guess.

Passionate attachments between young people can and do happen in any society as a byproduct of biological sexual attraction, but the social acceptability of the emotion has varied enormously over time and class and space, determined primarily by cultural norms and property arrangements. We are in a unique position today in that our culture is dominated by romantic notions of passionate love as the only socially admissible reason for marriage; sexual fulfillment is accepted as the dominant human drive and a natural right for both sexes; and contraception is normal and efficient. Behind all this lies a frenetic individualism, a restless search for a sexual and emotional ideal in human relationships, and a demand for instant ego gratification.

QUESTIONS FOR ANALYSIS

1. Explanatory writing does not merely bombard readers with information, but focuses the information around a main point or thesis. What point is Stone trying to get across to readers about the concept of romantic love?

2. How does Stone help readers follow his explanation? Make a scratch outline, noting the different strategies and cueing devices he uses. Then, decide whether Stone's organizational plan seems coherent and easy to follow for you, as one reader. (See Chapter 1 for guidelines on making a scratch outline.)

3. Apply the Chapter 1 critical reading strategy, Inventory of Oppositions, to discover how Stone uses opposing concepts to develop his explanation of romantic love. Here are a couple of oppositions to get you started making your own list: cultural vs. psychological; psychological vs. biochemical.

4. Stone refers to various sources in this essay—literary works, advice books, sermons, and research reports—but he doesn't give citations. Why do you think he chose not to document his sources, given the particular writing situation? How appropriate do you find his decision?

5. In paragraph 7, Stone discusses what he calls "a new development: the saturation of the whole culture—through every medium of communication—with the belief that sexuality is the predominant and overriding human drive." What is the relation between this point and the main point he is making about romantic love? What seem to you to be the advantages or disadvantages of concluding the essay in this way?

6. Review Exploring Your Personal Response in Chapter 1. Then write a 300–400-word personal response to the Stone selection, choosing one of the following topics:

   Write a letter to Stone, responding to anything in the essay that you found particularly unusual, interesting, or intriguing.
   Write about your personal associations with romantic or passionate love.

   After you have written your response, reread it thoughtfully. In two or three sentences, say what you learned about the Stone selection by writing an extended response to it.

IDEAS FOR YOUR OWN WRITING

What concept would you be interested in tracing through history? Make a list of possible topics using the following to get you started: work, education, the solar system, parent-child relationships, etiquette. Then, select one item from your list and write for five to ten minutes, getting down on paper what you now know about the concept and any questions you have about it.

David Quammen

David Quammen (b. 1948) was an English major at Yale and attended Oxford University as a Rhodes Scholar. He has published three novels: *To Walk the Line* (1970), *The Zolla Configuration* (1983), and *The Soul of Viktor Tronko* (1987). Even though he claims that his formal scientific training was "minuscule," Quammen is a prolific science writer. His essays have appeared in *Rolling Stone, Audubon, Esquire, Smithsonian,* the *New York Times Book Review, Montana Outdoors,* and *Outside* magazine, for which he writes a column called "Natural Acts." In 1985, he published a collection of these pieces, *Natural Acts: A Sidelong View of Science and Nature.*

Is Sex Necessary?
Virgin Birth and Opportunism
in the Garden

Beginning with the title, Quammen has some fun explaining this concept. Do you find anything amusing about the title? Some readers will recognize the allusion to the James Thurber and E. B. White classic parody of sex manuals, *Is Sex Necessary?* As you read and annotate the essay, pay special attention to Quammen's attempts to amuse as well as to inform. Think about his tone and how appropriate it is for the subject and his readers.

Birds do it, bees do it, goes the tune. But the songsters, as usual, would mislead us with drastic oversimplifications. The full truth happens to be more eccentrically nonlibidinous: Sometimes they *don't* do it, those very creatures, and get the same results anyway. Bees of all species, for instance, are notable to geneticists precisely for their ability to produce offspring while doing *without.* Likewise at least one variety of bird—the Beltsville Small White turkey, a domestic dinner-table model out of Beltsville, Maryland—has achieved scientific renown for a similar feat. What we are talking about here is celibate motherhood, procreation without copulation, a phenomenon that goes by the technical name *parthenogenesis.* Translated from the Greek roots: virgin birth.

And you don't have to be Catholic to believe in this one.

Miraculous as it may seem, parthenogenesis is actually rather common throughout nature, practiced regularly or intermittently by at least some

210

species within almost every group of animals except (for reasons still unknown) dragonflies and mammals. Reproduction by virgin females has been discovered among reptiles, birds, fishes, amphibians, crustaceans, mollusks, ticks, the jellyfish clan, flatworms, roundworms, segmented worms; and among insects (notwithstanding those unrelentingly sexy dragonflies) it is especially favored. The order Hymenoptera, including all bees and wasps, is uniformly parthenogenetic in the manner by which males are produced: Every male honeybee is born without any genetic contribution from a father. Among the beetles, there are thirty-five different forms of parthenogenetic weevil. The African weaver ant employs parthenogenesis, as do twenty-three species of fruit fly and at least one kind of roach. The gall midge *Miastor* is notorious for the exceptionally bizarre and grisly scenario that allows its fatherless young to see daylight: *Miastor* daughters cannibalize the mother from inside, with ruthless impatience, until her hollowed-out skin splits open like the door of an overcrowded nursery. But the foremost practitioners of virgin birth—their elaborate and versatile proficiency unmatched in the animal kingdom—are undoubtedly the aphids.

Now no sensible reader of even this can be expected, I realize, to care 4 faintly about aphid biology *qua* aphid biology. That's just asking too much. But there's a larger rationale for dragging you aphid-ward. The life cycle of these little nebbishy sap-sucking insects, the very same that infest rose bushes and house plants, not only exemplifies *how* parthenogenetic reproduction is done; it also very clearly shows *why*.

First the biographical facts. A typical aphid, which feeds entirely on 5 plant juices tapped off from the vascular system of young leaves, spends winter dormant and protected, as an egg. The egg is attached near a bud site on the new growth of a poplar tree. In March, when the tree sap has begun to rise and the buds have begun to burgeon, an aphid hatchling appears, plugging its sharp snout (like a mosquito's) into the tree's tenderest plumbing. This solitary individual aphid will be, necessarily, a wingless female. If she is lucky, she will become sole founder of a vast aphid population. Having sucked enough poplar sap to reach maturity, she produces—by *live birth* now, and without benefit of a mate— daughters identical to herself. These wingless daughters also plug into the tree's flow of sap, and they also produce further wingless daughters, until sometime in late May, when that particular branch of that particular tree can support no more thirsty aphids. Suddenly there is a change: The next generation of daughters are born with wings. They fly off in search of a better situation.

One such aviatrix lands on an herbaceous plant—say a young climbing 6 bean in some human's garden—and the pattern repeats. She plugs into the sap ducts on the underside of a new leaf, commences feasting destructively, and delivers by parthenogenesis a great brood of wingless daughters. The daughters beget more daughters, those daughters beget still more, and so on, until the poor bean plant is encrusted with a solid mob of these fat little elbowing greedy sisters. Then again, neatly triggered by the crowded conditions, a generation of daughters are born with wings. Away they fly, looking for prospects, and one of them lights on, say, a sugar beet. (The switch from bean to beet is fine, because our species of typical aphid is not inordinately choosy.) The sugar beet before long is covered, sucked upon mercilessly, victimized by a horde of mothers and nieces and granddaughters. Still not a single male aphid has appeared anywhere in the chain.

The lurching from one plant to another continues; the alternation between wingless and winged daughters continues. But in September, with fresh tender plant growth increasingly hard to find, there is another change. 7

Flying daughters are born who have a different destiny: They wing back to the poplar tree, where they give birth to a crop of wingless females that are unlike any so far. These latest girls know the meaning of sex! Meanwhile, at long last, the starving survivors back on that final bedraggled sugar beet have brought forth a generation of males. The males have wings. They take to the air in quest of poplar trees and first love. *Et voilà.* The mated females lay eggs that will wait out the winter near bud sites on that poplar tree, and the circle is thus completed. One single aphid hatchling—call her the *fundatrix*—in this way can give rise in the course of a year, from her own ovaries exclusively, to roughly a zillion aphids. 8

Well and good, you say. A zillion aphids. But what is the point of it? 9

The point, for aphids as for most other parthenogenetic animals, is (1) exceptionally fast reproduction that allows (2) maximal exploitation of temporary resource abundance and unstable environmental conditions, while (3) facilitating the successful colonization of unfamiliar habitats. In other words the aphid, like the gall midge and the weaver ant and the rest of their fellow parthenogens, is by its evolved character a galloping opportunist. 10

This is a term of science, not of abuse. Population ecologists make an illuminating distinction between what they label *equilibrium* and *opportunistic* species. According to William Birky and John Gilbert, from a paper in the journal *American Zoologist*: "Equilibrium species, exemplified by many vertebrates, maintain relatively constant population sizes, in part by being adapted to reproduce, at least slowly, in most of the environmental conditions which they meet. Opportunistic species, on 11 the other hand, show extreme population fluctuations; they are adapted to reproduce only in a relatively narrow range of conditions, but make up for this by reproducing extremely rapidly in favorable circumstances. At least in some cases, opportunistic organisms can also be categorized as colonizing organisms." Birky and Gilbert also emphasize that "The potential for rapid reproduction is the essential evolutionary ticket for entry into the opportunistic life style."

And parthenogenesis, in turn, is the greatest time-saving gimmick in 12 the history of animal reproduction. No hours or days are wasted while a female looks for a mate; no minutes lost to the act of mating itself. The female aphid attains sexual maturity and, bang, she becomes automatically pregnant. No waiting, no courtship, no fooling around. She delivers her brood of daughters, they grow to puberty and, zap, another generation immediately. If humans worked as fast, Jane Fonda today would be a great-grandmother. The time saved to parthenogenetic species may seem trivial, but it is not. It adds up dizzyingly: In the same time taken by a sexually reproducing insect to complete three generations for a total of 1,200 offspring, an aphid (assuming the *same* time required for each female to mature, and the *same* number of progeny in each litter), squandering no time on courtship or sex, will progress through six generations for an extended family of 318,000,000.

Even this isn't speedy enough for some restless opportunists. That 13 matricidal gall midge *Miastor*, whose larvae feed on fleeting eruptions of fungus under the bark of trees, has developed a startling way to cut further time from the cycle of procreation. Far from waiting for a mate, *Miastor* does not even wait for maturity. When food is abundant, it is the *larva*, not the adult female fly, who is eaten alive from inside by her own daughters. And as those voracious daughters burst free of the husk that was their mother, each of them already contains further larval daughters taking shape ominously within its own ovaries. While the food lasts, while opportunity endures, no *Miastor* female can live to adulthood without dying of motherhood.

The implicit principle behind all this nonsexual reproduction, all this 14 hurry, is simple: Don't argue with success. Don't tamper with a genetic blueprint that works. Unmated female aphids, and gall midges, pass on their own gene patterns virtually unaltered (except for the occasional mutation) to their daughters. Sexual reproduction, on the other hand, constitutes, by its essence, genetic tampering. The whole purpose of joining sperm with egg is to shuffle the genes of both parents and come up with a new combination that might perhaps be more advantageous. Give the kid something neither Mom nor Pop ever had. Parthenogenetic species, during their hurried phases at least, dispense with this genetic shuffle. They stick stubbornly to the gene pattern that seems to be working. They produce (with certain complicated exceptions) natural clones of themselves.

But what they gain thereby in reproductive rate, in great explosions of   15
population, they give up in flexibility. They minimize their genetic options. They lessen their chances of adapting to unforeseen changes of circumstance.

Which is why more than one biologist has drawn the same conclusion   16
as M. J. D. White: "Parthenogenetic forms seem to be frequently success-ful in the particular ecological niche which they occupy, but sooner or later the inherent disadvantages of their genetic system must be expected to lead to a lack of adaptability, followed by eventual extinction, or perhaps in some cases by a return to sexuality."

So it *is* necessary, at least intermittently (once a year, for the aphids,   17
whether they need it or not), this thing called sex. As of course you and I knew it must be. Otherwise surely, by now, we mammals and dragonflies would have come up with something more dignified.

QUESTIONS FOR ANALYSIS

1. Define *parthenogenesis* in your own words. What point does Quam-men make about it?

2. What information about parthenogenesis does Quammen present, and how does he arrange it? To discover his plan for this essay, make an outline following the guidelines in Chapter 1. Given his purpose and readers, what advantages or disadvantages do you see in this way of organizing the information?

3. In answering question 2, you analyzed how Quammen organizes his essay. Now, consider how he helps his readers follow this organization by providing cues to signal where they have been and where they are going. Annotate the essay, marking any cueing devices you find. Cueing devices include forecasting statements, transitional words and phrases, and summaries. How do these cues help to keep you, as one reader, oriented?

4. In paragraphs 5–8, Quammen narrates the process of parthenogenesis among aphids. Look closely at these paragraphs, circling the time markers (*now, next, then*) and the verbs used to denote shifts in tense (*produces, producing, produced, has produced,* and so forth). How effec-tively does this process narrative set out the order of events?

5. What adjectives would you use to characterize the persona Quammen projects in this essay? How does his use of *I* (in paragraphs 4 and 17)

contribute to this persona? How does Quammen's persona affect your reading of this essay?

IDEAS FOR YOUR OWN WRITING

"Lively writing about science and nature depends less on the offering of good answers," according to David Quammen, "than on the offering of good questions." The central question in this essay, for example, is stated in the title, "Is Sex Necessary?" In other essays Quammen has posed these questions: What are the redeeming merits, if any, of the mosquito? Are crows too intelligent for their station in life? Why do certain bamboo species wait 120 years before bursting into bloom?

Generate a list of questions about science or nature that you might like to explore further for an explanatory essay. Include questions to which you do not know the answers as well as questions whose answers you think will surprise or fascinate readers. Make the list as long as you can. Then, choose one question from your list to consider further.

If you already know the answer to this question, ask yourself how you might go about presenting what you know to readers. What basic concept is involved? What examples could you use to illustrate this concept? How could you make your explanation interesting to readers unfamiliar with the concept?

If you do not know the answer to the question you've chosen, ask yourself how you might go about gathering information about it. To what subject or field might it belong? Where should you look to find information on this subject or field? What related questions can you think of? If you can answer any of these questions, what do your answers tell you about your original question? Where should you look to find answers to these related questions?

Gary Zukav

Gary Zukav is a professional writer with broad interests in both the humanities and the sciences. During three years of work, in consultation with physicists in America and England, he wrote the book from which the following selection is taken. One of these physicists remarked that Zukav "puts the reader in touch with all the various ways that physicists have worked out for talking about what is so hard to talk about." This physicist also commented, "It is more stimulating to talk physics with him [Zukav] than with most professionals." Zukav seems to be one of those writers who can explain the work of specialists (in all fields) to nonspecialists, interested laypersons as well as college students taking their first course in an unfamiliar academic specialty.

Heisenberg's Uncertainty Principle

This selection comes from *The Dancing Wu Li Masters: An Overview of the New Physics* (1979), Zukav's book introducing nonspecialists to the new physics, quantum mechanics. In this selection, he attempts to explain a fundamental principle of the new physics, the uncertainty principle, first formulated in 1927 by the German physicist Werner Heisenberg.

Quantum mechanics studies physical properties of matter at the subatomic level. Since subatomic particles cannot be seen, physicists must study them with sensitive measuring instruments. The uncertainty principle explains what happens when physicists try to take these measurements.

As a prereading exercise, write for a few minutes about science. What is the scientific method? Why is it so important that scientists be able to take accurate measurements?

Heisenberg's remarkable discovery was that there are limits beyond   1
which we cannot measure accurately, at the same time, the processes of nature. These limits are not imposed by the clumsy nature of our measuring devices or the extremely small size of the entities that we attempt to measure, but rather by the very way that nature presents itself to us. In other words, there exists an ambiguity barrier beyond which we never can pass without venturing into the realm of uncertainty. For this reason, Heisenberg's discovery became known as the "uncertainty principle."

The uncertainty principle reveals that as we penetrate deeper and   2
deeper into the subatomic realm, we reach a certain point at which one

part or another of our picture of nature becomes blurred, and there is no way to reclarify that part without blurring another part of the picture! It is as though we are adjusting a moving picture that is slightly out of focus. As we make the final adjustments, we are astonished to discover that when the right side of the picture clears, the left side of the picture becomes completely unfocused and nothing in it is recognizable. When we try to focus the left side of the picture, the right side starts to blur and soon the situation is reversed. If we try to strike a balance between these two extremes, both sides of the picture return to a recognizable condition, but in no way can we remove the original fuzziness from them.

The right side of the picture, in the original formulation of the uncertainty principle, corresponds to the position in space of a moving particle. The left side of the picture corresponds to its momentum. According to the uncertainty principle, we cannot measure accurately, at the same time, both the position *and* the momentum of a moving particle. The more precisely we determine one of these properties, the less we know about the other. If we precisely determine the position of the particle, then, strange as it sounds, there is *nothing* that we can know about its momentum. If we precisely determine the momentum of the particle, there is no way to determine its position. 3

To illustrate this strange statement, Heisenberg proposed that we imagine a super microscope of extraordinarily high resolving power— powerful enough, in fact, to be able to see an electron moving around in its orbit. Since electrons are so small, we cannot use ordinary light in our microscope because the wavelength of ordinary light is much too long to "see" electrons, in the same way that long sea waves barely are influenced by a thin pole sticking out of the water. 4

If we hold a strand of hair between a bright light and the wall, the hair casts no distinct shadow. It is so thin compared to the wavelengths of the light that the light waves bend around it instead of being obstructed by it. To see something, we have to obstruct the light waves we are looking with. In other words, to see something, we have to illuminate it with wavelengths smaller than it is. For this reason, Heisenberg substituted gamma rays for visible light in his imaginary microscope. Gamma rays have the shortest wavelength known, which is just what we need for seeing an electron. An electron is large enough, compared to the tiny wavelength of gamma rays, to obstruct some of them: to make a shadow on the wall, as it were. This enables us to locate the electron. 5

The only problem, and this is where quantum physics enters the picture, is that, according to Planck's discovery, gamma rays, which have a much shorter wavelength than visible light, also contain much more energy than visible light. When a gamma ray strikes the imaginary 6 electron, it illuminates the electron, but unfortunately, it also knocks it out of its orbit and changes its direction and speed (its momentum) in an unpredictable and uncontrollable way. (We cannot calculate precisely the angle of rebound between a particle, like the electron, and a wave, like the gamma ray.) In short, if we use light with a wavelength short enough to locate the electron, we cause an undeterminable change in the electron's momentum.

The only alternative is to use a less energetic light. Less energetic light, however, causes our original problem: Light with an energy low enough not to disturb the momentum of the electron will have a wavelength so long that it will not be able to show us where the electron is! There is no way that we can know simultaneously the position *and* the momentum of a moving particle. All attempts to observe the electron alter the electron.   7

This is the primary significance of the uncertainty principle. At the subatomic level, *we cannot observe something without changing it.* There is no such thing as the independent observer who can stand on the sidelines watching nature run its course without influencing it.   8

In one sense, this is not such a surprising statement. A good way to make a stranger turn and look at you is to stare intently at his back. All of us know this, but we often discredit what we know when it contradicts what we have been taught is possible. Classical physics is based on the assumption that our reality, independently of us, runs its course in space and time according to strict causal laws. Not only can we observe it, unnoticed, as it unfolds, we can predict its future by applying causal laws to initial conditions. In this sense, Heisenberg's uncertainty principle is a *very* surprising statement.   9

We cannot apply Newton's laws of motion to an individual particle that does not have an initial location and momentum, which is exactly what the uncertainty principle shows us that we cannot determine. In other words, it is impossible, even in principle, ever to know enough about a particle in the subatomic realm to apply Newton's laws of motion which, for three centuries, were the basis of physics. *Newton's laws do not apply to the subatomic realm.*[1] (Newton's *concepts* do not even apply in the subatomic realm.) Given a beam of electrons, quantum theory can predict the probable distribution of the electrons over a given space at a given time, but quantum theory cannot predict, even in principle, the course of a single electron. The whole idea of a causal universe is undermined by the uncertainty principle.   10

---

[1]Strictly speaking, Newton's laws do not disappear totally in the subatomic realm: they remain valid as operator equations. Also, in some experiments involving subatomic particles Newton's laws may be taken as good approximations in the description of what is happening.

As Heisenberg wrote: 11

> What we observe is not nature itself, but nature exposed to our method of questioning. (*Physics and Philosophy*, p. 58).

The tables have been turned. "The exact sciences" no longer study an   12
objective reality that runs its course regardless of our interest in it or not,
leaving us to fare as best we can while it goes its predetermined way.
Science, at the level of subatomic events, is no longer exact, the distinction between objective and subjective has vanished, and the portals
through which the universe manifests itself are, as we once knew a long
time ago, those impotent, passive witnesses to its unfolding, the "I"s, of
which we, insignificant we, are examples. The Cogs in the Machine have
become the Creators of the Universe.

If the new physics has led us anywhere, it is back to ourselves, which,   13
of course, is the only place that we could go.

QUESTIONS FOR ANALYSIS

1. To demonstrate that you understand the uncertainty principle and
   why it's important, write a summary of the essay. (See the Guidelines
   for Summarizing in Chapter 1.)

2. Reread the essay, underlining any words that you would have liked
   Zukav to define. Then, look up each of these words in a college
   dictionary and write the definition in the margin next to the word.

   How adequate is the dictionary definition? Are there any cases in
   which you need still more information to understand the word in the
   context of the essay? What can you conclude about the need for
   explanatory essays to define unusual words or technical terms?

3. In paragraphs 2 and 3, Zukav uses an extended analogy to explain the
   uncertainty principle. What is this analogy, and why do you think it
   might be particularly helpful for nonspecialist readers trying to understand the concept?

4. In paragraphs 4–7, Zukav discusses Heisenberg's illustration of an
   imaginary microscope strong enough "to see an electron moving
   around in its orbit" to explain the uncertainty principle. How helpful
   do you find this illustration? Why?

5. You can learn much about explanatory writing by comparing and
   contrasting two related essays. Like the Quammen selection that
   precedes it, this essay attempts to explain a scientific concept to the
   general, nonspecialist reader.

   Reread the two selections, looking for ways they are alike and
   different. Then write a few paragraphs comparing and contrasting the

two selections. What conclusions can you draw about what makes explanations of technical concepts to nonspecialist readers effective? (For advice on Comparing and Contrasting Related Readings, see Chapter 1.)

IDEAS FOR YOUR OWN WRITING

Explaining concepts is a common writing assignment. What concepts have you learned that you think you could explain (with a little reviewing)? Write down the courses you've taken in the last year or two, skipping a few lines between each course. Then, under each course, list as many concepts as you can recall. Include in your list concepts you would need to look back over your notes and textbooks to explain, as well as those you could sit down and explain right now.

Choose one concept from your list, and consider how you would go about writing an explanatory essay on it for a particular set of readers. The readers you select may be ones who already know something about the concept or they may be totally unfamiliar with it. Given your readers and your purpose, how might you begin the essay? What examples or other specific detail might you include to make the abstract concept more understandable? To what other concept with which your readers might be more familiar could you compare or contrast the concept you're explaining?

Juan Bruce-Novoa

Juan Bruce-Novoa is a poet as well as a scholar. After receiving his Ph.D. in Spanish from the University of Colorado in 1974, he joined the faculty of Yale University as director of Latin American Studies. He is currently a professor at Trinity University in San Antonio, Texas. He has published a book of poems, *Innocencia Perversa/Perverse Innocence* (1977); a collection of interviews, *Chicano Authors* (1980); and a critical work, *Chicano Poetry: A Response to Chaos* (1982).

Interlingualism

This selection comes from Bruce-Novoa's book *Chicano Authors*. Written for students taking his course on Chicano culture, the book presents the thinking of fourteen leading Chicano poets, essayists, and fiction writers. *Chicano*, as you may know, is a term adopted by many Americans of Mexican descent to express pride in their Mexican heritage.

In the introduction, Bruce-Novoa discusses some common assumptions people have about Chicano authors and their writing. Before reading, review your own preconceptions by asking yourself the following questions: In what language do you suppose Chicano authors write? Would you expect Chicano authors to be much influenced by American and British writers?

Much attention has been given to what is usually termed bilingualism   1
in Chicano writing, the use of Spanish and English in the same work;
. . . but the language of Chicano literature is much more than a simple
mixing of languages. First, it should not be overlooked that many writers
use standard English and/or standard Spanish without mixing them. For
example, Bernice Zamora parodies Shakespeare's Sonnet CXVI, "Let me
not to the marriage of true minds," with a purposefully archaic English:

Do not ask, sir, why this weary woman
Wears well the compass of gay boys and men.
Masculinity is not manhood's realm
Which falters when ground passions overwhelm. (47)

Tino Villanueva utilizes an English reminiscent of Dylan Thomas in
"My Certain Burn toward Pale Ashes," yet later offers another tribute to
Thomas, this time in a Spanish which manages to echo the Welsh
master: "Un eco vago vibra del pasado / y aviso da que el tiempo con
presteza / al fin te vence, fuga, y no regresa" [A faint echo vibrates from

the past / giving notice that time, in its haste, / finally overcomes you, flees, and does not return] (15).

John Rechy is a master at approximating urban street language, especially in *City of Night*. His disrespect for grammar and spelling give his language the throbbing pulse and excitement of the rock-and-roll music that (one knows) blares in the background of his scenes. Alurista has continued the use of rock music and street language, though his context is much more interlingual. . . . Rolando Hinojosa is equally skilled with regional Mexican Spanish and its particular humor of the *albur* or phonetic word play. In "Al pozo con Bruno Cano," Cano y Melitón Burnias search for buried treasure in a cemetery at night; Burnias claims to know magic prayers for just such occasions. When Bruno, down in the pit, strikes something metallic, the following exchange takes place with the slightly deaf Melitón:

> Te digo que vamos cerca. [Bruno]
> Ah, sí, pues entonces, ¿qué rezo yo?
> ¿Qué?
> ¿Que qué rezo yo?
> ¿Cómo que qué resolló?
> ¿Qué resolló algo?
> ¿Que resolló algo dices?
> ¿Qué resolló? ¡ay, Diosito mío!
> Diciendo esto, Burnias voló, abandonó la pala y a su socio.[1]

Between the poles of standard usage we find some authors, like Alurista, who mix the languages. "Mis ojos hinchados / flooded with lágrimas / de bronze / melting on the cheek bones / of my concern" (poem 40); "must be the season of the witch / la bruja / la llorona / she lost her children / and she cries / en las barrancas of industry" (poem 26). Nick C. Vaca, one of the best writers from the early days of *El Grito*,

---

[1]In Spanish, ¿qué rezo yo?" [what prayer should I say?] and "¿qué resolló?" [what was that noisy breathing?] sound alike. The translator of *Estampas del Valle* has tried to approximate the effect by translating *rezar* as "chant" and *resollar* as "pant":

"'I said we're gettin' close.'
"'Okay, what should I chant?'
"'What?'
"'What do I chant?'
"'What do you mean, what do I chant?'
"'You heard something pant?'
"'Pant, you say?'
"'What panted? Omigod!'
"Saying this, Burnias fled, abandoning his shovel and his companion." (*Estampas del Valle*, p. 75)

does the same thing in prose: "y mis manos están heladas, con el frío y la fog of the morning. Chingado animal, even in the cold morning you don't leave me alone. Vete, antes que me mate, then you will have no home at all" (137).

This type of mixture, what linguists call code switching, was defined as a "binary phenomenon" by Philip Ortego: " . . . linguistic symbols of two languages are mixed in utterances using either language's syntactic structure" (306). Tino Villanueva takes this explanation further by attributing to the Chicano a *bisensitivity*, the feeling of experiencing something "from two points of reference: on one side from the dimension that the object can suggest within the Chicano context; and on the other side, from the dimension that the same reality suggests within an Anglosaxon context" (51). He goes on to give examples of experiences, such as playing marbles, that have two separate cultural contexts, implying that the particular context will determine the usage, producing the choice of code.

As convincing as these explanations seem, I disagree; they are misleading in their binary bound system. Chicanos do not function as constantly choice-making speakers; their language is a blend, a synthesis of the two into a third. Thus they are interlingual, not bilingual. The codes are not separate, but intrinsically fused. Taking, for instance, Villanueva's marbles example, the two contexts form a binary phenomenon only in a subjectless objectivity. As soon as the subject, the Chicano, appears, the two cease to be separate poles, blending together within the speaker. For the Chicano, within the *marble* there lurks the *canica* and vice versa. The feeling that one is saying more than the word means in either language, although the context can be entirely one or the other, is a common Chicano experience. A bilingual takes the meaning of a word such as *actual, ignore,* or *realize*[2] from the context of the language being spoken; the Chicano feels both, even though one may predominate, not simply because one language is being spoken, but because the entire semantic context is relevant. The bilingual will resist the "error"; the interlingual senses no "error." Chicano speech expands both the connotative and the denotative range of words in both languages, creating not a binary phenomenon, but a new phenomenon unfamiliar to the bilingual.

José Saldívar has demonstrated the interlingual phenomenon at work in Anaya's *Bless Me, Ultima,* explaining how the interlingual reader will sense in the word *moon* the word *luna*; they are one. So when, in a

---

[2]*Actual* means "of the present time" in Spanish; *ignorar* means "not to know"; *realizar* means "to achieve," as in English "to realize an action."

dream, the moon becomes Antonio's mother, a Luna by birth, the transformation is merely the adjustment of the surface representation, the word. The possibility was there all along.

The expert in this linguistic synthesis is José Montoya. His poetry 7 flows naturally, with no sensation of "code switching." He writes one language, his own, in which Spanish and English are no longer independent codes, but a single hybrid. Decoding his language in all its riches will be possible only for the interlingual reader, though the bilingual can come to "understand" his poems; the monolingual, of course, will be lost.

As long as we are bound by a linguistic science that insists on forcing 8 all languages into binary structures, Chicano speech will be misinterpreted. Yet finding another, more suitable approach is no easy task, as George Steiner clearly demonstrates in *After Babel*, while arguing convincingly for the need to rethink the nature of the bilingual and polyglot speaker as one who "undercuts lines of division between languages by reaching inward, to the symbiotic core" (119). He could be talking about the Chicano.

WORKS CITED

Alurista. "Must be the season of the witch." *Floricanto en Aztlan*. Los Angeles: Chicano Studies Research Center of UCLA, 1971.

———. "Mis ojos hinchados." *Floricanto en Aztlan*. Los Angeles: Chicano Studies Research Center of UCLA, 1971.

Hinojosa, Rolando R. "Al pozo con Bruno Cano." *Estampas del Valle y otras obras*. Berkeley: Quinto Sol, 1973.

Ortego, Philip. "The Chicano Renaissance." *Social Caseworker* 52 (May 1971): 306.

Salvídar, José. "Faulkner, Borges and Anaya." Unpublished Senior Essay, Yale University, 1978.

Steiner, George. *After Babel: Aspects of Language and Translation*. London: Oxford, 1975.

Vaca, N. C. "The Week of the Life of Manuel Hernandez." Ed. Octavio Romano. *El Espejo/The Mirror*. Berkeley: Quinto Sol, 1969.

Villanueva, Tino. "Apuntes sobre la poesia chicana." *Papeles de Son Armadans* 271–273 (October–December 1978): 51.

———. "Camino y capricho eterno." *Hay otra voz Poems*. Staten Island: Editorial Mansaje, 1972.

Zamora, Bernice. "Sonnet, Freely Adapted." *Restless Serpents*. Menlo Park, CA: Disenos Literarios, 1976.

QUESTIONS FOR ANALYSIS

1. Bruce-Novoa opposes the term *interlingualism* to another term, *bilingualism*. What is the difference between these two concepts? How

does comparing and contrasting these two concepts help him get across to readers his main point or thesis?

2. Bruce-Novoa divides Chicano writing into three subclasses. What are they? What purpose is served by this division?

3. As we indicated in the headnote, Bruce-Novoa initially wrote this book for his American college students, who could not be expected to know Chicano literature or the Spanish language. How does he accommodate to the special needs of his readers? How well, in your opinion, does he succeed?

4. Writers of explanation often quote from other texts. Bruce-Novoa quotes from the poems and stories he uses as illustration as well as from other scholars who have written about the concept he is explaining. Look closely at each quotation and notice how Bruce-Novoa makes it fit grammatically into his own sentence. Then, choose one quotation and rewrite Bruce-Novoa's sentence, trying out a different way of integrating the quotation into the sentence. Share your revised sentence with your classmates.

5. Review Exploring Your Personal Response in Chapter 1. Then write a 300–400-word personal response to this selection, choosing one of the following topics:

  Write about your personal associations with something in the reading, such as an image, idea, or example.

  Write to explore the meaning and implications of the central point made in the selection.

  After you have written your response, reread it thoughtfully. In two or three sentences, say what you have learned about this selection by writing an extended response to it.

IDEAS FOR YOUR OWN WRITING

The concept of interlingualism which Bruce-Novoa explains is a relatively original one. That is, it is not a concept that has already been written about extensively and strictly defined. Bruce-Novoa is, in a sense, conceiving the concept as he analyzes and groups together examples that demonstrate it.

Can you conceive of any emerging concepts in a field or area of interest to you—a new genre of television commercials or popular music, for example, or an evolving technique in a particular sport or an increasingly widespread use of language? List as many possibilities as you can think of. You may find it helpful to make a list with a classmate who has interests similar to yours. Then choose one concept and write for five minutes or so, listing examples and formulating definitions.

Sissela Bok

Born in Sweden in 1934, Sissela Bok grew up in Switzerland, France, and the United States. She received her B.A. and M.A. degrees in psychology from George Washington University and her Ph.D. in philosophy from Harvard. A former member of the Ethics Advisory Board to the Secretary of Health, Education, and Welfare, Bok also teaches ethics in the Harvard-MIT division of health sciences and technology.

In addition to numerous articles on medical ethics, she has written books on two interrelated moral issues: *Lying: Moral Choice in Public and Private Life* (1978) and *Secrets: On the Ethics of Concealment and Revelation* (1983). She is concerned with what we consider to be right and wrong, and how these moral judgments affect our everyday conduct.

Self-Deception

This selection, excerpted from *Secrets*, attempts to explain self-deception, a phenomenon with which we are all too familiar. The anorexic girl close to starving to death who thinks she looks fat and the alcoholic who denies having a drinking problem are two examples of self-deception Bok gives elsewhere in her book.

Before reading the selection, list other examples of self-deception from your own life and observation. Then, write nonstop for five minutes to explore your own understanding of this peculiar kind of deception. How do we deceive ourselves? Why?

To see the self as deceiving itself has seemed the only way to explain what might otherwise be incomprehensible: a person's failure to acknowledge what is too obvious to miss.[1] How, if not through such intentional misleading of self, can someone fail to notice that his work leads nowhere, that he lives beyond his means, that his marriage is a farce? How else can so many patients listen to a doctor's explanation of their life-threatening disease, respond as if they understood, yet know nothing about it a few hours later?

---

[1]For discussion of self-deception, see Raphael Demos, "Lying to Oneself," *Journal of Philosophy* 57 (1960):588–95; M. R. Haight, *A Study of Self-Deception* (Sussex: Harvester Press, 1980); Amélie Rorty, "Self-Deception, Akrasia, and Irrationality," *Social Science Information* 19 (Summer 1980):905–22; and my comment on this last article in the same journal, "The Self Deceived," pp. 923–35.

As helpful as such a view may be, it is also a troubling one. For exactly how can one be both insider and outsider thus, keeping secrets from oneself, even lying to oneself? How can one simultaneously know and ignore the same thing, hide it and remain in the dark about it? The paradoxical nature of such a view also seems to undercut reasoned choice *about* secrecy. If there is a deceiving and a deceived part in any one individual, then should one part only (and if so, which?) be considered responsible for choices made in such a state of self-deception? Which part is it that can exercise discretion or any other form of moral judgment? And how can we know that it is not deceiving itself in so doing? If we cannot, finally, then how can we even begin to sort out the moral problems of choice and responsibility?

On all counts, the view of the self keeping secrets from itself seems paradoxical. In this, it is not merely problematic, as are so many concepts concerning relations *between* people when used instead with respect to the self: duties to oneself, for example, or promises to oneself. These do not have the element of paradox inherent in the notion of keeping secrets from oneself. For while we can envision so construing duties and prom-ises that they apply, in somewhat different form, to oneself as well as to others, it is much harder to envision just how one goes about keeping a secret from oneself—being at once included and shut out.

The most sustained effort to overcome this seeming paradox has been that of psychoanalysis. Its view of human defense mechanisms is surely much more complex than the standard versions of self-deception. Freud's therapy was based on the assumption that people repress much of what they seem not to know, or to have forgotten, and that this material is capable of being retrieved. Heinz Hartmann (1937/1958) argued that "a great part of psychoanalysis can be described as a theory of self-deceptions and of misjudgments of the external world" (p. 64). And a number of psychiatrists have described all unconscious material as se-crets kept from the self by the self.[2] They have categorized as secret all that they could infer a person to have forgotten or repressed, relying on Freud's partitioning of the psyche, and on his imagery of strata, resist-ances, censors, and conflicting forces ranging back and forth across regions of differing accessibility.

The very profusion of metaphors that Freud brought in to convey such a picture of internal, self-imposed secrecy or deceit has not escaped

---

[2]See, for instance, Carl Fullerton Sulzberger, "Why It Is Hard To Keep Secrets," *Psychoanalysis* 2 (Fall 1953):37–43; Russell Meares, "The Secret," *Psychiatry* 39 (1976):258–65; and Rudolf Eckstein and Elaine Caruth, "Keeping Secrets," in Giovacchini, ed. *Tactics and Techniques in Psychoanalytic Therapy*, pp. 200–15.

criticism. Sartre (1943), among others, has derided the idea of the unconscious keeping secrets from the conscious; he has argued that Freud needed to postulate a process complete with "censor, conceived of as a line of demarcation, with customs, passport division, currency control, etc.," in order to re-establish within the self the duality of deceiver and deceived (p. 88). Freud, he argued, has merely interposed these barriers in order to overcome the paradox, and must then in turn overcome the duality itself through recourse to a "magic unity" (p. 92).

Having criticized Freud's attempt to overcome the contradiction inher-   6
ent in attributing self-deception and concealment from self, Sartre proceeded to set forth an even more improbable theory of self-deception as "bad faith." It is the denial that consciousness directs toward itself, and results from the fear of facing the abyss of one's own freedom. Sartre did nothing to overcome the paradox inherent in such bad faith; instead he underlined it by claiming, "I must know, as deceiver, the truth that is masked from me as deceived. . . . Better still, I have to know this truth very precisely in order to hide it from myself the more carefully" (p. 87).

"Bad faith," for Sartre, carried a stronger overtone of blame than "self-   7
deception." Because it is something one intends and is aware of, one is morally responsible for being in such a state, and for what one does or avoids as a result. . . . The concept of bad faith combined fluidity and blame in such a way as to allow him to assign moral responsibility without indicating just how he had arrived at his conclusions.[3]

Not only did Sartre not offer criteria for determining when bad faith is   8
and is not present; he never explained how he could retain the paradox of lying to oneself without contradiction. Rather than weakening the paradox, as Freud had, and introducing some distance between deceiver and deceived by means of the unconscious and of the processes of censorship, Sartre merely blurred it. He attributed to bad faith a mysterious quality of "evanescence" and described it as oscillating in perpetuity between good faith and cynicism. Many, he argued, live in a continuous state of bad faith with intermittent and sudden awakenings in either direction.

Freud, on the other hand, remained profoundly concerned   9
throughout his career to overcome the paradox. He was still struggling to do so in the last article he wrote, which he had to leave unfinished. In

---

[3]For a discussion of "bad faith" in Sartre's philosophy and of his stance toward moral philosophy, see Peter Caws, *Sartre* (London: Routledge & Kegan Paul, 1979); John King-Farlow, "Self-Deceivers and Sartrian Seducers," *Analysis* 23 (1963):131–36; Mary Warnock, *The Philosophy of Sartre* (London: Hutchinson & Co., 1965), pp. 50–60.

this article, Freud (1938/1957) postulated that the ego of a person in analysis must, when young, "have behaved in a remarkable manner" under the influence of "a powerful trauma" (p. 372). The child must have been tormented both by the desire to satisfy a strong instinct and by fear of the dangers that might ensue through doing so. The response is a split whereby the child both satisfies the instinct symbolically and rejects any knowledge concerning the matter:

> The two contrary reactions to the conflict persist as the center-point of a split in the ego. The whole process seems so strange to us because we take for granted the synthetic nature of the workings of the ego. But we are clearly at fault in this. The synthetic function of the ego, though it is of such extraordinary importance, is subject to particular conditions and is liable to a whole series of disturbances. (p. 373)

By means of the split ego, Freud thought to do away with the paradox 10 while allowing that the process did seem strange. Others have argued, in a similar vein, that a split self or even several selves are at work in self-deception to guard against anxiety-producing knowledge (Fingarette, 1969; Rorty, 1972).

Yet on closer inspection the contradiction remains. The view of the 11 split ego or self is but another metaphor—and an even more personalized one—for the mind in conflict. No more than the image of the self keeping secrets from itself or the unconscious from the conscious can it explain the complex defense mechanisms to which human beings resort, nor avert the paradox of both knowing and not knowing the same thing at the same time, both keeping a secret and ignoring it.

Neither such mutually secretive parts of the ego or the self, nor even 12 the deception by a split ego or self, can be shown to be either present or absent in any one person. As a result, someone presumed to be lying to himself—about incestuous fantasies, for example, or hatred too painful to confront—has no convincing way to deny the fact. Every effort at refuting the notion can arguably be seen as further proof of resistance, and of the force with which one part of the self is suppressing the secret truth. Anyone can then impute such "secrets" to anyone else, and point to a disavowal as further proof of their existence. A glance at the psychiatric literature will yield innumerable examples of such reasoning. A person's secrets, in such an extended view, may then turn out to encompass not only all that he knowingly conceals but also what he has forgotten or never noticed, and even all that he is imagined to be keeping from consciousness or from part of his ego.

The concept of "self-deception," and those of "split self," "bad faith," 13 "false consciousness," and "defense mechanisms" are nevertheless compelling metaphors. They point to internal conflicts and self-imposed defeats that we all recognize as debilitating. These metaphors are surely not empty ones: they remind us of all that stands in the way of perceiving and thinking. We cannot easily do without these metaphors; the danger comes when we begin to take them for *explanations*. As metaphors, they help us to see the paradoxes of human failure to perceive and react; as explanations of how the paradoxes are overcome, they short-circuit understanding and become misleading in their own right—one more way in which we avoid trying to understand the complexity that underlies our experience of paradox. They function then as what I. A. Richards (1925) called "premature ultimates," bringing inquiry to an end too suddenly (p. 40).

At such times, these concepts blur the distinction between intentional 14 concealment and ignorance; between lies and all the other ways in which one can influence perception and action; and between deceiving and being deceived. As a result, they permit some people to impute clear-cut intention, directness, and simplicity to the intricate processes of coping with information, while at the same time allowing others to dismiss the questions of responsibility and intention altogether. Each of the two responses obstructs the effort to sort out just what part individuals do play in what we take for self-deception.

REFERENCES

Bok, S. (1980). The self deceived. *Social Science Information, 19*, 923–935.
Caws, P. (1979). *Sartre.* London: Routledge & Kegan Paul.
Demos, R. (1960). Lying to oneself. *Journal of Philosophy, 57*, 588–595.
Eckstein, R., & Caruth, E. (1972). Keeping secrets. In P. L. Giovacchini (Ed.), *Tactics and techniques in psychoanalytic therapy* (pp. 200–215). London: Hogarth House.
Fingarette, H. (1969). *Self-deception.* London: Routledge & Kegan Paul.
Freud, S. (1957). Splitting of the ego in the defensive process. In J. Strachey (Ed. and Trans.), *Collected papers* (Vol. 5, pp. 372–75). London: Hogarth Press. (Original work published 1938).
Haight, M. R. (1980). *A study of self-deception.* Sussex: Harvester Press.
Hartmann, H. (1958). *Ego psychology and adaptation* (D. Rapaport, Trans.). New York: International Universities Press. (Original work published 1937).
King-Farlow, J. (1963). Self-deceivers and sartrian seducers. *Analysis, 23*, 131–136.
Meares, R. (1976). The secret. *Psychiatry, 39*, 258–265.
Richards, I. A. (1925). *Principles of literary criticism.* London: Kegan Paul, Trench, Trubner & Co.
Rorty, A. (1972). Belief and self-deception. *Inquiry, 15*, 387–410.
Rorty, A. (1980). Self-deception, akrasia, and irrationality. *Social Science Information, 19*, 905–922.
Sartre, J. P. (1943). *L'Etre et le neant* (Being and nothingness). Paris: Gallimard.
Sulzberger, C. F. (1953). Why it is hard to keep secrets. *Psychoanalysis, 2*, 37–43.
Warnock, M. (1965). *The philosophy of Sartre.* London: Hutchinson & Co.

QUESTIONS FOR ANALYSIS

1. Bok opens this selection with a series of questions (paragraphs 1 and 2). Reread the selection with these questions in mind, and then explain what role you think they play.

2. In paragraph 3, Bok contrasts self-deception with other "concepts concerning relations *between* people" (author's emphasis). What is the point of this contrast?

3. Throughout the essay, Bok uses terms associated with psychoanalysis, such as *defense mechanisms* and *repress*. Skim the essay, looking for these terms and noting whether they are defined adequately for you, as one reader. What conclusions can you draw from this selection about the importance of defining technical terms for readers?

4. Summarize Sartre's criticism of Freud's explanation of self-deception and Bok's criticism of Sartre's alternative explanation (in paragraphs 5–8). (For guidance in summarizing, see Chapter 1.)

5. To examine how writers of explanation use sources, apply the critical reading strategy of comparing and contrasting related readings to the essays by Bok and by Juan Bruce-Novoa. Notice how each writer integrates information from sources by paraphrasing or quoting. Also compare their documentation styles—how they cite sources parenthetically within the essay and in a list at the end of the essay. Write a couple of paragraphs presenting the results of your analysis.

IDEAS FOR YOUR OWN WRITING

What concepts related to human psychology would you consider trying to explain? Here are a few possibilities to get you started making your own list: depression, codependency, addiction, pleasure principle, sibling rivalry.

Choose one concept from your list that you think would be especially interesting to work with. Then write a few sentences saying what you already know about the concept, why you're interested in it, and why it might interest your readers. Write down any questions about the concept that you have as well as questions readers unfamiliar with the concept could be expected to have.

Laura Knapp

Laura Knapp wrote this explanatory essay for a freshman composition class at California State University, San Bernardino. She chose eating disorders as her topic because of her personal experience. Having suffered from anorexia for many years, she is now cured and counsels others.

My True Self Is Thin

Previewing this essay, you will notice that it opens with a quotation from a poem, an epigraph. Pause now before reading the whole essay to read and think about the epigraph. Take a few minutes to jot down your reactions. What feeling comes through to you? What does the speaker seem to want? What does she think of herself?

Then, after reading and annotating the essay, look at what you wrote about the epigraph and add any new ideas you now have. Finally, comment on the appropriateness of the quotation for this particular explanatory essay.

I love sweets, —
> heaven
would be dying on a bed of vanilla ice cream . . .

But my true self
is thin, all profile

and effortless gestures, the sort of blond
elegant girl whose
> body is the image of her soul.

FROM "ELLEN WEST," FRANK BIDART

Every day she wakes up, goes to the kitchen and grabs an apple from the refrigerator. She takes a knife and begins to cut the apple. An hour later, after cutting the apple into two hundred pieces, she starts to arrange it creatively on the table. Another hour passes and finally she starts to eat the mutilated piece of fruit. This will be the only thing she will eat except for a few pieces of celery, just enough to keep her from passing out when running five miles.

A prize-winning high-school wrestler wakes up in the morning and is consumed by the thought of what food he will binge on today. He plans the binge carefully, deciding where he will binge and on what foods. He knows that after binging he will be so uncomfortable that he will have to vomit. Besides, if he doesn't vomit, he will not make the weight for the meet today.

What these two people suffer from are eating disorders, the first from anorexia and the second from bulimia. The severity of eating disorders is easily understood if looked at on a scale from normal to pathological. Schizophrenia, the total breakdown of ordered thought, is at the extreme end of pathology. Eating disorders are not a total breakdown but they lie next to schizophrenia because they are self-deluding as well as self-destructive. The behavior of anorexics and bulimics can lead to death if they are not corrected.

The first classification of eating disorders is anorexia nervosa. Anorexia affects one in one hundred women and one in four hundred men, according to statistics compiled by the *Medical Journal* in 1983. The statistics perhaps don't seem alarming, but the disorders ought to be.

This subclass of disorders is characterized by gross disturbances in eating behaviors. Those who have anorexia refuse to maintain their body weight at a minimal normal weight for their height and age. Anorexics have an unrelenting, intense fear of gaining weight or becoming fat. Even though they are tremendously underweight, they are plagued by a distorted body image. The disturbance in body image is manifested by the way in which a person perceives his or her body weight, size, or shape. All anorexics are preoccupied with their body size. People with this disorder say they "feel fat" or that parts of their body "feel fat" even when they are obviously underweight.

Physical changes, which harm the body, occur when the anorexic does not maintain at least 85 percent of normal body weight. For example, the anorexic may suffer from amenorrhea, the condition in which women no longer menstruate. When a woman suffers from amenorrhea, her body is unable to absorb precious minerals, like calcium. Calcium deficiency leads to rheumatism, the painful swelling of the joints. Anorexics are also more likely to break their bones because of gross calcium deficiency. Hypothermia, subnormal body temperature, is another potential result of extensive weight loss. Hypothermia can be very serious because it slows the heart rate, which decreases the circulation of blood to the vital organs. The body goes into shock and the person can die.

With anorexics, weight loss is accomplished by a severe reduction in food, coupled with extensive exercise. In one instance, a girl who was hospitalized for anorexia fought with the orderlies about a piece of lettuce. The lettuce had been served as part of the lunch but the girl refused to eat it because it was four more calories than the hospital diet required. Later that day, she slipped away to run the hospital stairs. She had to burn off those extra calories.

A few other peculiar behaviors concerning food are common to   8
anorexics. For example, anorexics often prepare elaborate meals for other
people, but limit themselves to a narrow selection of low-calorie food. It
is not uncommon for them to hoard what little food they do eat and to
conceal, crumble, or throw food away.

Most anorexics firmly deny or minimize the severity of their disorder   9
and are uninterested or unwilling to seek therapy. For those who do
come forth, the ones with a body weight of more than 15 percent below
normal are hospitalized so as to prevent death from starvation. Approximately 4 percent of all anorexics that are hospitalized die of starvation.

Bulimia nervosa is not quite as well known as anorexia nervosa. For   10
years, bulimia was categorized with anorexia. Only recently has it been
recognized as a separate eating disorder. Bulimia is characterized by
recurrent episodes of binging and purging. Binging is rapid consumption
of a large amount of food in a relatively short period of time. Purging is
the consequent removal of the food ingested either by self-induced
vomiting, diuretics, or laxatives. Bulimics also engage in strict diets,
fasting, and rigorous exercise to lose weight. Bulimics are aware that
binging does not help in the weight loss process, but   binge nonetheless. They are overconcerned with their body weight   l a great lack
of control over their eating behavior during binge   ilimic's life is
dominated by these conflicts about eating.

Binges are usually planned. Food for binging i   erally high in   11
calories and sweet-tasting, and has a texture that facilitates fast eating.
Binging is done inconspicuously and in secret. The food is gobbled down
with little chewing and once the eating has begun, the binger may seek
out more food to continue the binge. What stops the bulimic? The binge
may be terminated by abdominal discomfort, sleep, or a social interrup-
tion. Following a binge, bulimics feel compelled to purge themselves.
Induced vomiting is the most common way to release the food. It
decreases the pain and allows for more eating and ofte   educes the post-
binge anguish. The actual binges to bulimics are p   able, but self-
criticism and depression often follow.

Those with bulimia are rarely significantly unde   . They main-   12
tain a weight slightly above or below a normal w   r their body.
Bulimics rarely die of starvation but that does not   they are free
from life-threatening problems. A bulimic's heart can stop beating due to
an electrolyte imbalance. The electrolytes in our bodies are essential to
the proper functioning of our hearts. The consistent cycle of binge/
vomit/fast/binge throws off the electrolytes. When electrolyte imbalance
occurs along with dehydration and low-calorie intake the result may be
death. In one instance, a young bulimic girl joined a diet center to lose

weight. She purged herself after every meal of the low-calorie diet. The girl died a few weeks after starting the diet because of an electrolyte imbalance. Other results of severe cases of bulimia are dental erosion from the acid of the vomit and esophageal tears and strains. Bulimia is often chronic and intermittent over a number of years.

While it has not yet been established what makes an anorexic stop eating or a bulimic binge, studies have shown that the majority of the people who have eating disorders are very intelligent and bright; many were model children. It is the perfectionist in them that exaggerates the flaws in their bodies. They associate their imperfect body with failure. These people feel that if they don't have control over their bodies and eating habits, they have no control over any part of their lives. Part of the battle of fighting anorexia and bulimia could be won by educating ourselves about the disorders. Aware of the disorders and their characteristics, we could perhaps save someone from self-destruction.

QUESTIONS FOR ANALYSIS

1. Following the epigraph, Knapp begins the essay with two brief anecdotes. What purpose do these anecdotes serve? What advantages or disadvantages do you see in opening an explanatory essay in this way?

2. Knapp divides eating disorders into two subclasses—anorexia nervosa and bulimia nervosa—but explains that the two used to be categorized together. List the differences and similarities between them, and then offer your own conclusions about whether they ought to be classified as a single disorder or two distinct types of eating disorders. On what basis have you made your decision?

3. Skim the essay, looking for places where Knapp explains causes or effects. How do you know whether these causal explanations are based on certain knowledge or speculation? Why is causal explanation needed in this particular essay?

4. Reread the final paragraph and explain why you think it is or is not a good way to conclude this explanation.

5. Review Exploring Your Personal Response in Chapter 1. Then write a 300–400-word personal response to the Knapp selection, choosing one of the following topics:

    Write about your personal associations with anything in the reading, such as an image, idea, or example.

    Write about this essay and another reading, book, or movie it reminded you of.

After you have written your response, reread it thoughtfully. In two or three sentences, say what you have learned about this selection by writing an extended response to it.

IDEAS FOR YOUR OWN WRITING

Knapp chose to write about eating disorders because she knows about it firsthand. What do you know about that you could explain to your classmates? You don't have to be an expert—you can always do some research—but choosing a topic that you know something about increases the chances that your explanatory writing will be interesting to readers because it is interesting to you.

Make a list of possible topics you could write about. It might help first to list categories such as sports, music, and other hobbies. Also list phenomena relating to personal experience, like twinship, cultural customs, and Alzheimer's disease. Under these headings, list anything you'd like to try to explain. Under music, for example, you might include harmony and fusion. Think about which items on your list other readers are likely to want to learn more about.

A GUIDE TO EXPLANATORY WRITING

As the selections you have read in this section suggest, essays explaining concepts are both informative and interesting to read. They help us understand unfamiliar ideas or learn more about things with which we may already be familiar. Writers of explanation avoid entering into controversy or asserting arguable points of their own; their purpose is to present information that is primarily factual. Clear organization is crucial, as is careful definition of what readers need to know, review of what they are likely to know already, and clarification of what may be confusing to them.

Explaining concepts can be particularly satisfying as a way of exploring your own knowledge of a topic and becoming expert in your understanding. The guide to writing that follows will help you at every stage in the process of composing an explanatory essay, from choosing a concept and organizing your strategies to evaluating and revising your draft.

The Writing Task

Write an essay that explains a concept to particular readers unfamiliar with the concept. The concept may be one that you are already familiar with or one that you are just now learning about yourself. Your purpose is to help your readers understand the concept and to give them some sense of why it is important that they make the effort to learn about it.

Invention

The following activities can help you get started gathering the information you will need to explain a concept. Work deliberately through these preliminary stages of invention. The more time and thought you put in now, the closer your first draft will come to satisfying your own and your readers' needs and expectations. Beginning with choosing a concept, these activities will help you to explore what you already know, consider what your readers need to know in order to understand the concept and appreciate its importance, gather and sort through your information, decide on which strategies to use in presenting your information, and find a tentative thesis or main point to focus your explanation.

CHOOSING A CONCEPT. Since explanations of concepts encompass nearly any subject you could imagine, the possibilities may seem dizzying. How do you go about finding a concept? Experienced writers begin the process by listing possibilities.

Before you start your own list, first review the Ideas for Your Own Writing that follow each reading selection in this chapter. On your list, include concepts that you already know about as well as those you would like to learn about. Try listing possible concepts in the following categories, which other students have found very helpful:

- a concept you studied in a course: photosynthesis, socialization, democracy, symbolism, auteurism
- a concept related to your personal experience or connected to a hobby or sport you enjoy: dyslexia, vertigo, floating, balance, contrapuntal harmony, monsters
- a concept related to an ordinary event or activity or phenomenon you are curious about: bird migration, internal combustion, allergies, optical illusions, dream interpretation
- a concept related to a current danger to public health, the environment, or the social order: poverty, acid rain, winter depression, alcoholism, safe sex

Once you have compiled a list of possible concepts, choose one that truly interests you, one you feel eager to write about and to learn more about.

EXPLORING YOUR CONCEPT. When writers are drawn to a concept, they will often invest some time exploring it in writing before they begin drafting. In this way, they can discover what they already know about the concept and determine what they need to find out. Take a few minutes now to write down whatever you know about the topic you have chosen. Write quickly, without planning or organizing. Feel free to write in phrases or word lists, as well as in sentences. You might also want to make drawings or charts. Write without stopping for several minutes, putting down everything you know about this concept and why you find it interesting and worth knowing about.

ANALYZING YOUR READERS. Since you will be writing for particular readers, you need to consider what they already know and think about the concept. Remember that your aim is not merely to explain it to them, but also to arouse their interest in it and to make them appreciate its significance.

One way to anticipate readers' needs and expectations is to write an imaginary dialogue between you and one of your readers. This requires you to play both roles: asking the kinds of questions you would ask if you were in the same position as your reader and trying to answer the questions. Keep your dialogue going for at least one full page, but push to sustain it for several pages. The longer you can make it, the more territory you will cover.

FINDING OUT MORE ABOUT YOUR CONCEPT. You may already have all the information you need to explain the concept to your particular readers. If, however, you need more information, you can get it by doing research at the library or interviewing an expert on the topic. Before you begin, check with your instructor to discover whether there are any special requirements such as that you turn in photocopies of all your written sources or use a particular documentation style.

Finding information at the library. The best place to start your research is your college library. Figure out the subject headings that you should consult for information on your topic, and then look in the card catalog, in encyclopedias (both general and specialized), in bibliographies, and in periodical indexes. If your library has open stacks, you can probably find a lot of information just by finding the right area and browsing. The appendix Strategies for Research and Documentation provides detailed guidance for finding information at a library.

One thing you should look for in your research is authoritative opinions and information. Once you have identified the experts on your topic, look for articles, books, and interviews by and with them. Find out their opinions, and see if anything they have said helps you understand your concept better. You can quote them directly, or you can summarize or paraphrase their words.

Consulting an expert. Is there someone very knowledgeable about your subject who might be helpful? If you are writing about a concept from another college course, for example, the teaching assistant or professor might be someone to consult. Not only could such a person answer questions, but also he or she might direct you to important or influential articles or books. (See the section on Interviews in the appendix.)

DECIDING WHICH STRATEGIES TO USE. Once you have some idea of what your readers need to know about the concept and you have gathered a wealth of information about it, you need to sort through the information and make some decisions about your presentation. The following questions correspond to particular explaining strategies (listed in parentheses). Answer these questions by writing a sentence or two on each. Not only will answering them help you determine which strategies to use, but it also will highlight any areas of information you might consider researching further.

> What term or terms are used to name the concept and what do they mean? (Defining)
>
> With what other concepts does it belong and how can it be broken down into classes? (Classifying and dividing)
>
> How is it like and unlike related concepts? (Comparing and contrasting)
>
> What is a particular example or instance of it? (Illustrating)
>
> How does it happen or how do you do it? (Narrating the process)
>
> What are its known causes or effects? (Explaining causes or effects)

FINDING A TENTATIVE MAIN POINT OR THESIS. Although your thesis may change as you draft and revise your explanation, stating it now will help you to make decisions as you plan your draft.

Begin by rereading what you have already written. As you read, keep your readers' needs and expectations in mind. Write nonstop for ten minutes, trying to answer these questions as you write: What makes this concept interesting to me? What is most important about it? Why should my readers bother to read about it? What significance or implications might it have for their lives? When you have finished writing, read over what you have written, and write one or two sentences that sum up the point you want to get across to your readers.

Drafting

Before you begin drafting, pause to review what you have written in response to the invention activities. Mark anything you think is especially interesting in your notes, anything you think will help readers understand the concept and appreciate its importance. Look for specifics—examples, anecdotes, facts, comparisons—that you could use to clarify the concept for readers. If you've researched the concept, note any quotations that are particularly apt for your discussion. Make a list of any additional information you think you might need. As you plan and draft the essay, you may find that you can do without this additional information or that it really is essential. In drafting, you will be making all kinds of decisions; the following guidelines are designed to help you begin by setting goals and planning the organization of your essay.

SETTING GOALS. Setting goals involves considering carefully what you want to accomplish in the essay and deciding on how you might achieve these goals. You will find that keeping your goals in mind as you plan and draft will make the writing go easier and faster. Here are some questions you might want to consider.

- What do my readers know about the concept? How do I present information that will be new to them? If you assume that your readers are somewhat familiar with the concept, you might follow Stone's lead and review what is certain knowledge and what is still unknown about the concept. Or you might do as Bok does and demonstrate the problematic nature of the concept by showing how attempts to explain it fall short. If, on the other hand, you assume as Seebohm does that the concept will be brand new to readers, your challenge is to find ways to make it relate to what they do know.

- How do I begin? What kind of opening is likely to capture my readers' attention? Quammen uses a witty title and song lyrics to capture readers' attention. Knapp uses an arresting epigraph followed by two quick anecdotes Seebohm begins with an anecdote. Bok and Stone pose questions for readers to consider.

- What persona is it appropriate for me to adopt in this particular writing situation? Seebohm plays the role of the interpreter and synthesizer. Quammen entertains as he explains. Zukav is a kind of enthusiast, trying to instill in readers his own sense of the concept's significance.

- How can I orient readers so that they don't get confused or bogged down? Two of the most common orienting devices are forecasting statements and transitions between key points and strategies. Good examples of forecasting can be found in the selections by Bruce-Novoa and Knapp. Transitions appear in every essay. You might look, for example, at Seebohm, Stone, and Bok. Many of the writers, such as Quammen and Seebohm, also use rhetorical questions to lead readers from one point to the next. When the explanation is especially complicated, writers like Zukav and Quammen insert summary statements to help readers clarify their understanding.

- How do I conclude the explanation? Some explanations conclude with summary statements, but most reemphasize the thesis. Seebohm, for instance, concludes by encouraging readers to put this new concept to use. Quammen reminds readers of what parthenogenesis is and why it is important, but he manages to end as he began, on a humorous note. Stone brings his history up to the modern age and suggests how the concept is being changed. Knapp suggests that understanding of eating disorders could lead readers to help someone suffering from one.

PLANNING YOUR ORGANIZATION. The goals you have set should help you decide what points you want to make and how to sequence them. You might want to try out different plans, but don't feel committed to any of them since drafting can itself lead you in new directions.

Having set specific goals, you are ready to plan the organization of your essay. Begin by making a tentative outline of the points you will want to make. Then consider carefully the order of these points in light of what your readers are likely to know about the concept. You could plan your essay around a series of implicit or explicit questions as Quammen does, follow a simple chronological plan as Stone does, or take up alternate explanations as Bok does.

You might want to try out different plans before drafting, but be sure that the plan you decide to follow is appropriate to your readers and focuses on the main point you want to get across.

Revising

You might begin your revision by analyzing your draft in light of the questions for analyzing basic features at the beginning of this chapter. If possible, ask someone else to analyze your draft in the same way. As you revise, be especially attentive to ways in which you can strengthen your focus, organization, content, and readability.

REVISING TO SHARPEN THE FOCUS. Read your draft carefully, looking for ways to sharpen the focus of your essay. As you were drafting, you may have decided to make a different main point about the information. If necessary, remove any information not directly related to your main point.

REVISING TO CLARIFY THE ORGANIZATION. Make an outline of your draft so that you can consider its underlying structure. Decide whether this structure is appropriate for your information, readers, and main point. Consider other ways in which the essay might be organized. Try moving parts of your essay around to determine if another organization might be more effective.

REVISING TO STRENGTHEN THE CONTENT. Your draft should be complete and authoritative, telling readers everything they need to know— but no more than they need to know—to convey your point about the concept. Determine whether you have provided enough substance in your essay or whether you should do further research in order to locate additional information. Decide whether all the material in your present draft is relevant and informative. Consider replacing overly familiar content with new or surprising content.

REVISING TO IMPROVE READABILITY. In order to grasp and remember the new information presented, readers should be able to proceed through an explanation of a concept efficiently. Consider whether your beginning helps readers to understand the plan of your essay. Be sure you have provided enough cues in the body of the essay to keep readers on track— timely paragraphing, forecasts, transitions, brief summaries. Read your draft slowly, sentence by sentence, looking for gaps and digressions. Do whatever you can to help your readers move smoothly through your essay.

When you have a revision, proofread to correct all errors in punctuation, usage, and spelling. Careless mistakes will detract from the readability of your essay.

CHAPTER SIX

Evaluation

Should we see the new Steven Spielberg film? Is Alice Walker's latest novel as good as *The Color Purple*? Does the assistant manager where you work deserve a promotion? Which of these textbook explanations of tropism is better, and why? How's the food in that new Vietnamese restaurant? If I buy a Toyota Tercel, will I get my money's worth? Which college is best for me?

These are some of the many occasions when evaluations are made—at home, at work, in school. We evaluate people, films, books, ideas, restaurants, events, objects, and places; often we are the ones being evaluated—by teachers, employers, the IRS.

Most of these everyday evaluations are casual, offhand expressions of taste such as "I really liked *Batman*. It's a great film." Usually, we state what we like or dislike without bothering to explain our judgment. Occasionally, however, someone asks the reason for one of our judgments and we can either say, "I don't know—I just know what I like," or we can give reasons and support and in so doing discover the basis for our judgment.

As a college student, you will be asked to write evaluations in many situations. You might be asked to evaluate a book or an article, judge a scientific hypothesis against the results of an experiment, evaluate the impact of a theory, or assess the value of two conflicting interpretations. You will also undoubtedly read evaluative writing in your courses and be tested on what you have read.

Written evaluations will almost certainly play an important part in your work. On the job, you will probably be evaluated periodically and may have to evaluate people whom you supervise. It is also likely that you will be asked your opinion of various plans or proposals under consideration, and your ability to make fair and reasonable evaluations will affect your chances for promotion.

Learning to write and read evaluative writing is valuable in a more general way as well. Writing evaluations builds your confidence in your own judgment. By supporting your opinions instead of merely asserting them, you gain practice in reasoning systematically. You learn to examine your own assumptions, to discover what you think and why, and come to understand better your own values.

A GUIDE TO READING EVALUATIVE WRITING

To begin your study of evaluative writing, you will first look closely at an essay by journalist and essayist Michael Kinsley. Closely analyzing Kinsley's writing will provide a foundation for the serious study of evaluative writing this chapter encourages. As you become a more critical, insightful reader of evaluations, your own evaluative writing will be more vivid and engaging.

As the initial step in your analysis, you will annotate the Kinsley selection. The next exercise asks you to take inventory of your annotations in order to disclose a pattern of meaning you have discovered. In the third exercise, guided by special questions, you will report what you have learned in analyzing the unique features of evaluative writing. Finally, the concluding exercise invites you to write a brief exploratory essay, consolidating what you have learned about the Kinsley selection and trying out your own ideas about it or extending your personal response to it.

The time you invest now in annotating, analyzing, and writing will pay off richly as you read, write about, and discuss the essays in this chapter. It will also give you confidence that you can successfully complete your own evaluative essay.

Annotating As You Read

Perhaps the most basic, and most useful, strategy for reading attentively and critically is annotating. Pencil in hand as you read, you are ready to record on the page any comments, questions, definitions, or insights—whatever crosses your mind—about a piece of writing. As an illustration, note how we have annotated the following brief passage from an evaluation, by Jason Thornton of rock band REM and their album *Document*, that appears in its entirety later in this chapter:

Reason for judgment contrasts paradoxes (Criterion: style?)	REM has always been a band of contrasts and paradoxes. Their first album, Murmur, sounded like folk music, a style that generally uses acoustic instruments, except that REM used electric guitars. By all rights, the
Example	
Example	music of their past five albums would be ideal for keyboards or synthesizers, but REM rarely uses a single keyboard track. Instead, they rely on the simple trio of Peter Buck's wide range of guitar playing, Mike Mill's rough
Contrast: "simple"/"complex"	bass lines, and Bill Berry's droning, occasionally militant drums. Despite the simple methods, REM forges complex songs through a mixture of melodies, simple chords, numerous rhythms, and staggering vocal harmonies. Once
Is this convincing?	together, this mixture forms a swirly, moody track that manages not to sound muddy, bogged down, or inconsistent. Sometimes with REM their finest points seem to be
"finest points"/ "roughest edges"	their roughest edges: each feedback whine from the guitar amp and rough vocal from singer Michael Stipe seems well planned and strategically placed.
	Often REM shows its originality in the sharp contrast between song lyrics and their music. Many times REM
"bitter"/"upbeat"	will use bitter lyrics along with upbeat music. There is Document's "Disturbance at the Heron House" which is
Example	made up of a catchy, popular tune while its lyrics describe a democracy gone mad by way of mob rule. The band
"cheerful"/"dark"	plays a cheerful-sounding, sixties-influenced tune as Stipe discusses a darker subject. . . .

For more on annotating, pause now to review the guidelines in Chapter 1 and the model annotations on the excerpt from "Letter from Birmingham Jail." Note particularly the Checklist for Annotating.

Exercise 1

Annotate Michael Kinsley's "Saint Ralph" as you read. Reread it at least once, continuing to annotate as you reread. Your purpose is to focus your attention on the text, to read as thoughtfully—as critically—as possible. Annotate details you admire as well as things you question or challenge, mark noteworthy stylistic devices or writing strategies, and write down any personal responses. Record your insights and reactions directly on and around the text itself.

"Saint Ralph," by Michael Kinsley, is an evaluation of Ralph Nader, the attorney and self-appointed consumer advocate, who began his career in 1965 by attacking auto industry executives for marketing a car (the Chevrolet Corvair) that they knew to be a safety hazard. Nader's book, *Unsafe at Any Speed*, contributed to the commercial failure of the Corvair and led to a series of laws mandating auto safety features. His activities spawned a generation of idealistic young consumer advocates, dubbed Nader's Raiders.

Kinsley, a former Nader's Raider, is a writer for the *New Republic*, the journal in which this essay was first published. "Saint Ralph" is not a piece of personal reminiscence, however, but a hard-nosed evaluation of Nader as a public figure, written on the twentieth anniversary of Nader's landmark exposé of the auto industry. Even though Kinsley takes Nader seriously, he can't resist poking fun at him. As you read, notice the way he has seasoned his praise with a few grains of satire.

Saint Ralph
Michael Kinsley

1   I worked several years for Ralph Nader, and he's actually quite warm and funny in person. Nevertheless, his is the classic zealot's worldview, paranoid and humorless, and his vision of the ideal society—regulations for all contingencies of life, warning labels on every french fry, and a citizenry on hair-trigger alert for violations of its personal space—is not one many others would care to share with him.

2   But reasonable people don't move the world. On the 20th anniversary of *Unsafe at Any Speed*, his tract against dangerous automobiles, no living American is responsible for more concrete improvements in the society we actually do inhabit than Ralph Nader.

3   In all statistical probability, at least several dozen of you who are reading this . . . would be dead today if Nader hadn't single-handedly invented the issue of auto safety. His long campaign for mandatory air bags may bore most people and enrage a few. But would even these people want cars without seat belts, padded dashboards, collapsible steering wheels, and shatter-resistant glass? On matters ranging from the Occupational Safety and Health

Administration to the Freedom of Information Act (just two of his monuments), Nader stands accused—sometimes justly—of going "too far." But without the people who go too far, we wouldn't go far enough.

Although Nader's personal popularity has diminished, and the causes he favors are out of fashion, his achievements are as immutable as FDR's. President Reagan may inveigh against burdensome government regulation, just as he inveighs against government spending. He may attempt changes at the margin. But he would no more get the government out of the business of protecting consumers, workers and the environment than he would dismantle Social Security. Americans like clean air and water, safe transportation, open government, honest advertisements, uncontaminated meat. No electable politician would attempt to push back the clock by 20 years.

I wonder how many conservative businessmen, even, would care to return to the days when anyone could light up a cigarette next to you on a long airplane flight, and when an airline could overbook and bump you with no explanation or compensation. No-smoking sections and airline bumping rules—minor bits of Naderism—seemed like quixotic obsessions when first proposed. Now they are taken for granted.

. . . Nader knows little of ordinary human appetites. This gives him his fanatic's strength of purpose. But it also sometimes leads him astray by blinding him to the benefits that come with the risks he campaigns against. The pleasure of a hot dog means nothing to Ralph. (He calls it "America's most dangerous unguided missile.") If everyone lived like Ralph Nader, we could dispense with nuclear power and not worry about replacing the energy. In this world of sinners, though, not everyone wants to live on raw vegetables and set the thermostat at 60. Intelligent public policy requires trade-offs that the fanatic is ill-equipped and indisposed to make.

Nader's other great weakness as a reformer is that he's a prisoner of the legal mind-set. He believes in the infinite power of lawyers to achieve both bad and good. "The ultimate goal of this movement," says a recent Nader press release, "is to give all citizens more rights and remedies for resolving their grievances and for achieving a better society." But it's open to doubt, to say the least, whether the better society is one where all grievances are thought of as a matter of legal rights and remedies, to be enforced by lawyers and judges.

These days Ralph Nader is something less than a colossus bestriding American society, but still something more than another colorful Washington character. Over two decades he and his ever-replenished band of disciples have operated out of a series of ratty offices, generally moving in shortly before the developers arrive to tear the place down and put up another fancy building for fancy lawyers (some of them, no doubt, getting rich off the very laws and agencies Ralph created).

He still wears those awful suits and lives in that same   9 studio apartment. Some cynics think the asceticism is an act. And it's true that his story about wearing shoes bought at the Army PX in 1959 is wearing as thin as those shoes must be. But if a good marketing sense were a bar to canonization, there would be few saints.

At age 52, Nader may be softening a little. He some-   10 times shows up at those business parties that pass for social life in Washington. I even think I saw him eating a piece of cheese at one a few weeks ago. His narrow lapels, pointy shoes, and skinny ties are now the height of fashion, offering some hope that the day will come when his clothes will be out again and his politics will be back.

For 20 years Washington has been wondering, Where's   11 the catch? Will he sell out for money, or will he run for office? Those are the normal options. But Ralph Nader is not a normal person. Operating on the mental fringe where self-abnegation blurs into self-obsession, Ralph is living proof that there isn't much difference between a fanatic and a saint. I'll bet you Mother Teresa is impossible to deal with, too.

Inventorying Your Annotations

Once you have annotated a reading with your insights and thoughts, you'll want to study your annotations for their special meaning. The best way to do this is by taking inventory of your annotations, to discover any patterns or key repetitions.

Before completing Exercise 2, review the guidelines and illustration for the Inventory of Annotations in Chapter 1.

Exercise 2

Inventory the annotations you made on "Saint Ralph," looking for meaningful patterns in your response to the selection.

Analyzing the Basic Features
of Evaluative Writing

In addition to annotating a text to record your initial impressions and inventorying your annotations to discover their patterns of meaning, you can analyze the basic features of a piece of writing, in this case those qualities that make it distinctively evaluative.

Look back at Identifying and Evaluating Basic Features in Chapter 1. Although the questions there are different from the ones you will find in this chapter, the answers illustrate what a thoughtful analysis of basic features might look like.

Exercise 3

Analyze "Saint Ralph" by answering the following questions. You will want to reread the selection with each question in mind, and you may want to annotate further.

Write out your answers to the questions.

1. *How successfully does the writer orient readers to the subject of the evaluation?* If readers and the writer know the subject being evaluated equally well—they all just saw the same movie, went to the same restaurant, or listened to the same record album—the writer need only announce the subject. Nearly always in evaluative writing situations, however, readers know little if anything about the subject being evaluated. Consequently, the writer must present or describe the subject to readers, giving them adequate context for following the evaluation. Since the writer's purpose is to evaluate the subject, not report on it, the presentation of the subject should be no longer than necessary to orient readers to the evaluation.

Ask yourself the following: How does the writer present the subject at the beginning (or soon after the beginning) of the essay? What kind of information is presented? What does the writer seem to assume readers already know about the subject? Given the writing situation and intended readers, how successfully does the writer's presentation of the subject orient readers to the evaluation?

2. *What is the writer's judgment?* The writer's judgment can be considered the thesis in evaluative writing: it indicates whether the writer approves or disapproves of the subject being evaluated. Some evaluations, however, discuss both good and bad qualities of their subjects, without at first appearing to make a judgment. Such evaluations, to

qualify as evaluations, must nevertheless indicate the writer's judgment. Most evaluations assert their judgments explicitly, sometimes even restating them several times. In these cases, you will have little difficulty indentifying the writer's judgment.

Ask yourself: Does the writer waffle (merely discussing good and bad points), or clearly make a judgment? Where in the essay is the judgment presented? Is the judgment stated explicitly, or only implied? Should the judgment be stated sooner? Should it be repeated? where?

3. *What are the criteria on which the judgment is based? How appropriate are they for the readers?* Criteria underlie every evaluation. They provide the basis for the evaluation or the standards by which the subject can be judged. For example, a film reviewer might evaluate a movie for a general adult readership on the basis of acting, story line, unity, cinematography, and direction.

Criteria must be appropriate to the subject: you would not evaluate an off-road vehicle and a sports car or a gourmet restaurant and a fast-food restaurant on the basis of exactly the same criteria. Criteria must also be appropriate to the readers: criteria for evaluating a movie could be technical for readers who make films or are film buffs, but nontechnical for the average moviegoer. Writers may sometimes state explicitly or even justify their criteria, but usually they are implicit. The writer's argument supporting the judgment—the reasons and evidence that may convince readers to consider the writer's judgment—derive from the criteria.

Ask yourself the following questions: What are the criteria underlying the evaluation? (One or more criteria may be stated or implied.) Which criteria, if any, seem inappropriate to the subject or readers? Which criteria, if any, has the writer failed to consider? Does the writer need to define or justify any of the criteria?

4. *What reasons does the writer give to justify the judgment? How convincing are the reasons?* With reasons, the writer answers the reader's question, Why did you make this judgment about this subject? Reasons and their supporting evidence are the heart of the writer's argument to justify the judgment. For example, a reviewer might praise a movie because the actors seem well suited for their roles, the actors performed uniformly well, one actor performed superbly, the theme was troubling but important for viewers to confront, and the conclusion was ambiguous but still satisfying and appropriate. (Notice that reasons related to acting derive from the criterion "acting," while reasons concerned with theme and conclusion derive from different criteria. A single criterion can generate one or several reasons.)

What reasons does the writer give to justify the judgment? List them. For the writer's purpose and readers, which are the most convincing reasons? the least convincing?

5. *What kinds of evidence does the writer collect to support the reasons? Is the evidence appropriate and relevant? Is there enough of it?* Evaluators must go well beyond listing reasons to create a convincing argument. They must also amass relevant evidence to support the reasons. In fact, the bulk of an evaluative essay is taken up by evidence. Evidence comes primarily from the subject being evaluated, but also from other subjects it may be compared to and from the writer's experience. Evidence from the subject provides examples that support the reasons. These examples may appear in an evaluative essay as facts, details, quotations, or paraphrases and summaries. The writer's experience may provide observations, anecdotes, and inventive analogies.

What kinds of evidence does the writer offer? For the intended readers, does the evidence seem appropriate and convincing? Which evidence seems most supportive of a reason? Which seems least supportive?

6. *If comparisons are used, what do they add to the argument?* Writers of evaluations typically use comparison to assess the subject's value relative to the value of another well-known subject. Comparison may be used in this way to praise or to condemn.

What comparisons does the writer make? What role does each comparison play in the essay? Is each one well developed enough to be convincing to readers?

7. *How confident are you of the writer's authority? What impression do you have of the writer from the tone of the essay?* When you read an evaluative piece, you make your own evaluation of the subject, and you do this partially by judging the writer. If you trust that the writer knows the subject and is fair and unbiased, then you will be likely to accept the judgment. As a critical reader, therefore, you form an opinion of the writer both from what is said and how it is said.

How would you describe the tone of the essay? (Is it skeptical, mocking, cautious, enthusiastic, humorous, or something else?) Does this seem to you the appropriate tone, given the writer's subject and readers? If you find the writing unauthoritative, how would you account for this failure? If you find it authoritative, how would you account for the writer's success? What is your general impression of the writer?

8. *How effectively is the evaluation organized?* There are no formats or simple rules that writers of evaluation can follow. In general, they try to emphasize their strongest arguments by placing them either at the beginning or at the ending of the essay. Most evaluations set out their

judgment early in the essay and restate it at the end. A brief description of the subject may open the essay. To guide the reader—particularly if the essay is long and complicated—statements forecasting the main points of the argument and signaling shifts from one point to another may be injected at crucial intervals.

How is the essay organized? For the intended readers, what advantages or disadvantages do you see in this organization? Would the evaluation be more convincing if the reasons were in a different order? Do the reasons form a logical sequence? What strategies does the writer adopt to keep the reader on track? Where, if anywhere, did you get off track? How effective are the opening and closing?

Exploring Your Personal Response

One other way of focusing your response to an evaluative essay is by taking the time to record your thoughts in a more extended piece of writing. Basically, such an exercise can help you to consider how the evaluation relates to your own impressions, to explore your understanding and define further your unique perspective on what you've read.

Exercise 4

Write 300–400 words (two or three handwritten pages) about "Saint Ralph." Choose one of the suggestions listed in Exploring Your Personal Response in Chapter 1.

James Agee

James Agee (1909–1955) was a major American writer, famous for his reportage, reviews, plays, and novels. Born in Knoxville, he is perhaps best known for his poetic novel *A Death in the Family*, which was awarded the Pulitzer Prize in 1958. Among his other works are *Let Us Now Praise Famous Men* (1941), a textual commentary accompanying Walker Evans's photographs of poor tenant farmers; and a posthumous collection of movie reviews, *Agee on Film*.

The Treasure
of the Sierra Madre

For many years, Agee was a celebrated film critic for the *Nation*, a weekly magazine still in circulation today. In 1944, W. H. Auden called Agee's reviews "the most remarkable regular event in American journalism today." This selection is Agee's *Nation* review of *The Treasure of the Sierra Madre*, a classic American movie frequently shown on television and in revival houses, usually as part of a series of films honoring its director, John Huston, or showcasing one of its stars, Humphrey Bogart.

Reviews are one of the most common forms of written evaluations. Because reviews date quickly, though, we've chosen to include a review of a classic rather than a more contemporary film. Consequently, we recommend that, if you haven't seen it already, you view *The Treasure* on videotape. (Check with a video rental store in your area or your college video library.) Doing so will increase your ability to analyze Agee's review and also introduce you to some of the decisions and choices evaluative writers face.

Before you begin reading Agee's review, recall any John Huston films you've seen—*The Maltese Falcon* (1941), *The African Queen* (1952), *Annie* (1982), *Prizzi's Honor* (1985). Also reflect on likely standards or criteria that might guide an experienced film reviewer's evaluation of a film for adult moviegoers. Take a moment to list these before you start reading.

Several of the best people in Hollywood grew, noticeably, during their years away at war; the man who grew most impressively, I thought, as an artist, as a man, in intelligence, in intransigence, and in an ability to put through fine work against difficult odds, was John Huston, whose *San Pietro* and *Let There Be Light*[1] were full of evidence of this many-sided

---

[1]*San Pietro* and *Let There Be Light* are documentaries Huston made as part of an Army film unit during World War II. [Eds.]

growth. I therefore looked forward with the greatest eagerness to the work he would do after the war.

His first movie since the war has been a long time coming, but it was certainly worth waiting for. *The Treasure of the Sierra Madre* is Huston's adaptation of B. Traven's novel of the same title. It is not quite a completely satisfying picture, but on the strength of it I have no doubt at all that Huston, next only to Chaplin,[2] is the most talented man working in American pictures, and that this is one of the movie talents in the world which is most excitingly capable of still further growth. *The Treasure* is one of very few movies made since 1927 which I am sure will stand up in the memory and esteem of qualified people alongside the best of the silent movies. And yet I doubt that many people will fully realize, right away, what a sensational achievement, or plexus of achievement, it is. You will seldom see a good artist insist less on his artistry; Huston merely tells his story so straight and so well that one tends to become absorbed purely in that; and the story itself—a beauty—is not a kind which most educated people value nearly enough, today.

This story and Huston's whole handling of it are about as near to folk art as a highly conscious artist can get; both also approach the global appeal, to the most and least sophisticated members of an audience, which the best poetic drama and nearly all the best movies have in common. Nominally an adventure story, this is really an exploration of character as revealed in vivid action; and character and action yield revelations of their own, political, metaphysical, moral, above all, poetic. The story unfolds so pleasurably on the screen that I will tell as little as possible of it here. Three American bums of the early 1920s (Walter Huston, Humphrey Bogart, Tim Holt) run into lottery luck in Tampico and strike into the godforsaken mountains of Mexico in search of gold. The rest of the story merely demonstrates the development of their characters in relation to hardship and hard work, to the deeply primitive world these modern primitives are set against, to the gold they find, and to each other. It is basically a tragic story and at times a sickeningly harsh one; most of it is told as cheerfully brutal sardonic comedy.

This may be enough to suggest how rich the story is in themes, semi-symbols, possible implications, and potentialities as a movie. Huston's most wonderful single achievement is that he focuses all these elements as simply as rays in a burning-glass: all you see, unless you look sharp, is a story told so truly and masterfully that I suspect the picture's best audience is the kind of men the picture is about, who will see it only by chance.

---

[2]Charlie Chaplin, a celebrated silent filmmaker and clown. [Eds.]

But this single achievement breaks down into many. I doubt we shall ever see a film more masculine in style; or a truer movie understanding of character and of men; or as good a job on bumming, a bum's life, a city as a bum sees it; or a more beautiful job on a city; or a finer portrait of Mexico and Mexicans (compare it with all the previous fancy-filter stuff for a definitive distinction between poetry and poeticism); or a crueler communication of absolute desolateness in nature and its effect on men (except perhaps in *Greed*[3]); or a much more vivid communication of hardship, labor, and exhaustion (though I wish these had been brutally and meticulously presented rather than skillfully sketched); or more intelligent handling of amateurs and semi-professionals (notably the amazing character who plays Gold-Hat, the bandit leader); or a finer selective eye for location or a richer understanding of how to use it; or scenes of violence or building toward violence more deeply authentic and communicative (above all in Huston's terrific use of listlessness); or smarter casting than that of Tim Holt as the youngest bum and that of Bruce Bennett as an intrusive Texan; or better acting than Walter Huston's beautiful performance; or subtler and more skillful collusions and variations of tempo (two hours have certainly never been better used in a movie); or a finer balance, in Ted McCord's perfect camera work, in every camera set-up, in every bit of editing, of unaffectedness, and sensitiveness. (As one fine example of that blend I recommend watching for the shot of Gold-Hat reflected in muddy water, which is so subtly photographed that in this noncolor film the hat seems to shed golden light.) There is not a shot-for-shot's sake in the picture, or one too prepared-looking, or dwelt on too long. The camera is always where it ought to be, never imposes on or exploits or over-dramatizes its subject, never for an instant shoves beauty or special meaning at you. This is one of the most visually alive and beautiful movies I have ever seen; there is a wonderful flow of fresh air, light, vigor, and liberty through every shot, and a fine athlete's litheness and absolute control and flexibility in every succession and series of shots. Huston shows that he is already capable of literally anything in movies except the profoundest kind of movie inventiveness, the most extreme kind of poetic concentration, artiness, soft or apathetic or sloppy or tasteless or excessive work, and rhetoric whether good or bad. His style is practically invisible as well as practically universal in its possible good uses; it is the most virile movie style I know of; and is the purest style in contemporary movies, here or abroad.

I want to say a little more about Walter Huston; a few thousand words would suit me better. Rightly or wrongly, one thing that adds to my

---

[3]*Greed* (1924), a silent epic, directed by Erich von Stroheim. [Eds.]

confidence that the son, so accomplished already, will get better and better, is the fact that the father has done that, year after year. I can think of nothing more moving or happier than every instance in which an old man keeps right on learning, and working, and improving, as naturally and eagerly as a child learns the fundamentals of walking, talking, and everything else in sight until his parents and teachers destroy his appetite for learning. Huston has for a long time been one of the best actors in the world and he is easily the most likable; on both counts this performance crowns a lifetime. It is an all but incredible submergence in a role, and transformation; this man who has credibly played Lincoln looks small and stocky here, and is as gaily vivacious as a water bug. The character is beautifully conceived and written, but I think it is chiefly Walter Huston who gives it its almost Shakespearean wonderfulness, charm, and wisdom. In spite of the enormous amount of other talent at large in the picture, Huston carries the whole show as deftly and easily as he handles his comedy lines.

There are a few weaknesses in the picture, most of which concern me   7 so little I won't even bother to mention them. Traven's Teutonic or Melvillean[4] excitability as a poet and metaphysician sometimes, I think, misleads him—and John Huston; magnificently as Walter Huston does it, and deeply as he anchors it in flesh and blood, the Vast Gale of Purifying Laughter with which he ends the picture strikes me as unreal stuck-onto-the-character, close to arty; yet I feel tender toward this kind of cliché, if I'm right that it is one. One thing I do furiously resent is the intrusion of background-music. There is relatively little of it and some of it is better than average, but there shouldn't be any, and I only hope and assume that Huston fought the use of it. The only weakness which strikes me as fundamental, however, is deep in the story itself: it is the whole character of the man played by Bogart. This is, after all, about gold and its effects on those who seek it, and so it is also a fable about all human life in this world and about much of the essence of good and evil. Many of the possibilities implicit in this fable are finely worked out. But some of the most searching implications are missed. For the Bogart character is so fantastically undisciplined and troublesome that it is impossible to demonstrate or even to hint at the real depth of the problem, with him on hand. It is too easy to feel that if only a reasonably restrained and unsuspicious man were in his place, everything would be all right; we wouldn't even have wars. But virtually every human being carries sufficient of that character within him to cause a great deal of trouble, and

---

[4]American writer Herman Melville wrote *Moby Dick* (1851) and other heavily symbolic tales.

the demonstration of that fact, and its effects, could have made a much greater tragicomedy—much more difficult, I must admit, to dramatize. Bogart does a wonderful job with this character as written (and on its own merits it is quite a character), miles ahead of the very good work he has done before. The only trouble is that one cannot quite forget that this is Bogart putting on an unbelievably good act. In all but a few movies one would thank God for that large favor. In this one it stands out, harmfully to some extent, for everything else about the picture is selfless.

It seems worth mentioning that the only thing which holds this movie 8 short of unarguable greatness is the failure of the story to develop some of the most important potentialities of the theme. In other words, "Hollywood," for once, is accountable only for some minor flaws. This is what it was possible to do in Hollywood, if you were talented enough, had standing enough, and were a good enough fighter. . . . God knows what can be done now. But if anybody can hope to do anything, I count on Huston, who made *San Pietro* and *Let There Be Light* as an army officer and *The Treasure of the Sierra Madre* as a Hollywood writer-director.

QUESTIONS FOR ANALYSIS

1. Agee gives many reasons why he likes the movie. Some reasons he merely mentions, but others he develops with specific illustrations from the movie. What are those reasons? (Skim the review, listing each reason briefly in a phrase.) Which are mentioned, and which are developed? Why do you suppose Agee chooses to develop the ones he does?

2. Film reviewers nearly always draw comparisons between movies. What comparisons does Agee make? Would further comparisons strengthen the review? If so, what kinds of comparisons would you like to have seen?

3. Agee wrote this review shortly after the movie was released. Because readers of such reviews must be assumed to be unfamiliar with the movie, the writer must describe it before evaluating it, yet without telling any more than he or she has to. What does Agee choose to summarize from the movie? Where does he place this summary? How much space does he devote to it?

4. In paragraph 7, Agee points out some of the movie's weaknesses. Why do you think he mentions its weaknesses? How does paragraph 7 affect your response to the review?

5. How does Agee begin and end his review? How effective do you find this beginning and ending?

IDEAS FOR YOUR OWN WRITING

If you consider writing a review essay of a film, keep in mind that it is best to evaluate a film in relation to one or more other films. We recommend writing about two or more films of the same type (horror, gangster, romance, slapstick comedy, fantasy) or about two or more films by the same director or about two or more films featuring the same actor or about two or more films in a completed or continuing series (the Indiana Jones films, the Godfather films). If you limit yourself to two films, choose any two that are notably comparable or the two that are the most recent. In any of these cases you would be asserting a judgment that one film is better (or worse) than another or that one film is the best (or worst) of a group of three or more.

There is one basic requirement for a good essay review: after choosing the films, *you must see them and take careful notes.* If at all possible, see each film twice—the second time after you have chosen the criteria for your evaluation and perhaps have completed a first rough draft of your essay. Relying solely on your memory of a film will produce a thin essay that any reader will recognize as lacking authority. Fortunately, home video rentals and college video libraries make it possible for you to view (and review) all but the most recent films.

You might also consider reviewing a play or concert at a theater on campus or in your community. You would want to see the play twice, taking careful notes each time. Since concerts may not be repeated, you would want to prepare carefully, take especially comprehensive notes during the concert, and then add notes and reflections immediately after the concert. Use good judgment: it would be unwise to review a piano recital or orchestral concert if you are not closely familiar with classical music, or a rock or jazz group if you have never played one of its instruments or listened to several of its recordings.

Stan Sesser

Stan Sesser has been a reporter for the *Wall Street Journal* and has taught business reporting in the Graduate School of Journalism at the University of California, Berkeley. In 1989, for the *New Yorker* magazine, Sesser profiled a student rebellion in Burma, which unfolded in much the same way as the student rebellion in China in the spring of 1989. Besides presently undertaking diverse writing projects for several national magazines, Sesser is the Friday restaurant columnist for the *San Francisco Chronicle*.

Bayon's Incredible Deal

Newspapers and certain magazines feature restaurant reviews as readily as movie and book reviews. In this restaurant review for his *San Francisco Chronicle* column, Sesser evaluates Bayon, a local Cambodian-French restaurant. It is easy to imagine how much pleasure restaurant reviewers find in their work, but have you ever speculated about how they go about doing that work? Must they remain unknown, using a pseudonym and taking notes surreptitiously; or do they announce themselves, take photographs of the food, and interview the chef? Do they take notes at all? Do they sneak a menu out? Do they visit a restaurant more than once? How much must they know about other restaurants of a type they review? Do they need any special knowledge about the cuisine (Mexican, French, Italian, or some other) of a restaurant they review? Do they go with someone else in order to sample a greater number of menu items? As you read Sesser's review, watch for clues to how he went about evaluating Bayon.

1   While it's a common occurrence to feel ripped off by a restaurant's prices, it's a rarity indeed to discover the other side of the coin—a restaurant that's such a bargain you feel guilty enough to contemplate leaving a 50 percent tip.

2   That's exactly what happened to me when I found myself eating a $9.95 French dinner that included soup, salad, entree and dessert. It was not only good; it was actually terrific. If the chef gave lessons to cooks at many of the restaurants where the same sort of dinner is $30, the caliber of the San Francisco French food scene would rise several notches.

3   This hard-to-believe bargain is to be found at Bayon on Lombard Street, a restaurant that has always been unusual. When I first reviewed it two years ago, it was serving Franco-Khmer cuisine—the food inspired by the French colonials in Cambodia who adapted French recipes to the

necessity of using Asian ingredients. I loved every bite, but didn't love the time it took to eat a meal, since chef Dean Leng prepared the complicated dishes entirely from scratch. I think lots of others shared my sentiments, because Bayon was crowded on weekends but largely empty weeknights, when few of us feel like lingering over food for three hours.

Since Leng had had extensive training in French cooking, he got the idea of changing over most of the menu to French food, limiting the number of entrees, and standardizing the cooking to the extent that the dishes could come out quickly. Now there are two appetizers and four entrees carried over from the old Franco-Khmer menu, five French entrees that can be ordered as part of the $9.95 dinner and a few a la carte French dishes.

The verdict after two dinners at Bayon: The Franco-Khmer food is as good as ever, and all the French entrees are wonderful. Even the soup and salad are excellent—at more expensive French restaurants you wouldn't complain about spending $9.95 for that quality of soup and salad alone. My only complaint involves the baguettes (terrible) and the desserts (too sweet, except for a spectacular creme caramel). As for the time problem, now things are arriving as quickly as anyone would want them; any faster and you'd feel rushed.

Like his Franco-Khmer food, Leng's French cuisine doesn't come from cookbooks. He develops his recipes with a Cambodian eye for lightness, using no cream apart from the soup and never more than a touch of butter or oil. The unthickened sauces manage to be extremely light but at the same time filled with flavor from the intensively reduced stocks. Leng makes his sauces by grilling vegetables to carmelize the sugars and simmering them with bones of either duck, beef, pork or chicken. Lemon grass is a secret Asian ingredient used in the French sauces with great success.

Except for the grilled chicken, which while good was not quite as interesting as everything else, the entrees on the $9.95 dinner are so perfect I'd be hard-pressed to recommend any one over the others. The choices are duck confit, catfish filet meuniere, grilled pork chops, or medallions of beef in a shiitake mushroom sauce. If duck is a good test of a restaurant, confit—where it's cooked in its own fat—is even better, since the duck can easily end up a greasy mess. At Bayon, however, the two duck legs emerged tender and fat-free, accompanied by a duck liver (which in French is "foie," not "foie gras," or fattened liver, as the menu advertises). In sharp contrast to the sweet, gluey sauces so often served with duck, the confit came with a light, aromatic sauce made from duck stock, garlic, shallots, Madeira, and a tiny bit of Asian fish sauce.

Leng pays lots of attention to the quality of ingredients, something you [8] can tell immediately when you taste the pork. The two charcoal-grilled chops have been marinated in a mixture that includes rosemary, thyme, bay leaves and lemon grass, and they're served with a tangy light sauce of chopped fresh mint added to Madeira, Marsala, and a stock made from pork and chicken bones. The beef is equally high quality, a marinated skirt steak grilled and accompanied by a rich beefy sauce thickened with sauteed shiitake mushrooms. The final entree is a very fresh-tasting catfish filet, dusted with flour, cooked quickly in a skillet, and served in a version of meuniere sauce that's a vast improvement over the usual lemon and butter. To these, Leng also adds apple cider vinegar, fresh ginger and a touch of fish sauce.

The fixed-price dinner starts with soup; at both meals I had a creamy [9] vegetable soup that reflected Leng's insistence on buying organic vegetables from farmers. The salad is simple butter lettuce, with a wonderfully tangy dressing of olive oil, lemon juice, vinegar, mustard, and dill seeds, thickened by a puree of red pepper. Dessert is often jackfruit custard, a blend of this tropical fruit with coconut milk and rice flour. And if all that isn't enough for your $9.95, each entree comes with an array of vegetables, usually including yellow squash, blue lake beans and a puree of carrots with garlic and shallots.

It's definitely worth venturing from the $9.95 menu, though, to try a [10] couple of the Cambodian dishes. At least start your meal with an appetizer of the crispy little spring rolls ($5.50), or the remarkable salad of shredded steamed chicken breast tossed with shredded cabbage, carrots, and bell peppers, in a tangy, oil-free dressing ($5.50). Among the Cambodian entrees, the chicken curry ($10.25) is as good as you'll find anywhere.

Some of the French a la carte dishes are worth considering, too. The [11] snails ($5.25) have such a fine garlic butter you'll wish for better bread to mop it up. Duck a l'orange ($13.50) is a hack American/French dish I'd tend to avoid, but at Bayon for once the sauce is light and pungent instead of sickly sweet and the crisp-skinned duck couldn't be better.

Bayon even offers a good and reasonably priced wine list. The 1986 [12] Estancia cabernet is a bargain for $14, and the $18 Shadow Creek Brut, something I'd never heard of, turned out to be the best California sparkling wine I've ever tasted.

How does a restaurant manage to offer a wonderful full-course French [13] dinner for $9.95 and manage to stay in business? I'm not sure it's possible but in the end it doesn't matter. Bayon could double the price, and it would still be one of the great bargains in San Francisco.

QUESTIONS FOR ANALYSIS

1. What is Sesser's purpose in this review? In considering this question, assume that his purpose goes beyond convincing readers to try Bayon. What evidence do you find in the review to support your conclusion about Sesser's purpose? After considering Sesser's purpose, speculate about different purposes restaurant reviews might exhibit.

2. Readers are never in doubt about Sesser's judgment, mainly because he reiterates it in so many ways. Annotate the review for all words and phrases of praise for Bayon or its chef. Does the reiterated praise seem to you appropriate or excessive for Sesser's newspaper readers?

3. What criteria seem to underlie Sesser's review? (His criteria would be abstract and general standards for evaluating any multicourse French restaurant.) List the criteria. For his subject and readers, do these criteria seem appropriate? Do you think he should have justified or explained any of his criteria?

4. List the reasons Sesser offers to support his judgment. Although his reasons derive from general criteria, they are particular to Bayon—its unique strengths and weaknesses. Do Sesser's reasons seem to you to provide the basis for a convincing evaluation? Speculate about reasons he might have overlooked. For his purposes and readers, can you imagine a different sequence for the reasons?

5. Select one paragraph in which you find Sesser's backing for a reason particularly convincing. Describe this backing and explain why you find it so convincing.

IDEAS FOR YOUR OWN WRITING

Consider evaluating a restaurant. You can tell from Sesser's review that for a restaurant review to be authoritative the reviewer needs some experience with the cuisine of the restaurant being evaluated. You would not, therefore, want to evaluate a Mexican restaurant unless you regularly go to Mexican restaurants. Since comparisons can play an important role in a restaurant review, you may want to select a restaurant to review favorably and then also go to another restaurant of its type, a restaurant that offers it some competition. You could then argue how much better your favored restaurant is than another good restaurant like it. Like Sesser, you should visit your favored restaurant twice.

What criteria would be appropriate to guide your analysis and evaluation? What purposes might you attempt to achieve with your readers?

Instead of evaluating a single restaurant, you might evaluate an entire cuisine—Mexican, Italian, Thai, traditional American. You would want to visit at least two restaurants serving the cuisine you are evaluating. You could also research the history of the cuisine and skim a popular cookbook, as well as interview others who share your enthusiasm for the cuisine. Your judgment could assert that one particular cuisine is superior to other currently popular cuisines or that it is the best choice for certain occasions.

Still another writing possibility would be to set out to find the single best example of a type of food—hamburger, low-fat frozen yogurt, salad bar—in your community. You would need to sample the food from several restaurants. Your exploration of appropriate criteria could lead to a rating scale which you—and even some of your friends—could complete as you sample each example of a type of food. Your survey would lead to the best example whose virtues you could extol, with convincing reasons and backing, in an evaluative essay.

Carlos Baker

Carlos Baker (b. 1909) is a respected literary scholar and English professor. Now retired, he held for many years the prestigious position of Woodrow Wilson Professor of Literature at Princeton University. He devoted most of his career to studying the American writer Ernest Hemingway, who won the Nobel Prize for Literature in 1954. Hemingway is probably best known for his novels *The Sun Also Rises* and *For Whom the Bell Tolls* and for his short stories. Baker has written numerous articles and three books on Hemingway: the critical study *Hemingway: The Writer as Artist* (1952), the definitive biography *Ernest Hemingway: A Life Story* (1968), and the collection *Ernest Hemingway: Selected Letters* (1981). Baker is also a novelist and a poet, with two novels and one collection of poetry to his credit.

The Way It Was

This selection opens the third chapter of *Hemingway: The Writer as Artist*. In this book, Baker analyzes Hemingway's writing and assesses his development as an artist. In this excerpt, Baker focuses on Hemingway's craft, evaluating it in terms of the author's own aesthetic principles. To illustrate his judgments, Baker draws examples from two major Hemingway works: *The Sun Also Rises*, a story of American expatriates traveling from Paris through the Spanish countryside that is generally believed to be Hemingway's best novel; and *Death in the Afternoon*, a nonfiction treatment of bullfighting that has been called the best book on the subject in any language.

Before you begin reading, pause to reflect on stories or novels by Hemingway you may have read. What do you know about his life and reputation as a writer? Have you studied or written about any of Hemingway's novels or stories? What do you recall of your impression of him as a writer?

"A writer's job is to tell the truth," said Hemingway in 1942. He had 1 believed it for twenty years and he would continue to believe it as long as he lived. No other writer of our time had so fiercely asserted, so pugnaciously defended, or so consistently exemplified the writer's obligation to speak truly. His standard of truth-telling remained, moreover, so high and so rigorous that he was ordinarily unwilling to admit secondary evidence, whether literary evidence or evidence picked up from other sources than his own experience. "I only know what I have seen," was a statement which came often to his lips and pen. What he had personally done, or what he knew unforgettably by having gone through one version of it, was what he was interested in telling about. This is not to say that he refused to invent freely. But he always made it a sacrosanct point to invent in terms of what he actually knew from having been there.

The primary intent of his writing, from first to last, was to seize and project for the reader what he often called "the way it was." This is a characteristically simple phrase for a concept of extraordinary complexity, and Hemingway's conception of its meaning subtly changed several times in the course of his career—always in the direction of greater complexity. At the core of the concept, however, one can invariably discern the operation of three esthetic instruments: the sense of place, the sense of fact, and the sense of scene.

The first of these, obviously a strong passion with Hemingway, is the sense of place. "Unless you have geography, background," he once told George Antheil,[1] "you have nothing." You have, that is to say, a dramatic vacuum. Few writers have been more place-conscious. Few have so carefully charted out the geographical groundwork of their novels while managing to keep background so conspicuously unobtrusive. Few, accordingly, have been able to record more economically and graphically the way it is when you walk through the streets of Paris in search of breakfast at a corner café. Or when your footfalls echo among surrounding walls on the ancient cobblestones of early morning Venice, heading for the market-place beside the Adriatic. Or when, at around six o'clock of a Spanish dawn, you watch the bulls running from the corrals at the Puerta Rochapea through the streets of Pamplona towards the bullring.

"When I woke it was the sound of the rocket exploding that announced the release of the bulls from the corrals at the edge of town. . . . Down below the narrow street was empty. All the balconies were crowded with people. Suddenly a crowd came down the street. They were all running, packed close together. They passed along and up the street toward the bullring and behind them came more men running faster, and then some stragglers who were really running. Behind them was a little bare space, and then the bulls, galloping, tossing their heads up and down. It all went out of sight around the corner. One man fell, rolled to the gutter, and lay quiet. But the bulls went right on and did not notice him. They were all running together."

---

[1]George Antheil was an American composer of Hemingway's generation. [Eds.]

This scene is as morning-fresh as a design in India ink on clean white ₅ paper. First is the bare white street, seen from above, quiet and empty. Then one sees the first packed clot of runners. Behind these are the thinner ranks of those who move faster because closer to the bulls. Then the almost comic stragglers, who are "really running." Brilliantly behind these shines the "little bare space," a desperate margin for error. Then the clot of running bulls—closing the design, except of course for the man in the gutter making himself, like the designer's initials, as inconspicuous as possible.

The earliest of his published work, descriptively speaking, shows an ₆ almost neoclassical restraint. Take a sample passage from *The Sun Also Rises*, not his earliest but fairly representative. This one concerns the Irati Valley fishing-trip of Jake Barnes and Bill Gorton.

"It was a beech wood and the trees were very old. Their roots bulked ₇ above the ground and the branches were twisted. We walked on the road between the thick trunks of the old beeches and the sunlight came through the leaves in light patches on the grass. The trees were big, and the foliage was thick but it was not gloomy. There was no undergrowth, only the smooth grass, very green and fresh, and the big gray trees were well spaced as though it were a park. 'This is country,' Bill said." . . .

For all the restraint, the avoidance of color-flaunting adjectives, and ₈ the plainsong sentences (five compound to one complex), the paragraph is loaded with precisely observed fact: beech wood, old trees, exposed roots, twisted branches, thick trunks, sun-patches, smooth green grass, foliage which casts a shade without excluding light. One cannot say that he has been given a generalized landscape—there are too many exact factual observations. On the other hand, the uniquenesses of the place receive no special emphasis. One recognizes easily the generic type of the clean and orderly grove, where weeds and brush do not flourish because of the shade, and the grass gets only enough light to rise to carpet-level. Undoubtedly, as in the neoclassical esthetic, the intent is to provide a generic frame within which the reader is at liberty to insert his own uniqueness—as many or as few as his imagination may supply.

Along with the sense of place, and as a part of it, is the sense of fact. ₉ Facts march through all his pages in a stream as continuous as the refugee wagons in Thrace or the military camions on the road from the Isonzo. Speculation, whether by the author or by the characters, is ordinarily kept to a minimum. But facts, visible or audible or tangible facts, facts baldly stated, facts without verbal paraphernalia to inhibit their striking power, are the stuff of Hemingway's prose.

Sometimes, especially in the early work, the facts seem too many for ₁₀ the effect apparently intended, though even here the reader should be on guard against misconstruing the intention of a given passage. It is hard to discover, nevertheless, what purpose beyond the establishment of the sense of place is served by Barnes's complete itinerary of his walk with Bill Gorton through the streets of Paris. The direction is from Madame Lecomte's restaurant on the Île St. Louis across to the left bank of the Seine, and eventually up the Boulevard du Port Royal to the Café Select. The walk fills only two pages. Yet it seems much longer and does not further the action appreciably except to provide Jake and Bill with healthy after-dinner exercise. At Madame Lecomte's (the facts again), they have eaten "a roast chicken, new green beans, mashed potatoes, a salad, and some apple pie and cheese." To the native Parisian, or a foreigner who knows the city, the pleasure in the after-dinner itinerary would consist in the happy shock of recognition. For others, the inclusion of so many of the facts of municipal or gastronomic geography—so many more than are justified by their dramatic purpose—may seem excessive.

Still, this is the way it was that time in Paris. Here lay the bridges and ₁₁ the streets, the squares and the cafés. If you followed them in the prescribed order, you came to the café where Lady Brett Ashley sat on a high stool at the bar, her crossed legs stockingless, her eyes crinkling at the corners.

If an imaginative fusion of the sense of place and the sense of fact is to ₁₂ occur, and if, out of the fusing process, dramatic life is to arise, a third element is required. This may be called the sense of scene. Places are less than geography, facts lie inert and uncoordinated, unless the imagination runs through them like a vitalizing current and the total picture moves and quickens. How was it, for example, that second day of the San Fermin fiesta in the Pamplona bullring after Romero had killed the first bull?

"They had hitched the mules to the dead bull and then the whips ₁₃ cracked, the men ran, and the mules, straining forward, their legs pushing, broke into a gallop, and the bull, one horn up, his head on its side, swept a swath smoothly across the sand and out the red gate."

Here are a dead bull, men, mules, whips, sand, and a red gate like a ₁₄ closing curtain—the place and the facts. But here also, in this remarkably graphic sentence, are the seven verbs, the two adverbs, and the five adverbial phrases which fuse and coordinate the diverse facts of place and thing and set them in rapid motion. If one feels that the sentence is very satisfying as a scene, and wishes to know why, the answer might well lie where it so often lies in a successful lyric poem—that is, in our sense of difficulty overcome. Between the inertness of the dead bull when he is merely *hitched* (a placid verb) and the smooth speed with which the body finally *sweeps* across the sand and out of sight, come the verbs of sweating effort: *crack, run, strain,* and *break*. It is precisely at the verb *broke* that the sentence stops straining and moves into the smooth glide of its close. The massing, in that section of the sentence, of a half-dozen *s*'s, compounded with the *th* sounds of *swath* and *smoothly,* can hardly have been inadvertent. They ease (or grease) the path of the bull's departure.

The pattern in the quoted passage is that of a task undertaken, striven   15 through, and smoothly completed: order and success. For another graphic sentence, so arranged as to show the precise opposites—total disorder and total failure—one might take the following example from *Death in the Afternoon*. The protagonist is a "phenomenon," a bullfighter who has lost his nerve.

"In your mind you see the phenomenon, sweating, white-faced, and   16 sick with fear, unable to look at the horn or go near it, a couple of swords on the ground, capes all around him, running in at an angle on the bull hoping the sword will strike a vital spot, cushions sailing down into the ring and the steers ready to come in."

In this passage, place has become predicament. The facts, thrown in   17 almost helter-skelter, imply the desperate inward fear which is responsible for the creation of the outward disorder. Verbs are held to a minimum, and their natural naked power is limited with qualifications. The phenomenon is *unable to look,* and *hoping to strike,* not *looking* and *striking*. He runs, but it is at a bad angle. The disorder of the swords on the ground and the capes all around is increased by the scaling-in of seat cushions from the benches, the audience's insult to gross cowardice. The author-spectator's crowning insult is the allusion to the steers, who by comparison with the enraged bull are bovine, old-womanly creatures. On being admitted to the ring, they will quiet and lead away the bull the phenomenon could not kill.

The sense of place and the sense of fact are indispensable to Heming-   18 way's art. But the true craft, by which diversities are unified and compelled into graphic collaboration, comes about through the operation of the sense of scene.

QUESTIONS FOR ANALYSIS

1. In this selection, Baker distinguishes among Hemingway's three aesthetic senses. Find the passages where Baker discusses each sense, and briefly summarize it in your own words. (Pause to review Summarizing in Chapter 1.) How does Baker use these senses to argue for his judgment of Hemingway's work?

2. Several times in the essay, Baker quotes a passage from a Hemingway work and then spends a paragraph or two discussing it. Choose one such passage, and its accompanying discussion. How does Baker use this passage as evidence to support his argument? To what details in the passage does he call attention in his discussion? What kinds of points does he make? How much of this discussion seems to you to be necessary or useful?

3. In paragraph 10, Baker qualifies his praise of Hemingway's allegiance to the truth. How does he do this? How does it influence your assessment of Baker's authority to evaluate Hemingway?

4. To discover how Baker organized his evaluation, outline it, following the plan for scratch outlining in Chapter 1. What advantages or disadvantages do you see in Baker's organization?

5. What do you think Hemingway means by "truth"? Is truth necessarily limited to empirical fact—firsthand observation and experience—or can it be acquired some other way? Do you agree that truth telling should be a criterion of fiction as well as nonfiction?

IDEAS FOR YOUR OWN WRITING

Consider evaluating an author's work. You would need to have read carefully several, but certainly not all, of that author's books or stories. It is certainly *not* essential that you read what others have written about the author.

With the help of your instructor and other students, you could list criteria appropriate for evaluating the author's work. You might then select only two or three criteria as the basis for your evaluation. What reasons would you give for evaluating this author's work? What readers would you have in mind, and what would you hope to achieve with them?

One way to focus your evaluation of an author's work is to evaluate a single-author anthology of stories or poems, concentrating only on the work in the anthology. Because many students have had notable success with such an assignment, we especially recommend it.

Still another way to make good use of a single-author anthology is to evaluate one poem or story as the best (or weakest) in the collection or the better of two comparable poems or stories. Whatever your thesis, other works in the anthology provide a basis for comparison—a strategy which readers find especially convincing. Your instructor could suggest anthologies by contemporary writers.

You could, of course, evaluate a single work—a novel, story, or play—as in a newspaper or magazine book review, asserting that it is an excellent (or awful) work of its type or the best (or worst) work of its type you have read. Even in this case, however, comparison to other works enhances the authority of your review.

Once you have decided on a text or collection of texts, you must read and reread them in order to review them authoritatively. Reasons and backing to support your judgment can be convincing only if they emerge from critical rereadings and thoughtful analysis.

John Crewdson

John Crewdson is chief of the *Chicago Tribune*'s Los Angeles bureau. A series of articles he wrote on the immigrant experience in America won the Pulitzer Prize in 1981 and served as the basis for his book *The Tarnished Door*. During the mid-1980s Crewdson reported extensively about two highly publicized child sexual abuse trials, in the course of which he interviewed a wide variety of legal personnel, investigators, and therapists, as well as many victims of child sexual abuse. The information he collected in this process provides the basis for his most recent book, *By Silence Betrayed: Sexual Abuse of Children in America* (1988).

An Evaluation of Materials Designed to Prevent Child Sexual Abuse

In this selection from *By Silence Betrayed*, Crewdson evaluates a diverse collection of materials designed to alert children to the possibility of sexual abuse. Crewdson writes not for specialists in child sexual abuse but for adult readers who may have interest in or concern about his subject. Reflect on what you know about this growing problem. Do you recall seeing or reading any materials cautioning children about the dangers of sexual abuse from adults?

America sometimes seems to be the most prevention-minded nation on earth. It's practically impossible to turn on a television or radio without being overwhelmed by appeals for help in preventing everything from heart attacks to forest fires to accidents in the home. As reports of child sexual abuse continue to rise faster than those of any other crime, many who are concerned for the welfare of children have begun a campaign to prevent child sexual abuse. At the moment, the most popular approach is teaching children how to protect themselves from child abusers. If children can only be taught to say no to adults who want sex, or so the thinking goes, the problem will be solved of its own accord. But most sexual-abuse prevention programs have serious shortcomings, not the least of which is their squeamishness about the subject at hand, and there are questions about how well even the best of them work.

271

There are hundreds of prevention materials available, most produced 2
by child therapists, rape crisis centers, teachers, hospitals, and writers of
children's books. New programs arrive on the market each week in such
numbers that newsletters are now being published to help keep track of
them all. In attempting to convey their message, they use every device
imaginable—storybooks, movies, videotapes, television programs, film-
strips, comic and coloring books, puppets, even live theater. A few have
enlisted Hollywood stars such as John Houseman and Henry Winkler to
instruct children on how to protect themselves. Most of the programs are
produced by nonprofit organizations, but some writers and publishers
have discovered that they can cash in on parents' fears, and the competition is so intense that a few authors have resorted to hucksterism and
outright scare tactics.

Though prevention programs differ widely in approach, nearly all 3
attempt to establish three fundamental ideas: that a child's body is the
child's "property," that a child can "say no" to an abusive adult, and that
a child who is molested must immediately tell someone who will take
action. Such messages are hard to argue with on their face, but they are
conveyed in a variety of ways. Some are silly, like Trooper B. Safe, a
fifteen-thousand-dollar robot with a flashing red light and siren that is
used by police in several states to teach children to avoid child molesters.
Dressed in a state trooper's uniform and speaking through a voice
synthesizer, the robot promises to protect "humanoids who live in the
intergalactic space-sphere called Earth," paying special attention to the
"small, younger human units." Most prevention programs adopt a more
serious tone, but many are flawed in other ways, and some are downright
dangerous.

One of the best-selling books on the subject is *Never Talk to Strangers*, 4
first published by Golden Books in 1967 and reissued last year. The book
uses what its publisher describes as fantasy and humor to convey its
message "in a nonthreatening way." The illustrations it contains show
children in familiar settings—at home, at the store, at the bus stop, at the
playground—when an unfamiliar and presumably threatening character
appears on the scene. None of these strangers, however, is human. "If you
are hanging from a trapeze," the book begins, "and up sneaks a camel
with bony knees, remember this rule, if you please—Never talk to
strangers!" It goes on to warn children about grouchy grizzly bears,
parachuting hawks, a rhinoceros waiting for a bus, coyotes who ask the
time, cars with a whale at the wheel, and bees carrying bass bassoons.

The use of animals to represent potential abusers is no doubt inspired 5
by the idea that children will be less frightened by a picture of a
rhinoceros wearing a tutu than by one of a malevolent stranger in a

raincoat, and other prevention programs use chipmunks, mice, or bears to make their point. The problem with such anthropomorphic presentations is illustrated by a filmstrip featuring Penelope Mouse, who has an otherwise unidentified "strange experience" at her Uncle Sid's house. When a group of schoolchildren who had been shown the filmstrip were asked later what its message was, they agreed that sexual abuse must be a serious problem among mice.

Another best-selling book is *It's O.K. to Say No!*, endorsed by the Catholic Youth & Community Service and the Children's Justice Foundation. The book mostly contains warnings about "child molesters" who frequent public restrooms and video arcades, with a few cautionary words about neighbors, teachers, and baby-sitters thrown in. But *It's O.K. to Say No!* never says what it's OK to say no to. In one story, a girl named Tina spends the night at the home of Lucy, her friend. After Tina's in bed, Lucy's big brother comes into her room and starts saying "strange things" that make Tina feel "uncomfortable." But what things? Why does Tina feel uncomfortable? The reader never finds out. Because *It's O.K. to Say No!* and similar storybooks are designed for parents to share with their children, their squeamishness may be an acknowledgment that many parents feel uneasy talking with their children about any aspect of sex. But those programs designed for presentation in the classroom or to youth groups by trained instructors are scarcely more forthcoming.

One of the most popular is *Red Flag, Green Flag*, a multimedia program developed by the Rape and Abuse Crisis Center of Fargo-Moorhead, North Dakota, the centerpiece of which is a coloring book that helps children learn the difference between a "green flag touch" and a "red flag touch." The program is typical of those that, in seeking ways to avoid actually talking about sex, distinguish between "good" touches, such as a hug or a pat on the head, and "bad" touches. Such jargon involves a number of potential contradictions, such as the possibility that a child whose genitals are being fondled might find the sensation pleasant. A few programs have tried to resolve such contradictions by introducing a third category called "confusing" touch, which they define as a touch that might feel good but is bad nonetheless. But the idea of confusing touches is just that, because it doesn't address what often happens in the real world.

Nor do such programs recognize that children often take things literally. Is an abuser who asks a child to perform fellatio touching the child, or is the child touching the abuser? Programs that warn children about adults who might "bother" or "hurt" them are equally misleading, since a child who's being sexually abused is probably not being physically hurt.

"We're giving children an outrageous double message," says Cordelia Anderson of the Illusion Theater in Minneapolis, which produced the first live-theater prevention program back in 1979. "We're saying that we want to talk to you about *it*, that if you have any questions about *it* I want you to ask me about *it*, that it's not OK if someone does *it* to you, and that if *it* happens it's not your fault. But what *it* means is so bad that I can't even say the words."

With the same misguided decorum they reserve for talking about "touching," most prevention programs refuse to call penises and vaginas by their proper names, referring instead to mysterious "private zones" or "places where your bathing suit covers." The *Red Flag, Green Flag* coloring book contains a drawing of an androgynous child whose arms, legs, chest, and other body parts are identified for what they are, while the region beween the child's legs is merely labeled "genitals (private parts)." Upon closer inspection, it becomes apparent that the child in the drawing has no genitals or private parts.

Another serious shortcoming is the exclusive focus of many prevention programs on the danger posed by strange adults. One film, produced by the Boulder, Colorado, police department, shows a shady-looking character luring a little girl into some bushes, where she is heard to scream—the same sort of "stranger danger" movie that American schoolchildren have been watching for decades with no noticeable effect on the incidence of sexual abuse. There's nothing really wrong with warning children never to accept candy or a ride from adults they don't know or never to open the door for a stranger, since some pedophiles do abuse strange children. It's just that most of them do not. Of the adult victims surveyed by the *Los Angeles Times*, only a quarter recalled having been abused by someone they didn't know.

Programs that teach children to memorize their home telephone number or that of the local police department might be helpful for a child who becomes lost, but they have very little to do with preventing sexual abuse. Some programs feature "assertiveness training" for children, teaching them to defend themselves physically by stomping on an abuser's foot or bending his pinky. But the idea that a child can repulse an attack by an adult is both ludicrous and dangerous to the child. Those who promote such programs maintain that, while warning children about strangers may not cover the spectrum of child abuse, such advice cannot hurt. Apart from the possibility that such messages may frighten some children unduly, the distinctions they draw about which adults should be trusted and which should not are often vague.

Never Talk to Strangers suggests that it's fine for a child to talk to any adult who is introduced by someone the child knows. "If your father introduces you to a roly-poly kangaroo," the book advises, "say politely, 'How do you do?' That's not talking to strangers because your family knows her." Or: "If your teacher says she'd like you to meet a lilac llama who's very sweet, invite her over and serve a treat. That's not talking to strangers because your teacher knows her." Worst of all: "If a pal of yours you've always known brings around a prancing roan, welcome him in a friendly tone. That's not talking to strangers because your pal knows him."

Prevention programs may give those who prepare and produce them a 13 sense that they're doing something about child abuse, but there are serious questions about whether even the best programs are worth the effort. When children who have been exposed to prevention programs are asked later about what they remember, the answer is usually "Not very much," and the level of recall doesn't seem to depend on the quality of the program. One study found that children who were exposed to one of the better programs had forgotten much of the information it contained after only two months, and nearly all of it after less than a year.

Even when children do remember a particular concept, they're less 14 than likely to be able to apply it to a real-life situation. Another study found that, while nearly all the children exposed to an assertiveness program could later repeat the definition of "assertiveness," fewer than half could give an example of an assertive reply to be used in an abusive situation. Younger children especially tend to parrot the answers they've been taught. When they're asked whom they'd tell about being abused, they may say their mother or their father, but when the time comes, there may be a gap between saying and doing.

It is a basic principle of education that people, especially young people, 15 learn much more efficiently if they have some personal experience that bears on what they're learning. Trying to explain the dangers of sexual abuse to a child who hasn't been abused is difficult, particularly when the presentation is not straightforward. A child who *has* been abused, on the other hand, is likely to understand immediately what is being said. If prevention programs have any real value, it may be that they prompt some victims to come forward. "We know that these programs are good for one thing," says a pediatrician who has studied the question. "They're good for identifying kids who have already been sexually abused. When you do one of these shows, inevitably one or two kids out of a group will come forward and say, 'Well, that happened to me.'"

Even in such cases, however, sexual-abuse prevention programs are 16 likely to be effective primarily with younger children who are being abused by someone outside their families. Far less clear is the value of such programs in preventing the most prevalent kinds of abuse, mainly *[handwritten margin notes: "Programs should continue?"] [arrow]*

incest and voluntary relationships between older children and pedophiles. The fact that such programs do encourage some victims to report
may be reason enough to continue with them. But the content of most
programs needs to be vastly improved to reflect what happens in the real
world. In view of some of the testimony in recent child abuse cases, for
example, one thing children should be taught is how to overcome the
fear created by watching small animals killed before their eyes. But no
matter what information the prevention programs contain, teaching
children to "say no" to sexual abuse is a simplistic answer to an extraordinarily complicated problem.

[handwritten margin notes: "Is, stated" "is it" "Isn't that simple"]

QUESTIONS FOR ANALYSIS

1. What criteria underlie Crewdson's evaluation? Since he does not state
   them explicitly, you will have to infer them. These criteria should
   provide the basis for evaluating any collection of materials designed to
   prevent child sexual abuse, those that Crewdson evaluates as well as
   any others. For his purpose and readers, do Crewdson's criteria seem
   adequate? Has he overlooked any important criteria?

2. What reasons does Crewdson give for disapproving the materials he
   reviews? List these reasons and decide whether they make a complete
   and convincing argument and whether they are in the best possible
   sequence.

3. What kinds of backing or evidence does Crewdson select to support
   his reasons? List the different kinds. What advantages do you think
   he saw in such a wide range of evidence?

4. Analyze the logical appeal of Crewdson's argument in paragraphs 13–
   16. Outline the argument first and then evaluate it. (Take a few
   minutes to review the discussion of Outlining and Evaluating the
   Argument under Analyzing an Argument in Chapter 1.) Write up
   the results of your analysis. Your purpose is to demonstrate that you
   recognize both the strengths and weaknesses of Crewdson's logic.

5. Review Exploring Your Personal Response in Chapter 1. Then write a
   300–400-word personal response to Crewdson's essay, choosing one of
   the following topics:

   > Write about your personal associations with something in the
   > reading, such as an idea or example.

   > Write to explore the meaning and implications of a particular point
   > Crewdson makes.

   After you have written your response, reread it thoughtfully. In two or three sentences, say what you learned about Crewdson's evaluation by writing an extended response to it.

IDEAS FOR YOUR OWN WRITING

Crewdson's evaluation suggests a writing idea you might consider: evaluating a collection of similar materials. Possibilities include books on child care or books introducing children to a particular historical period; magazines concerned with homes, fashion, food, motorcycles; specialized outdoor activities, professional sports, or news; coverage of a particular event by a variety of newspapers, newsmagazines, and other print sources; instructional videos on sailing, skiing, playing tennis or golf; materials cautioning about the dangers of smoking, drinking, drugs, venereal disease, AIDS, obsessive gambling, unwanted pregnancy, obesity; or materials explaining how to cope with pain, grief, alcoholism in the family, divorce, childlessness. You and your classmates will think of many more possibilities.

You may approve or disapprove of the collection as a whole, giving reasons why you find it valuable or not valuable for its intended readers; like Crewdson, you should go on to present evidence from individual items to back your reasons. To what kinds of readers might you direct your evaluation? How would you go about evaluating the collection for them—that is, what criteria would be appropriate for the collection and for your readers?

You might also consider evaluating a collection of materials like one of those listed above for the purpose of singling out one item as the best or worst in the collection.

Kim Marshall

An authority on education, Kim Marshall (b. 1948) was educated at Harvard and then taught sixth grade at Martin Luther King School in Boston, where he also served as curriculum coordinator. Since 1980, he has been curriculum director for the Boston public school system. In addition to teaching and developing school curricula, Marshall is a contributing editor to *Learning* magazine and has written several books on education, including *Law and Order in Grade 6E* (1972) and *The Story of Life* (1980). "The inspiration of my writing," Marshall explains, "has come from my eleven years of work in an inner-city Boston public school. I have become fascinated with classroom organization, kids, and curriculum, and have been anxious to share my experiences with others."

Literacy: The Price of Admission

The following selection is a book review—another common kind of evaluation. Marshall reviews *Illiterate America* by Jonathan Kozol, also a well-known educator. (An excerpt from Kozol's book can be found in Chapter 7 of this text.) Published in 1985, this book calls attention to the fact that many Americans can neither read nor write, a situation that produces enormous problems not only for the illiterate individuals but also for the nation as a whole. Kozol does not seek merely to establish illiteracy as a major problem; he also suggests ways of solving it. In his review, which appeared in *Harvard Magazine* shortly after Kozol's book was published, Marshall evaluates Kozol's book on the basis of how it succeeds as a proposal—how well it establishes the existence of the problem and how convincing a case it makes for the proposed solution.

Book reviewers, like film reviewers, usually assume that their readers are unfamiliar with the books they are evaluating and therefore describe their subjects in some detail. As you read Marshall's essay, notice how much he reveals about the contents of Kozol's book. But before you begin, ask yourself what Marshall's title, "Literacy: The Price of Admission," might mean. To what does knowing how to read and write gain admission? What happens to people in our society who don't know how to read and write? Why should illiteracy be a social as well as a personal problem?

"A third of the nation cannot read these words." So begins the first chapter of Jonathan Kozol's new book, *Illiterate America*, and we are immediately skeptical of the figure. But in short order, Kozol produces a blizzard of statistics showing that 25 million adult Americans can barely read at all, while another 35 million are "semi-literate," that is, unable to read at the level demanded by our technological society. That adds up to

60 million illiterate or marginally literate adults, disproportionately black and other minority, who are "substantially excluded from the democratic process and the economic commerce of a print society." Kozol argues that even these shocking figures are conservative estimates, since the census and other surveys tend to underestimate this mute population in our midst.

Kozol acknowledges that the first category—true illiteracy—has shrunk in recent years, but the second—functional illiteracy—has grown because of the steadily increasing demands of our society. Kozol ticks off the benchmarks of literacy: a ninth-grade reading level is required to understand the antidote instructions on a bottle of corrosive kitchen lye; a tenth-grade level is needed to understand the instructions on federal income tax forms; many newspapers are written at a tenth- to twelfth-grade level; and a twelfth-grade level is required to understand life insurance forms and the national newsmagazines. He quotes the educational director of the AFL-CIO as saying that by the 1990s, anyone who doesn't have at least a twelfth-grade reading, writing, and calculating level will be absolutely lost.

None of this material is accessible to 60 million adult Americans. The illiterate do not have access to important information on nutrition, bargains, travel, safety, work, entertainment, health insurance, medical consent forms, and educational and political choices. They are unable to make intelligent decisions to better their lives. Illiterate people are easy marks for consumer fraud, and don't have the skills to catch errors and prevent themselves from being cheated.

The illiterate are also saddled with shame and self-hatred. People who emerge from schools without the ability to read have to ask themselves, as Kozol frames it, "Am I inherently deficient? Am I lacking in intelligence? in energy? in will? If the answer is yes, I am inferior. If the answer is no, I am the victim of injustice." It is an unusual person who will draw the second conclusion, and for this reason, the illiterate are less likely than any other disadvantaged group to organize politically to improve their lot.

Most devastating is the effect of illiteracy on the next generation. The children of poor and marginal readers begin school with a tremendous disadvantage, and it is a remarkable school that can make up for these deficits. In addition, illiterate parents are hesitant to visit their children's classrooms, having developed a distaste for schools from having done poorly themselves, and are often ineffective in bringing their concerns to the attention of teachers and principals.

Kozol argues that the price we pay for this extraordinary level of illiteracy includes child welfare; the costs of crime (the prison population, Kozol says, represents the single highest concentration of adult illiterates); unemployment benefits; health costs; worker's compensation due to damage to equipment and accidents attributable to poor reading skills; and much more.

What is being done about illiteracy now? Kozol puts the four major 7 efforts under his analytical lens and finds them all wanting. He does give credit to several good initiatives, and is especially complimentary of a 1983 alliance of a number of adult literacy groups with the American Library Association and B. Dalton, the bookseller. But he feels that these efforts are grossly underfunded and are reaching far too few people. He calculates that present efforts to combat illiteracy are spending only $1.65 for each needy person.

Kozol finds the definition of literacy used by most programs wanting. 8 Teaching the skills needed to fill out job applications and welfare forms, he states, is a trivialization of literacy. His list of desiderata for true literacy aims much higher (and is, incidentally, something any public high school curriculum should contain). This book is impressive for the number of practical suggestions it offers for solving the illiteracy problem. The specific ideas give credibility to Kozol's oft-repeated assertion that we do not need another blue-ribbon commission to study this problem; we know what to do right now. He believes that, with the proper programs and a real national commitment, we could substantially conquer illiteracy by the year 2000.

Kozol believes that illiterate people desperately want to escape their 9 condition, and could be persuaded to participate in literacy programs that have a number of important characteristics:

—Carefully chosen people recruiting door-to-door in target neighborhoods

—Noninstitutional settings (church basements, vacant apartments), which students would refurbish

—Day care, potluck dinners, and other community-building devices; concrete rewards (a bookshelf for a child, for example); and occasional guest speakers

—Teachers who work with collegial groups of six or seven, not one-on-one

—Active participation of the elderly, and of college and high school students who would receive academic credit for tutoring

—"Two-way tutoring" of less skillful readers (both tutor and tutee improve in such situations)

—Teachers from public schools, whose long-term interests are at stake

—An integrated approach to the teaching of reading, writing, and critical thinking

—The use of language experience and new oral history methods

—The use of politically charged words ("rent," "landlord," "eviction") to draw on people's experience and engage and empower them (Kozol sees the process of motivating nonreaders as inherently political)

—The "one-way library," giving out overstock hardcover books that publishers shred by the thousands.

Kozol describes one Boston program using these ideas which in sixty 10 days of three-hour sessions in a church basement brought 250 adolescents from the third- to the sixth-grade reading level. But he is under no illusions that neighborhood barn raisings are enough to fund a nationwide network of such centers. He knows that the literacy problem must be put on a par with health care, environmental concerns, and defense. He calculates that meeting the needs of the thirty million worst-off illiterates would cost $10 billion a year and would require five million workers, as well as in-kind contributions from publishers, more action-oriented research, and universities encouraging their students to serve as volunteers. Kozol admits that none of these goals is realistic now, but thinks even a partial implementation of his proposal could make a substantial dent in the problem, reducing the number of illiterate people by one half. His book is a rousing call to arms for such a commitment.

Unfortunately, Kozol doesn't demand nearly enough of the institu- 11 tions responsible for teaching people to read in the first place—the public schools. Most Americans feel it is nothing short of a national scandal when children drift through school without learning to read, but Kozol throws up his hands and concentrates all his energy on adult literacy efforts. He does not mention an exciting wave of positive thinking and effective methodology in urban public school systems stemming from the work of Ronald Edmonds, Michael Rutter, and others. This research has found schools in urban areas that get excellent (and equitable) results despite the odds, and identified the factors that seem to be making a difference. Public school educators are increasingly taking responsibility for the learning of their least advantaged students, rather than making excuses for their not learning because of home environment, television, and so forth. Kozol has much to offer us in our uphill battle. I just wish there was more of a feeling in his book that we are all in this together, working toward the same goal.

Kozol's blanket indictment of computers and television as useless tools 12 for improving literacy is valid up to a point; many educators agree that most current instructional software is dreadful, and television remains a cold and one-way medium ill-suited to the needs of the illiterate. But he totally fails to mention word processing—a splendid application of computers to classrooms. There is growing evidence that the ability to edit one's writing so readily is having a very positive effect on the writing of millions of schoolchildren (as well as adults), and that in this respect computers are a liberating and empowering tool.

Kozol also minimizes the value of the rich nonprint environment in   13
which we all move—radio, television, movies, and conversation. An illiterate person *can* make reasonably intelligent voting decisions by watching speeches, press conferences, newscasts, debates, and competing advertisements, and so is not totally disenfranchised. Kozol also does not discuss the phenomenon of *aliteracy*, where millions of Americans know how to read but choose not to, and survive very well.

Kozol is a powerful and brilliant writer, but he sometimes gets carried   14
away and weakens his case. (At several points he comes dangerously close to implying that every industrial accident and billing error in the United States can be traced to illiterate workers.) He is prone to ringing words of a radical bent, and some readers who need to hear his message might close their minds because of this. (An example: "We do know this: Democracy is a mendacious term when used by one third of our electorate.") And Kozol's explanation of why we have the illiteracy problem we do hardly points toward the kind of nitty-gritty solution he proposes:

> Illiteracy among the poorest in our population is a logical consequence of the kinds of schools we run, the cities that starve them, the demagogues who segregate them, and the wealthy people who escape them altogether to enroll their kids in better funded, up-to-date, and more proficient institutions. It is a consequence, too, of economic planning which for many decades has regarded certain sectors of the population as expendable, or at least extraneous to the perpetuation of the social order.

All this notwithstanding, Kozol's is a tremendously important book   15
that deserves to make a difference. Almost twenty years ago, his first book, *Death at an Early Age*, led many idealistic young Americans to think of urban teaching as a high calling and got some of them into public education. My sense is that this tenacious visionary has again put his finger on a national issue of compelling moral importance. I only hope that *Illiterate America* will stir the current generation of latent idealists toward adult literacy action—and toward work in the beleaguered public schools. Our children deserve no less.

QUESTIONS FOR ANALYSIS

1. Marshall begins his review by quoting a statistic from Kozol but then is "immediately skeptical of [this] figure." Skim the essay, noting other places where Marshall cites statistics from Kozol's book. How does Kozol use these statistics? Does Marshall really treat them skeptically? Should he? Why, or why not?

2. Among the criteria for a good proposal is that the proposed solution be workable and not too expensive. What is Marshall's view of the feasibility of Kozol's proposal? What is your view?

3. What are Marshall's chief criticisms of Kozol's proposal? How does Marshall try to convince the reader that these criticisms are well taken? To what extent do Marshall's criticisms seriously undermine your confidence in Kozol's proposal?

4. Marshall suggests that literacy to Kozol has a political component. Why might Kozol think there is a connection between literacy and politics? Do you see such a connection? How does Marshall treat this idea in his evaluation of Kozol's book?

5. How would you characterize the tone of this essay? Is it consistent throughout, or does it modulate? How does Marshall's tone (or tones) contribute to or detract from the persuasiveness of his evaluation?

IDEAS FOR YOUR OWN WRITING

You may consider reviewing a nonfiction book. If you do so, be careful at the outset to concentrate on a book that covers a subject about which you feel relatively expert (as Marshall is an expert on education, the subject of Kozol's book). Then, be certain that you have defined very clearly for yourself the criteria on which an evaluation of this particular kind of book should be based. For example, if you choose to review a how-to book on improving college study skills or playing the guitar, you will need to think about issues like clarity of presentation, assumptions about the audience's skill level, practical information offered, and depth of coverage.

Like Marshall, you will probably want to summarize the book, although you may be able to do so more briefly than he does Kozol's book. You will also need to make your overall judgment (positive or negative) quite clear and to offer specific reasons—examples from the book and your own knowledge—to back your opinions.

1. Liked by Population
2. Top on the Charts
3. Other albums of group
4.

Jason Thornton

Jason Thornton wrote this essay as a freshman at the University of California, San Diego.

Documenting *Document*

In this essay, Thornton evaluates a 1987 recording by the rock group REM. As you read, notice Thornton's contrasts between REM's *Document*, the recording he is evaluating, and the rock group U2's recording, *The Joshua Tree*. Thornton wrote this review for his classmates, who he assumed had some knowledge of current rock music and at least a casual interest in these new recordings.

Before you read, jot down some criteria upon which you think an evaluation of an album of popular music might be based. As you read, consider whether Thornton uses the same criteria.

U2's *The Joshua Tree* may well become the best-remembered rock album of 1987. Certainly it is one of the best-selling and one of the most talked-about LPs of the year. But often the biggest isn't always the best, and the one album released this year that surpasses U2's epic is REM's current masterpiece, *Document*. Although REM, "America's most successful fringe band," according to rock critic David Fricke, is often overshadowed by bigger, more pop-oriented bands, this four-man band from Athens, Georgia, has a large cult following. Their first release, 1981's *Murmur*, was recently voted as one of the top 100 albums of the past twenty years by *Rolling Stone* rock critics. REM makes music like no one else, incorporating a large range of sounds from punk to country and western, from Aerosmith-like hard rock to folkish melodies to a style not unlike Andy Warhol's art-rock band, the Velvet Underground. Many bands try to be as diverse as REM, but no one does it as well. Like U2's *Joshua Tree*, *Document* is an eleven-song collection of straightforward rock 'n' roll and whimsical lyrics that are easy to relate to.

The music on *Document*, like that on last year's *Life's Rich Pageant*, is catchier and more pop-oriented than older albums like *Reckoning* or this year's strange B-side compilation *Dead Letter Office*. REM's songs have become more vivid, forceful, and straightforward. The group had a hand in producing *Document* (along with Scott Litt) and they show they can handle this task as well as they handle their instruments. They also show

How it affects public

Background of REM & their critique

Similarity

Description of songs

Support of album

284

they can bring more life and energy to their vinyl sound than their past producers could. Singer Michael Stipe's stinging, haunting lyrics are still there, though more prominent than on past REM LPs, creating a wonderful verbal hodgepodge, bringing forth images that vary from listener to listener. Stipe's words on *Document*, much like those of Bono Vox on *The Joshua Tree*, are loaded with symbolism of America and its people. But while U2 sees America as a distant land and relates to it in an almost spiritual sense, REM *is* American and their lyrics show a vivid sense of our land that the Irish U2 could never fully grasp.

REM has always been a band of contrasts and paradoxes. Their first album, *Murmur*, sounded like folk music, a style that generally uses acoustic instruments, except that REM used electric guitars. By all rights, the music of their past five albums would be ideal for keyboards or synthesizers, but REM rarely uses a single keyboard track. Instead, they rely on the simple trio of Peter Buck's wide range of guitar playing, Mike Mill's rough bass lines, and Bill Berry's droning, occasionally militant, drums. Despite the simple methods, REM forges complex songs through a mixture of melodies, simple chords, numerous rhythms, and staggering vocal harmonies. Once together, this mixture forms a swirly, moody track that manages not to sound muddy, bogged down, or inconsistent. Sometimes with REM their finest points seem to be their roughest edges: each feedback whine from the guitar amp and rough vocal from singer Michael Stipe seems well planned and strategically placed.

Often REM shows its originality in the sharp contrast between song lyrics and their music. Many times REM will use bitter lyrics along with upbeat music. There is *Document's* "Disturbance at the Heron House" which is made up of a catchy, popular tune while its lyrics describe a democracy gone mad by way of mob rule. The band plays a cheerful-sounding, sixties-influenced tune as Stipe discusses a darker subject:

> They gathered up the cages
> The cages and courageous,
> The followers of chaos
> Out of control.

Throughout the song Bill Berry pounds out a foot-stomping drum beat that keeps the rhythm while Stipe sings about a "stampede at the monument"—a symbol of a large mass of people assaulting their government.

One of the best traits of *Document* is the constant theme of social reform. *Document* opens with "Finest Worksong," a riveting rock anthem on which Stipe sings, "The time to rise / Has been engaged / We're better / Best to rearrange," a call for an uprising by the lower classes of

---

Handwritten margin annotations:
- Part of group
- More similar w/ U2
- U2 is unAmeri. REM is Ameri.
- 3
- Old style
- other men
- Explanation of sounds
- Mistakes are good
- 4
- Again — the Americ way
- examples of lyrics; descript. of democracy
- 5

society. As the song progresses, Stipe continues to discuss the faults of society until he finally comes to a conclusion on what he feels is the basis for America's social and economic difficulties: "What we want / What we need, / Has been confused."

Greed is expressed as a single three-line concept, as Peter Buck's 6 guitars, sounding almost heavy-metal–like, carry the song along with Mills's and Berry's rhythms.

On *Document*, REM also assaults the American government. On 7 "Exhuming McCarthy," with its sleazy bass line and instances of trumpeting horn playing by guest musician Steve Berlin, REM reminds Americans of an embarrassing event in American history, the McCarthy communist "Witch Hunts" of the 1950s. Stipe sings about McCarthy's belief that he was able to spot and uproot the communist dragon in society: "Enemy sighted, enemy met / I'm addressing the real politic." "Exhuming McCarthy" starts off with a strange typewriter sound, contains the actual taped voice of Senator McCarthy mixed into the guitar solo, and ends with an excellently harmonized double vocal, where two tracks of Michael Stipe's voice sing drastically different things yet blend together wonderfully.

There have been a few criticisms of the album. Although most of 8 REM's lyrics tend to be abstract, the ones on "Fireplace" seem almost too abstract. The song is made up of confusing extracts from a speech by Mother Ann Lee, a leader of the eighteenth-century American Shakers, a religious sect that believed all people should be celibate. The song's meaning is garbled and confused. The song's mixture of slow rock and waltz rhythms struggles to carry the song along, showing that REM can be less than perfect at times. Also, their version of "Strange" on side one, a song originally performed by the British band The Wire, seems out of place with its lyrical style different from Stipe's norm; but Buck, Mills, and Berry still manage to create a reasonably decent version of the song. Their song "It's the End of the World As We Know It (And I Feel Fine)" has been considered by many to be only an imitation of Bob Dylan's "Subterranean Homesick Blues."

Despite whatever shortcomings *Document* might possess, REM makes 9 up for them on other songs, such as on the album's ballads. No REM album would be complete without a few ballads. An example of one on *Document* is "Oddfellows Local 151," REM's strange but appealing salute to alcohol. In this song Stipe creates a character more typical of John Steinbeck than of a modern rock star. This character is Pee-Wee, a small-town storyteller who has taken to drinking but still manages to impress his townmates with his tales and "wisdom."

The most important song on this album, however, is "The One I 10

Love," REM's finest song to date. "The One I Love" starts off as a melancholy, regretful love song relying on lyrics such as:

> This one goes out to the one I love,
> This one goes out to the one I left behind,
> A simple prop to occupy my time.

Slowly, the song goes beyond the simple boy/girl relationships of most love songs and introduces the complex problem of distance and time spent away from a loved one affecting a relationship. In the end, "The One I Love" becomes an expression of the pain and guilt one feels because of unfaithfulness to a loved one.

> This one goes out to the one I love,
> This one goes out to the one I left behind,
> Another prop has occupied my time.

11 "The One I Love" and the other songs on *Document* constitute the best REM album yet and one of the best LPs of the year. With the catchy songs, contrasting lyrics mixed with upbeat tunes, themes of governmental and social reform, and touching ballads on *Document*, REM justly deserves to be classified as being in league with some of the top bands around today, such as U2. *Document* may not end up getting as much airplay as *The Joshua Tree* and it may not sell as many copies, but artistically, *Document* equals or betters *The Joshua Tree*, breaking through the boundaries of conventional songwriting and record making, taking rock music to a plateau never before achieved.

QUESTIONS FOR ANALYSIS

1. Do you find Thornton's review authoritative? If so, how does it seem to you that he establishes his authority as a reviewer of a rock recording?
2. To discover Thornton's organizational plan, outline his essay. (Pause to review Outlining in Chapter 1.) Given his purpose and readers, what advantages or disadvantages do you see in Thornton's plan?
3. Annotate the review for all comparisons and contrasts—both to other rock groups and their recordings and to REM's other records. (For this annotation, ignore comparisons between songs on *Document*.) Inventory your annotations to discover how Thornton makes use of contrasts in his essay. (Take a few minutes to review the Inventory of Annotations in Chapter 1.) What can you conclude about the role of contrasts in evaluative essays?

4. Thornton quotes song lyrics as backing for his reasons. Examine each instance of quoted lyrics. What advantages or disadvantages do you see in this sort of backing in a record review?

5. What criteria seem to underlie Thornton's review? For his subject and readers, do these criteria seem appropriate? Do you think he has overlooked any important criteria?

6. Reread Thornton's opening and closing. How do you evaluate their effectiveness? Can you think of an alternative opening or closing?

IDEAS FOR YOUR OWN WRITING

You, too, might evaluate a recently released recording. If you do, you will want to listen to the recording several times and also listen to other recordings by the same group. Tentatively identify a recording and think about what criteria would be appropriate for evaluating it. Which of Thornton's evaluative strategies would be relevant to your review?

A GUIDE TO EVALUATIVE WRITING

Although all evaluations argue for a judgment, they vary a great deal in how they present the subject and how they make their argument. There may be wide variation, for example, in how much information about the subject is imparted to readers. Sometimes writers describe their subjects in detail; at other times, they may assume that readers are already familiar with the subject.

As the readings in this chapter suggest, evaluations may also differ on whether they identify and justify their criteria and how they support their reasons. Some writers assume that readers will accept their standards of judgment, while others argue these standards explicitly. An argument may be constructed around several reasons with specific evidence provided for each reason, or it may be centered on a single reason.

However you finally decide to present your subject and argue for your judgment, you will need to do some thoughtful planning. The following brief guide suggests some things to consider as you plan, draft, and revise your own evaluative essay.

The Writing Task

Write an essay in which you evaluate some subject. Consider carefully the criteria on which your evaluation might be based.

From these criteria, come up with convincing reasons for your judgment. In your essay, amass enough specific evidence from your subject to make your evaluation seem authoritative.

Invention

Writing is a process of discovery—of learning what you already know about a subject and what you still need to know; of trying out ideas and arguments to see which are most effective; and of finding a voice, a tone that suits your subject and your readers. The following invention activities will help you to make these discoveries in a systematic way.

CHOOSING A SUBJECT. The readings in this chapter suggest different types of subjects you could write about—public figures, films, an author's work, restaurants, recordings. There are also countless other possibilities, as the Ideas for Your Own Writing that follow each reading suggest.

To find a subject, first list specific subjects in several of the following categories. Although you may be inclined to pick the first idea that comes to mind, try to make your list as long as you can. This will ensure that you have a variety of subjects from which to choose and also encourage you to think of unique subjects.

> a noteworthy person—a teacher or professor, political figure, artist, athlete, counselor, medical doctor, minister (Like Kinsley, you could consider both strong and weak points, but you should evaluate a person as the best or worst of his or her profession.)
>
> a film or a group of films by the same director
>
> a restaurant or type of cuisine
>
> a literary work or a collection of works by the same author
>
> a live or videotaped concert or performance
>
> a musical recording
>
> an essay in this text (arguing that it is a strong or weak example of its type) or any two essays (arguing that one is better)
>
> two games of the same sports team or a player's performance in two games (Both games should be videotaped so that you could analyze them closely.)

community institutions, services, or agencies—child-care centers, learning or tutorial centers, private schools or specialized public "magnet" schools, little league teams, summer recreational or academic programs (Personal experience with two or more examples in each category would permit comparisons and thereby enhance the authority of your evaluation.)

workplace equipment—word-processing or spread-sheet programs, safety equipment, operating equipment (Your evaluation will be more authoritative if two pieces of equipment, one superior to the other, are still in operation so that you can analyze both and directly compare them.)

local professionals—auto mechanic, teacher, dentist, gynecologist, pediatrician, psychological counselor, veterinarian, allergist, masseuse, chiropractor, dog trainer, gardener, tennis or sailing or rock climbing coach (Personal experience with at least two in a category will enable comparison and strengthen your evaluation.)

Once you have a list of possibilities, consider the following questions as you make your final selection:

Do I already know enough about this subject, or can I get the information I need in time? If, for instance, you decide to review a film, you should be able to see it soon. If you choose to evaluate a piece of workplace equipment, you should already be somewhat expert with it or have time to learn enough about it to be able to write with some authority.

Do I already have strong feelings and a firm judgment about this subject? It is always easier to write about subjects on which you have formed opinions, although it is conceivable that you could change your mind as you write. If you choose a subject that leaves you cold, your readers will probably have the same reaction. The more sure you are of your judgment, the more persuasive you are likely to be.

EXPLORING YOUR SUBJECT. Before you can go much further, you must ascertain what you already know about the subject and what additional information you may need. To do this, list everything you now know about the subject and all the questions you still have, or write about the subject for ten or fifteen minutes without stopping, putting down anything that enters your mind. If you discover that you need to gather more information, find out where you can get it and whether you have enough time for research.

ANALYZING YOUR READERS. To decide how much information about the subject to include in your essay, you will need to estimate how much your readers know about the subject and how much they need to know in order to accept your judgment. In planning your argument, you will also need to anticipate readers' attitudes and opinions. Take some time to think about the readers you will be addressing, what they might already know about the subject and what you will need to tell them, and also how they are likely to judge your subject.

SELECTING CRITERIA. Your evaluation can succeed only if you have a good understanding of the criteria or standards appropriate for judging your subject. Criteria apply not to your particular subject but to the class or category to which it belongs—all psychological films, not just *The Treasure of the Sierra Madre*; all French restaurants, not just Bayon; all pediatricians, not just your child's; all professional football games, not just the two Raiders' games you are comparing. Which criteria are appropriate for evaluating the class of things to which your subject applies? List as many as may be appropriate. You may want to enlist the help of other students, your instructor, or a campus expert on your subject. You could even read sources which attempt to establish criteria for evaluating the class of things to which your subject belongs.

SUPPORTING YOUR REASONS. To develop your arguments systematically, make a chart of your reasons and the backing you might use to support them. Divide a piece of paper into two columns. In the left-hand column, list the reasons you think are most appropriate for judging your subject; in the right-hand column, indicate the backing you could cite— examples, illustrations, quotations, facts, authorities—to support each reason.

Drafting

After you have made a fairly detailed chart of your argument, you are probably ready to set your goals, plan the organization of your essay, and decide how to begin.

SETTING GOALS. The decisions you make about what to include and how to order your ideas should be guided by some specific goals that reflect your purpose and your understanding of the readers' needs and expectations. Considering the following questions may help you to clarify your goals: What do I want to accomplish with this particular evaluation? Is my primary purpose to make a recommendation as Agee and Sesser do? Do I want readers to reexamine something they may have taken for granted, like a famous writer's style, as in Baker's essay on

Hemingway? Am I trying to expose my subject's flaws like Crewdson or weigh its good and bad points like Kinsley?

How much experience evaluating a subject of this kind can I expect my readers to have? Will they share my criteria or will I have to argue for them? For example, Baker indirectly argues for his criteria by showing that they are also Hemingway's.

How much information about the subject do my readers need to understand my evaluation? Obviously, reviews of new books, films, and albums should assume little or no familiarity on the part of readers.

PLANNING YOUR ORGANIZATION. Once you have decided how much your readers know and need to know, what reasons and backing you will use, and how best to present them, select a plan of organization that best reflects these decisions. For example, you may, like Marshall, begin by describing the subject and then move on to your evaluation, or you may weave the description, point by point, throughout your evaluation, as Thornton does.

BEGINNING. How you decide to begin your essay will depend on how familiar your readers are with your subject. If you are writing about something that is entirely new and unfamiliar, you will naturally want to begin with a description or summary of the subject.

AVOIDING LOGICAL FALLACIES. Evaluative writing is particularly susceptible to certain kinds of faulty logic. To avoid these logical fallacies, ask yourself the following questions as you plan and draft your essay:

- Am I basing my argument on personal *taste* instead of general criteria (praising a story, for example, because it reminds me of my own experience)?

- Am I basing my argument on *trivial criteria* and ignoring important ones (condemning a film because it has subtitles, for example)?

- Am I guilty of *hasty generalization* (for instance, criticizing a public figure because he or she once said something with which I disagree)?

- Am I making *weak comparisons* (failing to acknowledge weaknesses of subjects I praise and strengths of those I criticize)?

- Am I accepting the *burden of proof* (giving reasons and backing instead of merely asserting my opinions)?

- Am I guilty of *either/or thinking* (seeing only the good or only the bad in my subject)?

- Am I setting up a *straw man* (rebutting an obviously weak argument that is an easy target and ignoring stronger arguments that are harder to rebut)?

See the discussion of logical appeal under Analyzing an Argument in Chapter 1 for more on fallacies.

Revising

Once you have completed a rough draft, consider how the argument might be strengthened and the writing made clearer. Begin by reading your draft in light of the questions for analyzing basic features at the beginning of this chapter. As you read, be particularly aware of how you might make your argument clearer and more convincing for your prospective readers. If possible, have someone else read your draft critically as well.

REVISING YOUR ARGUMENT. When revising, keep your purpose and your readers in mind. If necessary, add more backing from the subject itself. Reconsider the criteria on which you have based your judgment, and decide if they are appropriate, if they need to be justified, if any are trivial. Study your reasons, looking for weak ones that should be improved or thrown out. Examine your backing to decide whether you have provided enough support. Look at the organization of your argument— the order of reasons, the proportion of good to bad qualities, the arguments you anticipate and rebut. Listen to the voice in your draft. Is it sufficiently authoritative? Is it appropriate for your readers?

REVISING TO IMPROVE READABILITY. If any part of your essay seems confusing, add forecasts, transitions, and other orienting cues to help your readers. Look for unclear writing—words that need to be defined, language that is too abstract, sentences that are hard to read—and revise to make your writing more understandable. Finally, proofread carefully for mistakes in usage, spelling, and punctuation.

CHAPTER SEVEN

Analysis of Cause or Effect

When something surprising happens, we automatically ask, "How did that happen?" The human brain seems to demand this explanation, as though incapable of leaving a mystery unresolved. We also ask ourselves what might result, sometimes for our own safety and at other times just from natural human curiosity. From these basic human responses to events, phenomena, and trends—from our compulsion to know what *caused* them and what *effects* they might have—comes the motive for writing about causes and effects.

Analysis of cause or effect involves conjecturing about an event, phenomenon, or trend that has no obvious or certain causes or effects and arguing in support of a proposed explanation. For example, a newspaper columnist might propose causes for a surprising election defeat, a decline in new housing construction, an increase in the trade deficit with Japan, or a decline in interest rates. A sportswriter might try to explain why a high-school soccer team lost a game it was favored to win, why a professional baseball-team owner was unable to sign a high draft pick, or why the Pacific Ten nearly always defeats the Big Ten in the Rose Bowl.

In government, business, and education, causal argument plays an important role. The secretary of state might request an analysis of the causes of political unrest in a Latin American country from the State Department's Latin American bureau. The chief executive officer of a computer-manufacturing firm could ask the sales manager to submit a report explaining the decline in sales of a low-priced personal computer. A school superintendent might draft a statement proposing several possible causes for falling test scores in math.

Analysis of cause or effect is also important in college study. For example, you might hear a lecture by an oceanographer speculating about an unexplained warming trend in the ocean, or you might read a history essay in which a noted scholar evaluates other scholars' proposed causes of the Civil War in order to argue for a never-before-considered cause. (If the historian merely summarized other scholars' proposed causes, he or she would be reporting established information, not speculating about new possibilities.) You might also encounter a sociological report conjecturing about the recent increase in suicides among the elderly. The writer could have no way of knowing for certain why more and more older people take their own lives but could only conjecture about it—and then argue with relevant facts, statistics, or anecdotes to support the conjectures.

Writing your own essays analyzing causes or effects will engage you in some of the most challenging problem-solving and decision-making situations a writer can experience. You will be able to test your powers of concentration and creativity as you speculate about the causes or effects of an event, phenomenon, or trend, searching out the hidden causes behind the obvious ones, differentiating among precipitating, remote, and perpetuating causes, and attempting to discover results that are surprising and yet still plausible.

You will also have the opportunity to research the causes or effects that have been proposed by others. After evaluating their conjectures and speculations, you can experiment with strategies of integrating them into your essay, accepting some and refuting others. As in all kinds of argument, you will continue to develop your sensitivity to your readers' knowledge and attitudes, anticipating their objections to your conjectures and discovering ways to be authoritative and convincing without alienating your reader. All of the thinking, planning, and writing strategies involved in this kind of writing will make you a better writer in general and will prepare you for many reading and writing situations you will encounter in other college classes.

A GUIDE TO READING ABOUT ANALYSIS OF CAUSE OR EFFECT

To begin your study of causal analysis, you will first look closely at an essay by horror-fiction writer Stephen King. Closely analyzing King's essay will provide a foundation for the serious study of arguments speculating about causes or effects this chapter encourages. As you become a more critical, insightful reader of cause/effect analysis, your own writing will be more confident and convincing.

As the initial step in your analysis, you will annotate the King selection. The next exercise asks you to take inventory of your annotations in order to disclose a pattern of meaning you have discovered. In the third exercise, guided by special questions, you will report what you have learned in analyzing the unique features of writing about cause or effect. Finally, the concluding exercise invites you to write a brief exploratory essay, consolidating what you have learned about the King selection and trying out your own ideas about it or extending your personal response to it.

The time you invest now in annotating, analyzing, and writing will pay off richly as you read, write about, and discuss the essays in this chapter. It will also give you more confidence that you can successfully complete your own essay, arguing convincingly for possible causes or effects of an event, trend, or phenomenon.

Annotating As You Read

As we have discussed, the most basic, and most useful, strategy for reading attentively and critically is annotating. Pencil in hand as you read, you are ready to record on the page any comments, questions, definitions, or insights—whatever crosses your mind—about a piece of writing. As an illustration, note how we have annotated the final paragraph from "Why Married Mothers Work," a causal analysis by economist Victor Fuchs that appears in its entirety later in this chapter.

Summary:
2 primary *causes*

Doesn't elaborate on *effects* **here, but implied: (1) number & timing of children (2) divorce more probable**

Interesting: "effects" *reinforce* **trend, becoming secondary "causes"**

I conclude that the growth of real wages and the expansion of the service sector have been the most important reasons for the growth of female labor force participation. This participation, in turn, has had important effects on marriage, fertility, and divorce, but there is also some feedback from fertility and divorce to labor force participation. Better control of fertility makes a career in the labor market more promising to women, not only because of a reduction in the number of children but also because women now have better control over the timing of births. The increase in the probability of divorce contributes to the rise in female labor force participation because women recognize that complete commitment to home and husband can leave them in a perilous economic position if the marriage should dissolve. Alimony and child support payments are often inadequate, and are not paid at all in a large proportion of cases. An old song says that

Quoting sexist song seems flippant, jarring, not effective.

"diamonds are a girl's best friend," but today the ability to earn a good wage is likely to prove a more reliable asset.

For more on annotating, pause now to review the guidelines in Chapter 1 and the model annotations on the excerpt from "Letter from Birmingham Jail." Note particularly the Checklist for Annotating.

Exercise 1

Annotate Stephen King's "Why We Crave Horror Movies" as you read. Reread it at least once, continuing to annotate as you reread. Your purpose is to focus your attention on the text, to read as thoughtfully—as critically—as possible. Annotate details you admire as well as things you question or challenge, mark noteworthy stylistic devices or writing strategies, write down any personal responses. Record your insights and reactions directly on and around the text itself.

Stephen King (b. 1947), a native of Portland, Maine, and a graduate of the University of Maine, is the United States' best-known writer of horror fiction. His most recent novels include *Skeleton Crew* (1985), *The Tommyknockers* (1987), and *Misery* (1989). Many of his novels—including *Carrie*, *The Shining*, and *Pet Sematary*—have been made into movies.

Writing for *Playboy* magazine, King speculates in the following essay about the popular appeal of horror movies. *Playboy*'s readers are predominantly men in their twenties and thirties. Given that readership, how would you predict King would argue for the appeal of horror movies? Before you begin reading, think about your own attitude toward horror films. Would you say you enjoy or even "crave" them? Are you repulsed by them? Indifferent?

Why We Crave Horror Movies
Stephen King

I think that we're all mentally ill; those of us outside the asylums only hide it a little better—and maybe not all that much better, after all. We've all known people who talk to themselves, people who sometimes squinch their faces into horrible grimaces when they believe no one is watching, people who have some hysterical fear—of snakes, the dark, the tight place, the long drop . . . and, of course, those final worms and grubs that are waiting so patiently underground.

When we pay our four or five bucks and seat ourselves at tenth-row center in a theater showing a horror movie, we are daring the nightmare.

Why? Some of the reasons are simple and obvious. To show that we can, that we are not afraid, that we can ride this roller coaster. Which is not to say that a really good horror movie may not surprise a scream out of us at some point, the way we may scream when the roller coaster twists through a complete 360 or plows through a lake at the bottom of the drop. And horror movies, like roller coasters, have always been the special province of the young; by the time one turns 40 or 50, one's appetite for double twists or 360-degree loops may be considerably depleted.

We also go to re-establish our feelings of essential normality; the horror movie is innately conservative, even reactionary. Freda Jackson as the horrible melting woman in *Die, Monster, Die!* confirms for us that no matter how far we may be removed from the beauty of a Robert Redford or a Diana Ross, we are still light-years from true ugliness.

And we go to have fun.

Ah, but this is where the ground starts to slope away, isn't it? Because this is a very peculiar sort of fun, indeed. The fun comes from seeing others menaced—sometimes killed. One critic has suggested that if pro football has become the voyeur's version of combat, then the horror film has become the modern version of the public lynching.

It is true that the mythic, "fairy-tale" horror film intends to take away the shades of gray. . . . It urges us to put away our more civilized and adult penchant for analysis and to become children again, seeing things in pure blacks and whites. It may be that horror movies provide psychic relief on this level because this invitation to lapse into simplicity, irrationality and even outright madness is extended so rarely. We are told we may allow our emotions a free rein . . . or no rein at all.

If we are all insane, then sanity becomes a matter of degree. If your insanity leads you to carve up women like Jack the Ripper or the Cleveland Torso Murderer, we clap you away in the funny farm (but neither of those two amateur-night surgeons was ever caught, heh-heh-heh); if, on the other hand, your insanity leads you only to talk to yourself when you're under stress or to pick your nose on your morning bus, then you are left alone to go about your business . . . though it is doubtful that you will ever be invited to the best parties.

The potential lyncher is in almost all of us (excluding   9 saints, past and present; but then, most saints have been crazy in their own ways), and every now and then, he has to be let loose to scream and roll around in the grass. Our emotions and our fears form their own body, and we recognize that it demands its own exercise to maintain proper muscle tone. Certain of these emotional muscles are accepted—even exalted—in civilized society; they are, of course, the emotions that tend to maintain the status quo of civilization itself. Love, friendship, loyalty, kindness—these are all the emotions that we applaud, emotions that have been immortalized in the couplets of Hallmark cards and in the verses (I don't dare call it poetry) of Leonard Nimoy.

When we exhibit these emotions, society showers us   10 with positive reinforcement; we learn this even before we get out of diapers. When, as children, we hug our rotten little puke of a sister and give her a kiss, all the aunts and uncles smile and twit and cry, "Isn't he the sweetest little thing?" Such coveted treats as chocolate-covered graham crackers often follow. But if we deliberately slam the rotten little puke of a sister's fingers in the door, sanctions follow—angry remonstrance from parents, aunts and un-cles; instead of a chocolate-covered graham cracker, a spanking.

But anticivilization emotions don't go away, and they   11 demand periodic exercise. We have such "sick" jokes as, "What's the difference between a truckload of bowling balls and a truckload of dead babies?" (You can't unload a truckload of bowling balls with a pitchfork . . . a joke, by the way, that I heard originally from a ten-year-old). Such a joke may surprise a laugh or a grin out of us even as we recoil, a possibility that confirms the thesis: If we share a brotherhood of man, then we also share an insanity of man. None of which is intended as a defense of either the sick joke or insanity but merely as an explanation of why the best horror films, like the best fairy tales, manage to be reactionary, anarchistic, and revolutionary all at the same time.

The mythic horror movie, like the sick joke, has a dirty   12 job to do. It deliberately appeals to all that is worst in us. It is morbidity unchained, our most base instincts let free, our nastiest fantasies realized . . . and it all happens, fittingly enough, in the dark. For those reasons, good liberals often shy away from horror films. For myself, I like to see the most aggressive of them—*Dawn of the Dead*, for instance—as lifting a trap door in the civilized fore-brain and throwing a basket of raw meat to the hungry alligators swimming around in that subterranean river beneath.

Why bother? Because it keeps them from getting out, 13 man. It keeps them down there and me up here. It was Lennon and McCartney who said that all you need is love, and I would agree with that.

As long as you keep the gators fed. 14

Inventorying Your Annotations

Once you have annotated a reading with your insights and thoughts, you'll want to study your annotations for their special meaning. The best way to do this is by taking inventory of your annotations, to discover any patterns or key repetitions.

Before completing Exercise 2, review the guidelines for the Inventory of Annotations in Chapter 1.

Exercise 2

Inventory the annotations you made on "Why We Crave Horror Movies," looking for meaningful patterns.

Analyzing the Basic Features
of Analysis of Cause or Effect

In addition to annotating a text to record your initial impressions and inventorying your annotations to discover patterns of meaning, you can analyze the basic features of a piece of writing, in this case those qualities that make it distinctively cause-or-effect analysis.

Look back at Identifying and Evaluating Basic Features in Chapter 1. Although the questions there are different from the ones you will find in this chapter, the answers illustrate what a thoughtful analysis of basic features might look like.

Exercise 3

Analyze "Why We Crave Horror Movies" by answering the following questions. You will want to reread the selection with each question in mind, and you may want to annotate further.

Write out your answers to the questions.

1. *How does the writer present the event, trend, or phenomenon?* Writers analyzing causes or effects have in mind a particular subject, usually an event, trend, or phenomenon. *Events* occur at a particular time and place—for example, a favored candidate loses a senate race, an airliner crashes, or an underdog soccer team wins a match. Events that are unlikely and puzzling especially invite speculation about their causes or effects. A *trend* is a noticeable change extending over many months or years. It can be identified by an increase or decrease, such as a rise in the birthrate or a decline in test scores. A *phenomenon* is a fact of life or an existing state of things, not a one-time event. It is something you or others have noticed about the human condition or the social order— for instance, low voter turnout for elections, workaholic syndrome, or cheating on exams. In some writing situations, the writer might safely assume that readers already know a great deal about the subject and thus simply announce the subject and immediately begin the analysis. For most subjects, however, writers must present the subject in enough detail so that readers understand fully what is to be analyzed. In some cases, the writer may even need to convince readers that the subject is important and worth analyzing.

To evaluate the writer's presentation of the subject, ask yourself whether the writer has provided enough information. Do you know all you need to know about the event, trend, or phenomenon? If you have not heard of the event, does the writer describe it adequately? If the subject is a phenomenon, has the writer demonstrated that it exists— with facts, statistics, or anecdotes? If the subject is a trend, has the writer presented statistics or other evidence to establish the existence of the trend?

2. *What causes or effects does the writer propose, and how comprehensive and logical are they?* The proposed causes or effects are the main points of the essay. These points can appear anywhere in the essay and are usually easy to identify. They may be listed at the beginning, or they may be introduced one at a time as the argument develops. They may also be summarized or restated at the end of the essay. Make a list of the proposed causes or effects.

Evaluate the proposed causes or effects by first determining whether they are plausible. Then decide whether the writer has ignored other equally plausible causes or results. In the case of *causes,* has the writer argued only predictable or obvious causes and overlooked not-so-obvious or hidden ones? Has the writer ignored background causes, instigating causes, or perpetuating causes? Are any proposed causes results or side-effects rather than actual causes? *Obvious causes* do not surprise readers—they might have predicted them before reading the argument. *Background causes* prepare the way for an event, trend, or phenomenon; *instigating causes* create it or set it in motion; and *perpetuating causes* sustain a trend or phenomenon. For example, in an argument that fewer and fewer children can read or write competently, a background cause could be that children are naturally drawn to visual media and prefer them over print or verbal media, which are less accessible and require instruction. An instigating cause could be that nearly every home has a television, and a perpetuating cause could be that parents are unwilling to limit their children's television viewing.

3. *What strategies does the writer adopt to argue for the proposed causes, and how effective are the strategies?* In arguing directly for the proposed causes or effects, does the writer rely on facts (statements widely accepted as true), statistics, authorities, personal anecdotes, scenarios (stories about something that might happen), or cases (typical people)? Are the facts current, reliable, and from trustworthy sources? Do the statistics come from reliable sources? Are authorities believable? Are the anecdotes and cases relevant and convincing? Do the cases ring true?

Does the writer use imaginative examples that may include surprising comparisons or contrasts, analogies, apt word images, or inventive hypothetical situations ("if . . . , then . . . ." "what if . . .")?

What strategies that might strengthen the argument has the writer overlooked? Where does the writer's direct argument for the proposed causes or effects seem most inventive or imaginative? Where does it seem predictable or superficial? Where is it most convincing and least convincing? Given the writer's purpose and readers, how might the writer argue the causes or effects more convincingly?

4. *How does the writer anticipate and refute objections and counterarguments?* When the causes or consequences of an event or trend are not certain but only probable, then there is sure to be disagreement. Readers will undoubtedly be able to think of objections to the best-argued explanations. Consequently, writers try to anticipate these objections and perhaps even attempt to refute them. Although it might seem strange that writers would acknowledge a possible objection to their arguments, they in fact increase their credibility and the plausibility of their arguments by anticipating possible objections.

Locate places in the essay where the writer has anticipated possible objections. Does the writer handle these objections tactfully and convincingly? Can you think of any other objections the writer should have anticipated?

5. *How does the writer consider alternative causes or effects?* In addition to

anticipating possible objections, writers may also consider alternative causes or effects that others have proposed, of which readers may or may not already be aware. Writers mention these alternatives in their essays, describing and evaluating them, accepting or refuting them. Such a strategy strengthens the writer's credibility and nearly always makes the writers's own proposed causes or effects seem more thoughtful and better informed and hence more trustworthy.

Does the writer present alternative causes or effects in the essay? If so, are they presented fairly? Does the writer incorporate them into his or her own argument or attempt to refute them? How successful is the writer in dealing with these alternatives? Can you think of alternative causes or results the writer may have overlooked?

6. *How does the writer establish an authoritative voice?* Although there are events and trends about which there can never be any certainty, through critical reading and evaluation we do finally have to accept certain explanations. Otherwise, we would be paralyzed by indecision over important governmental, social, educational, and personal matters.

To win our trust, writers must establish their authority by appearing informed, thoughtful, and reasonable. They must argue for their proposed causes or effects in a convincing way, anticipate readers' objections, and consider alternative causes or effects.

Consider how the writer establishes his or her authority in the essay. What strategies does the writer adopt to increase his or her credibility? What kind of voice do you hear in the essay?

7. *How is the essay organized?* To discover the organization, outline the essay, listing brief phrases to indicate the sequence of the argument. Include extended considerations of objections or alternatives in your outline. Then consider whether the essay is organized as well as it might be, given the writer's purpose and argument. Would a different sequence make the argument more convincing? Could the writer have created a chain of reasoning, with each cause or effect following logically from the preceding one? Are refutations of objections or alternatives located strategically? Is the argument easy to follow, with evidence and reasoning coherently arranged? Do you find the beginning engaging and effective? Imagine alternative beginnings for the essay. Is the ending the best possible conclusion to a convincing argument? Imagine alternative endings.

Exploring Your Personal Response

One other way of focusing your response to an analysis of cause or effect is by taking the time to record your thoughts in a more extended piece of writing. Basically, such an exercise can help you to consider how the cause or effect analysis relates to your own impressions of the subject, to explore your understanding and define further your unique perspective on what you've read.

Exercise 4

Write 300–400 words (two or three handwritten pages) about "Why We Crave Horror Movies." Choose one of the suggestions listed in Exploring Your Personal Response in Chapter 1.

K. C. Cole

K. C. Cole (b. 1946) began her writing career in the late 1960s as a reporter in Czechoslovakia, Hungary, and the Soviet Union. Returning to the United States in the early 1970s, she specialized in writing about education, science, and women. She has published articles in many newspapers and magazines, including *Saturday Review* and *Newsday*, where she held editorial and writing positions. Cole has published several books with the Exploratorium, a San Francisco science museum, including *Facets of Light: Colors and Images and Things That Glow in the Dark* (1980). Her more recent books include *Between the Lines* (1982), a collection of essays on women's issues, and *Sympathetic Vibrations: Physics as a Way of Life* (1984), an account of physicists' work and the impact of physics on our world.

Why Are There So Few Women in Science?

Like Stephen King in "Why We Crave Horror Movies," Cole speculates about the causes of a familiar phenomenon. Writing for the *New York Times* in 1981, Cole seeks to understand better why so few women go into science.

Before you begin reading, consider what causes occur to you to explain why only a small number of women become scientists, mathematicians, or engineers. Reflect on your own experience with science. Did you like or dislike science in high school? How would you explain your attraction or repulsion? Can you recall specific incidents that influenced your attitude? Which college majors do you associate with men and which with women?

I know few other women who do what I do. What I do is write about science, mainly physics. And to do that, I spend a lot of time reading about science, talking to scientists and struggling to understand physics. In fact, most of the women (and men) I know think me quite queer for actually liking physics. "How can you write about that stuff?" they ask, always somewhat askance. "I could never understand that in a million years." Or more simply, "I hate science." 1

I didn't realize what an odd creature a woman interested in physics was until a few years ago when a science magazine sent me to Johns Hopkins University in Baltimore for a conference on an electrical phenomenon known as the Hall effect. We sat in a huge lecture hall and listened as physicists talked about things engineers didn't understand, 2 and engineers talked about things physicists didn't understand. What *I* didn't understand was why, out of several hundred young students of physics and engineering in the room, less than a handful were women.

Sometime later, I found myself at the California Institute of Technology reporting on the search for the origins of the universe. I interviewed physicist after physicist, man after man. I asked one young administrator why none of the physicists were women. And he answered: "I don't know, but I suppose it must be something innate. My seven-year-old daughter doesn't seem to be much interested in science."

It was with that experience fresh in my mind that I attended a conference in Cambridge, Mass., on science literacy, or rather the worrisome lack of it in this country today. We three women—a science teacher, a young chemist and myself—sat surrounded by a company of august men. The chemist, I think, first tentatively raised the issue of science illiteracy in women. It seemed like an obvious point. After all, everyone had agreed over and over again that scientific knowledge these days was a key factor in economic power. But as soon as she made the point, it became clear that we women had committed a grievous social error. Our genders were suddenly showing; we had interrupted the serious talk with a subject unforgivably silly.

For the first time, I stopped being puzzled about why there weren't any women in science and began to be angry. Because if science is a search for answers to fundamental questions then it hardly seems frivolous to find out why women are excluded. Never mind the economic consequences.

A lot of the reasons women are excluded are spelled out by the Massachusetts Institute of Technology experimental physicist Vera Kistiakowsky in a recent article in *Physics Today* called "Women in Physics: Unnecessary, Injurious and Out of Place?" The title was taken from a nineteenth-century essay written in opposition to the appointment of a female mathematician to a professorship at the University of Stockholm. "As decidedly as two and two make four," a woman in mathematics is a "monstrosity," concluded the writer of the essay.

Dr. Kistiakowsky went on to discuss the factors that make women in science today, if not monstrosities, at least oddities. Contrary to much popular opinion, one of those is *not* an innate difference in the scientific ability of boys and girls. But early conditioning does play a stubborn and subtle role. A recent *Nova* program, "The Pinks and the Blues," documented how girls and boys are treated differently from birth—the boys always encouraged in more physical kinds of play, more active explorations of their environments. Sheila Tobias, in her book, *Math Anxiety*, showed how the games boys play help them to develop an intuitive understanding of speed, motion and mass.

The main sorting out of the girls from the boys in science seems to   8
happen in junior high school. As a friend who teaches in a science
museum said, "By the time we get to electricity, the boys already have
had some experience with it. But it's unfamiliar to the girls." Science
books draw on boys' experiences. "The examples are all about throwing a
baseball at such and such a speed," said my stepdaughter, who barely
escaped being a science drop-out.

The most obvious reason there are not many more women in science is   9
that women are discriminated against as a class, in promotions, salaries
and hirings, a conclusion reached by a recent analysis by the National
Academy of Sciences.

Finally, said Dr. Kistiakowsky, women are simply made to feel out of   10
place in science. Her conclusion was supported by a Ford Foundation
study by Lynn H. Fox on the problems of women in mathematics. When
students were asked to choose among six reasons accounting for girls'
lack of interest in math, the girls rated this statement second: "Men do
not want girls in the mathematical occupations."

A friend of mine remembers winning a Bronxwide mathematics com-   11
petition in the second grade. Her friends—both boys and girls—warned
her that she shouldn't be good at math: "You'll never find a boy who
likes you." My friend continued nevertheless to excel in math and
science, won many awards during her years at Bronx High School of
Science, and then earned a full scholarship to Harvard. After one year of
Harvard science, she decided to major in English.

When I asked her why, she mentioned what she called the "macho   12
mores" of science. "It would have been O.K. if I'd had someone to talk
to," she said. "But the rules of comportment were such that you never
admitted you didn't understand. I later realized that even the boys didn't
get everything clearly right away. You had to stick with it until it had
time to sink in. But for the boys, there was a payoff in suffering through
the hard times, and a kind of punishment—a shame—if they didn't. For
the girls it was O.K. not to get it, and the only payoff for sticking it out
was that you'd be considered a freak."

Science is undeniably hard. Often, it can seem quite boring. It is   13
unfortunately too often presented as laws to be memorized instead of
mysteries to be explored. It is too often kept a secret that science, like art,
takes a well-developed esthetic sense. Women aren't the only ones who
say, "I hate science."

That's why everyone who goes into science needs a little help from   14
friends. For the past ten years, I have been getting more than a little help
from a friend who is a physicist. But my stepdaughter—who earned the

highest grades ever recorded in her California high school on the math Scholastic Aptitude Test—flunked calculus in her first year at Harvard. When my friend the physicist heard about it, he said, "Harvard should be ashamed of itself."

What he meant was that she needed that little extra encouragement 15 that makes all the difference. Instead, she got that little extra discouragement that makes all the difference.

"In the first place, all the math teachers are men," she explained. "In 16 the second place, when I met a boy I liked and told him I was taking chemistry, he immediately said: 'Oh, you're one of those science types.' In the third place, it's just a kind of a social thing. The math clubs are full of boys and you don't feel comfortable joining."

In other words, she was made to feel unnecessary, injurious and out of 17 place.

A few months ago, I accompanied a male colleague from the science 18 museum where I sometimes work to a lunch of the history of science faculty at the University of California. I was the only woman there, and my presence for the most part was obviously and rudely ignored. I was so surprised and hurt by this that I made an extra effort to speak knowledgeably and well. At the end of the lunch, one of the professors turned to me in all seriousness and said: "Well, K.C., what do the women think of Carl Sagan?" I replied that I had no idea what "the women" thought about anything. But now I know what I should have said: I should have told him that his comment was unnecessary, injurious and out of place.

QUESTIONS FOR ANALYSIS

1. Cole writes for educated newspaper readers like you. Does she seem to be writing primarily to men or to women or to both equally? What do you think is her purpose in this essay? Point to specific evidence in the essay to support your answer.

2. In paragraphs 1–5, how does Cole present the phenomenon she speculates about? Given her readers and purpose, what advantages or disadvantages do you see in her beginning?

3. List all of the causes Cole mentions. Which are Kistiakowsky's and which are Cole's? How does Cole go beyond simply summarizing Kistiakowsky's causes in paragraphs 6–10?

4. What seem to you to be the most convincing and least convincing parts of Cole's causal analysis?

5. Cole does not directly acknowledge any objections readers may have to her argument, nor does she consider any alternative causes some

readers may prefer (except for dismissing in paragraph 7 the idea that differences might be innate). Why do you suppose she does not acknowledge objections or consider alternative causes? How might she have done it? Would it have strengthened her argument? Consider your answer in light of Cole's purpose and readers.

6. Evaluate the emotional and ethical appeals in Cole's essay. First, take a moment to review the discussion of emotional and ethical appeals under Evaluating the Argument in Chapter 1 (pp. 37–45). Then, as you reread Cole's essay with these appeals in mind, you may want to annotate the essay for evidence of such appeals. As in the Chapter 1 examples, present the results of your evaluations in separate paragraphs, one for emotional and one for ethical appeals.

7. Review Exploring Your Personal Response in Chapter 1. Then write a 300–400-word personal response to Cole's article, choosing one of the topics below:

Write to explore the implications of a particular point made in Cole's essay.

Write a letter to Cole in which you respond to anything in the essay you found particularly unusual, interesting, or troubling.

IDEAS FOR YOUR OWN WRITING

Like Cole, you might consider writing about a well-recognized social and educational problem. List several social or educational problems you are aware of. Consider especially problems in your college or community. Your list might include white-collar crime, failure or success of an urban renewal project in your community, teenage rebellion, lack of leadership from your state governor or legislature, discrimination in hiring and promotion, couples who divorce after many years of marriage, noisy college libraries, or cheating on exams. Choose a phenomenon from your list, and consider how you might go about speculating convincingly about its causes. Would you need to do research in order to learn more about the problem? What plausible causes can you think of now? How might you convince readers to take your speculations seriously? You do not have to propose a solution to the problem; rather, you only need to speculate about how it came about and why it remains a problem.

Robert Jastrow

Robert Jastrow (b. 1925) is a leading American physicist who has had a distinguished career as a teacher, researcher, science administrator, and writer. From 1958 to 1961 he was Chief of Theoretical Design for the National Aeronautics and Space Administration and from 1961 to 1981 founder and director of the Goddard Institute for Space Studies. His books include *Until the Sun Dies* (1977), *Red Giants & White Dwarfs* (1979), *The Enchanted Loom: Mind in the Universe* (1981), and *How to Make Nuclear Weapons Obsolete* (1985).

Man of Wisdom

This selection comes from Jastrow's book *Until the Sun Dies*. Unlike King and Cole, who speculate about the causes of a phenomenon, Jastrow ponders the causes of a trend: the gradual increase in the size of the human brain over a half million years. Jastrow writes for educated readers who may not be knowledgeable in science but who have an interest in what scientists are learning. Before you begin reading, preview the selection by reading the first paragraph, the first sentence or two in each subsequent paragraph, and all of the final paragraph.

Starting about one million years ago, the fossil record shows an accelerating growth of the human brain. It expanded at first at the rate of one cubic inch[1] of additional gray matter every hundred thousand years; then the growth rate doubled; it doubled again; and finally it doubled once more. Five hundred thousand years ago the rate of growth hit its peak. At that time the brain was expanding at a phenomenal rate of ten cubic inches every hundred thousand years. No other organ in the history of life is known to have grown as fast as this.[2]

What pressures generated the explosive growth of the human brain? A change of climate that set in about two million years ago may supply that part of the answer. At that time the world began its descent into a great Ice Age, the first to afflict the planet in hundreds of millions of years. The trend toward colder weather set in slowly at first, but after a million years patches of ice began to form in the north. The ice patches thickened into glaciers as more snow fell, and then the glaciers merged into great sheets of ice, as much as two miles thick. When the ice sheets reached their maximum extent, they covered two-thirds of the North American continent, all of Britain and a large part of Europe. Many mountain ranges were buried entirely. So much water was locked up on the land in the form of ice that the level of the earth's oceans dropped by three hundred feet.

These events coincided precisely with the period of most rapid expan-   3
sion of the human brain. Is the coincidence significant, or is it happen-
stance?

The story of human migrations in the last million years provides a clue   4
to the answer. At the beginning of the Ice Age Homo [man] lived near
the equator, where the climate was mild and pleasant. Later he moved
northward. From his birthplace in Africa[3] he migrated up across the
Arabian peninsula and then turned to the north and west into Europe,
as well as eastward into Asia.

When these early migrations took place, the ice was still confined to   5
the lands in the far north; but eight hundred thousand years ago, when
man was already established in the temperate latitudes, the ice moved
southward until it covered large parts of Europe and Asia. Now, for the
first time, men encountered the bone-chilling blasts of freezing winds
that blew off the cakes of ice to the north. The climate in southern
Europe had a Siberian harshness then, and summers were nearly as cold
as European winters are today.

In those difficult times, the traits of resourcefulness and ingenuity   6
must have been of premium value. Which individual first thought of
stripping the pelt from the slaughtered beast to wrap around his shivering
limbs? Only by such inventive flights of the imagination could the naked
animal survive a harsh climate. In every generation, the individuals
endowed with the attributes of strength, courage, and improvisation
were the ones more likely to survive the rigors of the Ice Age; those who
were less resourceful, and lacked the vision of their fellows, fell victims to
the climate and their numbers were reduced.

The Ice Age winter was the most devastating challenge that Homo had   7
ever faced. He was naked and defenseless against the cold, as the little
mammals had been defenseless against the dinosaurs one hundred million years ago. Vulnerable to the pressures of a hostile world, both
animals were forced to live by their wits; and both became, in their time,
the brainiest animals of the day.

The tool-making industry of early man also stimulated the growth of   8
the brain. The possession of a good brain had been one of the factors
that enabled Homo to make tools at the start. But the use of tools
became, in turn, a driving force toward the evolution of an even better
brain. The characteristics of good memory, foresight, and innovativeness
that were needed for tool-making varied in strength from one individual
to another. Those who possessed them in the greatest degree were the

[Marginal handwritten notes:]
Effect: already stated earlier but questions it now

Ice Age Homo helps support mate theory

explanation of precise weather

Because of cold weather with rate raised (how adults to?) in growth

answer, needed more rains to survive

Another Cause: tool-making industry

making and using tools built knowledge

practical heroes of their day; they were likely to survive and prosper, while the individuals who lacked them were more likely to succumb to the pressures of the environment. Again these circumstances pruned the human stock, expanding the centers of the brain in which past experiences were recorded, future actions were contemplated, and new ideas were conceived. As a result, from generation to generation the brain grew larger.

The evolution of speech may have been the most important factor of all. When early man mastered the loom of language, his progress accelerated dramatically. Through the spoken word a new invention in tool-making, for example, could be communicated to everyone; in this way the innovativeness of the individual enhanced the survival prospects of his fellows, and the creative strength of one became the strength of all. More important, through language the ideas of one generation could be passed on to the next, so that each generation inherited not only the genes of its ancestors but also their collective wisdom, transmitted through the magic of speech.

A million years ago, when this magic was not yet perfected, and language was a cruder art, those bands of men who possessed the new gift in the highest degree were strongly favored in the struggle for existence. But the fabric of speech is woven out of many threads. The physical attributes of a voice box, lips, and tongue were among the necessary traits; but a good brain was also essential, to frame an abstract thought or represent an object by a word.

Now the law of the survival of the fittest began to work on the population of early men. Steadily, the physical apparatus for speech improved. At the same time, the centers of the brain devoted to speech grew in size and complexity, and in the course of many generations the whole brain grew with them. Once more, as with the use of tools, reciprocal forces came into play in which speech stimulated better brains, and brains improved the art of speech, and the curve of brain growth spiraled upward.

Which factor played the most important role in the evolution of human intelligence? Was it the pressure of the Ice-Age climate? Or tools? Or language? No one can tell; all worked together, through Darwin's law of natural selection, to produce the dramatic increase in the size of the brain that has been recorded in the fossil record in the last million years. The brain reached its present size about one hundred thousand years ago, and its growth ceased. Man's body had been shaped into its modern form several hundred thousand years before that. Now brain and body were complete. Together they made a new and marvelous creature, charged with power, intelligence, and creative energy. His wits had been

brings ex honed by the fight against hunger, cold, and the natural enemy; his form
ll causes
the effect
o to mark
reader stand
understand
had been molded in the crucible of adversity. In the annals of anthropology his arrival is celebrated by a change in name, from Homo erectus—
the Man who stands erect—to Homo sapiens—the Man of wisdom.

NOTES

1. One cubic inch is a heaping tablespoonful.

2. If the brain had continued to expand at the same rate, men would be far brainier today than they actually are. But after several hundred thousand years of very rapid growth the expansion of the brain slowed down and in the last one hundred thousand years it has not changed in size at all.

3. Until recently, the consensus among anthropologists placed the origin of man in Africa. However, some recent evidence suggests that Asia may have been his birthplace.

QUESTIONS FOR ANALYSIS

1. Writers speculating about the causes of trends must first demonstrate to their readers that the trend actually exists, that it is increasing (or increased) or is decreasing (or decreased) over time. How does Jastrow demonstrate that human brain size actually increased during the time period he discusses?

2. Jastrow argues for three possible causes of increasing brain size. What are they? Why do you think he presents these causes in the order he does?

3. Which of the three causes are both causes *and* results of increasing brain size? How is this possible? What problems do you suppose writers of causal analyses face when they propose causes that are also results?

4. Jastrow's argument illustrates three important kinds of causes: *background* causes, *instigating* causes, and *perpetuating* or *sustaining* causes. Which causes play each of these roles in his essay? (These three types of causes are defined in question 2 of the Analyzing Basic Features section earlier in this chapter.)

5. Narrative plays an important part in Jastrow's argument. Look for the various places where he uses narrative. What role does each narrative play? Why is this strategy especially useful in Jastrow's essay?

6. In paragraphs 2, 3, 6, and 12, Jastrow asks questions. What function do these questions serve? How do they contribute to your understanding of the analysis?

IDEAS FOR YOUR OWN WRITING

Consider writing about a completed prehistoric or historic trend that interests you. List as many as you can, keeping in mind various types of trends: evolutionary, social, political, economic, artistic, agricultural, recreational. Consider trends from any century, trends of many years or just a few years. Your list might include trends like these: the decline of dinosaurs, of U.S. federalism, of vaudeville, or of corporal punishment, or the rise of human life expectancy, of nationalism, of impressionism, or of intelligence testing. Choose one trend from your list, and conjecture about its possible causes: How could you interest readers in your analysis of this trend?

Victor Fuchs

Victor R. Fuchs (b. 1934) is a professor of economics at Stanford University and research associate at the National Bureau of Economic Research. He has been elected a member of the Institute of Medicine of the National Academy of Sciences and appointed a Fellow of the American Academy of Arts and Sciences. His books include *Who Shall Live? Health, Economics, and Social Choice* (1975), *The Economics of Physician and Patient Behavior* (1978), *How We Live: An Economic Perspective on Americans from Birth to Death* (1983), and *The Health Economy* (1986).

Why Married Mothers Work

Like the Jastrow piece, the following selection from Fuchs's book *How We Live* is an example of causal analysis of a trend—the thirty-five-year increase in the numbers of married mothers who work.

Certain explanations and arguments, especially research reports and college textbooks, provide predictable cues to keep readers on track. For example, paragraph topics are usually announced in the first sentence of a paragraph. This sentence may also provide an obvious transition from one topic to the next. Consequently, you can usefully preview this kind of writing by skimming the selection, stopping to read only the first sentence of each paragraph. Preview the Fuchs selection in this way to learn as much as you can about it before you begin reading. Then pause to reflect on the title. Why do you think married mothers work? What reasons do you think an economist like Fuchs might give?

As you read this selection, notice how Fuchs documents the existence of the trend he discusses. You may be surprised to discover how long he waits to explain what he thinks has caused the trend. What is he doing instead?

Among single women ages 25–44 four out of five work for pay, and this proportion has not changed since 1950. Divorced and separated women have also traditionally worked, and their participation rates (about 75 percent) have grown only slightly. The truly astonishing changes have taken place in the behavior of married women with children, as shown in Figure 1. . . . 1

Why has the participation of married mothers grown so *rapidly* and so *steadily?* Popular discussions frequently attribute this growth to changes in attitudes that were stimulated by the feminist movement, but the time pattern portrayed in Figure 1 does not lend much support to this view. Betty Friedan's *The Feminine Mystique*, which is often credited with 2

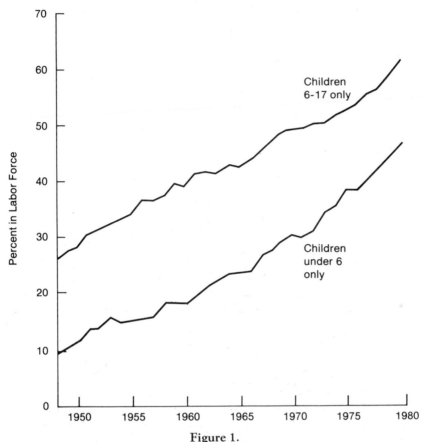

Figure 1.
Labor Force Participation Rates of Married Women with Husband Present, by Presence and Age of Own Children, 1948–1980
(Sources: Employment and Training Administration, *Employment and Training Report of the President, 1980*, table B-4; idem, *Employment and Training Report of the President, 1981*, table B-7.)

sparking the modern feminist movement, was published in 1963, long after the surge of married mothers into the labor force was under way. Moreover, there is no evidence of any sudden acceleration in response to this movement. Similarly, widespread public expressions of feminism *followed* rather than preceded the rise in the age of marriage and the fall in the birth rate. Divorce is the one variable whose change coincided with the burgeoning feminist movement, rising rapidly between 1965 and 1975. Thus, the feminist writings and discussion, valid as they may be in their own terms, will probably not be viewed by future historians as a basic cause of social change but primarily as a rationale and a rhetoric for changes that were already occurring for other reasons.

Government affirmative action programs are regarded by many as ₃
fostering female employment, but the timing again suggests that too
much has been claimed for this explanation. These programs, which did
not gain force until well into the 1960s, cannot explain the rapid rise in
participation of married mothers in the 1950s—a rise that was even more
rapid for older women with grown children. The timing of changes in the
occupational distribution of employed married women is also contrary to
what one would expect if the feminist movement or government affirmative action had a great deal of effect. The proportion who were in
professional and technical occupations rose rapidly between 1948 and
1965, from 7.7 percent to 14.7 percent, but thereafter the rate of increase
was more modest, only to 17.7 percent by 1979.

One of the most popular explanations for the two-earner family is that ₄
the wife's earnings are "needed to help make ends meet." This answer is
the one most frequently given by women to survey researchers, and it
receives some support from analytical studies that attempt to explain
why, at any particular time, some wives work and some don't. There is a
strong consensus among economists that, other things held constant, the
higher the husband's income, the less likely it is that the wife will work
for pay.

This explanation, however, does not contribute much to an under- ₅
standing of changes over time. "Need," in an absolute sense, can hardly
be the reason for the rapid rise in labor force participation of married
mothers in the 1950s, when the real hourly earnings of their husbands
were increasing at an unprecedented pace. Nathan Keyfitz (1980) observed that when women are asked why they work outside the home,
they tend to reply that they need the money. "But," he writes, "the
answer cannot be correct, since in earlier decades their husbands were
earning less, presumably families needed money, and yet wives were
content to stay home. Needing money is a universal, a constant, and a
first rule of method is that one cannot explain a variable . . . with a
constant."

One frequently mentioned but inadequately evaluated explanation for ₆
the surge of women into paid employment is the spread of time-saving
household innovations such as clothes washers and dryers, frozen foods,
and dishwashers. There is little doubt that it is easier to combine paid
employment with home responsibilities now than it was fifty years ago,
but it is not clear whether these time-saving innovations were the *cause* of
the rise in female labor force participation or whether they were largely a
response to meet a demand created by working women. Confusion about
this point is most evident in comments that suggest that the rapid growth
of supermarkets and fast-food outlets is a cause of women going to work.

Similar time-saving organizations were tried at least sixty years ago, but with less success because the value of time was much lower then. The absence of supermarkets and fast-food eating places in low-income countries today also shows that their rapid growth in the United States is primarily a *result* of the rising value of time and the growth of women in the work force, not the reverse.

Within the economics profession the explanation that commands the widest consensus is that *higher wages* have attracted more married mothers into the labor force. This explanation is more firmly grounded in economic theory than many of the others and is reasonably consistent with observed behavior, both over time and among families at a given point in time. Ever since the pioneering work of Jacob Mincer (1962), numerous cross-section analyses—studies that examine differences among individual families or groups of families—uniformly report that the probability of a wife's working is *positively* related to her potential wage rate, holding constant spouse's education. This is the opposite of the previously noted *negative* effect of the husband's wage rate on the wife's labor force participation. . . .

In addition to higher wages, the rapid expansion of jobs in the service sector has contributed to the rise in female labor force participation (Fuchs 1968). The service industries (retail trade, financial service, education, health, personal services, public administration) have traditionally offered much greater employment opportunities for women than have mining, manufacturing, construction, and other branches of the industrial sector. For instance, 73 percent of nonfarm female employment was in the service sector in 1960, whereas the comparable figure for males was only 44 percent.

There are many reasons for this large differential. First, most occupations in the service sector do not place a premium on physical strength. Second, hours of work are frequently more flexible in service industries and there are many more opportunities for part-time work. Other things held constant, mothers of small children are more likely to be working in those metropolitan areas where there is large variation in the weekly hours of men (King 1978). This variation is a good indicator of the existence of part-time employment opportunities, and women are much more likely than men to seek part-time employment. Third, service sector jobs are more likely to be located in or near residential areas, thus making them more attractive to women who bear large responsibilities for child care and homemaking.

The propensity of women to seek service sector employment is par- 10 ticularly relevant because it is this sector that has provided nearly all of the additional job opportunities in the U.S. economy since the end of

World War II. Between 1947 and 1980 U.S. employment expanded by 39 million; the service sector provided 33 million of these additional jobs. To be sure, some of the growth of service employment is the *result* of the increase in female labor force participation rather than the cause (Fuchs 1981a). Families with working mothers are more likely to eat out, to send their children to nursery school, and to purchase a wide range of personal and professional services. This feedback effect, however, accounts for only a part of the growth of service employment. The major explanation is that rapid increases in output per worker in agriculture and industry cut the demand for labor in those sectors and shifted employment to services. A secondary reason is that consumer demand shifted slightly toward services in response to the growth of real income.

I conclude that the growth of real wages and the expansion of the service sector have been the most important reasons for the growth of female labor force participation. This participation, in turn, has had important effects on marriage, fertility, and divorce, but there is also some feedback from fertility and divorce to labor force participation. Better control of fertility makes a career in the labor market more promising to women, not only because of a reduction in the *number* of children but also because women now have better control over the *timing* of births. The increase in the *probability* of divorce contributes to the rise in female labor force participation because women recognize that complete commitment to home and husband can leave them in a perilous economic position if the marriage should dissolve. Alimony and child support payments are often inadequate, and are not paid at all in a large proportion of cases. An old song says that "diamonds are a girl's best friend," but today the ability to earn a good wage is likely to prove a more reliable asset.

QUESTIONS FOR ANALYSIS

1. How does Fuchs demonstrate that the trend exists, that there has been a long-term increase in numbers of working married mothers? How convincing do you find this demonstration?

2. What causes would you propose for the increase in working married mothers? Does Fuchs anticipate and refute any of your causes? If so, how does he argue that they are mistaken? Are you convinced that your speculations are unconvincing?

3. Fuchs argues for two causes of the increase in numbers of married mothers who work. How specifically does he argue for these two causes? What do you find most convincing and least convincing in his argument?

4. In paragraphs 7–11, Fuchs argues for his own proposed causes. What does he seem to be doing in paragraphs 2–6? What advantages or disadvantages do you see in his strategy in those paragraphs?

5. Look closely at Fuchs's strategy for refuting the argument that married mothers work because their families need the income (paragraphs 4 and 5). Just how does he go about supporting his refutation? How well does he succeed?

6. To discover how Fuchs has organized and sequenced his argument, outline the essay from beginning to end. Take a moment to review the Guidelines for Outlining in Chapter 1. What advantages do you see in the way he has sequenced the parts of his argument? Can you imagine a different sequence?

IDEAS FOR YOUR OWN WRITING

If you're not already working full-time, you probably will be within a few years. Besides the trend Fuchs analyzes, many other current work-force developments will influence your employment opportunities. From your own experience or reading, are you aware of any significant trends? You could research these patterns or read to discover trends you may not be aware of. If you were to write about a work-force trend, you would need to demonstrate to your readers that it is actually a trend—increasing or decreasing over time. You could, like Fuchs, demonstrate it graphically. You might want to write about causes others have proposed for this trend; but, most important, you would offer your own speculations about the causes of the trend and argue for them inventively and convincingly.

Alternatively, consider currently changing patterns in leisure, entertainment, life-style, religious affiliation, political behavior, technology, or incidence of disease. Choose one changing pattern or trend, and consider what causes you might propose for it. Assume some readers might question your proposed causes, and imagine how you might answer their questions.

Jonathan Kozol

A well-known critic of American schools, Jonathan Kozol (b. 1936) has been in the forefront of educational reformers during the 1970s and 1980s. He has taught in the Boston and Newton, Massachusetts, public schools, as well as at Yale University and the University of Massachusetts at Amherst. To support his writing and research, he has been awarded numerous prestigious fellowships from the Guggenheim, Ford, and Rockefeller foundations. Kozol's books include *Death at an Early Age* (1967), for which he won the National Book Award, *Free Schools* (1972), *Children of the Revolution* (1978), *On Being a Teacher* (1981), and *Illiterate America* (1985).

The Human Cost
of an Illiterate Society

This selection is a complete chapter from Kozol's *Illiterate America*, a comprehensive study of the nature, causes, and consequences of illiteracy. In this chapter, Kozol speculates about the human consequences of illiteracy, outlining the limitations and dangers in the lives of adults who cannot read or write. Elsewhere in the book, Kozol conjectures about the causes of illiteracy, but here he concentrates on the results of the phenomenon, speculating about what life is like for an illiterate. He adopts this strategy of arguing the results of illiteracy in order to demonstrate that the human costs of the problem pose a moral dilemma for our country.

Since the selection is relatively lengthy, you can profitably review it before reading. Unlike textbooks with their helpful headings and subheadings, book chapters make more demands on readers. Following the previewing strategies in Chapter 1, first reflect on the title (What do you know about illiteracy? What might be its human costs?), and then read the first two or three paragraphs, the first sentence in the following paragraphs, and all of the final paragraph or two.

PRECAUTIONS. READ BEFORE USING.
Poison: Contains sodium hydroxide (caustic soda-lye).
Corrosive: Causes severe eye and skin damage, may cause blindness.
Harmful or fatal if swallowed.
If swallowed, give large quantities of milk or water.
Do not induce vomiting.
Important: Keep water out of can at all times to
prevent contents from violently erupting . . .

—*warning on a can of Drano*

[margin annotation: Effects]

We are speaking here no longer of the dangers faced by passengers on Eastern Airlines or the dollar costs incurred by U.S. corporations and taxpayers. We are speaking now of human suffering and of the ethical dilemmas that are faced by a society that looks upon such suffering with qualified concern but does not take those actions which its wealth and ingenuity would seemingly demand.

[margin annotation: 2 What are we doing to prevent illiterate Non-Americans worry about the dangers instead]

Questions of literacy, in Socrates' belief, must at length be judged as matters of morality. Socrates could not have had in mind the moral compromise peculiar to a nation like our own. Some of our Founding Fathers did, however, have this question in their minds. One of the wisest of those Founding Fathers (one who may not have been most compassionate but surely was more prescient than some of his peers) recognized the special dangers that illiteracy would pose to basic equity in the political construction that he helped to shape.

[margin annotation: 3 Socrates- knew of illiterate Founding Fathers realized it no]

"A people who mean to be their own governors," James Madison wrote, "must arm themselves with the power knowledge gives. A popular government without popular information or the means of acquiring it, is but a prologue to a farce or a tragedy, or perhaps both."

[margin annotation: Madison - how can we form a govern no one will be stable to read or understand]

Tragedy looms larger than farce in the United States today. Illiterate citizens seldom vote. Those who do are forced to cast a vote of questionable worth. They cannot make informed decisions based on serious print information. Sometimes they can be alerted to their interests by aggressive voter education. More frequently, they vote for a face, a smile, or a style, not for a mind or character or body of beliefs.

[margin annotation: When voting- they go for appearance which puts the wrong people in government]

The number of illiterate adults exceeds by 16 million the entire vote cast for the winner in the 1980 presidential contest. If even one third of all illiterates could vote, and read enough and do sufficient math to vote in their self-interest, Ronald Reagan would not likely have been chosen president. There is, of course, no way to know for sure. We do know this: Democracy is a mendacious term when used by those who are prepared to countenance the forced exclusion of one third of our electorate. So long as 60 million people are denied significant participation, the government is neither of, nor for, nor by, the people. It is a government, at best, of those two thirds whose wealth, skin color, or parental privilege allows them opportunity to profit from the provocation and instruction of the written word.

[margin annotation: Illiterate adults change the whole course of this nation. only 2/3 coun]

The undermining of democracy in the United States is one "expense" that sensitive Americans can easily deplore because it represents a contradiction that endangers citizens of all political positions. The human price is not so obvious at first.

[margin annotation: 7 Political price - cle human price - uncle]

Since I first immersed myself within this work I have often had the following dream: I find that I am in a railroad station or a large department store within a city that is utterly unknown to me and where I

[margin annotation: 8]

cannot understand the printed words. None of the signs or symbols is familiar. Everything looks strange: like mirror writing of some kind. Gradually I understand that I am in the Soviet Union. All the letters on the walls around me are Cyrillic. I look for my pocket dictionary but I find that it has been mislaid. Where have I left it? Then I recall that I forgot to bring it with me when I packed my bags in Boston. I struggle to remember the name of my hotel. I try to ask somebody for directions. One person stops and looks at me in a peculiar way. I lose the nerve to ask. At last I reach into my wallet for an ID card. The card is missing. Have I lost it? Then I remember that my card was confiscated for some reason, many years before. Around this point, I wake up in a panic.

This panic is not so different from the misery that millions of adult 9 illiterates experience each day within the course of their routine existence in the U.S.A.

Illiterates cannot read the menu in a restaurant. 10

They cannot read the cost of items on the menu in the *window* of the 11 restaurant before they enter.

Illiterates cannot read the letters that their children bring home from 12 their teachers. They cannot study school department circulars that tell them of the courses that their children must be taking if they hope to pass the SAT exams. They cannot help with homework. They cannot write a letter to the teacher. They are afraid to visit in the classroom. They do not want to humiliate their child or themselves.

Illiterates cannot read instructions on a bottle of prescription medi- 13 cine. They cannot find out when a medicine is past the year of safe consumption; nor can they read of allergenic risks, warnings to diabetics, or the potential sedative effect of certain kinds of nonprescription pills. They cannot observe preventive health care admonitions. They cannot read about "the seven warning signs of cancer" or the indications of blood-sugar fluctuations or the risks of eating certain foods that aggravate the likelihood of cardiac arrest.

Illiterates live, in more than literal ways, an uninsured existence. They 14 cannot understand the written details on a health insurance form. They cannot read the waivers that they sign preceding surgical procedures. Several women I have known in Boston have entered a slum hospital with the intention of obtaining a tubal ligation and have emerged a few days later after having been subjected to a hysterectomy. Unaware of their rights, incognizant of jargon, intimidated by the unfamiliar air of fear and atmosphere of ether that so many of us find oppressive in the confines even of the most attractive and expensive medical facilities, they have signed their names to documents they could not read and which nobody, in the hectic situation that prevails so often in those overcrowded hospitals that serve the urban poor, had even bothered to explain.

Childbirth might seem to be the last inalienable right of any female citizen within a civilized society. Illiterate mothers, as we shall see, already have been cheated of the power to protect their progeny against the likelihood of demolition in deficient public schools and, as a result, against the verbal servitude within which they themselves exist. Surgical denial of the right to bear that child in the first place represents an ultimate denial, an unspeakable metaphor, a final darkness that denies even the twilight gleamings of our own humanity. What greater violation of our biological, our biblical, our spiritual humanity could possibly exist than that which takes place nightly, perhaps hourly these days, within such overburdened and benighted institutions as the Boston City Hospital? Illiteracy has many costs; few are so irreversible as this.

Even the roof above one's head, the gas or other fuel for heating that protects the residents of northern city slums against the threat of illness in the winter months become uncertain guarantees. Illiterates cannot read the lease that they must sign to live in an apartment which, too often, they cannot afford. They cannot manage check accounts and therefore seldom pay for anything by mail. Hours and entire days of difficult travel (and the cost of bus or other public transit) must be added to the real cost of whatever they consume. Loss of interest on the check accounts they do not have, and could not manage if they did, must be regarded as another of the excess costs paid by the citizen who is excluded from the common instruments of commerce in a numerate society.

"I couldn't understand the bills," a woman in Washington, D.C., reports, "and then I couldn't write the checks to pay them. We signed things we didn't know what they were."

Illiterates cannot read the notices that they receive from welfare offices or from the IRS. They must depend on word-of-mouth instruction from the welfare worker—or from other persons whom they have good reason to mistrust. They do not know what rights they have, what deadlines and requirements they face, what options they might choose to exercise. They are half-citizens. Their rights exist in print but not in fact.

Illiterates cannot look up numbers in a telephone directory. Even if they can find the names of friends, few possess the sorting skills to make use of the yellow pages; categories are bewildering and trade names are beyond decoding capabilities for millions of nonreaders. Even the emergency numbers listed on the first page of the phone book— "Ambulance," "Police," and "Fire"—are too frequently beyond the recognition of nonreaders.

Many illiterates cannot read the admonition on a pack of cigarettes. 20
Neither the Surgeon General's warning nor its reproduction on the
package can alert them to the risks. Although most people learn by word
of mouth that smoking is related to a number of grave physical disorders,
they do not get the chance to read the detailed stories which can
document this danger with the vividness that turns concern into determination to resist. They can see the handsome cowboy or the slim
Virginia lady lighting up a filter cigarette; they cannot heed the words
that tell them that this product is (not "may be") dangerous to their
health. Sixty million men and women are condemned to be the un-
alerted, high-risk candidates for cancer.

Illiterates do not buy "no-name" products in the supermarkets. They 21
must depend on photographs or the familiar logos that are printed on
the packages of brand-name groceries. The poorest people, therefore, are
denied the benefits of the least costly products.

Illiterates depend almost entirely upon label recognition. Many labels, 22
however, are not easy to distinguish. Dozens of different kinds of Camp-
bell's soup appear identical to the nonreader. The purchaser who cannot
read and does not dare to ask for help, out of the fear of being stigmatized (a fear which is unfortunately realistic), frequently comes home
with something which she never wanted and her family never tasted.

Illiterates cannot read instructions on a pack of frozen food. Packages 23
sometimes provide an illustration to explain the cooking preparations;
but illustrations are of little help to someone who must "boil water, drop
the food—*within* its plastic wrapper—in the boiling water, wait for it to
simmer, instantly remove."

Even when labels are seemingly clear, they may be easily mistaken. A 24
woman in Detroit brought home a gallon of Crisco for her children's
dinner. She thought that she had bought the chicken that was pictured
on the label. She had enough Crisco now to last a year—but no more
money to go back and buy the food for dinner.

Recipes provided on the packages of certain staples sometimes tempt a 25
semiliterate person to prepare a meal her children have not tasted. The
longing to vary the uniform and often starchy content of low-budget
meals provided to the family that relies on food stamps commonly leads
to ruinous results. Scarce funds have been wasted and the food must be
thrown out. The same applies to distribution of food-surplus produce in
emergency conditions. Government inducements to poor people to "explore the ways" by which to make a tasty meal from tasteless noodles,
surplus cheese, and powdered milk are useless to nonreaders. Intended as
benevolent advice, such recommendations mock reality and foster
deeper feelings of resentment and of inability to cope. (Those, on the

other hand, who cautiously refrain from "innovative" recipes in preparation of their children's meals must suffer the opprobrium of "laziness," "lack of imagination . . .")

Illiterates cannot travel freely. When they attempt to do so, they encounter risks that few of us can dream of. They cannot read traffic signs and, while they often learn to recognize and to decipher symbols, they cannot manage street names which they haven't seen before. The same is true for bus and subway stops. While ingenuity can sometimes help a man or woman to discern directions from familiar landmarks, buildings, cemeteries, churches, and the like, most illiterates are virtually immobilized. They seldom wander past the streets and neighborhoods they know. Geographical paralysis becomes a bitter metaphor for their entire existence. They are immobilized in almost every sense we can imagine. They can't move up. They can't move out. They cannot see beyond. Illiterates may take an oral test for drivers' permits in most sections of America. It is a questionable concession. Where will they go? How will they get there? How will they get home? Could it be that some of us might like it better if they stayed where they belong?

Travel is only one of many instances of circumscribed existence. Choice, in almost all its facets, is diminished in the life of an illiterate adult. Even the printed TV schedule, which provides most people with the luxury of preselection, does not belong within the arsenal of options in illiterate existence. One consequence is that the viewer watches only what appears at moments when he happens to have time to turn the switch. Another consequence, a lot more common, is that the TV set remains in operation night and day. Whatever the program offered at the hour when he walks into the room will be the nutriment that he accepts and swallows. Thus, to passivity, is added frequency—indeed, almost uninterrupted continuity. Freedom to select is no more possible here than in the choice of home or surgery or food.

"You don't choose," said one illiterate woman. "You take your wishes from somebody else." Whether in perusal of a menu, selection of highways, purchase of groceries, or determination of affordable enjoyment, illiterate Americans must trust somebody else: a friend, a relative, a stranger on the street, a grocery clerk, a TV copywriter.

"All of our mail we get, it's hard for her to read. Settin' down and writing a letter, she can't do it. Like if we get a bill . . . we take it over to my sister-in-law . . . My sister-in-law reads it."

Billing agencies harass poor people for the payment of the bills for purchases that might have taken place six months before. Utility companies offer an agreement for a staggered payment schedule on a bill past due. "You have to trust them," one man said. Precisely for this reason, you end up by trusting no one and suspecting everyone of possible deceit. A submerged sense of distrust becomes the corollary to a constant need to trust. "They are cheating me . . . I have been tricked . . . I do not know . . ."

Not knowing: This is a familiar theme. Not knowing the right word for the right thing at the right time is one form of subjugation. Not knowing the world that lies concealed behind those words is a more terrifying feeling. The longitude and latitude of one's existence are beyond all easy apprehension. Even the hard, cold stars within the firmament above one's head begin to mock the possibilities for self-location. Where am I? Where did I come from? Where will I go?

"I've lost a lot of jobs," one man explains. "Today, even if you're a janitor, there's still reading and writing . . . They leave a note saying, 'Go to room so-and-so . . .' You can't do it. You can't read it. You don't know."

"The hardest thing about it is that I've been places where I didn't know where I was. You don't know where you are . . . You're lost."

"Like I said: I have two kids. What do I do if one of my kids starts choking? I go running to the phone . . . I can't look up the hospital phone number. That's if we're at home. Out on the street, I can't read the sign. I get to a pay phone. 'Okay, tell us where you are. We'll send an ambulance.' I look at the street sign. Right there, I can't tell you what it says. I'd have to spell it out, letter for letter. By that time, one of my kids would be dead . . . These are the kinds of fears you go with, every single day . . ."

"Reading directions, I suffer with. I work with chemicals . . . That's scary to begin with . . ."

"You sit down. They throw the menu in front of you. Where do you go from there? Nine times out of ten you say, 'Go ahead. Pick out something for the both of us.' I've eaten some weird things, let me tell you!"

Menus. Chemicals. A child choking while his mother searches for a word she does not know to find assistance that will come too late. Another mother speaks about the inability to help her kids to read: "I can't read to them. Of course that's leaving them out of something they should have. Oh, it matters. You *believe* it matters! I ordered all these books. The kids belong to a book club. Donny wanted me to read a book to him. I told Donny: 'I can't read.' He said: 'Mommy, you sit down. I'll read it to you.' I tried it one day, reading from the pictures. Donny looked at me. He said, 'Mommy, that's not right.' He's only five. He knew I couldn't read . . ."

A landlord tells a woman that her lease allows him to evict her if her baby cries and causes inconvenience to her neighbors. The consequence of challenging his words conveys a danger which appears, unlikely as it

(Margin annotations, handwritten:)
Distrust comes common because you just don't know

you don't know anything

you can't hold jobs of the lowest anymore

Lost location

People with these problems. It's real

your kids are embarrassed. You are their limiting knowledge

seems, even more alarming than the danger of eviction. Once she admits
that she can't read, in the desire to maneuver for the time in which to
call a friend, she will have defined herself in terms of an explicit importance that she cannot endure. Capitulation in this case is preferable to
self-humiliation. Resisting the definition of oneself in terms of what one
cannot do, what others take for granted, represents a need so great that
other imperatives (even one so urgent as the need to keep one's home in
winter's cold) evaporate and fall away in face of fear. Even the loss of
home and shelter, in this case, is not so terrifying as the loss of self.

[margin: You lose your dignity]

"I come out of school. I was sixteen. They had their meetings. The
directors meet. They said that I was wasting their school paper. I was
wasting pencils . . ."

[margin: 39]
[margin: Do school take the time to help]

Another illiterate, looking back, believes she was not worthy of her
teacher's time. She believes that it was wrong of her to take up space
within her school. She believes that it was right to leave in order that
somebody more deserving could receive her place.

[margin: 40]

Children choke. Their mother chokes another way: on more than
chicken bones.

[margin: 41 — meaning within itself]

People eat what others order, know what others tell them, struggle not
to see themselves as they believe the world perceives them. A man in
California speaks about his own loss of identity, of self-location, definition:

[margin: 42 — more examples]

"I stood at the bottom of the ramp. My car had broke down on the
freeway. There was a phone. I asked for the police. They was nice. They
said to tell them where I was. I looked up at the signs. There was one that
I had seen before. I read it to them: ONE WAY STREET. They thought it was a
joke. I told them I couldn't read. There was other signs above the ramp.
They told me to try. I looked around for somebody to help. All the cars
was going by real fast. I couldn't make them understand that I was lost.
The cop was nice. He told me: 'Try once more.' I did my best. I couldn't
read. I only knew the sign above my head. The cop was trying to be nice.
He knew that I was trapped. 'I can't send out a car to you if you can't tell
me where you are.' I felt afraid. I nearly cried. I'm forty-eight years old. I
only said: 'I'm on a one-way street . . .'"

[margin: 43 — Can't even talk right — Loss of direction brings humiliation]

Perhaps we might slow down a moment here and look at the realities
described above. This is the nation that we live in. This is a society that
most of us did not create but which our President and other leaders have
been willing to sustain by virtue of malign neglect. Do we possess the
character and courage to address a problem which so many nations,
poorer than our own, have found it natural to correct?

[margin: 44 — How do we correct a prob such everyone can Everyone help thems help just give a little effor]

The answers to these questions represent a reasonable test of our belief
in the democracy to which we have been asked in public school to swear
allegiance.

[margin: 45 — Vahy we need better education & better mor]

[bottom handwritten notes: Democracy is not helping those who do not want to be helped. Another, We put people in prison by noncriminals so they can get out an kill again]

QUESTIONS FOR ANALYSIS

1. Kozol relies on a strategy of enumerating, or listing, effects. Count the effects to discover just how many he lists. Instead of arguing at length the importance of a few effects, he lists many effects, pausing to argue a few of them briefly. Given Kozol's purpose in this chapter and its importance in his book, what advantages or disadvantages do you see in his strategy of enumeration?

2. List the effects in order, identifying each with a word or brief phrase. Why do you think Kozol sequenced the effects in just this way? Do they form related clusters? Do they form a chain of reasoning, with one effect leading to the next? Why do you think Kozol begins with certain effects and concludes with others?

3. Paragraphs 20–25 assert various reasons why Kozol would like readers to accept his claim that illiteracy results in unbearable and immoral human suffering. Take a moment to review the discussion of evaluating logical appeals under Evaluating an Argument in Chapter 1, and then apply the ABC test to the reasons and backing Kozol supplies in these paragraphs. Where are Kozol's reasons and backing appropriate, believable, or consistent? Where are they inappropriate, unbelievable, or inconsistent? Does he commit any of the logical fallacies discussed in Chapter 1? As you evaluate Kozol's argument, make notes. Then organize your notes, and write up the results of your evaluation. Your purpose is to demonstrate that you recognize both the strengths and weaknesses of Kozol's logic.

4. Kozol insists that illiteracy is a moral problem. What does he mean by this claim, and how does he go about establishing it? Given his purpose and readers, what advantages do you see in his linking of illiteracy with morality? Are you convinced of this link?

5. Writers often frame an essay or book chapter by referring at the end to something from the beginning. How does Kozol use framing in this selection? (Contrast paragraphs 2–7 with paragraphs 44 and 45.) What advantages do you see in this framing?

6. Review Exploring Your Personal Response in Chapter 1. Then write a 300–400-word personal response to Kozol's chapter, choosing one of the following topics:

> Write about your personal associations with something in Kozol's essay, such as an image, idea, example, or assertion.
> Play devil's advocate and challenge Kozol's analysis.

IDEAS FOR YOUR OWN WRITING

Consider speculating, like Kozol, about the results of a significant social problem. List some of the major social problems (local or national) that concern you. Your list might include the high pregnancy rate among unmarried teenagers, high dropout rates from schools, or high costs of a college education; unsafe working conditions or high employee turnover at your job; poor academic advising at your college or too many required courses; congested traffic or uncontrolled development in your community; or lack of good bookstores in your area or limited access to local news because there is only one daily newspaper. Choose one and consider how you might go about speculating about its effects. What effects might you argue for? How could you convince your readers to consider your proposed effects plausible? Would you need to research the problem in order to write about it more authoritatively? You need not propose a solution to this problem, but only speculate about its possible effects.

Alternatively, recall recent controversial decisions by college or community leaders. Perhaps there have been controversial decisions about campus life (convenience, safety, recreation, tutoring, or other special services) or about the future of your community (growth, transportation, safety). Make a list of specific decisions, and choose one you might write about. Consider how you would write a letter to your college or community newspaper speculating about the effects or consequences of the decision. What short-term and long-term consequences would you propose? How would you convince readers to take your ideas seriously?

I calculated 6l SI to 39 SO. Due to this, the conclusion I must make is that the author is very imaginative and uncertain. She uses many statements which can be true William Kowinski *and can be false or both.*

William Kowinski is a free-lance writer who has been the book review editor and managing arts editor of the Boston *Phoenix*. He has written articles for many newspapers and magazines, including *Esquire* and the *New York Times Magazine*. He lives in Greensburg, Pennsylvania.

Mallaise: How to Know
If You Have It

This selection is taken from *The Malling of America* (1985), a wide-ranging study of the history, architecture, and social significance of shopping malls. In this chapter, Kowinski speculates about the effects of malls on people who visit them, speculations based on seven years of visiting malls and interviewing people there. Since you too have probably repeatedly visited malls, you will be in a good position to evaluate Kowinski's speculations.

As you begin reading, notice how Kowinski engages readers' interest. Then, as you read further, pay special attention to the proposed effects of malls. Kowinski's title is a pun on the word *malaise*, which refers to a feeling of discomfort or uneasiness.

Malls make some people sick. Literally, sometimes. They feel feverish, their eyes glaze, their stomachs tumble, they fall down, they throw up. 1

Some people are just annoyed by one or another aspect of a mall, or a nonspecific quality of a particular mall, or malls in general. "That mall makes me *sick!*" they say. Or "I don't like malls—I *hate* them." Malls make people angry. Some of these people are shoppers, but some are people who work in malls or even own mall stores. 2

Malls affect people. They're designed to. But in some ways, either by their nature or by a side effect caused by their main ingredients, they do things to people that people are unaware of or don't understand, but if they knew or understood, they probably wouldn't like it. 3

There are other more obvious things that happen to people in malls that they don't or wouldn't like. Crime, for instance. 4

This section of *The Malling of America* is about some of the negative aspects of malls that affect people and that people perceive. Does the mall make you tired? Set your nerves on edge? Do you find it difficult to concentrate? Do you feel the absence of certain phenomena—weather, for 5

332

example, or civil liberties? Do you sometimes wonder if you are really as safe as mall management would like you to believe?

If you're a parent, do you fear for your children's ability to survive outside comfort control because they spend so much time in the mall? And if you're an adolescent, do you feel your horizons becoming limited to a hundred chain-store outlets and three anchor department stores? Or are you worried that this is precisely the world your parents do live in, and where they want you always to remain?

These are some of the symptoms of mallaise. Perhaps you have one or two, or know someone who does, or perhaps you want to be prepared, just in case. Then perhaps you should read on.

I had my first attack of *mal de mall*[1] in Columbia, Maryland. I was in a restaurant in the Columbia Mall having coffee. The attack was characterized by feverishness, sudden fatigue, and high anxiety, all recurring whenever I glanced out at the mall itself. The thought of going out there again made me sweat and swoon, and I had to fight the hallucinatory certainty that when I left the restaurant I would be in Greengate mall, or maybe Woodfield, or Tysons Corner. Or *all* of them.

Mal de mall, or mall sickness, is one of the classifications of mallaise, the general term for physical and psychological disturbances caused by mall contact. I know because I made them all up. Among the symptoms I have personally observed or heard about from their victims are these:

Dismallcumbobulation: "I don't like to go to malls because I always get lost," a woman told me, "and that's embarrassing. I feel stupid. It makes me mad." The hyped-up overabundance of similar products plus the bland sameness of many mall environments make people feel lost even when they aren't. Even familiar malls relocate stores and reconfigure themselves, which adds to the feeling of a continuous featureless space. And the similarity of one mall to another is disorienting. You walk out of the Stuft Potato and you not only don't remember which way your car is, you might not remember what mall this is. There are other kinds of dismallcumbobulation: the loss of a sense of time as well as place, and forgetting one's purpose in coming to the mall—all of which can lead to apathy and hopelessness, loss of consciousness, or fainting. Some victims recommend deep-breathing exercises every fifteen minutes while at the mall.

Inability to Relate to Others: "It's impossible to talk to someone when you're shopping at the mall," a friend told me, explaining why she prefers

---

[1] *Mal de mall* is a play on the French expression *mal de mer* ("seasickness"). [Eds.]

to shop alone. "I notice it at the mall all the time—you see two people together but they aren't really talking to each other. They're talking, but they're staring off in different directions, and pretty soon they just wander away from each other." Among the possible effects of this symptom are disenchantment and divorce.

Plastiphobia, or the fear of being enclosed in a cocoon of blandness. "Suddenly I just stood still and looked around," a young man said. "I saw all the people and what we were all doing there, what we were spending our day doing, and I suddenly just couldn't wait to get out. I was in a plastic place with plastic people buying plastic products with plastic charge cards. I had to escape." Sometimes this reaction is accompanied by severe anxiety, alienation from the human race, and in at least one very severe case I know of, by all the usual manifestations of a drug overdose.

All of these, and their variations, are unfortunate side effects (or perhaps just extreme cases) of the main psychological effects that the mall intends. Excitement may become overstimulation; relaxation may drift into confusion and torpor. The combination is what I call the Zombie Effect.

There is, in fact, a fine line between the ideal mall shopper and the dismayed mall shopper, between mall bliss and mallaise, between the captivated shopper and the Zombie Effect. The best description of the Zombie Effect I've heard was Barbara Lambert's, which she imparted while we toured the malls of Chicagoland.

It hits you, Barbara said, when you're standing there naked, looking in the mirror of the dressing room. Your clothes are in a pile on the floor or draped over a chair. Maybe it's just a little cubicle with a curtain, and you can still hear the hum and buzz of the mall and the tiny timbres of Muzak. You're about to try something on, in an effortless repetition of what you've been doing since you came to the mall. And suddenly you realize *you've been here all day*. Time has in fact been passing while you've been gliding through store after store in a tender fuzz of soft lights and soft music. The plash of fountains, the glow of people, but almost no intrusive sound has broken your floating—no telephone, no demands, nothing to dodge or particularly watch out for. Just a gentle visual parade of clothes, fabric tags, and washing instructions. Racks, displays, cosmetics, brisk signs, flowing greenery, and spasms of color in the dream light. An ice-cream cone, a cup of coffee. Other figures have glided by: walking models of the mall's products, or walking models of the weird. An old man who reminds you of your grandfather, sitting on a blondwood bench under a potted palm. A woman who may or may not have been your best friend's other best friend in high school, striding by on strange shoes—or maybe that's a new style and yours are strange? You're looking at your naked image in a bare little room, and a little breeze touches you. Whatever you actually came here for is in the distant past. You've been floating here . . . for hours.

But that's the whole idea of this psychological structure: to turn off your mind and let you float; to create a direct and unfettered connection between eyeing and buying; and the more you do, the easier it becomes. Malls make for great eye/hand-on-credit-card coordination.

The way it's done is with a combination of peacefulness and stimulation. The environment bathes you in sweet neutrality with soft light, candied music, and all the amenities that reassure and please without grabbing too much individual attention. At the same time, the stores and products dance for you with friendly smiles and colorful costumes. The sheer number of products and experiences you pay for and their apparent variety are in themselves factors that excite and focus.

Once again, it's all a lot like television. TV lulls and stimulates simultaneously. The medium itself is familiar and comfortable and friendly; the programs can be interesting but it is not really by accident that they are not as compact, colorful, dramatic, or insistent as the commercials. Watching television we are everywhere and nowhere in particular, just as at the mall. Suddenly you might realize that you've been watching it all day, just floating for hours. And if you look at people watching television—especially their eyes—they look pretty much like mall shoppers: the Zombie Effect.

But these effects are all supposed to be pleasant and unconscious. When either the lulling or stimulating quality—or especially the combination and conflict between them—is strongly felt, then it's no longer pleasant. Overstimulation causes anxiety, and sometimes an intense focus on heavy-duty, no-nonsense, get-out-of-my-way shopping, or else a frenzied need to get out of there, fast and forever. The lulling and sense deprivation cause listlessness and confusion, and occasionally rebellion at being Muzaked into implacable mushy madness. The conflict of both going on at the same time can cause the sense of dislocation and exhaustion that is the clearest indicator of the Zombie Effect. The victim shuffles and mumbles, is distant or unduly preoccupied, doesn't listen, acts automatically, and not only can't remember where the car is parked but often doesn't care.

There are ancillary symptoms and causes as well: headaches caused by guilt at buying too much; depression at not being able to buy everything; the walking emptiness caused by consistently emphasized, endless greed.

The cure for all forms of mallaise is theoretically simple: The victim leaves the mall. There are no laws requiring people to stay in the mall, or even to go there in the first place. It isn't anyone's civic, moral, spiritual, or intellectual duty. The mall may be the best place—or even the only place—to shop for certain products, but that doesn't mean the shopper has to stay there for hours. Nevertheless, it isn't always easy to leave.

For that is another aspect of the Zombie Effect: Victims stay for no 22 good or apparent reason, and even beyond their conscious desire to be there. Shoppers mallinger partly because of the mall's psychological apparatus, its implicit promise of safety, sanctuary, and salvation. Of Nirvana! The Crystal City! A New Heaven on a New Earth! The mall hasn't become the most successful artificial environment in America for nothing.

With its real walls and psychological illusions, the mall protects against 23 so many hazards and uncertainties that the mallaise sufferer may well mallinger a little longer to ponder the consequences of walking out. Such a person may fear trading the malladies of the Zombie Effect for the perils of mall withdrawal, which is characterized by shaking in downtown areas, fear of crossing streets, inordinate terror in the presence of rain or sunshine, confusion when actual travel is required between purchases, and the feeling of estrangement when wearing a coat.

I wish I could say that medical science is on top of this new set of 24 malladies, but the truth is that it is scandalously behind the times. Right now, there may be many thousands of Zombie Effect sufferers, untreated and undiagnosed. If you find this hard to believe—well, have you been to the mall lately?

QUESTIONS FOR ANALYSIS

1. Reread carefully Kowinski's introduction to his speculations (paragraphs 1–7). What strategies does he use to engage readers' interest and draw them into his selection? How did his introduction influence the way you read the selection?

2. In paragraphs 9 through 14, Kowinski presents the main effect of malls, along with its symptoms. How does Kowinski organize this section? What advantages or disadvantages do you see in his way of organizing?

3. Throughout the chapter, Kowinski contrasts the intended effects of malls with the unintended side effects. Skim the essay, annotating places where he makes this contrast explicit. Given his purpose, why do you think he relies on this contrast?

4. What kind of evidence for the Zombie Effect does Kowinski offer? Why do you think he chose this kind of evidence?

5. Writers speculating about effects often use analogies, which can be quite tricky to use convincingly because they may not stand up under critical analysis. Analyze Kowinski's analogy comparing mall visits to television watching (paragraph 18). What are the points of comparison in the analogy? How successful do you think it is?

6. Compare the voice or tone in the Kowinski and Kozol selections. (Pause to review Comparing and Contrasting Related Readings in Chapter 1.) Account for the tone in each selection by referring to specific words, phrases, and sentences. What can you conclude about the tone of the two selections?

IDEAS FOR YOUR OWN WRITING

Consider, like Kowinski, the effects of familiar activities not generally considered harmful, such as studying, praying, jogging, napping, vacationing, or dancing. Choose one of these activities, and come up with some possible harmful effects. How might you go about writing an essay—either serious or humorous—speculating about these effects? Could you arrange to participate in the activity again, observing closely what goes on and talking to others who participate?

Alternatively, think about public or commercial institutions with which you are familiar, such as a sports stadium, church, college, swimming pool, golf course, or summer camp. Choose one of these as a possible essay topic. How might you go about writing a humorous essay speculating about its unexpected harmful effects on those who visit it? What strategies of Kowinski's might you adopt?

Lori Weichenthal

Lori Weichenthal wrote this essay as a freshman at the University of California, San Diego.

The Rise of Regional Theater

Weichenthal's essay is ambitious, well argued, and carefully documented. As serious an effort as it is, it began with her personal interest in regional theaters in Ashland and San Jose. Writing the essay enabled her to combine personal experience (memory, reflection), reporting (interviews with regional theater directors), and library research.

As you begin reading the essay, notice how she demonstrates that the trend does exist. Then notice how many different kinds of causes she proposes to explain the trend.

In 1956, theater lovers in San Jose, California, and Cleveland, Ohio, had something in common: a long and often futile wait to see professionally produced plays. The dramatic world of the United States was centered in the theaters along New York's Broadway. Few quality theater companies existed elsewhere. The only opportunity most Americans had to see a polished production was when the Broadway companies traversed the country with the top shows of the season. Even then, many theatergoers were left without a ticket: the tours usually covered only major cities; and many regions of the country, especially in the Northwest, were entirely overlooked. In the mid-sixties, however, permanent professional theaters began to appear in places as diverse as Miami, Florida, and Anchorage, Alaska. Today, in 1986, this movement has developed into a thriving trend, and audiences in San Jose and Cleveland have to wait no more. Each city now possesses its own professional theater, which produces upwards of six plays a year. Both cities have benefited from the trend toward new regional theaters.

The rise of regional theater was at first very slow. In 1956, *Theatre World*, the yearbook of the theatrical industry, recognized only two professional theaters beyond the boundaries of New York City, although in actuality a few more existed (Blums 6). Most were small, struggling companies, attempting to maintain a limited summer session on a shoestring budget. In 1965, however, a call went forth to establish a National Endowment for the Arts. The Ford Foundation and the federal govern-

338

ment responded, allocating a substantial sum of money to advance regional theater and to deal with the "theatrical wilderness" that existed in many parts of the country, especially in the Northwestern and Southern states (Ross ix). With this money, new companies slowly began to emerge, and existing companies grew stronger. In 1968, twenty-eight professional theaters outside of New York were recorded in *Theatre World* (Willis vol. 25).[1] In 1974, the number doubled, reaching fifty-nine (Willis vol. 31). In addition, interesting notes began to appear in the once Broadway-monopolized book, commenting on the possible values of the emerging companies:

> The importance of these regional companies for experimental purposes, and for developing new talent and audiences is obvious. They are deserving indeed of any encouragement that may be given them. Perhaps the future of the Broadway theater may depend upon their continuing productivity. (Willis 6 vol. 31)

The established dramatic community was beginning to take notice that professional theater no longer existed only within the confines of New York City.

With the arrival of the eighties, the number of regional theaters took an amazing leap, rising to a recorded 152 (Zeisler iv). This number continued to increase throughout the early eighties, even as Broadway began to experience a decline. As the number of new regional theaters increased on an average of ten per year, the number of Broadway productions declined by ten. Attendance at Broadway theaters decreased by 5 percent, as the number of individuals attending regional productions climbed to twelve million (all data are from Willis). Broadway, it seemed, could no longer be considered the center of the dramatic universe. Regional theater had risen and was taking some of the glow from the Broadway sun. What caused this change? What force fueled and maintained the ascent of regional theater?

The most apparent explanation for the appearance of local professional theaters is the establishment of the National Endowment for the Arts (NEA). Before the NEA's founding, financial support simply was not available for dramatic pursuits beyond Broadway. Theater was an investment into which producers put money in order to extract profits. Regional theaters presented little chance for monetary gain and, consequently, attracted few investors. The few companies that existed before the Endowment did so through "great determination, a tight budget, and a great deal of begging" (Ruben 94).

With the money from NEA, however, regional theater could develop and expand. It is no surprise that the first jump in the number of regional theaters corresponds directly with the establishment of NEA. In addition, NEA allocated money to establish communication and exchange networks among the isolated companies throughout the country. This increased the growth potential of new companies, who could now rely on the experience of more established theatrical groups. Thus, NEA was vital to the original establishment of the trend toward regional theater. Money alone, however, cannot explain the increase in local companies; money does not ensure success or the existence of an audience, a necessity for theatrical survival. Yet, most of the theaters founded with the assistance of the Endowment have survived, developed significant audiences and even managed to make a profit. A more intensive search, then, is necessary to explain properly the trend toward regional theater.

One deeper cause for the rise of regional theater is that, in recent decades, there has been a general increase in demand for live entertainment. In 1982, the amount of income that the average United States citizen spent on live entertainment increased 5 percent over 1973 (Census Bureau 205). In the category of live entertainment, theater was a major contributor, behind only rock concerts. Thus, regional theater has benefited from people's increasing interest in live entertainment. Even as technology brings inexpensive electronic media into the home, the special exchange between audience and performer that constitutes live theater is growing in importance. Paul Barnes, director of educational outreach at the Oregon Shakespearean Festival (OSF), noted that the young especially are excited by live theater and the many levels of response it provides: "They are not just sitting in front of a sterile tube. They are sitting with a group of vibrant people, watching fellow humans act. The possibilities are limitless" (Barnes).

Regional theater is uniquely capable of fulfilling the need for live entertainment. Many theaters, including OSF, have even experimented with participatory plays, further servicing their audiences' desire for live interaction. Such plays have become increasingly popular, playing to sellout audiences in many local theaters throughout the country. Thus, the modern need for personal involvement in entertainment, so naturally fulfilled by theatrical productions, has encouraged the rise of regional companies in the United States. A purely economic explanation for the success of permanent professional theaters is also available: regional theaters are more financially feasible than the Broadway-centered system. For less money, regional theater reaches more people than Broadway and its touring companies could ever manage. In 1980, the 152 regional theaters reached 12 million theatergoers at an average cost of $2.53 (Zeisler iv). For a touring company to reach only a tenth of this audience cost an average of $4.61 (Willis 5 vol. 37).[2]

This great price gap is largely due to the fact that regional theaters are   8
more cost effective. As mostly nonprofit organizations, they stick to tight
budgets and rarely run into the overexpenditures that are legendary on
Broadway. In 1983, OSF had a budget of $2,354,000 for the production
of eleven plays, an average cost of $214,000 a play. The company took in
$2,476,000 that year, leaving a profit of $122,000 to reinvest (Ross 105).
The same year, it cost $5,000,000 to produce one Broadway play (*My One
and Only*), and investment returns were not good (Brustein 23).

This difference in fiscal responsibility ultimately shows up in ticket   9
prices. The average ticket price to a Broadway production in 1983 was
$25; the high was $50 (Willis 5). In contrast, a subscription for five plays
at one newly formed regional theater, the San Jose Repertory, cost $36,
an obvious savings (Isenberg 95). Such differences in price regional
theater far more consumer attractive. As a New York critic put it,
Broadway is "trying to sell a million Cadillacs when only a fraction of the
populace has the means to buy them!" (Brustein 26). Many theatergoers
are choosing the economy model provided by regional theater and are
discovering a much smoother ride.

Beyond economics, the success of regional theater can be attributed to   10
its early realization of its role in the community. Beyond providing
quality performances, a Broadway company has no commitment to the
cities at which it stops on tour. This is not true of a local permanent
theater, which, in order to survive, must maintain positive relations
within the region it serves. From the start, many local companies realized
their calling to be more than just producers of plays; they took on some
extra responsibility and established outreach programs to tap unfound
audiences and to develop new audiences and artists for the future.

OSF has maintained an outreach program almost from its founding.   11
Originally simply a service where actors traveled to surrounding colleges
to teach Shakespeare, the program expanded in 1975 to involve two
actor teams that traverse the Pacific Coast from Alaska to central California, instructing school-age students and getting them "into Shakespeare." In addition, the festival offers specials to all its audiences,
including backstage tours and round-table discussions with actors and
production stage hands. Paul Barnes, the director of these outreach
programs, says that they are all ways to provide for the theater of the
future. He believes the positive effects of the program are already trace-
able. People from new areas, tapped by the traveling actors, have begun
attending the festival; and young theatergoers have increased markedly,
adding to the total audience gain of 100,000 over ten years (all data are
from Barnes interview).

Newer regional theaters have also established outreach programs. The   12
San Jose Repertory, in its first year of existence, established a magnet
program with a local high school to encourage artistic talent. It also
established a touring program visiting local schools, to introduce young
children to theater. The initial expense drained their limited funds;
however, director David Lemos called it an investment that paid off.
Such programs made the public aware of the theater and helped to triple
audience size, as well as serving to develop fresh talent that has already
appeared in several company productions (Lemos).

OSF and San Jose Repertory are the rule, not the exception. Almost   13
all regional theaters today have some type of outreach program, and the
dividends they have received have been many. The programs have found
the audience to maintain the theaters now, as well as the audience and
actors of tomorrow. Regional theaters' realization of the necessity of their
outreach role has contributed significantly to their survival.

Another possible cause of the increasing numbers of regional theaters   14
is that these companies can design their productions to meet the specific
interests of the local citizenry. In 1984, OSF produced a play, *Dream-
house*, about California life (located in Ashland, Oregon, near the California border, the festival draws largely a California clientele). The play,
which probably would not have sold well in Ohio, had a 96 percent box
office return, largely because it was a play that dealt with immediate
issues important to Californians (Ruben 96). Similarly, the San Jose
Repertory produced a play, *Yup!*, about the lives of Yuppies, young urban
professionals in the surrounding Silicon Valley. The show was sold out
throughout the summer while a Broadway musical in town at the same
time attracted only half an audience (Lemos). Such productions meet the
needs of the local audiences and have regional theaters popular with
wide ranges of audiences. This popularity has helped to maintain the
regional theaters and has convinced many communities to establish their
own theaters, furthering the trend of regional theater in the United
States.

All of these causes help explain the trend toward regional theater. The   15
establishment of NEA clearly contributed to the initial stages of the
movement, and the economic advantages and unique service capacity of
regional companies have helped in their development and maintenance.
However, even all these aspects together do not provide a complete
picture as to why regional theater has risen, and they certainly do not
explain the sudden surge in the trend during the eighties. There must
still be a deeper, more fundamental, explanation of the ascent of regional
companies. Taking into account the proverbial saying that "art mirrors
life," a look at the nation as a whole provides a clue: this theatrical

movement is merely a part of a larger, more general, trend toward decentralization.

In his popular book *Megatrends*, John Naisbitt documents this trend as it affects every aspect of American life from politics to television. The main aspect of the trend is that now and in the future important movements will come from the grass roots. The rise of regional theater fits perfectly into this megatrend, taking the power away from the center of Broadway and giving it to the regions, just as important political activity is now centered in the states, not the nation's capital. In addition, the megatrend of decentralization explains the sudden rise in regional theater in the eighties, as this is when Naisbitt documents the real force of the trend beginning. [16]

Thus, the best explanation of the rise of regional theater is that it is part of the larger movement toward decentralization that the country is undergoing. All the other causes contributed toward regional theaters' rise, and probably other causes too, but it is this single cause which gives the theatrical movement meaning. The strength of the local theaters does not mean the death of Broadway as some critics may contend. Rather, it signals a new age, where the vitality and talent will come from the regions to Broadway and other national centers. [17]

NOTES

1. Data cited with no page number were obtained by counting the entries contained within one volume.
2. These costs are based on data from the cited text, calculated using the formula (cost of production)/(total audience attendance).

WORKS CITED

Barnes, Paul. [Personal interview]. 3 May and 6 May 1986.

Blums, Daniel, ed. *Theatre World*. New York: Grenburg, 1957.

Brustein, Robert. "The Broadway Slump." *The New Republic* (7 March 1983): 25–26.

Census Bureau. *Census of Sports and Leisure*. Washington, D.C.: Census, 1982.

Isenberg, Barbara, ed. *California Theatre Annual*. California: Performing Arts Network, 1982.

Lemos, David. (Personal interview). 3 May 1986.

Naisbitt, John. *Megatrends: Ten New Directions Transforming Our Lives*. New York: Warner Books, 1982.

Ross, Laura, ed. *Theatre Profiles 5*. New York: Theatre Communications, 1982.

Rubin, Margaret, ed. *Ashland, Oregon, Shakespearean Festival*. Ashland: Oregon Shakespearean Festival, 1984.

Willis, John, ed. *Theatre World*. Vols. 25–39. New York: Crown, 1984.

Zeisler, Peter. *Theatre Profiles 3*. New York: Theatre Communications, 1980.

QUESTIONS FOR ANALYSIS

1. Do you find Weichenthal's argument for the increase in regional theaters convincing? What part of her argument do you find most convincing? least convincing?

2. How does Weichenthal demonstrate that the trend exists, that there has indeed been an increase in the number of regional theaters? What do you find convincing or unconvincing about this demonstration?

3. List in order the causes Weichenthal proposes to explain the rise of regional theaters. What kinds of causes does she propose, and how does she argue for each one? Can you imagine a better order for the causes? Can you think of any causes she has overlooked?

4. Writers often have difficulty integrating sources smoothly into their essays. Choose one paragraph in which Weichenthal cites several outside sources. How successfully does she integrate these sources into the paragraph?

5. Compare the causal arguments in the King, Cole, Fuchs, Jastrow, and Weichenthal selections. (Pause to review Comparing and Contrasting Related Readings in Chapter 1.) Pay particular attention to the ways in which these authors support their proposed causes and anticipate readers' possible objections. From these comparisons, what can you conclude about the nature of causal argument?

IDEAS FOR YOUR OWN WRITING

List recent trends in entertainment and the arts, like the increase in jazz groups and recordings or the growing preference for watching movies at home. Choose one whose causes you would be interested in exploring in an essay. How would you demonstrate that you have identified a trend (which continues over a period of time) and not a fad (which lasts for no more than a year or two)? What causes might enlighten your readers about the origins of this trend? You would want to go beyond obvious causes to search out hidden and unexpected causes.

A GUIDE TO WRITING ABOUT ANALYSIS OF CAUSE OR EFFECT

From the readings in this chapter, you have learned a great deal about writing that analyzes causes or effects and are in a good position to understand the problems and possibilities of this kind of writing. This section offers guidance for writing an essay of this type. You will find activities to help you identify a topic and discover what to say about it, organize your ideas and draft the essay, and revise your draft to strengthen your argument and improve readability.

The Writing Task

Write an essay that presents a well-thought-out argument speculating about why a phenomenon, trend, or event has occurred, or discussing its significant effects. The phenomenon, trend, or event may be one you have observed firsthand, one you learned about in the news, or one you are learning about now in a course. If your essay is an analysis of causes, it should do two things: demonstrate the existence of the phenomenon, trend, or event and offer possible causes for it. In this case your purpose is to convince your particular readers that your proposed causes are plausible. If your essay is an analysis of effects, it should introduce the reader to the phenomenon, trend, or event and enumerate some of its effects or results—positive, negative, or both. In this case your purpose is to convince your reader to accept your speculations about the effects of the subject.

Invention

The following activities can help to get you started and enable you to explore your subject fully. A few minutes spent completing each of these writing activities will improve your chances of producing a detailed and convincing first draft. You can decide on a subject for your essay, review what you presently know about the subject, conjecture about possible causes or effects, evaluate others' proposed causes or effects, and analyze how you might convince readers that you have a plausible argument.

CHOOSING A SUBJECT. The subject of a cause or effect essay may be a trend, an event, or a phenomenon. Essays about trends and phenomena are illustrated by the readings in this chapter. Before considering a subject for your essay, you might want to review the Ideas for Your Own Writing that follow each reading. These varied possibilities for cause or effect essays may suggest an essay you would like to write.

After reviewing the ideas for writing, you may still need to identify an appropriate subject for an essay. A good way to begin is to list as many possibilities as you can think of. List-making generates ideas: as soon as you start a list, you will think of possibilities you cannot imagine now.

Even if you feel confident that you already have a subject, listing other possibilities will help you to test your choice. Make separate lists for *trends, events,* or *phenomena.* List specific subjects suggested by the possibilities included here for each category.

For *trends,* consider the following possibilities:

changes in men's or women's roles and opportunities in marriage, education, or work

changing patterns in leisure, entertainment, life-style, religious life, health, technology

completed artistic or historical trends (various art movements or historical changes)

long-term changes in economic conditions or political behavior

For *events,* these possibilities might help you to get your own list under way:

a recent college, community, national, or international event about which there is puzzlement or controversy

a recent surprising event at your college like the closing of a tutorial or health service, cancellation of popular classes, changes in library hours or dormitory regulations, the loss of a game by a favored team, or some violent act by one student against another

a recent puzzling or controversial event in your community like the abrupt resignation of a public official, a public protest by an activist group, a change in traffic laws, a zoning decision, or the banning of a book from school libraries

a historical event about which there is still some dispute as to its causes or effects

For *phenomena,* there are many possibilities:

social problems like discrimination, homeless people, child abuse, illiteracy, high-school dropouts, youth suicides, teenage pregnancy

various aspects of college life like libraries too noisy to study in, classes too large, lack of financial aid, difficulties in scheduling the classes you want, shortcomings in student health services, unavailability of housing (in this essay you will not need to solve these problems, but only to analyze their causes or effects)

human traits like anxiety, selfishness, fear of success, fear of failure, leadership, jealousy, lack of confidence, envy, opportunism, curiosity, openness, health or fitness

After you have completed your lists, reflect on the possibilities you have compiled. Since an authoritative essay analyzing causes or effects requires sustained thinking, drafting, revising, and possibly even research, you will want to choose a subject to which you can commit yourself enthusiastically for a week or two. Choose a subject that interests you, even if you feel uncertain about how to approach it. The writing and research activities that follow will enable you to test your subject choice and to discover what you have to say about it.

EXPLORING YOUR SUBJECT. You may discover you know more about your topic than you suspected if you write about it for a few minutes without stopping. This brief sustained writing stimulates memory search, helps you probe your interest in the subject, and enables you to test your subject choice. As you write, consider questions such as these: What interests me in this subject? What is there about it that might interest readers? What do I already know about it? Why don't we already have an accepted explanation for this subject? What causes or effects have people already suggested for this subject? How can I learn more about it?

CONSIDERING CAUSES OR EFFECTS. Before you research your subject (should you need to), you will want to discover what causes (or effects) of it you can already imagine. Make a list of possible causes or effects. Consider background, instigating, and perpetuating causes; try to think not only of obvious causes or effects, but also of ones that are likely to be overlooked in a superficial analysis of your subject. These types of causes are defined in question 2 of the Analyzing Basic Features section earlier in this chapter.

Reflect on your list, identifying the most convincing causes or effects. Do you have enough to make a strong argument? Could a friend help you to extend your list? Imagine how you might convince readers of the plausibility of some of these causes or effects.

RESEARCHING YOUR SUBJECT. When developing an essay analyzing causes or effects, you can often gain great advantage by researching your subject. (See the appendix on Strategies for Research and Documentation.) You can review and evaluate others' proposed causes or effects, in case you want to present any of these alternatives in your own essay. Reviewing others' causes or effects may suggest to you plausible causes or effects you have overlooked. You may also find evidence and arguments to use in your own counterarguments to readers' objections.

ANALYZING YOUR READERS. Your purpose is to convince readers with a plausible argument for your proposed causes or effects. To succeed, you will need to choose causes or effects, evidence, and arguments that will convince your particular readers. You will want to anticipate objections these readers may have to any of your proposed causes or effects and to identify alternatives they may favor.

To analyze your readers, you might find it helpful to write for a few minutes, identifying who they are, what they know about the subject, and how they can be convinced by your proposed causes or effects.

REHEARSING YOUR ARGUMENT. The heart of your essay will be the argument you make for the plausibility of your proposed causes or effects. Like a ballet dancer or baseball pitcher warming up for a performance, you can prepare for your first draft by rehearsing the argument you will make. Write for a few minutes about each cause or effect, trying out an argument for your particular readers. This writing activity will focus your thinking and encourage you to keep discovering new arguments up until the time you start drafting. It may also lead you to search for additional evidence to support your arguments.

Drafting

Review the lists, writings, and notes you produced in the preceding invention activities. Note the most promising material. You may realize that you need further information, a deeper analysis, or a better understanding of your readers. If you have the time, stop now to fill in these gaps. If you feel reasonably confident about your material, however, you may be ready to begin drafting. Remember that you will solve some problems and make further discoveries as you draft. The following guidelines will help you to set goals for your draft and to plan your organization.

SETTING GOALS. If you establish goals for your draft before you begin writing, you will find that you can move ahead more quickly. With general goals in mind, you can make particular writing decisions more confidently. Consider these questions now and keep them in mind as you draft in order to maintain your focus:

How will I convince my readers that my proposed causes or effects are plausible? Shall I marshal scientific evidence like Jastrow, quote authorities and give several reasons like Fuchs, or include personal anecdotes and cases like Kozol and Cole?

How should I anticipate readers' objections to my argument? What should I do about alternative causes or effects? Shall I consider alternative causes carefully and refute each one like Fuchs, or review alternative causes and incorporate all of them into my own explanation like Weichenthal?

How much will my readers need to know about my subject—the event, trend, or phenomenon? Will I need to describe my subject in some detail in the way that Cole shows how women are excluded from science, or can I assume that my readers have personal experience with my subject just as Weichenthal seems to assume that her readers have all seen a play at some regional theater? If my subject is a trend, can I demonstrate that the trend exists with a chart like Fuchs or by quoting authoritative sources like Weichenthal?

How can I begin engagingly and end conclusively? Shall I begin by emphasizing the importance or timeliness of my subject like Cole and Kozol? Might I begin with a personal anecdote in the way that Kozol relates his recurring dream of being in Russia and unable to read the Cyrillic alphabet or Cole tells of noticing few women at scientific conferences?

How will I establish my authority to argue the causes or effects of my subject? Shall I do this by citing personal experience and presenting a carefully researched consideration of others' proposed causes like Weichenthal, by showing a comprehensive understanding of the effects of a phenomenon like illiteracy as does Kozol, or by displaying a breadth of scientific knowledge like Jastrow and Fuchs?

PLANNING YOUR ORGANIZATION. With goals in mind and invention notes at hand, you are ready to make a tentative outline of your draft. The sequence of proposed causes or effects will be at the center of your outline, but you may also want to plan where you will consider alternatives or counterargue objections. Notice that some writers in this chapter who conjecture about causes (Fuchs and Weichenthal) consider alternative causes—evaluating, refuting, or accepting them—before they present their own. Much of an essay analyzing causes may be devoted to considering alternatives. Both writers who conjecture about causes and writers who speculate about effects usually consider readers' possible objections to their causes or effects along with the argument for each cause or effect. If you must provide readers with a great deal of information about your subject as context for your argument, you may want to outline this information carefully. For your essay, this part of the outline may be a major consideration. Your plan should make the information readily accessible to your readers. Remember that this outline is merely tentative; you may decide to change it once you start drafting.

AVOIDING LOGICAL FALLACIES. Speculating about trends, phenomena, and events poses special challenges. Reasons and evidence must be thoughtfully selected, and certain common errors in causal reasoning must be avoided. To avoid making errors in your reasoning, ask yourself the following questions as you plan and draft your essay:

- How can I avoid the *post hoc, ergo propter hoc* (Latin for "after this, therefore because of this") fallacy? Have I mistakenly assumed that something that occurred prior to the beginning of the phenomenon or trend was therefore a cause?

- How can I be sure not to *confuse causes with effects*? Sometimes effects can be sustaining causes of a trend, but if that is so, I should acknowledge it as such. Are any of my causes also results? Are any of my causes actually results and not causes at all?

- How can I show readers that I have *accepted the burden of proof*? I must offer proof for all my assertions and not *shift the burden of proof* to my readers by assuming they will automatically understand certain assertions.

- How can I refute counterarguments without committing the *ad hominem* (Latin for "to the man") fallacy? Can I argue against them without ridiculing their proponents?

- How can I consider and reject alternative causes without committing the *straw man* fallacy? (A straw man is easy to push over.)

- Can I argue for one cause only without being accused of the *either/or* fallacy? Might readers find my argument more convincing if I acknowledge alternative causes?

Revising

Once you have a complete first draft, you will almost certainly be able to find ways to improve it. With your purpose and readers in mind, read your draft critically, using the questions about basic features at the beginning of this chapter. (If possible, have someone else read your draft critically, too.) As you revise, you will be primarily concerned with strengthening your argument and improving the readability of your essay.

REVISING TO STRENGTHEN THE ARGUMENT. Decide whether you have adequately considered your readers' needs. Your argument should be aimed at particular readers, not to manipulate them, but to convince them that your conjectures or speculations are plausible. Make sure that your readers will not feel that you have ignored obvious alternatives or failed to anticipate predictable objections. Be certain, too, that you have not assumed readers know more about your subject than they in fact do. Try to develop and strengthen the argument for each proposed cause or effect, adding further evidence or anecdotes. Or perhaps you should drop a weakly argued cause or effect entirely and rearrange the sequence in which you present the causes or effects. You may even find that you want to do further research on your subject in order to gain a better understanding and to discover still other possible causes or effects.

REVISING TO IMPROVE READABILITY. Reconsider your beginning and ending. Can you think of another beginning that would more effectively orient your readers and draw them into your essay? Can you improve your ending so that it brings your argument to a more emphatic and memorable close? Examine each sentence closely to ensure that it says what you intend it to say. Cut any unnecessary words or phrases. Try to improve the flow from sentence to sentence, and consider adding transitions or other cues and signals to keep the reader on track.

Once you have completed your revision, proofread your essay with extreme care in order to catch any errors of mechanics, usage, punctuation, or style. Try to have someone else proofread the essay as well.

CHAPTER EIGHT

Proposal

Proposals, one of the most common kinds of writing in the workplace and in government, are written every day to analyze problems and to recommend practical solutions. Some of these proposals have immediate pragmatic ends, particularly those written in the workplace. Several engineering firms, for example, might write proposals to compete for a contract to build an intraurban rail system. The business manager of a small firm might write a memo to the company president proposing an upgrading of the computing system to include electronic mail and networking. Seeking funding to support her research on the American poet Walt Whitman, a university professor might write a proposal to the National Endowment for the Humanities.

Other proposals address social problems and have more long-range ends in that they attempt to influence the direction of public policy. The United Nations, for instance, might form a task force to recommend ways to eliminate acid rain. The College Entrance Examination Board might sponsor a commission to suggest how the decline in Scholastic Aptitude Test (SAT) scores could be reversed. A private institution such as the Carnegie Foundation might ask a group of respected academic, government, and business leaders to propose ways to improve high schools.

Still other proposals are written by individuals who want to solve problems plaguing communities or groups to which they belong. A student living in a college dormitory might make a proposal to reduce the noise level at certain hours so that students can study. Another student might propose that an escort service be created to prevent rape on campus. A sorority member might recommend rescheduling rush week so that it will not interfere with midterm exams.

Problem solving is a way of thinking basic to many academic disciplines. For example, historians, psychologists, anthropologists, and philosophers all proceed by identifying important questions or problems and by examining various ways of understanding or solving them. Scientists use a systematic form of problem solving—the scientific method. Problem solving involves critical thinking along with creativity. It combines analysis with synthesis, questioning with inventing answers.

Learning to read proposals and to write a proposal of your own will help you hone your problem-solving abilities. You will also find that much of the work you have already done in this book—mastering the critical reading strategies and writing many of the kinds of essays— contributes directly to your work with proposals. Proposal writers often discuss the problem in terms of their personal experience or firsthand observation. They explain concepts, evaluate alternative solutions, speculate on a problem's causes or a proposed solution's possible effects. When you write a proposal, therefore, you have the opportunity to bring together much of what you have learned in this course.

A GUIDE TO READING PROPOSALS

To begin your study of proposals, you will first look closely at a proposal by educator Mark Kleiman. Closely analyzing Kleiman's proposal will provide a foundation for the serious study of proposal writing this chapter encourages. As you become a more critical, insightful reader of proposals, your own writing will become more confident and convincing.

As the initial step in your analysis, you will annotate the Kleiman selection. The next exercise asks you to take inventory of your annotations in order to disclose a pattern of meaning you have discovered. In the third exercise, guided by special questions, you will report what you have learned in analyzing the unique features of proposal writing. Finally, the concluding exercise invites you to write a brief exploratory essay, consolidating what you have learned about the Kleiman selection and trying out your own ideas about it or extending your personal response to it.

The time you invest now in annotating, analyzing, and writing will pay off richly as you read, write about, and discuss the essays in this chapter.

It will also give you confidence that you can write an effective proposal of your own.

Annotating As You Read

As we have discussed, perhaps the most basic, and most useful, strategy for reading attentively and critically is annotating. Pencil in hand as you read, you are ready to record on the page any comments, questions, definitions, or insights—whatever crosses your mind—about a piece of writing. As an illustration, note how we have annotated the following brief passage from a proposal for second-language education in American schools by educator Daniel Shanahan that appears in its entirety later in this chapter:

myopic: "shortsighted" *regressive:* "going backwards"

It is nothing less than criminal for a country so admittedly language poor and so strapped for competitive advantages in the international marketplace to be adopting myopic and regressive language laws that reinforce the naïve monolingual bias that threatens to isolate and weaken it. Yet it is also understandable that Americans want clarity and perhaps a degree of reassurance in our increasingly volatile and shifting ethnic and linguistic environment. A compromise addressing both sides of the problem must be found, and I believe it will not be as hard to come by as some people might imagine.

Problem: Americans want "linguistic reassurance" but must avoid "monolinguistic bias" to remain competitive internationally (2 sides)

2-pronged solution = "compromise"

Let Congress pass a law designating English the "standard" language of the United States, but let the measure also include the appropriation of sufficient money to insure that 20 years from now, all Americans graduating from high school will be proficient in a second language.

Not defined: How proficient?

Let a high-school diploma and college admission be denied to anyone without a sufficient level of proficiency. And let proficiency in a second language—at the level of a native speaker—be required for graduation from college and entry into civil-service and private-sector white-collar employment. In other words, let us put our money

Not very specific here: how *much* money and from where?

where our mouths are. The price tag for instituting such requirements—including the cost of training the needed teachers over five years—would be less than the budget for the Strategic Defense Initiative for two fiscal years. Moreoever, the benefits would be far greater. For only with such determined policies can we hope to calm fears

Continues 2-pronged approach

about language plurality and insure that we do not become a culture of monolingual dinosaurs.

For more on annotating, pause now to review the guidelines in Chapter 1 and the model annotations on the excerpt from "Letter from Birmingham Jail." Note particularly the Checklist for Annotating.

Exercise 1

Annotate Mark Kleiman's "Grant Bachelor's Degrees by Examination" as you read. Reread it at least once, continuing to annotate as you reread. Your purpose is to focus your attention on the text, to read as thoughtfully—as critically—as possible. Annotate details you admire as well as things you question or challenge, mark noteworthy stylistic devices or writing strategies, highlight important points and key terms, write down any personal responses. Record your insights and reactions directly on and around the text itself.

People usually read proposals because they are troubled by a problem and want to solve it. Occasionally, proposals alert them to new problems. They respond most positively to proposals that are thoughtful, thorough, and innovative. They especially admire the creativity displayed in a proposal that reconceives an old problem in an altogether new way or finds solutions no one has considered.

The following sample proposal takes an iconoclastic view of higher education. Mark Kleiman, a research fellow at Harvard University, argues that since getting a college degree represents a problem for some people, it should be possible to receive a degree without the education. Before you begin reading, think about why and for whom the traditional means of getting a college degree might be a problem.

Kleiman did not address his proposal to educators but published it in the *Wall Street Journal*, a daily newspaper primarily for businesspeople. To accept this proposal, readers must change their way of thinking about college education. Kleiman attempts to affect this change by describing the college degree in language associated with business rather than with education. As you read, notice how he is able to make his proposal seem quite reasonable and practical.

Grant Bachelor's Degrees by Examination
Mark Kleiman

Colleges and universities offer their undergraduate students two distinct commodities: an education (or rather   1 the opportunity for one) and a degree. The offer is what antitrust lawyers call a "tie sale": They won't sell you the diploma unless you buy the whole package.

As fall approaches and parents dig into their pockets (or apply to their banks) for the $15,000 a year it now costs to send a child to a "prestige" institution such as the one where I work, it's time to ask why the education-and-degree package shouldn't be unbundled. If a student can achieve on his own, and demonstrate to the faculty, knowledge and competence higher than, say, the median of a school's graduating class, why shouldn't he be able to buy a certificate testifying as much?

Such a certificate—a B.A. by examination—would qualify its holder for employment, or for graduate or professional study, without costing him four years of forgone earnings plus the cash price of a small house.

Rather than thinking of this proposal as unbundling credential-granting from education, one might prefer to consider it as substituting a performance standard for a technical-specification standard in the award of degrees.

There are three arguments for such a proposal.

First, it would save resources.

Second, it would make a valuable credential available to some who cannot now afford it, thus contributing to social mobility. (In addition to those earning their first degrees in this way, B.A.-by-exam programs at high-prestige schools might attract students who feel, often correctly, that their obscure sheepskins are holding them back.)

Third, and more speculatively, it might free high-powered but unconventional high-school graduates to pursue a self-education more useful to them than any pre-packaged education, without shutting themselves out of jobs and advanced-degree programs.

There are two obvious objections. Those who took their B.A.s by examination might miss out on the opportunities college provides for social interaction and other forms of personal and intellectual development. It might also be said that, since no examination could capture the richness of an undergraduate education, B.A.s by exam would have incentives to become, and would in fact be, narrower and shallower than their eight-semesters-in-residence counterparts.

The first objection is probably true but not conclusive. Some who would choose the exam route over the regular undergraduate course would probably be wise not to buy the nonacademic attributes of college for four years' income plus $60,000; others will not, in fact, choose the more expensive option, even if it is the only one offered.

To the second objection there are two solutions: high   11
standards and resource-intensive examinations. A process lasting a month and costing $3,000 to administer and
score, testing both general knowledge and competence in
a major field, and involving written, oral and practical
components and the preparation of a thesis or the equivalent, should suffice to evaluate breadth and depth at
least as well as the current system does. The interests of
the group running an examination program would run
parallel with those of the rest of the institution in keeping
standards high, and the social and moral pressure to
award degrees in borderline cases ought to be much less
for exam students than for ordinary undergraduates. By
setting standards for examination B.A.s above the me-
dian of the eight-semester graduates, an institution could
ensure that the exam program raised the average educational level of its degree-holders.

The price to candidates could reflect fully loaded cost   12
plus a substantial contribution to overhead and still look
like a bargain. To deal with the unwillingness of potential
candidates to gamble several thousand dollars on their
chances of success, it might make sense to administer a
fairly cheap ($200) screening test and give anyone who
passed a money-back guarantee on the more thorough
(and expensive) degree exam. The failure rate could be
built into the price, or some insurance company might be
willing to administer the screening test and sell failure
insurance.

This proposal should not be confused with college   13
credit for "life experience," "urban semesters" or other
moves to substitute the pragmatic for the scholarly in
undergraduate education. The point is to tie the degree
more rather than less tightly to specific academic competence, to certify the result—an educated person—rather
than the *process* leading to that result.

If this idea required a consensus in order to be tried   14
out, it would never stand a chance. Fortunately, no such
consensus is needed. All it takes is one undeniably first-
rate institution willing to break the credential cartel.

Inventorying Your Annotations

Once you have annotated a reading with your insights and thoughts,
you'll want to study your annotations for their special meaning. The best
way to do this is by taking inventory of your annotations, to discover any
patterns or significant repetitions.

Before completing Exercise 2, review the guidelines and illustration for the Inventory of Annotations in Chapter 1.

Exercise 2

Inventory the annotations you made on "Grant Bachelor's Degrees by Examination," looking for meaningful patterns in your response to the selection.

Analyzing the Basic Features
of Proposals

In addition to both annotating a text to record your initial impressions and inventorying your annotations to discover their patterns of meaning, you can analyze the basic features of a piece of writing, in this case those qualities that make it distinctively a proposal.

Look back at Identifying and Evaluating Basic Features in Chapter 1. Although the questions there differ from those you will find in this chapter, the answers illustrate what a thoughtful analysis of basic features might look like.

Exercise 3

Analyze "Grant Bachelor's Degrees by Examination" by answering the following questions. You will want to reread the selection with each question in mind, and you may want to annotate further.

Write out your answers to the questions.

1. *How convincing is the claim that the problem exists and is serious? How well defined is the problem?* Proposals make two claims, one having to do with the problem, the other with the proposed solution. This pair of questions deals with the problem claim—that is, a claim that a particular problem exists and is serious enough to require a solution.

The problem must be one that can be pointed to and not some vague complaint. It usually needs to be defined in some detail to convince readers of its existence and seriousness. To support their way of defining the problem, writers often provide backing in the form of concrete evidence—facts, statistics, testimony of witnesses and authorities. They may also include general information indicating the type of problem it is, how it came about, who is affected by it, and what its consequences might be.

As you read a proposal, pay special attention to how the problem is defined. Proposals dealing with commonly acknowledged problems may not need to define the problem in detail, but all proposals should describe the problem to some extent. In cases where the problem is new or defined in an unusual way, the need for definition is especially great. Notice too how the writer classifies and analyzes the problem. Finally, consider how the writer explains the causes of the problem.

Ask yourself these questions: What is the problem? What key terms does the writer use to define the problem? What attitudes and values do these terms imply? What does the writer seem to assume readers already know and think about the problem? How might the writer improve the definition of the problem? What more do readers need to know about the problem?

2. *What exactly is the proposed solution?* Beyond establishing that a problem exists and is serious, a proposal must also suggest a way to solve that particular problem. The assertion of this solution is the proposal's primary claim or thesis. Proposal writers usually offer original solutions, but they may also support the ideas of others, perhaps ideas that have been suggested but not taken seriously.

The proposed solution should not be hard to find since it is usually restated several times. Summarizing the proposed solution, particularly if it seems complicated, can be a useful critical reading strategy. Noting your first reaction to the solution enables you to anticipate objections and judge the argument.

Ask yourself: Where in the essay is the solution initially proposed? Is this an appropriate point to set out the solution, or must the problem be explained more before readers can grasp it? Does the solution seem obvious or surprising? Have you heard it before?

3. *What reasons and backing does the writer give to convince readers to accept the proposed solution? How effective is the argument that the proposed solution is a feasible way of solving the problem?* It is not enough to merely propose or assert a solution; good reasons must be given to convince readers to accept the proposed solution. The most obvious reason for accepting a proposed solution is that it will indeed remedy the problem or, at least, contribute to its solution. Occasionally, the connection between the proposed solution and the way that the problem has been

defined makes further backing unnecessary. But more often, the writer has to show readers that the proposed solution will, in fact, help solve the problem. A common way writers make this case is by arguing that the proposed solution will eliminate the problem's root causes or avoid its detrimental effects. As a critical reader, you need to determine whether the writer makes a convincing argument that the proposed solution will actually solve the problem.

Another reason for accepting a proposed solution is that it is feasible and can be implemented. Not all proposals need to demonstrate how the proposed solution would work, but as a critical reader you should consider whether such an explanation is necessary and, if it is provided, whether it is adequate. The easier the proposed solution is to implement, the more likely it is to win readers' support. Therefore, writers usually set out the steps needed to implement the solution, attempting to convince readers that implementation will be neither too hard nor too costly.

Begin your analysis by determining whether the proposal outlines specific actions for implementing the proposed solution. If it does, ask yourself how workable the plan seems. If the proposal does not set out a specific plan, ask yourself whether such a plan should have been spelled out or if you can imagine how the solution could be put into effect.

Also ask, how does the writer establish that the proposed solution will indeed solve the problem? If the writer simply asserts that it will, should readers accept the assertion without support? If the writer gives a reason—for example, that the proposed solution will remove the problem's causes—look for the backing or evidence, and evaluate the writer's reasoning by applying the ABC test described and illustrated in Chapter 1 under Analyzing an Argument.

4. *How effectively does the writer refute objections to the proposed solution and alternative solutions?* In addition to giving readers reasons to accept the proposed solution, proposal writers must also anticipate readers' responses. Proposal writers must consider how critical readers might object to their argument. For example, critics might question the way the problem has been defined, pointing out that if it were defined in another way, the proposed solution would be less convincing. Or they might argue that the proposed solution would be more difficult or expensive to implement than the writer has acknowledged.

Because there is seldom only one way of solving a problem, proposal writers also must anticipate alternative solutions that have been made or could be made. By comparing the proposed solution to the alternatives, they can indicate the advantages of their own proposal and the relative disadvantages of the others. Sometimes writers make a point-by-point comparison, showing that their solution is strong where the others are weak; or they might show that all the possible solutions have their own strengths and weaknesses, but that the strengths of the proposed solution outweigh its weaknesses.

As a critical reader, you will want to pay close attention to how the writer handles objections and alternative solutions. Look for places where possible objections are raised. Are they represented fairly? Has the writer ignored objections that might present a serious challenge and acknowledged only weak or frivolous objections? If so, the writer may have committed a logical fallacy, pretending the argument is stronger than it really is by setting up a *straw man* that can be easily knocked down.

Notice also the alternative solutions the writer acknowledges. Are these fairly represented? What other alternatives could the writer have brought up? Now consider the points of comparison. Has the writer left out any important points? Has the writer fairly weighed the advantages and disadvantages of the various solutions? To evaluate the refutation and determine whether it is free of logical fallacies, apply the ABC test. (See Analyzing an Argument in Chapter 1.)

5. *Where in the proposal does the writer try to arouse readers' emotions? Given the purpose and readers, how convincing is this emotional appeal? Is it manipulative or fair?* Since proposals are designed to move readers to action, writers often appeal to their readers' emotions as well as to their sense of logic. Appealing to emotion is not necessarily bad. For example, a writer trying to show readers how serious the problem of homelessness is might tell the story of a family living in an abandoned car. Or the writer might cite statistics indicating just how many families actually live on the streets. On the other hand, stories and statistics such as these might distort the facts. They may be designed to scare readers or make them feel guilty.

As a critical reader, you have to determine whether this kind of evidence or backing is manipulative. Ask yourself: Has enough information been presented to indicate whether examples are representative or isolated? Are characters made to seem pitiful because of the way the stories are written? Does the choice of words and their connotations—especially analogies, similes, and metaphors—elicit an exaggerated or inappropriate emotional response in readers?

6. *What is the tone or image of the writer projected by the proposal? Given the purpose and readers, how effective is the proposal's ethical appeal?* Since the aim of all proposals is to get readers to agree, proposal writers never

adopt a querulous or quarrelsome tone. They always strive to be perceived as reasonable and accommodating. Even when they criticize other people's proposals or refute objections, they avoid attacking people personally or unfairly. Proposal writers also try to impress readers with their command of the subject. By appearing knowledgeable, they hope to win readers' confidence in their authority. In addition, they need to convince readers that they have no personal interest in the outcome. If the proposed solution will be of personal benefit to the writer, readers are likely to be distrustful and suspicious.

Begin your analysis of the ethical appeal by describing the writer's ethos or persona. Ask yourself: What kind of person does the writer seem to be? How does the writer's handling of objections and alternative solutions contribute to the ethical appeal?

What seems to you, as one reader, to be the dominant tone of the essay? Given the purpose and readers of this proposal, how appropriate does this tone seem? Does the writer come across as disinterested, knowledgeable, flexible, caring, practical?

7. *How effectively are the parts of the proposal arranged?* Because proposals contain many parts and are often complicated, they should be clearly organized and easy to follow.

Poor organization and inadequate orienting devices make reading difficult and are likely to put off readers, especially those who are busy and basically unsympathetic. Proposal writers generally use the following orienting devices: forecasting statements (that let readers know what to expect in the essay), transitions (that show how each point is logically connected), headings (that identify the major parts of the proposal), and summary statements (that review what's been said, emphasizing the most important points).

Outline the proposal to see how well it is organized. Also notice any cueing devices the writer uses. How effective are they in keeping you, as one reader, on track?

Exploring Your Personal Response

Another way of focusing your response to a proposal is by taking the time to record your thoughts in a more extended piece of your own writing. Extended writing can help you to consider how the piece relates to your own experience, to explore your impressions, and define further your unique perspective on what you've read.

Exercise 4

Write 300–400 words (two or three handwritten pages) about "Grant Bachelor's Degrees by Examination." Choose one of the suggestions listed in Exploring Your Personal Response in Chapter 1.

Alan Wertheimer

Alan Wertheimer is a political scientist. His publications include *Contemporary Political Theory* (1970), edited with Anthony de Crespigny, and *Coercion* (1987), a book in a series of studies in moral, philosophical, and legal philosophy.

Compulsory Voting

This proposal first appeared in 1976 in the *New York Times*, but it is hardly out of date since the problem of low voter turnout is still very much with us.

Take a few minutes before reading the selection to consider what you currently know and think about this problem. Consider these previewing questions: What reasons do people usually give for not voting? Do you think that it is important that everyone in a democracy vote? Why or why not?

As the Presidential election approaches we will no doubt be asked to   1
recall that it was, in part, the demand for the "right to vote" that led to independence. Editorial writers throughout America will predictably bemoan the low level of participation and implore us to feel doubly guilty for failing to vote in this Bicentennial and Presidential election year.

Rather than conduct these ritual "get-out-the-vote" dances, why not   2
simply make voting compulsory?

That we even seem compelled to urge citizens to exercise a right (what   3
other *rights* do we need to urge citizens to exercise?) indicates that we may err in thinking of voting as a *right* at all. If citizens have a duty to vote, we should penalize those who fail to do their duty.

My argument for compulsory voting makes several (I think uncon-   4
troversial) assumptions: Competitive elections are desirable—for all their problems and deficiencies they are preferable to alternative methods of obtaining political leaders; it is technically possible to administer a compulsory-voting program (nonvoters would pay a tax or fine as in Belgium, the Netherlands, and Australia); compulsory voting works—it *does* increase the percentage of eligible voters who actually vote.

Elections can be understood as "public goods." A public good is any   5
good that if made available to *any* member of a community must be made available to *all* members, generally because there is no feasible way to

exclude noncontributors from enjoying the good. Public highways, national defense and police protection are examples of public good.

Now if the benefit of a public good is available to all, it is irrational for one to *voluntarily* contribute to its provision, in terms of money, time or energy. The rational citizen will attempt to "free ride," to enjoy the benefits while minimizing or avoiding the cost, as when we attempt to pay the lowest tax possible (or none at all). 6

All Americans benefit from the peaceful change of leadership and the fact that elections keep all elected officials (even those we do not support) at least somewhat responsive to our preferences. Voters and nonvoters alike receive these benefits and receive additional benefits if their preferred candidate wins. It follows that the rational citizen will not vote but will ride by avoiding the costs (including information cost) involved in voting. 7

I am not suggesting that we should not vote, merely that it is not in one's *individual interest* to vote, because no single vote will affect the outcome of the election and the electoral system will not crumble if any one of us fails to vote. We get the same benefits regardless of what we do. 8

It is not surprising that many citizens fail to vote. Rather, why do so many act irrationally (if altruistically) and vote? 9

First, some people are simply willing to sacrifice their interest for the public good. 10

Second, many people overestimate the importance of their vote. Third, many vote to assuage their sense of guilt. But this hardly happens spontaneously. We systematically encourage citizens to overestimate the importance of their vote and to feel guilty when they do not vote—and it works. 11

What would compulsory voting do? First we would be spared the ritual propaganda campaigns in which we lie to ourselves about the significance of our individual votes and drum up our feelings of guilt. Second, we could be allowed to abstain, and thus citizens could specifically indicate that no candidate was satisfactory. Third, because it is largely the poor who tend not to vote, compulsory voting would increase their political power, as candidates would be forced to become more responsive to their interests. Fourth, since those who prefer candidates who are unlikely to win often do not vote, elections would provide a more accurate description of the nation's political preferences. 12

QUESTIONS FOR ANALYSIS

1. Begin your analysis of this proposal by making an outline according to the guidelines under Outlining in Chapter 1. Then, consider how well

organized it is and how well it helps readers follow from one point to the next.

2. What problem does Wertheimer address in this proposal? Given his purpose and the *New York Times* readership he could expect, how well does he establish that the problem exists and is serious? What other kinds of backing or evidence could he have used to support this problem claim?

3. In paragraph 3, Wertheimer asserts that voting should be regarded as a "duty" instead of as a "right." How does defining the problem in this way set the stage for the proposed solution? If you accept Wertheimer's assertion, how would you support it? If you reject it, what objections do you have?

4. In paragraph 4, Wertheimer identifies three of his "assumptions." What are they? How do they contribute to his argument?

   Notice also that he calls these assumptions "uncontroversial" and provides backing for only one of them. Are they really uncontroversial? What kind of backing would convince you, as a critical reader, to accept these assumptions as true?

5. Why do you suppose Wertheimer spends so much space (paragraphs 5–8) explaining why people fail to vote? How convincing do you find this causal argument?

6. What purpose does the last paragraph serve? If making voting compulsory would increase voter turnout (as Wertheimer assumes in the fourth paragraph), why argue that it would also have these additional advantages?

IDEAS FOR YOUR OWN WRITING

Low voter turnout is one important problem faced by our democracy. List other electoral problems that could be addressed in a proposal. Here are a few possibilities to get you started: the financing of campaigns primarily by special-interest groups, the use of television sound bites in place of thoughtful debate, uninvolvement of young people.

From your list choose one problem about which you think you have some insight. To creatively solve this problem, consider how it has been defined traditionally. Can you think of a new, unconventional way of defining it? What implications might this new definition have for solving the problem? What causes are usually given for the problem? Can you think of any others? What potential solutions do these causes suggest?

Allen L. Sack

Allen L. Sack is a sociology professor at the University of New Haven. As a college student at Notre Dame, he played on a championship football team.

What We Need Is Real Collegiate Sports Reform

As this selection illustrates, some proposals are written in response to others. In this case, Sack offers his own proposal to improve the new policy established by the National Collegiate Athletic Association (NCAA) to reform collegiate sports. Sack's essay was published in November 1986 in the *New York Times*.

Before you begin reading, preview this proposal by skimming the essay. Read the first and last paragraphs completely, and the opening sentences of every other paragraph. Then reflect for a moment on what this previewing reveals about the proposal.

The practice of setting lower admissions standards for athletes than for other students has become commonplace. As a result, athletes with extremely limited verbal and mathematical skills have become a standard feature at almost all Division I schools. Under the best of circumstances, marginal students such as these would have difficulty with college-level work. When they are also expected to meet the high-pressure demands of college sport, it is not surprising that they often fail to make satisfactory academic progress. The low graduation rates of Division I athletes have become a national scandal.

Given the public perception that there has been a total breakdown of academic standards for athletes, it is understandable that the National Collegiate Athletic Association's new eligibility requirements, known as Proposition 48, has been received by many with considerable enthusiasm. Most media references to the new rules credit the N.C.A.A. with "setting tough new academic standards" or with "restoring academic integrity" in college sport. The general impression is that a bold new initiative has been taken to insure that college athletes can compete in the classroom as well as on the playing field.

Unfortunately, a close look at Proposition 48 reveals that it is more of an exercise in skillful public relations than a serious effort to institute academic reform. The gist of this legislation is that athletes at Division I schools must meet certain minimum academic standards in order to be eligible for freshman sports. To be eligible, athletes must have a 2.0 average in a core curriculum of high school courses and scores of at least 700 on the Scholastic Aptitude Test (S.A.T.) or 15 on the American College Testing Program's examination (A.C.T.).

The most serious loophole in Proposition 48, and what renders it 4 virtually worthless as a mechanism for raising academic standards, is that it is merely concerned with freshman eligibility. What many people fail to realize is that under this new rule, schools can continue to admit athletes who fail to meet the N.C.A.A.'s freshman eligibility requirements and can grant them scholarships. All that Proposition 48 says is that these athletes will not be eligible for freshman sports. After sitting out a year, athletes who were not eligible as freshmen are free to enter the high-pressure world of commercial college sport.

I cannot for the life of me see how Proposition 48 raises academic 5 standards or constitutes a bold new initiative. All it really does is bar extremely marginal students, many of whom do not belong in college in the first place, from playing freshman sports. When I played football at Notre Dame in the mid-1960's, freshmen, including National Merit Scholars, were not eligible for varsity sports. In this respect, Proposition 48 fails to come up to standards that existed two decades ago.

If the N.C.A.A. and its member institutions had really been com- 6 mitted to substantive reforms, they could, at the very least, have made a combined score of 700 on the S.A.T. exam (or the equivalent A.C.T. score) a minimum eligibility requirement for participation in Division I sports, regardless of year in college. This would, in effect, bar students who cannot meet the N.C.A.A. minimum from ever participating in big-time college sports. Such a rule would not interfere with an individual school's admission policies, but merely extend the N.C.A.A.'s freshman eligibility requirements to the sophomore, junior and senior years. The University of Georgia has already adopted this policy. The N.C.A.A. could easily do likewise.

I obviously disagree with those who say that admissions exams like the 7 S.A.T. are meaningless. It is true that they do not measure innate intelligence. But they do give a rough idea of what kind of educational background a student has had. A combined score of below 700 on the S.A.T.'s, for instance, suggests that a student has either attended inferior schools or comes from a neighborhood or family that lacks the material and cultural resources to emphasize the development of skills needed for success in college. Such a student may also have spent more time and energy on sports than on school work while in primary or secondary school.

Remedial programs can help these poorly prepared students to make   8
up for valuable time lost in lower grades. However, it takes more than two semesters of not playing college sports to make up for 17 years of rotten schools, nonsupportive educational environments, and other disadvantages caused by discrimination, poverty, unemployment, and centuries of educational neglect. Our nation's universities have a moral obligation to recruit and to provide financial aid for academically motivated students from educationally disadvantaged backgrounds. This includes students who perform poorly on admissions tests. But it is educationally insane for such students to be allowed to enter the high-pressure world of big-time college sports.

Even athletes who score 700 and above and are highly motivated will   9
need all the help they can get to juggle the contradictory demands of sports and school work. No single reform would do more to give athletes the education they were promised in return for athletic services than providing a fifth year of scholarship aid beyond four years of athletic eligibility. The N.C.A.A. currently requires athletes to complete 12 credits of course work a semester in order to maintain satisfactory academic progress. This is probably as many courses as an athlete can handle and still meet the demands of sports. The problem is that an athlete who meets the N.C.A.A.'s satisfactory progress guidelines over a four-year period will end up with only 96 credits, far short of the approximately 120 needed to graduate.

N.C.A.A. legislation guaranteeing a fifth year of scholarship aid to   10
athletes who have competed for their schools for four years would meet this problem head on. Such a proposal would make it unnecessary to debate the issue of freshman eligibility. Athletes could sit out their freshman year, if this seemed academically advisable. Or they could finish school in four years, or they could complete their educations after their athletic responsibilities were ended. Many schools already provide athletes with a fifth year of aid. This simple reform, coupled with the extension of the freshman eligibility requirement to the sophomore, junior, and senior years, would demonstrate a genuine commitment to academic reform. Such reforms would also send shock waves down into the high schools and junior high schools.

If colleges simply stopped recruiting athletes whose verbal and mathe-   11
matical abilities are extremely limited, the message would be clear. Kids who presently spend all of their time bouncing basketballs and dreaming of athletic stardom would have to confront the reality that exceptional

athletic ability will not guarantee college admission. Proposition 48 sends out no such message. This fall, hundreds of star athletes who failed to meet the N.C.A.A.'s new requirements were admitted to Division I schools, and almost all of them received athletics scholarships. After sitting out a year, these athletes will represent their schools in sports and demonstrate to America's young people that colleges will never turn away a talented athlete, even if he or she can barely read and write. This, unfortunately, is the message of Proposition 48.

It should be noted, in closing, that if universities really wanted to 12 restore academic integrity in their athletic programs, they would simply enforce the admissions requirements they already have on the books. This would mean that athletes would have to meet the same standards as other students. As a result, schools with highly competitive admissions standards would no longer be able to recruit talented "blue-chip" athletes who are only marginal students. And this would severely disrupt the competitive balance within the college sports industry. Academically competitive schools like Notre Dame and Michigan would no longer be athletic powers, and less selective state universities would corner the market on "blue-chip" athletes, as well as on national championships. Over all, the quality of play would suffer and commercial college sport, as we know it, would probably not survive.

Given this reality, it is not reasonable to expect those who control 13 college sport to make academic integrity a top priority. As long as universities function as centers for mass commercial entertainment, athletic ability will continue to take precedence over academic standard. Nonetheless, I am not convinced that the survival of college sport as a business necessitates the almost total abandonment of standards that is given legitimacy by a rule like Proposition 48. What is desperately needed in American education today is a return to higher standards. Young people need to be prodded and goaded to higher levels of achievement. Extending the N.C.A.A.'s new freshman eligibility rules to sophomore, junior, and senior years would be a modest step in the right direction. Giving athletes five years to finish their degrees would be a giant step.

QUESTIONS FOR ANALYSIS

1. What exactly is the problem, and who is responsible for it? If the problem is defined in terms of too low admissions standards, it would seem that the N.C.A.A. and what Sack calls "the college sports industry" (paragraph 12) are responsible. On the other hand, if the problem is defined as too low graduation rates for Division I athletes, the student athletes themselves are apparently responsible for their

own failure. How do you think Sack defines the problem? How would you?

2. In paragraphs 2–5, Sack discusses the solution proposed by the N.C.A.A. Since his aim is to convince supporters of the N.C.A.A. proposal that it does not go far enough and that they should support his proposal instead, how effective is his refutation of the N.C.A.A. proposal? What shared values and beliefs does he appeal to?

3. In the opening sentence of paragraph 6, Sack offers his own solution. How does he argue in favor of this solution in paragraphs 6–8? What reasons does he give, and how does he back them? What objections does he acknowledge, and how does he refute them? Outline this argument, and then evaluate its logical, emotional, and ethical appeals. (For guidelines on outlining and evaluating an argument, see Analyzing an Argument in Chapter 1.)

4. In paragraph 9, Sack offers a second solution—guaranteeing five years of scholarship aid to athletes—to go along with his first. Whereas he calls his first solution "a modest step in the right direction," he calls the second "a giant step" (paragraph 13). What is so special about Sack's second solution? How does he argue in its support?

5. In paragraph 11, Sack discusses yet another possible solution: that "colleges simply [stop] recruiting athletes whose verbal and mathematical abilities are extremely limited." Why do you think he introduces this possibility? How does it contribute to the argument for his own proposed solutions?

6. Review Exploring Your Personal Response in Chapter 1. Then, write a 300–400-word personal response to this selection. Choose either one of the following topics:

Write an essay about your personal associations with something in the reading.

Write a letter to Sack in which you respond to anything in the essay that you found unusual, interesting, intriguing, or objectionable.

After you have written your response, reread it thoughtfully. In two or three sentences, say what you have learned about the Sack proposal by writing an extended response to it.

IDEAS FOR YOUR OWN WRITING

What other problems relating to collegiate sports or to college in general can you think of? List as many problems as you can. Here are a few suggestions to get you started. What could be done financially for college athletes who suffer injuries that plague them throughout their lives? How could women's sports be supported better? How could college campuses be made safer? What could be done to prevent date rape? How could dorm food be improved?

From your list, choose one problem that you would like to examine further. What might be the causes of this problem? How could they be eliminated? Consider various ways the problem could be defined. Who seems to be responsible for the problem? Who has the power to take action? What kinds of action do you think might help solve the problem?

Daniel Shanahan

Daniel Shanahan heads the Program in English Studies at the Monterey Institute of International Studies.

A Proposal for
a Multilingual America

This proposal orginally appeared in 1989 as an editorial in the *Chronicle of Higher Education*, a journal read primarily by college administrators and instructors. Like the Sack proposal on collegiate sports reform, Shanahan's proposal centers on the refutation of an alternative solution—the "official language" proposition that, according to Shanahan, already has been passed into law in seventeen states.

To preview this proposal, consider what you now know about the movement to establish English as the official language in the United States. What problem is it designed to remedy? What objections to it would Shanahan or anyone else be likely to have? Does a legal solution to the problem seem called for or even possible? What special interest would educators be likely to have in the question of whether English should be the official language?

In 1904, at a hearing on the mistreatment of immigrant laborers, the 1 president of the Reading Railroad told a Congressional committee: "These workers don't suffer—they don't even speak English."

Working conditions in the United States have come a long way since 2 then, but the attitude in this country toward people who do not speak English hasn't changed very much. While few of us would support the contention that non-English speakers somehow have no right to equal protection under the law, it has become more acceptable in recent years to oppose such things as bilingual education and bilingual ballots that attempt to address problems faced by speakers of languages other than English.

The issue is a relatively simple one, but it has a complex social and 3 historical background. Before the revival of ethnic pride in the 1960's and 70's, most immigrants who came to this country tried to "launder" much of their cultural past, and their native languages were among the first things to go. For them, learning English was an act of faith in the new land they had adopted. Although the price was steeper than many of them realized at the time, most were willing, even happy, to pay it.

But in the 1960's, the civil-rights movement forced a reassessment of   4
what was "American," and many once-acceptable means of distinguishing among groups were seen as undemocratic, to be ferreted out and
eliminated wherever they were found. It is unfortunate that during that
period the issue of language (largely as it applied to Hispanic Americans)
became fused with the issue of civil rights.

As a result, bilingual issues were overwhelmed by emotional baggage,   5
first the liberal guilt of the 60's and 70's and then the conservative
reaction of the Reagan era. Lost in the shuffle was a much more vital
issue, and one which pivots, not on questions of deprivation of civil
rights, but on America's ability to remain a viable actor in the increasingly global environment by becoming more competent linguistically.

The "official language" propositions that have been passed in 17 states   6
in recent years—three in last fall's elections—are clear signs that the
electorate does not understand the true effect of the language issue on
the national interest. Most such propositions pass because of fear and
resentment on the part of the majority language group. While the
campaign advertisements run by supporters of the proposals do not
overtly express resentment over money spent to serve those who do not
speak English, the sentiments expressed by voters who support the
initiatives often can be summed up in some variation of the statement:
"My parents had to learn English when they came to this country. . . ."

Resentment is, of course, a more or less unacceptable basis for policy   7
analysis, so supporters' justifications of English-only initiatives usually
play on fears: of social disunity, of economic hardship, of the cost of
cultural plurality. Canada is most frequently cited as an example of the
way cultural plurality, maintained through linguistic plurality, can lead to
social instability. Putting aside for the moment the fact that Canada not
only survived Quebec's "quiet revolution" but also profited from it, as
the economic boom in Quebec is now demonstrating, such analysis of the
language issue ignores the extent to which the entire world is rapidly
becoming a stage on which the players must speak more than one
language to survive and compete economically.

The Japanese have led the way in learning second—and third—   8
languages to further their economic competitiveness. It can be argued
that the difficulty of their own language made it unlikely that foreigners
would learn it and forced them to learn the languages of others, but it
can just as easily be argued that this apparent liability simply led them to
see the handwriting on the wall more quickly than others, and it thus
became a competitive advantage.

Europeans have always been proficient in other languages, largely   9
because of the high concentration of different languages in their rela-

tively small geographic space. Being multilingual is helping them establish an economic union that looms as a powerful force in the already crowded and competitive global marketplace.

Even in developing countries, where one might expect lack of education to limit multilingualism, many people speak a regional dialect at home and the language of the dominant cultural group in the workplace; some also speak the European language of the colonial period as well. Against this international backdrop, the spectacle of Americans passing laws to limit the languages used in their country can only be seen as self-destructive.

Of course, there must be a standard language in a country, if only for the purpose of efficiency, but the language is designated by practice, not by law. In the United States, the standard language is and always has been English. The question should not be whether we should spend money to make it possible for immigrants to use their native languages in official situations, nor should it be whether we encourage others, children especially, to maintain a language other than English. Quite clearly, the question ought to be whether we should undertake a nationwide effort to encourage, enhance, and expand multilingual proficiency among native speakers of English, as well as among non-natives.

The answer to that question must be a resounding and unequivocal Yes.

It is nothing less than criminal for a country so admittedly language poor and so strapped for competitive advantages in the international marketplace to be adopting myopic and regressive language laws that reinforce the naïve monolingual bias that threatens to isolate and weaken it. Yet it is also understandable that Americans want clarity and perhaps a degree of reassurance in our increasingly volatile and shifting ethnic and linguistic environment.

A compromise addressing both sides of the issue must be found, and I believe it will not be as hard to come by as some people might imagine.

Let Congress pass a law designating English the "standard" language of the United States, but let the measure also include the appropriation of sufficient money to insure that 20 years from now, all Americans graduating from high school will be proficient in a second language.

Let a high-school diploma and college admission be denied to anyone without a sufficient level of proficiency. And let proficiency in a second language—at the level of a native speaker—be required for graduation from college and entry into civil-service and private-sector white-collar employment. In other words, let us put our money where our mouths are. The price tag for instituting such requirements—including the cost of training the needed teachers over five years—would be less than the budget for the Strategic Defense Initiative for two fiscal years. Moreover, the benefits would be far greater. For only with such determined policies can we hope to calm fears about language plurality and insure that we do not become a culture of monolingual dinosaurs.

We have 20 years, nearly triple the time President Kennedy allowed 17 when he committed us to reaching the moon. By comparison, the expenditures required to create a linguistically proficient nation would be insignificant. The benefits, not only in economic terms but also in terms of enhancing our understanding of other cultures and of ourselves, would be beyond measure. The costs, should we fail to act decisively, could eventually prove to be catastrophic.

QUESTIONS FOR ANALYSIS

1. Begin your analysis of this proposal by making an outline of it following the guidelines in Chapter 1 under Outlining.

2. Shanahan opens this proposal with an analysis of the historical background of the problem, or "issue," at hand. Given his purpose and readers, what advantages or disadvantages do you see in this opening strategy?

3. How has this problem been defined traditionally? How does Shanahan define it? What key terms does he use in his definition, and what values do these terms imply?

4. In paragraph 6, Shanahan begins his refutation of the "official language" solution. Outline his refutation, and evaluate it on the basis of its logical, emotional, and ethical appeals. (Review Analyzing an Argument in Chapter 1 for help in outlining and evaluating.)

5. In paragraphs 15–17, Shanahan offers his own solution. How well-reasoned is his argument that this solution is a feasible way of solving the problem as he has defined it? Evaluate the logical appeal of his argument by applying the ABC test. (The ABC test of sound reasoning is discussed under Analyzing an Argument in Chapter 1.)

6. Look closely at Shanahan's proposal, annotating the places where you sense that he is making an emotional appeal. Then, consider the appropriateness of each appeal. Does Shanahan's appeal to his readers' emotions seem to you, as one critical reader, to be manipulative or fair?

7. Review Exploring Your Personal Response in Chapter 1. Then, write a 300–400-word personal response to this selection. Choose either one of the following topics:

Write an essay about your personal associations with something in the reading.

Write a letter to Shanahan in which you respond to anything in the essay that you found unusual, interesting, intriguing, or objectionable.

After you have written your response, reread it thoughtfully. In two or three sentences, say what you have learned about Shanahan's proposal by writing an extended, personal response to it.

IDEAS FOR YOUR OWN WRITING

We may often find that solutions offered for particular social problems are "myopic" or "regressive," much as Shanahan sees the "official language" propositions passed by several states. Offering alternative proposals can provide an effective means of countering proposals that we find misguided.

List some current social problems—teenage drinking, for example, or disorder in public schools—and solutions currently being proposed or enacted with which you may disagree—such as raising the legal drinking age or imposing strict dress codes in schools. Choose a problem and solution that you feel strongly about. On what basis would you refute the solution? How might your definition of the problem differ from that of the solution's advocates? What values do you think are involved? How else could the problem, as you define it, be solved?

Edward L. Palmer

Edward Palmer, one of the founders of Children's Television Workshop, was for several years its vice president for research. The Workshop, which began in 1968, is perhaps best known for "Sesame Street." Palmer has organized international conferences on children's television and has traveled to study children's television programming in Britain, Japan, Germany, and Australia. From this work and travel came Palmer's book, *Television and America's Children: A Crisis of Neglect* (1988).

Improving Television for America's Children

This selection, from *Television and America's Children*, outlines a proposal for improving the amount and quality of television programming for children. In it, Palmer seeks to convince policymakers and concerned adults that there is a serious problem with children's television, yet a problem which has a feasible solution. Before you read his proposal, give some thought to the problem. Which programs do you remember best from your childhood? What might have made them more entertaining or informative? What reasons might legislators and educators have for seeking general improvements in the quality of children's television programs?

All the ingredients to create and air a full schedule of high-quality educational shows for children are in place. America has the expertise, the production capability, the pedagogical and research skills, the audience, and the need. Public television [PTV] has abundant air space, and might be prevailed upon by parents and outside underwriters to become a willing host. Parents, children, and educators have shown great enthusiasm for all the fine quality programs so far made available.

Thanks to the many outstanding successes of the past twenty years, we have fashioned our own unique national vision of quality. Why, then, have we lacked the will to carry it through? Why is our government so short-sighted in failing to create the national policy and provide the funding to make full and effective use of the most cost-efficient teaching medium ever invented—broadcast television?

The lapses we countenance in our own television institutions are seen in cross-cultural comparisons to be woefully shortsighted, or even bizarre. For instance, the Japanese Broadcasting Corporation, NHK, reports that in 85 percent of all Japanese schools, every classroom has a color television. The NHK reports further that each year 97 percent of all classrooms in Japan make some use of NHK's school television service. Yet, by contrast, the U.S. Department of Education places almost no priority whatsoever on television's development and use to advance learning for America's children. The bizarre part is that where another country's provision for the use of television in education is so vital and so far advanced, we are utterly without any well-informed, long-term, or dependable policy to guide our own educational uses of television, and this is true in spite of the unarguable fact that U.S. schools are drastically and chronically burdened by performance demands that exceed their capacity to deliver, and that television languishes as a proven but neglected cost-efficient ally.

It is fitting that we begin exploring a minimally adequate PTV children's schedule that places children's needs first, and, only then, keeping in mind the same high standard, turn to explore an agenda for legislated regulation on the commercial side. . . . The schedule most likely to attract funding support must be modest—minimally adequate to serve all children aged two through thirteen—and, I believe, must consist of programs geared to our most urgent national education problems. Moreover, for each educational outcome sought, television must be seen to be more effective, and substantially more cost-efficient, than any other means available. This high standard is well within broadcast television's capability. 4

The schedule which will be proposed here in detailed outline calls for a multi-year program build-up, in phases, eventually yielding a one-hour weekday schedule, year round, for each of three child age-groups: 2- to 5-year-olds, 6- to 9-year-olds, and 10- to 13-year-olds. The scale of yearly funding support is $62.4 million. Although modest, this amount is about double the current expenditure from all sources for children's PTV programming. Anything more ambitious to begin is unrealistic; anything less ambitious short-changes children by drastically under-utilizing this powerful educational resource. 5

This yearly budget, as shown below, will buy enough programming at today's rates to continue the preschool service and provide a quarter of a full year's schedule each for 6- to 9- and 10- to 13-year-olds. By simple arithmetic, this yearly program build-up rate will fill a year's schedule for each age group in four years. "Simple arithmetic" is misleading in this case, however, because not all programming will bear up well in repeats— some will be topical, for instance—so that perhaps five or more build-up years will be required to fill a year-long program schedule. 6

Children stay in an age band for four years before they "graduate" and move on to the next higher level. The second phase in the build-up process, therefore, will be to provide the children in each four-year age band with a four-year cycle of programming. This must be done to ensure that during the four-year period of time children spend in each age band, they will encounter fresh information and ideas—and not just repeats of the same programs—year after year. A realistic (efficient, affordable) third phase is then to institute a provision for perpetual renewal, by adding each year a quarter of a year's new programming—amounting to 65 hours for each of three age bands. The need for perpetual renewal results from program attrition, which can happen due to shifting educational practices and priorities, or topicality of subject matter, or because some experiments do not work or require revision. 7

The near-term pattern, if new productions are created at the rate of 25 percent of a four-year schedule each year, will be to accumulate a program backlog to fill first a full year's offering, then a two-year cycle, and then a three-year cycle, and so on. The eventual aim is to achieve a state of equilibrium wherein a quarter of the year's program schedule is produced anew each year, and an equal amount drops out of use. We need to program for 260 weekdays each year. 8

Whether one's concern may be with funding or with managing a children's schedule, the following summary suggests some desirable schedule conditions: 9

- *Fill the children's TV schedule through the entire calendar year.* Children of all ages watch TV and can learn from it all year round. There are no "school vacations" with at-home television. A constantly fresh program offering maintains a loyal audience, allowing the children's schedule to be its own best promotion. Television can help counteract the well-known drop-off in achievement which occurs in the summer between school years. During school years, those programs not actually used in the classroom can be assigned as homework.

- *Make optimum use of previously broadcast materials each year.* This practice is the key to schedule building. It is an important factor not only in creating an adequate quantity and diversity of programs but also in achieving the best possible cost-efficiency.

- *Aim to provide each four-year child age band with a full, four-year cycle of programs.*

- *Provide a sensible ratio of new to repeat programming.* Preschool children, as compared with their school-age counterparts, both enjoy repeat exposure to the same programs and derive greater educational benefit from it. Older children, like adults, have little tolerance for program repetition. The minimum renewal rate which will allow new educational needs to be met, and fresh new approaches taken, is a quarter of a year's new programming annually.

• *Slot children's programs at convenient and appropriate viewing times.*

Table 1 outlines the budget figures for a proposed national children's   10
TV schedule. This proposal assumes that we will incorporate, and build upon, the backlog of excellent and durable programs which already exists, eventually to provide an hour each weekday for each of the three age groups. The total amount of programming required to fill this schedule is 780 hours a year.

Children grow up with this amount of programming in Japan and   11
Great Britain and thereby enjoy an opportunity to encounter new and useful information and ideas each weekday. Over the important twelve-year learning period between two and thirteen, they grow up "through" programs geared to successive levels of interest and understanding, "graduating" every three to five years from one level of difficulty and interest to the next.

Sesame Street is an excellent case study to show how a sustained   12
investment over several years can create a backlog of reusable programming. This reuse only improves the series' already highly favorable cost-efficiency, as programs and program elements are played again and again for successive "generations" of preschool children. *Sesame Street* in 1987 costs more than $11 million annually to produce. The actual expenditure for its first season was $7.2 million in 1979 dollars. Each year since, a

TABLE 1
Initial Yearly Costs for Proposed National Children's TV Schedule[a,b]

AGE GROUP	SCHEDULED HOURS EACH YEAR	NEW HOURS EACH YEAR	COST PER NEW HOUR[c] (thousands)	YEARLY TOTAL (millions)	ANNUAL COST PER CHILD
2–5	260	60	$200	$12.0	$0.86
6–9	260	65	$375	$24.4	$1.74
10–13	260	65	$400	$26.0	$1.86
Total	780	190		$62.4	$14.9 (avg)

[a]The calculations in the table are based on 14 million children per four-year age group, for a total of 42 million, as a convenient approximation. (Population source: U.S. Bureau of the Census, Current Population Reports Series, P-25, No. 952.)
[b]A factor of 50 percent has been added to production, to cover the activities of series development, curriculum planning, pre-production research and child testing, pilot production and review, and audience building.
[c]The cost per hour is based on prevailing mid-1980s production costs in U.S. public TV in general and in children's PTV programming in particular.

substantially renewed series of 130 hour-long programs has been produced and broadcast. Today, however, expensively produced films, animation, and Muppet segments, reused from previous years, make up about two-thirds of each hour-long program. In times of inflated costs the savings are significant.

Only a fraction of the many hundreds of pieces of carefully crafted film 13 and videotapes contained in this treasure store are called into use each year to assemble what is, for the children, a largely fresh 130-hour series. Most of the new program elements created consist of less costly studio-produced scenes.

Without doing a detailed cost analysis, one could estimate that the 14 cost today to inaugurate a wholly new, 130-hour *Sesame Street* series from scratch would easily exceed $25 million. This means that the replacement value of the program segments that are now carried forward into each new *Sesame Street* season from previous years is more than $15 million.

This system of building a backlog of reusable programs and program 15 elements is the key to creating an efficient and affordable children's schedule.

Sesame Street and its successors among CTW [Children's Television 16 Workshop] productions represent a massive number of program hours, outstanding in technical and artistic quality. By renewing *Sesame Street* each year as a 130-hour series, the Workshop is able to provide for an uninterrupted year-round presence in the weekday PTV schedule—and make learning an everyday pastime in preschool children's lives. This continuity is accomplished to some degree with mirrors, as it were, because each year's 130 programs exactly fill a six-month broadcast schedule, then are repeated one time in their entirety to fill out the year. This rate of repeat will not hold up in audience appeal with older children or with programs designed other than with *Sesame Street*'s largely unthemed, variety format.

Sesame Street is seen by many as a model of collaborative production 17 and research activities, but as the above illustration makes clear, it also offers some important lessons on how to develop and manage a TV schedule. This realm of concern will become especially important if and when we enter a new and expanded phase in quality children's television.

The CTW experience is instructive and may be looked upon as the 18 model for an even larger national program package for all children. The *Sesame Street* case has shown that judicious reuse of programs and program elements can introduce major cost savings without any compromise of educational benefits.

QUESTIONS FOR ANALYSIS

1. To analyze the organization of this proposal, begin by making an outline of it following the guidelines in Chapter 1 under Outlining. How well organized does it seem to you as one reader? What kinds of cueing devices—forecasting statements, transitions, summaries—are provided to help you follow from point to point?

2. How does Palmer define the problem? How well does he demonstrate that the problem exists and is serious?

3. In paragraphs 5–8, Palmer explains what he calls the programming "build-up process." Summarize this process in your own words. What role does the explanation of this process play in the proposal? (Review the advice under Summarizing in Chapter 1.)

4. Palmer lists in paragraph 9 the criteria he thinks should apply to any proposal for a schedule of children's educational television programming. How reasonable do these criteria seem to you as a general reader? Is anything important left out? How well does Palmer's own proposal stand up when you apply these criteria to it?

5. Palmer concludes his proposal with what he calls a "case study." How does this case study help support his argument?

6. Review Exploring Your Personal Response in Chapter 1. Then, write a 300–400-word personal response to this selection. Choose either one of the following topics:

    Write about your personal associations with something in the reading.

    Play devil's advocate and challenge the writer's ideas or argument.

    After you have written your response, reread it thoughtfully. In two or three sentences, say what you have learned about Palmer's proposal by writing an extended, personal response to it.

IDEAS FOR YOUR OWN WRITING

Make a list of problems relating to popular forms of entertainment such as television, film, theater, musical performance and recording. To get you started, here are two problems that have been raised recently: the lyrics of some rock songs encourage drug use, suicide, or other antisocial behavior; several prime-time television programs are too violent or sexually explicit for children. Choose one problem from your list. How could you define this problem so that others would have to acknowledge that it exists and is serious? Who could take action to solve the problem?

Do you think you would address your proposal specifically to these individuals or to a general audience in order to mobilize public opinion? How might you argue differently if you were writing to those able to take direct action rather than to the public at large?

Charles C. Moskos

Charles C. Moskos is a sociologist who specializes in studying the military. He is currently Professor of Sociology at Northwestern University and Chairman of the Inter-University Seminar on Armed Forces and Society. He has lectured at the Army Research Institute and has been a fellow at the Woodrow Wilson International Center for Scholars. His most recent publications include *The Military—More Than Just a Job?* (1988) and *A Call to Civic Service: National Service for Country and Community* (1988).

A Practical Proposal for National Service

In the following excerpt from *A Call to Civic Service*, Charles C. Moskos proposes a plan for voluntary civil service. As you will see, civil service involves a wide range of activities, including replastering and painting homes for the poor, bringing food to the homes of elderly and infirm people, teaching adults to read and write, and reseeding forest land after a fire. What kind of service work would you be interested in doing? What advantages would this kind of work have for you?

You might want to preview this long and complicated proposal by skimming it. Note that Moskos provides headings and a figure. What do you learn from them? How helpful are they?

National-service proposals have failed to attract sustained policy attention to date for two seemingly contradictory reasons. On the one hand, many of the proposals come across as vague and incomplete; they omit any serious discussion of such crucial matters as administration and budget. Other proposals suffer from just the opposite: too formal and detailed, they tend to ignore both political realities and the historical experience of actual youth service programs.

In order to reach a higher plane, the debate requires new types of proposals that are neither too grand nor too rigid. While surveys have indicated a broad approval among Americans for some form of national service, long-term support will inevitably depend on the particulars of any plan that is actually enacted. Nothing would more rapidly undermine public support than a scheme that ignores real-world problems. Poorly framed proposals by enthusiasts can inadvertently lead to public disillusionment, even cynicism, about national service. This is all to say that the program itself becomes a defining factor in the course of general debate on national service.

To start, any practical service proposal must take into account some basic features of the national mood. Many Americans seem convinced that our society is rapidly losing its civic underpinnings and that, as a result, important social needs are going unmet. At the same time, the public does not seem prepared to support any program that would be compulsory in nature or would require the creation of a huge bureaucracy. Building on such sentiments, a successful national-service program would have to be both voluntary and comprehensive; it should be neither federal nor local but something of both.

A concrete proposal must begin with some numbers. Some 4 million Americans per year turned age eighteen in the 1970s. This figure declined to 3.6 million in the 1980s and is projected to reach a low of 3.2 million in 1992. The number is then expected to begin climbing again, approaching 4 million by the end of the century. But the proportion of youth aged eighteen to twenty-four years will steadily decline as a percentage of the total population, from 12 percent in 1985 to 10 percent in 1990 to 9 percent in the year 2000.

The proposal outlined here would involve about one million young people a year; about 600,000 would enter civilian service and about 400,000 would join the military. One million young people doing national service is a tremendous number, but, because the program would be noncompulsory, this would still be only one-quarter to one-third of the total youth cohort. The focus here will be entirely on civilian service, the most novel component of any comprehensive program. . . .

Meeting Society's Needs. For any national-service program to work, it must perform tasks that neither the marketplace nor government can provide. There is work to be done that remains undone because there is no profit in it for the private sector and the public sector cannot afford it. The focus in national service must always be on the services provided. If a national-service program cannot provide services more effectively or more cheaply than private enterprise or employees of public agencies, then there is no basis for it.

The most detailed estimates on the number of tasks that could be performed by short-term volunteers with no specialized training is found in a 1986 Ford Foundation report on national service. Based on the informed analyses of specialists in various fields, the report concluded that nearly 3.5 million positions could be filled by unskilled young people.[1] Most of these slots are located in education, the health sector, and child care, but several hundred thousand youth could be employed in such fields as conservation, criminal justice, and libraries and museums.

A partial listing of specific tasks within the general categories given   8 above are: education—tutors, teachers' aides; health care—aides for inpatient care in hospitals, nursing homes, hospices, mental institutions, ambulatory care in outpatient facilities, also providers of home care, including meals on wheels, and transportation services; child care—workers for home care, center-based care, and care in work sites; conservation—forestry planting, soil conservation, construction and maintenance in recreation areas; criminal justice—police reserves, civilian patrols, police staff support; libraries and museums—preservers of library and museum collections, makers of braille and talking books, deliveries to homebound and institutionalized borrowers. This list could be extended almost indefinitely by incorporating the many, many services undertaken by nonprofit organizations across the country. . . .

Administrative Organization. National service emphasizes the   9 ethic of citizenship duty rather than employment. National servers would receive a stipend, say $100 weekly, along with health and life insurance; room and board would be provided if need be with corresponding reductions in the stipend. The normal workweek would be forty hours. The basic length of service would be one year, though certain specialized programs would involve longer terms and some local programs might possibly require less. Although in-service compensation would be minimal, generous postservice educational and job-training benefits would be available to those who completed their term of service. The long-term goal is that only national servers would be eligible for such benefits.

Administering the overall program would be a Corporation for Na-   10 tional Youth Service.[2] It would function as a public corporation in the mold of the Corporation for Public Broadcasting. The president and Congress would jointly appoint the board, taking due care to make sure that major interest groups are represented (given concerns that national servers might displace workers, union representation would be essential). Congress would appropriate funds for the corporation, which would then award grants to state and local youth corps. The corporation would establish guidelines for acceptable levels of expenditures per enrollee and also would set standards to preclude exploitation of youth servers. The corporation would also coordinate programs administered by federal agencies, serve as a clearinghouse for national-service initiatives, and have a small research staff. The corporation itself would not directly supervise national servers or carry out national-service functions.

The corporation would have no control over the Peace Corps (to be 11 moderately expanded, with perhaps some cultural-exchange programs with industrialized countries) or VISTA (to be greatly expanded), both of which would retain their current structure.[3] However, the corporation would be responsible for newly created "signature" programs, each with a specific mission. Such programs might involve working with the United States Border Patrol or civil-defense programs. A signature program could be matched to the needs of those afflicted with a particular disease, Alzheimer's and AIDS being preeminent examples. By meeting clear needs not served by the marketplace, signature programs would help dramatize the civic content of national service.

The great majority of civilian youth servers, however, would not be in 12 federal programs. Most activity would occur at the state and local levels. By awarding block grants, the corporation would afford local units considerable autonomy in planning their programs. The rule of thumb ought to be that larger and higher agencies should not deliver services that can be performed by smaller and lower agencies. National responsibility would be limited to insuring that fund recipients meet certain basic standards pertaining to such matters as compensation, the kind of work performed, the terms of agreement between enrollees and employers, the prevention of job displacements, and the screening out of sectarian and political advocacy.

Once funded, state and local units would set up their own corps. They 13 would also be free to choose their own organizational format—panels appointed by the governor or mayor, an add-on to a government youth

FIGURE 1.

Model of Administrative Organization for National Service

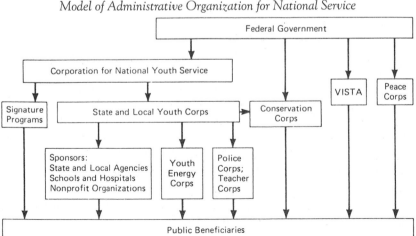

office, a new office agency entirely, or a single individual. In some instances, servers would enroll directly in state and local youth corps, as is now the case with the California Conservation Corps and the New York City Volunteer Corps. In other (and probably the majority of) cases, state and local youth corps enrollees would be assigned to "sponsors" and live at home. The sponsors—public agencies, schools, hospitals, and nonprofit organizations—would be the backbone of the delivery of human services. The sponsor system would be modeled after the old Seattle Program for Local Service and its successor, the state of Washington Service Corps.

A national program could also set aside funds for staff-intensive (and 14 therefore expensive) programs that would seek to involve disadvantaged youth who might not otherwise enroll. The prototype is the Youth Energy Corps in New York City, where enrollees receive basic education and hands-on training while undertaking such tasks as weatherizing tenements and rehabilitating public facilities. Such projects are consistent with the civic content of national service because, unlike the Job Corps, enrollees not only acquire training but also serve a community need.

Rounding out the national-service program would be that old stand- 15 by, conservation work. Building on the model of the Young Adult Conservation Corps of the 1970s and the proposed American Conservation Corps, the federal government would distribute funds among three administrative entities: the Forest Service of the Department of Agriculture, the Department of the Interior, and the individual states. Because this table of organization has proven itself in modern conservation history, there is no reason for the National Service Corporation to become involved. The federal programs would be mainly residential, as would most of the state programs. But a sizable amount of conservation work in or near metropolitan areas could also be nonresidential.

It is impossible to predict the exact shape a national-service program 16 would take in practice. America does not stand still, and no such program can be cast in finite detail. But the plan outlined here has several distinct advantages. One is that because it is based on programs already in place, national service could be implemented in a relatively short period of time. Within a year, it could accommodate 100,000 people. Positions for another 100,000 could be added each year, with the final goal of 600,000 being reached in five years or so. Another advantage is that a minimal administrative structure overlays existing and expandable organizations. Yet with its decentralized structure, the proposed national service has an overreaching civic content that will give local programs a chance to feel a part of the whole. . . .

Costs. Overall, the direct costs of the national-service program would 17
come to about $7 billion. With 600,000 enrollees, this works out to a per-
slot annual cost of about $11,700. This does not take into account,
however, cost sharing by state and local governments. These would be
expected to assume 25 percent of the costs of all nonfederal projects. (The
exception would be the Police and Teacher Corps, for which cost sharing
would be on a 50/50 basis, on the presumption of special arrangements
being made with public universities and colleges.) Overall, the state and
local governments would contribute an estimated $1.3 billion and the
federal government $5.7 billion. The annual costs to the federal govern-
ment would thus come to about $9,500 per enrollee (not counting
postservice educational benefits described below).

Furthermore, the nonprofit sponsors responsible for the delivery of 18
human services would contribute $1,000 a year for each young person
they enrolled. As Seattle's Public Local Service program demonstrated in
the 1970s, this arrangement is both effective and enforceable. The
purpose is not only to help defray expenses but also to insure that young
enrollees are not simply treated as free labor. Requiring sponsors to pay
enrollees would also make them less reluctant to discharge those who do
not perform up to standard.

Although prediction of exact dollar figures in such a large and untried 19
program is a risky business, the general principles of cost accounting of
national service are clear. Costs are higher to the degree that programs
are more residential, managed by public agencies, directed toward high-
risk youth, and staff-intensive. Correspondingly, costs are lower to the
degree that national service is nonresidential, managed by nonprofit
organizations, untargeted, and low on staff. The spreadsheet given in
Table 1 can be varied by changing the weights given to each of these
factors. [Table not included.—*Eds.*]

To be really complete, a budgeting exercise on national service must 20
include the value of the work performed. What is the final value of
preserving our physical resources, cleaning up the environment, caring
for the elderly and handicapped, rescuing our research collections, staffing our public institutions with citizen servers, and opening new avenues
for dead-end youth? There is no ready answer. Even though evaluation
studies on service programs indicate that for every dollar expended at
least one dollar of value is gained, such studies can go only so far. By
focusing either on short-term impacts on program participants or economic analyses of specific services delivered, evaluation researchers typically fail to include the more general societal benefits that a national-
service program would provide. The gains in civic culture and social
consensus, though difficult to measure, would surely be sizable.[4]

Any large-scale national-service program will cost money, and it is best 21 to say so up front. Even the costs presented [here] do not include capital expenditures or purchases of equipment, although in many cases these will already be taken care of because most national servers will be working in existing organizations. But we should also place the financial outlays of a national-service program in context. For instance, the program outlined here would (in constant dollars) cost the federal government about two-thirds of the annual funds expended on the unlamented CETA.[5] That a comprehensive national-service program could be had at such a price should make the idea all the more appealing.

Postsecondary-School Aid and National Service. Educational 22 benefits for youth who complete a term of duty is a keystone of any national-service program. In return for one year of civilian service at subsistence wages, postservice benefits are a proper response to an accomplishment of civic duty. The GI Bill following World War II was a nation's way of expressing its gratitude for those who served in its military. It is time to extend this principle to those who perform civilian service as well.[6] When I first proposed this linkage a decade ago, I was virtually alone. Increasingly, however, the notion of a "GI Bill" for civilian national service is attracting serious attention. I stress that connecting student aid to national service is not adding another expenditure on the federal treasury; rather, the proposal is to shift present appropriations to national service.

In its initial stages, a national-service program should guarantee all 23 enrollees postsecondary-school benefits that feature much more favorable terms than those available to nonservers. Student loan forgiveness for national service is one obvious and easily implemented policy. In time, participation in national service would become a prerequisite for federal educational and vocational training assistance. Such an approach would fit nicely with the recommendations of the 1985 Newman report issued by the Carnegie Foundation for the Advancement of Teaching. That report urged that federal student aid move away from loan programs toward outright grants and work-study arrangements.

Imagine if the $8 billion that Congress authorized for federal educa- 24 tional assistance in 1986 were divided equally among 600,000 national servers; each enrollee would receive a $14,000 scholarship! Even if only half that amount were disbursed, each individual would receive $7,000. Think of it still another way: generous scholarship aid could be offered to national servers simply by paying them out of the $4 billion that the taxpayer now spends for bank subsidies and loan defaults in the present student-aid program.

The principal argument raised against linking national service and [25] federal educational aid is that it would have a regressive effect. According to this line of reasoning, students from wealthy families who do not need aid would be unaffected, while poor students would have to enter national service in order to get aid. Without assistance, poor students intent on staying in college would be forced to take more part-time jobs, rely on family and other personal sources, and attend less expensive (mainly public) colleges.

Such a line of reasoning has a certain surface plausibility, but really [26] cannot stand up to scrutiny. The fact of the matter is that the present shift away from grants toward loans in student aid heightens the class division between those who can afford to pay for college and those who cannot. From 1980 to 1986, the proportion of students from working-class families who enrolled in college dropped by one-fifth.[7] The percentage of black high-school graduates entering college dropped from 34 in 1976 to 25 in 1985; for Hispanics the decline was from 36 to 27 percent.[8] The prospect of student-incurred debt is undoubtedly a major factor in the declining number of poor youth entering and completing college.[9] Thus replacing the present student-aid program with one that links national service to a GI Bill-type grant would most likely widen rather than restrict access to higher education.[10] Also important, a movement toward a service-based rather than a needs-based aid program would almost surely strengthen public support for the whole concept of federal assistance to college students.[11]

The argument that linking student aid to national service is regressive [27] also misses on a deeper point. Student aid by its very nature is regressive. Only about half of all young people even enter college, so at the very outset aid goes to those students with the best career prospects.[12] A national service that has special programs for poor youth facing otherwise dead-end prospects is infinitely more progressive than the status quo. Finally, the grossest inequities in our society are found in the differential treatment one can expect in terms of day care for children, primary and secondary school education, and how the aged, sick, and infirm are handled. Youth participation in delivery of human services would reduce such inequities more than any other feasible policy.

We are still left, however, with the question of how a nonmandatory [28] system can bring the most privileged youth into national service. In the end, there is no voluntary scheme that can insure the participation of the very rich in national service.[13] We must acknowledge we are a capitalist society, with all that implies in terms of class advantages. But a comprehensive national-service program linked with student aid would at least introduce the concept of civic responsibility to a very large portion of American youth, thereby helping raise the nation's standards of citizenship. We should not lose sight of the fact that educational costs are a heavy burden for almost all American families. Few readers of these pages look lightly upon college expenses, either their own or their children's. Regarding those who choose not to serve because they are both rich enough to dismiss student aid and unaffected by civic considerations, one feels regret for them and the country.

Throughout this discussion, I have steadfastly focused on that which is practicable. To be successful, a national-service system should build on present trends rather than take a great leap into the unknown. Organizational structures must remain flexible, because they will surely be affected by the social circumstances and political compromises of the real world. As with all programs of this scope, we can expect incidents of fraud and abuse. There will probably be national-service "horror stories." But the program will avoid a negative image largely to the degree it attracts a cross section of American youth early on. Such youth in turn will become the "alumni" supporters of national service for their juniors.

It is within our reach to establish a comprehensive youth program to serve national needs without compulsion, without a Brobdingnagian bureaucracy, and without massive costs. The real key is to link governmental subsidies of higher education and postsecondary job training to voluntary service. The goal is nothing less than making civic duty an intrinsic part of growing up in America.

NOTES

1. Richard Danzig and Peter Szanton, *National Service: What Would It Mean?* (Lexington, Mass.: Lexington Books, 1986), pp. 17–40.

2. The idea of a public corporation to be the administrative agency of national service originates with Donald J. Eberly. See Eberly, "A Model for Universal Youth Service," unpublished paper prepared for the Eleanor Roosevelt Institute, 1976; also Eberly, "An Administrative Model: National Youth Service (NYS)," in Michael W. Sherraden and Donald J. Eberly, eds., *National Service: Social, Economic and Military Impacts* (New York: Pergamon, 1982), pp. 122–24.

3. The Peace Corps might be revamped to include volunteers serving (most likely as aids to English instructors) in countries where long-term American interests would be advanced by developing a future cadre of Americans with knowledge of the host country's language and culture. Japan, China, the USSR, Israel, and most of the countries of Europe and the Arab world come quickly to mind. In the more industrialized nations, a cost-sharing feature might be introduced.

4. A penetrating critique of how evaluation studies deal only with short-term and directly quantifiable outcomes is Harold L. Wilensky, "Political Legitimacy and

Consensus: Missing Variables in the Assessment of Social Policy," in S. E. Spiro and E. Yuchtman-Yaar, eds., *Evaluating the Welfare State* (New York: Academic Press, 1983), pp. 51–74.

5. On CETA costs, see Grace A. Franklin and Randall B. Ripley, *CETA: Politics and Policy, 1973–1982* (Knoxville, Tenn.: University of Tennessee Press, 1984), p. 24.

6. National servers who choose not to go to college or obtain vocational training should be eligible for GI Bill–type home loans on the post–World War II model and/or some kind of modest bonus upon completion of service.

7. Robert Kuttner, "The Patrimony Society," *The New Republic*, May 11, 1987, p. 20.

8. Edward B. Fiske, "Colleges Open New Minority Drives," *New York Times*, November 18, 1987, p. 18.

9. Kathryn Mohrman, "Unintended Consequences of Federal Student Aid Policies," *Brookings Review* (Fall 1987), pp. 24–30; Jane S. Hansen, *Student Loans: Are They Overburdening a Generation?* Report prepared for the Joint Economic Committee, U.S. Congress, December 1986.

10. The probable effect of limiting college student aid to national servers might go something like the following. Some number of middle-class students who do not presently receive student aid would receive such aid because of their enrollment in national service. But we also know that poor youth greatly oversubscribe youth corps. Thus some number of poor youth who otherwise would not go on to college will do so because of their newly acquired eligibility for student aid. I am indebted for this formulation to Richard Danzig.

11. On the political implications of means versus non-means tested social programs, see Robert Kuttner, *The Life of the Party* (New York: Elisabeth Sifton/Viking, 1987).

12. *The Forgotten Half: Non-College Youth in America* (Washington, D.C.: William T. Grant Foundation Commission on Work, Family, and Citizenship, 1988).

13. William F. Buckley, Jr., has proposed a voluntary national service in which elite colleges and universities would only accept applicants who had completed "one year in public service." As quoted in Sherraden and Eberly, eds., *National Service*, p. 116.

QUESTIONS FOR ANALYSIS

1. This is a longer, more complicated proposal than the ones that precede it in this chapter. To get a sense of how Moskos organizes it, make an outline following the procedures given in Chapter 1 under Outlining. Notice particularly the cueing devices—forecasting statements, transitions, summaries, and headings—Moskos provides to help readers follow from one point to another. How well organized does this proposal seem to you as one reader?

2. What problems is the proposed civilian-service program designed to help solve? How does Moskos argue that the program he proposes

would indeed help solve these problems? How convincing for you, as one reader, is this argument?

3. Moskos devotes many paragraphs to explaining the administrative organization of his proposed civilian service, but he spends only one (paragraph 16) arguing its advantages. Are you surprised by this allotment of space? What seem to you to be the advantages or disadvantages of this strategy?

4. The costs of any program are likely to be the center of concern. How does Moskos justify the costs for his civilian-service program? Which arguments seem to you to be the strongest and the weakest? Explain.

5. If the aim of establishing a voluntary civilian service is, at least in part, to reestablish a national commitment to civic duty, then why does Moskos think it is necessary to reward civil servers with a postservice "GI Bill"? Is this a contradiction? What advantages and disadvantages do you see in making postsecondary-school aid a part of the package?

6. How would you characterize the dominant tone of this essay? How does Moskos come across? Does he seem trustworthy? Point to one or more places in the essay to support your opinion.

7. In the first five paragraphs, Moskos defines criteria for a good proposal. What are they? Judged on the basis of his own criteria, how well does Moskos's proposal fare?

IDEAS FOR YOUR OWN WRITING

Moskos identifies a wide variety of social problems ranging from child care to forest planting. Choose one of the problems he names—or one of your own—and do some creative problem solving. You might want to begin by considering what the causes of the problem are so that you can consider ways of removing them. Another strategy is to think analogically: Ask yourself, what is this problem like? A third strategy is to try to imagine what the result of a solution would look like and then to work back from there to see how such a solution might be achieved.

Jonathan Swift

Jonathan Swift (1667–1745) is best known as the author of *Gulliver's Travels* (1726), a book that is often regarded as a children's story but which is actually a sweeping satire of the age. As befits a clergyman—Swift was dean of an Anglican church in Dublin, Ireland—the butt of much of Swift's satire is moral obtuseness. Born in Ireland of English parents, he was also particularly sensitive to injustices resulting from British rule of Ireland. The situation in Ireland at the time was grim. The Irish Catholic peasants, charged excessive rents by the British absentee landlords, were desperately poor. With the exception of Swift, few spoke out on behalf of the Irish, and the British Parliament simply ignored the problem. Swift is still revered in Ireland for his series of letters opposing England's plan to impose new coins, a plan that would have further debased the value of Irish currency and worsened the already extreme poverty in Ireland.

A Modest Proposal

"A Modest Proposal (For Preventing the Children of Poor People in Ireland from Being a Burden to Their Parents or Country, and for Making Them Beneficial to the Public)" was originally published as an anonymous pamphlet in 1729. At the time, some readers took it at face value, thinking it was a serious proposal to solve the problem of poverty in Ireland. It is not hard to see how readers could have been duped since it is a textbook example of proposal writing—defining and establishing the problem with a multitude of facts and systematically expounding the advantages of the proposed solution over the alternatives. But it is also a masterful piece of irony. Conjecture, as you read, how readers could have mistaken the tone. What does Swift do to make his persona believable at the same time that he is making such an outrageous proposal?

It is a melancholy object to those who walk through this great town[1] or travel in the country, when they see the streets, the roads, and cabin doors, crowded with beggars of the female sex, followed by three, four, or six children, all in rags and importuning every passenger for an alms. These mothers, instead of being able to work for their honest livelihood, are forced to employ all their time in strolling to beg sustenance for their helpless infants, who, as they grow up, either turn thieves for want of

---

[1]Dublin. [Eds.]

work, or leave their dear native country to fight for the Pretender in Spain, or sell themselves to the Barbados.[2]

I think it is agreed by all parties that this prodigious number of children in the arms, or on the backs, or at the heels of their mothers, and frequently of their fathers, is in the present deplorable state of the kingdom a very great additional grievance; and therefore whoever could find out a fair, cheap, and easy method of making these children sound, useful members of the commonwealth would deserve so well of the public as to have his statue set up for a preserver of the nation.

But my intention is very far from being confined to provide only for the children of professed beggars; it is of a much greater extent, and shall take in the whole number of infants at a certain age who are born of parents in effect as little able to support them as those who demand our charity in the streets.

As to my own part, having turned my thoughts for many years upon this important subject, and maturely weighed the several schemes of other projectors,[3] I have always found them grossly mistaken in their computation. It is true, a child just dropped from its dam may be supported by her milk for a solar year, with little other nourishment; at most not above the value of two shillings, which the mother may certainly get, or the value in scraps, by her lawful occupation of begging; and it is exactly at one year that I propose to provide for them in such a manner as instead of being a charge upon their parents or the parish, or wanting food and raiment for the rest of their lives, they shall on the contrary contribute to the feeding, and partly to the clothing, of many thousands.

There is likewise another great advantage in my scheme, that it will prevent those voluntary abortions, and that horrid practice of women murdering their bastard children, alas, too frequent among us, sacrificing the poor innocent babes, I doubt, more to avoid the expense than the shame, which would move tears and pity in the most savage and inhuman breast.

The number of souls in this kingdom being usually reckoned one million and a half, of these I calculate there may be about two hundred thousand couples whose wives are breeders; from which number I subtract thirty thousand couples who are able to maintain their own children, although I apprehend there cannot be so many under the present

---

[2]Rebellious Irish citizens had joined an army to help James Stuart, the Pretender, reclaim the throne of England. Many others had gone to Barbados as indentured servants because they could find no other way to emigrate to the new world. [Eds.]

[3]Planners or those making proposals. [Eds.]

distress of the kingdom; but this being granted, there will remain an hundred and seventy thousand breeders. I again subtract fifty thousand for those women who miscarry, or whose children die by accident or disease within the year. There only remain an hundred and twenty thousand children of poor parents annually born. The question therefore is, how this number shall be reared and provided for, which, as I have already said, under the present situation of affairs, is utterly impossible by all the methods hitherto proposed. For we can neither employ them in handicraft or agriculture; we neither build houses (I mean in the country) nor cultivate land. They can very seldom pick up a livelihood by stealing till they arrive at six years old, except where they are of towardly parts;[4] although I confess they learn the rudiments much earlier, during which time they can however be looked upon only as probationers, as I have been informed by a principal gentleman in the country of Cavan, who protested to me that he never knew above one or two instances under the age of six, even in a part of the kingdom so renowned for the quickest proficiency in that art.

I am assured by our merchants that a boy or girl before twelve years old is no salable commodity; and even when they come to this age they will not yield above three pounds, or three pounds and half a crown at most on the Exchange; which cannot turn to account either to the parents or the kingdom, the charge of nutriment and rags having been at least four times that value.

I shall now therefore humbly propose my own thoughts, which I hope will not be liable to the least objection.

I have been assured by a very knowing American of my acquaintance in London, that a young healthy child well nursed is at a year old a most delicious, nourishing, and wholesome food, whether stewed, roasted, baked, or boiled; and I make no doubt that it will equally serve in a fricassee or a ragout.[5]

I do therefore humbly offer it to public consideration that of the hundred and twenty thousand children, already computed, twenty thousand may be reserved for breed, whereof only one fourth part to be males, which is more than we allow to sheep, black cattle, or swine; and my reason is that these children are seldom the fruits of marriage, a circumstance not much regarded by our savages, therefore one male will be sufficient to serve four females. That the remaining hundred thousand may at a year old be offered in sale to the persons of quality and

---

[4]Innate abilities. [Eds.]
[5]Stew. [Eds.]

fortune through the kingdom, always advising the mother to let them suck plentifully in the last month, so as to render them plump and fat for a good table. A child will make two dishes at an entertainment for friends; and when the family dines alone, the fore or hind quarter will make a reasonable dish, and seasoned with a little pepper or salt will be very good boiled on the fourth day, especially in winter.

I have reckoned upon a medium that a child just born will weigh 11
twelve pounds, and in a solar year if tolerably nursed increaseth to twenty-eight pounds.

I grant this food will be somewhat dear, and therefore very proper for 12
landlords, who, as they have already devoured most of the parents, seem to have the best title to the children.

Infant's flesh will be in season throughout the year, but more plentiful 13
in March, and a little before and after. For we are told by a grave author, an eminent French physician,[6] that fish being a prolific diet, there are more children born in Roman Catholic countries about nine months after Lent than at any other season; therefore, reckoning a year after Lent, the markets will be more glutted than usual, because the number of popish infants is at least three to one in this kingdom; and therefore it will have one other collateral advantage, by lessening the number of Papists among us.

I have already computed the charge of nursing a beggar's child (in 14
which list I reckon all cottagers, laborers, and four-fifths of the farmers) to be about two shillings per annum, rags included; and I believe no gentleman would repine to give ten shillings for the carcass of a good fat child, which, as I have said, will make four dishes of excellent nutritive meat, when he hath only some particular friend or his own family to dine with him. Thus the squire will learn to be a good landlord, and grow popular among the tenants; the mother will have eight shillings net profit, and be fit for work till she produces another child.

Those who are more thrifty (as I must confess the times require) may 15
flay the carcass; the skin of which artificially[7] dressed will make admirable gloves for ladies, and summer boots for fine gentlemen.

As to our city of Dublin, shambles[8] may be appointed for this purpose 16
in the most convenient parts of it, and butchers we may be assured will not be wanting; although I rather recommend buying the children alive, and dressing them hot from the knife as we do roasting pigs.

A very worthy person, a true lover of his country, and whose virtues I 17

---

[6]The French humorist, François Rabelais. [Eds.]

[7]Artfully. [Eds.]

[8]Slaughterhouses. [Eds.]

highly esteem, was lately pleased in discoursing on this matter to offer a refinement upon my scheme. He said that many gentlemen of his kingdom, having of late destroyed their deer, he conceived that the want of venison might be well supplied by the bodies of young lads and maidens, not exceeding fourteen years of age nor under twelve, so great a number of both sexes in every country being now ready to starve for want of work and service; and these to be disposed of by their parents, if alive, or otherwise by their nearest relations. But with due deference to so excellent a friend and so deserving a patriot, I cannot be altogether in his sentiments; for as to the males, my American acquaintance assured me from frequent experience that their flesh was generally tough and lean, like that of our schoolboys, by continual exercise, and their taste disagreeable; and to fatten them would not answer the charge. Then as to the females, it would, I think with humble submission, be a loss to the public, because they soon would become breeders themselves; and besides, it is not improbable that some scrupulous people might be apt to censure such a practice (although indeed very unjustly) as a little bordering upon cruelty; which, I confess, hath always been with me the strongest objection against any project, how well soever intended.

But in order to justify my friend, he confessed that this expedient was 18 put into his head by the famous Psalmanazar,[9] a native of the island Formosa, who came from thence to London above twenty years ago, and in conversation told my friend that in his country when any young person happened to be put to death, the executioner sold the carcass to persons of quality as a prime dainty; and that in his time the body of a plump girl of fifteen, who was crucified for an attempt to poison the emperor, was sold to his Imperial Majesty's prime minister of state, and other great mandarins of the court, in joints from the gibbet, at four hundred crowns. Neither indeed can I deny that if the same use were made of several plump young girls in this town, who without one single groat to their fortunes cannot stir abroad without a chair, and appear at the playhouse and assemblies in foreign fineries which they never will pay for, the kingdom would not be the worse.

Some persons of a desponding spirit are in great concern about that 19 vast number of poor people who are aged, diseased, or maimed, and I have been desired to employ my thoughts what course may be taken to ease the nation of so grievous an encumbrance. But I am not in the least pain upon that matter, because it is very well known that they are every day dying and rotting by cold and famine, and filth and vermin, as fast

---

[9]Frenchman George Psalmanazar wrote a fictional description of Formosa and duped London society into believing he was Japanese. [Eds.]

as can be reasonably expected. And as to the younger laborers, they are now in almost as hopeful a condition. They cannot get work, and consequently pine away for want of nourishment to a degree that if any time they are accidentally hired to common labor, they have not strength to perform it; and thus the country and themselves are happily delivered from the evils to come.

I have too long digressed, and therefore shall return to my subject. I think the advantages by the proposal which I have made are obvious and many, as well as of the highest importance. 20

For first, as I have already observed, it would greatly lessen the number of Papists, with whom we are yearly overrun, being the principal breeders of the nation as well as our most dangerous enemies; and who stay at home on purpose to deliver the kingdom to the Pretender, hoping to take their advantage by the absence of so many good Protestants, who have chosen rather to leave their country than to stay at home and pay tithes against their conscience to an Episcopal curate. 21

Secondly, the poorer tenants will have something valuable of their own, which by law may be made liable to distress,[10] and help to pay their landlord's rent, their corn and cattle being already seized and money a thing unknown. 22

Thirdly, whereas the maintenance of an hundred thousand children, from two years old and upwards, cannot be computed at less than ten shillings a piece per annum, the nation's stock will be thereby increased fifty thousand pounds per annum, besides the profit of a new dish introduced to the tables of all gentlemen of fortune in the kingdom who have any refinement in taste. And the money will circulate among ourselves, the goods being entirely of our own growth and manufacture. 23

Fourthly, the constant breeders, besides the gain of eight shillings sterling per annum by the sale of their children, will be rid of the charge of maintaining them after the first year. 24

Fifthly, this food would likewise bring great custom to taverns, where the vintners will certainly be so prudent as to procure the best receipts for dressing it to perfection, and consequently have their houses frequented by all the fine gentlemen, who justly value themselves upon their knowledge in good eating; and a skillful cook, who understands how to oblige his guests, will contrive to make it as expensive as they please. 25

Sixthly, this would be a great inducement to marriage, which all wise nations have either encouraged by rewards or enforced by laws and penalties. It would increase the care and tenderness of mothers toward 26

---

[10]Open to repossession by creditors. [Eds.]

their children, when they were sure of a settlement for life to the poor babes, provided in some sort by the public, to their annual profit instead of expense. We should see an honest emulation among the married women, which of them could bring the fattest child to the market. Men would become as fond of their wives during the time of their pregnancy as they are now of their mares in foal, their cows in calf, or sows when they are ready to farrow; nor offer to beat or kick them (as is too frequent a practice) for fear of a miscarriage.

Many other advantages might be enumerated. For instance, the addition of some thousand carcasses in our exportation of barreled beef, the propagation of swine's flesh, and improvements in the art of making good bacon, so much wanted among us by the great destruction of pigs, too frequent at our tables, which are no way comparable in taste or magnificence to a well-grown, fat, yearling child, which roasted whole will make a considerable figure at a lord mayor's feast or any other public entertainment. But this and many others I omit, being studious of brevity. 27

Supposing that one thousand families in this city would be constant customers for infants' flesh, besides others who might have it at merry meetings, particularly weddings and christenings, I compute that Dublin would take off annually about twenty thousand carcasses, and the rest of the kingdom (where probably they will be sold somewhat cheaper) the remaining eighty thousand. 28

I can think of no one objection that will possibly be raised against this proposal, unless it should be urged that the number of people will be thereby much lessened in the kingdom. This I freely own, and it was indeed one principal design in offering it to the world. I desire the reader will observe, that I calculate my remedy for this one individual kingdom of Ireland and for no other that ever was, is, or I think ever can be upon earth. Therefore let no man talk to me of other expedients: of taxing our absentees at five shillings a pound: of using neither clothes nor household furniture except what is of our own growth and manufacture: of utterly rejecting the materials and instruments that promote foreign luxury: of curing the expensiveness of pride, vanity, idleness, and gaming in our women: of introducing a vein of parsimony, prudence, and temperance: of learning to love our country, in the want of which we differ even from Laplanders and the inhabitants of Topinamboo:[11] of quitting our animosities and factions, nor acting any longer like the Jews, who were murdering one another at the very moment their city was taken:[12] 29

---

[11]In Brazil. [Eds.]

[12]During the Roman siege of Jerusalem (70 A.D.), some Jews were murdered for conspiring with the enemy. [Eds.]

of being a little cautious not to sell our country and conscience for nothing: of teaching landlords to have at least one degree of mercy toward their tenants: lastly, of putting a spirit of honesty, industry, and skill into our shopkeepers; who, if a resolution could now be taken to buy only our native goods, would immediately unite to cheat and exact upon us in the price, the measure, and the goodness, nor could ever yet be brought to make one fair proposal of just dealing, though often and earnestly invited to it.[13]

Therefore I repeat, let no man talk to me of these and the like expedients, till he hath at least some glimpse of hope that there will ever be some hearty and sincere attempt to put them in practice.

But as to myself, having been wearied out for many years with offering vain, idle, visionary thoughts, and at length utterly despairing of success, I fortunately fell upon this proposal, which, as it is wholly new, so it hath something solid and real, of no expense and little trouble, full in our own power, and whereby we can incur no danger in disobliging England. For this kind of commodity will not bear exportation, the flesh being of too tender a consistence to admit a long continuance in salt, although perhaps I could name a country which would be glad to eat up our whole nation without it.[14]

After all, I am not so violently bent upon my own opinion as to reject any offer proposed by wise men, which shall be found equally innocent, cheap, easy, and effectual. But before something of that kind shall be advanced in contradiction to my scheme, and offering a better, I desire the author or authors will be pleased maturely to consider two points. First, as things now stand, how they will be able to find food and raiment for an hundred thousand useless mouths and backs. And secondly, there being a round million of creatures in human figure throughout this kingdom, whose sole subsistence put into a common stock would leave them in debt two millions of pounds sterling, adding those who are beggars by profession to the bulk of farmers, cottagers, and laborers, with their wives and children who are beggars in effect; I desire those politicians who dislike my overture, and may perhaps be so bold to attempt an answer, that they will first ask the parents of these mortals whether they would not at this day think it a great happiness to have been sold for food at a year old in this manner I prescribe, and thereby have avoided such a perpetual scene of misfortunes as they have since gone through by the oppression of landlords, the impossibility of paying rent without money or trade, the want of common sustenance, with neither house nor

---

[13]Swift made these proposals in other pamphlets. [Eds.]
[14]England. [Eds.]

clothes to cover them from the inclemencies of the weather, and the most inevitable prospect of entailing the like or greater miseries upon their breed forever.

I profess, in the sincerity of my heart, that I have not the least personal 33 interest in endeavoring to promote this necessary work, having no other motive than the public good of my country, by advancing our trade, providing for infants, relieving the poor, and giving some pleasure to the rich. I have no children by which I can propose to get a single penny; the youngest being nine years old, and my wife past childbearing.

QUESTIONS FOR ANALYSIS

1. Begin your analysis of Swift's proposal by outlining it according to the procedures in Chapter 1 under Outlining. Mark on your outline where the following basic features are presented: problem definition, refutation of alternative solutions, the proposed solution, the reasons and backing in support of the proposed solution, and refutation of possible objections.

2. As an ironist, Swift has an ulterior or concealed purpose as well as an ostensible or pretended purpose. What is his ostensible purpose? His ulterior purpose? How do you know what his ulterior purpose is if it is concealed? What clues does he give readers that would enable them to see through the pretense?

3. Where in the proposal does Swift argue that the problem exists and is serious? Which of the three kinds of appeals—logical, emotional, ethical—does he make? Point to an example of each kind of appeal you find in this part of the proposal.

4. Swift considers various alternative solutions in paragraphs 6–7 and 29. Which of these alternatives seem to you to be serious, and which seem ironic? Given his ulterior purpose and readers, how does Swift's treatment of alternative solutions support his argument?

5. A characteristic of this proposal is its overwhelming use of statistics. What are these statistics used to prove? How convincing are they?

6. Skim the essay, annotating and taking inventory of instances in which human beings are referred to in terms usually used for live-stock. What does such labeling of people imply? (Chapter 1 gives guidance for taking Inventory of Annotations.)

7. How do you know, just from reading the proposal, that it is ironic? To answer this question, you might focus your attention on the proposal's ethical appeal. How does the persona demonstrate that he is a trustworthy, moral person? What is wrong with this demonstration?

IDEAS FOR YOUR OWN WRITING

Although this proposal was written many years ago, the problems it addresses—poverty, hunger, moral stupidity—unfortunately remain. How would you awaken your neighbors to the plight of the less fortunate? Write some notes suggesting a way to increase the awareness of people in your own community about a specific social problem.

Alternatively, consider how you might use irony to ridicule attitudes held by your contemporaries. Think of proposed solutions you find repellent, and use irony and exaggeration to write your own "modest proposal."

Will Scarvie

Will Scarvie wrote this proposal for a freshman composition course at the University of California, San Diego.

Proposal to Increase Efficiency

Like many students, Will Scarvie worked while he was attending college. He was a computer operator at a small firm of certified public accountants. Although he wrote this proposal for his composition course, he eventually sent it to the company president and, with some modification, the proposal was implemented. As you will see from quickly skimming it, this proposal is written in the form of an interoffice memo.

As you might imagine, Scarvie found himself in a delicate rhetorical situation as he wrote this proposal. As you read, put yourself in Scarvie's place and consider these questions: What tone would you take? How would you present your proposal without appearing to be telling the president how to run the company? How would you avoid appearing to be out for brownie points? How would you avoid placing blame on people with whom you must continue to work, even if you think they are responsible for the problem?

TO: Rubin L. Gorewitz, President
FROM: Will Scarvie, Computer Operator
SUBJECT: Proposal to Increase Efficiency

As you may know, Rubin L. Gorewitz & Co. CPA has had an 1 inordinate number of projects backlogged in the computer section. Although some of us in the section have been blamed, we are not the cause. The problem stems from the increase in workload given us by the accountants, each of whom now handles more than seventy clients in the course of a year. I feel confident we could manage the increased workload efficiently, if we had a priority system in place.

Every day, accountants give us projects that must be finished "right 2 away." We have no criteria to help us decide which of these projects to do first. The accountants have equal authority and seem always to be in a rush. Their need is undoubtedly real, since I am sure that meeting with a client without the promised document could lead the client to question the firm's reliability. To remedy this problem, we need to improve communication between the accountants and the computer section, and to

407

make clear to the computer operators which jobs have priority over the others.

I propose that we design a chart, which would be posted near the door 3 of the computer section, and would let operators know what jobs need to be done and when. The sheet would consist of six columns. The first, titled "Client/Accountant," would contain the names of the client and accountant so that routing would be clear and we would know who to get in touch with if there were a problem. The next, "Job Type," would indicate precisely what needs to be done. At the same time that we make up this form, we also might take the opportunity to update the list of job types and have a meeting of the computer section staff and the account- ants to make sure that we're all using the same language.

The third column, "Date and Time Needed," would identify clearly 4 what the deadline is for the project. The fourth, "Job Notes," would be used by accountants to notify the computer operators of any special changes or additions to the standard job type. The fifth, "Number of Checks," would help the computer operator estimate how long the project will actually take. It is a crucial bit of information that we do not currently get. The final column, "Operator/Time In-Out," would indi- cate which computer operator (or operators in cases where two or more people work on a project) is doing the project, as well as when the project began and ended. Accountants needing to update instructions would be able simply to check the chart to see whom to talk to. The in/out time could be used for a study of the time it takes to complete different types of projects; such a study would help us make more realistic estimates for future projects.

I would urge one further change in the current system: Assign one 5 computer operator the job of coordinating the work of the computer section. The coordinator would be responsible for ranking projects in order of priority and seeing that the operators team up when a large project needs immediate action. Important criteria for the job of coordi- nator obviously would include experience dealing with a wide range of job types and problems. The person chosen for the job should also need good people skills, since he or she will need to negotiate with account- ants to resolve conflicts about whose project has priority. Since this job involves more responsibility than the normal computer operator has, I would think it should be a somewhat higher-paid position.

One of the accountants offered an alternative solution you might 6 consider. She recommended that the company purchase additional com- puters and hire more computer operators to work them. She didn't specify how many new computers and operators should be added. Al- though this solution may become necessary as the company continues to expand and the workload increases, I do not think we are at the point yet where an expenditure of this kind is required. I believe that the problem we are having lies not in staffing but in organization. As it is, we are able to finish most projects on time. Centralizing the management of the workload and improving communication would, I think, enable us to get all projects done on time.

You may object that my solution is cumbersome and would take too long to institute, but I think that all it would take is a brief meeting between the accountants and computer operators to explain the procedure. The chart itself would require little time to prepare and photocopy. Of course, you would have to select a coordinator, and that might take some time and money. I'd recommend that we have at least a one-week trial period to make sure that we all understand how the new system works and to make whatever revisions become necessary.

The chief difficulty I foresee is in estimating the time projects take, but that is a problem we have with the current system as well. If we conduct the study I mentioned earlier, I am sure our ability to estimate will eventually improve. As we become more efficient, I also think the accountants will become more confident in our ability to do the job and therefore will be more realistic in prioritizing their projects. Given these benefits and the minimal costs, I respectfully urge you to give this proposal your immediate consideration.

QUESTIONS FOR ANALYSIS

1. How does Scarvie establish the problem as worthy of the company president's attention? How well do you think he avoids placing blame? Why is it important that proposal writers need to think carefully about blaming others?

2. In paragraphs 3 and 4, Scarvie gives a detailed description of the chart he's proposing. Are there any places where the description could be clearer? What do you see as the advantages or disadvantages of going into this much detail?

3. Why do you think Scarvie mentions the alternative solution (paragraph 6)? How effectively does he refute this solution?

4. In the last two paragraphs, Scarvie anticipates possible objections to his proposal. How well does he refute them? Why do you think he includes objections to his own proposal, and what do you think of concluding a proposal in this way?

5. How would you describe Scarvie's tone? If you were the company president, what would be your opinion of him based on this memo?

IDEAS FOR YOUR OWN WRITING

Make a list of the organizations—at work or school, in athletic or social activities—to which you belong and the various problems they each have. Then choose one problem that you think you might be able to help solve. How would you define the problem? What are your ideas for solving it? To whom would you send this proposal? What kinds of arguments would be likely to convince your reader to adopt your solution?

A GUIDE TO PROPOSAL WRITING

As the proposals in this chapter illustrate, a proposal has two basic features: the problem and the solution. To establish that the problem exists and is serious, the proposal writer usually offers a detailed analysis of the problem, including facts, examples, and statistics. To convince readers to accept the solution offered, the writer presents an argument, often anticipating possible objections, rejecting alternative solutions, and demonstrating how the proposed solution can be easily implemented.

Proposal writing requires careful planning. The writer must not only determine exactly what the problem is and how to solve it, but must also consider how readers will respond to the argument. The following guide to invention, drafting, and revising divides this complex writing task into smaller, more manageable parts and leads you systematically through each stage of the process.

The Writing Task

Write an essay proposing a solution to a clearly defined problem affecting a group or community to which you belong. Your task is to establish that the problem exists, to offer a solution that can reasonably be implemented, to lay out the particulars by which your proposal would be put into effect, and to consider objections and alternative solutions as necessary.

Invention

Invention refers to the process of discovery and planning by which you generate something to say. The following invention activities will help you to choose a problem to write about, analyze it and identify a solution, consider your readers, develop an argument for your proposed solution, and research your proposal.

CHOOSING A PROBLEM. The readings in this chapter offer solutions to a range of challenging social and political problems, and various Ideas for Your Own Writing follow each one. Unless you have either special knowledge of a social or political problem or adequate time to conduct research, you should choose a problem that concerns a local group in which you now participate.

Begin the selection process by listing several groups to which you presently belong—for instance, your neighborhood, film society, dormitory, sports team, biology class, or church group. For each group, list as many problems facing it as you can. If you cannot think of any problems for a particular organization, consult with other members. Then reflect on your list of problems, and choose the one for which you would most like to find a solution. It can be a problem that everyone already knows about or one that only you are aware of.

ANALYZING THE PROBLEM AND IDENTIFYING A SOLUTION. You can profitably analyze the problem by exploring it in writing. Jot down what you now know about the problem, how you know it is a problem, and why you think it is serious. Compare this problem to others you know about. Consider how it came about and what ill effects it produces by remaining unsolved.

This analysis of the problem will probably lead you to possible solutions. If no solution is apparent, one of the following creative problem-solving procedures may help:

Solve one small aspect of the problem.

Find out how a comparable problem has been solved.

Develop a solution that eliminates one or more of the problem's causes.

Think of another way to categorize the problem.

Envision the problem in another medium or context.

Consider how another person you respect (someone you know personally or a historical or fictional figure) might solve the problem.

If you cannot think of an original solution, investigate ones that others have proposed. At some point, you will need to consider alternative solutions anyway and how they compare to your own. Remember that your solution does not have to be original, but it should be one you feel strongly about.

To test the feasibility of your solution, try listing the steps that would be necessary in order to implement it. Such an outline of steps might be used later to convince readers that the solution will indeed work.

CONSIDERING YOUR READERS. Since you want your proposal to be persuasive, you first need to have some idea of who your readers will be and what they will find convincing. Will you be writing to other members of your group, to an outside committee, to an individual in a position of authority? Once you have particular readers in mind, you can decide how much they already know about the problem and what solutions they might prefer. Consider what values and attitudes you share with your readers and how they have responded in the past to similar problems.

DEVELOPING AN ARGUMENT. In order for your proposal to succeed, it must present a convincing argument based on sound reasoning and solid backing. Begin constructing an argument by listing reasons and evidence—facts, statistics, examples, testimony from witnesses or authorities—backing each reason. Try to imagine how your prospective readers will respond. If it helps, pretend to be one particular person (real or imaginary) responding to each reason. Defend your solution against objections such as these: it won't really solve the problem, we can't afford it, there isn't enough time, no one will cooperate, it's already been tried, I don't see how to even get started, you're making this proposal because it will benefit you personally.

As part of your argument, compare your solution to alternative solutions by weighing the strengths and weaknesses of each. Then, demonstrate to readers that your solution has more advantages and fewer disadvantages. Also, show readers how relatively easy it will be to implement your solution.

RESEARCHING YOUR PROPOSAL. If you are writing about a problem in a group to which you belong, talk to other members of the group to learn more about their understanding of the problem. You might even try out your solution on one or two people; their objections and questions will help you sharpen your own ideas.

If you are writing about a larger social or political problem, you should do research in order to confirm what you remember and to learn more about the problem. You can probably locate all the information you need in a good research library; you could also interview an expert on the problem. Readers will not take you seriously unless you seem well informed.

Drafting

Once you have completed the invention activities, you can use your exploratory writing and the notes you have compiled as the basis for a rough draft. Before you begin writing, however, you should set goals and decide on a tentative plan for your draft.

SETTING GOALS. Before writing you should set some goals for your essay that reflect your readers' concerns and your purpose for writing. Consider, for example, how your readers are likely to view the problem. If they are unfamiliar with it, you will have to inform them. If they are vaguely aware of the problem but not inclined to take it seriously, you will have to demonstrate its seriousness, as Palmer does by comparing Japanese classroom television to American. If readers have a narrow understanding of the problem, you may have to redefine it for them, as Shanahan does in showing that the solution being followed is itself a problem. Consider also, in arguing for your proposed solution, how you can acknowledge your readers' legitimate concerns. Notice how Moskos, recognizing that many readers would oppose mandatory national service, makes his proposal noncompulsory.

Given your readers and purpose, you should also consider what tone to adopt. Scarvie takes a businesslike tone. Swift uses irony to get readers to see the horrific dimensions of the problem and the false beneficence of some would-be problem solvers.

PLANNING YOUR ORGANIZATION. Determining what your readers presently think and what you want them to think will help you not only formulate goals but also determine how to organize your proposal. If your readers are already familiar with the problem, for example, you may need only to refer to it in passing. If, however, they have never thought about the problem or have not perceived it in the way you want them to, you should probably spend some time right away explaining the problem.

Here is a general plan you might follow if your prospective readers have already considered other solutions to the problem:

Identify the problem.

Describe your proposed solution.

Discuss the advantages of your solution as compared to other solutions.

Restate the primary advantage of your proposed solution.

Swift and Palmer follow this basic outline, while Sack centers his essay around his refutation of alternative solutions and Shanahan devotes most of his essay to an analysis of the problem.

BEGINNING. Most proposal writers begin by presenting the problem. They may, like Shanahan, assert its seriousness. They usually describe the problem in vivid detail to impress readers, often presenting examples to dramatize the problem. Shanahan opens his essay with an arresting story that calls attention to the paradoxical nature of the problem. Among our selections, only Wertheimer begins with the solution.

AVOIDING LOGICAL FALLACIES. As you plan and draft your proposal, be particularly careful to avoid these logical fallacies:

Am I committing an *either/or fallacy* by presenting my solution as the only possible solution (ignoring or dismissing alternative solutions out of hand)?

Am I setting up alternative solutions or objections to my proposal as *straw men* (mentioning only the weak alternatives or objections that are easy to knock down)?

Am I guilty of *oversimplifying* (suggesting that the problem is less complicated and easier to solve than it really is)?

Am I making an *ad hominem* (Latin for "to the man") attack (criticizing or satirizing my opponents instead of addressing their ideas and arguments)?

Revising

No amount of invention and planning can ensure that a draft will be complete and well organized. In fact, as you draft you are likely to discover new and important points and also to encounter problems that you could not have anticipated. Therefore, you should be prepared to do some rethinking and restructuring of your draft, particularly when you are writing a proposal or any other complicated essay.

Begin by reading your draft thoughtfully and critically, using the questions for analyzing basic features at the beginning of this chapter. If possible, try to have someone else read your draft too.

REVISING TO STRENGTHEN YOUR ARGUMENT. When revising, keep in mind the dual purpose of your proposal: to inform readers about the problem and to convince them to accept your solution. Try to be even more specific in presenting the problem, demonstrating that it exists and explaining why it is serious. Always keep your readers in mind as you work to strengthen your argument. Show that your solution really solves the problem, and describe in detail how it can be implemented. Compare the proposed solution to alternative solutions in order to argue the advantages of your own. Reconsider your assumptions. Identify your underlying values and beliefs and determine whether your readers share them. If they do, try to make this bond even stronger by stating the assumptions directly. If they do not share your values, determine the values and beliefs you do share and try to build your argument on these.

REVISING TO IMPROVE READABILITY. Make an outline of your draft in order to see its organization more objectively. If you think readers will find the structure too complicated or confusing, reorganize your points or make the connections between one part and the next more obvious. Rewrite any unclear writing—language that is too abstract, indirect, or garbled. Finally, proofread your draft carefully; check for any mistakes in usage, spelling, and punctuation.

CHAPTER NINE

Position Paper

Chapter 8 focused on proposals, a pragmatic kind of writing used to solve problems and to get things accomplished. This chapter introduces the position paper, a related kind of writing that plays a central role in civic life. While the proposal solves problems, the position paper debates opinions on controversial issues. Proposals have a specific, practical purpose; position papers tend to be more general and philosophical. If you were concerned, for example, about the problem of drug abuse on high-school campuses, you might write a proposal recommending that students' lockers be searched. If, however, you were concerned about the issue of whether schools have the right to infringe on students' privacy by searching their lockers without permission, you would write a position paper instead. Debating such issues produces many of the laws that govern our lives, determine the kinds of schools we attend, the sort of medical care we receive, the quality of life we enjoy. Entering the debate on these issues is a sign of full, responsible citizenship.

Position papers are written on issues that are controversial, issues upon which reasonable people disagree, sometimes vehemently. Simply gathering information will not settle these disputes, although the more that is known about an issue, the more informed the opinions on the issue will be. What is needed is an airing of the arguments on all sides of the issue. Only when debate is open and vigorous can we fully understand what is at stake and hope to reach a consensus of opinion.

As citizens in a democracy, we have a duty to inform ourselves about the issues and to participate actively in the public debate over them. As college students, you can expect to read and write position papers in many of your courses, particularly in philosophy, history, and political science. Even in biology, you may have the opportunity to explore the issue of creationism or animal experimentation. By arguing for your opinion and defending it against possible objections, you learn to think critically. You not only examine the opinions and reasoning of others but also look objectively at your own values and assumptions. Writing position papers brings you into communication with other people. It leads you to discover ways to bridge the gap between yourself and others, to recognize where you disagree and where there might be common ground for agreement.

In addition to the readings in this chapter, you will find a variety of position papers arguing aspects of civil disobedience in the casebook of materials in Chapter 10.

A GUIDE TO READING POSITION PAPERS

To begin your work with position papers, you will first look closely at an essay by Paula Skreslet. Closely analyzing Skreslet's writing will provide a foundation for the serious study of position-paper writing this chapter encourages. As you become a more critical, insightful reader of position papers, your own writing will become more confident and convincing.

As the initial step in your analysis, you will annotate the Skreslet selection. The next exercise asks you to take inventory of your annotations in order to disclose a pattern of meaning you have discovered. In the third exercise, guided by special questions, you will report what you have learned in analyzing the basic features of position papers. Finally, the concluding exercise invites you to write a brief exploratory essay, consolidating what you have learned about the Skreslet selection and trying out your own ideas about it or extending your personal response to it.

The time you invest in annotating, analyzing, and writing will pay off richly as you read, write about, and discuss the essays in this chapter. It will also give you confidence that you can successfully write a position paper of your own.

Annotating As You Read

Perhaps the most basic, and most useful, strategy for reading attentively and critically is annotating. Pencil in hand as you read, you are ready to record on the page any comments, questions, definitions, or insights—whatever crosses your mind—about a piece of writing. As an illustration, note how we have annotated the following concluding paragraphs from an essay by Michael Kirby arguing against hasty legislative responses to the AIDS (acquired immunodeficiency syndrome) epidemic. The essay appears in its entirety later in this chapter.

Many jurisdictions have enacted laws to provide screening for the presence of HIV. China, for example, has recently extended its compulsory testing to all foreigners who apply to live in the country for more than six months. Many other countries, particularly those reporting a low incidence of AIDS and HIV, have drawn up similar laws.

Reason
"Compulsory testing laws likely to be discriminatory": groups to be tested **"already stigmatized"** and **"lack effective voice":** several supporting examples **(Logical appeal)**

One of the trickiest problems AIDS presents to lawmakers is that groups initially infected with the HIV virus in developed countries were already stigmatized and, in some sense, outcast. I refer to homosexual or bisexual men, intravenous drug users and prostitutes. In Australia, public opinion polls suggest wide support for mandatory testing of such groups.

Good reasons exist for testing drug users and prostitutes.

Democratically elected governments, under the pressure to do *something* in the face of a major epidemic, may be tempted to legislate against particular groups. Migrants, prisoners, drug users and prostitutes, in particular, lack effective voice to dissuade lawmakers from making laws discriminating against them. To test migrants but

Could quarantine prisoners with AIDS to prevent spread.

not tourists would seem unjustifiable, since the latter may indeed have greater exposure to AIDS. Testing prisoners without making arrangements for their care if found to be HIV-positive is pointless. Yet in prisons around the world, compulsory testing is now increasing.

Reason
"Laws generate pain": strong supporting example **(Emotional appeal)**

Sadly, hysteria can generate pain for the dying and the grieving. In New South Wales, regulations require that a person known to have AIDS—or reasonably suspected to have suffered it—be placed at time of death in double plastic bags, heat sealed, with the words "Infectious Disease-Handle with Care" placed on the body. This procedure only exacerbates grief, betraying the right of a deceased person not to disclose the nature of his illness. There is no scientific basis for the regulation. AIDS is not transmitted by handling a body. The regulation was, I regret, nothing more than response to a trade-union demand grounded in irrational fear. We will see many more such laws before this epidemic is over.

Scary
Invoking authority

An Australian judge once said that the law "limps after medicine . . . at the rear of the line." For the health of society and the practical containment of AIDS and HIV,

Claim restated

Nicely personal conclusion: tone is engaging

that is where I would generally keep the law for the present. <u>Overenthusiasm in enacting laws on AIDS may make some people feel better, but such laws will have precious little impact on controlling the epidemic. For the time being, control in countries like Australia and the United States depends primarily on community and individual education</u>. That may seem a strange conclusion for a lawyer to reach. But I am sure that it is right.

For more on annotating, pause now to review the guidelines in Chapter 1 and the model annotations on the excerpt from "Letter from Birmingham Jail." Note particularly the Checklist for Annotating.

Exercise 1

Annotate Paula Skreslet's "The Prizes of First Grade" as you read. Reread it at least once, continuing to annotate as you reread. Your purpose is to focus your attention on the text, to read as thoughtfully—as critically—as possible. Annotate details you admire as well as things you question or challenge, mark noteworthy stylistic devices or writing strategies, and write down any personal responses. Record your insights and reactions directly on and around the text itself.

Paula Skreslet's "The Prizes of First Grade" was originally published in the "My Turn" section of *Newsweek* on November 30, 1987. "My Turn" features brief essays on contemporary issues written by *Newsweek* readers. Like many position papers, this one comes out of the writer's personal experience and observation. Skreslet, an instructor at the College of Idaho, a liberal arts school, and the mother of triplets, writes both as a parent and as an educator concerned about the practice of using material rewards as incentives.

Before reading Skreslet's position paper, consider what you think about the use of reward—and punishment—in school. Reflect on your own education. Have there been any systems of rewards and punishments? What are the advantages and disadvantages of such systems?

The Prizes of First Grade
Paula Skreslet

In the first 10 days of the school year my triplets   1
brought home the following from their first-grade classes:

one candy bar, one peanut-butter-and-chocolate-chip cookie, two bags of popcorn, two "Very Important Person" badges, three "Constitutional Knowledge" stickers, one "I Know the Alphabet" award, two drawing prizes, 31 Nature Trail tickets, nine Lincoln play dollars, several music awards, some library awards, "Neater Eater" awards, playground-behavior awards and innumerable Scratch N Sniff stickers, stamps, stars and smile faces. What an introduction to the Lincoln School's positive-incentive program!

It's unusual, I know, for one family to have three six-year-olds, and perhaps that's why the prizes seem so excessive. But I'm troubled by the fact that well-behaved, attentive children are being bombarded with rewards for doing what schools routinely expect. My children are bewildered by the riches they've earned merely for being themselves.

My husband and I have taught them that politeness, learning and order are good things, and something good is to be desired and developed for its own sake. But at school they learned, and very quickly, that children earn Nature Trail tickets for running the quarter-mile track during lunch recess. Or Lincoln Dollars for picking up trash on the playground or for helping a younger child find the bathroom—deeds that used to be called "good citizenship." Furthermore, the school keeps score. The children can redeem trail tickets and play dollars for group prizes, like a free recess. Thanks to the involvement of local merchants, students can also earn a free order of french fries or free admission to the roller-skating rink.

Why is it necessary to buy the minimal cooperation of children with rewards and treats? Our school is no detention chamber. It is a bright, tidy building surrounded by acres of lawn where pupils follow their teachers into classrooms in a line like little ducks. And Caldwell, Idaho, is so homogeneous a town that we still teach kindergartners the story of Jesus at Christmas time, and nobody thinks twice about it. What is new to me, what I question philosophically, is the idea that good behavior must be reinforced so systematically—that without tangible incentives, first graders won't return their library books when due. Or that they won't learn the alphabet without stickers, stars and candy bars.

An inner-city high school in Cleveland received a lot of press attention recently when it began to experiment with a program of paying students for their grades. Each student is to receive $40 for an A, $20 for a B and $10 for a C. The amount earned will be credited toward a scholarship fund that students can apply to college tuition or for vocational training. In that respect financial aid based on performance is no shocking innovation. But the commercialism of paying for *each* notch on the grade-point average seems a bit much. It shamelessly assigns a dollar value to levels of learning that can scarcely be measured symbolically, much less in coin. It also says that students are so materialistic, so unmotivated and lazy that they will not learn without a bribe. I find that an insulting idea.

What I think we're seeing in Cleveland and at the   6
Lincoln School is the well-meant but distorted application of a current business principle—the vogue that stresses "excellence" and its corollary, "competitiveness." We've convinced ourselves that the way to safeguard America's position in commerce and science is to appeal to young people's hunger for the rewards the marketplace can provide. Thomas J. Peters, in his influential book, "In Search of Excellence," writes: "Get the incentives right and productivity will follow. If we give people big, straightforward monetary incentives to do right and work smart, the productivity problem will go away." . . .

Peters lists McDonalds, AT&T, Tupperware, IBM as   7
companies that use "pins, buttons, badges and medals" to boost performance. He especially applauds programs that reward the majority of workers who can be tempted to perform a bit better than before. I don't know enough about the application of this principle in the business world, but I do know it's inappropriate in the first grade. Public and nonprofit institutions are not widget factories. Learning involves developing the intellect and character of a child—it's not a productivity problem that can be solved solely by a particular performance.

What I'm trying to do with my children is to teach   8
them how to respond to challenges, how to contribute to the community even at their own expense. Secretary of Education William Bennett visited Caldwell last year and presented Lincoln with a plaque for being an exemplary school—an honor given to just 270 grade schools in the United States. Yet I'm afraid that with the best of intentions, the school may be my adversary instead of my ally. If children are taught to behave decently because they will profit from it, I wonder what principle will guide them as adults when they see how easy it is to profit from wrong behavior.

Some children at the Lincoln School have already   9
discovered that they can skip running the quarter-mile track and simply pressure younger children into handing over their Nature Trail tickets. It isn't the ideal of healthy

exercise that's motivating them. I believe that's what happens if we are taught to value a prize, a payoff, rather than a good that is to be sought without any accessory advantage—such as justice, or honor.

I've lost count of the prizes my triplets have earned so far. They are well on their way to coming out winners in this scramble of enhanced self-interest. But I can't forget about the little boy who didn't remember to return his book and kept the whole class from getting its library star, or the girl who talked in line so the class didn't get a playground award. The winners will also suffer if they don't discover for themselves that they can gain the pleasure of health and strength from exercise, the joy of music from songs, the power of mathematics from counting and all of human wisdom from reading. I'm going to do my utmost to teach my children about these rewards.

Inventorying Your Annotations

Once you have annotated a reading with your insights and ideas, you'll want to study your annotations for their special meaning. The best way to do this is by taking inventory of your annotations, to discover any patterns or significant repetitions.

Before completing Exercise 2, review the guidelines and illustration for the Inventory of Annotations in Chapter 1.

Exercise 2

Inventory the annotations you made on "The Prizes of First Grade," looking for meaningful patterns in your response to the selection.

Analyzing the Basic Features of Position Papers

In addition to annotating a text to record your initial impressions and inventorying your annotations to discover their patterns of meaning, you can analyze the basic features of a piece of writing, in this case those qualities that characterize position papers.

Look back at Identifying and Evaluating Basic Features in Chapter 1. The questions there are the same ones you will find in this chapter, and the answers suggest what a thoughtful analysis of basic features might look like.

Exercise 3

Analyze "The Prizes of First Grade" by answering the following questions. You will want to reread the selection with each question in mind, and you may want to annotate further.

Write out your answers to the questions.

1. *How does the writer define the issue? Is it clearly arguable? What is at stake?* At the heart of the position paper is the controversial issue; what makes an issue controversial is that people disagree about it. The disagreement often stems from different ways of defining the issue. Take the issue of capital punishment, for example. If the writer defines it as a question of what kind of punishment fits the crime, he or she might decide that the death penalty is appropriate punishment for murder. If, on the other hand, the writer defines the issue in terms of deterring people from committing murder rather than punishing them after they do so, he or she might decide that fear of death does not prevent people from committing murder. As a critical reader, you will want to identify the issue and determine whether or not you can accept the writer's way of defining it.

In addition, you should consider whether the issue, as it is defined, is even arguable. Some issues upon which there is considerable debate are not arguable because they can either be resolved by fact or are so deeply rooted in belief that they are impervious to fact or reason. For example, arguing over which river is the longest in the world is pointless because the answer is a simple matter of fact that can be easily demonstrated. Arguing over matters of faith is just as pointless, for somewhat more subtle reasons. The issue of whether abortion should be legal, for example, is not arguable for those who oppose abortion on religious grounds. The best issues for position papers are matters of opinion—judgments rather than certainties. Facts and beliefs should be brought to bear on these issues but cannot easily resolve them.

Ask yourself: How does the writer present the issue? How does the writer establish that the issue is important? What key terms does the writer use to define the issue? What does the writer seem to assume readers already know and think about the issue? Given the writing situation, how effectively does the writer define the issue for the intended readers?

2. *What exactly is the writer's position on this issue? How well is this position distinguished from opposing positions? Are the opposing positions presented fairly?* A position paper makes explicit the opinion, or claim, it advocates by announcing it directly in a thesis statement, which may appear at any point in the essay. In long, complicated essays, the claim may even be restated several times. Although it should be stated emphatically, the claim can be modified in the course of the argument. In fact, qualifying a position to accommodate objections or limiting the conditions under which it is true strengthens rather than weakens an argument. What writers should avoid is equivocation, backing away or hedging so much that readers cannot determine what position is being taken. The claim must be clear—neither ambiguous nor vague.

Occasionally an issue is so complicated that the writer's position must be placed in the context of several different positions. As a critical reader, you must first identify where the writer stands on the issue and the relation of the writer's position to the opposing positions. Then, decide whether the writer has represented the range of opinion on this issue fairly. If the opposing position is exaggerated or oversimplified, for example, the writer may have set up the opposition as a straw man, an unfair target established simply because it is so easily knocked down.

Ask yourself: Does the writer waffle (merely discussing the pros and cons of different positions) or take a position? Where in the essay is the writer's claim most clearly stated? How does the writer present other positions on the issue? Are these presentations fair and accurate?

3. *Does the writer merely assert that the position is true? Or does the writer provide an argument to support the position? Given the purpose and readers, how convincing is the reasoning or logical appeal of the argument?* Position papers that merely state and restate the position without providing reasons why readers should accept it commit a logical fallacy called *begging the question.* To have any chance of convincing readers that the claim is true or, at the very least, worthy of their thoughtful attention, writers must share their reasoning. They must support their position with reasons and back them with various kinds of evidence, such as examples, facts, quotations from authorities, statistics, and analogies. Writers also must anticipate both objections that might be made to their argument and counterarguments that might be given to support opposing claims; they must acknowledge those that make sense and refute those that do not. Like reasons, refutations also depend on the strength of their backing.

As a critical reader, you should apply to any position paper you read the ABC test of sound reasoning described in Chapter 1 and assure yourself that the argument is free of logical fallacies. Determine whether the reasons, refutation, and backing given to support the claim are *appropriate, believable,* and *consistent.*

Begin by analyzing the argument to see how it works. What reasons are given to support the claim? How are they backed? Has the writer anticipated possible objections or counterarguments? Which are accepted as valid? Which are refuted? How is the refutation backed?

To evaluate the logical appeal, test for *appropriateness* by asking yourself: Does the support justify the claim? Test for *believability* by asking: Is the backing authoritative and credible? Test for *consistency* by asking: Are the supporting statements contradictory? Has the writer committed any fallacies under any of these categories? (For a list of fallacies, see the section on Analyzing an Argument in Chapter 1.)

4. *Where in the argument does the writer try to arouse the reader's emotions? Given the purpose and readers, how convincing is this emotional appeal? Is it manipulative or fair?* In addition to appealing to the reader's sense of logic, writers of position papers may also appeal to the reader's emotions. Some emotional appeals may be appropriate, reminding readers, for example, of cherished values and beliefs related to the issue. But many emotional appeals are clearly manipulative, elicited by the writer's distorting of evidence or using slanted or highly charged language.

As a critical reader, you will want to be alert to manipulative arguments. Look for extreme or isolated examples, melodramatic anecdotes, alarming statistics, exaggerated warnings, and other scare tactics. Notice the choice of words and their connotations, especially analogies and figures of speech like metaphor and simile. Ask yourself: Do I feel manipulated by anything in the argument? Does the writer use highly emotive or slanted language, one-sided or loaded language, belittling or exaggerated language?

5. *What is the ethos or image of the writer that is conveyed through the writing? Given the purpose and readers, how effective is this ethical appeal?* In debating controversial issues, writers naturally assume that their readers will either disagree with them or be skeptical. Because they seek to build bridges between their own opinions and those of others, writers of position papers typically try to project an image or persona that will be perceived as reasonable and trustworthy. Even when challenging their readers' basic assumptions about deeply felt issues, writers try to inspire respect and confidence by making ethical appeals to readers. They attempt to demonstrate their goodwill and understanding by anticipating objections and counterarguments to their argument and, whenever possible, by making concessions and qualifying their position to accommodate reasonable objections and counterarguments. Even when they

cannot agree with readers' objections, writers of position papers none-theless acknowledge legitimate objections and explain their reasons for rejecting them.

To evaluate the ethical appeal, first look at what the writer says and then look at how the writer says it. This close analysis of the essay's tone will give you a sense of the writer's unexpressed attitudes and feelings. If the tone contradicts the persona the writer consciously projects, you might wonder if the writer is being sincere. Ask yourself: Has the writer accepted the burden of proof and presented a well-supported, reasonable argument for the claim? Has the writer acknowledged legitimate objec-tions and counterarguments? What is the tone of the writing? For example, is it sarcastic, impassioned, defiant, ironic, snooty, aloof? Is the tone consistent throughout, or does it change? If there are shifts in tone, where do they occur? What might these shifts in tone signify about the writer's attitudes and feelings?

6. *How well organized is the essay?* Since position papers tend to be fairly complicated and the reasoning somewhat hard to follow, it is particularly important that they be carefully organized and provide cues to keep readers on track. Most position papers forecast their argument by listing the main reasons for the position taken before developing them. They also usually separate the parts of the argument—distinguishing the definition of the issue from the arguments pro and con—and offer transitions to label the divisions clearly. In especially complex arguments, writers may number the points or summarize before going on to the next part of the argument.

Ask yourself: How is the essay organized? (To discover the overall organization, make an outline of the essay following the guidelines for Outlining the Argument under Analyzing an Argument in Chapter 1.) Given the particular readers and purpose, how effective is this organiza-tional plan? Point to any places in the essay where you felt confused or lost. How well did the opening of the essay prepare you for what was to come? How helpful were the cueing devices—forecasting statements, transitions, and summaries?

Exploring Your Personal Response

One other way of focusing your response to a position paper is by taking the time to record your thoughts in a more extended piece of writing. Basically, such an exercise can help you to consider how the argument relates to your own experience, to explore your understanding and define further your unique perspective on what you've read.

Exercise 4

Write 300–400 words (two or three handwritten pages) about "The Prizes of First Grade." Choose one of the suggestions listed in Exploring Your Personal Response in Chapter 1.

Michael Kirby

Michael Kirby is a member of the World Health Organization's Global Commission on AIDS. He is also president of the Court of Appeals of the Supreme Court of New South Wales, Australia.

AIDS Hysteria

This article from the *Los Angeles Times* was originally published in a somewhat longer form in the July 1989 issue of *Daedalus*, a scholarly journal dedicated to the arts and sciences. As a judge and a World Health Organization Commission member, Michael Kirby naturally is concerned about laws that are being considered to quarantine or register those who test positive for HIV (human immunovirus), the virus believed to be the cause of AIDS.

Before you begin reading, preview the selection by reading the first and last paragraphs. Then reflect for a moment on what this previewing reveals about the rhetorical situation in which Kirby is writing.

There are limits on what the law can and should do in response to AIDS. It never ceases to surprise me how otherwise intelligent people (including some lawyers) assume that when society has a problem, all it need do is make new law and the problem will be solved.

But obedience to a law, even if everyone is familiar with it, cannot be assumed. The law may entirely miss its mark because of ambiguity or sanctions that cannot be enforced. Want of resources, discriminatory prosecution or ineffective design of enforcement mechanisms frequently torpedo a law that looked fine when first passed but just did not work on the streets.

Our objective in proposing new laws on AIDS must be to contain the epidemic. Australian Health Minister Dr. Neal Blewett has a clear criterion for AIDS-related measures. I take it as my text: "Whether it will or will not impede the spread of the disease, whether it will be productive or counterproductive in containing the dissemination of the virus; any action, however well intentioned, which impedes efforts to monitor, contain and assess the spread of the disease should be rejected."

The policies adopted to cope with earlier epidemics lie in the history books as warnings about human pain and cruelty but, above all, about general ineffectiveness. The best-known administrative measure of earlier times, quarantine, is said to have been developed in 14th-Century Italy.

Such isolation was followed by the temporary removal of suspects, the creation of plague barriers, the use of purifying fires in public places and vicious actions against minorities who were already stigmatized by factors other than disease.

King Philip of France ordered the extraction of the tongues of all blasphemers. He believed, ever so sincerely, that blasphemy had brought the bubonic plague on his country.

Reporting, incarcerating, disenfranchisement, privation and deprivation of civil rights have been the usual legal companions of infections over the centuries. As late as 1832 in Paris, numberless innocent people stricken with cholera were lynched by fearful mobs.

In this age of computer science and biotechnology, can we do better? Only if we acknowledge the limited function of law as a response to AIDS and realize that laws will not be effective until they are based on good data concerning the nature of AIDS and the precise conduct that encourages or diminishes transmission. We must recognize the counterproductive effects of laws that limit the supply of condoms or the availability of sterile needles.

We may decide that we prefer a society that clings to the ideals of sexual chastity to a society that teaches young school children explicitly about the dangers of AIDS and facilitates the provision of condoms to all who want them. We may prefer prosecuting the "war on drugs" rather than legalizing the provision of sterile needles or bleach to users at risk. But we should do so with our eyes open.

A frightened community concerned about the spread of a dangerous virus may be impatient indeed with the human-rights context. But any review of law on this subject which ignores human rights will be empty of principle.

There is no human right to spread a deadly virus, whether knowingly or recklessly. The right to the protection of life is primary. But it must be achieved with the protection of other relevant human rights, such as the right to privacy, the right to marry and found a family, the right to work and the right to freedom from inhuman or degrading treatment. We must harmonize legal responses with fundamental values that will endure even after the AIDS peril has been overcome.

It is possible that in some places knowingly spreading HIV to another person—or being recklessly indifferent to the consequences of sexual or other conduct—already violates general provisions of criminal law. Such conduct might amount to murder, manslaughter or assault occasioning grievous bodily harm. Calls are now being made for the provision of specific criminal offenses permitting courts to penalize the deliberate or reckless spread of this lethal virus.

Responding to such calls, a number of states in Australia and the 12 United States have enacted laws to provide a specific penalty in the case of unprotected sexual intercourse by an infected person. Such law does not prohibit an infected person from having sexual intercourse. It applies the law's sanction for failing to inform and secure the consent of the other person.

All such laws should be seen as having a symbolic rather than a 13 practical value. Proof and enforcement would be extremely difficult. The offender may be dead or very ill by the time of prosecution. Proof that he or she caused the infection may be next to impossible. Moreover, such laws may have a counterproductive effect, even though unintended. If an element in such crimes is knowledge of one's own HIV status, the law may actually discourage persons from taking the HIV test, particularly if there are provisions for reporting persons who prove positive.

Quarantine laws are generally categorized as civil rather than criminal, 14 yet they may impose restrictions on individual freedom as severe as penal laws. Sometimes they do so without the protections typically built into criminal process.

So far, only Cuba has a specific law to quarantine persons with HIV 15 infection. Such a law would be unjust and ineffective in the most developed nations. The antibody test does not disclose all who are infected. It would be difficult, if not impossible, to provide resources to house, feed, guard and isolate all such persons. The impact of removing from an economy people with 8, 10 or more years of valuable contribution would be crippling.

Clearly, the target of laws and policies should be the behavior that 16 spreads the risk, not the individual as such. Laws focused on individuals or groups may carry the risk of unjust discrimination or may be too heavy-handed in their operation. That is why a general policy of quarantine has been described, rightly in my view, as a brutal and unrealistic approach to the containment of HIV.

Nevertheless, calls for quarantine and identification of the infected 17 will become more common as the infection spreads. In a number of jurisdictions, already existing powers of quarantine have been enhanced and made specific to include AIDS. Fortunately, lessons have been learned from the ways communities earlier tackled syphilis, also a potentially lethal sexually transmissible disease. An English Royal Commission report in 1913 made the point that the public health objectives of identifying the infected, counseling them and giving them such treatment as was available were more likely to contain the disease than were punishment and quarantine. As with syphilis, so with AIDS. Winning the support of those who bear the burden of infection and modifying their behavior is the strategy that offers most promise at this time, at least in developed countries.

Many jurisdictions have enacted laws to provide screening for the presence of HIV. China, for example, has recently extended its compulsory testing to all foreigners who apply to live in the country for more than six months. Many other countries, particularly those reporting a low incidence of AIDS and HIV, have drawn up similar laws. 18

One of the trickiest problems AIDS presents to lawmakers is that groups initially infected with the HIV virus in developed countries were already stigmatized and, in some sense, outcast. I refer to homosexual or bisexual men, intravenous drug users and prostitutes. In Australia, public opinion polls suggest wide support for mandatory testing of such groups. 19

Democratically elected governments, under the pressure to do *something* in the face of a major epidemic, may be tempted to legislate against particular groups. Migrants, prisoners, drug users and prostitutes, in particular, lack effective voice to dissuade lawmakers from making laws discriminating against them. To test migrants but not tourists would seem unjustifiable, since the latter may indeed have greater exposure to AIDS. Testing prisoners without making arrangements for their care if found to be HIV-positive is pointless. Yet in prisons around the world, compulsory testing is now increasing. 20

Sadly, hysteria can generate pain for the dying and the grieving. In New South Wales, regulations require that a person known to have AIDS—or reasonably suspected to have suffered it—be placed at time of death in double plastic bags, heat sealed, with the words "Infectious Disease-Handle with Care" placed on the body. This procedure only exacerbates grief, betraying the right of a deceased person not to disclose the nature of his illness. There is no scientific basis for the regulation. AIDS is not transmitted by handling a body. The regulation was, I regret, nothing more than response to a trade-union demand grounded in irrational fear. We will see many more such laws before this epidemic is over. 21

An Australian judge once said that the law "limps after medicine . . . at the rear of the line." For the health of society and the practical containment of AIDS and HIV, that is where I would generally keep the law for the present. Overenthusiasm in enacting laws on AIDS may make some people feel better, but such laws will have precious little impact on controlling the epidemic. For the time being, control in countries like Australia and the United States depends primarily on community and individual education. That may seem a strange conclusion for a lawyer to reach. But I am sure that it is right. 22

QUESTIONS FOR ANALYSIS

1. What issue does Kirby address in this position paper, and what is his position on it? Annotate the essay, marking where the issue is explained and where Kirby's position is most explicitly stated.

2. In paragraphs 4–6, Kirby refers to historical situations that he claims are analogous to the current AIDS epidemic. Arguing by analogy may be effective as backing if it passes the test of appropriateness—that is, the lesson learned from one case must be applicable to the other case. Examine each of Kirby's analogies to see whether they are appropriate.

3. In paragraphs 14–17, Kirby gives his reasons for opposing quarantine. What are his reasons? How does he back them? How convincing do you find this part of the argument?

4. Beginning with the choice of the word *hysteria* in the title, Kirby makes a series of emotional appeals to the reader. Reread the essay, and annotate these emotional appeals. Then, evaluate their use in this essay. Given the writer's purpose and readers, which of the appeals seem to be appropriate and which seem manipulative? Why?

5. What adjective would you use to describe the image Kirby projects in this essay? Point to one place in the essay where this image comes across most strongly.

6. Studying the oppositions in a position paper can give you insight into the conflicting values and concerns that underlie the debate. Take inventory of the oppositions in this essay following the procedures described in Chapter 1 under Inventory of Oppositions. To get you started, here's one opposition we found: the ideal of chastity versus the need for explicit information about how the AIDS virus is transmitted (paragraph 8).

IDEAS FOR YOUR OWN WRITING

Position papers often deal with legal issues, arguing for or against laws to control certain kinds of behavior or to solve particular social problems. Make a list of controversial laws that have been enacted or proposed. Recent issues raised in the press include whether a mother who takes cocaine during pregnancy should be prosecuted for child abuse; whether high-school dropouts should be denied a driver's license until age twenty-one; whether gay couples should be allowed to marry; whether smoking should be banned in public; whether government arts funding should be denied to "offensive" works or exhibits; whether homeless people should be forced into shelters. From your list, choose one topic about which you have a strong opinion. Jot down some arguments, both pro and con, about the issue. How would you go about doing further research on this topic? Chapter 10's Casebook on Civil Disobedience might provide some useful ideas.

Frederick A. King

Frederick A. King is the director of Emory University's primate research center. At the time he wrote the essay reprinted here, King was also chair of the American Psychological Association's Committee on Animal Research and Experimentation.

Animals in Research: The Case for Experimentation

This selection was written in 1984 for *Psychology Today*, a magazine published by the American Psychological Association to popularize writing and research in psychology. At that time, the animal-rights movement was just gaining momentum. To preview this essay, take a few minutes to recall what you know about the debate over the use of animals in scientific research. What's at issue? What arguments do opponents of animal research usually make? What arguments do proponents offer? Which side do you think makes the better case?

The Mobilization for Animals Coalition (MFA) is an international network of more than 400 animal-protectionist organizations that address themselves to a variety of issues, including hunting, trapping, livestock protection, vegetarianism, and pets. Their primary concern, however, is an adamant opposition to animal research. Some groups within the movement want to severely curtail research with animals, but the most visible and outspoken faction wants to eliminate it.

The astonishing growth of this activist movement during the past three years has culminated this year in an intense attack on the use of animals in psychological research. This past spring, John McArdle of the Humane Society of the United States charged that torture is the founding principle and fundamental characteristic of experimental psychology, and that psychological experimentation on animals among all the scientific disciplines is "the ideal candidate for elimination. No major scientific endeavor would suffer by such an act." A recent pamphlet published by the MFA stated, "Of all these experiments, those conducted in psychology are the most painful, pointless, and repulsive."

The following specific allegations have been made by the MFA: Animals are given intense, repeated electric shocks until they lose the ability even to scream in pain; animals are deprived of food and water and allowed to suffer and die from hunger and thirst; animals are put in isolation until they are driven insane or die from despair and terror; animals are subjected to crushing forces that smash their bones and rupture their internal organs; the limbs of animals are mutilated or amputated to produce behavioral changes; animals are the victims of extreme pain and stress, inflicted out of idle curiosity, in nightmarish experiments designed to make healthy animals psychotic.

Such irresponsible accusations of research cruelty have consistently   4
characterized the publications of the MFA. However, a recent study by psychologists D. Caroline Coile and Neal E. Miller of Rockefeller University counters these charges. Coile and Miller looked at every article (a total of 608) appearing in the past five years in journals of the American Psychological Association that report animal research. They concluded that none of the extreme allegations made by the MFA could be supported.

Coile and Miller admit that charges of cruelty may have gone unre-   5
ported or been reported elsewhere but, they say, if such studies did occur, "they certainly were infrequent, and it is extremely misleading to imply that they are typical of experimental psychology."

Furthermore, there are standards and mechanisms to ensure that   6
research animals are treated in a humane and scientifically sensible way. These mechanisms include the Federal Animal Welfare Act of 1966 (amended in Congress in 1970, 1976, and 1979); periodic inspection of all animal-research facilities by the Department of Agriculture; visits by federal agencies that fund animal research and are increasingly attentive to the conditions of animal care and experimental procedures that could cause pain or distress; and a comprehensive document, "Guide for the Care and Use of Laboratory Animals," prepared by the National Academy of Sciences. In addition, virtually every major scientific society whose members conduct animal research distributes guidelines for such research. Above and beyond all of this, most universities and research institutes have animal-care committees that monitor animal research and care.

The United States Public Health Service is revising its guidelines to   7
require institutions that do research with animals to designate even clearer lines of authority and responsibility for animal care. This will include detailed information about how each institution complies with the new regulations as well as a requirement that animal-research committees include not only the supervising laboratory veterinarian and scientists but also a nonscientist and a person not affiliated with the

institution. These committees will review programs for animal care, inspect all animal facilities, and review and monitor all research proposals before they are submitted to agencies of the United States Public Health Service. The committees will also have the power to disapprove or terminate any research proposal.

This is not to say that research scientists are perfect. There will be occasional errors, cases of neglect, and instances of abuse—as is the case with any human endeavor, whether it be the rearing of children, the practicing of a trade or profession, or the governing of a nation. But a high standard of humane treatment is maintained.

The choice of psychological research for special attack almost certainly stems from the fact that such research is viewed as more vulnerable than are studies of anatomy, physiology, or microbiology. In the minds of many, psychology is a less well-developed science than the biological sciences and the benefits that have accrued from psychological research with animals are less well known. Hence, it is more difficult to grasp the necessity for animal research in behavioral studies than it is in biomedical studies.

Anyone who has looked into the matter can scarcely deny that major advances in medicine have been achieved through basic research with animals. Among these are the development of virtually all modern vaccines against infectious diseases, the invention of surgical approaches to eye disorders, bone and joint injuries and heart disease, the discovery of insulin and other hormones, and the testing of all new drugs and antibiotics.

The benefits to humans of psychological research with animals may be less well known than those of medical research but are just as real. Historically, the application of psychological research to human problems has lagged considerably behind the applied use of medical research. Mental events and overt behavior, although controlled by the nervous system and biology of an organism, are much more difficult to describe and study than are the actions of tissues or organ systems. To describe the complex interplay of perceptions, memories, cognitive and emotional processes with a physical and social environment that changes from moment to moment, elaborate research designs had to be developed. Since even a single type of behavior, such as vocalization, has so many different forms, a wide variety of ways of measuring the differences had to be developed. Finally, because much psychological research makes inferences from behavioral observations about internal states of an organism, methods were needed to insure that the interpretations were valid. Such complexities do not make the study of animal or human behavior less scientific or important than other kinds of research, but they do make it more difficult and slow its readiness for clinical applications.

Basic psychological research with animals has led to important [12] achievements in the interest of human welfare. Examples include the use of biofeedback, which has its origin in studies of behavioral conditioning of neuromuscular activities in rats and other animals. Today, biofeedback can be used to control blood pressure and hypertension and help prevent heart attacks. In the case of paralyzed patients, it can be used to elevate blood pressure, enabling those who would otherwise have to spend their lives lying down to sit upright. Biofeedback techniques also are used in the reduction and control of severe pain and as a method of neuromuscular control to help reverse the process of scoliosis, a disabling and disfiguring curvature of the spine. Biofeedback can also be a cost-effective alternative to certain medical treatments and can help avoid many of the complications associated with long-term drug use.

Language studies with apes have led to practical methods of teaching [13] language skills to severely retarded children who, prior to this work, had little or no language ability. Patients who have undergone radiation therapy for cancer can now take an interest in nutritious foods and avoid foods that have little nutritional value, thanks to studies of conditioned taste aversion done with animals. Neural and behavioral studies of early development of vision in cats and primates—studies that could not have been carried out with children—have led to advances in pediatric ophthalmology that can prevent irreversible brain damage and loss of vision in children who have cataracts and various other serious eye problems.

Behavioral modification and behavioral therapy, widely accepted tech- [14] niques for treating alcohol, drug, and tobacco addiction, have a long history of animal studies investigating learning theory and reward systems. Programmed instruction, the application of learning principles to educational tasks, is based on an array of learning studies in animals. These are but a few examples of the effectiveness and usefulness for humans of psychological research with animals.

Those opposed to animal research have proposed that alternatives to [15] animal research, such as mathematical and computer models and tissue cultures, be used. In some cases, these alternatives are both feasible and valuable. Tissue cultures, for example, have been very effective in certain toxicological studies that formerly required live animals. For psychological studies, however, it is often necessary to study the whole animal and its relationship to the environment. Visual problems, abnormal sexual behavior, depression, and aggression, for example, are not seen in tissue cultures and do not lend themselves to computer models. When human subjects cannot be used for such studies, animals are necessary if the research is to be done at all.

Extremists within the animal-rights movement take the position that animals have rights equal to or greater than those of humans. It follows from this that even if humans might benefit from animal research, the cost to animals is too high. It is ironic that despite this moral position, the same organizations condone—and indeed sponsor—activities that appear to violate the basic rights of animals to live and reproduce. Each year 10,000,000 dogs are destroyed by public pounds, animal shelters, and humane societies. Many of these programs are supported and even operated by animal-protectionist groups. Surely there is a strong contradiction when those who profess to believe in animal rights deny animals their right to life. A similar situation exists with regard to programs of pet sterilization, programs that deny animals the right to breed and to bear offspring and are sponsored in many cases by antivivisectionists and animal-rights groups. Evidently, animal-rights advocates sometimes recognize and subscribe to the position that animals do not have the same rights as humans. However, their public posture leaves little room for examining these subtleties or applying similar standards to animal research. 16

Within the animal-protectionist movement there are moderates who have confidence in scientists as compassionate human beings and in the value of research. Their primary aims are to insure that animals are treated humanely and that discomfort in animal experimentation is kept to a minimum. It is to this group that scientists and scientific organizations have the responsibility to explain what they do, why and how they do it and what benefits occur. 17

I believe that the values guiding contemporary animal research represent prevailing sentiment within the scientific community and, indeed, within society at large. And I believe that these values are congruent with those of the moderates within the animal-protectionist movement. As articulated by ethicist Arthur Caplan, rights, in the most realistic sense, are granted by one group to another based on perceived similarities between the groups. Plainly, animals lack those characteristics that would allow them to share in the rights we grant to humans. We do not grant domestic animals the right to go where they wish or do what they want because they are obviously unable to comprehend the responsibilities and demands of human society. In fact, we do not as a society even grant all domestic animals and pets the right to live. 18

This does not mean, however, that we do not have a moral responsibility to animals. I believe, along with Caplan and the scientific re- 19 search community at large, that we hold a moral stewardship for animals and that we are obliged to treat them with humane compassion and concern for their sentience. Many animal forms can and do feel pain and are highly aware of their environment. This awareness makes them worthy of our respect and serious concern. Caplan is certainly correct when he says that this moral obligation ought to be part of what it means to be a scientist today.

Science must proceed. The objective quest for knowledge is a treasured   20 enterprise of our heritage and culture. Scientific inquiry into the nature of our living world has freed us from ignorance and superstition. Scientific understanding is an expression of our highest capacities—those of objective observation, interpretive reasoning, imagination, and creativity. Founded on the results of basic research, often conducted with no goal other than that of increased understanding, the eventual practical use of this knowledge has led to a vastly improved well-being for human-kind.

Extremists in the animal-rights movement probably will never accept   21 such justifications for research or assurances of humane treatments. They may reject any actions, no matter how conscientious, that scientists take in realistically and morally reconciling the advance of human welfare with the use of animals. But, fortunately, there are many who, while deeply and appropriately concerned for the compassionate treatment of animals, recognize that human welfare is and should be our primary concern.

QUESTIONS FOR ANALYSIS

1. Describe the rhetorical situation in which King is writing. What seems to be his purpose? What do you think he assumes about his readers? Given his purpose and audience, what seems to be his overall plan or argumentative strategy?

2. King opens the essay with three paragraphs reporting charges of cruelty to animals that have been made against psychological researchers. Then in paragraphs 4–8, he tries to refute these charges. Outline this part of the argument, and evaluate it by applying the ABC test. (See Analyzing an Argument in Chapter 1.)

3. Summarize paragraphs 9–14. What is the purpose of this part of the argument? How well do you think this purpose is accomplished? (For guidelines, review the Chapter 1 discussion of Summarizing.)

4. King begins the essay by talking about so-called extremists within the animal-rights movement. Then, in paragraphs 16–19, he draws a distinction between these extremists and moderates like ethicist Arthur Caplan, with whom King says he agrees. What is the purpose of making this distinction? How does it contribute to the overall argument?

5. As you can see from the headnote, King has the appropriate credentials for writing on this issue. But writers of position papers cannot rely on their credentials alone; their writing must also inspire confidence in their readers. How does King attempt to win his readers' trust? Describe the ethical appeal of this essay. Given the rhetorical situation in which he is writing, how well do you think this ethical appeal is likely to work?

6. Review Exploring Your Personal Response in Chapter 1. Then, write a 300–400-word personal response to this selection. Choose one of the following topics:

> Write a letter to the author in which you respond to anything in the essay that you found unusual, interesting, intriguing, or objectionable.

> Write an essay comparing what King says with what others have said about the subject.

After you have written your response, reread it thoughtfully. In two or three sentences, say what you have learned about the King selection by writing an extended response to it.

IDEAS FOR YOUR OWN WRITING

In this essay, King sings the praises of science. And yet, he admits that scientists are not perfect, and thus "[t]here will be occasional errors, cases of neglect, and instances of abuse." What do you think the role of the scientist ought to be? List controversial issues involving scientific or medical ethics. Here are a few to get you started: Are scientists justly criticized for their lack of moral leadership in relation to the development of the atomic bomb? Should scientists be allowed to experiment with humans by transplanting mechanical and animal hearts? Should doctors refuse to treat dangerously infectious patients? Should doctors help terminally ill patients to die? Choose one topic from your list about which you have a strong opinion. Jot down some arguments, both pro and con, about the issue. How would you go about doing further research on this topic?

David Hoekema

Formerly a philosophy professor at St. Olaf College in Minnesota, David Hoekema is currently the executive secretary of the American Philosophical Association. Hoekema has written extensively on the ethical dimension of contemporary social issues such as apartheid, hunger, and nuclear war. In 1979, he addressed the issue of capital punishment in a speech delivered at a forum sponsored by the Citizens' Committee for Criminal Justice. This selection is a revised version that appeared in a journal called the *Christian Century*.

Capital Punishment: The Question of Justification

Hoekema, as you know, is a philosophy professor. What does this fact lead you to expect about his argument? How does the added fact that it was published in the *Christian Century* influence your expectations? What do you think might be a "Christian" position on this issue? What kind of argument might support this position?

In 1810 a bill introduced in the British Parliament sought to abolish capital punishment for the offense of stealing five shillings or more from a shop. Judges and magistrates unanimously opposed the measure. In the House of Lords, the chief justice of the King's Bench, Lord Ellenborough, predicted that the next step would be abolition of the death penalty for stealing five shillings from a house; thereafter no one could "trust himself for an hour without the most alarming apprehension that, on his return, every vestige of his property [would] be swept away by the hardened robber" (quoted by Herbert B. Ehrmann in "The Death Penalty and the Administration of Justice," in *The Death Penalty in America*, edited by Hugo Adam Bedau [Anchor, 1967], p. 415).

During the same year Parliament abolished the death penalty for picking pockets, but more than 200 crimes remained punishable by death. Each year in Great Britain more than 2,000 persons were being sentenced to die, though only a small number of these sentences were actually carried out.

I

In this regard as in many others, the laws of the English colonies in North America were much less harsh than those of the mother country.

442

At the time of the Revolution, statutes in most of the colonies prescribed hanging for about a dozen offenses—among them murder, treason, piracy, arson, rape, robbery, burglary, sodomy and (in some cases) counterfeiting, horse theft and slave rebellion. But by the early nineteenth century a movement to abolish the death penalty was gaining strength.

The idea was hardly new: czarist Russia had eliminated the death penalty on religious grounds in the eleventh century. In the United States the movement had been launched by Benjamin Rush in the eighteenth century, with the support of such other distinguished citizens of Philadelphia as Benjamin Franklin and Attorney General William Bradford. By the 1830s, bills calling for abolition of capital punishment were being regularly introduced, and defeated, in several state legislatures. In 1846 Michigan voted effectively to abolish the death penalty— the first English-speaking jurisdiction in the world to do so.

In the years since, twelve states have abolished capital punishment entirely. Although statutes still in effect in some states permit the death penalty to be imposed for a variety of offenses—ranging from statutory rape to desecration of a grave to causing death in a duel—murder is virtually the only crime for which it has been recently employed. There are about 400 persons in U.S. prisons under sentence of death, but only one execution (Gary Gilmore's) has been carried out in this country in the past eleven years.

However, the issue of whether capital punishment is justifiable is by no means settled. Since the Supreme Court, in the case of *Furman* v. *Georgia* in 1972, invalidated most existing laws permitting capital punishment, several states have enacted new legislation designed to meet the court's objections to the Georgia law. And recent public-opinion surveys indicate that a large number, possibly a majority, of Americans favor imposing the death penalty for some crimes. But let us ask the ethical question: Ought governments to put to death persons convicted of certain crimes?

II

First, let us look at grounds on which capital punishment is defended. Most prominent is the argument from *deterrence*. Capital punishment, it is asserted, is necessary to deter potential criminals. Murderers must be executed so that the lives of potential murder victims may be spared.

Two assertions are closely linked here. First, it is said that convicted murderers must be put to death in order to protect the rest of us against those individuals who might kill others if they were at large. This argument, based not strictly on deterrence but on incapacitation of known offenders, is inconclusive, since there are other effective means of protecting the innocent against convicted murderers—for example, imprisonment of murderers for life in high-security institutions.

Second, it is said that the example of capital punishment is needed to 9
deter those who would otherwise commit murder. Knowledge that a
crime is punishable by death will give the potential criminal pause. This
second argument rests on the assumption that capital punishment does
in fact reduce the incidence of capital crimes—a presupposition that must
be tested against the evidence. Surprisingly, none of the available empirical data shows any significant correlation between the existence or use of
the death penalty and the incidence of capital crimes.

When studies have compared the homicide rates for the past fifty years 10
in states that employ the death penalty and in adjoining states that have
abolished it, the numbers have in every case been quite similar; the death
penalty has had no discernible effect on homicide rates. Further, the
shorter-term effects of capital punishment have been studied by examining the daily number of homicides reported in California over a ten-year
period to ascertain whether the execution of convicts reduced the number. Fewer homicides were reported on days immediately following an
execution, but this reduction was matched by an increase in the number
of homicides on the day of execution and the preceding day. Executions
had no discernible effect on the weekly total of homicides. (Cf. "Death
and Imprisonment as Deterrents to Murder," by Thorsten Sellin, in
Bedau, op. cit., pp. 274–284, and "The Deterrent Effect of Capital
Punishment in California," by William F. Graves, in Bedau, op. cit., pp.
322–332.)

The available evidence, then, fails to support the claim that capital 11
punishment deters capital crime. For this reason, I think, we may set
aside the deterrence argument. But there is a stronger reason for rejecting
the argument—one that has to do with the way in which supporters of
that argument would have us treat persons.

Those who defend capital punishment on grounds of deterrence would 12
have us take the lives of some—persons convicted of certain crimes—
because doing so will discourage crime and thus protect others. But it is a
grave moral wrong to treat one person in a way justified solely by the
needs of others. To inflict harm on one person in order to serve the
purposes of others is to use that person in an immoral and inhumane
way, treating him or her not as a person with rights and responsibilities
but as a means to other ends. The most serious flaw in the deterrence
argument, therefore, is that it is the wrong *kind* of argument. The
execution of criminals cannot be justified by the good which their deaths
may do the rest of us.

III

A second argument for the death penalty maintains that some crimes, 13
chief among them murder, *morally require* the punishment of death. In

particular, Christians frequently support capital punishment by appeal to the Mosaic code, which required the death penalty for murder. "The law of capital punishment," one writer has concluded after reviewing relevant biblical passages, "must stand as a silent but powerful witness to the sacredness of God-given life" ("Christianity and the Death Penalty," by Jacob Vellenga, in Bedau, op. cit., pp. 123–130).

In the Mosaic code, it should be pointed out, there were many capital [14] crimes besides murder. In the book of Deuteronomy, death is prescribed as the penalty for false prophecy, worship of foreign gods, kidnapping, adultery, deception by a bride concerning her virginity, and disobedience to parents. To this list the laws of the book of Exodus add witchcraft, sodomy, and striking or cursing a parent.

I doubt that there is much sentiment in favor of restoring the death [15] penalty in the United States for such offenses. But if the laws of Old Testament Israel ought not to govern our treatment of, say, adultery, why should they govern the penalty for murder? To support capital punishment by an appeal to Old Testament law is to overlook the fact that the ancient theocratic state of Israel was in nearly every respect profoundly different from any modern secular state. For this reason, we cannot simply regard the Mosaic code as normative for the United States today.

But leaving aside reference to Mosaic law, let me state more strongly [16] the argument we are examining. The death penalty, it may be urged, is the only just penalty for a crime such as murder; it is the only fair *retribution*. Stated thus, the argument at hand seems to be the right *kind* of argument for capital punishment. If capital punishment can be justified at all, it must be on the basis of the *seriousness of the offense* for which it is imposed. Retributive considerations *should* govern the punishment of individuals who violate the law, and chief among these considerations are the principle of proportionality between punishment and offense and the requirement that persons be punished only for acts for which they are truly responsible. I am not persuaded that retributive considerations are sufficient to set a particular penalty for a given offense, but I believe they do require that in comparative terms we visit more serious offenses with more severe punishment.

Therefore, the retributive argument seems the strongest one in support [17] of capital punishment. We ought to deal with convicted offenders not as we want to, but as they deserve. And I am not certain that it is wrong to argue that a person who has deliberately killed another person deserves to die.

But even if this principle is valid, should the judicial branch of our [18] governments be empowered to determine whether individuals deserve to die? Are our procedures for making laws and for determining guilt sufficiently reliable that we may entrust our lives to them? I shall return to this important question presently. But consider the following fact: During the years from 1930 to 1962, 466 persons were put to death for the crime of rape. Of these, 399 were black. Can it seriously be maintained that our courts are administering the death penalty to all those and only to those who deserve to die?

IV

Two other arguments deserve brief mention. It has been argued that, 19 even if the penalty of life imprisonment were acceptable on other grounds, our society could not reasonably be asked to pay the cost of maintaining convicted murderers in prisons for the remainder of their natural lives.

This argument overlooks the considerable costs of retaining the death 20 penalty. Jury selection, conduct of the trial, and the appeals process become extremely time-consuming and elaborate when death is a possible penalty. On the other hand, prisons should not be as expensive as they are. At present those prisoners who work at all are working for absurdly low wages, frequently at menial and degrading tasks. Prisons should be reorganized to provide meaningful work for all able inmates; workers should be paid fair wages for their work and charged for their room and board. Such measures would sharply reduce the cost of prisons and make them more humane.

But these considerations—important as they are—have little relevance 21 to the justification of capital punishment. We should not decide to kill convicted criminals only because it costs so much to keep them alive. The cost to society of imprisonment, large or small, cannot justify capital punishment.

Finally, defenders of capital punishment sometimes support their case 22 by citing those convicted offenders—for example, Gary Gilmore—who have asked to be executed rather than imprisoned. But this argument, too, is of little relevance. If some prisoners would prefer to die rather than be imprisoned, perhaps we should oblige them by permitting them to take their own lives. But this consideration has nothing to do with the question of whether we ought to impose the punishment of death on certain offenders, most of whom would prefer to live.

V

Let us turn now to the case *against* the death penalty. It is sometimes 23 argued that capital punishment is unjustified because those guilty of crimes cannot help acting as they do: the environment, possibly interacting with inherited characteristics, causes some people to commit crimes.

It is not moral culpability or choice that divides law-abiding citizens from criminals—so Clarence Darrow argued eloquently—but the accident of birth or social circumstances.

If determinism of this sort were valid, not only the death penalty but 24 all forms of punishment would be unjustified. No one who is compelled by circumstances to act deserves to be punished. But there is little reason to adopt this bleak view of human action. Occasionally coercive threats compel a person to violate the law; and in such cases the individual is rightly excused from legal guilt. Circumstances of deprivation, hardship and lack of education—unfortunately much more widely prevalent— break down the barriers, both moral and material, which deter many of us from breaking the law. They are grounds for exercising extreme caution and for showing mercy in the application of the law, but they are not the sole causes of crimes: they diminish but do not destroy the responsibility of the individual. The great majority of those who break the law do so deliberately, by choice and not as a result of causes beyond their control.

Second, the case against the death penalty is sometimes based on the 25 view that the justification of punishment lies in the reform which it effects. Those who break the law, it is said, are ill, suffering either from psychological malfunction or from maladjustment to society. Our responsibility is to treat them, to cure them of their illness, so that they become able to function in socially acceptable ways. Death, obviously, cannot reform anyone.

Like the deterrence argument for capital punishment, this seems to be 26 the wrong *kind* of argument. Punishment is punishment and treatment is treatment, and one must not be substituted for the other. Some persons who violate the law are, without doubt, mentally ill. It is unreasonable and inhumane to punish them for acts which they may not have realized they were doing; to put such a person to death would be an even more grievous wrong. In such cases treatment is called for.

But most persons who break the law are not mentally ill and do know 27 what they are doing. We may not force them to undergo treatment in place of the legal penalty for their offenses. To confine them to mental institutions until those put in authority over them judge that they are cured of their criminal tendencies is far more cruel than to sentence them to a term of imprisonment. Voluntary programs of education or vocational training, which help prepare prisoners for noncriminal careers on release, should be made more widely available. But compulsory treatment for all offenders violates their integrity as persons; we need only look to the Soviet Union to see the abuses to which such a practice is liable.

VI

Let us examine a third and stronger argument, a straightforward moral 28 assertion; the state ought not to take life unnecessarily. For many reasons—among them the example which capital punishment sets, its effect on those who must carry out death sentences and, above all, its violation of a basic moral principle—the state ought not to kill people.

The counterclaim made by defenders of capital punishment is that in 29 certain circumstances killing people is permissible and even required, and that capital punishment is one of those cases. If a terrorist is about to throw a bomb into a crowded theater, and a police officer is certain that there is no way to stop him except to kill him, the officer should of course kill the terrorist. In some cases of grave and immediate danger, let us grant, killing is justified.

But execution bears little resemblance to such cases. It involves the 30 planned, deliberate killing of someone in custody who is not a present threat to human life or safety. Execution is not necessary to save the lives of future victims, since there are other means to secure that end.

Is there some vitally important purpose of the state or some fundamen- 31 tal right of persons which cannot be secured without executing convicts? I do not believe there is. And in the absence of any such compelling reason, the moral principle that it is wrong to kill people constitutes a powerful argument against capital punishment.

VII

Of the arguments I have mentioned in favor of the death penalty, only 32 one has considerable weight. That is the retributive argument that murder, as an extremely serious offense, requires a comparably severe punishment. Of the arguments so far examined against capital punish-ment, only one, the moral claim that killing is wrong, is, in my view, acceptable.

There is, however, another argument against the death penalty which I 33 find compelling—that based on the imperfection of judicial procedure. In the case of *Furman* v. *Georgia*, the Supreme Court struck down existing legislation because of the arbitrariness with which some convicted offenders were executed and others spared. Laws enacted subsequently in several states have attempted to meet the court's objection, either by making death mandatory for certain offenses or by drawing up standards which the trial jury must follow in deciding, after guilt has been estab-lished, whether the death penalty will be imposed in a particular case. But these revisions of the law diminish only slightly the discretion of the jury. When death is made the mandatory sentence for first-degree murder, the question of death or imprisonment becomes the question of whether to find the accused guilty as charged or guilty of a lesser offense, such as second-degree murder.

When standards are spelled out, the impression of greater precision is often only superficial. A recent Texas statute, for example, instructs the jury to impose a sentence of death only if it is established "beyond a reasonable doubt" that "there is a probability that the defendant would commit criminal acts of violence that would constitute a continuing threat to society" (Texas Code of Criminal Procedure, Art. 37.071; quoted in *Capital Punishment: The Inevitability of Caprice and Mistake*, by Charles L. Black, Jr. [Norton, 1974], p. 58). Such a law does not remove discretion but only adds confusion. 34

At many other points in the judicial process, discretion rules, and arbitrary or incorrect decisions are possible. The prosecutor must decide whether to charge the accused with a capital crime, and whether to accept a plea of guilty to a lesser charge. (In most states it is impossible to plead guilty to a charge carrying a mandatory death sentence.) The jury must determine whether the facts of the case as established by testimony in court fit the legal definition of the offense with which the defendant is charged—a definition likely to be complicated at best, incomprehensible at worst. From a mass of confusing and possibly conflicting testimony the jury must choose the most reliable. But evident reliability can be deceptive: persons have been wrongly convicted of murder on the positive identification of eyewitnesses. 35

Jurors must also determine whether at the time of the crime the accused satisfied the legal definition of insanity. The most widely used definition—the McNaghten Rules formulated by the judges of the House of Lords in 1843—states that a person is excused from criminal responsibility if at the time of his act he suffered from a defect of reason which arose from a disease of the mind and as a result of which he did not "know the nature and quality of his act," or "if he did know it . . . he did not know he was doing what was wrong" (quoted in *Punishment and Responsibility*, by H. L. A. Hart [Oxford University Press, 1968], p. 189). Every word of this formula has been subject to legal controversy in interpretation, and it is unreasonable to expect that juries untrained in law will be able to apply it consistently and fairly. Even after sentencing, some offenders escape the death penalty as a result of appeals, other technical legal challenges, or executive clemency. 36

Because of all these opportunities for arbitrary decision, only a small number of those convicted of capital crimes are actually executed. It is hardly surprising that their selection has little to do with the character of their crimes but a great deal to do with the skill of their legal counsel. 37

And the latter depends in large measure on how much money is available for the defense. Inevitably, the death penalty has been imposed most frequently on the poor, and in this country it has been imposed in disproportionate numbers on blacks.

To cite two examples in this regard: All those executed in Delaware 38 between 1902 and the (temporary) abolition of the state's death penalty in 1958 were unskilled workers with limited education. Of 3,860 persons executed in the United States between 1930 and the present, 2,066, or 54 percent, were black. Although for a variety of reasons the per capita rate of conviction for most types of crime has been higher among the poor and the black, that alone cannot explain why a tenth of the population should account for more than half of those executed. Doubtless prejudice played a part. But no amount of goodwill and fair-mindedness can compensate for the disadvantage to those who cannot afford the highly skilled legal counsel needed to discern every loophole in the judicial process.

VIII

Even more worrisome than the discriminatory application of the death 39 penalty is the possibility of mistaken conviction and its ghastly consequences. In a sense, any punishment wrongfully imposed is irrevocable, but none is so irrevocable as death. Although we cannot give back to a person mistakenly imprisoned the time spent or the self-respect lost, we can release and compensate him or her. But we cannot do anything for a person wrongfully executed. While we ought to minimize the opportunities for capricious or mistaken judgments throughout the legal system, we cannot hope for perfect success. There is no reason why our mistakes must be fatal.

Numerous cases of erroneous convictions in capital cases have been 40 documented; several of those convicted were put to death before the error was discovered. However small their number, it is too large. So long as the death penalty exists, there are certain to be others, for every judicial procedure—however meticulous, however compassed about with safeguards—must be carried out by fallible human beings.

One erroneous execution is too many, because even lawful executions 41 of the indisputably guilty serve no purpose. They are not justified by the need to protect the rest of us, since there are other means of restraining persons dangerous to society, and there is no evidence that executions deter the commission of crime. A wrongful execution is a grievous injustice that cannot be remedied after the fact. Even a legal and proper execution is a needless taking of human life. Even if one is sympathetic—

as I am—to the claim that a murderer deserves to die, there are compelling reasons not to entrust the power to decide who shall die to the persons and procedures that constitute our judicial system.

QUESTIONS FOR ANALYSIS

1. To discover the general plan of this position paper, make an outline of it. (See the guidelines for Outlining in Chapter 1.) Look particularly at the numbered sections to determine why Hoekema divided the essay into parts. Also notice the cueing devices—forecasting statements, transitions, and summaries—to see how Hoekema helps the reader follow his argument. Given his purpose and audience, what seem to be the advantages and disadvantages of this organization?

2. What is the purpose of the first six paragraphs? What would be lost—or gained—if Hoekema had begun instead with paragraph 7?

3. According to Hoekema, the "most prominent" defense of capital punishment is the "argument from deterrence" (paragraphs 7–12). How convincing is his refutation of this important argument? Is he correct to call it the "wrong kind" of argument? Evaluate its logical, emotional, and ethical appeals. (Review the procedures under Analyzing an Argument in Chapter 1.)

4. In paragraph 32, Hoekema concludes that the "fair retribution" argument is the strongest in favor of the death penalty, while the "moral claim that killing is wrong" is the strongest argument against it. Examine closely Hoekema's treatment of both arguments. On what basis does he reach this conclusion? What reasons, refutation, and backing does he bring up? Is his evaluation of these arguments based on their logical, emotional, or ethical appeals?

5. At various points in the essay, Hoekema quotes or summarizes publications on capital punishment. Find these references, and examine the way he uses them. Why does he quote some sources and summarize others? For example, in paragraph 33 he uses his own words to report the Supreme Court decision in *Furman* v. *Georgia*, while he quotes a Texas statute in paragraph 34. What seem to you to be the relative advantages and disadvantages of quoting and summarizing sources?

6. Review Exploring Your Personal Response in Chapter 1. Then, write a 300–400-word personal response to the Hoekema selection, choosing one of the following topics:

    Play devil's advocate and challenge the writer's ideas or argument.

    Write about the history of your reading of this essay. That is, tell a story about your impressions and reactions during first and later readings. Reflect on how your response to the essay changed.

After you have written your response, reread it thoughtfully. In two or three sentences, state what you have learned about Hoekema's position paper by writing an extended response to it.

IDEAS FOR YOUR OWN WRITING

Hoekema asserts that punishment ought to be meted out on the basis of "fair retribution," in other words, that punishment should fit the crime. How do we decide what is fair retribution? For example, is it fair for a student who plagiarizes to be dismissed from school or for a student to be suspended for a year for drug possession? What is fair retribution for child abuse, drunk driving, rape? Choose one of these crimes or one that you've thought of, and speculate on what would be a fair punishment. Consider various possibilities, and give your reasons for and against each possible punishment. How might you go about discovering what the typical punishment is for this type of crime?

A Debate on Cultural Literacy

The next two essays—"Culture Gives Us a Sense of Who We Are" by Robert Solomon and "We Can't Dance Together" by María Rosa Menocal—are paired because they take opposing positions on an issue. The subject of their debate has concerned educators throughout the twentieth century and has been argued under different names, such as "liberal arts," "great books," and most recently "cultural literacy."

Whatever it is called, the debate revolves around the question of what should be taught in higher education. Should all students study the same basic curriculum before they go on to specialize in a major? If so, what should be included in this core curriculum? While some argue that the curriculum should center on the "great" works of Western civilization, others question the basis for selecting the works that have been traditionally considered "great." One line of argument focuses on the question of whether the prevailing idea of culture is too limited by male-dominated European tradition, while another insists that this tradition is fundamental to a liberal education.

In recent years, the issue has come into the spotlight with efforts to change the curriculum at colleges across the nation. Two popular and controversial books have helped focus attention on the issue: *The Closing of the American Mind: How Higher Education Has Failed Democracy and Impoverished the Souls of Today's Students* (1987) by Allan Bloom and *Cultural Literacy: What Every American Needs to Know* (1987) by E. D. Hirsch. Both books advocate a "return" to a core of studies emphasizing traditional works and have come under fire as elitist, sexist, racist, and regressive.

Robert C. Solomon

Robert C. Solomon (b. 1942) is a philosopher and a college professor who has had firsthand experience at public and private colleges across the nation. As an undergraduate, he studied at the University of Pennsylvania and received his Ph.D. from the University of Michigan. Before assuming his present position at the University of Texas at Austin, he taught at Princeton University, the University of Southern California, and the University of Pittsburgh.

Solomon has written many books on the history of philosophy, including *Nietzsche* (1973), *Introducing Philosophy* (1977), and *History and Human Nature: A Philosophical Review of European History and Culture, 1750–1850* (1979). His experience as a student and a teacher, together with his study of philosophy, led him to conclude that the average college student desperately needs a broad liberal education. Because he felt the issue should be of interest to the general public and not just to academics, Solomon published his essay "Culture Gives Us a Sense of Who We Are" (1981) in the *Los Angeles Times*, a newspaper read by over a million people.

Culture Gives Us a Sense of Who We Are

Solomon wrote this essay for a broad general audience in order to raise people's awareness of the issue of cultural literacy. Knowing Solomon's audience and his purpose for writing should lead you as a critical reader to anticipate his writing strategies. What tone will he adopt? What assumptions will he make about his readers and their knowledge of liberal arts education?

As the title indicates, Solomon uses the idea of culture as the crux of his argument. Obviously, he will have to define what he means by this central term. Before you begin reading, take a moment to define the term for yourself. What do *you* mean by *culture*? How important is culture to you? Then, as you read the essay, pay close attention to the way Solomon uses the word. How does he define *culture*? Does he assume there is only one culture or several subcultures? Can culture really be taught? Should it?

In our aggressively egalitarian society, "culture" has always been a suspect word, suggesting the pretensions of an effete and foolish leisure class, like the grand dames spoofed in Marx Brothers' films. But the pretensions of a self-appointed cultural elite notwithstanding, "culture" actually refers to nothing more objectionable than a system of shared symbols and examples that hold a society together. Within a culture we are kindred spirits, simply because we understand one another.

A recent and somewhat frightening Rockefeller Foundation study on the state of the humanities in American life reported that the vast majority of even our most educated citizens are ignorant of the common literature and history that reinforce not only cultural identity but also moral choices. Doctors, lawyers and business executives are in positions of great responsibility, but often have little or no training in the ethical background that makes their critical choices meaningful.

Across our society in general, we find ourselves increasingly fragmented, split into factions and "generation gaps"—which now occur at two- or three-year intervals—just because the once-automatic assumption of a shared culture, something beyond shared highways, television programming and economic worries, is no longer valid.

In our schools, according to the Rockefeller report, the problem lies   4
largely in what has recently been hailed as the "back to basics" movement, which includes no cultural content whatsoever, just skills and
techniques. Reading is taught as a means of survival in the modern
world, not as a source of pleasure and of shared experience. The notion
of "great books" is viewed by most educators as an archaic concept,
relegated to the museum of old teaching devices, such as the memoriza-
tion in Greek of passages from Homer.

But are "great books" (and legends, poems, paintings and plays)   5
indeed the only conduit of culture, or have they been replaced by more
accessible and effortless media of transmission—television, for example,
and films?

Films, to be sure, have entered into our cultural identity in an ex-   6
tremely powerful way; indeed, it is not clear that a person who knows
nothing of Bogart or Chaplin, who has never seen (young) Brando or
watched a Western could claim to be fully part of American culture. But
these are classics, and they have some of the same virtue as great books;
their symbols, characters and moral examples have been around long
enough to span generations and segments of our population, and to
provide a shared vocabulary, shared heroes and shared values. No such
virtue is to be found in television series that disappear every two years (or
less), films that survive but a season or "made-for-TV" movies with a
lifetime of two hours minus commercial breaks.

"Television culture" is no culture at all, and it is no surprise that, when   7
kids change heroes with the season, their parents don't (and couldn't
possibly) keep up with them. The symbolism of *Moby Dick* and *The
Scarlet Letter*, however much we resented being force-fed them in school,
is something we can all be expected to share. The inanities of *The Dukes
of Hazzard*, viewed by no matter how many millions of people, will not
replace them.

The same is true of our musical heritage. The Beatles are only a name   8
to most 12-year-olds. Beethoven, by contrast, continues to provide the
musical themes we can assume (even if wrongly) that all of us have heard,
time and time again. This isn't snobbery; it's continuity.

A professor recently wrote in the *Wall Street Journal* that he had   9
mentioned Socrates in class (at a rather prestigious liberal arts college)
and had drawn blanks from more than half the students. My colleagues
and I at the University of Texas swap stories about references that our
students don't catch. Even allowing generous leeway for our own professional prejudices and misperceptions of what is important, the general
picture is disturbing. We are becoming a culture without a culture,
lacking fixed points of reference and a shared vocabulary.

It would be so easy, so inexpensive, to change all that; a reading list for
high school students; a little encouragement in the media; a bit more
enlightenment in our college curricula.

With all of this in mind, I decided to see just what I could or could not
assume among my students, who are generally bright and better educated than average (given that they are taking philosophy courses, hardly
an assumed interest among undergraduates these days). I gave them a
name quiz, in effect, of some of the figures that, on most people's list,
would rank among the most important and often referred to in Western
culture. Following are some of the results, in terms of the percentage of
students who recognized them:

Socrates, 87%; Louis XIV, 59%; Moses, 90%; Hawthorne, 42%; John
Milton, 35%; Trotsky, 47%; Donatello, 8%; Copernicus, 47%; Puccini,
11%; Charlemagne, 40%; Virginia Woolf, 25%; Estes Kefauver, 8%;
Debussy, 14%; Giotto, 4%; Archduke Ferdinand, 21%; Lewis Carroll,
81%; Charles Dodgson, 5%; Thomas Aquinas, 68%; Spinoza, 19%;
Moliere, 30%; Tchaikovsky, 81%; Darwin, 56%; Karl Marx, 65%;
Faulkner, 43%; George Byron, 18%; Goethe, 42%; Raphael, 17%; Eu-
ripides, 8%; Homer, 39%; T.S. Eliot, 25%; Rodin, 24%; Mozart, 94%;
Hitler, 97%; Wagner, 34%; Dante, 25%; Louis XVI, 25%; Kafka, 38%;
Stravinsky, 57%; John Adams, 36%.

A friend who gave the same quiz to his English composition class got
results more than 50% lower on average.

I suppose that many people will think the quiz too hard, the names
often too obscure—but that, of course, is just the point. The students,
interestingly enough, did not feel this at all—not one of them. They "sort
of recognized" most of the names and felt somewhat embarrassed at not
knowing exactly who these people were. There was no sense that the quiz
was a "trivia" contest (as in, "What's the name of Dale Evans' horse?")
and there were no accusations of elitism or ethnocentrism. The simple
fact was that they knew these names were part of their culture, and in
too many cases they knew that they weren't—but should be—conversant
with them. Maybe that, in itself, is encouraging.

QUESTIONS FOR ANALYSIS

1. What position does Solomon take on the issue? Where does he state
   his claim most explicitly?

2. What does Solomon mean by the key term *culture*? Why do you think
   he refers to the fact that, for some, culture is a "suspect word"? Why
   might it be considered suspect? How does he try to define the issue by
   redefining culture as "nothing more objectionable than a system of
   shared symbols and examples that hold a society together"?

3. In paragraphs 2–4, Solomon refers to a Rockefeller Foundation study. How does he use this outside source? What role does it play in his argument?

4. In paragraphs 6 and 7, Solomon draws a distinction between the cultural values of film versus those of television. But he offers only a single example of television—*The Dukes of Hazzard.* To evaluate this backing, consider whether this example is representative of the programs available on television. In your own experience, does television lack "classics" whose "symbols, characters and moral examples . . . provide a shared vocabulary, shared heroes and shared values"?

5. Take the name quiz (paragraph 12) yourself. Then review the three possible objections to his argument that Solomon alludes to in his final paragraph: (1) that it is not a fair test of culture but merely a trivia contest, (2) that such a listing of names is elitist, and (3) that it is ethnocentric. How effectively does Solomon handle these objections? How would you refute or defend them?

6. Evaluate Solomon's argument on the basis of its logical, emotional, or ethical appeal. (Review the discussion of evaluating these appeals under Analyzing an Argument in Chapter 1.)

IDEAS FOR YOUR OWN WRITING

Critical readers might argue that what Solomon is addressing is not whether a liberal education is valuable or whether cultural literacy is important, but whether the humanities—philosophy, literature, the arts, and history—should have an equal place with the sciences in our increasingly technological society. List arguments for and against required study of the humanities for all students, including those majoring in the sciences. What is your position on this issue?

Solomon characterizes television programs like *The Dukes of Hazzard* as "inane"; others go farther and call such programs harmful because they teach young, impressionable children that it is fun to disobey the law. At the heart of the controversy is the question of whether parents should limit or censor their children's television watching. This is only one of many controversial issues revolving around the role of television in contemporary life. List as many others as you can. Here are a few possibilities to get you started: Is the minority experience fairly represented? Should programs that offend particular sensibilities be banned or limited to particular times? Does television contribute to crime or violence in any way? Choose one item from your list, and consider reasons to support both sides, pro and con.

María Rosa Menocal

María Rosa Menocal is a professor in the Department of Spanish and Portuguese at Yale University.

"We Can't Dance Together"[1]

Like Robert Solomon's essay, the following selection also deals with the issue of cultural literacy, particularly the cultural value of rock and roll. It was originally published in *Profession 88*, a journal read primarily by professors of English and other languages, in an edition devoted to the controversy generated by the books by Allan Bloom and E. D. Hirsch. Menocal responds directly to Bloom's critique of rock music, an argument she summarizes in paragraph 2 of her essay.

Before reading Menocal's refutation of Bloom's criticism, review the argument made by Robert Solomon in "Culture Gives Us a Sense of Who We Are." Like Bloom, Solomon sees little cultural value in rock music. He writes in paragraphs 7–8: "'Television culture' is no culture at all. . . . The same is true of our musical heritage. The Beatles are only a name to most 12-year-olds. Beethoven, by contrast, continues to provide musical themes we can assume (even if wrongly) that all of us have heard, time and again. This isn't snobbery; it's continuity."

Take a few minutes to consider how you would respond to this kind of argument. What is the difference between "snobbery" and "continuity"? Do you agree with Solomon that most 12-year-olds know the Beatles only by name but do not know their music? Is there a sense of tradition or continuity within rock music itself?

> *Maybe this small attachment to my past is only another case of what Frank Zappa calls a bunch of old guys sitting around playing rock'n'roll. But as we all know, rock'n'roll will never die, and education too, as Henry Adams always sez, keeps going on forever.*

THOMAS PYNCHON, INTRODUCTION TO *SLOW LEARNER*, xxxiv

Anyone who teaches Petrarch's lyric magnum opus, vulgarly known as the *Canzoniere*, is eventually bound to reveal to his or her students the rather delicious irony that Petrarch actually thought—or at least said, repeatedly—that writing in the vernacular, the language of the masses and the vulgar, was not a particularly worthwhile or dignified enterprise. [1]

I, at least, get a somewhat malicious pleasure from pointing out that it is, of course, because of his magnificently "vulgar" collection of love songs that Petrarch is at all remembered—and that he is such an integral part of canonical Western culture. The irony is a double one: first, if his statements can be taken at face value, Petrarch was terribly wrong in his assessments of the relative merits of his vernacular versus his "classical" writings; second, we have now, following his obviously misguided thinking on the matter and in blatant disregard of the historical lesson, "classicized" the love songs—which were so successful precisely because they weren't "classical" in the first place.[2] When one reads Allan Bloom's derisive comments about music in *The Closing of the American Mind*, which are characterized by a remarkably similar disdain for popular love lyrics and the accompanying reverence for the "great tradition," one can't help but wonder, at least for a split second, if Bloom doesn't have a manuscript of rock lyrics stashed away someplace. Well, it was just a split second.

In fact, a first reading of Bloom, of the chapter entitled "Music" in particular, should logically lead one merely to shrug one's shoulders at his stereotypically retrograde views. I spent several months ticking off all the reasons why writing a response to Bloom's book was, is, even on the face of it, a waste of time and a somewhat self-indulgent exercise. It struck me as significant, however, that other reviewers, no matter how negative, rarely mentioned his ravings about music, tending to be concerned with the more "serious" issues about education he raises. Even the witty and intelligent review in *Rolling Stone*, which lays many of Bloom's pretenses bare ("he is peddling fundamentalism for highbrows" [Greider 39]) essentially passes over Bloom's substantive comments about music— in great measure, no doubt, because for anyone reading that journal his comments are too ludicrous even to require a response, their silliness exposed just by their being quoted. But because, as the example of Petrarch so clearly indicates, the multiple and complex issues revolving around the question of "vulgar" love lyrics and the canonical literary tradition are much too important to and central in our profession to be left to the occasional college newspaper refutation by a student music reviewer, I decided to respond.

I do so acknowledging the following limitations. First, I do not pretend to be in any way comprehensive or systematic in my treatment of rock, and the examples I have chosen are idiosyncratic, personal, and relatively random, the music that happened to come to mind. I am not a scholar or an expert in this area, nor is this a research paper on rock.[3] I am a middling to average, at best, connoisseur of the genre. But my examples are not unrepresentative (although they in fact represent a minuscule selection of the full range), and someone else's personal sampling would have comparable validity. Second, I will not address in any great detail the much larger issues Bloom raises, although they are, perforce, the backdrop for the music chapter and, more important, they reflect an ideology within which his rejection of rock must be understood. But those are other reviews.[4] And for the sake of my argument—in sum, that Bloom is, from a scholarly point of view, wrong about what rock and roll is—I will attempt to suspend any sustained rebuttal that involves opinion as to what culture (and thus rock and roll) ought to be.

Bloom's argument about rock has three major elements: (1) that rock music and its lyrics are limited to "sex, hate and a smarmy, hypocritical version of brotherly love" (74), with an emphasis on sex: "rock music has one appeal only, a barbaric appeal, to sexual desire—not love, not *eros*, but sexual desire undeveloped and untutored" (73); (2) that rock's values (or lack thereof) are, at worst, antagonistic to fundamental cultural values and, at best, lie well outside other lasting cultural pursuits: "Rock music encourages passions and provides models that have no relation to any life the young people . . . can possibly lead, or to the kinds of admiration encouraged by liberal studies. . . . [A]s long as they have the Walkman on, they cannot hear what the great tradition has to say" (80–81); (3) that rock is a musical-lyrical genre that concerns youth and children overwhelmingly: "Never was there an art form directed so exclusively to children" (74). Let's take these elements in that order.

Bloom's assertions about the poverty and limitations of rock's themes are perhaps the most excruciating in their simple lack of factualness—and there is such an embarrassment of riches available as counterargument that it is difficult to know where to start. What *is* true, certainly, is that the richest thematic mine is that of love—and more often than not, love that is in some way unsatisfying, unhappy, or unfulfilled. But many, if not most, of rock's classic love songs are about a great deal more—or less—than sex. From the Beatles' basically silly "Michelle, my belle, these are words that go together well" (which reveals the metaliterary preoccupation of rock as well) to Dylan's charming ditty "You're Gonna Make Me Lonesome When You Go," which includes a refusal of other types of love poetry ("Situations have ended sad / Relationships have all been bad / Kind of been like Verlaine's and Rimbaud's / But there's no way I can compare / All them scenes to this affair / You're gonna make me lonesome when you go"), to the troubled and tortured love of Neil Young's "Now that you've made yourself love me / Do you think I can change it in a day?" there are few, if any, of the variations and variegations of "classical" love poetry that have not found lyrics in the rock canon.

Even if we limit ourselves to the writing of the artists mentioned 6
above, Bloom's generalization not only crumbles but has to be replaced
by the realization that rock's obsession with love and with its own
expressions of the longing for love are next of kin to those same obsessions in all other lyrical schools. Thus, the Beatles's hymn to enduring,
perfect, and as yet unfound love in "I Will" ("Who knows how long I've
loved you? / You know I love you still / Will I wait a lonely lifetime? / If
you want me to I will / For if I ever saw you / I didn't catch your name /
But it never really mattered / I will always feel the same") is neatly
counterbalanced by their wistful and hopeful projection about a perhaps
nonexistent future in the classic "When I'm Sixty-Four" ("Will you still
need me? / Will you still feed me? / When I'm sixty-four"). Dylan's
repertoire of love songs (although it is fair to say that he is far from being
known as a love lyricist) is scarcely less representative of these ties to lyric
antecedents. From the early, bittersweet "Don't Think Twice It's All
Right" about the pain of failed love ("Well it ain't no use to sit and
wonder why, babe / If you don't know by now . . . When your rooster
crows at the break of dawn / Look out your window and I'll be gone /
You're the reason that I'm traveling on / But don't think twice, it's all
right . . . But I wish there was something you would do or say / To try
and make me change my mind and stay . . .") to the famous "Just like a
Woman" (satirized by Woody Allen in *Annie Hall*) to other, much more
difficult and hermetic songs such as "Queen Jane Approximately"
("When all the flower girls want back what they have lent you / And the
smell of their roses does not remain / And all of your children start to
resent you / Won't you come see me, Queen Jane?"), his long and varied
career as a lyricist is reminiscent of a poetic ancestry he is quite conscious
of following.[5] And the centrality of the broken heart to the lyric tradition
is simply and touchingly reflected in Neil Young's "Only Love Can Break
Your Heart" ("When you were young and on your own / How did it feel
to be alone? . . . But only love can break your heart / Try to be sure right
from the start / Yes only love can break your heart / What if your world
should fall apart?").

The interesting question, of course, is why and how the preoccupation 7
with love and its expression in rock is so reminiscent of other lyrical
traditions, so like other schools and canons that are now studied, by and
large, in a more rarefied atmosphere. From twelfth-century Persian
courtly poetry to Petrarchism in Renaissance Europe to opera in the last
century, love and its many problems—sometimes sexual, sometimes
not—are of overwhelming and enduring fascination and are perhaps the
ultimate inspiration for poetry and lyrics—an inspiration that all these
lyrical schools are also explicitly conscious of and that is often the focus

of metaliterary interest itself. Taken as a whole, rock exhibits, theme for theme, much the same concerns as those of the traditions we have now classicized. In one example, the preoccupation with unsatisfactory love becomes the subject or object of poetry and creates, in turn, the association between the lyricist or singer and the lover. Self-reflection and metalyrical concerns include the glory and fame that will be achieved through the singing or poetry: some examples are "So You Want to Be a Rock 'n' Roll Star," "Do You Believe in Magic?" and that early and enduring anthem of rock, "Johnny B. Goode" ("My father told me some day you will be a man / And you will be the leader of a big old band / Many people coming from miles around / To hear you play your music when the sun goes down / Maybe someday your name will be in lights / Saying Johnny B. Goode tonight"). Thus, what is critical is not merely that Bloom (and others) have got it wrong but that ignorance prevents them from seeing that rock is in so many ways like parts of the "great tradition." And one is then, indeed, led to the question of whether rock resembles these traditions because it is descended from them or because some sort of universal parallelism is at work—a question that, because of our Bloom-like prejudices, has scarcely been asked, let alone answered.[6] As for the sexuality, well, indeed, some rock lyrics are sexual, even, perhaps, exclusively and pointedly and vulgarly sexual. But sexuality, too, is far from uniquely modern, and Mick Jagger's "Satisfaction" and "Let's Spend the Night Together" pale, in both vulgarity and explicitness, beside some of the songs of the venerated William of Aquitaine.

But while rock may thus mimic earlier lyric schools in its fascination with the generative power of unhappy love, it has exploited a much fuller range of themes, including the historicopolitical one that Bloom dismisses as "a smarmy, hypocritical version of brotherly love." Once again the generalization alarmingly misrepresents the remarkable range of topics covered and views expressed. Many of rock's earliest masterpieces, written in the late sixties and early seventies, were, in fact, politically committed, and opposition to the war (and the draft) and sympathy for the civil rights movements were major conditioning and influential currents. But as often as not, the lyrics produced in this climate were most conspicuously informed by and interwoven with the other musical and lyrical traditions that are such important components of rock: black, particularly spiritual, music and the sort of folk tradition that Joan Baez's songs rely on so heavily. Remnants of these strains, pervasive in rock even today, explain the centrality of the Talking Heads's "Take Me to the River" and Eric Clapton's (and others') recordings of "Swing Low, Sweet Chariot." And while there are plenty of examples of virtually unmediated protest (Country Joe and the Fish's "What are we fighting for? /

Don't ask me I don't give a damn / Next stop is Viet Nam . . ." is a classic, certainly, as is Dylan's even more famous "The Times They Are A-Changin' "), much of the "political" lyrics of rock are infinitely more complex.

The Band, for example, specialized in songs that reflected back on the Civil War South, and by giving the poet a Confederate voice in "The Night They Drove Old Dixie Down," they brilliantly underscored, without ever being explicit, the universal tragedy of war. The currently popular U2 plumbs the complex problems and no-win situation of Northern Ireland in equally subtle ways. Finally, many rock lyricists have made their points by merely taking over or only slightly rewriting "classics" from other traditions: Prince sings the Lord's Prayer with remarkable effect; the Byrds sang Ecclesiastes in "Turn, Turn, Turn." If these are smarmy versions of brotherly love, so be it. In fact, what is stunning here is that rock's connections with the "great tradition" are often quite explicit, markedly intertextual, and ultimately impossible to ignore. The extent to which Bloom's second major objection to rock— that it has no cultural ties or links or avenues beyond itself—is simply mistaken comes very much to the fore here.[7]

But above and beyond specific songs that are strictly and obviously tied, intertextually, to any number of classic texts outside the rock tradition, rock's place in contemporary society is a major link to a number of cultural phenomena that we now, from a safe distance, view as canonical. In fact, it is telling that Bloom does acknowledge the great impact of rock: at the outset of the chapter he goes on at some length, and with considerable accuracy, about the unique role rock plays in society and about rock's importance, unparalleled in recent history. He begins the chapter, in fact, noting that "[n]othing is more singular about this generation than its addiction to music. This is the age of music and the states of soul that accompany it. To find a rival to this enthusiasm, one would have to go back at least a century to Germany and the passion for Wagner's operas" (68). And, having remarked that one crucial difference between rock and the German passion of the last century is that rock is much less elitist (i.e., it cuts across class boundaries more), he goes on to note the great change that has occurred in the role music and its lyrics play in this century: "The power of music in the soul . . . has been recovered after a long period of desuetude" (69). In acknowledging this rather remarkable turn of events, this existence in the late twentieth century of a status for music and its lyrics that did not always exist and when it did was a major cultural institution and a central part of the culture, Bloom is implicitly recognizing what he will explicitly deny later on: the cultural centrality of the rock phenomenon. In fact, Bloom even goes on to note that this is the first generation he has taught that fully understands Plato's opposition to music, something earlier generations, for whom music was "background," were incapable of understanding. And since Bloom explicitly recognizes the enormous impact per se of the phenomenon, his refusal to see its cultural impact is grounded, explicitly, in what he sees as its failure to address issues other than sex—an opinion that, as I have tried to suggest, cannot be substantiated.

What can be substantiated is the perhaps radical-sounding assertion, already implicit in Bloom's comments, that the rock phenomenon is a twentieth-century version, in many if not in most of its details, of what at other times and in other places have been major lyrical schools with resounding impact in the cultures that produced them. Poetry, after all, had long ago ceased to be "lyrical" in the etymological sense of the word, an integral part of music. For most people—and many scholars—poetry is what was and is written down to be read and what is published in poetry journals or in the *New Yorker* or in anthologies. Poetry in that form not only is substantively different from lyrics but is rarely (and then only for a minuscule percentage of the population, now or in any other period of history) a living part of one's cultural or spiritual experience. But rock is much like opera and even more like the phenomenon of the troubadours in twelfth- and thirteenth-century Europe, when lyricists started singing in the vernaculars rather than in the long-dead Latin. Rock is poetry that is aggressively and self-consciously a part of the living tradition that, in great measure because it is attached to music, plays a fundamental and vital cultural role for many more people. In this regard, as in various others, Bloom's assertion that rock makes it difficult for young people to have a passionate relationship to the art and thought that are the substance of a liberal education is almost perversely skewed.

The truth is the opposite: the person, young or otherwise, for whom poetry is a living form that resonates daily in the mind and soul is quite capable of appreciating not only the poetry of the troubadours or of Petrarch, so similar in other ways, but, more important, the great lyrical power of poetry in and of itself. Members of this generation, as Bloom likes to put it, are the first in a long time, thanks to rock, to be in a position to understand the impact and repercussions of many earlier lyrical phenomena. They should be able to grasp, for example (particularly if we as mediators can simply point out the parallels), what is moving, rather than dusty and mechanical and arcane, in a previous generation's songs—much more so, I would argue, than people who don't know why tears have been shed at Lennon's "Imagine" or who don't think of love in the haunting structures of "Here, There, and Everywhere," or who might not hear the ecstasy and triumph of the Grateful

Dead's "Touch of Grey" ("I will survive"), so often sung last summer by Jerry Garcia, who could have been grandfather to many in the audience. For those whose poetic sensibilities have incubated in the heart and soul and tapping feet, Puccini's sentimental arias can be truly moving and Verdi's triumphal choruses can stir, vicariously if nothing else, the same sentiments stirred at Woodstock.[8] The list of ways in which the experience of rock is enlightening vis-à-vis the "great tradition" is seemingly endless: students who know full well that a strong lyric tradition thrives on the seemingly paradoxical combination of parameters and restraints, and the individual creativity that thrives within the tradition and the repetition of commonplaces, can eventually read the medieval and Renaissance lyric traditions with a fuller appreciation of their astonishing repetitiousness. And those same "students" of rock, because rock has included, and continues to include, a substantial "trobar clus" strain, those students who have learned instinctively to appreciate everything from "Lucy in the Sky with Diamonds" ("with tangerine trees and marmalade skies") to "Third World Man," by Steely Dan ("When he's crying out / I just think that Ghana Rondo / E l'era del terzo mondo / He's a third world man"), bring an important background to the study of the myriad canonical schools of hermetic lyrics that have produced poets as varied as Arnaut Daniel, the Spanish mystics, Mallarmé, and that fellow splicer of lines from the Italian, Ezra Pound.

Bloom's third major misapprehension is actually rather touching—or pathetic: that rock's appeal is exclusively to the young, that rock is a phenomenon of a "generation," that it affects his "students," and so on. This notion is belied by the simple facts of chronologies, celebrated every year as one great rock star after another turns forty or fifty and as those who grew up on rock are now bringing up children of their own. Toward the end of this chapter Bloom depicts a pathetic scenario where the poor parents who have struggled to provide a good life and who wish only the best for their child watch on, terrified and helpless, as their thirteen-year-old boy is mesmerized by MTV and its attendant horrors. This is a remarkable fantasy; the parents are, likely as not, especially if they are highbrow and college-educated, the ones who watch MTV and who introduced rock to their child in the first place. And while they may care less for their child's currently preferred groups and lyrics than for their own classics, they are probably not much concerned since it has become clear that their classics are becoming *the* classics and that their child will be listening to the Beatles, as well as to the Beatles's progeny. But more telling than even those fundamentals are columns on contemporary music that now appear regularly in the *New Yorker*, that holy sanctum of haute culture, and articles in academic journals that reflect the extent to which the centrality of rock can no longer be defined in generational terms at all.[9]

In fact, many of Bloom's (and others') misapprehensions about rock   14
and its impact are rooted in remarkably clichéd notions about the general poverty of "youth culture" and a commensurate (and I believe equally illusory) aggrandizement of the degree of "high culture" in earlier societies and generations. Thus, to take but one example, Bloom dismisses the powerful argument that, in fact, there is a significant revival of interest in classical music by saying that even if there is, only five to ten percent of the population is affected. Does he believe that much more than that has ever had a serious interest in classical music? The serious listener does, indeed, listen seriously to all sorts of music. And not only is "Roll Over, Beethoven" tongue-in-cheek, ultimately, but twenty or so years down the line it may well end up on the same shelf as the Ninth. Likewise, it is obvious that, as with all other schools or cultural phenomena, there is a lot of trash out there and a part of the audience at every concert has never heard of Ecclesiastes. So what else is new? Are we to pretend that everyone who listened avidly to Wagner knew all the allusions? Don't we all know that for every Mozart there were hundreds of Salieris? Rock is no better and probably no worse. There is little doubt that many people who listen to much that is marvelously lyrical in rock, that is poetic and moving, never get past the beat, and, also undoubtedly, much of what has been written and will continue to be written will never amount to anything in posterity.

But it is nonsense—or wishful thinking—to say, as Bloom does, that   15
when we take the Walkmans off after years of listening to rock there will be nothing left. *Au contraire*. It is a pity Bloom has listened so little, for, given the great concern for culture and the educational tradition he claims to be championing, he is thus almost perversely depriving himself of access to a richly variegated and (in the very cultural terms he wishes to see the "liberal tradition") an enormously influential phenomenon. We cannot afford to ignore Bloom's misapprehensions about music, because the nature of his misunderstanding is so intimately tied with the debates now raging, not just at Stanford but nearly everywhere, about what constitutes the canon of "Western civilization." And the educator, particularly in the field of literature and literary culture, who like Bloom walks about deaf to our living lyric tradition is a less able explicator and mediator of the literary traditions and canonized poets that are the fundamental intertexts for the troubadours of our own time. It might alter both the tenor and the substance of these discussions considerably if we were to recognize that a great deal of what is being listened to on the Walkmans is the great tradition very much alive and well—and as

Pynchon sez, rock'n'roll will never die, and education keeps going on forever.

NOTES

1. "Hey nineteen / That's Retha Franklin / She don't remember / The Queen of Soul / It's hard times befallen / The sole survivors / She thinks I'm crazy / But I'm just growing old. . . . Hey nineteen / No we can't dance together / No we can't talk at all . . ." (Steely Dan, "Hey Nineteen").

   This paper is written in memory of Clifton Cherpack, who did not quite make it to sixty-four.

2. See Vickers's extraordinary article for a much fuller discussion of these issues. Her appreciation of the parallels between Petrarch's work and that of one rock group, Survivor, as well as her detailed and sensitive exploration of the complexities of the relationship between popular and "classical" culture is exemplary. I am indebted to her for allowing me to read a prepublication version of the article.

3. Nevertheless, I have been asked to provide scholarly documentation for the songs and lyrics I quote. This is both perfectly reasonable and appropriate, given that I am, in part, claiming that much of rock and its lyrics is a cultural phenomenon to be treated like any other—and thus a song should be quoted as we would quote a poem. It is also true, however, and also part of my argument, that "everyone" knows that, for example, "When I'm Sixty-Four" is on the Beatles's *Sgt. Pepper* that came out in 1967 and that the lyrics of a remarkable body of rock are part of the active memory of many people. Thus the citations and quotations that follow are representative of the communal knowledge and memory of rock—a reflection of the living lyrical tradition. The "Works Cited" listings reflect ex post facto documentation, in some cases incomplete. Note that many artists avoid putting dates on their albums.

4. See especially David Rieff's scathing comments about Bloom's cultural-ideological posture.

5. Dylan, who changed his name from Robert Zimmerman to one that linked him explicitly with the great tradition, has written dozens of songs whose lyrics explicitly harken back to all manner of poetic schools, from the Bible ("God said to Abraham give me a son / Abe said, 'Man, you must be putting me on'" ["Highway 61 Revisited"]) to Petrarch ("Then she opened up a book of poems / And handed it to me / Written by an Italian poet / From the fourteenth century" ["Tangled Up in Blue"]) to the great poetic struggle of modernism ("Everybody's shouting: / Which side are you on? / Ezra Pound and T. S. Eliot / Fighting in the captain's tower . . ." ["Desolation Row"]).

6. The one exception I know of is Vickers's article.

7. The British punk tradition, which I know scarcely at all and thus do not discuss more fully, includes a number of "singings" of important texts. I am grateful to a student, Kirsten Thorne, for bringing to my attention "The Wasteland," by The Mission U.K., and "*In Dulce Decorum*," by The Damned, where the text is a speech of Winston Churchill's.

8. Lest the connection appear farfetched I note that in the movie *The Killing Fields* the two most emotionally wrenching scenes are accompanied by Puccini's "Nessun dorma" and Lennon's "Imagine."

9. A recent issue of *Stanford French Review* contains an article entitled "The Grateful Dead: Corneille's Tragedy and the Illusion of History."

WORKS CITED

The Band. "The Night They Drove Old Dixie Down." *The Band.* Capitol, CDP 7 46493 2, n.d. on original album.

Beatles. "Here, There and Everywhere." *Revolver.* Capitol, CDP 7 46441 2, 1966.

————."I Will." No title [*White Album*]. EMI-Capitol, CDP 7 46443 2, 1968.

————. "Michelle." *Rubber Soul.* EMI-Capitol, CDP 7 46440 2, 1965.

————. "When I'm Sixty-Four." "Lucy in the Sky with Diamonds." *Sgt. Pepper's Lonely Hearts Club Band.* EMI, CDP 7 46442 2, 1967.

Berry, Chuck. "Johnny B. Goode."

————. "Roll Over, Beethoven."

Bloom, Allan. *The Closing of the American Mind: How Higher Education Has Failed Democracy and Impoverished the Souls of Today's Students.* New York: Simon, 1987.

Byrds. "So You Want to Be a Rock'n' Roll Star." *The Byrds.* Columbia, G 30127, n.d.

————. "Turn, Turn, Turn." *Turn, Turn, Turn.* Columbia, CG 33645, n.d.

Clapton, Eric. "Swing Low, Sweet Chariot." *Time Pieces.* RSO, 800 014–2, 1975.

Country Joe McDonald. "I-Feel-like-I'm-Fixin'-to-Die Rag." *Woodstock.* Atlantic-Cotillion, SD 3–500, 1970.

Dylan, Bob. "Don't Think Twice It's All Right." *The Freewheelin' Bob Dylan.* Columbia, CK 8786, n.d.

————. "Highway 61 Revisited." "Desolation Row." "Queen Jane Approximately." *Highway 61 Revisited.* Columbia, CK 9189, 1965.

————. "Just like a Woman." *Blonde on Blonde.* Columbia, CK 841, n.d.

————. "Tangled Up in Blue." "You're Gonna Make Me Lonesome When You Go." *Blood on the Tracks.* Columbia, X 698, 1974.

————. "The Times They Are a-Changin'."

Grateful Dead. "Touch of Grey." *In the Dark.* Arista, ARCD 8452, 1987.

Greider, William. "Bloom and Doom." *Rolling Stone* 8 Oct. 1987: 39–40.

Lennon, John. "Imagine."

Lovin' Spoonful. "Do You Believe in Magic?"

Pynchon, Thomas. *Slow Learner.* New York: Bantam, 1984.

Rieff, David. "The Colonel and the Professor." *Times Literary Supplement* 4–11 Sept. 1987: 950, 960.

Rolling Stones. "Let's Spend the Night Together." *Flowers.* Abkco, 75092, 1966.

————. "Satisfaction."

Steely Dan. "Hey Nineteen." "Third World Man." *Gaucho.* MCA Records, MCAD-37220, 1980.

Talking Heads. "Take Me to the River." *Stop Making Sense*. Sire, 25186–1, 1984.

Vickers, Nancy. "Vital Signs: Petrarch and Popular Culture." *Romanic Review*, forthcoming.

Young, Neil. "Only Love Can Break Your Heart." "I Believe in You." *After the Gold Rush*. Reprise, 2283–2, 1970.

QUESTIONS FOR ANALYSIS

1. To discover the organizational plan for this position paper, make an outline of it. (Review the procedure for Outlining in Chapter 1.) Notice where Menocal provides cueing devices—forecasting statements, transitions, summaries—to guide readers through her argument. Given the rhetorical situation in which she is writing, how effectively is the essay organized?

2. In the opening paragraphs, Menocal explains why she has written this essay. Why do you think she makes this explanation? What do you think are the advantages or disadvantages of doing so?

3. Choose Menocal's refutation of *one* of Bloom's points. Then, evaluate the logical appeal of her argument by applying the ABC test described and illustrated under Analyzing an Argument in Chapter 1.

4. In supporting an argument, writers have to consider what kinds of backing or evidence are likely to carry weight with their particular readers. Menocal relies primarily on song lyrics as the backing for her argument. Skim the essay to see when and how she uses this evidence. Does she appear to assume that readers will be familiar with the songs she refers to or quotes? Given her purpose and readers, what advantages or disadvantages do you see in her use of this kind of backing?

5. Menocal frames her essay by beginning with an epigraph from Thomas Pynchon's novel *Slow Learner* and referring to it again at the end of the essay. How apt and effective is this framing device?

6. Review Exploring Your Personal Response in Chapter 1. Then, write a 300–400-word personal response to the Menocal selection, choosing one of the following topics:
   Write an essay comparing what Menocal says with what others have said about the subject.
   Write an essay exploring the meaning and implications of a particular point made in the reading.

   After you have written your response, reread it thoughtfully. In two or three sentences, say what you have learned about Menocal's position by writing an extended response to it.

IDEAS FOR YOUR OWN WRITING

Consider extending Menocal's argument to other aspects of popular culture: movies, sports, television, advertising, video games, or anything you can think of. Choose a genre that you would be interested in writing about. Can you relate specific examples of this genre of popular culture to a historical tradition? Can you suggest any ways in which this genre of popular culture can contribute to one's appreciation of more traditional areas of academic study? Can you find examples to suggest the value of this kind of popular culture?

Jill Kuhn

Jill Kuhn wrote a version of this essay for a freshman composition course at California State University, San Bernardino.

Sex Education in Our Schools

The issue of sex education is not a new one, and it is likely that you are already familiar with some of the arguments advanced by both sides. You may even have a strong opinion on this issue yourself, possibly influenced by experience with sex education courses. Before reading Kuhn's essay, take a few minutes to record your thoughts on this issue. Try to recall the various arguments you've heard over the years and what you've felt and thought about it.

Even though sex education courses have been taught in many public schools since 1967, the debate still rages over whether it is appropriate to teach sex in the schools. Now that the AIDS epidemic is upon us, we have no choice. As Surgeon General C. Everett Koop said in a report on AIDS: "we have to be as explicit as necessary to get the message across. You can't talk of the dangers of snake poisoning and not mention snakes" (Qtd. in Leo 138).

Everyone agrees that ideally sex education ought to be taught at home by parents. But apparently it is either not taught at all or taught ineffectively. The Sorenson report found, for example, that over 70 percent of the adolescents studied do not talk freely about sex with their parents (Gordon 5). They complain that while their parents tend to lecture them on morality and speak in abstractions, what they need is to learn specific facts about sex and contraception. A study done on 1,873 youths found that 67 percent of the boys and 29 percent of the girls had never been given any advice on sex by their parents and, moreover, "of those who were 'advised' more than two-thirds of the boys and one-fourth of the girls felt that neither of their parents had helped them to deal effectively with the problem of sex" (Gordon 8).

Many people oppose sex education courses because they assume that students are more likely to have sex after taking a course in it. Phyllis Schlafly, for example, claims that "the way sex education is taught in the schools encourages experimentation" (Leo 138). A study by Laurie Schwab Zabin comparing sexually inexperienced female high-school students with access to sex education and those without access found, however, that those with sex education tended to postpone their first sexual experience until they were an average of seven months older than those without sex education (Leo 140).

According to the statistics, teenagers have sex, and nothing their 4 parents or anyone else says is going to stop them. "Of the 29 million teenagers between the ages of thirteen and nineteen," according to Madelon Lubin Finkel and Steven Finkel, "12 million (41.1%) are esti-mated to have had sexual intercourse" (49). Moreover, they estimate that "more than one-fifth of first premarital pregnancies among teenagers occurred within the first month of initiating sex."

Surely it is preferable for sexually active adolescents to have accurate   5 information about sex and contraception than to live in ignorance. And they are amazingly ignorant. Takey Crist administered a questionnaire on sexual anatomy to 600 female students at the University of North Carolina at Chapel Hill, and found that among sexually active women, over one-fourth could not answer any of the questions (Gordon 19). In a nationwide study, 41 percent of the pregnant unmarried teenagers polled said that they had thought they could not get pregnant because, as they put it, "it was the wrong time of the month" (Finkel and Finkel 49). A study of unwed pregnant teenagers in Baltimore found that less than half could name three kinds of birth control and that one-third of those who did not use contraceptives were unaware that they could have used them (Gordon 19). An astonishing 91 percent of those questioned felt that they lacked adequate knowledge about how to use birth control.

Sex education courses dispel myths and misconceptions about sexual   6 behavior in general and birth control in particular. A course taught in twenty-three Atlanta public schools entitled "Postponing Sexual Involve-ment" was developed specifically in answer to students' requests for help in learning how to say no without hurting anyone's feelings (Leo 142). Adrienne Davis, a health educator at UCLA, makes self-esteem the central issue in her sex education teaching (Leo 141). Although as Marilyn Hurwitz explains, adolescent sex tends to be "spontaneous, based on passion and the moment, not thought and reason," a Johns Hopkins University study of sexually active teenagers concluded that teaching about birth control "significantly increases the likelihood" that they will use contraceptives (Leo 140).

The advent of AIDS makes sex education a necessity rather than a   7 luxury. Surgeon General Koop's report on AIDS calls for sex education to begin "at an early age, so that children can grow up knowing the behaviors to avoid to protect themselves from exposure to the AIDS virus" (Qtd. in Lewis 348). But he also emphasizes the need to focus sex education on teenagers because even though they may consider them-selves invulnerable, they are actually at great risk: "adolescents and preadolescents are those whose behavior we wish especially to influence because of their vulnerability when they are exploring their own sex-uality (heterosexual and homosexual) and perhaps experimenting with drugs." At least 2.5 million teenagers, according to the American Social Health Association, contract a sexually transmitted disease every year, including AIDS (Lewis 348). In fact, comparisons between Army recruits in the New York City area and the general population show that a much higher proportion of young people test positive for HIV, the virus believed to cause AIDS, and that the incidence of positive tests is "stunningly high" among minority recruits.

Parents can no longer afford to be overprotective. If they truly want to protect their children, they must give up the fantasy that what their sons and daughters don't know, won't hurt them. Sex kills, and we must teach our children how to defend themselves. It is not enough to preach, "Just say no!" Adolescents always have and will continue to explore their own sexuality. What they need from us is information and openness. Parents certainly have a key role to play, but they cannot do it alone. Sex education must be taught in the schools and, as the Surgeon General urges, it should begin in the early grades.

WORKS CITED

Finkel, Madelon Lubin, and Steven Finkel. "Sex Education in High School." *Society* (November/December 1985): 48–51.

Gordon, Sol. *The Sexual Adolescent.* North Scituate, MA: Duxbury Press, 1973.

Leo, John. "Should Schools Offer Sex Education?" *Reader's Digest* (March 1987): 138–42.

Lewis, Ann C. "A Dangerous Silence." *Phi Delta Kappan* (June 1987): 348–49.

QUESTIONS FOR ANALYSIS

1. Begin your analysis of Kuhn's argument by making an outline of it. (Follow the guidelines under Analyzing an Argument in Chapter 1.) Identify the claim, reasons, refutations, and backing. Label the kinds of backing.

2. How does Kuhn define the issue? Why do you think Kuhn spends so much time trying to impress upon readers the seriousness of the issue? How effective do you think she is? Why?

3. You will see by skimming your outline of Kuhn's argument that she relies heavily on statistical studies. Look closely at the places where she cites statistics. What advantages or disadvantages do you see in this particular kind of backing or evidence and the way Kuhn uses it?

4. How does Kuhn acknowledge the feelings and opinions of those with opposing views? How does this strategy contribute to the ethical appeal of her argument?

5. Compare and contrast one particular aspect of Kuhn's position paper to one other selection in this chapter. Look, for example, at the authors' ways of organizing their essays, their opening or closing paragraphs, their ways of defining the issue, their handling of anticipated objections and counterarguments, or their use of particular kinds of backing such as statistics or examples. (For an illustration, see Comparing and Contrasting Related Readings in Chapter 1.)

IDEAS FOR YOUR OWN WRITING

What other controversial issues that relate to adolescence can you think of? List issues you think you might want to know more about. Here are a few possibilities to get you started: bilingual education, affirmative action for underrepresented students, minimum wage, censorship of popular recordings, competency testing. Choose an issue from your list to explore as a possible topic for an essay. How would you go about researching both sides of the issue?

A GUIDE TO WRITING POSITION PAPERS

As the selections in this chapter indicate, the position paper can be quite an intricate piece of writing or it can be simple and direct. The complexity of a particular essay will depend on how complicated the issue is and how the argument is constructed. Writers of position papers must be very much aware of their readers. Since they may be writing to people with whom they disagree on the issue, they must make a special effort to gain their readers' confidence and respect. Probably the best way of doing this is by presenting a coherent, well-reasoned argument. The following brief guide suggests activities to help you invent, draft, and revise a position paper of your own.

The Writing Task

Write an essay that argues a position on a controversial issue. Take close and fair account of opposing viewpoints and counter-arguments, but remember that your purpose is to state your own position clearly and, if not to change your readers' minds, at least to convince those who disagree with you that they must deal objectively with the arguments you raise.

Invention

Invention is especially important in writing a position paper because there are so many things to consider as you write: how you might define—or redefine—the issue, what other opinions you should discuss and how you should represent them, what reasons and evidence you could offer to support your opinion and in what order, and what tone would be most appropriate for the particular subject and audience. These invention activities will help you to focus your thinking on these writing issues.

CHOOSING A CONTROVERSIAL ISSUE. Most authors of position papers choose issues about which they feel strongly and already know a good deal. If you do not have a specific issue in mind, you might want to consider the issues that appear in the Ideas for Your Own Writing that follow each reading in this chapter. You can discover other possibilities by reading newspapers or newsmagazines.

Make a list of the possibilities you are considering, indicating what you think each issue involves and what position you are presently inclined to take on it. The ideal issue will be one about which you have already formed an opinion; in writing about this issue you will have an opportunity to examine your own point of view critically. Also, your writing task will be easier if you can choose an issue upon which there is a clear division of opinion.

Once you have selected an issue, you may need to do some background research on it, particularly if the issue is one that you have not thought very much about until now. If you think you need more information at this point, go to the library or interview some people. You should not get too caught up in the process of doing research, however, until you are fairly sure of your audience, because knowledge of your readers will influence the kind of information you decide to use in your paper. Remember too that you are planning to write a persuasive essay, not a report of what others think about the issue. You can certainly cite authorities, but the essay should represent your best thinking on the subject, not someone else's.

The Casebook on Civil Disobedience in Chapter 10 is a good source of ideas for a position paper.

ANALYZING YOUR READERS. Most position papers are set up as a debate in which the writer addresses readers who hold the opposing position. You may, however, choose to address your essay to readers who are undecided about the issue. At this stage in your planning, you should try to identify your prospective audience. Write a few sentences profiling your readers. What are their views on the issue? What reasons do they most often give for their opinions? What kinds of backing or evidence do they use to support their opinions? What basic assumptions or values underlie their claims? What are the historical, political, or ideological dimensions to their views? What kinds of personal experiences and beliefs are you likely to have in common with these readers? On what basis might you build a bridge of shared concerns with them? What kinds of arguments might carry weight with them?

STATING YOUR THESIS. Having identified the issue and audience, try stating what you now think will be the claim, or thesis, of your position paper. You will undoubtedly need to refine this statement as you clarify your position and explore your argument, but stating it tentatively here will help focus the rest of your invention.

EXPLORING YOUR REASONS. Now that you have chosen a promising issue and analyzed your prospective readers, you should devote your energies to exploring your own reasons for holding your position. Do this with your readers in mind, setting up a debate between yourself and your readers.

Divide a page in half vertically and list your reasons in the left-hand column and your readers' possible responses to each reason in the right-hand column. You may not know how your readers will respond to every point you make, of course, but you should try to put yourself in their place and decide whether there are any objections they could make or on what grounds they might accept the point. Leave a space of about five lines between each of your reasons. Then use that space to develop the reason and to indicate what kinds of evidence you might use to support it. Planning an argument this way is likely to be messy, particularly if you move frequently from one column to the other. Although it may seem chaotic, this can be a very productive invention activity. These notes may serve later as a rough outline after you have decided which are your best arguments and in what order you should arrange them.

DEVELOPING BACKING FOR YOUR BEST REASONS. This activity is really an extension of the previous one. It involves reviewing your notes and selecting the reasons you now think are the most promising. These should be reasons that might actually persuade your readers, reasons that you believe in and that you can support with specific backing. Take each reason in turn and try to develop it as fully as you can. You may need more information, and you can either locate it now or make a note to do so later. The important thing is to clarify for yourself how this particular reason justifies your position. In addition, you should identify the kinds of backing you can use to support each reason. Do you have examples? facts? statistics? authorities you can quote? anecdotes you can relate? Instead of simply listing possible backing, try actually drafting a few sentences.

For each of your reasons, you should also acknowledge any strong objections readers might make. If you can accommodate any of these objections by making concessions or qualifying your position, it's a good idea to do so. If not, rehearse your refutation, explaining why you must disagree.

RESTATING YOUR CLAIM. Look back at your earlier tentative thesis statement and revise it to conform with what you have discovered in exploring your argument. You may only need to make minor revisions to signal how you have modified or qualified your position. Or you may need to rewrite the entire statement to account for your new understanding of the issue.

Drafting

After a thoughtful and thorough invention process, you are ready to set goals for drafting, plan your organization, and consider how to begin the essay and avoid logical fallacies.

SETTING GOALS. Before writing, reorient yourself by setting goals that reflect your purpose and audience. Ask yourself specifically what you want to accomplish by writing to these readers about this issue. Are you chiefly interested in presenting your opinion, or do you want to change your readers' minds? If your goal is the latter, consider whether you are being realistic. Remember that some issues—capital punishment, for example—are so deeply rooted in values and beliefs that it is very hard to get people to change their minds. The most you can hope to do is either present your own best argument or get readers to reexamine the issue from a more objective point of view.

Consider how familiar your readers already are with the issue. If you think it is new to them, you will need to help them understand why it is important. Because Solomon assumes that his readers have not thought deeply about cultural literacy, he tries to demonstrate its importance. If, on the other hand, you assume readers are familiar with the issue, you might try to get them to see it in a new light. It is usually safe to assume that your readers have not explored the issue as thoroughly as you, and you will therefore need to identify the main issues at stake and define the key terms.

Consider also which of your readers' values and assumptions correspond to your own. If, for example, you are writing about something your readers are likely to fear or detest, acknowledge their feelings as legitimate and show that you share their concerns.

Finally, think of the kinds of arguments that would be most likely to convince your particular readers on this issue. Will they respect the judgment of authorities or expert witnesses on this issue, as Solomon seems to think? Do they need facts and statistics to better understand the dimensions of the issue, as Hoekema and Kuhn apparently assume? Will they be especially responsive to arguments based on principle, as Kirby believes?

PLANNING YOUR ORGANIZATION. With these goals in mind, reread the invention writing you did under the exploring and developing your reasons sections. They should give you the perspective to order your reasons and outline your argument. Writers often begin and end with the strongest reasons, putting weaker ones in the middle. This organization gives the best reasons the greatest emphasis. Hoekema more or less follows this pattern. Another common plan is to begin with a definition like Solomon does, letting the definition carry most of the argument's weight. Menocal organizes her essay around a point-by-point refutation of an opponent's argument, while Hoekema systematically examines the arguments raised by both sides.

BEGINNING. The opening of a position paper sets the tone, identifies the issue, and usually establishes the writer's position. In deciding how to begin, think again about your readers and their attitudes toward the issue. Solomon, for example, must get over two obstacles—his readers' ignorance of the liberal arts and their pejorative associations with the word *culture*. Menocal appeals to her "cultured" readers' familiarity with the poet Petrarch before launching into her argument about rock music.

AVOIDING LOGICAL FALLACIES. Arguing about controversial issues demands probably the most difficult kind of reasoning because emotions run high and issues tend to be extremely complex. To avoid making errors in your argument, ask yourself the following questions as you plan and draft your essay:

Am I making *sweeping generalizations* (for instance, assuming that if killing is morally wrong, then state-licensed murder must also be wrong)?

Am I committing an *ad hominem attack* on my opponents (criticizing their intelligence or motives rather than their arguments)?

Am I *oversimplifying* the issue (making a complex issue seem simple)?

Am I guilty of *either-or reasoning* (assuming that there are only two positions on an issue, the right one and theirs)?

Am I building a *straw man* (representing the opposition's argument unfairly so that I can knock it down easily)?

Revising

Even the most experienced writers revise their drafts. No amount of invention and planning can ensure that a draft will be complete and perfectly organized. In fact, as you draft you are likely to discover new and important points to make. You may also encounter unanticipated problems that require radical rethinking or restructuring of your essay. This is particularly true for a complicated essay like a position paper.

Begin your revision by reading your draft critically, using the questions for analyzing basic features at the beginning of this chapter. In addition, try to get someone else to read your draft critically. Following are suggestions for revising to strengthen your argument and to improve readability.

REVISING TO STRENGTHEN YOUR ARGUMENT. As you revise, keep in mind your purpose: to persuade readers that your opinion is valid and reasonable. Consider how well you have managed your tone and accommodated your readers. Look for places where you might modify your language or provide more information. If you can make any concessions without renouncing your position, try to do so. Also, examine closely how you represent and react to opposing opinions. Are you fair and objective? Could you explain your objections any better? Can you emphasize the areas where you and your readers agree rather than where you disagree? How might this strategy strengthen your argument?

Focus on your reasons and supporting evidence. Is each reason developed sufficiently, or can you add more detail for your readers? Ask yourself why your readers should be convinced by each reason. Then consider how you might bring the point home more dramatically. Study the evidence you provide to see whether it is as convincing as you had hoped. How else might you support your point? What other examples or facts could you mention? What authorities could you cite?

Look again at your definition of the issue, and try to modify this definition so as to win readers to your side. Remember that defining the issue is part of your argument, and that it establishes the way the argument might be resolved. Does your definition polarize opinion unnecessarily? Could it be less extreme and more conciliatory?

REVISING TO IMPROVE READABILITY. Begin by outlining your draft to determine whether your argument is coherent and well organized. Consider inserting forecasting statements, summaries, or transitions to make the organization clearer. Look for any unclear writing. Be especially critical of abstract and indirect language. Long, convoluted sentences do not impress readers; they depress and confuse them. Finally, proofread your draft carefully, and correct any errors in usage, punctuation, and spelling.

CHAPTER TEN

Casebook on
Civil Disobedience

Pro-democracy student protesters lead nearly three months of demonstrations, marches, hunger strikes, boycotts, and sit-ins at Tiananmen Square in Beijing, China. Tens, sometimes hundreds of thousands of citizens demonstrate their support for the students. Early morning on June 4, 1989, troops fire on the demonstrators, killing hundreds, perhaps thousands.

Two hundred and fifty pro-life protesters are arrested June 10, 1989, for blocking the entrance to a Los Angeles Medical Clinic at which legal abortions are performed.

After trying for two years to get the city to tear down abandoned and decaying houses that had become a haven for prostitution and drug trafficking, residents of Chatham Street in Detroit demolished a clapboard house themselves and were arrested for breaking at least ten laws.

As these summaries of recent news reports indicate, civil disobedience is not simply a thing of the past. You may associate civil disobedience with the civil rights movement and anti–Vietnam War protests of the sixties and early seventies, or with acts of civil disobedience over abortion, apartheid, animal rights, environmental issues, and political freedom in the United States and throughout the world in the 1980s.

This chapter brings together historical documents with recent writing on issues of civil disobedience. It divides into three sections: an introduction featuring excerpts from the great tradition of writing on civil disobedience; a selection of longer pieces, including an abridgment of Sophocles' tragedy *Antigone* and various American essays from the nineteenth and twentieth centuries; and a concluding debate on a recent instance of civil disobedience—flag burning.

Studying this chapter will exercise your skills as a critical reader. You will find opportunity to use many of the critical reading strategies you have practiced in preceding chapters; you will find examples of some of the genres you have been reading and writing; and, upon your instructor's request, you will be given the opportunity to join in the conversation by writing an essay of your own on some aspect of civil disobedience. Among the kinds of essays you may be asked to write are these:

- an autobiographical piece about your own experience with an act of civil disobedience
- a reflective essay occasioned by a particular reminiscence, reading, or conversation about the topic
- an observational essay reporting what you witnessed
- an explanation, possibly based on analysis of a particular document on civil disobedience or on research into the history of civil disobedience in a particular country or period
- an evaluation of a film, television program, or piece of writing on some aspect of civil disobedience
- an essay speculating about the causes or effects of an actual or a hypothetical act of civil disobedience
- a proposal to resolve some problem which engendered acts of civil disobedience
- a position paper arguing your own view on an issue related to civil disobedience

The tradition of writing on civil disobedience dates back to the ancient Greeks. It was addressed by Sophocles in *Antigone*, by Plato in the *Apology* and *Crito*, by the seventeenth-century philosophers Thomas Hobbes in *Leviathan* and John Locke in *The Second Treatise on Civil Government*, by Thomas Jefferson in the Declaration of Independence, and by the Indian political and spiritual leader Mohandas Gandhi in *Non-Violent Resistance*.

The discussion centers on the question of whether disobeying the law can be justified. Socrates, who was accused of corrupting youth through his teachings, declares in the *Apology* that to conform to the wishes of the state "would be a disobedience to God." This justification, generally referred to as the "higher-law argument," has become the clarion call of civil disobedients. In response, opponents usually invoke the argument developed by Hobbes that because social order is founded on a social contract, everyone must follow the laws of the state. The reasoning goes that if each individual followed the dictates of conscience, anarchy would result.

Socrates was unconventional in many ways: He renounced material possessions and social position, taught through conversation, and took provocative positions to generate discussion and lead students to examine their own assumptions and prejudices. In 399 B.C., an Athenian court tried and convicted Socrates, condemning him to death. His crime was corrupting the city's youth through his teaching of philosophy and undermining their faith in the gods recognized by the state (Zeus, Athena, Apollo, for example).

We include here two excerpts written by Socrates' student, the philosopher Plato. The first comes from the *Apology*, which reconstructs Socrates' defense at his trial. Here, Socrates sets forth his position on civil disobedience.

> If now, when, as I conceive and imagine God orders me to fulfill the philosopher's mission of searching into myself and other men, I were to desert my post through fear of death, or any other fear, that would indeed be strange, and I might justly be arraigned in court for denying the existence of the gods. . . . I do know that injustice and disobedience to a better, whether God or man, is evil and dishonorable, and I will never fear or avoid a possible good rather than a certain evil. And therefore if you say to me, Socrates, you shall be let off, but upon one condition, that you are not to enquire and speculate in this way any more, and that if you are caught doing so again you shall die; if this was the condition on which you let me go, I should reply: Men of Athens, I honor and love you, but I shall obey God rather than you, and while I have life and strength I shall never cease from the practice and teaching of philosophy . . . [for] the unexamined life is not worth living.*

The second excerpt comes from one of Plato's later dialogues, *Crito*, which takes place after the trial when Socrates is in prison awaiting execution. His friend Crito visits him in prison and urges him to escape. Socrates refuses. In this passage, Socrates reveals why he feels he must accept his punishment:

> *Soc.* Then consider the matter in this way:—Imagine that I am about to play truant (you may call the proceeding by any name which you like), and the laws and the government come and interrogate me: "Tell us, Socrates," they say; "what

---

*Translated by Benjamin Jowett.

are you about? are you not going by an act of yours to overturn us—the laws, and the whole state, as far as in you lies? Do you imagine that a state can subsist and not be overthrown, in which the decisions of law have no power, but are set aside and trampled upon by individuals?" What will be our answer, Crito, to these and the like words? Any one, and especially a rhetorician, will have a good deal to say on behalf of the law which requires a sentence to be carried out. He will argue that this law should not be set aside; and shall we reply, "Yes; but the state has injured us and given an unjust sentence." Suppose I say that?

Cr. Very good, Socrates.

Soc. "And was that our agreement with you?" the law would answer; "or were you to abide by the sentence of the state?" And if I were to express my astonishment at their words, the law would probably add: "Answer, Socrates, instead of opening your eyes—you are in the habit of asking and answering questions." . . . Then the laws will say, "Consider, Socrates, if we are speaking truly that in your present attempt you are going to do us an injury. For, having brought you into the world, and nurtured and educated you, and given you and every other citizen a share in every good which we had to give, we further proclaim to any Athenian by the liberty which we allow him, that if he does not like us when he has become of age and has seen the ways of the city, and made our acquaintance, he may go where he pleases and take his goods with him. None of our laws will forbid him or interfere with him. Any one who does not like us and the city, and who wants to emigrate to a colony or to any other city, may go where he likes, retaining his property. But he who has experience of the manner in which we order justice and administer the state, and still remains, has entered into an implied contract that he will do as we command him."†

This idea that an "implied contract" exists between the individual and the state is central to the argument over civil disobedience. Seventeenth-century political philosophers Thomas Hobbes (1588–1679) and John Locke (1632–1704) both accept the idea of a social contract but differ on the question of whether the individual is bound to obey the state in matters of conscience.

Hobbes argues in *Leviathan* (1651) that without absolute obedience to the state, people would be at one another's throats because, in his view, people are naturally selfish—"solitary, poor, nasty, brutish." While this selfishness impels people to pursue pleasure, he noted that it also leads them to try to avoid pain. They are willing, therefore, to enter into a contract that gives absolute power to the state in return for its protection:

The generation of a commonwealth. The definition of a commonwealth. The only way to erect such a common power, as may be able to defend them from the invasion of foreigners, and the injuries of one another, and thereby to secure them in such sort, as that by their own industry, and by the fruits of the earth, they may

---

†Translated by Benjamin Jowett.

nourish themselves and live contentedly; is, to confer all their power and strength upon one man, or upon one assembly of men, that may reduce all their wills, by plurality of voices, unto one will: which is as much as to say, to appoint one man, or assembly of men, to bear their person; and every one to own, and acknowledge himself to be author of whatsoever he that so beareth their person, shall act, or cause to be acted, in those things which concern the common peace and safety; and therein to submit their wills, every one to his will, and their judgments, to his judgment. This is more than consent, or concord; it is a real unity of them all, in one and the same person, made by covenant of every man with every man, in such manner, as if every man should say to every man, *I authorize and give up my right of governing myself, to this man, or to this assembly of men, on this condition, that thou give up thy right to him, and authorize all his actions in like manner.* This done, the multitude so united in one person, is called a COMMONWEALTH, in Latin CIVITAS. This is the generation of that great LEVIATHAN, or rather, to speak more reverently, of that *mortal god*, to which we owe under the *immortal God*, our peace and defence. For by this authority, given him by every particular man in the commonwealth, he hath the use of so much power and strength conferred on him, that by terror thereof, he is enabled to form the wills of them all, to peace at home, and mutual aid against their enemies abroad. And in him consisteth the essence of the commonwealth; which, to define it, is *one person, of whose acts a great multitude, by mutual covenants one with another, have made themselves every one the author, to the end he may use the strength and means of them all; as he shall think expedient, for their peace and common defence.*

•   •   •

. . . *No man can without injustice protest against the institution of the sovereign declared by the major part.* Thirdly, because the major part hath by consenting voices declared a sovereign; he that dissented must now consent with the rest; that is, be contented to avow all the actions he shall do, or else justly be destroyed by the rest. For if he voluntarily entered into the congregation of them that were assembled, he sufficiently declared thereby his will, and therefore tacitly covenanted, to stand to what the major part should ordain: and therefore if he refuse to stand thereto, or make protestation against any of their decrees, he does contrary to his covenant, and therefore unjustly. And whether he be of the congregation, or not; and whether his consent be asked, or not, he must either submit to their decrees, or be left in the condition of war he was in before; wherein he might without injustice be destroyed by any man whatsoever.

John Locke's view of the natural condition of human beings differs markedly from Hobbes's. Instead of being driven by selfish desires and thus continuously warring with one another, as Hobbes thought, people are governed by reason, according to Locke. Reason teaches them that "no one ought to harm another in his life, health, liberty, or possessions." The people establish the state to protect their rights and authorize it to make and enforce laws. But if the state ever violates their rights, Locke believed, the people have the right to refuse their obedience to it.

Here are two brief excerpts from Locke's *Second Treatise on Civil Government* (1683):

Men being, as has been said, by Nature, all free, equal and independent, no one can be put out of this Estate, and subjected to the Political Power of another, without his own *Consent*. The only way whereby any one devests himself of his Natural Liberty, and *puts on the bonds of Civil Society* is by agreeing with other Men to joyn and unite into a Community, for their comfortable, safe, and peaceable living one amongst another, in a secure Enjoyment of their Properties, and a greater Security against any that are not of it. This any number of Men may do, because it injures not the Freedom of the rest; they are left as they were in the Liberty of the State of Nature. When any number of Men have so *consented to make one Community* or Government, they are thereby presently incorporated, and make *one Body Politick*, wherein the *Majority* have a Right to act and conclude the rest.

For when any number of Men have, by the consent of every individual, made a *Community*, they have thereby made that *Community* one Body, with a Power to Act as one Body, which is only by the will and determination of the *majority*. For that which acts any Community, being only the consent of the individuals of it, and it being necessary to that which is one body to move one way; it is necessary the Body should move that way whither the greater force carries it, which is the *consent of the majority*: or else it is impossible it should act or continue one Body, *one Community*, which the consent of every individual that united into it, agreed that it should; and so every one is bound by that consent to be concluded by the *majority*.

• • •

The Reason why Men enter into Society, is the preservation of their Property; and the end why they chuse and authorize a Legislative, is, that there may be Laws made, and Rules set as Guards and Fences to the Properties of all the Members of the Society, to limit the Power, and moderate the Dominion of every Part and Member of the Society. For since it can never be supposed to be the Will of the Society, that the Legislative should have a Power to destroy that, which every one designs to secure, by entering into Society, and for which the People submitted themselves to the Legislators of their own making; whenever the *Legislators endeavour to take away, and destroy the Property of the People*, or to reduce them to Slavery under Arbitrary Power, they put themselves into a state of War with the People, who are thereupon absolved from any farther Obedience, and are left to the common Refuge, which God hath provided for all Men, against Force and Violence.

But 'twill be said, this *Hypothesis* lays a *ferment* for frequent *Rebellion*. To which I Answer,

First, No more than any other *Hypothesis*. For when the *People* are made *miserable*, and find themselves *exposed to the ill usage of Arbitrary Power*, cry up their Governours, as much as you will for Sons of *Jupiter*, let them be Sacred and Divine, descended or authoriz'd from Heaven; give them out for whom or what you please, the same will happen, *The People generally ill treated*, and contrary to right, will be ready upon any occasion to ease themselves of a burden that sits heavy upon them. They will wish and seek for the opportunity, which, in the change, weakness, and accidents of humane affairs, seldom delays long to offer it self.

The American Revolution was one of history's most dramatic acts of civil disobedience. Thomas Jefferson wrote the Declaration of Independence to justify the actions of the American colonists. Notice, as you read, echoes of John Locke's argument and refutation of Hobbes's.

When in the Course of human events, it becomes necessary for one people to dissolve the political bands which have connected them with another, and to assume among the Powers of the earth, the separate and equal station to which the Laws of Nature and of Nature's God entitle them, a decent respect to the opinions of mankind requires that they should declare the causes which impel them to the separation.

We hold these truths to be self-evident, that all men are created equal, that they are endowed by their Creator with certain unalienable Rights, that among these are Life, Liberty and the pursuit of Happiness. That to secure these rights, Governments are instituted among Men, deriving their just powers from the consent of the governed. That whenever any Form of Government becomes destructive of these ends, it is the Right of the People to alter or to abolish it, and to institute new Government, laying its foundation on such principles and organizing its powers in such form, as to them shall seem most likely to effect their Safety and Happiness. Prudence, indeed, will dictate that Governments long established should not be changed for light and transient causes; and accordingly all experience hath shown, that mankind are more disposed to suffer, while evils are sufferable, than to right themselves by abolishing the forms to which they are accustomed. But when a long train of abuses and usurpations, pursuing invariably the same Object evinces a design to reduce them under absolute Despotism, it is their right, it is their duty, to throw off such Government, and to provide new Guards for their future security.—Such has been the patient sufferance of these Colonies; and such is now the necessity which constrains them to alter their former Systems of Government. The history of the present King of Great Britain is a history of repeated injuries and usurpations, all having in direct object the establishment of an absolute Tyranny over these States. To prove this, let Facts be submitted to a candid world.

He has refused his Assent to Laws, the most wholesome and necessary for the public good.

He has forbidden his Governors to pass Laws of immediate and pressing importance, unless suspended in their operation till his Assent should be obtained; and when so suspended, he has utterly neglected to attend to them.

He has refused to pass other Laws for the accommodation of large districts of people, unless those people would relinquish the right of Representation in the Legislature, a right inestimable to them and formidable to tyrants only.

He has called together legislative bodies at places unusual, uncomfortable, and distant from the depository of their public Records, for the sole purpose of fatiguing them into compliance with his measures.

He has dissolved Representative Houses repeatedly for opposing with manly firmness his invasions on the rights of the people.

He has refused for a long time, after such dissolutions, to cause others to be elected; whereby the Legislative Powers, incapable of Annihilation, have returned to the People at large for their exercise; the State remaining in the mean time exposed to all the dangers of invasion from without, and convulsions within.

He has endeavoured to prevent the population of these States; for that purpose obstructing the Laws of Naturalization of Foreigners; refusing to pass others to encourage their migration higher, and raising the conditions of new Appropriations of Lands.

He has obstructed the Administration of Justice, by refusing his Assent to Laws for establishing Judiciary powers.

He has made Judges dependent on his Will alone, for the tenure of their offices, and the amount and payment of their salaries.

He has erected a multitude of New Offices, and sent hither swarms of Officers to harass our People, and eat out their substance.

He has kept among us in times of peace, Standing Armies without the Consent of our legislature.

He has affected to render the Military independent of and superior to the Civil power.

He has combined with others to subject us to a jurisdiction foreign to our constitution, and unacknowledged by our laws; giving his Assent to their acts of pretended Legislation.

For quartering large bodies of armed troops among us:

For protecting them, by a mock Trial, from punishment for any Murders which they should commit on the inhabitants of these States:

For cutting off our Trade with all parts of the world.

For imposing taxes on us without our Consent:

For depriving us in many cases, of the benefits of Trial by Jury:

For transporting us beyond Seas to be tried for pretended offences:

For abolishing the free System of English Laws in a neighbouring Province, establishing therein an Arbitrary government, and enlarging its Boundaries so as to render it at once an example and fit instrument for introducing the same absolute rule into these Colonies.

For taking away our Charters, abolishing our most valuable Laws, and altering fundamentally the Forms of our Governments:

For suspending our own Legislature, and declaring themselves invested with Power to legislate for us in all cases whatsoever.

He has abdicated Government here, by declaring us out of his Protection and waging War against us.

He has plundered our seas, ravaged our Coasts, burnt our towns, and destroyed the lives of our people.

He is at this time transporting large Armies of foreign Mercenaries to compleat the works of death, desolation and tyranny, already begun with circumstances of Cruelty & perfidy scarcely paralleled in the most barbarous ages, and totally unworthy the Head of a civilized nation.

He has constrained our fellow Citizens taken Captive on the high Seas to bear Arms against their Country, to become the executioners of their friends and Brethren, or to fall themselves by their Hands.

He has excited domestic insurrections amongst us, and has endeavoured to bring on the inhabitants of our frontiers, the merciless Indian Savages, whose known rule of warfare, is an undistinguished destruction of all ages, sexes and conditions.

In every stage of these Oppressions We have Petitioned for Redress in the most humble terms: Our repeated Petitions have been answered only by repeated injury. A Prince, whose character is thus marked by every act which may define a Tyrant, is unfit to be the ruler of a free People.

Nor have We been wanting in attention to our British brethren. We have warned them from time to time of attempts by their legislature to extend an unwarrantable jurisdiction over us. We have reminded them of the circumstances of our emigration and settlement here. We have appealed to their native justice and magnanimity, and we have conjured them by the ties of our common kindred to disavow these usurpations, which, would inevitably interrupt our connections and correspondence. They too have been deaf to the voice of justice and of consanguinity. We must, therefore, acquiesce in the necessity, which denounces our Separation, and hold them, as we hold the rest of mankind, Enemies in War, in Peace Friends.

We, therefore, the Representatives of the United States of America, in General Congress, Assembled, appealing to the Supreme Judge of the world for the rectitude of our intentions, do, in the Name, and by Authority of the good People of these Colonies, solemnly publish and declare, That these United Colonies are, and of Right ought to be Free and Independent States; that they are Absolved from all Allegiance to the British Crown, and that all political connection between them and the State of Great Britain, is and ought to be totally dissolved; and that as Free and Independent States, they have full Power to levy War, conclude Peace, contract Alliances, establish Commerce, and to do all other Acts and Things which Independent States may of right do. And for the support of this Declaration, with a firm reliance on the protection of divine Providence, we mutually pledge to each other our Lives, our Fortunes and our sacred Honor.

This introduction concludes with a brief passage that draws a distinction between criminal disobedience and civil disobedience. It was written by Mohandas Gandhi, the Indian spiritual and political leader who led his nation to independence. In *Non-Violent Resistance* (Satyagraha), Gandhi set forth the principles and tactics of modern civil disobedience.

I wish I could persuade everybody that civil disobedience is the inherent right of a citizen. He dare not give it up without ceasing to be a man. Civil disobedience is never followed by anarchy. Criminal disobedience can lead to it. Every State puts down criminal disobedience by force. It perishes, if it does not. But to put down civil disobedience is to attempt to imprison conscience. Civil disobedience can only lead to strength and purity. A civil resister never uses arms and hence he is harmless to a State that is at all willing to listen to the voice of public opinion. He is dangerous for an autocratic State, for he brings about its fall by engaging public opinion upon the matter for which he resists the State. Civil disobedience therefore becomes a sacred duty when the State has become lawless, or which is the same thing, corrupt. And a citizen that barters with such a State shares its corruption or lawlessness.

It is therefore possible to question the wisdom of applying civil disobedience in respect of a particular act or law; it is possible to advise delay and caution. But the right itself cannot be allowed to be questioned. It is a birthright that cannot be surrendered without surrender of one's self-respect.

Sophocles

Sophocles (c. 496–406 B.C.), most famous of the tragedians from the golden age of ancient Greek drama, is survived by seven plays, including *Oedipus the King*, *Electra*, and *Antigone*—all of which continue to excite and stimulate audiences almost 2500 years after they were written. Sophocles' plays center on issues of human responsibility and on individuals whose tragic fates are determined by the decisions that result from their own most basic traits of character.

Antigone

Set in Thebes, *Antigone* relates the legendary story of the children of the dead king Oedipus—Antigone, her sister Ismene, and her brothers Eteocles and Polyneices—and their uncle Creon, brother-in-law to Oedipus. After Oedipus' demise, Eteocles and Polyneices have struggled to assume his power, finally killing each other in battle. When Creon, who had sided with Eteocles, succeeds to the throne, he declares Polyneices a traitor and issues an edict forbidding his burial. Antigone, who is to marry Creon's son Haimon, insists on defying Creon's order, even though she knows the penalty will be death.

The following version of the play is an abridgment of the translation by Dudley Fitts and Robert Fitzgerald. We have deleted some dialogue, several entire scenes, and the poetic choral odes in order to focus this reading on the debate regarding civil disobedience that is at the heart of the play.

Scene: *Before the palace of Creon, King of Thebes. A central double door, and two lateral doors. A platform extends the length of the façade, and from this platform three steps lead down into the "orchestra," or chorus-ground.*
Time: *Dawn of the day after the repulse of the Argive army from the assault on Thebes.*

Antigone and Ismene enter from the central door of the Palace.

Antigone. Listen, Ismene:
Creon buried our brother Eteocles
With military honors, gave him a soldier's funeral,
And it was right that he should; but Polyneices,
Who fought as bravely and died as miserably,—
They say that Creon has sworn
No one shall bury him, no one mourn for him,
But his body must lie in the fields, a sweet treasure

For carrion birds to find as they search for food.
That is what they say, and our good Creon is coming here   10
To announce it publicly; and the penalty—
Stoning to death in the public square! There it is,
And now you can prove what you are:
A true sister, or a traitor to your family.
Ismene. Antigone, you are mad! What could I possibly do?
Antigone. You must decide whether you will help me or not.
Ismene. I do not understand you. Help you in what?
Antigone. Ismene, I am going to bury him. Will you come?
Ismene. Bury him! You have just said the new law forbids it.
Antigone. He is my brother. And he is your brother, too.   20
Ismene. But think of the danger! Think what Creon will do!
Antigone. Creon is not strong enough to stand in my way.
Ismene. Ah sister!

 The law is strong, we must give in to the law
 In this thing, and in worse. I beg the Dead
 To forgive me, but I am helpless: I must yield
 To those in authority. And I think it is dangerous business
 To be always meddling.
Antigone.   If that is what you think,
 I should not want you, even if you asked to come.   30
 You have made your choice, you can be what you want to be.
 But I will bury him; and if I must die,
 I say that this crime is holy: I shall lie down
 With him in death, and I shall be as dear
 To him as he to me.
     It is the dead,
 Not the living, who make the longest demands:
 We die for ever . . .
     You may do as you like,
 Since apparently the laws of the gods mean nothing to you.   40
Ismene. They mean a great deal to me; but I have no strength
 To break laws that were made for the public good.
Antigone. That must be your excuse, I suppose. But as for me,
 I will bury the brother I love.
Ismene.   Antigone,
 I am so afraid for you!
Antigone. Go away, Ismene:
 I shall be hating you soon, and the dead will too,
 For your words are hateful. Leave me my foolish plan:
 I am not afraid of the danger; if it means death,   50
 It will not be the worst of deaths—death without honor.

Ismene. Go then, if you feel that you must.
  You are unwise,
  But a loyal friend indeed to those who love you.
  [*Exit into the Palace. Antigone goes off.*]

. . . .

Enter Creon from the Palace. He addresses the Chorus from the top step.

Creon. Gentlemen: I have the honor to inform you that our Ship of
State, which recent storms have threatened to destroy, has come safely
to harbor at last, guided by the merciful wisdom of Heaven. I have
summoned you here this morning because I know that I can depend
upon you: your devotion to King Laïos was absolute; you never
hesitated in your duty to our late ruler Oedipus; and when Oedipus   60
died, your loyalty was transferred to his children. Unfortunately, as
you know, his two sons, the princes Eteocles and Polyneices, have
killed each other in battle; and I, as the next in blood, have succeeded
to the full power of the throne.
    I am aware, of course, that no Ruler can expect complete loyalty
from his subjects until he has been tested in office. Nevertheless, I say
to you at the very outset that I have nothing but contempt for the kind
of Governor who is afraid, for whatever reason, to follow the course
that he knows is best for the State; and as for the man who sets private
friendship above the public welfare,—I have no use for him, either. I   70
call God to witness that if I saw my country headed for ruin, I should
not be afraid to speak out plainly; and I need hardly remind you that I
would never have any dealings with an enemy of the people. No one
values friendship more highly than I; but we must remember that
friends made at the risk of wrecking our Ship are not real friends at all.
    These are my principles, at any rate, and that is why I have made
the following decision concerning the sons of Oedipus: Eteocles, who
died as a man should die, fighting for his country, is to be buried with
full military honors, with all the ceremony that is usual when the   80
greatest heroes die; but his brother Polyneices, who broke his exile to
come back with fire and sword against his native city and the shrines
of his fathers' gods, whose one idea was to spill the blood of his blood
and sell his own people into slavery—Polyneices, I say, is to have no
burial: no man is to touch him or say the least prayer for him; he shall
lie on the plain, unburied; and the birds and the scavenging dogs can
do with him whatever they like.
    This is my command, and you can see the wisdom behind it. As
long as I am King, no traitor is going to be honored with the loyal man.

But whoever shows by word and deed that he is on the side of the 90
State,—he shall have my respect while he is living, and my reverence
when he is dead.

Choragos. * If that is your will, Creon son of Menoiceus,
  You have the right to enforce it: we are yours.
Creon. That is my will. Take care that you do your part.
Choragos. We are old men: let the younger ones carry it out.
Creon. I do not mean that: the sentries have been appointed.
Choragos. Then what is it that you would have us do?
Creon. You will give no support to whoever breaks this law.
Choragos. Only a crazy man is in love with death!   100
Creon. And death it is; yet money talks, and the wisest
  Have sometimes been known to count a few coins too many.

Enter Sentry.

Sentry. I'll not say that I'm out of breath from running, King, because
  every time I stopped to think about what I have to tell you, I felt like
  going back. And all the time a voice kept saying, "You fool, don't you
  know you're walking straight into trouble?"; and then another voice:
  "Yes, but if you let somebody else get the news to Creon first, it will be
  even worse than that for you!" . . .

Creon. Come to the point. What have you to say? . . .
Sentry. A dreadful thing . . . I don't know how to put it—   110
Creon. Out with it!
Sentry.   Well, then;
  The dead man—
                    Polyneices—

Pause. The Sentry is overcome, fumbles for words. Creon waits impassively.

                                        out there—
                                                someone,—
  New dust on the slimy flesh!

Pause. No sign from Creon.

  Someone has given it burial that way, and
  Gone . . .

---

*Chorus. [Eds.]

Long pause. Creon finally speaks with deadly control.

Creon. And the man who dared do this? 120
Sentry. I swear I
  Do not know! You must believe me!
Creon [*furiously*]. I swear by God and by the throne of God,
  The man who has done this thing shall pay for it!
  Find that man, bring him here to me, or your death
  Will be the least of your problems.

Exit Sentry.

. . . .

Re-enter Sentry leading Antigone.

Choragos. What does this mean? Surely this captive woman
  Is the Princess, Antigone. Why should she be taken?
Sentry. Here is the one who did it! We caught her
  In the very act of burying him. 130
  Take her, then; question her; judge her as you will.
  I am through with the whole thing now, and glad of it.
Creon. But this is Antigone! Why have you brought her here?
Sentry. She was burying him, I tell you!
Creon [*severely*]. Is this the truth?
Sentry. I saw her with my own eyes. Can I say more?
Creon [*slowly, dangerously*]. And you, Antigone?
  You with your head hanging,—do you confess this thing?
Antigone. I do. I deny nothing.
Creon [*to Sentry*]. You may go. 140

[*Exit Sentry.*]

  [*To Antigone.*] Tell me, tell me briefly:
  Had you heard my proclamation touching this matter?
Antigone. It was public. Could I help hearing it?
Creon. And yet you dared defy the law.
Antigone. I dared.
  It was not God's proclamation. That final Justice
  That rules the world below makes no such laws.
  Your edict, King, was strong,
  But all your strength is weakness itself against
  The immortal unrecorded laws of God. 150

They are not merely now: they were, and shall be,
Operative for ever, beyond man utterly.
I knew I must die, even without your decree:
I am only mortal. And if I must die
Now, before it is my time to die,
Surely this is no hardship: can anyone
Living, as I live, with evil all about me,
Think Death less than a friend? This death of mine
Is of no importance; but if I had left my brother
Lying in death unburied, I should have suffered.   160
Now I do not.
               You smile at me. Ah Creon,
Think me a fool, if you like; but it may well be
That a fool convicts me of folly.

Choragos. Like father, like daughter: both headstrong, deaf to reason!
    She has never learned to yield.

Creon.   She has much to learn.
    The inflexible heart breaks first, the toughest iron
Cracks first, and the wildest horses bend their necks
At the pull of the smallest curb.   170
                  Pride? In a slave?
This girl is guilty of a double insolence,
Breaking the given laws and boasting of it.
Who is the man here,
She or I, if this crime goes unpunished?
Sister's child, or more than sister's child,
Or closer yet in blood—she and her sister
Win bitter death for this!
[*To Servants.*]   Go, some of you,
Arrest Ismene. I accuse her equally.   180
Bring her: you will find her sniffling in the house there.
Her mind's a traitor: crimes kept in the dark
Cry for light, and the guardian brain shudders;
But how much worse than this
Is brazen boasting of barefaced anarchy!

Antigone. Creon, what more do you want than my death?

Creon.   Nothing.
    That gives me everything.

Antigone. Then I beg you: kill me.
    This talking is a great weariness: your words   190
Are distasteful to me, and I am sure that mine
Seem so to you. And yet they should not seem so:

I should have praise and honor for what I have done.
All these men here would praise me
Were their lips not frozen shut with fear of you.
[*Bitterly.*] Ah the good fortune of kings,
Licensed to say and do whatever they please!
Creon. You are alone here in that opinion.
Antigone. No, they are with me.
   But they keep their tongues in leash.   200
Creon. Maybe. But you are guilty, and they are not.
Antigone. There is no guilt in reverence for the dead.
Creon. But Eteocles—was he not your brother too?
Antigone. My brother too.
Creon.   And you insult his memory?
Antigone [*softly*]. The dead man would not say that I insult it.
Creon. He would: for you honor a traitor as much as him.
Antigone. His own brother, traitor or not, and equal in blood.
Creon. He made war on his country.
   Eteocles defended it.   210
Antigone. Nevertheless, there are honors due all the dead.
Creon. But not the same for the wicked as for the just.
Antigone. Ah Creon, Creon.
   Which of us can say what the gods hold wicked?
Creon. An enemy is an enemy, even dead.
Antigone. It is my nature to join in love, not hate.
Creon [*finally losing patience*]. Go join them, then; if you must have
   your love,
   Find it in hell!

Exit Antigone and Guards.

. . . .

Choragos. But here is Haimon, King, the last of all your sons.   220
   Is it grief for Antigone that brings him here,
   And bitterness at being robbed of his bride?

Enter Haimon.

Creon. We shall soon see, and no need of diviners.
                              —Son,
   You have heard my final judgment on that girl:
   Have you come here hating me, or have you come
   With deference and with love, whatever I do?

Haimon. I am your son, father. You are my guide.
　You make things clear for me, and I obey you.
　No marriage means more to me than your continuing wisdom.　　230
Creon. Good. That is the way to behave: subordinate
　Everything else, my son, to your father's will.
　This is what a man prays for, that he may get
　Sons attentive and dutiful in his house,
　Each one hating his father's enemies,
　Honoring his father's friends. But if his sons
　Fail him, if they turn out unprofitably,
　What has he fathered but trouble for himself
　And amusement for the malicious?
　　　　　　　　　　　　So you are right　　240
　Not to lose your head over this woman.
　Your pleasure with her would soon grow cold, Haimon,
　And then you'd have a hellcat in bed and elsewhere.
　Let her find her husband in Hell!
　Of all the people in this city, only she
　Has had contempt for my law and broken it.
　Do you want me to show myself weak before the people?
　Or to break my sworn word? No, and I will not.
　The woman dies.
　I suppose she'll plead "family ties." Well, let her.　　250
　If I permit my own family to rebel,
　How shall I earn the world's obedience?
　Show me the man who keeps his house in hand,
　He's fit for the public authority.
　　　　　　　　　　　　I'll have no dealings
　With law-breakers, critics of the government:
　Whoever is chosen to govern should be obeyed—
　Must be obeyed, in all things, great and small,
　Just and unjust! O Haimon,
　The man who knows how to obey, and that man only,　　260
　Knows how to give commands when the time comes.
　You can depend on him, no matter how fast
　The spears come: he's a good soldier, he'll stick it out.
　Anarchy, anarchy! Show me a greater evil!
　This is why cities tumble and the great houses rain down,
　This is what scatters armies!
　No, no: good lives are made so by discipline.
　We keep the laws then, and the lawmakers,
　And no woman shall seduce us. If we must lose,
　Let's lose to a man, at least! Is a woman stronger than we?　　270

Choragos. Unless time has rusted my wits,
  What you say, King, is said with point and dignity.
Haimon [*boyishly earnest*].   Father.
  Reason is God's crowning gift to man, and you are right
  To warn me against losing mine. I cannot say—
  I hope that I shall never want to say—that you
  Have reasoned badly. Yet there are other men
  Who can reason, too; and their opinions might be helpful.
  You are not in a position to know everything
  That people say or do, or what they feel: 280
  Your temper terrifies them—everyone
  Will tell you only what you like to hear.
  But I, at any rate, can listen; and I have heard them
  Muttering and whispering in the dark about this girl.
  They say no woman has ever, so unreasonably,
  Died so shameful a death for a generous act:
  "She covered her brother's body. Is this indecent?
  "She kept him from dogs and vultures. Is this a crime?
  "Death?—She should have all the honor that we can give her!"
  This is the way they talk out there in the city.   290
  You must believe me:
  Nothing is closer to me than your happiness.
  What could be closer? Must not any son
  Value his father's fortune as his father does his?
  I beg you, do not be unchangeable:
  Do not believe that you alone can be right.
  The man who thinks that,
  The man who maintains that only he has the power
  To reason correctly, the gift to speak, the soul—
  A man like that, when you know him, turns out empty.   300
  It is not reason never to yield to reason!
  In flood time you can see how some trees bend,
  And because they bend, even their twigs are safe,
  While stubborn trees are torn up, roots and all.
  And the same thing happens in sailing:
  Make your sheet fast, never slacken,—and over you go,
  Head over heels and under: and there's your voyage.
  Forget you are angry! Let yourself be moved!
  I know I am young; but please let me say this:
  The ideal condition   310
  Would be, I admit, that men should be right by instinct;
  But since we are all too likely to go astray,
  The reasonable thing is to learn from those who can teach.

Choragos. You will do well to listen to him, King,
  If what he says is sensible. And you, Haimon,
  Must listen to your father.—Both speak well.
Creon. You consider it right for a man of my years and experience
  To go to school to a boy?
Haimon.   It is not right
  If I am wrong. But if I am young, and right,   320
  What does my age matter?
Creon. You think it right to stand up for an anarchist?
Haimon. Not at all. I pay no respect to criminals.
Creon. Then she is not a criminal?
Haimon. The City would deny it, to a man.
Creon. And the City proposes to teach me how to rule?
Haimon. Ah. Who is it that's talking like a boy now?
Creon. My voice is the one voice giving orders in this City!
Haimon. It is no City if it takes orders from one voice.
Creon. The State is the King!   330
Haimon. Yes, if the State is a desert.

Creon. This boy, it seems, has sold out to a woman.
Haimon. If you are a woman: my concern is only for you.
Creon. So? Your "concern"! In a public brawl with your father!
Haimon. How about you, in a public brawl with justice?
Creon. With justice, when all that I do is within my rights?
Haimon. You have no right to trample on God's right.
Creon [*completely out of control*]. Fool, adolescent fool! Taken in by a
  woman!
Haimon. You'll never see me taken in by anything vile.   340
Creon. Every word you say is for her!
Haimon [*quietly, darkly*]. And for you.
  And for me. And for the gods under the earth.
Creon. You'll never marry her while she lives.
Haimon. Then she must die.—But her death will cause another.
Creon. Another?
  Have you lost your senses? Is this an open threat?
Haimon. There is no threat in speaking to emptiness.
Creon. I swear you'll regret this superior tone of yours!
  You are the empty one!   350
Haimon. If you were not my father, I'd say you were perverse.
Creon. You girlstruck fool, don't play at words with me!
Haimon. I am sorry. You prefer silence.
Creon.   Now, by God—!

I swear, by all the gods in heaven above us,
You'll watch it, I swear you shall!
[*To the Servants*]   Bring her out!
Bring the woman out! Let her die before his eyes!
Here, this instant, with her bridegroom beside her!

Haimon. Not here, no; she will not die here, King.   360
   And you will never see my face again.
   Go on raving as long as you've a friend to endure you.

[*Exit Haimon.*]

Choragos.   Gone, gone.
   Creon, a young man in a rage is dangerous!
Creon. Let him do, or dream to do, more than a man can.
   He shall not save these girls from death.
Choragos.   These girls?
   You have sentenced them both?
Creon.   No, you are right.
   I will not kill the one whose hands are clean.   370
Choragos. But Antigone?
Creon [*somberly*].   I will carry her far away
   Out there in the wilderness, and lock her
   Living in a vault of stone. She shall have food,
   As the custom is, to absolve the State of her death.
   And there let her pray to the gods of hell:
   They are her only gods:
   Perhaps they will show her an escape from death,
   Or she may learn, though late,
   That piety shown the dead is piety in vain.   380

. . . .

Antigone enters guarded.

Choragos. . . . Here is Antigone, passing to that chamber
   Where all find sleep at last.

Antigone. Look upon me, friends, and pity me
   Turning back at the night's edge to say
   Goodbye to the sun that shines for me no longer;
   Now sleepy Death
   Summons me down to Acheron, that cold shore:
   There is no bridesong there, nor any music.

Creon interrupts impatiently.

Creon. If dirges and planned lamentations could put off death,
   Men would be singing for ever.   390
   [*To the Servants*]   Take her, go!
   You know your orders: take her to the vault
   And leave her alone there. And if she lives or dies,
   That's her affair, not ours: our hands are clean.
Antigone. O tomb, vaulted bridebed in eternal rock,
   Soon I shall be with my own again
   Where Persephone welcomes the thin ghosts underground:
   And I shall see my father again, and you, mother,
   And dearest Polyneices—
                  dearest indeed   400
   To me, since it was my hand
   That washed him clean and poured the ritual wine:
   And my reward is death before my time!
   And yet, as men's hearts know, I have done no wrong,
   I have not sinned before God. Or if I have,
   I shall know the truth in death. But if the guilt
   Lies upon Creon who judged me, then, I pray,
   May his punishment equal my own.
Choragos.   O passionate heart,
   Unyielding, tormented still by the same winds!   410
Creon. Her guards shall have good cause to regret their delaying.
Antigone. Ah! That voice is like the voice of death!
Creon. I can give you no reason to think you are mistaken.
Antigone. Thebes, and you my fathers' gods,
   And rulers of Thebes, you see me now, the last
   Unhappy daughter of a line of kings,
   Your kings led away to death. You will remember
   What things I suffer, and at what men's hands,
   Because I would not transgress the laws of heaven.
   [*To the Guards, simply*] Come: let us wait no longer.   420

Exit Antigone, guarded, and Creon.

· ·

Enter Messenger.

Messenger. Men of the line of Cadmos, you who live
   Near Amphion's citadel:
              I cannot say

Of any condition of human life "This is fixed,
This is clearly good, or bad." Fate raises up,
And Fate casts down the happy and unhappy alike:
No man can foretell his Fate.
                                        Take the case of Creon:
Creon was happy once, as I count happiness:
Victorious in battle, sole governor of the land,   430
Fortunate father of children nobly born.
And now it has all gone from him! Who can say
That a man is still alive when his life's joy fails?
He is a walking dead man. Grant him rich,
Let him live like a king in his great house:
If his pleasure is gone, I would not give
So much as the shadow of smoke for all he owns.

Choragos. Your words hint at sorrow: what is your news for us?

Messenger. They are dead. The living are guilty of their death.

Choragos. Who is guilty? Who is dead? Speak!   440

Messenger.   Haimon.
    Haimon is dead; and the hand that killed him
    Is his own hand.

Choragos. His father's? or his own?

Messenger. His own, driven mad by the murder his father had
    done. . . .
        . . . We ran
    To the vault where Antigone lay on her couch of stone.
    One of the servants had gone ahead,
    And while he was yet far off he heard a voice   450
    Grieving within the chamber, and he came back
    And told Creon. And as the King went closer,
    The air was full of wailing, the words lost,
    And he begged us to make all haste. "Am I a prophet?"
    He said, weeping, "And must I walk this road,
    "The saddest of all that I have gone before?
    "My son's voice calls me on. Oh quickly, quickly!
    "Look through the crevice there, and tell me
    "If it is Haimon, or some deception of the gods!"
    We obeyed; and in the cavern's farthest corner   460
    We saw her lying:
    She had made a noose of her fine linen veil
    And hanged herself. Haimon lay beside her,
    His arms about her waist, lamenting her,
    His love lost under ground, crying out
    That his father had stolen her away from him.

When Creon saw him the tears rushed to his eyes
And he called to him: "What have you done, child? Speak to me.
"What are you thinking that makes your eyes so strange?
"O my son, my son, I come to you on my knees!"   470
But Haimon spat in his face. He said not a word,
Staring—
          And suddenly drew his sword
And lunged. Creon shrank back, the blade missed; and the boy,
Desperate against himself, drove it half its length
Into his own side, and fell. And as he died
He gathered Antigone close in his arms again,
Choking, his blood bright red on her white cheek.
And now he lies dead with the dead, and she is his
At last, his bride in the houses of the dead.   480

Enter Creon with attendants, bearing Haimon's body.

Choragos. But here is the King himself: oh look at him,
  Bearing his own damnation in his arms.
Creon. Nothing you say can touch me any more.
  My own blind heart has brought me
  From darkness to final darkness. Here you see
  The father murdering, the murdered son—
  And all my civic wisdom!
  Haimon my son, so young, so young to die,
  I was the fool, not you; and you died for me.
Choragos. That is the truth; but you were late in learning it.   490
Creon. This truth is hard to bear. Surely a god
  Has crushed me beneath the hugest weight of heaven,
  And driven me headlong a barbaric way
  To trample out the thing I held most dear.
  The pains that men will take to come to pain!
  Lead me away. I have been rash and foolish. . . .
  I look for comfort; my comfort lies here dead.
  Whatever my hands have touched has come to nothing.
  Fate has brought all my pride to a thought of dust.

*As Creon is being led into the house, the Choragos advances and speaks directly
to the audience.*

Choragos. There is no happiness where there is no wisdom;   500
  No wisdom but in submission to the gods.
  Big words are always punished,
  And proud men in old age learn to be wise.

Henry David Thoreau

Henry David Thoreau (1817–1862) is probably best known for *Walden* (1854), a book that tells of his experience living alone at Walden Pond, in Massachusetts. The book is a work of philosophy as well as literature, in which Thoreau establishes a world view based on release from the burden of material possessions.

Civil Disobedience

An outspoken opponent of slavery, Thoreau was active in a variety of abolitionist efforts. His essay "Civil Disobedience" (1849) was occasioned by a small but symbolic act of civil disobedience Thoreau performed. He refused to pay his taxes to protest the government's pro-slavery policies, particularly the war with Mexico conducted to gain more land in the southwest for the expansion of slavery, and consequently spent a night in jail.

I heartily accept the motto, "That government is best which governs least;" and I should like to see it acted up to more rapidly and systematically. Carried out, it finally amounts to this, which also I believe— "That government is best which governs not at all;" and when men are prepared for it, that will be the kind of government which they will have. Government is at best but an expedient; but most governments are usually, and all governments are sometimes, inexpedient. The objections which have been brought against a standing army, and they are many and weighty, and deserve to prevail, may also at last be brought against a standing government. The standing army is only an arm of the standing government. The government itself, which is only the mode which the people have chosen to execute their will, is equally liable to be abused and perverted before the people can act through it. Witness the present Mexican war, the work of comparatively a few individuals using the standing government as their tool; for, in the outset, the people would not have consented to this measure.

This American government—what is it but a tradition, though a recent one, endeavoring to transmit itself unimpaired to posterity, but each instant losing some of its integrity? It has not the vitality and force of a single living man; for a single man can bend it to his will. It is a sort of wooden gun to the people themselves. But it is not the less necessary for this; for the people must have some complicated machinery or other, and hear its din, to satisfy that idea of government which they have. Governments show thus how successfully men can be imposed on, even impose on themselves, for their own advantage. It is excellent, we must all allow. Yet this government never of itself furthered any enterprise, but by the alacrity with which it got out of its way. *It* does not keep the country free. *It* does not settle the West. *It* does not educate. The character inherent in the American people has done all that has been accomplished; and it would have done somewhat more, if the government had not sometimes got in its way. For government is an expedient by which men would fain succeed in letting one another alone; and, as has been said, when it is most expedient, the governed are most let alone by it. Trade and commerce, if they were not made of india-rubber, would never manage to bounce over the obstacles which legislators are continually putting in their way; and, if one were to judge these men wholly by the effects of their actions and not partly by their intentions, they would deserve to be classed and punished with those mischievous persons who put obstructions on the railroads.

But, to speak practically and as a citizen, unlike those who call themselves no-government men, I ask for, not at once no government, but *at once* a better government. Let every man make known what kind of government would command his respect, and that will be one step toward obtaining it. 3

After all, the practical reason why, when the power is once in the hands of the people, a majority are permitted, and for a long period continue, to rule is not because they are most likely to be in the right, nor because this seems fairest to the minority, but because they are physically the strongest. But a government in which the majority rule in all cases cannot be based on justice, even as far as men understand it. Can there not be a government in which majorities do not virtually decide right and wrong, but conscience?—in which majorities decide only those questions to which the rule of expediency is applicable? Must the citizen ever for a moment, or in the least degree, resign his conscience to the legislator? Why has every man a conscience, then? I think that we should be men first, and subjects afterwards. It is not desirable to cultivate a respect for the law, so much as for the right. The only obligation which I have a right to assume is to do at any time what I think right. It is truly enough said that a corporation has no conscience; but a corporation of conscientious men is a corporation *with* a conscience. Law never made men a whit more just; and, by means of their respect for it, even the well-disposed are daily made the agents of injustice. A common and natural result of an undue respect for law is, that you may see a file of soldiers, colonel, captain, corporal, privates, powder-monkeys, and all, marching 4 in admirable order over hill and dale to the wars, against their wills, ay, against their common sense and consciences, which makes it very steep marching indeed, and produces a palpitation of the heart. They have no doubt that it is a damnable business in which they are concerned; they are all peaceably inclined. Now, what are they? Men at all? or small movable forts and magazines, at the service of some unscrupulous man in power? Visit the Navy-Yard, and behold a marine, such a man as an American government can make, or such as it can make a man with its black arts—a mere shadow and reminiscence of humanity, a man laid out alive and standing, and already, as one may say, buried under arms with funeral accompaniments, though it may be,—

> Not a drum was heard, not a funeral note,
> As his corse to the rampart we hurried;
> Not a soldier discharged his farewell shot
> O'er the grave where our hero was buried.

The mass of men serve the state thus, not as men mainly, but as ⁵ machines, with their bodies. They are the standing army, and the militia, jailers, constables, *posse comitatus*, etc. In most cases there is no free exercise whatever of the judgment or of the moral sense; but they put themselves on a level with wood and earth and stones; and wooden men can perhaps be manufactured that will serve the purpose as well. Such command no more respect than men of straw or a lump of dirt. They have the same sort of worth only as horses and dogs. Yet such as these even are commonly esteemed good citizens. Others—as most legislators, politicians, lawyers, ministers, and office-holders—serve the state chiefly with their heads; and, as they rarely make any moral distinctions, they are as likely to serve the devil, without *intending* it, as God. A very few— as heroes, patriots, martyrs, reformers in the great sense, and *men*—serve the state with their consciences also, and so necessarily resist it for the most part; and they are commonly treated as enemies by it. A wise man will only be useful as a man, and will not submit to be "clay," and "stop a hole to keep the wind away," but leave that office to his dust at least:—

> I am too high-born to be propertied,
> To be a secondary at control,
> Or useful serving-man and instrument
> To any sovereign state throughout the world.

He who gives himself entirely to his fellow-men appears to them useless ⁶ and selfish; but he who gives himself partially to them is pronounced a benefactor and philanthropist.

How does it become a man to behave toward this American govern- ⁷ ment today? I answer, that he cannot without disgrace be associated with it. I cannot for an instant recognize that political organization as *my* government which is the *slave's* government also.

All men recognize the right of revolution; that is, the right to refuse   8 allegiance to, and to resist, the government, when its tyranny or its inefficiency are great and unendurable. But almost all say that such is not the case now. But such was the case, they think, in the Revolution of '75. If one were to tell me that this was a bad government because it taxed certain foreign commodities brought to its ports, it is most probable that I should not make an ado about it, for I can do without them. All machines have their friction; and possibly this does enough good to counterbalance the evil. At any rate, it is a great evil to make a stir about it. But when the friction comes to have its machine, and oppression and robbery are organized, I say, let us not have such a machine any longer. In other words, when a sixth of the population of a nation which has undertaken to be the refuge of liberty are slaves, and a whole country is unjustly overrun and conquered by a foreign army, and subjected to military law, I think that it is not too soon for honest men to rebel and revolutionize. What makes this duty the more urgent is the fact that the country so overrun is not our own, but ours is the invading army.

Paley, a common authority with many on moral questions, in his   9 chapter on the "Duty of Submission to Civil Government," resolves all civil obligation into expediency; and he proceeds to say that "so long as the interest of the whole society requires it, that is, so long as the established government cannot be resisted or changed without public inconveniency, it is the will of God . . . that the established government be obeyed—and no longer. This principle being admitted, the justice of every particular case of resistance is reduced to a computation of the quantity of the danger and grievance on the one side, and of the probability and expense of redressing it on the other." Of this, he says, every man shall judge for himself. But Paley appears never to have contemplated those cases to which the rule of expediency does not apply, in which a people, as well as an individual, must do justice, cost what it may. If I have unjustly wrested a plank from a drowning man, I must restore it to him though I drown myself. This, according to Paley, would be inconvenient. But he that would save his life, in such a case, shall lose it. This people must cease to hold slaves, and to make war on Mexico, though it cost them their existence as a people.

In their practice, nations agree with Paley; but does any one think that   10 Massachusetts does exactly what is right at the present crisis?

A drab of state, a cloth-o'-silver slut,
To have her train borne up, and her soul trail in the dirt.

Practically speaking, the opponents to a reform in Massachusetts are not a hundred thousand politicians at the South, but a hundred thousand merchants and farmers here, who are more interested in commerce and agriculture than they are in humanity, and are not prepared to do justice to the slave and to Mexico, *cost what it may.* I quarrel not with far-off foes, but with those who, near at home, cooperate with, and do the bidding of, those far away, and without whom the latter would be harmless. We are accustomed to say, that the mass of men are unprepared; but improvement is slow, because the few are not materially wiser or better than the many. It is not so important that many should be as good as you, as that there be some absolute goodness somewhere; for that will leaven the whole lump. There are thousands who are *in opinion* opposed to slavery and to the war, who yet in effect do nothing to put an end to them; who, esteeming themselves children of Washington and Franklin, sit down with their hands in their pockets, and say that they know not what to do, and do nothing; who even postpone the question of freedom to the question of free trade, and quietly read the prices-current along with the latest advices from Mexico, after dinner, and, it may be, fall asleep over them both. What is the price-current of an honest man and patriot today? They hesitate, and they regret, and sometimes they petition; but they do nothing in earnest and with effect. They will wait, well disposed, for others to remedy the evil, that they may no longer have it to regret. At most, they give only a cheap vote, and a feeble countenance and God-speed, to the right, as it goes by them. There are nine hundred and ninety-nine patrons of virtue to one virtuous man. But it is easier to deal with the real possessor of a thing than with the temporary guardian of it.

All voting is a sort of gaming, like checkers or backgammon, with a slight moral tinge to it, a playing with right and wrong, with moral questions; and betting naturally accompanies it. The character of the voters is not staked. I cast my vote, perchance, as I think right; but I am not vitally concerned that that right should prevail. I am willing to leave it to the majority. Its obligation, therefore, never exceeds that of expediency. Even voting *for the right* is *doing* nothing for it. It is only expressing to men feebly your desire that it should prevail. A wise man will not leave the right to the mercy of chance, nor wish it to prevail through the power of the majority. There is but little virtue in the action of masses of men. When the majority shall at length vote for the abolition of slavery, it will be because they are indifferent to slavery, or because there is but little slavery left to be abolished by their vote. *They* will then be the only slaves. Only *his* vote can hasten the abolition of slavery who asserts his own freedom by his vote.

I hear of a convention to be held at Baltimore, or elsewhere, for the   12
selection of a candidate for the Presidency, made up chiefly of editors,
and men who are politicians by profession; but I think, what is it to any
independent, intelligent, and respectable man what decision they may
come to? Shall we not have the advantage of his wisdom and honesty,
nevertheless? Can we not count upon some independent votes? Are
there not many individuals in the country who do not attend conventions? But no: I find that the respectable man, so called, has immediately
drifted from his position, and despairs of his country, when his country
has more reason to despair of him. He forthwith adopts one of the
candidates thus selected as the only *available* one, thus proving that he is
himself *available* for any purposes of the demagogue. His vote is of no
more worth than that of any unprincipled foreigner or hireling native,
who may have been bought. O for a man who is a *man*, and, as my
neighbor says, has a bone in his back which you cannot pass your hand
through! Our statistics are at fault: the population has been returned too
large. How many *men* are there to a square thousand miles in this
country? Hardly one. Does not America offer any inducement for men
to settle here? The American has dwindled into an Odd Fellow—one
who may be known by the development of his organ of gregariousness,
and a manifest lack of intellect and cheerful self-reliance; whose first and
chief concern, on coming into the world, is to see that the almshouses are
in good repair; and, before yet he has lawfully donned the virile garb, to
collect a fund for the support of the widows and orphans that may be;
who, in short, ventures to live only by the aid of the Mutual Insurance
company, which has promised to bury him decently.

It is not a man's duty, as a matter of course, to devote himself to the   13
eradication of any, even the most enormous, wrong; he may still properly
have other concerns to engage him; but it is his duty, at least, to wash his
hands of it, and, if he gives it no thought longer, not to give it practically
his support. If I devote myself to other pursuits and contemplations, I
must first see, at least, that I do not pursue them sitting upon another
man's shoulders. I must get off him first, that he may pursue his
contemplations too. See what gross inconsistency is tolerated. I have
heard some of my townsmen say, "I should like to have them order me
out to help put down an insurrection of the slaves, or to march to
Mexico;—see if I would go"; and yet these very men have each, directly
by their allegiance, and so indirectly, at least, by their money, furnished a
substitute. The soldier is applauded who refuses to serve in an unjust war
by those who do not refuse to sustain the unjust government which
makes the war; is applauded by those whose own act and authority he

disregards and sets at naught; as if the state were penitent to that degree that it hired one to scourge it while it sinned, but not to that degree that it left off sinning for a moment. Thus, under the name of Order and Civil Government, we are all made at last to pay homage to and support our own meanness. After the first blush of sin comes its indifference; and from immoral it becomes, as it were, *unmoral*, and not quite unnecessary to that life which we have made.

The broadest and most prevalent error requires the most disinterested 14 virtue to sustain it. The slight reproach to which the virtue of patriotism is commonly liable, the noble are most likely to incur. Those who, while they disapprove of the character and measures of a government, yield to it their allegiance and support are undoubtedly its most conscientious supporters, and so frequently the most serious obstacles to reform. Some are petitioning the State to dissolve the Union, to disregard the requisitions of the President. Why do they not dissolve it themselves—the union between themselves and the State—and refuse to pay their quota into its treasury? Do not they stand in the same relation to the State that the State does to the Union? And have not the same reasons prevented the State from resisting the Union which have prevented them from resisting the State?

How can a man be satisfied to entertain an opinion merely, and enjoy 15 *it*? Is there any enjoyment in it, if his opinion is that he is aggrieved? If you are cheated out of a single dollar by your neighbor, you do not rest satisfied with knowing that you are cheated, or with saying that you are cheated, or even with petitioning him to pay you your due; but you take effectual steps at once to obtain the full amount, and see that you are never cheated again. Action from principle, the perception and the performance of right, changes things and relations; it is essentially revolutionary, and does not consist wholly with anything which was. It not only divides States and churches, it divides families; ay, it divides the *individual*, separating the diabolical in him from the divine.

Unjust laws exist: shall we be content to obey them, or shall we 16 endeavor to amend them, and obey them until we have succeeded, or shall we transgress them at once? Men generally, under such a government as this, think that they ought to wait until they have persuaded the majority to alter them. They think that, if they should resist, the remedy would be worse than the evil. But it is the fault of the government itself that the remedy *is* worse than the evil. *It* makes it worse. Why is it not more apt to anticipate and provide for reform? Why does it not cherish its wise minority? Why does it cry and resist before it is hurt? Why does it not encourage its citizens to be on the alert to point out its faults, and *do* better than it would have them? Why does it always crucify Christ, and excommunicate Copernicus and Luther, and pronounce Washington and Franklin rebels?

One would think, that a deliberate and practical denial of its authority 17
was the only offence never contemplated by government; else, why has it not assigned its definite, its suitable and proportionate, penalty? If a man who has no property refuses but once to earn nine shillings for the State, he is put in prison for a period unlimited by any law that I know, and determined only by the discretion of those who placed him there; but if he should steal ninety times nine shillings from the State, he is soon permitted to go at large again.

If the injustice is part of the necessary friction of the machine of 18
government, let it go, let it go: perchance it will wear smooth—certainly the machine will wear out. If the injustice has a spring, or a pulley, or a rope, or a crank, exclusively for itself, then perhaps you may consider whether the remedy will not be worse than the evil; but if it is of such a nature that it requires you to be the agent of injustice to another, then, I say, break the law. Let your life be a counter friction to stop the machine. What I have to do is to see, at any rate, that I do not lend myself to the wrong which I condemn.

As for adopting the ways which the State has provided for remedying 19
the evil, I know not of such ways. They take too much time, and a man's life will be gone. I have other affairs to attend to. I came into this world, not chiefly to make this a good place to live in, but to live in it, be it good or bad. A man has not everything to do, but something; and because he cannot do *everything*, it is not necessary that he should do *something* wrong. It is not my business to be petitioning the Governor or the Legislature any more than it is theirs to petition me; and if they should not hear my petition, what should I do then? But in this case the State has provided no way: its very Constitution is the evil. This may seem to be harsh and stubborn and unconciliatory; but it is to treat with the utmost kindness and consideration the only spirit that can appreciate or deserves it. So is all change for the better, like birth and death, which convulse the body.

I do not hesitate to say, that those who call themselves Abolitionists 20
should at once effectually withdraw their support, both in person and property, from the government of Massachusetts, and not wait till they constitute a majority of one, before they suffer the right to prevail through them. I think that it is enough if they have God on their side, without waiting for that other one. Moreover, any man more right than his neighbors constitutes a majority of one already.

I meet the American government, or its representative, the State 21
government, directly, and face to face, once a year—no more—in the
person of its tax-gatherer; this is the only mode in which a man situated
as I am necessarily meets it; and it then says distinctly, Recognize me; and
the simplest, the most effectual, and, in the present posture of affairs, the
indispensablest mode of treating with it on this head, of expressing your
little satisfaction with and love for it, is to deny it then. My civil
neighbor, the tax-gatherer, is the very man I have to deal with—for it is,
after all, with men and not with parchment that I quarrel—and he has
voluntarily chosen to be an agent of the government. How shall he ever
know well what he is and does as an officer of the government, or as a
man, until he is obliged to consider whether he shall treat me, his
neighbor, for whom he has respect, as a neighbor and well-disposed man,
or as a maniac and disturber of the peace, and see if he can get over this
obstruction to his neighborliness without a ruder and more impetuous
thought or speech corresponding with his action. I know this well, that if
one thousand, if one hundred, if ten men whom I could name—if ten
honest men only—ay, if *one* HONEST man, in this State of Massachusetts,
ceasing to hold slaves, were actually to withdraw from this copartnership,
and be locked up in the county jail therefor, it would be the abolition of
slavery in America. For it matters not how small the beginning may seem
to be: what is once well done is done forever. But we love better to talk
about it: that we say is our mission. Reform keeps many scores of
newspapers in its service, but not one man. If my esteemed neighbor, the
State's ambassador, who will devote his days to the settlement of the
question of human rights in the Council Chamber, instead of being
threatened with the prisons of Carolina, were to sit down the prisoner of
Massachusetts, that State which is so anxious to foist the sin of slavery
upon her sister—though at present she can discover only an act of
inhospitality to be the ground of a quarrel with her—the Legislature
would not wholly waive the subject the following winter.

Under a government which imprisons any unjustly, the true place for a 22
just man is also a prison. The proper place to-day, the only place which
Massachusetts has provided for her freer and less desponding spirits, is in
her prisons, to be put out and locked out of the State by her own act, as
they have already put themselves out by their principles. It is there that
the fugitive slave, and the Mexican prisoner on parole, and the Indian
come to plead the wrongs of his race should find them; on that separate,
but more free and honorable, ground, where the State places those who
are not *with* her, but *against* her—the only house in a slave State in which
a free man can abide with honor. If any think that their influence would

be lost there, and their voices no longer afflict the ear of the State, that they would not be as an enemy within its walls, they do not know by how much truth is stronger than error, nor how much more eloquently and effectively he can combat injustice who has experienced a little in his own person. Cast your whole vote, not a strip of paper merely, but your whole influence. A minority is powerless while it conforms to the majority; it is not even a minority then; but it is irresistible when it clogs by its whole weight. If the alternative is to keep all just men in prison, or give up war and slavery, the State will not hesitate which to choose. If a thousand men were not to pay their tax-bills this year, that would not be a violent and bloody measure, as it would be to pay them, and enable the State to commit violence and shed innocent blood. This is, in fact, the definition of a peaceable revolution, if any such is possible. If the tax-gatherer, or any public officer, asks me, as one has done, "But what shall I do?" my answer is, "If you really wish to do anything, resign your office." When the subject has refused allegiance, and the officer has resigned his office, then the revolution is accomplished. But even suppose blood should flow. Is there not a sort of blood shed when the conscience is wounded? Through this would a man's real manhood and immortality flow out, and he bleeds to an everlasting death. I see this blood flowing now.

I have contemplated the imprisonment of the offender, rather than the seizure of his goods—though both will serve the same purpose—because they who assert the purest right, and consequently are most dangerous to a corrupt State, commonly have not spent much time in accumulating property. To such the State renders comparatively small service, and a slight tax is wont to appear exorbitant, particularly if they are obliged to earn it by special labor with their hands. If there were one who lived wholly without the use of money, the State itself would hesitate to demand it of him. But the rich man—not to make any invidious comparison—is always sold to the institution which makes him rich. Absolutely speaking, the more money, the less virtue; for money comes between a man and his objects, and obtains them for him; and it was certainly no great virtue to obtain it. It puts to rest many questions which he would otherwise be taxed to answer; while the only new question which it puts is the hard but superfluous one, how to spend it. Thus his moral ground is taken from under his feet. The opportunities of living are diminished in proportion as what are called the "means" are increased. The best thing a man can do for his culture when he is rich is to endeavor to carry out those schemes which he entertained when he was poor. Christ answered the Herodians according to their condition. "Show me the tribute-money," said he;—and one took a penny out of his pocket;—if you use money which has the image of Caesar on it, and which he has made current and valuable, that is, *if you are men of the State*, and gladly enjoy the advantages of Caesar's government, then pay him back some of his own when he demands it. "Render therefore to Caesar that which is Caesar's, and to God those things which are God's" —leaving them no wiser than before as to which was which; for they did not wish to know.

When I converse with the freest of my neighbors, I perceive that, 24 whatever they may say about the magnitude and seriousness of the question, and their regard for the public tranquillity, the long and the short of the matter is, that they cannot spare the protection of the existing government, and they dread the consequences to their property and families of disobedience to it. For my own part, I should not like to think that I ever rely on the protection of the State. But, if I deny the authority of the State when it presents its tax-bill, it will soon take and waste all my property, and so harass me and my children without end. This is hard. This makes it impossible for a man to live honestly, and at the same time comfortably, in outward respects. It will not be worth the while to accumulate property; that would be sure to go again. You must hire or squat somewhere, and raise but a small crop, and eat that soon. You must live within yourself, and depend upon yourself always tucked up and ready for a start, and not have many affairs. A man may grow rich in Turkey even, if he will be in all respects a good subject of the Turkish government. Confucius said: "If a state is g erned by the principles of reason, poverty and misery are subjects of shame; if a state is not governed by the principles of reason, riches and honors are the subjects of shame." No: until I want the protection of Massachusetts to be extended to me in some distant Southern port, where my liberty is endangered, or until I am bent solely on building up an estate at home by peaceful enterprise, I can afford to refuse allegiance to Massachusetts, and her right to my property and life. It costs me less in every sense to incur the penalty of disobedience to the State than it would to obey. I should feel as if I were worth less in that case.

Some years ago, the State met me in behalf of the Church, and 25 commanded me to pay a certain sum toward the support of a clergyman whose preaching my father attended, but never I myself. "Pay," it said, "or be locked up in the jail." I declined to pay. But, unfortunately, another man saw fit to pay it. I did not see why the schoolmaster should be taxed to support the priest, and not the priest the schoolmaster; for I was not the State's schoolmaster, but I supported myself by voluntary subscription. I did not see why the lyceum should not present its tax-bill, and have the State to back its demand, as well as the Church. However, at the request of the selectmen, I condescended to make some such statement as this in writing:— "Know all men by these presents, that I, Henry Thoreau, do not wish to be regarded as a member of any incorporated society which I have not joined." This I gave to the town clerk; and he has it. The State, having thus learned that I did not wish to be regarded as a member of that church, has never made a like demand on me since; though it said that it must adhere to its original presumption that time. If I had known how to name them, I should then have signed off in detail from all the societies which I never signed on to; but I did not know where to find a complete list.

I have paid no poll-tax for six years. I was put into a jail once on this account, for one night; and, as I stood considering the walls of solid stone, two or three feet thick, the door of wood and iron, a foot thick, and the iron grating which strained the light, I could not help being struck with the foolishness of that institution which treated me as if I were mere flesh and blood and bones to be locked up. I wondered that it should have concluded at length that this was the best use it could put me to, and had never thought to avail itself of my services in some way. I saw that, if there was a wall of stone between me and my townsmen, there was a still more difficult one to climb or break through before they could get to be as free as I was. I did not for a moment feel confined, and the walls seemed a great waste of stone and mortar. I felt as if I alone of all my townsmen had paid my tax. They plainly did not know how to treat me, but behaved like persons who are underbred. In every threat and in every compliment there was a blunder; for they thought that my chief desire was to stand the other side of that stone wall. I could not but smile to see how industriously they locked the door on my meditations, which followed them out again without let or hindrance, and *they* were really all that was dangerous. As they could not reach me, they had resolved to punish my body; just as boys, if they cannot come at some person against whom they have a spite, will abuse his dog. I saw that the State was half-witted, that it was timid as a lone woman with her silver spoons, and that it did not know its friends from its foes, and I lost all my remaining respect for it, and pitied it.

Thus the State never intentionally confronts a man's sense, intellectual or moral, but only his body, his senses. It is not armed with superior wit or honesty, but with superior physical strength. I was not born to be forced. I will breathe after my own fashion. Let us see who is the strongest. What force has a multitude? They only can force me who obey a higher law than I. They force me to become like themselves. I do not hear of *men* being *forced* to live this way or that by masses of men. What sort of life were that to live? When I meet a government which says to me, "Your money or your life," why should I be in haste to give it my money? It may be in a great strait, and not know what to do: I cannot help that. It must help itself; do as I do. It is not worth the while to snivel about it. I am not responsible for the successful working of the machinery of society. I am not the son of the engineer. I perceive that, when an acorn and a chestnut fall side by side, the one does not remain inert to make way for the other, but both obey their own laws, and spring and grow and flourish as best they can, till one, perchance, overshadows and destroys the other. If a plant cannot live according to its nature, it dies; and so a man.

The night in prison was novel and interesting enough. The prisoners 28 in their shirt-sleeves were enjoying a chat and the evening air in the doorway, when I entered. But the jailer said, "Come, boys, it is time to lock up"; and so they dispersed, and I heard the sound of their steps returning into the hollow apartments. My room-mate was introduced to me by the jailer as "a first-rate fellow and a clever man." When the door was locked, he showed me where to hang my hat, and how he managed matters there. The rooms were whitewashed once a month; and this one, at least, was the whitest, most simply furnished, and probably the neatest apartment in the town. He naturally wanted to know where I came from, and what brought me there; and, when I had told him, I asked him in my turn how he came there, presuming him to be an honest man, of course; and, as the world goes, I believe he was. "Why," said he, "they accuse me of burning a barn; but I never did it." As near as I could discover, he had probably gone to bed in a barn when drunk, and smoked his pipe there; and so a barn was burnt. He had the reputation of being a clever man, had been there some three months waiting for his trial to come on, and would have to wait as much longer; but he was quite domesticated and contented, since he got his board for nothing, and thought that he was well treated.

He occupied one window, and I the other; and I saw that if one stayed 29 there long, his principal business would be to look out the window. I had soon read all the tracts that were left there, and examined where former prisoners had broken out, and where a grate had been sawed off, and heard the history of the various occupants of that room; for I found that even here there was a history and a gossip which never circulated beyond the walls of the jail. Probably this is the only house in the town where verses are composed, which are afterward printed in a circular form, but not published. I was shown quite a long list of verses which were composed by some young men who had been detected in an attempt to escape, who avenged themselves by singing them.

I pumped my fellow-prisoner as dry as I could, for fear I should never 30 see him again; but at length he showed me which was my bed, and left me to blow out the lamp.

It was like travelling into a far country, such as I had never expected to 31 behold, to lie there for one night. It seemed to me that I never had heard the town clock strike before, nor the evening sounds of the village; for we slept with the windows open, which were inside the grating. It was to see my native village in the light of the Middle Ages, and our Concord was turned into a Rhine stream, and visions of knights and castles passed before me. They were the voices of old burghers that I heard in the streets. I was an involuntary spectator and auditor of whatever was done and said in the kitchen of the adjacent village inn—a wholly new and rare experience to me. It was a closer view of my native town. I was fairly inside of it. I never had seen its institutions before. This is one of its peculiar institutions; for it is a shire town. I began to comprehend what its inhabitants were about.

In the morning, our breakfasts were put through the hole in the door, 32 in small oblong-square tin pans, made to fit, and holding a pint of chocolate, with brown bread, and an iron spoon. When they called for the vessels again, I was green enough to return what bread I had left; but my comrade seized it, and said that I should lay that up for lunch or dinner. Soon after he was let out to work at haying in a neighboring field, whither he went every day, and would not be back till noon; so he bade me good-day, saying that he doubted if he should see me again.

When I came out of prison—for some one interfered, and paid that 33 tax—I did not perceive that great changes had taken place on the common, such as he observed who went in a youth and emerged a tottering and gray-headed man; and yet a change had to my eyes come over the scene—the town, and State, and country—greater than any that mere time could effect. I saw yet more distinctly the State in which I lived. I saw to what extent the people among whom I lived could be trusted as good neighbors and friends; that their friendship was for summer weather only; that they did not greatly propose to do right; that they were a distinct race from me by their prejudices and superstitions, as the Chinamen and Malays are; that in their sacrifices to humanity they ran no risks, not even to their property; that after all they were not so noble but they treated the thief as he had treated them, and hoped, by a certain outward observance and a few prayers, and by walking in a particular straight though useless path from time to time, to save their souls. This may be to judge my neighbors harshly; for I believe that many of them are not aware that they have such an institution as the jail in their village.

It was formerly the custom in our village, when a poor debtor came out 34 of jail, for his acquaintances to salute him, looking through their fingers, which were crossed to represent the grating of a jail window, "How do ye do?" My neighbors did not thus salute me, but first looked at me, and then at one another, as if I had returned from a long journey. I was put into jail as I was going to the shoemaker's to get a shoe which was mended. When I was let out the next morning, I proceeded to finish my errand, and, having put on my mended shoe, joined a huckleberry party, who were impatient to put themselves under my conduct; and in half an hour—for the horse was soon tackled—was in the midst of a huckleberry field, on one of our highest hills, two miles off, and then the State was nowhere to be seen.

This is the whole history of "My Prisons." 35

I have never declined paying the highway tax, because I am as desirous 36 of being a good neighbor as I am of being a bad subject; and as for supporting schools, I am doing my part to educate my fellow-countrymen now. It is for no particular item in the tax-bill that I refuse to pay it. I simply wish to refuse allegiance to the State, to withdraw and stand aloof from it effectually. I do not care to trace the course of my dollar, if I could, till it buys a man or a musket to shoot one with—the dollar is innocent—but I am concerned to trace the effects of my allegiance. In fact, I quietly declare war with the State, after my fashion, though I will still make what use and get what advantage of her I can, as is usual in such cases.

If others pay the tax which is demanded of me, from a sympathy with 37 the State, they do but what they have already done in their own case, or rather they abet injustice to a greater extent than the State requires. If they pay the tax from a mistaken interest in the individual taxed, to save his property, or prevent his going to jail, it is because they have not considered wisely how far they let their private feelings interfere with the public good.

This, then, is my position at present. But one cannot be too much on 38 his guard in such a case, lest his action be biased by obstinacy or an undue regard for the opinions of men. Let him see that he does only what belongs to himself and to the hour.

I think sometimes, Why, this people mean well, they are only ignorant; 39 they would do better if they knew how: why give your neighbors this pain to treat you as they are not inclined to? But I think again, This is no reason why I should do as they do, or permit others to suffer much greater pain of a different kind. Again, I sometimes say to myself, When many millions of men, without heat, without ill will, without personal feeling of any kind, demand of you a few shillings only, without the possibility, such is their constitution, of retracting or altering their present demand, and without the possibility, on your side, of appeal to any other millions, why expose yourself to this overwhelming brute force? You do not resist cold and hunger, the winds and the waves, thus obstinately; you quietly submit to a thousand similar necessities. You do not put your head into the fire. But just in proportion as I regard this as not wholly a brute force, but partly a human force, and consider that I have relations to those millions as to so many millions of men, and not of mere brute or inanimate things, I see that appeal is possible, first and instantaneously, from them to the Maker of them, and, secondly, from them to themselves. But if I put my head deliberately into the fire, there is no appeal to fire or to the Maker of fire, and I have only myself to blame. If I could convince myself that I have any right to be satisfied with men as they are, and to treat them accordingly, and not according, in some respects, to my requisitions and expectations of what they and I ought to be, then, like a good Mussulman and fatalist, I should endeavor to be satisfied with things as they are, and say it is the will of God. And, above all, there is this difference between resisting this and a purely brute or natural force, that I can resist this with some effect; but I cannot expect, like Orpheus, to change the nature of the rocks and trees and beasts.

I do not wish to quarrel with any man or nation. I do not wish to split 40 hairs, to make fine distinctions, or set myself up as better than my neighbors. I seek rather, I may say, even an excuse for conforming the laws of the land. I am but too ready to conform to them. Indeed, I have reason to suspect myself on this head; and each year, as the tax-gatherer comes round, I find myself disposed to review the acts and positions of the general and State governments, and the spirit of the people, to discover a pretext for conformity.

> We must affect our country as our parents,
> And if at any time we alienate
> Our love or industry from doing it honor,
> We must respect effects and teach the soul
> Matter of conscience and religion,
> And not desire of rule or benefit.

I believe that the State will soon be able to take all my work of this sort out of my hands, and then I shall be no better a patriot than my fellow-countrymen. Seen from a lower point of view, the Constitution, with all its faults, is very good; the law and the courts are very respectable; even this State and this American government are, in many respects, very admirable, and rare things, to be thankful for, such as a great many have described them; but seen from a point of view a little higher, they are what I have described them; seen from a higher still, and the highest, who shall say what they are, or that they are worth looking at or thinking of at all?

However, the government does not concern me much, and I shall 41 bestow the fewest possible thoughts on it. It is not many moments that I live under a government, even in this world. If a man is thought-free, fancy-free, imagination-free, that which *is not* never for a long time appearing *to be* to him, unwise rulers or reformers cannot fatally interrupt him.

I know that most men think differently from myself; but those whose 42 lives are by profession devoted to the study of these or kindred subjects content me as little as any. Statesmen and legislators, standing so completely within the institution, never distinctly and nakedly behold it. They speak of moving society, but have no resting-place without it. They may be men of a certain experience and discrimination, and have no doubt invented ingenious and even useful systems, for which we sincerely thank them; but all their wit and usefulness lie within certain not very wide limits. They are wont to forget that the world is not governed by policy and expediency. Webster never goes behind government, and so cannot speak with authority about it. His words are wisdom to those legislators who contemplate no essential reform in the existing government; but for thinkers, and those who legislate for all time, he never once glances at the subject. I know of those whose serene and wise speculations on this theme would soon reveal the limits of his mind's range and hospitality. Yet, compared with the cheap professions of most reformers, and the still cheaper wisdom and eloquence of politicians in general, his are almost the only sensible and valuable words, and we thank Heaven for him. Comparatively, he is always strong, original, and, above all, practical. Still, his quality is not wisdom, but prudence. The lawyer's truth is not Truth, but consistency or a consistent expediency. Truth is always in harmony with herself, and is not concerned chiefly to reveal the justice that may consist with wrong-doing. He well deserves to be called, as he has been called, the Defender of the Constitution. There are really no blows to be given by him but defensive ones. He is not a leader, but a follower. His leaders are the men of '87. "I have never made an effort," he says, "and never propose to make an effort; I have never countenanced an effort, and never mean to countenance an effort, to disturb the arrangement as originally made, by which the various States came into the Union." Still thinking of the sanction which the Constitution gives to slavery, he says, "Because it was a part of the original compact—let it stand." Notwithstanding his special acuteness and ability, he is unable to take a fact out of its merely political relations, and behold it as it lies absolutely to be disposed of by the intellect—what, for instance, it behooves a man to do here in America today with regard to slavery—but ventures, or is driven, to make some such desperate answer as the following, while professing to speak absolutely, and as a private man—from which what new and similar code of social duties might be inferred? "The manner," says he, "in which the governments of those States where slavery exists are to regulate it is for their own consideration, under their responsibility to their constituents, to the general laws of propriety, humanity, and justice, and to God. Associations formed elsewhere, springing from a feeling of humanity, or any other cause, have nothing whatever to do with it. They have never received any encouragement from me, and they never will."

They who know of no purer sources of truth, who have traced up its 43 stream no higher, stand, and wisely stand, by the Bible and the Constitution, and drink at it there with reverence and humility; but they who behold where it comes trickling into this lake or that pool, gird up their loins once more, and continue their pilgrimage toward its fountain-head.

No man with a genius for legislation has appeared in America. They 44 are rare in the history of the world. There are orators, politicians, and eloquent men, by the thousand; but the speaker has not yet opened his mouth to speak who is capable of settling the much-vexed questions of the day. We love eloquence for its own sake, and not for any truth which it may utter, or any heroism it may inspire. Our legislators have not yet learned the comparative value of free trade and of freedom, of union, and of rectitude, to a nation. They have no genius or talent for comparatively humble questions of taxation and finance, commerce and manufacturers and agriculture. If we were left solely to the wordy wit of legislators in Congress for our guidance, uncorrected by the seasonable experience and the effectual complaints of the people, America would not long retain her rank among the nations. For eighteen hundred years, though perchance I have no right to say it, the New Testament has been written; yet where is the legislator who has wisdom and practical talent enough to avail himself of the light which it sheds on the science of legislation?

The authority of government, even such as I am willing to submit to— 45 for I will cheerfully obey those who know and can do better than I, and in many things even those who neither know nor can do so well—is still an impure one: to be strictly just, it must have the sanction and consent of the governed. It can have no pure right over my person and property but what I concede to it. The progress from an absolute to a limited monarchy, from a limited monarchy to a democracy, is a progress toward a true respect for the individual. Even the Chinese philosopher was wise enough to regard the individual as the basis of the empire. Is a democracy, such as we know it, the last improvement possible in government? Is it not possible to take a step further towards recognizing and organizing the rights of man? There will never be a really free and enlightened State until the State comes to recognize the individual as a higher and independent power, from which all its own power and authority are derived, and treats him accordingly. I please myself with imagining a State at least which can afford to be just to all men, and to treat the individual with respect as a neighbor; which even would not think it inconsistent with its own repose if a few were to live aloof from it, not meddling with it, nor embraced by it, who fulfilled all the duties of neighbors and fellow-men. A State which bore this kind of fruit, and suffered it to drop off as fast as it ripened, would prepare the way for a still more perfect and glorious State, which also I have imagined, but not yet anywhere seen.

Martin Luther King, Jr.

Martin Luther King, Jr. (1929–1968) is a modern American hero for many people in this country and around the world. His birthday has been made a national holiday to commemorate both the man and the movement he led. A Baptist minister who became leader of the civil rights movement, King was awarded the Nobel Peace Prize in 1964 and was assassinated in 1968.

King graduated from Morehouse College and Grozer Theological Seminary and earned a Ph.D. from Boston University. He was pastor at a Montgomery, Alabama, church in 1955 when he first advocated civil disobedience, a citywide bus boycott protesting segregated seating on public transportation. In 1957 King organized the Southern Christian Leadership Conference, and a year later he moved the headquarters to Atlanta, Georgia, where he became pastor with his father of the Ebenezer Baptist Church.

King carried his campaign of civil disobedience throughout the South. In 1963 he went to Birmingham, Alabama, to lead protestors in a demonstration against segregation of restaurants, hotels, and department stores. Violence escalated and a black church was bombed, killing four little girls. King was arrested and jailed. In prison, he wrote the following selection, an expression of his moral philosophy and a justification of civil disobedience.

Letter from Birmingham Jail

King wrote this essay in response to a public statement published in a local newspaper. In fact, he began writing his reaction in the margins of the newspaper and eventually made it public. The statement, reprinted in Chapter 1, was signed by eight clergymen, and although it does not explicitly mention King or the Southern Christian Leadership Conference, it criticizes him for exporting civil disobedience to Birmingham. Before reading King's letter, look back at the clergymen's statement. Then ask yourself how you would have responded if you had been in King's place. How would you defend King's actions?

MY DEAR FELLOW CLERGYMEN:

While confined here in the Birmingham city jail, I came across your 1
recent statement calling my present activities "unwise and untimely." Seldom do I pause to answer criticism of my work and ideas. If I sought to answer all the criticisms that cross my desk, my secretaries would have little time for anything other than such correspondence in the course of

the day, and I would have no time for constructive work. But since I feel that you are men of genuine good will and that your criticisms are sincerely set forth, I want to try to answer your statement in what I hope will be patient and reasonable terms.

I think I should indicate why I am here in Birmingham, since you have   2
been influenced by the view which argues against "outsiders coming in." I have the honor of serving as president of the Southern Christian Leadership Conference, an organization operating in every southern state, with headquarters in Atlanta, Georgia. We have some eighty-five affiliated organizations across the South, and one of them is the Alabama Christian Movement for Human Rights. Frequently we share staff, educational, and financial resources with our affiliates. Several months ago the affiliate here in Birmingham asked us to be on call to engage in a nonviolent direct-action program if such were deemed necessary. We readily consented, and when the hour came we lived up to our promise. So I, along with several members of my staff, am here because I was invited here. I am here because I have organizational ties here.

But more basically, I am in Birmingham because injustice is here. Just   3
as the prophets of the eighth century B.C. left their villages and carried their "thus saith the Lord" far beyond the boundaries of their home towns, and just as the Apostle Paul left his village of Tarsus and carried the gospel of Jesus Christ to the far corners of the Greco-Roman world, so am I compelled to carry the gospel of freedom beyond my own home town. Like Paul, I must constantly respond to the Macedonian call for aid.

Moreover, I am cognizant of the interrelatedness of all communities   4
and states. I cannot sit idly by in Atlanta and not be concerned about what happens in Birmingham. Injustice anywhere is a threat to justice everywhere. We are caught in an inescapable network of mutuality, tied in a single garment of destiny. Whatever affects one directly, affects all indirectly. Never again can we afford to live with the narrow, provincial "outside agitator" idea. Anyone who lives inside the United States can never be considered an outsider anywhere within its bounds.

You deplore the demonstrations taking place in Birmingham. But your   5
statement, I am sorry to say, fails to express a similar concern for the conditions that brought about the demonstrations. I am sure that none of you would want to rest content with the superficial kind of social analysis that deals merely with effects and does not grapple with underlying causes. It is unfortunate that demonstrations are taking place in Birmingham, but it is even more unfortunate that the city's white power structure left the Negro community with no alternative.

In any nonviolent campaign there are four basic steps: collection of the   6 facts to determine whether injustices exist; negotiation; self-purification; and direct action. We have gone through all these steps in Birmingham. There can be no gainsaying the fact that racial injustice engulfs this community. Birmingham is probably the most thoroughly segregated city in the United States. Its ugly record of brutality is widely known. Negroes have experienced grossly unjust treatment in the courts. There have been more unsolved bombings of Negro homes and churches in Birmingham than in any other city in the nation. These are the hard, brutal facts of the case. On the basis of these conditions, Negro leaders sought to negotiate with the city fathers. But the latter consistently refused to engage in good-faith negotiation.

Then, last September, came the opportunity to talk with leaders of   7
Birmingham's economic community. In the course of the negotiations, certain promises were made by the merchants—for example, to remove the stores' humiliating racial signs. On the basis of these promises, the Reverend Fred Shuttlesworth and the leaders of the Alabama Christian Movement for Human Rights agreed to a moratorium on all demonstrations. As the weeks and months went by, we realized that we were the victims of a broken promise. A few signs, briefly removed, returned; the others remained.

As in so many past experiences, our hopes had been blasted, and the   8
shadow of deep disappointment settled upon us. We had no alternative except to prepare for direct action, whereby we would present our very bodies as a means of laying our case before the conscience of the local and the national community. Mindful of the difficulties involved, we decided to undertake a process of self-purification. We began a series of workshops on nonviolence, and we repeatedly asked ourselves: "Are you able to accept blows without retaliating?" "Are you able to endure the ordeal of jail?" We decided to schedule our direct-action program for the Easter season, realizing that except for Christmas, this is the main shopping period of the year. Knowing that a strong economic-withdrawal program would be the by-product of direct action, we felt that this would be the best time to bring pressure to bear on the merchants for the needed change.

Then it occurred to us that Birmingham's mayoral election was coming   9
up in March, and we speedily decided to postpone action until after election day. When we discovered that the Commissioner of Public Safety, Eugene "Bull" Connor, had piled up enough votes to be in the run-off, we decided again to postpone action until the day after the run-off so that the demonstrations could not be used to cloud the issues. Like many others, we wanted to see Mr. Connor defeated, and to this end we endured postponement after postponement. Having aided in this

community need, we felt that our direct-action program could be delayed no longer.

You may well ask, "Why direct action? Why sit-ins, marches, and so forth? Isn't negotiation a better path?" You are quite right in calling for negotiation. Indeed, this is the very purpose of direct action. Nonviolent direct action seeks to create such a crisis and foster such a tension that a community which has constantly refused to negotiate is forced to confront the issue. It seeks so to dramatize the issue that it can no longer be ignored. My citing the creation of tension as part of the work of the nonviolent-resister may sound rather shocking. But I must confess that I am not afraid of the word "tension." I have earnestly opposed violent tension, but there is a type of constructive, nonviolent tension which is necessary for growth. Just as Socrates felt that it was necessary to create a tension in the mind so that individuals could rise from the bondage of myths and half-truths to the unfettered realm of creative analysis and objective appraisal, so must we see the need for nonviolent gadflies to create the kind of tension in society that will help men rise from the dark depths of prejudice and racism to the majestic heights of understanding and brotherhood.

The purpose of our direct-action program is to create a situation so crisis-packed that it will inevitably open the door to negotiation. I therefore concur with you in your call for negotiation. Too long has our beloved Southland been bogged down in a tragic effort to live in monologue rather than dialogue.

One of the basic points in your statement is that the action that I and my associates have taken in Birmingham is untimely. Some have asked: "Why didn't you give the new city administration time to act?" The only answer that I can give to this query is that the new Birmingham administration must be prodded about as much as the outgoing one, before it will act. We are sadly mistaken if we feel that the election of Albert Boutwell as mayor will bring the millennium to Birmingham. While Mr. Boutwell is a much more gentle person than Mr. Connor, they are both segregationists, dedicated to maintenance of the status quo. I have hoped that Mr. Boutwell will be reasonable enough to see the futility of massive resistance to desegregation. But he will not see this without pressure from devotees of civil rights. My friends, I must say to you that we have not made a single gain in civil rights without determined legal and nonviolent pressure. Lamentably, it is an historical fact that privileged groups seldom give up their privileges voluntarily. Individuals may see the moral light and voluntarily give up their unjust posture; but, as Reinhold Niebuhr has reminded us, groups tend to be more immoral than individuals.

We know through painful experience that freedom is never voluntarily 13 given by the oppressor; it must be demanded by the oppressed. Frankly, I have yet to engage in a direct-action campaign that was "well timed" in the view of those who have not suffered unduly from the disease of segregation. For years now I have heard the word "Wait!" It rings in the ear of every Negro with piercing familiarity. This "Wait" has almost always meant "Never." We must come to see, with one of our distinguished jurists, that "justice too long delayed is justice denied."

We have waited for more than 340 years for our constitutional and 14 God-given rights. The nations of Asia and Africa are moving with jetlike speed toward gaining political independence, but we still creep at horse-and-buggy pace toward gaining a cup of coffee at a lunch counter. Perhaps it is easy for those who have never felt the stinging darts of segregation to say, "Wait." But when you have seen vicious mobs lynch your mothers and fathers at will and drown your sisters and brothers at whim; when you have seen hate-filled policemen curse, kick, and even kill your black brothers and sisters; when you see the vast majority of your twenty million Negro brothers smothering in an airtight cage of poverty in the midst of an affluent society; when you suddenly find your tongue twisted and your speech stammering as you seek to explain to your six-year-old daughter why she can't go to the public amusement park that has just been advertised on television, and see tears welling up in her eyes when she is told that Funtown is closed to colored children, and see ominous clouds of inferiority beginning to form in her little mental sky, and see her beginning to distort her personality by developing an unconscious bitterness toward white people; when you have to concoct an answer for a five-year-old son who is asking, "Daddy, why do white people treat colored people so mean?"; when you take a cross-country drive and find it necessary to sleep night after night in the uncomfortable corners of your automobile because no motel will accept you; when you are humiliated day in and day out by nagging signs reading "white" and "colored"; when your first name becomes "nigger," your middle name becomes "boy" (however old you are) and your last name becomes "John," and your wife and mother are never given the respected title "Mrs."; when you are harried by day and haunted by night by the fact that you are a Negro, living constantly at tiptoe stance, never quite knowing what to expect next, and are plagued with inner fears and outer resentments; when you are forever fighting a degenerating sense of "nobodiness"—then you will understand why we find it difficult to wait. There comes a time when the cup of endurance runs over, and men are no longer willing to be plunged into the abyss of despair. I hope, sirs, you can understand our legitimate and unavoidable impatience.

You express a great deal of anxiety over our willingness to break laws. 15 This is certainly a legitimate concern. Since we so diligently urge people to obey the Supreme Court's decision of 1954 outlawing segregation in the public schools, at first glance it may seem rather paradoxical for us consciously to break laws. One may well ask: "How can you advocate breaking some laws and obeying others?" The answer lies in the fact that there are two types of laws: just and unjust. I would be the first to advocate obeying just laws. One has not only a legal but a moral responsibility to obey just laws. Conversely, one has a moral responsibility to disobey unjust laws. I would agree with St. Augustine that "an unjust law is no law at all."

Now, what is the difference between the two? How does one determine 16 whether a law is just or unjust? A just law is a man-made code that squares with the moral law or the law of God. An unjust law is a code that is out of harmony with the moral law. To put it in the terms of St. Thomas Aquinas: An unjust law is a human law that is not rooted in eternal law and natural law. Any law that uplifts human personality is just. Any law that degrades human personality is unjust. All segregation statutes are unjust because segregation distorts the soul and damages the personality. It gives the segregator a false sense of superiority and the segregated a false sense of inferiority. Segregation, to use the terminology of the Jewish philosopher Martin Buber, substitutes an "I-it" relationship for an "I-thou" relationship and ends up relegating persons to the status of things. Hence segregation is not only politically, economically, and sociologically unsound, it is morally wrong and sinful. Paul Tillich has said that sin is separation. Is not segregation an existential expression of man's tragic separation, his awful estrangement, his terrible sinfulness? Thus it is that I can urge men to obey the 1954 decision of the Supreme Court, for it is morally right; and I can urge them to disobey segregation ordinances, for they are morally wrong.

Let us consider a more concrete example of just and unjust laws. An 17 unjust law is a code that a numerical or power majority group compels a minority group to obey but does not make binding on itself. This is *difference* made legal. By the same token, a just law is a code that a majority compels a minority to follow and that it is willing to follow itself. This is *sameness* made legal.

Let me give another explanation. A law is unjust if it is inflicted on a 18 minority that, as a result of being denied the right to vote, had no part in enacting or devising the law. Who can say that the legislature of Alabama which set up that state's segregation laws was democratically elected? Throughout Alabama all sorts of devious methods are used to prevent Negroes from becoming registered voters, and there are some counties in which, even though Negroes constitute a majority of the population, not a single Negro is registered. Can any law enacted under such circumstances be considered democratically structured?

Sometimes a law is just on its face and unjust in its application. For   19 instance, I have been arrested on a charge of parading without a permit. Now, there is nothing wrong in having an ordinance which requires a permit for a parade. But such an ordinance becomes unjust when it is used to maintain segregation and to deny citizens the First-Amendment privilege of peaceful assembly and protest.

I hope you are able to see the distinction I am trying to point out. In no   20 sense do I advocate evading or defying the law, as would the rabid segregationist. That would lead to anarchy. One who breaks an unjust law must do so openly, lovingly, and with a willingness to accept the penalty. I submit that an individual who breaks a law that conscience tells him is unjust, and who willingly accepts the penalty of imprisonment in order to arouse the conscience of the community over its injustice, is in reality expressing the highest respect for law.

Of course, there is nothing new about this kind of civil disobedience. It   21 was evidenced sublimely in the refusal of Shadrach, Meshach, and Abednego to obey the laws of Nebuchadnezzar, on the ground that a higher moral law was at stake. It was practiced superbly by the early Christians, who were willing to face hungry lions and the excruciating pain of chopping blocks rather than submit to certain unjust laws of the Roman Empire. To a degree, academic freedom is a reality today because Socrates practiced civil disobedience. In our own nation, the Boston Tea Party represented a massive act of civil disobedience.

We should never forget that everything Adolf Hitler did in Germany   22 was "legal" and everything the Hungarian freedom fighters did in Hungary was "illegal." It was "illegal" to aid and comfort a Jew in Hitler's Germany. Even so, I am sure that, had I lived in Germany at the time, I would have aided and comforted my Jewish brothers. If today I lived in a Communist country where certain principles dear to the Christian faith are suppressed, I would openly advocate disobeying that country's anti-religious laws.

I must make two honest confessions to you, my Christian and Jewish   23 brothers. First, I must confess that over the past few years I have been gravely disappointed with the white moderate. I have almost reached the regrettable conclusion that the Negro's great stumbling block in his stride toward freedom is not the White Citizen's Counciler or the Ku

Klux Klanner, but the white moderate, who is more devoted to "order" than to justice; who prefers a negative peace which is the absence of tension to a positive peace which is the presence of justice; who constantly says, "I agree with you in the goal you seek, but I cannot agree with your methods of direct action"; who paternalistically believes he can set the timetable for another man's freedom; who lives by a mythical concept of time and who constantly advises the Negro to wait for a "more convenient season." Shallow understanding from people of good will is more frustrating than absolute misunderstanding from people of ill will. Lukewarm acceptance is much more bewildering than outright rejection.

I had hoped that the white moderate would understand that law and order exist for the purpose of establishing justice and that when they fail in this purpose they become the dangerously structured dams that block the flow of social progress. I had hoped that the white moderate would understand that the present tension in the South is a necessary phase of the transition from an obnoxious negative peace, in which the Negro passively accepted his unjust plight, to a substantive and positive peace, in which all men will respect the dignity and worth of human personality. Actually, we who engage in nonviolent direct action are not the creators of tension. We merely bring to the surface the hidden tension that is already alive. We bring it out in the open, where it can be seen and dealt with. Like a boil that can never be cured so long as it is covered up but must be opened with all its ugliness to the natural medicines of air and light, injustice must be exposed, with all the tension its exposure creates, to the light of human conscience and the air of national opinion, before it can be cured. 24

In your statement you assert that our actions, even though peaceful, must be condemned because they precipitate violence. But is this a logical assertion? Isn't this like condemning a robbed man because his possession of money precipitated the evil act of robbery? Isn't this like condemning Socrates because his unswerving commitment to truth and his philosophical inquiries precipitated the act by the misguided populace in which they made him drink hemlock? Isn't this like condemning Jesus because his unique God-consciousness and never-ceasing devotion to God's will precipitated the evil act of crucifixion? We must come to see that, as the federal courts have consistently affirmed, it is wrong to urge an individual to cease his efforts to gain his basic constitutional rights because the quest may precipitate violence. Society must protect the robbed and punish the robber. 25

I had also hoped that the white moderate would reject the myth concerning time in relation to the struggle for freedom. I have just 26 received a letter from a white brother in Texas. He writes: "All Christians know that the colored people will receive equal rights eventually, but it is possible that you are in too great a religious hurry. It has taken Christianity almost two thousand years to accomplish what it has. The teachings of Christ take time to come to earth." Such an attitude stems from a tragic misconception of time, from the strangely irrational notion that there is something in the very flow of time that will inevitably cure all ills. Actually, time itself is neutral; it can be used either destructively or constructively. More and more I feel that the people of ill will have used time much more effectively than have the people of good will. We will have to repent in this generation not merely for the hateful words and actions of the bad people, but for the appalling silence of the good people. Human progress never rolls in on wheels of inevitability; it comes through the tireless efforts of men willing to be co-workers with God, and without this hard work, time itself becomes an ally of the forces of social stagnation. We must use time creatively, in the knowledge that the time is always ripe to do right. Now is the time to make real the promise of democracy and transform our pending national elegy into a creative psalm of brotherhood. Now is the time to lift our national policy from the quicksand of racial injustice to the solid rock of human dignity.

You speak of our activity in Birmingham as extreme. At first I was 27 rather disappointed that fellow clergymen would see my nonviolent efforts as those of an extremist. I began thinking about the fact that I stand in the middle of two opposing forces in the Negro community. One is a force of complacency, made up in part of Negroes who, as a result of long years of oppression, are so drained of self-respect and a sense of "somebodiness" that they have adjusted to segregation; and in part of a few middle-class Negroes who, because of a degree of academic and economic security and because in some ways they profit by segregation, have become insensitive to the problems of the masses. The other force is one of bitterness and hatred, and it comes perilously close to advocating violence. It is expressed in the various black nationalist groups that are springing up across the nation, the largest and best-known being Elijah Muhammad's Muslim movement. Nourished by the Negro's frustration over the continued existence of racial discrimination, this movement is made up of people who have lost faith in America, who have absolutely repudiated Christianity, and who have concluded that the white man is an incorrigible "devil."

I have tried to stand between these two forces, saying that we need 28 emulate neither the "do-nothingism" of the complacent nor the hatred and despair of the black nationalist. For there is the more excellent way of love and nonviolent protest. I am grateful to God that, through the influence of the Negro church, the way of nonviolence became an integral part of our struggle.

If this philosophy had not emerged, by now many streets of the South would, I am convinced, be flowing with blood. And I am further convinced that if our white brothers dismiss as "rabblerousers" and "outside agitators" those of us who employ nonviolent direct action, and if they refuse to support our nonviolent efforts, millions of Negroes will, out of frustration and despair, seek solace and security in black-nationalist ideologies—a development that would inevitably lead to a frightening racial nightmare. 29

Oppressed people cannot remain oppressed forever. The yearning for freedom eventually manifests itself, and that is what has happened to the American Negro. Something within has reminded him of his birthright of freedom, and something without has reminded him that it can be gained. Consciously or unconsciously, he has been caught up by the *Zeitgeist*, and with his black brothers of Africa and his brown and yellow brothers of Asia, South America, and the Caribbean, the United States Negro is moving with a sense of great urgency toward the promised land of racial justice. If one recognizes this vital urge that has engulfed the Negro community, one should readily understand why public demonstrations are taking place. The Negro has many pent-up resentments and latent frustrations, and he must release them. So let him march; let him make prayer pilgrimages to the city hall; let him go on freedom rides—and try to understand why he must do so. If his repressed emotions are not released in nonviolent ways, they will seek expression through violence; this is not a threat but a fact of history. So I have not said to my people, "Get rid of your discontent." Rather, I have tried to say that this normal and healthy discontent can be channeled into the creative outlet of nonviolent direct action. And now this approach is being termed extremist. 30

But though I was initially disappointed at being categorized as an extremist, as I continued to think about the matter I gradually gained a measure of satisfaction from the label. Was not Jesus an extremist for love: "Love your enemies, bless them that curse you, do good to them that hate you, and pray for them which despitefully use you, and persecute you." Was not Amos an extremist for justice: "Let justice roll down like waters and righteousness like an ever-flowing stream." Was not Paul an extremist for the Christian gospel: "I bear in my body the marks of the Lord Jesus." Was not Martin Luther an extremist: "Here I stand; I cannot do otherwise, so help me God." And John Bunyan: "I will stay in jail to the end of my days before I make a butchery of my conscience." And Abraham Lincoln: "This nation cannot survive half slave and half 31 free." And Thomas Jefferson: "We hold these truths to be self-evident, that all men are created equal. . . ." So the question is not whether we will be extremists, but what kind of extremists we will be. Will we be extremists for hate or for love? Will we be extremists for the preservation of injustice or for the extension of justice? In that dramatic scene on Calvary's hill three men were crucified. We must never forget that all three were crucified for the same crime—the crime of extremism. Two were extremists for immorality, and thus fell below their environment. The other, Jesus Christ, was an extremist for love, truth, and goodness, and thereby rose above his environment. Perhaps the South, the nation, and the world are in dire need of creative extremists.

I had hoped that the white moderate would see this need. Perhaps I 32 was too optimistic; perhaps I expected too much. I suppose I should have realized that few members of the oppressor race can understand the deep groans and passionate yearnings of the oppressed race, and still fewer have the vision to see that injustice must be rooted out by strong, persistent, and determined action. I am thankful, however, that some of our white brothers in the South have grasped the meaning of this social revolution and committed themselves to it. They are still all too few in quantity, but they are big in quality. Some—such as Ralph McGill, Lillian Smith, Harry Golden, James McBride Dabbs, Ann Braden, and Sarah Patton Boyle—have written about our struggle in eloquent and prophetic terms. Others have marched with us down nameless streets of the South. They have languished in filthy, roach-infested jails, suffering the abuse and brutality of policemen who view them as "dirty nigger-lovers." Unlike so many of their moderate brothers and sisters, they have recognized the urgency of the moment and sensed the need for powerful "action" antidotes to combat the disease of segregation.

Let me take note of my other major disappointment. I have been so 33 greatly disappointed with the white church and its leadership. Of course, there are some notable exceptions. I am not unmindful of the fact that each of you has taken some significant stands on this issue. I commend you, Reverend Stallings, for your Christian stand on this past Sunday, in welcoming Negroes to your worship service on a nonsegregated basis. I commend the Catholic leaders of this state for integrating Spring Hill College several years ago.

But despite these notable exceptions, I must honestly reiterate that I 34 have been disappointed with the church. I do not say this as one of those negative critics who can always find something wrong with the church. I say this as a minister of the gospel, who loves the church; who was nurtured in its bosom; who has been sustained by its spiritual blessings and who will remain true to it as long as the cord of life shall lengthen.

When I was suddenly catapulted into the leadership of the bus protest 35 in Montgomery, Alabama, a few years ago, I felt we would be supported by the white church. I felt that the white ministers, priests, and rabbis of the South would be among our strongest allies. Instead, some have been outright opponents, refusing to understand the freedom movement and misrepresenting its leaders; all too many others have been more cautious than courageous and have remained silent behind the anesthetizing security of stained glass windows.

In spite of my shattered dreams, I came to Birmingham with the hope 36 that the white religious leadership of this community would see the justice of our cause and, with deep moral concern, would serve as the channel through which our just grievances could reach the power structure. I had hoped that each of you would understand. But again I have been disappointed.

I have heard numerous southern religious leaders admonish their 37 worshipers to comply with a desegregation decision because it is the law, but I have longed to hear white ministers declare: "Follow this decree because integration is morally right and because the Negro is your brother." In the midst of blatant injustices inflicted upon the Negro, I have watched white churchmen stand on the sideline and mouth pious irrelevancies and sanctimonious trivialities. In the midst of a mighty struggle to rid our nation of racial and economic injustice, I have heard many ministers say: "Those are social issues, with which the gospel has no real concern." And I have watched many churches commit themselves to a completely otherworldly religion which makes a strange, un-Biblical distinction between body and soul, between the sacred and the secular.

I have traveled the length and breadth of Alabama, Mississippi, and all 38 the other southern states. On sweltering summer days and crisp autumn mornings I have looked at the South's beautiful churches with their lofty spires pointing heavenward. I have beheld the impressive outlines of her massive religious-education buildings. Over and over I have found myself asking: "What kind of people worship here? Who is their God? Where were their voices when the lips of Governor Barnett dripped with words of interposition and nullification? Where were they when Governor Wallace gave a clarion call for defiance and hatred? Where were their voices of support when bruised and weary Negro men and women decided to rise from the dark dungeons of complacency to the bright hills of creative protest?"

Yes, these questions are still in my mind. In deep disappointment I 39 have wept over the laxity of the church. But be assured that my tears have been tears of love. There can be no deep disappointment where there is not deep love. Yes, I love the church. How could I do otherwise? I am in the rather unique position of being the son, the grandson, and the great-grandson of preachers. Yes, I see the church as the body of Christ. But, oh! How we have blemished and scarred that body through social neglect and through fear of being nonconformists.

There was a time when the church was very powerful—in the time   40
when the early Christians rejoiced at being deemed worthy to suffer for what they believed. In those days the church was not merely a ther-mometer that recorded the ideas and principles of popular opinion; it was a thermostat that transformed the mores of society. Whenever the early Christians entered a town, the people in power became disturbed and immediately sought to convict the Christians for being "disturbers of the peace" and "outside agitators." But the Christians pressed on, in the conviction that they were "a colony of heaven," called to obey God rather than man. Small in number, they were big in commitment. They were too God-intoxicated to be "astronomically intimidated." By their effort and example they brought an end to such ancient evils as infan-ticide and gladiatorial contests.

Things are different now. So often the contemporary church is a weak,   41
ineffectual voice with an uncertain sound. So often it is an archdefender of the status quo. Far from being disturbed by the presence of the church, the power structure of the average community is consoled by the church's silent—and often even vocal—sanction of things as they are.

But the judgment of God is upon the church as never before. If today's   42
church does not recapture the sacrificial spirit of the early church, it will lose its authenticity, forfeit the loyalty of millions, and be dismissed as an irrelevant social club with no meaning for the twentieth century. Every day I meet young people whose disappointment with the church has turned into outright disgust.

Perhaps I have once again been too optimistic. Is organized religion too   43
inextricably bound to the status quo to save our nation and the world? Perhaps I must turn my faith to the inner spiritual church, the church within the church, as the true *ekklesia* and the hope of the world. But again I am thankful to God that some noble souls from the ranks of organized religion have broken loose from the paralyzing chains of conformity and joined us as active partners in the struggle for freedom. They have left their secure congregations and walked the streets of Albany, Georgia, with us. They have gone down the highways of the South on tortuous rides for freedom. Yes, they have gone to jail with us. Some have been dismissed from their churches, have lost the support of their bishops and fellow ministers. But they have acted in the faith that right defeated is stronger than evil triumphant. Their witness has been the spiritual salt that has preserved the true meaning of the gospel in

these troubled times. They have carved a tunnel of hope through the dark mountain of disappointment.

I hope the church as a whole will meet the challenge of this decisive 44 hour. But even if the church does not come to the aid of justice, I have no despair about the future. I have no fear about the outcome of our struggle in Birmingham, even if our motives are at present misunderstood. We will reach the goal of freedom in Birmingham and all over the nation, because the goal of America is freedom. Abused and scorned though we may be, our destiny is tied up with America's destiny. Before the pilgrims landed at Plymouth, we were here. Before the pen of Jefferson etched the majestic words of the Declaration of Independence across the pages of history, we were here. For more than two centuries our forebears labored in this country without wages; they made cotton king; they built the homes of their masters while suffering gross injustice and shameful humiliation—and yet out of a bottomless vitality they continued to thrive and develop. If the inexpressible cruelties of slavery could not stop us, the opposition we now face will surely fail. We will win our freedom because the sacred heritage of our nation and the eternal will of God are embodied in our echoing demands.

Before closing I feel impelled to mention one other point in your 45 statement that has troubled me profoundly. You warmly commended the Birmingham police force for keeping "order" and "preventing violence." I doubt that you would have so warmly commended the police force if you had seen its dogs sinking their teeth into unarmed, nonviolent Negroes. I doubt that you would so quickly commend the policemen if you were to observe their ugly and inhumane treatment of Negroes here in the city jail; if you were to watch them push and curse old Negro women and young Negro girls; if you were to see them slap and kick old Negro men and young boys; if you were to observe them, as they did on two occasions, refuse to give us food because we wanted to sing our grace together. I cannot join you in your praise of the Birmingham police department.

It is true that the police have exercised a degree of discipline in 46 handling the demonstrators. In this sense they have conducted themselves rather "nonviolently" in public. But for what purpose? To preserve the evil system of segregation. Over the past few years I have consistently preached that nonviolence demands that the means we use must be as pure as the ends we seek. I have tried to make clear that it is wrong to use immoral means to attain moral ends. But now I must affirm that it is just as wrong, or perhaps even more so, to use moral means to preserve immoral ends. Perhaps Mr. Connor and his policemen have been rather nonviolent in public, as was Chief Pritchett in Albany, Georgia, but they have used the moral means of nonviolence to maintain the immoral end of racial injustice. As T. S. Eliot has said, "The last temptation is the greatest treason: To do the right deed for the wrong reason."

I wish you had commended the Negro sit-inners and demonstrators of Birmingham for their sublime courage, their willingness to suffer, and their amazing discipline in the midst of great provocation. One day the South will recognize its real heroes. They will be the James Merediths, with the noble sense of purpose that enables them to face jeering and hostile mobs, and with the agonizing loneliness that characterizes the life of the pioneer. They will be old, oppressed, battered Negro women, symbolized in a seventy-two-year-old woman in Montgomery, Alabama, who rose up with a sense of dignity and with her people decided not to ride segregated buses, and who responded with ungrammatical profundity to one who inquired about her weariness: "My feets is tired, but my soul is at rest." They will be the young high school and college students, the young ministers of the gospel and a host of their elders, courageously and nonviolently sitting in at lunch counters and willingly going to jail for conscience' sake. One day the South will know that when these disinherited children of God sat down at lunch counters, they were in reality standing up for what is best in the American dream and for the most sacred values in our Judaeo-Christian heritage, thereby bringing our nation back to those great wells of democracy which were dug deep by the founding fathers in their formulation of the Constitution and the Declaration of Independence. [47]

Never before have I written so long a letter. I'm afraid it is much too long to take your precious time. I can assure you that it would have been much shorter if I had been writing from a comfortable desk, but what else can one do when he is alone in a narrow jail cell, other than write long letters, think long thoughts, and pray long prayers? [48]

If I have said anything in this letter that overstates the truth and indicates an unreasonable impatience, I beg you to forgive me. If I have said anything that understates the truth and indicates my having a patience that allows me to settle for anything less than brotherhood, I beg God to forgive me. [49]

I hope this letter finds you strong in the faith. I also hope that circumstances will soon make it possible for me to meet each of you, not as an integrationist or a civil-rights leader but as a fellow clergyman and a Christian brother. Let us all hope that the dark clouds of racial prejudice will soon pass away and the deep fog of misunderstanding will be lifted from our fear-drenched communities, and in some not too distant tomorrow the radiant stars of love and brotherhood will shine over our great nation with all their scintillating beauty. [50]

Yours for the cause of Peace and Brotherhood,
MARTIN LUTHER KING, JR.

Lewis H. Van Dusen, Jr.

Lewis H. Van Dusen, Jr. (b. 1910) is a Rhodes Scholar and a graduate of Harvard Law School. He practices law in Philadelphia and has served as the chancellor of the Philadelphia Bar Association. Van Dusen has also been active in the American Bar Association as chairman of the Committee on Ethics and Professional Responsibility, and as a member of the Committee on the Federal Judiciary.

Civil Disobedience: Destroyer of Democracy

In this essay, which first appeared in the *American Bar Association Journal*, Van Dusen argues against civil disobedience. He draws a sharp distinction between "conscientious disobedience of state law" as practiced by Antigone, Socrates, Gandhi, and Thoreau and "conscientious law testing" as practiced by Martin Luther King, Jr.

As Charles E. Wyzanski, Chief Judge of the United States District Court in Boston, wrote in the February, 1968, *Atlantic*: "Disobedience is a long step from dissent. Civil disobedience involves a deliberate and punishable breach of legal duty." Protesters might prefer a different definition. They would rather say that civil disobedience is the peaceable resistance of conscience.

The philosophy of civil disobedience was not developed in our American democracy, but in the very first democracy of Athens. It was expressed by the poet Sophocles and the philosopher Socrates. In Sophocles's tragedy, Antigone chose to obey her conscience and violate the state edict against providing burial for her brother, who had been decreed a traitor. When the dictator Creon found out that Antigone had buried her fallen brother, he confronted her and reminded her that there was a mandatory death penalty for this deliberate disobedience of the state law. Antigone nobly replied, "Nor did I think your orders were so strong that you, a mortal man, could overrun the gods' unwritten and unfailing laws."

Conscience motivated Antigone. She was not testing the validity of the law in the hope that eventually she would be sustained. Appealing to the judgment of the community, she explained her action to the chorus. She was not secret and surreptitious—the interment of her brother was open and public. She was not violent; she did not trespass on another

539

citizen's rights. And finally, she accepted without resistance the death sentence—the penalty for violation. By voluntarily accepting the law's sanctions, she was not a revolutionary denying the authority of the state. Antigone's behavior exemplifies the classic case of civil disobedience.

Socrates believed that reason could dictate a conscientious disobedience of state law, but he also believed that he had to accept the legal sanctions of the state. In Plato's *Crito*, Socrates from his hanging basket accepted the death penalty for his teaching of religion to youths contrary to state laws. 4

The sage of Walden, Henry David Thoreau, took this philosophy of nonviolence and developed it into a strategy for solving society's injustices. First enunciating it in protest against the Mexican War, he then turned it to use against slavery. For refusing to pay taxes that would help pay the enforcers of the fugitive slave law, he went to prison. In Thoreau's words, "If the alternative is to keep all just men in prison or to give up slavery, the state will not hesitate which to choose." 5

Sixty years later, Gandhi took Thoreau's civil disobedience as his strategy to wrest Indian independence from England. The famous salt march against a British imperial tax is his best-known example of protest. 6

But the conscientious law breaking of Socrates, Gandhi and Thoreau is to be distinguished from the conscientious law testing of Martin Luther King, Jr., who was not a civil disobedient. The civil disobedient withholds taxes or violates state laws knowing he is legally wrong, but believing he is morally right. While he wrapped himself in the mantle of Gandhi and Thoreau, Dr. King led his followers in violation of state laws he believed were contrary to the Federal Constitution. But since Supreme Court decisions in the end generally upheld his many actions, he should not be considered a true civil disobedient. 7

The civil disobedience of Antigone is like that of the pacifist who withholds paying the percentage of his taxes that goes to the Defense Department, or the Quaker who travels against State Department regulations to Hanoi to distribute medical supplies, or the Vietnam war protester who tears up his draft card. This civil disobedient has been nonviolent in his defiance of the law; he has been unfurtive in his violation; he has been submissive to the penalties of the law. He has neither evaded the law nor interfered with another's rights. He has been neither a rioter nor a revolutionary. The thrust of his cause has not been the might of coercion but the martyrdom of conscience. 8

Was the Boston Tea Party Civil Disobedience? Those who justify violence and radical action as being in the tradition of our Revolution show a misunderstanding of the philosophy of democracy. 9

James Farmer, former head of the Congress of Racial Equality, in defense of the mass action confrontation method, has told of a famous 10 organized demonstration that took place in opposition to political and economic discrimination. The protesters beat back and scattered the law enforcers and then proceeded to loot and destroy private property. Mr. Farmer then said he was talking about the Boston Tea Party and implied that violence as a method for redress of grievances was an American tradition and a legacy of our revolutionary heritage. While it is true that there is no more sacred document than our Declaration of Independence, Jefferson's "inherent right of rebellion" was predicated on the tyrannical denial of democratic means. If there is no popular assembly to provide an adjustment of ills, and if there is no court system to dispose of injustices, then there is, indeed, a right to rebel.

The seventeenth century's John Locke, the philosophical father of the　11 Declaration of Independence, wrote in his *Second Treatise on Civil Government*: "Wherever law ends, tyranny begins . . . and the people are absolved from any further obedience. Governments are dissolved from within when the legislative [chamber] is altered. When the government [becomes] . . . arbitrary disposers of lives, liberties and fortunes of the people, such revolutions happen. . . ."

But there are some sophisticated proponents of the revolutionary　12 redress of grievances who say that the test of the need for radical action is not the unavailability of democratic institutions but the ineffectuality of those institutions to remove blatant social inequalities. If social injustice exists, they say, concerted disobedience is required against the constituted government, whether it be totalitarian or democratic in structure.

Of course, only the most bigoted chauvinist would claim that America　13 is without some glaring faults. But there has never been a utopian society on earth and there never will be unless human nature is remade. Since inequities will mar even the best-framed democracies, the injustice rationale would allow a free right of civil resistance to be available always as a shortcut alternative to the democratic way of petition, debate and assembly. The lesson of history is that civil insurgency spawns far more injustices than it removes. The Jeffersons, Washingtons and Adamses resisted tyranny with the aim of promoting the procedures of democracy. They would never have resisted a democratic government with the risk of promoting the techniques of tyranny.

Legitimate Pressures and Illegitimate Results. There are many civil rights　14 leaders who show impatience with the process of democracy. They rely on the sit-in, boycott or mass picketing to gain speedier solutions to the problems that face every citizen. But we must realize that the legitimate pressures that won concessions in the past can easily escalate into the illegitimate power plays that might extort demands in the future. The victories of these civil rights leaders must not shake our confidence in the democratic procedures, as the pressures of demonstration are desirable only if they take place within the limits allowed by law. Civil rights gains should continue to be won by the persuasion of Congress and other legislative bodies and by the decision of courts. Any illegal entreaty for the rights of some can be an injury to the rights of others, for mass demonstrations often trigger violence.

Those who advocate taking the law into their own hands should 15 reflect that when they are disobeying what they consider to be an immoral law, they are deciding on a possibly immoral course. Their answer is that the process for democratic relief is too slow, that only mass confrontation can bring immediate action, and that any injuries are the inevitable cost of the pursuit of justice. Their answer is, simply put, that the end justifies the means. It is this justification of any form of demonstration as a form of dissent that threatens to destroy a society built on the rule of law.

Our Bill of Rights guarantees wide opportunities to use mass meetings, 16 public parades and organized demonstrations to stimulate sentiment, to dramatize issues and to cause change. The Washington freedom march of 1963 was such a call for action. But the rights of free expression cannot be mere force cloaked in the garb of free speech. As the courts have decreed in labor cases, free assembly does not mean mass picketing or sit-down strikes. These rights are subject to limitations of time and place so as to secure the rights of others. When militant students storm a college president's office to achieve demands, when certain groups plan rush-hour car stalling to protest discrimination in employment, these are not dissent, but a denial of rights to others. Neither is it the lawful use of mass protest, but rather the unlawful use of mob power.

Justice Black, one of the foremost advocates and defenders of the right 17 of protest and dissent, has said:

> . . . Experience demonstrates that it is not a far step from what to many seems to be the earnest, honest, patriotic, kind-spirited multitude of today, to the fanatical, threatening, lawless mob of tomorrow. And the crowds that press in the streets for noble goals today can be supplanted tomorrow by street mobs pressuring the courts for precisely opposite ends.

Society must censure those demonstrators who would trespass on the 18 public peace, as it must condemn those rioters whose pillage would destroy the public peace. But more ambivalent is society's posture toward the civil disobedient. Unlike the rioter, the true civil disobedient commits no violence. Unlike the mob demonstrator, he commits no trespass on others' rights. The civil disobedient, while deliberately violating a law, shows an oblique respect for the law by voluntarily submitting to its sanctions. He neither resists arrest nor evades punishment. Thus, he breaches the law but not the peace.

But civil disobedience, whatever the ethical rationalization, is still an [19] assault on our democratic society, an affront to our legal order and an attack on our constitutional government. To indulge civil disobedience is to invite anarchy, and the permissive arbitrariness of anarchy is hardly less tolerable than the repressive arbitrariness of tyranny. Too often the license of liberty is followed by the loss of liberty, because into the desert of anarchy comes the man on horseback, a Mussolini or a Hitler.

Violations of Law Subvert Democracy. Law violations, even for ends [20] recognized as laudable, are not only assaults on the rule of law, but subversions of the democratic process. The disobedient act of conscience does not ennoble democracy; it erodes it.

First, it courts violence, and even the most careful and limited use of [21] nonviolent acts of disobedience may help sow the dragon-teeth of civil riot. Civil disobedience is the progenitor of disorder, and disorder is the sire of violence.

Second, the concept of civil disobedience does not invite principles of [22] general applicability. If the children of light are morally privileged to resist particular laws on grounds of conscience, so are the children of darkness. Former Deputy Attorney General Burke Marshall said: "If the decision to break the law really turned on individual conscience, it is hard to see in law how [the civil rights leader] is better off than former Governor Ross Barnett of Mississippi who also believed deeply in his cause and was willing to go to jail."

Third, even the most noble act of civil disobedience assaults the rule of [23] law. Although limited as to method, motive and objective, it has the effect of inducing others to engage in different forms of law breaking characterized by methods unsanctioned and condemned by classic theories of law violation. Unfortunately, the most patent lesson of civil disobedience is not so much nonviolence of action as defiance of authority.

Finally, the greatest danger in condoning civil disobedience as a per- [24] missible strategy for hastening change is that it undermines our democratic processes. To adopt the techniques of civil disobedience is to assume that representative government does not work. To resist the decisions of courts and the laws of elected assemblies is to say that democracy has failed.

There is no man who is above the law, and there is no man who has a [25] right to break the law. Civil disobedience is not above the law, but against the law. When the civil disobedient disobeys one law, he invariably subverts all law. When the civil disobedient says that he is above the law, he is saying that democracy is beneath him. His disobedience shows a distrust for the democratic system. He is merely saying that since democracy does not work, why should he help make it work. Thoreau expressed well the civil disobedient's disdain for democracy:

> As for adopting the ways which the state has provided for remedying the evil, I know not of such ways. They take too much time and a man's life will be gone. I have other affairs to attend to. I came into this world not chiefly to make this a good place to live in, but to live in it, be it good or bad.

Thoreau's position is not only morally irresponsible but politically 26 reprehensible. When citizens in a democracy are called on to make a profession of faith, the civil disobedients offer only a confession of failure. Tragically, when civil disobedients for lack of faith abstain from democratic involvement, they help attain their own gloomy prediction. They help create the social and political basis for their own despair. By foreseeing failure, they help forge it. If citizens rely on antidemocratic means of protest, they will help bring about the undemocratic result of an authoritarian or anarchic state.

How far demonstrations properly can be employed to produce political 27 and social change is a pressing question, particularly in view of the provocations accompanying the National Democratic Convention in Chicago last August and the reaction of the police to them. A line must be drawn by the judiciary between the demands of those who seek absolute order, which can lead only to a dictatorship, and those who seek absolute freedom, which can lead only to anarchy. The line, wherever it is drawn by our courts, should be respected on the college campus, on the streets and elsewhere.

Undue provocation will inevitably result in overreaction, human emo- 28 tions being what they are. Violence will follow. This cycle undermines the very democracy it is designed to preserve. The lesson of the past is that democracies will fall if violence, including the intentional provocations that will lead to violence, replaces democratic procedures, as in Athens, Rome and the Weimar Republic. This lesson must be constantly explained by the legal profession.

We should heed the words of William James: 29

> Democracy is still upon its trial. The civic genius of our people is its only bulwark and . . . neither battleships nor public libraries nor great newspapers nor booming stocks: neither mechanical invention nor political adroitness, nor churches nor universities nor civil service examinations can save us from degeneration if the inner mystery be lost.

That mystery, at once the secret and the glory of our English-speaking race, consists of nothing but two habits. . . . One of them is habit of trained and disciplined good temper towards the opposite party when it fairly wins its innings. The other is that of fierce and merciless resentment toward every man or set of men who break the public peace. (James, *Pragmatism*, 127–28)

Alice Walker

Novelist, poet, and essayist Alice Walker is best known for her Pulitzer Prize–winning novel *The Color Purple* (1982), which—along with *Meridien* (1976), her highly regarded novel of the civil rights movement—has become a classic of American literature. Her essays have been collected in *In Search of Our Mothers' Gardens* (1983). More information about Walker can be found in the headnote to "Beauty: When the Other Dancer Is the Self" in Chapter 2.

The Civil Rights Movement: What Good Was It?

This essay, initially published in the *American Scholar* in 1967, evaluates the American civil rights movement of the early 1960s from Walker's personal perspective. This is how Walker describes it in her collection *In Search of Our Mothers' Gardens*: "I wrote the following essay in the winter of 1966–67 while sharing one room above Washington Square Park in New York with a struggling young Jewish law student who became my husband. It was my first published essay and won the three-hundred-dollar first prize in the annual *American Scholar* essay contest. The money was almost magically reassuring to us in those days of disaffected parents, outraged friends, and one-item meals, and kept us in tulips, peonies, daisies, and lamb chops for several months."

Someone said recently to an old black lady from Mississippi, whose 1
legs had been badly mangled by local police who arrested her for "disturbing the peace," that the Civil Rights Movement was dead, and asked, since it was dead, what she thought about it. The old lady replied, hobbling out of his presence on her cane, that the Civil Rights Movement was like herself, "if it's dead, it shore ain't ready to lay down!"

This old lady is a legendary freedom fighter in her small town in the 2
Delta. She has been severely mistreated for insisting on her rights as an American citizen. She has been beaten for singing Movement songs, placed in solitary confinement in prisons for talking about freedom, and placed on bread and water for praying aloud to God for her jailers' deliverance. For such a woman the Civil Rights Movement will never be over as long as her skin is black. It also will never be over for twenty

546

million others with the same "affliction," for whom the Movement can never "lay down," no matter how it is killed by the press and made dead and buried by the white American public. As long as one black American survives, the struggle for equality with other Americans must also survive. This is a debt we owe to those blameless hostages we leave to the future, our children.

Still, white liberals and deserting Civil Rights sponsors are quick to   3
justify their disaffection from the Movement by claiming that it is all over. "And since it is over," they will ask, "would someone kindly tell me what has been gained by it?" They then list statistics supposedly showing how much more advanced segregation is now than ten years ago—in schools, housing, jobs. They point to a gain in conservative politicians during the last few years. They speak of ghetto riots and of the survey that shows that most policemen are admittedly too anti-Negro to do their jobs in ghetto areas fairly and effectively. They speak of every area that has been touched by the Civil Rights Movement as somehow or other going to pieces.

They rarely talk, however, about human attitudes among Negroes that   4
have undergone terrific changes just during the past seven to ten years (not to mention all those years when there was a Movement and only the Negroes knew about it). They seldom speak of changes in personal lives because of the influence of people in the Movement. They see general failure and few, if any, individual gains.

They do not understand what it is that keeps the Movement from   5
"laying down" and Negroes from reverting to their former *silent* second-class status. They have apparently never stopped to wonder why it is always the white man—on his radio and in his newspaper and on his television—who says that the Movement is dead. If a Negro were audacious enough to make such a claim, his fellows might hanker to see him shot. The Movement is dead to the white man because it no longer interests him. And it no longer interests him because he can afford to be uninterested: he does not have to live by it, with it, or for it, as Negroes must. He can take a rest from the news of beatings, killings, and arrests that reach him from North and South—if his skin is white. Negroes cannot now and will never be able to take a rest from the injustices that plague them, for they—not the white man—are the target.

Perhaps it is naïve to be thankful that the Movement "saved" a large   6
number of individuals and gave them something to live for, even if it did not provide them with everything they wanted. (Materially, it provided them with precious little that they wanted.) When a movement awakens people to the possibilities of life, it seems unfair to frustrate them by then denying what they had thought was offered. But what was offered? What

was promised? What was it all about? What good did it do? Would it have been better, as some have suggested, to leave the Negro people as they were, unawakened, unallied with one another, unhopeful about what to expect for their children in some future world?

I do not think so. If knowledge of my condition is all the freedom I get   7
from a "freedom movement," it is better than unawareness, forgotten-ness, and hopelessness, the existence that is like the existence of a beast. Man only truly lives by knowing; otherwise he simply performs, copying the daily habits of others, but conceiving nothing of his creative pos-sibilities as a man, and accepting someone else's superiority and his own misery.

When we are children, growing up in our parents' care, we await the   8
spark from the outside world. Sometimes our parents provide it—if we are lucky—sometimes it comes from another source far from home. We sit, paralyzed, surrounded by our anxiety and dread, hoping we will not have to grow up into the narrow world and ways we see about us. We are hungry for a life that turns us on; we yearn for a knowledge of living that will save us from our innocuous lives that resemble death. We look for signs in every strange event; we search for heroes in every unknown face.

It was just six years ago that I began to be alive. I had, of course, been   9
living before—for I am now twenty-three—but I did not really know it. And I did not know it because nobody told me that I—a pensive, yearning, typical high-school senior, but Negro—existed in the minds of others as I existed in my own. Until that time my mind was locked apart from the outer contours and complexion of my body as if it and the body were strangers. The mind possessed both thought and spirit—I wanted to be an author or a scientist—which the color of the body denied. I had never seen myself and existed as a statistic exists, or as a phantom. In the white world I walked, less real to them than a shadow; and being young and well hidden among the slums, among people who also did not exist—either in books or in films or in the government of their own lives—I waited to be called to life. And, by a miracle, I was called.

There was a commotion in our house that night in 1960. We had   10
managed to buy our first television set. It was battered and overpriced, but my mother had gotten used to watching the afternoon soap operas at the house where she worked as maid, and nothing could satisfy her on days when she did not work but a continuation of her "stories." So she pinched pennies and bought a set.

I remained listless throughout her "stories," tales of pregnancy, abor-   11
tion, hypocrisy, infidelity, and alcoholism. All these men and women were white and lived in houses with servants, long staircases that they floated down, patios where liquor was served four times a day to "relax"

them. But my mother, with her swollen feet eased out of her shoes, her heavy body relaxed in our only comfortable chair, watched each movement of the smartly coiffed women, heard each word, pounced upon each innuendo and inflection, and for the duration of these "stories" she saw herself as one of them. She placed herself in every scene she saw, with her braided hair turned blond, her two hundred pounds compressed into a sleek size-seven dress, her rough dark skin smooth and *white.* Her husband became "dark and handsome," talented, witty, urbane, charming. And when she turned to look at my father sitting near her in his sweat shirt with his smelly feet raised on the bed to "air," there was always a tragic look of surprise on her face. Then she would sigh and go out to the kitchen looking lost and unsure of herself. My mother, a truly great woman who raised eight children of her own and half a dozen of the neighbors' without a single complaint, was convinced that she did not exist compared to "them." She subordinated her soul to theirs and became a faithful and timid supporter of the "Beautiful White People." Once she asked me, in a moment of vicarious pride and despair, if I didn't think that "they" were "jest naturally smarter, prettier, better." My mother asked this: a woman who never got rid of any of her children, never cheated on my father, was never a hypocrite if she could help it, and never even tasted liquor. She could not even bring herself to blame "them" for making her believe what they wanted her to believe: that if she did not look like them, think like them, be sophisticated and corrupt-for-comfort's-sake like them, she was a nobody. Black was not a color on my mother; it was a shield that made her invisible.

Of course, the people who wrote the soap-opera scripts always made   12
the Negro maids in them steadfast, trusty, and wise in a home-remedial sort of way; but my mother, a maid for nearly forty years, never once identified herself with the scarcely glimpsed black servant's face beneath the ruffled cap. Like everyone else, in her daydreams at least, she thought she was free.

Six years ago, after half-heartedly watching my mother's soap operas   13
and wondering whether there wasn't something more to be asked of life, the Civil Rights Movement came into my life. Like a good omen for the future, the face of Dr. Martin Luther King, Jr., was the first black face I saw on our new television screen. And, as in a fairy tale, my soul was stirred by the meaning for me of his mission—at the time he was being rather ignominiously dumped into a police van for having led a protest march in Alabama—and I fell in love with the sober and determined face of the Movement. The singing of "We Shall Overcome"—that song betrayed by nonbelievers in it—rang for the first time in my ears. The influence that my mother's soap operas might have had on me became

impossible. The life of Dr. King, seeming bigger and more miraculous than the man himself, because of all he had done and suffered, offered a pattern of strength and sincerity I felt I could trust. He had suffered much because of his simple belief in nonviolence, love, and brotherhood. Perhaps the majority of men could not be reached through these beliefs, but because Dr. King kept trying to reach them in spite of danger to himself and his family, I saw in him the hero for whom I had waited so long.

What Dr. King promised was not a ranch-style house and an acre of manicured lawn for every black man, but jail and finally freedom. He did not promise two cars for every family, but the courage one day for all families everywhere to walk without shame and unafraid on their own feet. He did not say that one day it will be us chasing prospective buyers out of our prosperous well-kept neighborhoods, or in other ways exhibiting our snobbery and ignorance as all other ethnic groups before us have done; what he said was that we had a right to live anywhere in this country we chose, and a right to a meaningful well-paying job to provide us with the upkeep of our homes. He did not say we had to become carbon copies of the white American middle class; but he did say we had the right to become whatever we wanted to become.   14

Because of the Movement, because of an awakened faith in the newness and imagination of the human spirit, because of "black and white together"—for the first time in our history in some human relationship on and off TV—because of the beatings, the arrests, the hell of battle during the past years, I have fought harder for my life and for a chance to be myself, to be something more than a shadow or a number, than I had ever done before in my life. Before, there had seemed to be no real reason for struggling beyond the effort for daily bread. Now there was a chance at that other that Jesus meant when He said we could not live by bread alone.   15

I have fought and kicked and fasted and prayed and cursed and cried myself to the point of existing. It has been like being born again, literally. Just "knowing" has meant everything to me. Knowing has pushed me out into the world, into college, into places, into people.   16

Part of what existence means to me is knowing the difference between what I am now and what I was then. It is being capable of looking after myself intellectually as well as financially. It is being able to tell when I am being wronged and by whom. It means being awake to protect myself and the ones I love. It means being a part of the world community, and being *alert* to which part it is that I have joined, and knowing how to change to another part if that part does not suit me. To know is to exist: to exist is to be involved, to move about, to see the world with my own eyes. This, at least, the Movement has given me.   17

The hippies and other nihilists would have me believe that it is all the 18 same whether the people in Mississippi have a movement behind them or not. Once they have their rights, they say, they will run all over themselves trying to be just like everybody else. They will be well fed, complacent about things of the spirit, emotionless, and without that marvelous humanity and "soul" that the Movement has seen them practice time and time again. "What has the Movement done," they ask, "with the few people it has supposedly helped?" "Got them white-collar jobs, moved them into standardized ranch houses in white neighbor-hoods, given them nondescript gray flannel suits?" "What are these people now?" they ask. And then they answer themselves, "Nothings!"

I would find this reasoning—which I have heard many, many times 19 from hippies and nonhippies alike—amusing if I did not also consider it serious. For I think it is a delusion, a cop-out, an excuse to disassociate themselves from a world in which they feel too little has been changed or gained. The real question, however, it appears to me, is not whether poor people will adopt the middle-class mentality once they are well fed; rather, it is whether they will ever be well fed enough to be able to choose whatever mentality they think will suit them. The lack of a movement did not keep my mother from *wishing* herself bourgeois in her daydreams.

There is widespread starvation in Mississippi. In my own state of 20 Georgia there are more hungry families than Lester Maddox would like to admit—or even see fed. I went to school with children who ate red dirt. The Movement has prodded and pushed some liberal senators into pressuring the government for food so that the hungry may eat. Food stamps that were two dollars and out of the reach of many families not long ago have been reduced to fifty cents. The price is still out of the reach of some families, and the government, it seems to a lot of people, could spare enough free food to feed its own people. It angers people in the Movement that it does not; they point to the billions in wheat we send free each year to countries abroad. Their government's slowness while people are hungry, its unwillingness to believe that there are Americans starving, its stingy cutting of the price of food stamps, make many Civil Rights workers throw up their hands in disgust. But they do not give up. They do not withdraw into the world of psychedelia. They apply what pressure they can to make the government give away food to hungry people. They do not plan so far ahead in their disillusionment with society that they can see these starving families buying identical ranch-style houses and sending their snobbish children to Bryn Mawr and Yale. They take first things first and try to get them fed.

They do not consider it their business, in any case, to say what kind of 21 life the people they help must lead. How one lives is, after all, one of the rights left to the individual—when and if he has opportunity to choose.

It is not the prerogative of the middle class to determine what is worthy of aspiration. There is also every possibility that the middle-class people of tomorrow will turn out ever so much better than those of today. I even know some middle-class people of today who are not *all* bad.

I think there are so few Negro hippies because middle-class Negroes, 22 although well fed, are not careless. They are required by the treacherous world they live in to be clearly aware of whoever or whatever might be trying to do them in. They are middle class in money and position, but they cannot afford to be middle class in complacency. They distrust the hippie movement because they know that it can do nothing for Negroes as a group but "love" them, which is what all paternalists claim to do. And since the only way Negroes can survive (which they cannot do, unfortunately, on love alone) is with the support of the group, they are wisely wary and stay away.

A white writer tried recently to explain that the reason for the 23 relatively few Negro hippies is that Negroes have built up a "super-cool" that cracks under LSD and makes them have a "bad trip." What this writer doesn't guess at is that Negroes are needing drugs less than ever these days for any kind of trip. While the hippies are "tripping," Negroes are going after power, which is so much more important to their survival and their children's survival than LSD and pot.

Everyone would be surprised if the Israelis ignored the Arabs and took 24 up "tripping" and pot smoking. In this country we are the Israelis. Everybody who can do so would like to forget this, of course. But for us to forget it for a minute would be fatal. "We Shall Overcome" is just a song to most Americans, *but we must do it*. Or die.

What good was the Civil Rights Movement? If it had just given this 25 country Dr. King, a leader of conscience, for once in our lifetime, it would have been enough. If it had just taken black eyes off white television stories, it would have been enough. If it fed one starving child, it would have been enough.

If the Civil Rights Movement is "dead," and if it gave us nothing else, 26 it gave us each other forever. It gave some of us bread, some of us shelter, some of us knowledge and pride, all of us comfort. It gave us our children, our husbands, our brothers, our fathers, as men reborn and with a purpose for living. It broke the pattern of black servitude in this country. It shattered the phony "promise" of white soap operas that sucked away so many pitiful lives. It gave us history and men far greater than Presidents. It gave us heroes, selfless men of courage and strength, for our little boys and girls to follow. It gave us hope for tomorrow. It called us to life.

Because we live, it can never die.   27

David R. Weber

A teacher at Phillips Exeter Academy, David R. Weber has contributed poems, essays, and reviews to a variety of publications, including the *New York Times*, the *Independent School Bulletin*, and the *Chronicle of Higher Education*. He is also the editor of *Civil Disobedience in America: A Documentary History* (1978), a collection of sermons, letters, essays, literary works, and transcripts representing America's long tradition of writing on civil disobedience. His purpose, he explains in the preface, "is to counter the widespread impression that the history of civil disobedience in the United States before the Vietnam period has only two figures of lasting interest, Henry David Thoreau and Martin Luther King."

Civil Disobedience in America

This selection is excerpted from the general introduction to *Civil Disobedience in America*. Weber explains that from the start America was torn over the issue of civil disobedience: "Many Americans have held attitudes or ideas that might have led them into conscientious lawbreaking; but most have had other, contradictory ideas and values—as well as strong practical motives—that have led them to avoid or oppose it."

The history of American civil disobedience falls into three broad and generally distinct traditions. The first is opposition, mainly by individual dissenters in the seventeenth and eighteenth centuries, to legal violations of the principle of religious liberty; the second is disobedience, mainly in the nineteenth century and among many twentieth-century war resisters, to statutes that seemed to implicate individual citizens in immoral actions; the third is the use of mass civil disobedience as a tactic to achieve social or legal change, mainly in the civil rights movement of the 1950s and 1960s. Each of these traditions has its own characteristic forms, its own internal logic, and its own problems. . . .

The first of the three traditions was a continuing part of the life of the Massachusetts Bay Colony, where dissenters against the orthodox (Congregational) Standing Order, mainly Quakers and then Baptists as well, were hanged, banished, or whipped. Later they were fined, imprisoned, or distrained (that is, their goods were seized and sold to raise the money they had refused to pay in taxes for the support of orthodox ministers). . . .

By the mid-eighteenth century the dissenters' lot had improved some-   3
what. The physical ferocity of the penalties meted out to them had
declined, but the milder punishments were severe enough: one woman in
Raynham, Massachusetts, was jailed for thirteen months when she
refused to pay a tax of nine pence (McLoughlin 713). Through a series of
laws passed in 1727 and the years following, an Anglican, Baptist, or
Quaker could obtain exemption from church taxes by filing "an annual
certificate signed by his minister and a committee of respectable lay
members of his church attesting that he was 'conscientiously' of their
persuasion" (McLoughlin 711). This attempt at statutory accommodation was fatally undermined, however, by a combination of factors:
social prejudice against the dissenters, with its resulting bitterness; the
readiness of parish tax assessors to deny the validity of many certificates
by exploiting legal technicalities, so that the dissenters' revenue wouldn't
be lost to the orthodox community; and finally, the dissenters' sense
(partly as a result of these pressures) that the mere requirement of the
certificate itself was a violation of religious liberty, since it granted to the
civil authority the power to sanction spiritual choices and to penalize
unacceptable religious views.

So the new laws did not bring the disobedience to an end. Instead the   4
Baptists, frustrated by continuing harassment after decades of more or
less patient suffering, felt driven to new measures. The manifesto of their
new mode of resistance was Isaac Backus's "Appeal to the Public for
Religious Liberty," which in its strategies is perhaps the nearest thing in
our earlier history to an anticipation of the mass civil disobedience
advocated in the twentieth century by A. Philip Randolph and Martin
Luther King. In its central principle, however, Backus's pamphlet looks
back rather than forward: for him what is at stake is still religious
freedom implemented by separation of church and state.

American civil disobedience begins, then, with resistance to specifi-   5
cally religious persecution or harassment, rather than with opposition to
injustice conceived in broader or more secular terms. In its tenacious
defense of the right to determine freely the forms and content of one's
own religious practice, this tradition looks back to the religious martyrs
of the Bible. It had numerous advocates and practitioners in the two
centuries before religious disestablishment was fully achieved.

This earlier tradition served and in some sense fostered its successors,   6
since religious experience, religious commitments, and religious logic
remained central to American civil disobedience. Throughout the ante
bellum period Protestant ministers advocated (and opposed) civil disobedience in sermons based on biblical texts; and disobedience as recent as
Dr. King's and the Berrigans' is of course informed by Christian faith

and passion. In one crucial respect, however, the early tradition had little help to offer subsequent disobedients: the resistance of Baptists and Quakers to religious taxes had scrupulously avoided any challenge to secular authority in most of its provinces; it had been merely an attempt to exempt religious worship from the realm of that authority. These early disobedients were, William McLoughlin observes, "radicals only in religion; their social and political views were virtually identical with their neighbors', and on moral issues . . . they were decidedly conservative" (717). So the newer strain of disobedience had in an important way a more delicate task; Jonathan Mayhew, John Woolman, and William Ellery Channing had carried the prohibitions and prescriptions of Christian revelation onto new ground. The challenge now was to vindicate the rights of the individual conscience in some secular areas without undermining the authority of human government generally. Those ministers who sought to extend the doctrine of religious liberty and obligation into social and political behavior were angrily challenged on the ground that they were now "preaching politics." Laymen who made the same arguments were accused of anarchy. This issue has been a live one ever since; so in considering the principal defenses developed by nineteenth-century disobedients, we shall anticipate as well some aspects of the twentieth-century debate.

Throughout much of our history, then, the advocates of civil disobedience have been accused of holding principles that lead straight to disorder, anarchy, or subversion, or at best to violations of law in support of less admirable causes than those of religious liberty, racial and sexual justice, and peace. The disobedients have generally replied to this charge in two ways. First, they have argued that the prediction is false, that it is only the "wise minority" that will brave legal and social sanctions in the name of conscience; they have suggested further that their own effort to maintain the connection between law and justice by opposing unjust legislation will do more in the long run to foster reverence for law than will the inflexible authoritarianism of their opponents. The latter, they have argued, will breed cynicism about the moral dimension of the law and thus, however paradoxically, will itself ultimately foster lawlessness. Second, they have simply maintained that the moral imperative under which they act transcends all concern for consequences. The abolition of slavery, Thoreau said, is one of those cases "in which a people, as well as an individual, must do justice, cost what it may. . . . This people must cease to hold slaves, and to make war on Mexico, though it cost them their existence as a people" (40–41). . . .

The second defense—that consequences should not be consulted in matters of overriding principle—is still less satisfactory, since it lends itself to a potentially dangerous level of romantic abstraction. To borrow terms from Richard Hofstadter, disobedients who hold their actions to be above a consideration of consequences have scorned "the rational calculus of tactical probabilities"; their "claims for therapy or sanctification . . . rest upon an arbitrary assumption of success" (34). For two reasons, however, the argument of the disobedients is less sinister than that of the advocates of "revolutionary" violence whom Hofstadter discusses. The first is simply that the risks of immediate harm are much smaller and less grave in the disobedients' case; the second is that their position is based upon a metaphysical optimism that they affirmed in innocence and good faith. In the nineteenth century they simply took for granted that since a benign divine providence ultimately determined the nature and course of human history, any truly conscientious action could not fail to have generally beneficial consequences. This was a central element in their world view, not an easy rationalization or a mask for self-indulgence. (Most of their nineteenth-century opponents in fact shared this premise, while drawing different conclusions from it.) Even if to us this perspective is no longer available, our grimmer sense of history ought not to impose a too hasty judgment of their personal choices. . . .

Another recurrent issue that disobedients have had to face from early on is the relation of their lawbreaking to violence. It is widely assumed that this problem has had a single solution—that nonviolence is a necessary aspect of civil disobedience—but the assumption is arbitrary and unhistorical. It has led among other things to a view of Thoreau which misrepresents him by making his civil disobedience far more similar to Gandhi's and King's than it actually is. Among nineteenth-century disobedients John Greenleaf Whittier is actually a much closer parallel: "the destruction of one human life," Whittier said categorically, "would be too great a price to pay for any social or political change" (qtd. in Pollard 600). Whittier generally held to this absolute nonviolence even during the turmoil over the Fugitive Slave Law; and many other nineteenth-century disobedients—Nathaniel Hall is an example—joined him in this stand. Their position is remote, however, from the one espoused by some others. Thomas Wentworth Higginson is perhaps the most overt exponent of a willingness to adopt physical violence as an aspect of his disobedience, but Theodore Parker and Thoreau embrace the same logic. . . .

Similarly Wendell Phillips, despite his long association with William Lloyd Garrison, argued in 1852 that fugitive slaves could legitimately use violence to prevent their recapture; his position is, he notes, "a new measure in the antislavery enterprise" (140–44). Phillips spoke for those abolitionists who were theoretically committed to nonviolence but who discovered under the pressure of events that their deepest feelings actually lay elsewhere and thus reluctantly came to accept the logic of a more militant position than they had wished to occupy.

Thoreau and Parker, however, had never adopted nonviolence as a 11 positive principle to begin with. Even in "Civil Disobedience" written before the fugitive slave cases of the 1850s had clarified the ways in which violence might be morally justified, Thoreau had separated himself from "those who call themselves no-government men"—that is, from the radical nonresistants. And once the fugitive slave issue had been posed, Parker was quick to add firearms to the resources of his Bible.

Perhaps it will be objected that Thoreau, Parker, and Higginson had 12 actually moved beyond civil disobedience into a form of revolution or at least of guerrilla warfare. It is true that Higginson and Parker were to be two of the Secret Six who raised funds for John Brown in the weeks before his attack on Harpers Ferry, and that some of the language of "Slavery in Massachusetts" and *Massachusetts in Mourning* has a paramilitary ring. Further, in the sermons in which Parker espouses civil disobedience he often appeals to the moral authority of the American Revolution. We may clarify this question, I think, by considering somewhat more closely the logic by which certain forms of violence justified themselves to these men.

They derived their ideas from two sources that seemed to them com- 13 plementary: the Bible and the Anglo-American tradition of natural rights and natural law by which the American Revolution had been justified. Parker liked to make the fusion symbolically explicit. When he married the escaped slaves William and Ellen Craft, members of his parish, he concluded the ceremony on a dramatic note: "he put a Bible and a sword into William's hands and bade him use both with all his might" (Schwartz 193).

A cornerstone of this position was the conviction that life, liberty, and 14 the pursuit of happiness—especially life and liberty—were values of fully equal authority. An implication of this view was that someone whose liberty was threatened by a slave-catcher had precisely the same right of capital self-defense as one menaced by a would-be murderer. It meant too that just as a fellow citizen should if necessary intervene forcibly to prevent a killing, so he should employ whatever force was necessary to frustrate an attempt to kidnap a fugitive slave. In both cases the aggressor had forfeited his own right to further life by threatening the inalienable natural rights of someone else. These views, Parker and the others thought, were sanctioned by both natural and revealed religion, as well as by their association with our successful revolution. But these ideas did not necessarily move beyond civil disobedience to general resistance or revolution. They were available to men who had no thought of a general overthrow of the government in power; they were accepted by some whose resistance to law remained steadily focused on what they saw as a single anomalous statute. When Higginson, Parker, and Thoreau spoke of revolution, they were articulating a conception that was more moral than political. In short, this way of thinking about violence lent itself very readily to militant theories of civil disobedience.

Nonviolence, then, has by no means always been a part of civil   15
disobedience. (The reverse is also true, of course: much of the tradition of nonviolent thought and nonviolent direct action—demonstrations, boycotts, protests, petitions—has no concern with lawbreaking.) Similarly, some but hardly all American disobedients have viewed an acceptance of legal penalties as an indispensable part of their illegal action. For some, going to jail has been an important symbol of their allegiance to the overall rule of law in the society; it has been a way of making clear the limits of their quarrel, of saying that though one particular statute compels their disobedience, the authority of secular law in general remains intact and binding. "Where duty to God and man required us to refuse active obedience to such enactments," Whitter said, "we would submit *as good citizens*, to the penalty incurred" (Pollard 600–601). On this point, as on nonviolence, Thoreau and many others take a different stance. Despite his famous night in the Concord jail, Thoreau seems to have regarded imprisonment as a risk to be run rather than as a symbolic experience to be embraced on principle. It is true that he calls jail "the only house in a slave State in which a free man can abide with honor" and that he argues for mass jailgoing by "all just men" as a means of bringing injustice to a halt. But just as his characteristic note is individualistic and not that of a participant in a movement, so his usual position about imprisonment is that it is an inconvenience imposed by the state, not an integral part of the act of civil disobedience. The disobedient in Thoreau's view has all the right on *his* side; he is not bound to make conciliatory bows to state authority. All the evidence seems to indicate that if Sam Staples had not come after him, Thoreau would not have sought out the jailhouse. Even in his hope of catalyzing resistance in many others, it is the readiness to face imprisonment—that is, the lawbreaking itself—which he emphasizes as the effective moral force. And in any case his rationale for the dissident's presence in jail is quite different from Whittier's and Hall's. For them it is a guarantee that civil disobedience will not tend to foster a breakdown of law and order. For Thoreau, when it isn't simply a price the disobedient has to pay for his moral freedom, it is an aggressive tactic by which the state can be made to give up its support of slavery. Thoreau believed that Massachusetts,

through its complicity in slavery, had forfeited its moral authority generally; his is a much more radical analysis than the emphasis of Whittier and Hall on reconciling civil disobedience with loyal citizenship. Thoreau would have been quick to say that his own behavior was also in the interests of true citizenship; but the role played by imprisonment in his thinking about civil disobedience has none of the social piety of more conservative disobedients.

The complexities of Thoreau's ["Civil Disobedience"] should help us   16
to see that American civil disobedience has often been ambiguously rooted in two distinguishable motives: the impulse to free oneself from guilt or sin and the impulse to end some social evil, to reform or remake the world. These objectives have sometimes been so harmonious that the disobedient has had no need to distinguish between them: Thoreau's essay—many other instances could be cited, especially from the nineteenth century—is shaped by the assumption that to act with maximum personal principle and integrity is also necessarily to act with maximum beneficial effect upon the social and political world (though such action may well involve a high price, possibly even martyrdom, for the disobedients themselves). Thoreau refused to pay his poll tax not only because a man could "not without disgrace be associated" with the government but because conscientious action was "essentially revolutionary" and held out far greater promise of bringing northern complicity in slavery to an end than political practicality could do.

In the twentieth century civil disobedience has tended to be inspired   17
less by a vision of individual innocence maintained in opposition to state decree than by a determination to influence the state and the society both—either to restrain them from doing evil or to lead them into a process of active regeneration. A. Philip Randolph's testimony before the Senate Armed Services Committee in 1948 is in this sense a major watershed in the history of American civil disobedience. In his advocacy of disobedience in response to segregation in the armed forces, Randolph makes use of the concept of a "higher law," but his ideas are cast in secular and political terms:

> In resorting to the principles of direct-action techniques of Gandhi, whose death was publicly mourned by many members of Congress and President Truman, Negroes will be serving a higher law than any passed by a national legislature in an era when racism spells our doom. . . . In refusing to accept compulsory military segregation, Negro youth will be serving their fellow men throughout the world.
>
> I feel qualified to make this claim because of a recent survey of American psychologists, sociologists and anthropologists. The survey revealed an overwhelming belief among these experts that enforced segregation on racial or religious lines has serious and detrimental psychological effects both on the segre-

gated groups *and on those enforcing segregation.* . . . Negro youth have a moral obligation not to lend themselves as world-wide carriers of an evil and hellish doctrine. (277)

Nothing in this appeal to the authority of modern science, however, would hinder an alliance between secular and religious disobedients. (Indeed, when Adam Clayton Powell supported Randolph's position before the committee, he envisioned a national movement of draft resistance led in the black community by its thousands of Protestant ministers.) Men of many different persuasions could share too in Randolph's appeal to the other authority on which his disobedience is based: the conceptions of equality and freedom at the center of our national political tradition.

At several points Randolph anticipates the thinking of Martin Luther 18 King, though for King it was "Christ [who] furnished the spirit and motivation, while Gandhi furnished the method" (85). Like King, Randolph looks to Gandhi for both practical and moral reasons; he sees in Gandhi's movement both an instance of success in the struggle of dispossessed groups against established power and a compelling example of moral superiority to the wielders of power. Randolph's tone, however, holds less love and more anger than King's. While King's emphasis is on the power of nonviolent direct action, as a manifestation of love, to bring about the "blessed community," Randolph's is on the tactical strength of organized direct action by blacks and on the psychological benefits for black people that will follow from their having seized an independent initiative to secure the dignity of equal status. In this sense his perspectives and tonalities are more in harmony with those of contemporary black activism than King's.

Both Randolph and King value civil disobedience chiefly for its prom- 19 ise of desirable social results; but this emphasis is still fully in harmony with the older one on personal innocence. In the last ten years, however, the two motives have been felt more and more to be distinct, or even to be in conflict with each other. John William Ward's ["To Whom Shall I Write a Letter?"], for example, makes no romantic assumptions about the identity of conscientious and effective action. Ward was moved to his action by a wish to bear personal witness against the war in Vietnam and also by frustration that conventional methods of protest had had no influence upon American policy, but he was under no illusion that civil disobedience would be effective where other means had failed.

In 1971 Allard Lowenstein invoked a different sense of the practical 20 probabilities to oppose civil disobedience, feeling that its effects were likely to be the reverse of what the disobedients wished. Since civil disobedience was too radical and threatening to be accepted by most

Americans, he argued, actions like the Berrigans' raid on the Catonsville draft board would tend to discredit rather than to galvanize popular opposition to the war. The citizen conscientiously opposed to the war, then, had to face an excruciating dilemma: he could end his own complicity through tax refusal or other illegal action, but only at the cost of futility or worse; or he could hope to play some role in turning public feeling against the war through more acceptable, conventional means, all the while paying taxes that would purchase automatic weapons and napalm. If he chose the latter course, he would probably be haunted by the possibility that his deepest motive for remaining within the law was the ignoble one of protecting himself from the penalties of disobedience. If he chose the former, he risked fearful personal consequences with very little assurance that he would achieve anything more than the semi-martyrdom of imprisonment.

This sort of approach to questions of personal political ethics is [21] perhaps distinctively modern in its fundamental lack of faith that goodness or justice will ultimately prevail in human affairs. Civil disobedience has never been an easy choice, because it has generally entailed great personal risks and has often been deeply troubling philosophically, even for its advocates. But in the latter part of the twentieth century, virtually bereft of political heroes and dominated by images (and not just images) of institutionalized power, it is perhaps harder than ever to sustain a sufficient sense of the reality and power of the individual conscience, a sense that makes civil disobedience an act of moral force and promise, not just of frustration or desperation. The wish or willingness to bear moral witness even at large personal cost must now contend with a malaise to which Thoreau and his contemporaries were generally immune: the sense that "in the vast impersonality of twentieth-century society and government, it has become almost impossible for individuals to affect the grinding course of things" (Wicker D13). In short, it seems harder now to hold to either of the assumptions that have historically been at the heart of civil disobedience. . . .

WORKS CITED

Backus, Isaac. "Appeal to the Public for Religious Liberty." In David R. Weber (ed.), *Civil Disobedience in America: A Documentary History*. Ithaca: Cornell UP, 1978: 49–54.

Berrigan, Daniel. *The Trial of the Catonsville Nine*. Boston: Beacon Press, 1970.

Channing, William Ellery. "Lecture on War" (1838). In David R. Weber (ed.), *Civil Disobedience in America: A Documentary History*. Ithaca: Cornell UP, 1978: 61–69.

Gandhi, Mohandas K. *Non-Violent Resistance*. New York: Schocken Books, 1961.

Hall, Nathaniel. *The Limits of Civil Disobedience* (1851). In David R. Weber (ed.), *Civil Disobedience in America: A Documentary History*. Ithaca: Cornell UP, 1978: 115–20.

Higginson, Thomas Wentworth. *Massachusetts in Mourning*. Boston: James Munroe, 1854.

Hofstadter, Richard. "Reflections on Violence in the United States." In Richard Hofstadter and Michael Wallace (eds.), *American Violence: A Documentary History*. New York: Vintage Books, 1971.

King, Martin Luther, Jr. *Stride toward Freedom*. New York: Harper & Row, 1958.

Mayhew, Jonathan. "Discourse Concerning Unlimited Submission and Non-Resistance to the Higher Powers" (1750). In David R. Weber (ed.), *Civil Disobedience in America: A Documentary History*. Ithaca: Cornell UP, 1978: 38–44.

McLoughlin, William G. "Massive Civil Disobedience as a Baptist Tactic in 1773." *American Quarterly* 21 (Winter 1989).

Parker, Theodore. *The Function and Place of Conscience, in Relation to the Laws of Men.* Boston: Crosby & Nichols, 1850.

Phillips, Wendell. Speech at the Melodeon on the First Anniversary of the Rendition of Thomas Sims (1852). In David R. Weber (ed.), *Civil Disobedience in America: A Documentary History*. Ithaca: Cornell UP, 1978: 140–44.

Pollard, John A. *John Greenleaf Whittier: Friend of Man*. Boston: Houghton Mifflin, 1949.

Randolph, A. Philip. "Testimony of A. Philip Randolph . . . before the Senate Armed Services Committee Wednesday, March 31, 1948." In August Meier, Elliot Rudwick, and Francis L. Broderick (eds.), *Black Protest Thought in the Twentieth Century*. Indianapolis: Bobbs-Merrill, 1971.

Schwartz, Harold. "Fugitive Slave Days in Boston." *New England Quarterly* 27 (1954).

Thoreau, Henry David. "Civil Disobedience." In Milton Meltzer (ed.), *Thoreau: People, Principles, and Politics*. New York: Hill & Wang, 1963.

Ward, John William. "To Whom Should I Write a Letter?" (1972). In David R. Weber (ed.), *Civil Disobedience in America: A Documentary History*. Ithaca: Cornell UP, 1978: 286–89.

Wicker, Tom. "The Malaise beyond Dissent." *New York Times* 12 March 1967.

Woolman, John. *John Woolman's Journal.* (c. 1760). Philadelphia: Friends' Book Association, 1892.

On June 22, 1989, the Supreme Court announced its five to four decision upholding a protester's right to burn the flag. The case, *Johnson v. Texas*, grew out of an incident in Dallas during the 1984 Republican National Convention when Gregory L. Johnson burned an American flag in front of the city hall as several dozen others chanted, "America, the red, white, and blue, we spit on you." The decision set off a storm of controversy and a movement to amend the Constitution to forbid explicitly desecration of the flag. Below are excerpts from the majority opinion and two dissenting opinions followed by a pair of newspaper editorials, one pro and one con.

Justice William J. Brennan

From the Opinion

After publicly burning an American flag as a means of political protest, Gregory Lee Johnson was convicted of desecrating a flag in violation of Texas law. This case presents the question whether his conviction is consistent with the First Amendment. We hold that it is not. 1

While the Republican National Convention was taking place in Dallas in 1984, respondent Johnson participated in a political demonstration dubbed the "Republican War Chest Tour." . . . 2

The demonstration ended in front of Dallas City Hall, where Johnson unfurled the American flag, doused it with kerosene and set it on fire. While the flag burned, the protestors chanted, "America, the red, white, and blue, we spit on you." After the demonstrators dispersed, a witness to the flag-burning collected the flag's remains and buried them in his backyard. No one was physically injured or threatened with injury, though several witnesses testified that they had been seriously offended by the flag burning. 3

Of the approximately 100 demonstrators, Johnson alone was charged with a crime. The only criminal offense with which he was charged was the desecration of a venerated object in violation of Texas Penal Code Ann. Sec. 42.09 (a)(3) (1989). ["Desecration of a Venerated Object"]. After a trial, he was convicted, sentenced to one year in prison and fined $2,000. The Court of Appeals for the Fifth District of Texas at Dallas affirmed Johnson's conviction, but the Texas Court of Criminal Appeals 4 reversed, holding that the State could not, consistent with the First Amendment, punish Johnson for burning the flag in these circumstances. . . .

State Asserted Two Interests. To justify Johnson's conviction for engaging in symbolic speech, the State asserted two interests: preserving the flag as a symbol of national unity and preventing breaches of the peace. The Court of Criminal Appeals held that neither interest supported his conviction.

Acknowledging that this Court had not yet decided whether the Government may criminally sanction flag desecration in order to preserve the flag's symbolic value, the Texas court nevertheless concluded that our decision in West Virginia Board of Education v. Barnette, 319 U.S. 624 (1943), suggested that furthering this interest by curtailing speech was impermissible.

• • •

The First Amendment literally forbids the abridgement only of "speech," but we have long recognized that its protection does not end at the spoken or written word. . . .

• • •

Especially pertinent to this case are our decisions recognizing the communicative nature of conduct relating to flags. Attaching a peace sign to the flag, Spence v. Washington, 1974; saluting the flag, Barnette, and displaying a red flag, Stromberg v. California (1931), we have held, all may find shelter under the First Amendment. . . . That we have had little difficulty identifying an expressive element in conduct relating to flags should not be surprising. The very purpose of a national flag is to serve as a symbol of our country; it is, one might say, "the one visible manifestation of two hundred years of nationhood." . . .

Pregnant with expressive content, the flag as readily signifies this nation as does the combination of letters found in "America."

• • •

The Government generally has a freer hand in restricting expressive conduct than it has in restricting the written or spoken word. . . . It may not, however, proscribe particular conduct *because* it has expressive elements. . . . It is, in short, not simply the verbal or nonverbal nature of the expression, but the governmental interest at stake, that helps to determine whether a restriction on that expression is valid.

• • •

If there is a bedrock principle underlying the First Amendment, it is 11
that the Government may not prohibit the expression of an idea simply
because society finds the idea itself offensive or disagreeable. . . .

We have not recognized an exception to this principle even where our 12
flag has been involved. In Street v. New York, 394 U.S. 576 (1969), we
held that a state may not criminally punish a person for uttering words
critical of the flag. . . .

• • •

Nor may the Government, we have held, compel conduct that would 13
evince respect for the flag. . . .

• • •

We never before have held that the Government may insure that a 14
symbol be used to express only one view of that symbol or its referents.
. . . To conclude that the Government may permit designated symbols to
be used to communicate only a limited set of messages would be to enter
territory having no discernible or defensible boundaries.

Which Symbols Warrant Unique Status? Could the Govern- 15
ment, on this theory, prohibit the burning of state flags? Of copies of the
Presidential seal? Of the Constitution? In evaluating these choices under
the First Amendment, how would we decide which symbols were sufficiently special to warrant this unique status? To do so, we would be
forced to consult our own political preferences, and impose them on the
citizenry, in the very way that the First Amendment forbids us to do.

There is, moreover, no indication—either in the text of the Constitu- 16
tion or in our cases interpreting—that a separate juridical category exists
for the American flag alone. Indeed, we would not be surprised to learn
that the persons who framed our Constitution and wrote the Amendment that we now construe were not known for their reverence for the
Union Jack.

The First Amendment does not guarantee that other concepts vir- 17
tually sacred to our nation as a whole—such as the principle that
discrimination on the basis of race is odious and destructive—will go
unquestioned in the marketplace of ideas. We decline, therefore, to
create for the flag an exception to the joust of principles protected by the
First Amendment.

• • •

We are fortified in today's conclusion by our conviction that forbid- 18
ding criminal punishment for conduct such as Johnson's will not endan-
ger the special role played by our flag or the feelings it inspires. . . .

A Reaffirmation of Principles. We are tempted to say, in fact, that 19 the flag's deservedly cherished place in our community will be strengthened, not weakened, by our holding today. Our decision is a reaffirmation of the principles of freedom and inclusiveness that the flag best reflects, and of the conviction that our toleration of criticism such as Johnson's is a sign and source of our strength.

•   •   •

The way to preserve the flag's special role is not to punish those who 20 feel differently about these matters. It is to persuade them that they are wrong. . . .

We can imagine no more appropriate response to burning a flag than 21 waving one's own, no better way to counter a flag-burner's message than by saluting the flag that burns, no surer means of preserving the dignity even of the flag that burned than by—as one witness here did—according its remains a respectful burial. We do not consecrate the flag by punishing its desecration, for in doing so we dilute the freedom that this cherished emblem represents.

Justice John Paul Stevens

From a Dissenting Opinion

Even if flag burning could be considered just another species of symbolic speech under the logical application of the rules that the Court has developed in its interpretation of the First Amendment in other contexts, this case has an intangible dimension that makes those rules inapplicable.

A country's flag is a symbol of more than "nationhood and national unity." It also signifies the ideas that characterize the society that has chose that emblem, as well as the special history that has animated the growth and power of those ideas. . . .

So it is with the American flag. It is more than a proud symbol of the courage, the determination and the gifts of nature that transformed 13 fledgling colonies into a world power. It is a symbol of freedom, of equal opportunity, of religious tolerance and of good will for other peoples who share our aspirations. . . .

The value of the flag as a symbol cannot be measured. Even so, I have no doubt that the interest in preserving that value for the future is both significant and legitimate. . . . The creation of a Federal right to post bulletin boards and graffiti on the Washington Monument might enlarge the market for free expression, but at a cost I would not pay.

Similarly, in my considered judgment, sanctioning the public desecration of the flag will tarnish its value—both for those who cherish the ideas for which it waves and for those who desire to don the robes of martyrdom by burning it. That tarnish is not justified by the trivial burden on free expression occasioned by requiring that an available, alternative mode of expression—including uttering words critical of the flag—be employed.

• • •

The ideas of liberty and equality have been an irresistible force in motivating leaders like Patrick Henry, Susan B. Anthony, and Abraham Lincoln, schoolteachers like Nathan Hale and Booker T. Washington, the Philippine Scouts who fought at Bataan, and the soldiers who scaled the bluff at Omaha Beach. If those ideas are worth fighting for—and our history demonstrates that they are—it cannot be true that the flag that uniquely symbolizes their power is not itself worthy of protection from unnecessary desecration.

Chief Justice William H. Rehnquist

From a Dissenting Opinion

In holding this Texas statute unconstitutional, the Court ignores 1
Justice Holmes's familiar aphorism that "a page of history is worth a
volume of logic." For more than 200 years, the American flag has
occupied a unique position as the symbol of our nation, a uniqueness
that justifies a governmental prohibition against flag burning in the way
respondent Johnson did here.

At the time of the American Revolution, the flag served to unify the 2
13 colonies at home while obtaining recognition of national sovereignty
abroad. Ralph Waldo Emerson's Concord Hymn describes the first skir-
mishes of the Revolutionary War in these lines:

"By the rude bridge that arched the flood,
Their flag to April's breeze unfurled,
Here once the embattled farmers stood,
And fired the shot heard round the world."

• • •

In the First and Second World Wars, thousands of our countrymen 3
died on foreign soil fighting for the American cause. At Iwo Jima in the
Second World War, United States Marines fought hand to hand against
thousands of Japanese. By the time the marines reached the top of
Mount Suribachi, they raised a piece of pipe upright and from one end
fluttered a flag. That ascent had cost nearly 6,000 American lives. . . .

• • •

The flag symbolizes the nation in peace as well as in war. It signifies 4
our national presence on battleships, airplanes, military installations and
public buildings from the United States Capitol to the thousands of
county courthouses and city halls throughout the country. . . .

No other American symbol has been as universally honored as the 5
flag. In 1931 Congress declared "The Star Spangled Banner" to be our
national anthem. In 1949 Congress declared June 14th to be Flag Day. In
1987 John Philip Sousa's "The Stars and Stripes Forever" was designated
as the national march. Congress has also established "The Pledge of
Allegiance to the Flag" and the manner of its deliverance. . . .

• • •

With the exception of Alaska and Wyoming, all of the states now have 6
statutes prohibiting the burning of the flag. . . .

•   •   •

The result of the Texas statute is obviously to deny one in Johnson's 7
frame of mind one of many means of "symbolic speech." Far from being a
case of "one picture being worth a thousand words," flag burning is the
equivalent of an inarticulate grunt or roar that, it seems fair to say, is
most likely to be indulged in not to express any particular idea, but to
antagonize others. . . .

The Texas statute deprived Johnson of only one rather inarticulate 8
symbolic form of protest—a form of protest that was profoundly offensive
to many—and left him with a full panoply of other symbols and every
conceivable form of verbal expression to express his deep disapproval of
national policy. . . .

Richard N. Goodwin

It's Our Right to Offend and Outrage

Not only do I fly the flag on the 4th of July, but ordinarily I celebrate   1
Independence Day with fireworks illegally smuggled from my neighboring state of New Hampshire.

For years I had a flag sticker affixed to a pickup truck. I belonged   2
briefly to the National Rifle Assn. And I still get an occasional lump in
my throat at the singing of "The Star Bangled Banner" before the Red
Sox begin another episode in their disastrous season. Loving the flag and
"the Republic for which it stands," I am not so much horrified (there are
more horrible things on every news broadcast) as I am shocked and
repelled when the flag is burned in public, usually as a gesture of protest
against the policies or values of the United States.

However I was not shocked, not even surprised, when the Supreme   3
Court—by an ominously close margin—decided that burning or "desecrating" the flag as an act of protest against America was an exercise of
freedom of speech protected by the First Amendment.

Of course it is.   4

Freedom of speech includes the right to attack America—verbally or   5
symbolically—or it is little more than an expression of mild good will
rather than the cornerstone of democratic liberty it has always been
thought to be.

The wording of the Founding Fathers is brief, direct and unequivocal: 6
"Congress [and the states, courtesy of the 14th Amendment] shall make
no law . . . abridging the freedom of speech . . ." "No law" means no law.
"Abridging," according to the Oxford English Dictionary, means to
"curtail, to lessen, to diminish." If there is any ambiguity at all, it is in
the word "speech," which does not include inciting to riot, rebellion or
other acts physically endangering our fellow citizens. But that was neither the purpose nor the result of Gregory Johnson's act when he doused
the flag with kerosene and ignited it in front of a few dozen demonstrators in Dallas during the 1984 Republican convention. He was trying to
make a point and chose to do so in a manner most Americans find
repulsive. But he was clearly acting within his rights . . . and ours.

Indeed, some of the most distinguished figures of American history   7
have gone much further than Johnson's futile, childish actions. Thomas
Jefferson, whose eloquent statement of human rights in the Declaration

of Independence has resounded through the centuries, spoke out in favor of periodic armed rebellion against the government, claiming that "a little rebellion now and then is a good thing . . . God forbid we should ever be 20 years without such a rebellion." And he meant not protest, but armed and bloody revolt to refresh "the tree of liberty."

A century later, William Lloyd Garrison—ultimately to be known as the Great Liberator—publicly burned the Constitution of the United States, calling it "an agreement with Death and a covenant with hell." In response to his abolitionist views, a Boston mob dragged Garrison through the streets. He would have been lynched were it not for the intervention of the mayor, who personally despised Garrison but felt it his duty to uphold the law and, not incidentally, Garrison's right to speak and to burn the most sacred of American documents—not merely a symbol of the country, but its substance. Not too many years later, Garrison was a guest of Abraham Lincoln at the White House—an honor that is unlikely to befall Gregory Johnson.   8

Today, scattered through the shelves of America's libraries are myriad books assaulting the policies, values and historical conduct of the United States. There are writers who have accused us of hypocrisy, and others of fascism. From the right are attacks on democracy itself and the liberties that make us a free nation.   9

Only a few years ago the American flag was removed from dozens of capitol and state buildings in the South, to be replaced by the banner of the old Confederacy. Over the centuries, from Jefferson to Johnson, the country has withstood the most ferocious verbal and symbolic assaults. It has done so because of the inherent strength of the free values that distinguish us as a nation; and, in part, because we have given every citizen the right to speak freely and act peacefully in opposition to government and country alike.   10

The core, the essence, of the First Amendment is to protect people whose views—however expressed—are "profoundly offensive" to the majority. We need no First Amendment to safeguard those who advocate motherhood, family and making money. It is designed as the guardian of those whose views are found offensive. The reason is twofold: First, the views of a small and despised minority may, in the marketplace of ideas, finally prevail, as was the case with the abolitionist. The second, and more important though less pragmatic, is that the right to express one's view, however offensive, is the heartbeat of a free society. A man who cannot say what he thinks or believes is not a free man.   11

Which leaves us only with the question whether there is something about the flag that should exempt it from the First Amendment. Here again, the answer is *no*. The flag is an established symbol of America. But   12 it is not the only one. There is the Great Seal of the United States, the Constitution, the Declaration of Independence, the President himself in his capacity as chief of state. Are these somehow lesser symbols that can be freely burned while the flag alone should be protected? Of course not. But why stop there? How about a satiric and mildly obscene version of the Star Spangled Banner recorded by the latest stars of heavy metal? Or the Pledge of Allegiance, substituting the word *hate* for *love*, chanted from the stage of an off-Broadway theater.

Offensive? Yes. Perhaps repulsive. But not criminal, not under the First   13
Amendment that includes the right to offend and outrage your fellow citizens.

The flag is not a religious icon, but one among many symbols of the   14
secular state. It ranks high on the list, but it is not alone. Indeed, it is irrational, although politically comprehensible, that the government is trying to change the Bill of Rights to protect the flag alone, ignoring the desecration of symbols far more transcendent. According to the Pledge of Allegiance, a principal plank in the platform last year of candidate George Bush, we are "One nation under God." Yet no one thinks to erect a barrier to protect the symbols of God who, even the most patriotic politician would admit, occupies a rank in the order of things many universes higher than the fragment of globe that is America. Still, the symbols of his earthly church—the cross, the Star of David, the Islamic crescent—can be burned and desecrated in public demonstration without punishment (with the exception of vandalism). It is true that the First Amendment protects freedom of religion (and irreligion) as well as speech. But if we intend to change it, why not protect the Divine—or at least his earthly body—as well as the country?

The suggestion is not absurd, not meant—wholly—as satire. It only   15
illustrates that if by constitutional amendment—hurried through by politicians anxious to kneel to the immediate wishes of their constituencies—we are making distinctions for which there is no warrant in reason, feeling or importance, then we are setting a hazardous precedent.

The Bill of Rights has served us well for two centuries. Let only those   16
of stature equal to the men who wrote it now act to change it. By that standard there is little cause for concern. The amendment *wouldn't get a single vote.*

George P. Fletcher

What about U.S. Unity?

In the Supreme Court's only significant liberal decision of this term, a majority of the justices interpreted the First Amendment broadly to protect flag burning as free speech. If Gregory Lee Johnson could only express his antipatriotic sentiments by burning the flag in Dallas, then the First Amendment affirms his constitutional right to assault the symbols of our national unity.

Liberals, with typical enthusiasm for free speech, took the court's decision to be self-evidently correct. Yet, the question raised by the Johnson case is not whether we believe in the First Amendment but how highly we regard national unity and pride as values competing with freedom of expression.

There is no question that the First Amendment provides the foundation for all of our political rights. Yet most of the arguments supporting Mr. Johnson's right to communicate his outrage through flag burning misrepresent the structure of the First Amendment.

One such argument is that it is simply too dangerous to recognize any exception to the First Amendment; once adrift from the absolute, there would be no place to moor. This conveniently overlooks the point that the Constitution recognizes numerous exceptions to the First Amendment, including those covering defamation of character, obscenity and copyright of creative works.

Nor does it make much sense to argue that the Court should read the First Amendment as protecting flag burning because protestors have no other way of presenting their message to the public. It's absurd to assert that any act necessary to make a political point (or that the speaker thinks is necessary) should be protected under the First Amendment.

Lee Harvey Oswald might have thought that his aggressive acts in Dallas were necessary to make a political point. But no one would suggest that he could therefore have taken refuge in the First Amendment. The necessity of making a political point hardly whitewashes otherwise illegal and harmful conduct.

The question then is whether flag burning is harmful conduct. Attacking a national symbol is not as egregious an act as endangering another's life or physical well-being. But encouraging a strong sense of national unity might be as important as other interests that take precedence over the value of free speech—such as protecting individuals from defamation and writers from copyright infringement.

If someone deliberately spills paint on a work of art, the artist should 8 have a remedy, notwithstanding the First Amendment, against the violation of his work. If someone deliberately spills paint on the flag, the public should have a comparable right to vindicate its sense of national pride.

Without a strong sense of community and common destiny, we as a 9 society will never be able to tackle the social ills of this country. The symbols of our unity have worn thin in the wake of the Vietnam War, the movements to overcome racism and sexism and the privatism of the Reagan years. Without symbols of our commonality we cannot foster a sense of reciprocal obligation that would make social action possible.

But we live in a country that has largely lost its sense of community 10 and nationhood. We have few ties to the past, virtually no concern about our future economic welfare and no sense of commitment to the poor among us. As we affirm the right to burn the flag, we hide behind the walls and guard dogs that separate us.

Liberal Democrats act at their peril when they abandon the flag and 11 treat issues of loyalty as the private reserve of the emotional right. Gov. Michael Dukakis foolishly ignored these issues in the 1988 Presidential campaign by pretending that our ambiguous Constitution settled the controversy about the Pledge of Allegiance. There is no excuse now for his party to repeat his mistakes.

This is not to say that we should send flag burners to jail. But as a 12 society we should express our disapproval—by punitive fines, if necessary—of attacks on the symbols that unite us as a country. A constitutional amendment is one option, but it might be more appropriate to begin a national campaign to intensify respect for the symbols of our interdependence.

The Johnson case stands virtually alone among the array of recent 13 Supreme Court decisions cutting back the protection of civil rights, curtailing the rights of criminal defendants and expanding capital punishment. Indulging in the highly individualistic, self-expression ethic of the First Amendment is an easy consolation prize for liberals. But the liberal agenda is compromised by accentuating individualism at the expense of our national identity and of our concern for the welfare of our fellow countrymen.

APPENDIX

Strategies for Research and Documentation

Many of the selections in this text are based on field and library research: writers have visited places and interviewed people, and have gone to the library to gather necessary information. Critical readers are often called upon to do research, following up on ideas or claims, looking firsthand at a source mentioned by the writer, or finding more information about a writer they admire. Writers also have occasion to do research: unless they write solely from memory, writers will rely in part on research for their essays, reports, and books.

Many of the Ideas for Your Own Writing in this text invite field or library research. As a writer at work using this text—and for writing you do for many of your college courses—you have to do research. You will often need to document your sources, indicating precisely where you found certain information. This appendix offers some strategies and guidelines for field and library research, along with instructions for documenting your sources.

FIELD RESEARCH

In universities, government agencies, and the business world, field research can be as important as library research or experimental research. In specialties such as sociology, political science, anthropology, polling, advertising, and news reporting, field research is the basic means of gathering information.

This appendix is a brief introduction to two of the major kinds of field research: observations and interviews. The writing activities involved are central to several academic specialties. If you major in education, journalism, or one of the social sciences, you probably will be asked to do writing based on observations and interviews. You will also read large amounts of information based on these ways of learning about people, groups, and institutions.

Observation
Planning the Observational Visit

GETTING ACCESS. If the place you propose to visit is public, you probably will have easy access to it. If everything you need to see is within view of anyone passing by or using the place, you can make your observations without any special arrangements. Indeed, you may not even be noticed. If you require special access, you will need to arrange your visit, calling ahead or making a get-acquainted visit, in order to introduce yourself and state your purpose. Find out the times you may visit, and be certain you can get to the place easily.

ANNOUNCING YOUR INTENTIONS. State your intentions directly and fully. Say who you are, where you are from, and what you hope to do. You may be surprised at how receptive people can be to a student on assignment from a college course. Not every place you wish to visit will welcome you, however. A variety of constraints on outside visitors exist in private businesses as well as public institutions. But generally, if people know your intentions, they may be able to tell you about aspects of a place or activity you would not have thought to observe.

TAKING YOUR TOOLS. Take a notebook with a firm back so that you will have a steady writing surface, perhaps a small stenographer's notebook with a spiral binding across the top. Remember to take a writing instrument. Some observers dictate their notes into portable tape recorders, a method you may wish to try.

Observing and Taking Notes

OBSERVING. Some activities invite multiple vantage points, whereas others seem to limit the observer to a single perspective. Take advantage of every perspective available to you. Come in close, take a middle position, and stand back. Study the scene from a stationary position and also try to move around it. The more varied your perspectives, the more you are likely to observe.

Your purpose in observing is both to describe the activity and to analyze it. You will want to look closely at the activity itself, but you will also want to think about what makes this activity special, what seems to be the point of it.

Try to be an innocent observer: pretend you have never seen anything like this activity before. Look for typical features of the activity as well as unusual features. Look at it from the perspective of your readers. Ask what details of the activity would surprise and inform and interest them.

TAKING NOTES. You undoubtedly will find your own style of note-taking, but here are a few pointers. (1) Write only on one side of the page. Later, when you organize your notes, you may want to cut up the pages and file notes under different headings. (2) Take notes in words, phrases, or sentences. Draw diagrams or sketches, if they help you see and understand the place. (3) Note any ideas or questions that occur to you. (4) Use quotation marks around any overheard conversation you take down.

Since you can later reorganize your notes quite easily, you do not need to take notes in any planned or systematic way. You might, however, want to cover these possibilities:

The Setting. The easiest way to begin is to name objects you see. Just start by listing objects. Then record details of some of these objects—color, shape, size, texture, function, relation to similar or dissimilar objects. Although your notes probably will contain mainly visual details, you might also want to record sounds and smells. Be sure to include some notes about the shape, dimensions, and layout of the place. How big is it? How is it organized?

The People. Record the number of people, their activities, their movements and behavior. Describe their appearance or dress. Record parts of overheard conversations. Note whether you see more men than women, more of one racial group rather than of another, more older than younger people. Most important, note anything surprising and unusual about people in the scene.

Your Personal Reactions. Include in your notes any feelings you have about what you observe. Also record, as they occur to you, any hunches or ideas or insights you have.

Reflecting on What You Saw

Immediately after your visit (within just a few minutes, if possible), find a quiet place to reflect on what you saw, review your notes, and add to them. Give yourself at least a half hour for quiet thought.

What you have in your notes and what you recall on reflection will suggest many more images and details from your observations. Add these to your notes.

Finally, review all your notes, and write a few sentences about your main impressions of the place. What did you learn? How did this visit change your preconceptions about the place? What surprised you most? What is the dominant impression you get from your notes?

Interviews

Interviewing tends to involve four basic steps: (1) planning and setting up the interview, (2) note-taking, (3) reflecting on the interview, and (4) writing up your notes.

Planning and Setting Up the Interview

CHOOSING AN INTERVIEW SUBJECT. The first step is to decide whom to interview. If you are writing about something in which several people are involved, choose subjects representing a variety of perspectives—a range of different roles, for example. If you are profiling a single person, most, if not all, of your interviews will be with that person.

You should be flexible because you may be unable to speak to the person you targeted and may wind up with someone else—the person's assistant, perhaps. You might even learn more from an assistant than you would from the person in charge.

ARRANGING AN INTERVIEW. You may be nervous about calling up a busy person and asking for some of his or her time. Indeed, you may get turned down. But if so, do ask if someone else might talk to you.

Do not feel that just because you are a student you do not have the right to ask for people's time. People are often delighted to be asked about themselves. And, since you are a student on assignment, some people may feel that they are doing a form of public service to talk with you.

When introducing yourself to arrange the interview, give a short and simple description of your project. If you say too much, you could prejudice or limit the person's response. It is a good idea to exhibit some enthusiasm for your project, of course.

Keep in mind that the person you are interviewing is donating time to you. Be certain that you call ahead to arrange a specific time for the interview. Be on time. Bring all the materials you need, and express your thanks when the interview is over.

PLANNING FOR THE INTERVIEW. Make any necessary observational visits and do any essential background reading before the interview. Consider your objectives. Do you want an orientation to the place (the "big picture") from this interview? Do you want this interview to lead you to other key people? Do you want mainly facts or information? Do you need clarification of something you have heard in another interview or observed or read? Do you want to learn more about the person, or learn about the place through the person, or both? Should you trust or distrust this person?

The key to good interviewing is flexibility. You may be looking for facts, but your interview subject may not have any to offer. In that case, you should be able to shift gears and go after whatever your subject has to discuss.

Prepare Some Questions in Advance. Take care in composing these questions; they can be the key to a successful interview. Bad questions rarely yield useful answers. A bad question places unfair limits on respondents. Two specific types to avoid are forced-choice questions and leading questions.

Forced-choice questions are bad because they impose your terms on your respondents. Consider this example: "Do you think rape is an expression of sexual passion or of aggression?" A person may think that neither sexual passion nor aggression satisfactorily explains rape. A better way to phrase the question would be to ask, "People often fall into two camps on the issue of rape. Some think it is an expression of sexual passion, while others argue it is really not sexual but aggressive. Do you think it is either of these? If not, what is your opinion?" This form of questioning allows you to get a reaction to what others have said at the same time it gives the person freedom to set the terms.

Leading questions are bad because they assume too much. An example of this kind of question is this: "Do you think the increase in the occurrence of rape is due to the fact that women are perceived as competitors in a severely depressed economy?" This question assumes that there is an increase in the occurrence of rape, that women are perceived (apparently by rapists) as competitors, and that the economy is severely depressed. A better way of asking the question might be to make the assumptions more explicit by dividing the question into its parts: "Do you think there is an increase in the occurrence of rape? What could have caused it? I've heard some people argue that the economy has something to do with it. Do you think so? Do you think rapists perceive women as competitors for jobs? Could the current economic situation have made this competition more severe?"

Good questions come in many different forms. One way of considering them is to divide them into two types: open and closed. *Open questions* give the respondent range and flexibility. They also generate anecdotes, personal revelations, and expressions of attitudes. The following are examples of open questions:

- I wonder if you would take a few minutes to tell me something about your early days in the business. I'd be interested to hear about how it got started, what your hopes and aspirations were, what problems you faced and how you dealt with them.
- Tell me about a time you were (name an emotion).
- What did you think of (name a person or event)?
- What did you do when (name an event) happened?

The best questions are those that allow the subject to talk freely but to the point. If the answer strays too far from the point, a follow-up question may be necessary to refocus the talk. Another tack you may want to try is to rephrase the subject's answer, to say something like: "Let me see if I have this right," or "Am I correct in saying that you feel. . . ." Often, a person will take the opportunity to amplify the original response by adding just the anecdote or quotation you've been looking for.

Closed questions usually request specific information. For example:

- How do you do (name a process)?
- What does (name a word) mean?
- What does (a person, object, or place) look like?
- How was it made?

Taking Your Tools

As for an observational visit, you will need a notebook with a firm back so that you can write on it easily without the benefit of a table or desk. We recommend a full-size (8½ x 11) spiral or ring notebook.

In this notebook, divide several pages into two columns with a line drawn vertically from a distance of about one third of the width of the page from the left margin. Use the left-hand column to note details about the scene, the person, the mood of the interview, other impressions. Head this column DETAILS AND IMPRESSIONS. At the top of the right-hand column, write several questions. You may not use them, but they will jog your memory. This column should be titled INFORMATION. In this column you will record what you learn from answers to your questions.

Taking Notes During the Interview

Because you are not taking a verbatim transcript of the interview (if you wanted a literal account, you would use a tape recorder or short-hand), your goals are to gather information and to record a few good quotations and anecdotes. In addition, because the people you interview may be unused to giving interviews and so will need to know you are listening, it is probably a good idea to do more listening than note-taking. You may not have much confidence in your memory, but, if you pay close attention, you are likely to recall a good deal of the conversation afterward. During the interview, you should take some notes: a few quotations; key words and phrases to jog your memory; observational jottings about the scene, the person, and the mood of the interview. Remember that *how* something is said is as important as *what* is said. Pick up material that will give the interview write-up texture—gesture, physical appearance, verbal inflection, facial expression, dress, hair-style, body language, anything that makes the person an individual.

Reflecting on the Interview

As soon as you finish the interview, find a quiet place to reflect on it, and review your notes. This reflection is essential because so much happens in an interview that you cannot record at the time. You need to spend at least a half hour, maybe longer, adding to your notes and thinking about what you learned.

At the end of this time, write a few sentences about your main impressions from the interview. What did you learn? What surprised you most? How did the interview change your attitude or understanding about the person or place? How would you summarize your main impressions of the person? How did this interview influence your plans to interview others or to reinterview this person? What do you want to learn from these next interviews?

LIBRARY RESEARCH

Library research involves a variety of diverse activities: checking the card catalog, browsing in the stacks, possibly consulting the *Readers' Guide to Periodical Literature*, asking the reference librarian for help. Although librarians are there to help in time of need, all college students should nevertheless learn basic library research skills. Here we present the search strategy, a systematic and efficient way of doing library research.

The search strategy was developed by librarians to make library research manageable and productive. Although specific search strategies will vary to fit the needs of individual research problems, the general process will be demonstrated here: how to get started; where to find sources; what types of sources are available and what sorts of information they provide; how to evaluate these sources; and, most important, how to go about this process of finding and evaluating sources *systematically*.

Library research can be useful at various stages of the writing process. How you use the library depends on the kind of essay you are writing and the special needs of your subject. You may, for example, need to do research immediately to choose a subject. Or you may choose a topic without the benefit of research but then use the library to find specific

Overview of a Search Strategy

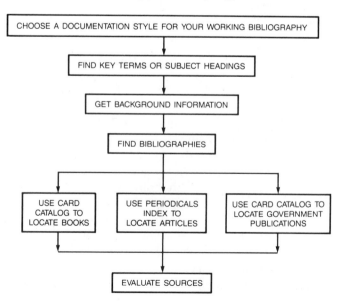

information to support your thesis. But no matter when you use library research, you will need to have a search strategy. This search strategy will guide you in setting up a working bibliography and a documentation style, in searching for key words or subject headings, in seeking background information, in finding bibliographies, and in using the card catalog and specialty indexes. Finally, it will help you evaluate the sources that you will use in your writing.

A Working Bibliography

A working bibliography is a preliminary, ongoing record of books, articles, pamphlets—all the sources of information you discover as you research your subject. (A final bibliography, on the other hand, lists only sources actually used in your paper.) Some of the sources in your working bibliography may turn out to be irrelevant, while others simply will be unavailable. In addition, you can use your working bibliography as a means of keeping track of any encyclopedias, bibliographies, and indexes you consult, even though you may not list these resources in your final bibliography.

Because you probably may have to cite many different sources, you must decide on a documentation style before you write. The next section presents the documentation styles sponsored by the Modern Language Association (MLA) and the American Psychological Association (APA). Other disciplines often have their own preferred styles of documentation, which your instructor may wish you to use. Decide on a style to use at the beginning, when you are constructing a working bibliography, as well as later, when you compile a final bibliography.

Practiced researchers keep their working bibliography either in a notebook or on index cards. They make a point of keeping bibliographical information separate from notes they take on the sources listed in their bibliography.

Many researchers find index cards more convenient because they are so easily alphabetized. Others find them too easy to lose and prefer, instead, to keep everything—working bibliography, notes, and drafts—in one notebook. Whether you use cards or a notebook, the important thing is to make your entries accurate and complete.

Key Subject Headings

To research a subject, you need to know how it is classified, what key words are used as subject headings in encyclopedias, bibliographies, and the card catalog. As you learn more about your subject, you will discover how other writers refer to it, how it usually is subdivided, and also what subjects are related to it. To begin your search, you should consult the *Library of Congress Subject Headings*. This reference book lists the standard subject headings used in card catalogs and in many encyclopedias and bibliographies. It usually can be found near the card catalog.

Sometimes, the words you think would be used for subject headings are not the ones actually used. For example, if you look up "World War I," you will find a cross-reference to "European War, 1914–1918." But, if you look up "bulimia," you will find neither a heading nor a cross-reference. Since many people call bulimia an "eating disorder," you might try that heading. But again you would draw a blank. If you tried "appetite," however, you would be referred to "anorexia," a related disorder. Here is the entry for "appetite":

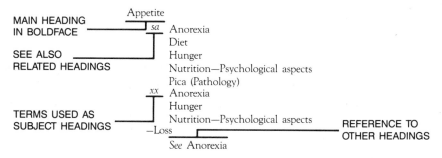

If you then look up "anorexia," you still will not find "bulimia," but you can expect some of the publications on anorexia to deal also with bulimia. In this process of trying possible headings and following up cross-references, you also will find related headings such as "nutrition," "obesity," and "psychological."

Background Information

Once you have decided on the form and style of a working bibliography and have found promising subject headings, your search strategy will lead you to the gathering of background sources of information. Such sources will give you a general understanding of the nature and scope of your research subject. They may also provide a historical perspective on the subject, helping you grasp its basic principles and ideas, suggesting what its major divisions or aspects might be, and identifying important people associated with it.

Encyclopedias are the best sources of background information. You have no doubt heard of the *Encyclopaedia Britannica*, probably the best-known general encyclopedia. But there are many specialized encyclopedias. To use encyclopedias effectively, you need to know what subject headings you are looking for. Check each encyclopedia's subject index to locate your subject.

General Encyclopedias

General encyclopedias are usually multivolume works that contain articles on all areas of knowledge. Written by experts, the articles frequently conclude with a list of important works and bibliographies. Most encyclopedias arrange their subjects alphabetically. Standard general encyclopedias include *Encyclopaedia Britannica*, *Encyclopedia Americana*, *Collier's Encyclopedia*, and *World Book Encyclopedia*.

Specialized Encyclopedias

Specialized encyclopedias focus on a single area of knowledge. To find specialized encyclopedias, look in the subject card catalog under the appropriate subject heading. Encyclopedias usually are cataloged under the subheading "Dictionaries" and are kept in the reference section of the library. Here is a partial list of specialized encyclopedias:

Encyclopedia of Education

Encyclopedia of Philosophy

Grove's Dictionary of Music and Musicians

International Encyclopedia of the Social Sciences

Harvard Encyclopedia of American Ethnic Groups

McGraw-Hill Dictionary of Art

McGraw-Hill Encyclopedia of Science and Technology

Oxford Classical Dictionary

Oxford Companion to American History

Bibliographies

A bibliography is simply a list of publications on a given subject. Whereas an encyclopedia gives you background information on your subject, a bibliography gives an overview of what has been published on the subject. Its scope may be broad or narrow. Some bibliographers try to be exhaustive, including every title they can find, while most are selective. To discover how selections were made, check the bibliography's preface or introduction. Occasionally, bibliographies are annotated; that is, they provide brief summaries of the entries and, sometimes, also evaluate them. Bibliographies may be found in a variety of places: in encyclopedias, in the card catalog, and in secondary sources. The best way to locate a comprehensive, up-to-date bibliography on your subject is to use the *Bibliographic Index*, a master list of bibliographies with fifty or more titles. It includes bibliographies from articles, books, and government publications. A new volume of *Bibliographic Index* is published every year. Because this index is not cumulative, you should check back over several years, beginning with the most current volume.

The Card Catalog

The card catalog tells you what books are in the library. Books are listed on three separate cards—by author, subject, and title. Author, subject, and title cards all give the same basic information. Each card includes a *call number* in the upper left-hand corner. You will want to take extreme care in copying down this number, for it guides you to the location in your library of the source you seek.

Periodicals Indexes and Abstracts

The most up-to-date information on a subject usually is not found in books, but in recently published articles that appear in journals and serials, or periodicals, as they often are called. Periodicals appear daily, weekly, quarterly, or annually (hence the name *periodical*). Articles in such publications usually are not listed in the card catalog; to find them, you must instead use periodicals indexes and abstracts. Indexes will only list articles, whereas abstracts summarize as well as list them. Like encyclopedias, periodicals indexes and abstracts exist in both general and specialized forms.

General Indexes

General indexes list articles in nontechnical, general interest publications. They cover a broad range of subjects. Most have separate author and subject listings as well as a list of book reviews. Following are some general indexes:

Readers' Guide to Periodical Literature (1905–present) covers more than 180 popular periodicals.

Humanities Index (1974–present) covers archaeology, history, classics, literature, performing arts, philosophy, and religion.

Social Sciences Index (1974–present) covers economics, geography, law, political science, psychology, public administration, and sociology.

Public Affairs Information Service Bulletin [PAIS] (1915–present) covers articles and other publications by public and private agencies on economic and social conditions, international relations, and public administration. Subject listing only.

Book Review Digest contains excerpts of book reviews which are alphabetized under the author's name. Published yearly.

Specialized Indexes

Specialized indexes list articles in periodicals devoted to technical or scholarly research reports. Following is a list of some specialized indexes:

Almanac of American Politics (1972–present)

American Statistics Index (1973–present)

Applied Science and Technology Index (1958–present)

Biological and Agricultural Index (1964–present)

Congressional Digest (1921–present)

Congressional Quarterly Weekly Reports (1956–present)

Education Index (1929–present)

Historical Abstracts (1955–present)

MLA International Bibliography of Books and Articles in the Modern Languages and Literature (1921–present)

Philosopher's Index (1967–present)

Psychology Abstracts (1927–present)

Statistical Abstracts of the United States (annual)

Statistical Yearbook (1949–present)

Newspaper Indexes

Newspapers often provide information unavailable elsewhere, especially accounts of current events, analyses of recent trends, texts of important speeches by public officials, obituaries, and film and book reviews. Libraries usually miniaturize newspapers and store them on microfilm (reels) or microfiche (cards), which must be placed in viewing machines in order to be read. Following are some general and specialized newspaper indexes:

General news indexes

Facts on File (1941–present)

Keesing's Contemporary Archives (1931–present)

Indexes to particular newspapers

Christian Science Monitor Index (1960–present)

(London) *Times Index* (1785–present)

New York Times Index (1851–present)

Wall Street Journal Index (1972–present)

Computerized or microfilm newspaper and periodical indexes

National Newspaper Index—lists items in the *New York Times, Wall Street Journal, Christian Science Monitor, Los Angeles Times,* and *Washington Post.*

Magazine Index—lists articles in nearly 400 general-interest periodicals.

Business Index—covers over 800 business publications.

Government Publications

The countless documents published by agencies of the United States government and by state governments and United Nations organizations may be an additional source of useful information. Most college research libraries have a government publications collection, usually cataloged and housed separately. The collection should include agency publications, statistics, research reports, and public service pamphlets. Following are some indexes of government publications:

Monthly Index to the United States Government Publications (1895–present)—separate cumulative index is published annually.

CIS Index and *CIS Abstracts* (1970–present)—Congressional Committee documents.

Public Affairs Information Service Bulletin [PAIS] (1915–present)—PAIS indexes government documents as well as books on political and social issues.

International Bibliography, Information, Documentation (1973–present)—indexes selected documents published by the United Nations and other international organizations.

United Nations Documents Index (1950–present)—comprehensive index to documents published by the United Nations.

ACKNOWLEDGING SOURCES

Much of the writing you will do in college requires you to use outside sources in combination with your own firsthand observation and reflection. When you get information and ideas from reading, lectures, and interviews, you are using sources. In college, using sources is not only acceptable, it is expected. Educated people nearly always base their original thought on the work of others. In fact, most of your college education is devoted to teaching you two things: (1) what Matthew Arnold called "the best that has been thought and said," and (2) the way to analyze the thoughts of others, integrate them into your own thinking, and effectively convey what you think to others.

Although there is no universally agreed-upon system for acknowledging sources, there is agreement on both the need for documentation and the items that should be included. Writers should acknowledge sources for two reasons—to give credit to those sources and to enable readers to consult the sources for further information. This information should be included when documenting sources: (1) name of author, (2) title of publication, and (3) publication source, date, and page.

Most documentation styles combine some kind of citation in the text with a separate list of references keyed to the textual citations. There are basically two ways of acknowledging sources: (1) citing sources within the essay, enclosing the citation in parentheses, and (2) footnotes (or endnotes) plus a bibliography. The Modern Language Association (MLA), a professional organization of English instructors, had until 1984 endorsed the footnote style of documentation. Since then, the *MLA Handbook* has prescribed the simpler parenthetical citation method similar to the style endorsed by the American Psychological Association (APA)—the style used by many social and natural science instructors.

If you have any questions, consult the *MLA Handbook for Writers of Research Papers*, Third Edition (1988), or the *Publication Manual of the American Psychological Association*, Third Edition (1983). The *MLA Handbook* includes both the new and old MLA styles.

Citing Sources within Your Essay

The MLA and APA styles both advocate parenthetical citations within an essay keyed to a works-cited list at the end. However, they differ on what should be included in the parenthetical citation. Whereas the MLA uses an author-page citation, the APA uses an author-year-page citation.

MLA   Dr. James is described as a "not-too-skeletal Ichabod Crane" (Simon 68).

APA   Dr. James is described as a "not-too-skeletal Ichabod Crane" (Simon, 1982, p. 68).

Notice that the APA style uses a comma between author, year, and page as well as "p." for page (Simon, 1982, p. 68), whereas the MLA puts nothing but space between author and page (Simon 68). For a block quotation, put the citation after the final period; otherwise, put the citation before the final period.

If the author's name is cited in the essay, put the page reference in parentheses as close as possible to the borrowed material, but without disrupting the flow of the sentence. For the APA style, cite the year in parentheses directly following the author's name, and place the page reference in parentheses before the period ending the sentence. In the case of block quotations for both MLA and APA, put the page reference in parentheses two spaces after the period ending the sentence.

MLA   Simon describes Dr. James as a "not-too-skeletal Ichabod Crane" (68).

APA   Simon (1982) describes Dr. James as a "not-too-skeletal Ichabod Crane" (p. 68).

To cite a source by two or more authors, the MLA uses all the authors' last names, unless the entry in the works-cited list gives the first author's name followed by "et al." The APA uses all the authors' last names the first time the reference occurs and the last name of the first author followed by "et al." subsequently.

MLA   Dyal, Corning, and Willows identify several types of students, including the "Authority-Rebel" (4).

APA   Dyal, Corning, and Willows (1975) identify several types of students, including the "Authority-Rebel" (p. 4).

MLA   The Authority-Rebel "tends to see himself as superior to other students in the class" (Dyal, Corning, and Willows 4).

APA   The Authority-Rebel "tends to see himself as superior to other students in the class" (Dyal et al., 1975, p. 4).

To cite one of two or more works by the same author(s), the MLA uses the author's last name, a shortened version of the title, and the page. The APA uses the author's last name plus the year and page.

MLA   When old paint becomes transparent, it sometimes shows the artist's original plans: "a tree will show through a woman's dress" (Hellman, *Pentimento* 1).

APA   When old paint becomes transparent, it sometimes shows the artist's original plans: "a tree will show through a woman's dress" (Hellman, 1973, p. 1).

To cite a work listed only by its title, both the MLA and the APA use a shortened verison of the title.

MLA   Lillian Hellman calls Dashiell Hammett: "my closest, my most beloved friend" (*Woman* 224).

APA   Lillian Hellman (1969) calls Dashiell Hammett: "my closest, my most beloved friend" (*Woman*, p. 224).

To quote material taken not from the original but from a secondary source that quotes the original, both the MLA and the APA give the secondary source in the works-cited list, and cite both the original and secondary sources within the essay.

MLA   E. M. Forster says "the collapse of all civilization, so realistic for us, sounded in [Matthew Arnold's] ears like a distant and harmonious cataract" (qtd. in Trilling 11).

APA   E. M. Forster says "the collapse of all civilization, so realistic for us, sounded in [Matthew Arnold's] ears like a distant and harmonious cataract" (cited in Trilling, 1955, p. 11).

Citing Sources at the End of Your Essay

Keyed to the parenthetical citations in the text, the list of works cited identifies all the sources you used in the essay. Every source cited in the text must refer to an entry in the works-cited list. And, conversely, every entry in the works-cited list must correspond to at least one parenthetical citation in the text.

Whereas the MLA style uses the title "Works Cited," the APA prefers "References." Both alphabetize the entries according to the first author's last name. When several works by an author are listed, the APA recommends these rules for arranging the list:

- Same-name single-author entries precede multiple-author entries:
  Aaron, P. (1985).
  Aaron, P., & Zorn, C. R. (1982).
- Entries with the same first author and different second author should be alphabetized according to the second author's last name:
  Aaron, P., & Charleston, W. (1979).
  Aaron, P., & Zorn, C. R. (1982).
- Entries by the same authors should be arranged by year of publication, in chronological order:
  Aaron, P., & Charleston, W. (1979).
  Aaron, P., & Charleston, W. (1984).
- Entries by the same author(s) with the same publication year should be arranged alphabetically by title (excluding *A, An, The*), and lowercase letters (*a, b, c,* and so on) should follow the year in parentheses:
  Aaron, P. (1985a). Basic . . . .
  Aaron, P. (1985b). Elements . . . .

The essential difference between the MLA and APA styles of listing sources is the order in which the information is presented. The MLA follows this order: author's name; title; publication source, year, and page. The APA puts the year after the author's name. Note, too, that APA style lists only initials for an author's first and middle names. The examples that follow indicate other minor differences in capitalization and arrangement between the two documentation styles.

Books

A book by a single author

MLA   Simon, Kate. *Bronx Primitive*. New York: Harper, 1982.

APA   Simon, K. (1982). *Bronx primitive*. New York: Harper & Row.

A book by an agency or corporation

MLA   Association for Research in Nervous and Mental Disease. *The Circulation of the Brain and Spinal Cord: A Symposium on Blood Supply*. New York: Hafner, 1966.

APA   Association for Research in Nervous and Mental Disease. (1966). *The circula-*
tion of the brain and spinal cord: A symposium on blood supply. New York:
Hafner Publishing Co.

A book by two or three authors

MLA   Strunk, W., Jr., and E. B. White. *The Elements of Style.* 4th ed. New York:
Macmillan, 1983.

Dyal, James A., William C. Corning, and Dale M. Willows. *Readings in*
Psychology: The Search for Alternatives. 3rd ed. New York: McGraw-Hill,
1975.

APA   Strunk, W., Jr., & White, E. B. (1983). *The elements of style.* (4th ed.). New
York: Macmillan.

Dyal, J. A., Corning, W. C., & Willows, D. M. (1975). *Readings in psychology:*
The search for alternatives. (3rd ed.). New York: McGraw-Hill.

A book by more than three authors

MLA   Belenky, Mary Field, et al. *Women's Ways of Knowing: The Development of Self,*
Voice, and Mind. New York: Basic, 1986.

APA   Belenky, M. F., Clinchy, B. M., Goldberger, N. R., & Tarule, J. M. (1986).
Women's ways of knowing: The development of self, voice, and mind. New
York: Basic Books.

A book by an unknown author

Use title in place of author.

MLA   *College Bound Seniors.* Princeton, NJ: College Board Publications, 1979.

APA   *College bound seniors.* (1979). Princeton, NJ: College Board Publications.

An edition prepared by a named editor

APA   Arnold, M. *Culture and anarchy.* (J. D. Wilson, Ed.). Cambridge: Cambridge
University Press, 1966. (Originally published, 1869.)

MLA has two formats. If you refer to the text itself, begin with the
author:

MLA   Arnold, Matthew. *Culture and Anarchy.* Ed. J. Dover Wilson, Cambridge:
Cambridge UP, 1966.

If you cite the editor in your text, begin with the editor:

MLA   Wilson, J. Dover, ed. *Culture and Anarchy.* By Matthew Arnold. Cambridge: Cambridge UP, 1966.

An anthology

MLA   Dertouzos, Michael L., and Joel Moses, eds. *The Computer Age: A Twenty-Year View.* Cambridge, MA: MIT, 1979.

APA   Dertouzos, M. L., & Moses, J. (Eds.). (1979). *The computer age: A twenty-year view.* Cambridge, MA: MIT Press.

A translation

APA   Tolstoy, L. (1972). *War and Peace.* (C. Garnett, Trans.). London: Pan Books. (Originally published 1868–1869).

MLA has two formats. If you are referring to the work itself, begin with the author:

MLA   Tolstoy, Leo. *War and Peace.* Trans. Constance Garnett. London: Pan, 1972.

If you cite the translator in your text, begin the entry with the translator's name:

MLA   Garnett, Constance, trans. *War and Peace.* By Leo Tolstoy. London: Pan, 1972.

A work in an anthology or collection

MLA   Bell, Daniel. "The Social Framework of the Information Society." *The Computer Age: A Twenty-Year View.* Ed. Michael L. Dertouzos and Joel Moses. Cambridge, MA: MIT, 1979. 163–211.

APA   Bell, D. (1979). The social framework of the information society. In M. L. Dertouzos & J. Moses (Eds.), *The computer age: A twenty-year view* (pp. 163–211). Cambridge, MA: MIT.

An essay in an anthology by the same author

MLA   Weaver, Richard. "The Rhetoric of Social Science." *Ethics of Rhetoric.* Ed. Richard Weaver. South Bend, Indiana: Gateway, 1953, 186–210.

APA   Weaver, R. (1953). The rhetoric of social science. In R. Weaver, *Ethics of rhetoric* (pp. 186–210). South Bend, Indiana: Gateway Editions.

Articles

An article in a journal with continuous annual pagination

MLA   Dworkin, Ronald. "Law as Interpretation." *Critical Inquiry* 9 (1982): 179–200.

APA   Dworkin, R. (1982). Law as interpretation. *Critical Inquiry, 9,* 179–200.

An article in a journal that paginates each issue separately

MLA   Festinger, Leon. "Cognitive Dissonance." *Scientific American* 2 (Oct. 1962): 93–102.

APA   Festinger, L. (1962, October). Cognitive dissonance. *Scientific American, 2,* 93–102.

An article from a daily newspaper

MLA   Lubin, J. S. "On Idle: The Unemployed Shun Much Mundane Work, at Least for a While." *Wall Street Journal* 5 Dec. 1980: 1, 25.

APA   Lubin, J. S. (1980, December 5). On idle: The unemployed shun much mundane work, at least for a while. *Wall Street Journal,* pp. 1, 25.

A review

MLA   Lehman, John. "Little John." Rev. of *The Lone Star: The Life of John Connally,* by James Reston, Jr. *Atlantic* Oct. 1989: 109–12.

   Rev. of *Keep the Change,* by Thomas McGuane. *Atlantic* Oct. 1989: 115.

APA   Lehman, J. (1989, October). Little john. [Review of *The lone star: the life of John Connally.*]. *Atlantic,* 109–112.

   Review of *Keep the change.* (1989, October). [Review of *Keep the change.*] *Atlantic,* 115.

An editorial

MLA   "Stepping Backward." Editorial. *Los Angeles Times* 4 July 1989, sec. II: 6.

APA   Stepping backward. (1989, July 4). [Editorial.]. *Los Angeles Times,* section II, p. 6.

Letter to the editor

MLA   Strain, Diana. Letter. *Los Angeles Times* 29 June 1989, sec. IV: 5.

APA   Strain, D. (1989, June 29). [Letter to the editor.]. *Los Angeles Times,* section IV, p. 5.

Other Sources

Computer software

MLA   Hogue, Bill. *Miner 2049er.* Computer Software. Big Five Software.

   Microsoft Word. Vers. 4.0. Computer Software. Microsoft, 1987.

APA   Hogue, B. (1982). *Miner 2049er.* [Computer program.]. Van Nuys, CA: Big Five Software.

   Microsoft Word 4.0 (1987). [Computer program.]. Bellevue, WA: Microsoft.

Records and tapes

MLA   Beethoven, Ludwig van. Violin Concerto in D Major, op. 61. Cond. Alexander Gauk, U.S.S.R. State Orchestra. David Oistrakh, violinist. Allegro, ACS 8044, 1980.

   Springsteen, Bruce. "Dancing in the Dark." *Born in the U.S.A.* Columbia, QC 38653, 1984.

APA   Beethoven, L. van. (Composer). (1980). *Violin concerto in D major, op. 61.* (Cassette Recording No. ACS 8044). New York: Allegro.

   Springsteen, B. (Singer and Composer). (1984). Dancing in the dark. *Born in the U.S.A.* (Record No. QC 38653). New York: Columbia.

Interviews

MLA   Lowell, Robert. "Robert Lowell." With Frederick Seidel. *Paris Review* 25 (Winter-Spring 1961): 56–95.

   Franklin, Anna. Personal Interview. 3 September 1983.

APA   Seidel, F. (1977, Winter-Spring). [Interview with Robert Lowell.]. *Paris Review, 25,* 56–95.

   Franklin, A. (1983, September 3). [Personal Interview.].

Film or videotape

MLA   *The Wizard of Oz.* Dir. Victor Fleming. With Judy Garland, Ray Bolger, Bert Lahr, and Jack Haley. MGM, 1939.

APA   Le Roy, M. (Producer), & Fleming, V. (Director). (1939). *Wizard of Oz* [Film]. Hollywood, CA: MGM.

Television or radio program

MLA   *Hill Street Blues.* Writ. Michael Kozoll and Stephen Bochco. With Daniel J. Travanti, Joe Spano, and Charles Haid. NBC, 15 Jan. 1981.

APA   Kozoll, M. & Bochco, S. (Writers). (1981, January 15) *Hill street blues*. NBC.

Live performance

MLA   *Orpheus Descending*. By Tennessee Williams. Dir. Peter Hall. With Vanessa
Redgrave. Neil Simon Theatre, New York. 13 Sept. 1989.

APA   Nederlander, J. (Producer), & Hall, P. (Director). (1989, September 13)
Orpheus descending [Play]. New York: Neil Simon Theatre.

Work of art

MLA   Van Gogh, Vincent. *Starry Night*. Museum of Modern Art. New York.

APA   Van Gogh, V. (Artist). (1889) *Starry night* [Painting]. New York: Museum of
Modern Art.

Acknowledgments *(continued from p. iv)*

Crewdson, John, "An Evaluation of Materials Designed to Prevent Child Sexual Abuse." From *Silence Betrayed: Sexual Abuse of Children in America* by John Crewdson © 1986 by John Crewdson. Reprinted by permission of Little, Brown and Company.

Didion, Joan, "On Self-Respect" from *Slouching Towards Bethlehem* by Joan Didion. Copyright © 1961, 1968 by Joan Didion. Reprinted by permission of Farrar, Straus and Giroux, Inc.

Dillard, Annie, "A Chase." Excerpts from *An American Childhood* by Annie Dillard. Copyright © 1987 by Annie Dillard. Reprinted by permission of Harper & Row, Publishers, Inc.

Erhlich, Gretel, "Saddle Bronc Riding at the National Finals." From *The Solace of Open Spaces* by Gretel Ehrlich. Copyright © Gretel Ehrlich, 1985. All rights reserved. Reprinted by permission of Viking Penguin, a division of Penguin Books USA, Inc.

Etzioni, Amitai, from "When Rights Collide." Copyright Amitai Etzioni, 1977.

Fitts, Dudley & Fitzgerald, Robert (eds.), "The Antigone of Sophocles." Abridgement from *The Antigone of Sophocles, English Version,* by Dudley Fitts and Robert Fitzgerald, copyright 1939 by Harcourt Brace Jovanovich, Inc. Reprinted by permission of the publisher. *Caution:* All rights, including professional, amateur, motion picture, recitation, lecturing, public reading, radio broadcasting, and television, are strictly reserved. Inquiries on all rights should be addressed to Harcourt Brace Jovanovich, Inc., Orlando, Florida 32887. Abridgement of *The Antigone of Sophocles* appearing in this volume may not be used without the permission of St. Martin's Press.

Fitzgerald, Frances, "Refugees." From *Fire in the Lake: The Vietnamese and the Americans in Vietnam* by Frances Fitzgerald © 1972 by Frances Fitzgerald. By permission of Little, Brown and Company.

Fletcher, George P., "What About U.S. Unity." Copyright © 1989 by The New York Times Company. Reprinted by permission.

Fuchs, Victor, "Why Married Mothers Work." From *How We Live* by Victor R. Fuchs, Harvard University Press, 1983. Copyright © 1983 by the President and Fellows of Harvard College.

Gandhi, Mohandas K., "Satyagraha or Passive Resistance." Reprinted with permission of the Navajivan Trust, Ahmedabad, India.

Goodman, Ellen, "Nouvelle Nutrition." © 1989, The Boston Globe Newspaper Company/The Washington Post Writers Group. Reprinted with permission.

Goodwin, Richard N., "Our Right to Offend and Outrage." Originally appeared in the *Los Angeles Times,* July 3, 1989. Reprinted by permission of author.

Gornick, Vivian, "Mrs. Kerner." Excerpt from *Fierce Attachments* by Vivian Gornick. Copyright © 1987 by Vivian Gornick. Reprinted by permission of Farrar, Straus and Giroux, Inc.

Hoekema, David, "Capital Punishment: The Question of Justification." Copyright © 1979 by Christian Century Foundation. Reprinted by permission from the March 28, 1979, issue of The Christian Century.

Jastrow, Robert, "Man of Wisdom." From *Until the Sun Dies,* W. W. Norton and Co. (1977) © Robert Jastrow. Reprinted with permission.

King, Frederick A., "Animals in Research: The Case for Experimentation." Reprinted with permission from *Psychology Today* magazine. Copyright © 1984 (PT Partners, LP).

King, Martin Luther, Jr., "Letter from Birmingham Jail" from *Why We Can't Wait* by Martin Luther King, Jr. Copyright © 1963, 1964 by Martin Luther King, Jr. Reprinted by permission of Harper & Row, Publishers, Inc.

King, Stephen, "Why We Crave Horror Movies." Originally appeared in *Playboy* Magazine. Reprinted by permission.

Kinsley, Michael, "Saint Ralph." Reprinted by permission of *The New Republic*, © 1985, The New Republic, Inc.

Kirby, Michael, "AIDS Hysteria." Reprinted by permission of *Daedalus*. Journal of the American Academy of Arts and Sciences, "Living with AIDS: Part II," Summer 1989, Cambridge, Massachusetts.

Kleiman, Mark, "Grant Bachelor's Degrees by Examination." Copyright © 1985, Mark A. R. Kleiman. Reprinted from the *Wall Street Journal*.

Kowinski, William Soverini, "Mallaise: How to Know If You Have It" from *The Malling of America* by William Kowinski. Copyright © 1985 by William Kowinski. By permission of William Morrow & Co.

Kozol, Jonathon, "The Human Cost of Illiteracy." Excerpt(s) from *Illiterate America* by Jonathan Kozol, copyright © 1985 by Jonathan Kozol. Used by permission of Doubleday, a division of Bantam, Doubleday, Dell Publishing Group, Inc.

Kumin, Maxine, "From a Journal." From *In Deep* by Maxine Kumin. Copyright © Maxine Kumin, 1987. All rights reserved. Reprinted by permission of Viking Penguin, a division of Penguin Books USA, Inc.

Marshall, Kim, "Literacy: The Price of Admission." Copyright © 1985 *Harvard Magazine*. Reprinted by permission.

McMurtry, John, "Kill 'Em! Crush 'Em! Eat 'Em Raw!" Dr. John McMurtry is Professor of Philosophy at the University of Guelph. His latest book is *Understanding War: A Philosophical Inquiry* (Samuel Stevens, University of Toronto Press, 1989). Copyright © 1971 by John McMurtry. Reprinted with permission.

McPhee, John, "The New York Pickpocket Academy." Excerpt from *Giving Good Weight* by John McPhee. Copyright © 1975, 1976, 1979 by John McPhee. Reprinted by permission of Farrar, Straus and Giroux, Inc.

Menocal, Maria Rosa, "We Can't Dance Together." Reprinted by permission of the Modern Language Association of America from *Profession 88*. Copyright © 1988 by the Modern Language Association of America.

Morris, Charles R., "Civil Disobedience." Excerpt from *A Time of Passion* by Charles R. Morris. Copyright © 1984 by Charles R. Morris as the Trustee for the benefit of Michael Morris, Kathleen Morris and Matthew Morris. Reprinted with permission of Harper & Row, Publishers, Inc.

Moskos, Charles C., "A Practical Proposal for National Service." Reprinted with permission of *The Free Press*, a division of Macmillan, Inc. from *A Call to Civic Service: National Service for Country and Community* by Charles C. Moskos. Copyright © 1988 by the Twentieth Century Fund.

Palmer, Edward L., "*Improving Television for America's Children*," from *Television and America's Children: A Crisis of Neglect*. © 1988, Oxford University Press.

Perera, Victor, "Kindergarten" from *Rites: A Guatemalan Boyhood*. Copyright © 1985 by Victor Perera, reprinted in this volume by permission of Harcourt Brace Jovanovich, Inc.

Quammen, David, "Is Sex Necessary? Virgin Birth and Opportunism in the Garden." Reprinted by permission of David Quammen. All rights reserved. Copyright © 1982 by David Quammen.

Rodriguez, Richard, "Gains at Losses." From *Hunger of Memory* by Richard Rodriguez. Copyright © 1982 by Richard Rodriguez. Reprinted by permission of David R. Godine, Publisher.

Sack, Allen L., "What We Need Is Real Collegiate Sports Reform." Copyright © 1986 by The New York Times Company. Reprinted by permission.

Seebohm, Caroline, "Lateral Thinking." Courtesy *House & Garden*. Copyright © 1974 by the Condé Nast Publications, Inc.

Sesser, Stan, "French Dinner on Incredible Bargain." © 1989 *San Francisco Chronicle*. Reprinted by permission.

Shames, Lawrence, "The Eyes of Fear." Reprinted with permission from *Esquire*. Copyright © 1982 by Esquire Associates.

Shanahan, Daniel, "A Proposal for a Multilingual America." Originally appeared in *The Chronicle of Higher Education*, May 31, 1989. Reprinted by permission of the author.

Skreslet, Paula, "The Prizes of First Grade." From *Newsweek*, November 30, 1987, and © 1987, Newsweek, Inc. All rights reserved. Reprinted with permission.

"Soup," reprinted by permission; © 1989 The New Yorker, Inc.

Solomon, Robert C., "Culture Gives Us a Sense of Who We Are." Reprinted with permission of Robert C. Solomon.

Staples, Brent, "Black Men and Public Space." Copyright © 1987 by The New York Times Company. Reprinted by permission.

Stone, Lawrence, "Passionate Attachments." Copyright © 1988 by Harper's Magazine. All rights reserved. Reprinted from the February issue by special permission.

Theroux, Phyllis, "Fear of Families." Copyright © 1982 by Phyllis Theroux. From the book *Peripheral Visions* by Phyllis Theroux, William Morrow and Company, Inc., 1982.

Van Dusen, Lewis H., Jr., "Civil Disobedience: Destroyer of Democracy." Reprinted with permission of the American Bar Association.

Walker, Alice, "Beauty: When the Other Dancer Is the Self" and "The Civil Rights Movement: What Good Was It?" from *In Search of Our Mothers' Gardens*, copyright © 1967, 1983 by Alice Walker, reprinted in her volume by permission of Harcourt Brace Jovanovich.

Weber, David R., "Civil Disobedience in America." Excerpted from pp. 18–30 from the "General Introduction" to *Civil Disobedience in America: A Documentary History*, edited by David R. Weber. Copyright © 1978 by Cornell University Press. Used with permission of Cornell University Press.

Wertheimer, Alan, "Compulsory Voting." Copyright © 1976 by The New York Times Company. Reprinted by permission.

Zukav, Gary, "Heisenberg's Uncertainty Principle." From *The Dancing Wu Li Masters* by Gary Zukav. Copyright © 1979 by Gary Zukav. By permission of William Morrow & Co.

Topical Index

This index classifies readings by topics in order to facilitate topic-centered discussions and special writing assignments.

Index of Authors, Titles, and Terms

NOV 25 1992